FEMINISM AND PHILOSOPHY

FEMINISM
AND PHILOSOPHY

*Essential Readings
in Theory, Reinterpretation,
and Application*

EDITED BY
Nancy Tuana
University of Oregon

Rosemarie Tong
Davidson College

c. 1995

Westview Press

BOULDER • SAN FRANCISCO • OXFORD

Copyright © 1995 by Westview Press, Inc.

Published in 1995 in the United States of America by Westview Press, Inc., 5500 Central Avenue, Boulder, Colorado 80301-2877, and in the United Kingdom by Westview Press, 36 Lonsdale Road, Summertown, Oxford OX2 7EW

Library of Congress Cataloging-in-Publication Data
Feminism and philosophy : essential readings in theory,
   reinterpretation, and application / [edited by] Nancy Tuana and
   Rosemarie Tong.
      p.   cm.
   Includes bibliographical references.
   ISBN 0-8133-2212-X — ISBN 0-8133-2213-8 (pbk.)
   1. Feminist theory.   I. Tuana, Nancy.   II. Tong, Rosemarie.
HQ1190.F42   1995
305.42'01—dc20
                                                                    94-21411
                                                                    CIP

Printed and bound in the United States of America

The paper used in this publication meets the requirements
of the American National Standard for Permanence of Paper
for Printed Library Materials Z39.48-1984.

10   9   8   7   6   5   4   3   2   1

*To members of the Society for Women
in Philosophy—past, present, and
future—in thanks for their support
and inspiration*

Contents

Preface

Our anthology has three fundamental goals. Its first and foremost goal is to enable readers to understand what differentiates each of the feminist perspectives we have chosen for discussion, if only to better appreciate the diversity of feminist thought. Liberal, Marxist, radical, socialist, psychoanalytic, ecological, phenomenological, postmodern, and anarcha feminists provide a number of distinct as well as intersecting explanations for women's personal, professional, and political conditions. They also provide a variety of differing recommendations for improving or transforming those conditions. Feminists disagree about which aspects of women's lives—work, sexual relations, or family relations—best explain women's oppression, repression, and suppression under patriarchy. They also disagree about which legal remedies, job opportunities, sexual experiments, reproductive technologies, and linguistic revisions are most likely to liberate women. Finally, they disagree about which forms of oppression other than gender oppression feminists must address: racism, classism, homophobia, ageism, or any and all forms of systematic discrimination.

The second basic aim of our anthology is to help readers challenge traditional philosophy with as many feminist perspectives as possible. As we see it, each feminist perspective sheds light on what is absent as well as what is present in traditional philosophy. All too often, traditional philosophers have neglected so-called women's issues: child care, housework, sexual relations, and family problems. In addition, traditional philosophers have embraced a metaphysics that dichotomizes reality into oppositional dyads such as culture/nature, mind/body, reason/emotion, self/other, male/female and that privileges the first member of each of these dyads over the other. Uncovering this metaphysic has enabled feminist philosophers to realize that it will not be sufficient to simply add women's concerns to the subject matter of traditional philosophy but that the very categories of traditional philosophy themselves are gender-marked and must therefore be reconceptualized.

The third and final goal of our anthology is to persuade readers that feminist philosophers make the kinds of distinctions that matter in women's everyday lives. Feminist philosophers do not simply engage in thought for thought's sake. They are committed to major social changes—to achieving equality between men and women—and they see their theories as contributing to such a fundamental transformation. Thus, feminist analyses of a wide range of personal, professional, and political issues not only reveal, for example, the uses, abuses, and misuses of power to which traditional philosophical analyses remain oblivious; they also prompt women and men to change themselves, others, and their mutual environment.

The subtitle of our book, *Essential Readings in Theory, Reinterpretation, and Application,* explains our method of organization. We believe that each feminist perspective we have chosen—liberal, Marxist, radical, psychoanalytic, socialist, anarcha, ecological, phenomenological, and postmodern—can be best understood by seeing the connections between its theory and its practice. Each section thus contains three essays. The first essay in each part gives readers a sense of the worldview and methodology that undergird that particular feminist perspective. The second essay represents an instance of the use of that perspective to criticize some aspect of traditional philosophy. The third essay provides a discussion of how that perspective would be used to address "real-life" problems that concern women.

Given our principle of organization, there are various ways in which this book can be read. One can read our anthology cover to cover, aiming to understand how each different feminist perspective weaves together elements of theory, reinterpretation, and application. Or one can read the essays in a more eclectic fashion. For example, by reading all the first essays from each section—the ones that offer theoretical descriptions of the various feminist perspectives—readers can better understand feminists' disagreements as well as agreements about the causes of and explanations for women's oppression. Similarly, by reading all the second essays across the various perspectives, readers can better appreciate how feminist philosophers specifically challenge some of the luminaries of traditional philosophy. Finally, by reading all the third essays together, readers can better sense the power of feminist philosophy—its ability to help women solve their everyday problems.

Although we have attempted to provide a wide range of feminist perspectives in this anthology, it is not exhaustive of the varieties of feminist approaches. Size limitations prohibited us from including more representatives of current feminist thought, such as analytic feminism and pragmatist feminism. We could not include, additionally, many exciting new directions in feminist writing, such as feminist aesthetic theory, feminist spirituality, feminist epistemology, and feminist ethics. Finally, a more profound set of limitations prohibited us from including more multicultural and global feminist articles. Sadly, feminist philosophy has tended to commit some of the same sins of omission that traditional philosophy has committed. Only recently have feminist philosophers seriously devoted themselves to filling in the gaps and holes in their works—absences that bespeak the fact that they have paid too little attention to matters of race, class, sexual identity, age, religion, and physical and psychological conditions in their works. As this state of affairs is remedied, we can expect to see feminist philosophy transformed, an event we hope to witness in our lifetime.

Nancy Tuana
Rosemarie Tong

Credits

Permissions to reprint are gratefully acknowledged.

Zillah R. Eisenstein, "The Sexual Politics of the New Right: Understanding the 'Crisis of Liberalism' for the 1980s," *Signs: Journal of Women in Culture and Society* 7, no. 3 (1982):567–588. © 1982 by The University of Chicago.

Melissa A. Butler, "Early Liberal Roots of Feminism: John Locke and the Attack on Patriarchy," *American Political Science Review* 72 (1978):135–150.

Mary Anne Warren, "The Moral Significance of Birth," *Hypatia: A Journal of Feminist Philosophy* 4, no. 3 (1989):46–65.

Nancy C.M. Hartsock, "The Feminist Standpoint: Developing the Ground for a Specifically Feminist Historical Materialism," in *Discovering Reality*, Sandra Harding and Merrill B. Hintikka, eds. (Dordrecht, Holland: D. Reidel, 1983), pp. 283–310. Copyright © 1983 by D. Reidel Publishing Co. Reprinted by permission of Kluwer Academic Publishers.

Mary O'Brien, "Reproducing Marxist Man," in *The Sexism of Social and Political Theory: Women and Reproduction from Plato to Nietzsche,* Lorenne M.G. Clark and Lynda Lange, eds. (Toronto: University of Toronto Press, 1979), pp. 99–116. Reprinted by permission of University of Toronto Press, publisher. Copyright © 1979 by University of Toronto Press.

Heidi I. Hartmann, "The Family as the Locus of Gender, Class, and Political Struggle: The Example of Housework," in *Signs: Journal of Women in Culture and Society* 6, no. 3 (1981):109–134. © 1981 by The University of Chicago.

Catharine A. MacKinnon, "Sexuality, Pornography, and Method: 'Pleasure Under Patriarchy,'" in *Feminism and Political Theory*, Cass R. Sunstein, ed. (Chicago: University of Chicago Press, 1990), pp. 207–239. Epigraph from "Dialogue" is reprinted from *The Fact of a Doorframe, Poems Selected and New, 1950–1984,* by Adrienne Rich, by permission of the author and W. W. Norton & Company, Inc. Copyright © 1984 by Adrienne Rich. Copyright © 1975, 1978 by W. W. Norton & Company, Inc. Copyright © 1981 by Adrienne Rich.

Introduction

The past twenty years have witnessed a blossoming of feminist philosophy. From an initial concern over traditional philosophy's negative descriptions of women, feminist philosophers have proceeded to an analysis of its tendency both to devalue women's intellectual efforts and to trivialize women's moral concerns. Having revealed the spaces in traditional philosophy that might have been occupied, populated, or otherwise filled by women and their thoughts, feminist philosophers have concluded that much of traditional philosophy is "male-biased"; its major concepts and theories, indeed its own self-understanding, reveal what Alison Jaggar simply summarizes as "a distinctively masculine way of approaching the world."[1]

Despite the fact that some traditional philosophers (Plato, Mill, and Marx) sought to validate women as men's equals, most traditional philosophers (including Aristotle, Aquinas, Kant, Hegel, and Nietzsche) expressed serious reservations about women's capacities, especially their rational capacities. Rather than viewing the misogynistic comments of these thinkers as causing no reason for alarm, feminist philosophers have read them as troubling signs that gender biases have permeated philosophical theorizing, often causing traditional philosophers to discredit women and all that is discernibly "female." Indeed, with few exceptions, traditional philosophers have treated, for example, the private realm of the family, generally associated with women, as a realm mired in the concrete, particular, and subjective and, thus, not worthy of sustained philosophical reflection.

Convinced that the issues that arise in the private domain are just as philosophically important as the issues that arise in the public work of government, finance, the sciences, and the arts, feminist philosophers have been committed to developing philosophical analyses of such topics as female sexuality, the experiences of female embodiment, childbearing and rearing, and housekeeping. In focusing on these topics, feminist philosophers have relied on the experiences of women. This emphasis on women's experience—on women's ways of knowing and making moral decisions as well as of perceiving reality and controlling their destiny—builds on the understanding that from time to time, what women feel, think, or do will differ from what men feel, think, or do. It also builds on the realization that there is no unitary explanation for these gender differences. Social conditioning, biological differences, or, more likely, a complex interaction of the two are all probable explanations for why women and men do not always experience things the same way. Indeed, they are also probable explanations for why *women* do not always see things in the same way. "Women's experience" is not shorthand for some sort of monolithic, female "groupthink" but for a vast array of thoughts, feelings, and activities mediated through the lenses of each individual woman's race, class, sexual preference, ethnicity, religion, age, physical condition, and state of mind.

Focused as they are on women's experiences, feminist philosophers have become painfully aware of the degree to which traditional philosophy overlooks or trivializes women's interests, issues, concerns, and persons. They have also come to see traditional philosophy's tendency first to identify women with the less valued half of its major dichotomies (for example, mind/body, self/other, and reason/emotion) and then to systematically neglect that less valued half of reality throughout the course of its own development. Thus, feminist philosophers have observed that among the neglected "female-associated" elements in many of traditional philosophy's canonical texts are the concrete, particular, and subjective, which are viewed as the enemies of the abstract, universal, and objective; the emotions and the body, which are set in opposition to reason and the mind; the human need for cooperation and community, which is viewed as far less urgent than the human desire to compete and to assert one's individuality; and, finally, the judgment that the lines between the disciplines, as well as between theory and practice and value and fact, should be blurred, hazy, and permeable as opposed to clear, distinct, and impenetrable. Feminist philosophers do not seek to justify the claim that the dimensions of reality that most traditional philosophers have deemphasized or totally ignored are *inherently* "female" or "feminine." Still, most feminist philosophers do agree with Alison Jaggar that many of these dimensions of reality are "gender-coded by being associated symbolically with maleness or femaleness, masculine or feminine."[2] It is apparent, for example, that in our culture women are associated with the emotions and the body, whereas men are associated with reason and the mind. Thus, feminist philosophers sometimes articulate the project they share with many other nontraditional philosophers—the project of transforming traditional philosophy by fully integrating what it is missing into its theoretical base—as either "adding" women's experience to traditional philosophy or "correcting for" male bias.

Despite the fact that many feminist philosophers want to reconceive traditional philosophy, it is important to note that they do not necessarily reject everything about it. On the contrary, the work of feminist philosophers has been greatly enriched by their training in various schools of philosophy. In fact, it is precisely by working *with* as well as *against* the "Tradition" that feminist philosophers have produced an amazing array of theories, each of which not only identifies the causes of women's oppression and possible ways to overcome it but also explains knowledge, reality, and action in general. Thus, if anything is clear, it is that feminist philosophers are an eclectic group. Although *as feminists* all feminist philosophers share a commitment to give voice to women's experiences and to remove women's subordination, *as philosophers* they adopt a variety of different strategies and methodologies to accomplish these goals. Questions such as "What is feminist philosophy's position on abortion?" "To what political theory do feminist philosophers subscribe?" or "Do feminist philosophers believe in the objectivity of science?" are based on a failure to understand the diversity among feminist philosophers.

Therefore, one of our goals in editing this anthology is simply to make clear the range of different approaches, perspectives, and frameworks that together constitute feminist philosophy. These differences affect the questions asked by individual theorists as well as the types of answers offered in their accounts; they also shape both the explanations for women's oppression and the solutions proposed for its elimination. To enable themselves and others to fully appreciate the scope of feminist thought, some feminist philosophers have sought to identify and name the general theoretical commitments of its major schools. Alison M. Jaggar, in *Feminist Politics and Human Nature,* carefully delineates the similarities and differences in the descriptions and prescriptions of the politics of liberal feminism, traditional Marxism, radical feminism, and socialist feminism. We have added to her list by including anarcha, phenomenological, psychoanalytic, and postmodern feminist perspectives.

Not all feminists find these names appropriate. Indeed, they find some of them misleading. Feminist thought, they insist, resists categorization, especially categorization based on the "Father's" labels—as if liberal feminism were only a variation on John Stuart Mill's treatise "On Liberty," Marxist feminism an improvement on Karl Marx's *Das Kapital,* and psychoanalytic feminism an addendum to Sigmund Freud's essays on female sexuality.

We respect such objections. It would be a tragedy if these labels masked the variety of ways in which feminist philosophy often transforms the very methods and core assumptions of the traditional philosophical schools of thought with which they are identified. It would also be a mistake if these labels detracted from the efforts of radical feminists, for example, to do philosophy de novo without relying on any patriarch's thought—a daunting, even perilous task, but one that has much to recommend it. Still, feminist thought is old enough to have a history complete with its own set of labels. Additionally, individual feminist philosophers are often more indebted to one of the traditional schools of thought than to others. Thus, the descriptors "liberal," "Marxist," "radical," "psychoanalytic," "socialist," "anarcha," "ecological," "phenomenological," and "postmodern" help mark a history that borrows from the old in its struggle to create the new. A time will perhaps come when feminist thought will shed these labels for others that better express its intellectual and political commitments to women. Until this transition, we believe that on balance, the old labels remain useful in signaling to the broader public that feminism is not a monolithic ideology, that all feminists do not think alike, and that, like all other time-honored modes of thinking, feminist thought has a past as well as a present and a future.

Significantly, most feminist philosophers tend to wear comfortably the clothes of several schools of feminist thought. Iris Marion Young, whose essay "Pregnant Embodiment: Subjectivity and Alienation" appears in the section on phenomenological feminist perspectives, also writes from a socialist feminist perspective. Nancy Fraser, who identifies herself as developing a socialist feminist critical theory, has published numerous essays in which she seeks to apply the methods of certain postmodern thinkers to the concerns of feminists. And these are only two of many examples—examples that suggest that the interdisciplinary nature of feminist inquiry lends itself to a shifting between methodological approaches as the content of one's analysis shifts.

Despite all of its successes, feminist philosophy is not without its failures. Recently, feminist philosophers have come to recognize *as a problem* the sociological fact that the majority of them are white, middle-class, and, to a lesser extent, heterosexual women; they have come to acknowledge *as a mistake* any attempt to articulate "Woman's Experience," to discuss the things all women supposedly have in common without also acknowledging women's differences. Although it requires a very delicate balance, feminist philosophers increasingly seek to investigate what separates women from each other without diminishing the affinities that women generally feel for each other. The final section of this anthology, which focuses on the intersections of racism, sexism, and classism, is devoted to a discussion of some of these issues. We urge readers to approach this concluding section not as a postscript to what has preceded it but as a promissory note of types of discourses that must eventually permeate all schools of feminist thought.

Feminist philosophy is particularly exciting because of its dynamism; it is rapidly evolving in a variety of ways, some of which elude us precisely because we do not have the words to capture them. We hope that readers of this anthology will be stimulated to apply a variety of feminist perspectives to their everyday problems, to reinterpret the traditional philosophers they may have read, and, most important, to conceive their own feminist theories—their own explanations for women's different experiences. Creating feminist philosophy should not be the prerogative of a few privileged thinkers. On the contrary, it should be both the right and the duty of each and every woman and man who has the sense and sensibilities of a feminist.

Notes

1. Alison M. Jaggar, "How Can Philosophy Be Feminist?" American Philosophical Association *Newsletter on Feminism and Philosophy* (April 1988):6.
   2. Ibid.

ONE

LIBERAL FEMINIST

PERSPECTIVES

Liberal feminist theory has enjoyed a long history, originally promulgated in the eighteenth and nineteenth centuries by such thinkers as Mary Wollstonecraft (1759–1797), Harriet Taylor (1807–1858), John Stuart Mill (1806–1873), Elizabeth Cady Stanton (1815–1902). These feminists embraced the values of liberalism but argued that its main proponents—John Locke (1632–1704) and Jean Jacques Rousseau (1712–1778)—failed to recognize the full implications of liberal political theory for the position of women in society.

The values of liberalism, including the core belief in the importance and autonomy of the individual, developed in the seventeenth century. In fact, liberal political theory began as a rejection of patriarchal political theory: the view that certain people—the monarchs—were inherently superior to others—the subjects—who were to be their subordinates. In opposition to patriarchalism, liberals advanced a belief in the natural equality and freedom of human beings and advocated the creation of a social structure that would recognize the uniqueness of individuals and provide them with equality of opportunity. Nevertheless, liberal political theory developed alongside an acceptance of one structure of patriarchalism, the patriarchal family, in which wives were subject to their husbands. This, in the words of Zillah R. Eisenstein, constitutes the residual patriarchal bias of liberalism in which "the ideology of liberal individualism and personal freedom applied only to men in the market ... [and] did not extend to the sexual hierarchy of patriarchy within the family."[1] Although agreeing with Eisenstein that Locke embraced the patriarchal family, Melissa A. Butler contends in her "Early Liberal Roots of Feminism: John Locke and the Attack on Patriarchy" that he nevertheless anticipated later feminist elaborations of liberal theory in that he "believed that women shared the basic freedom and equality characteristic of all members of the species." Any feminist examination of a liberal political theorist, such as Butler's of Locke, must consider whether the theory's residual patriarchalism is an inherent part of it. If so, its sexist biases cannot be simply eradicated but will require radical transformations.[2]

Contemporary liberals, who emphasize the model of the rational, self-determining individual, advocate the development of social, economic, and political institutions that optimize the autonomy of individual citizens. Classical liberals focus on civil liberties such as voting rights, freedom of speech, and property rights; welfare liberals emphasize economic justice by supporting such programs as Social Security, food stamps, Medicaid and Medicare, and low-cost housing.

Many social commentators interpret as a liberal feminist movement the so-called second wave of feminism, which began in the 1960s with the work of such women as Bella Abzug, Betty Friedan, Elizabeth Holtzman, Patsy Mink, Pat Schroeder, and Eleanor Smeal. Although liberal feminist platforms have received the most publicity and public recognition—perhaps because of the National Organization for Women's support of the Equal Rights Amendment—the women's movement in the 1960s was also strongly influenced by many of the other varieties of feminism we include in this anthology.

Initially, contemporary liberal feminists focused on gender justice by working to eradicate oppressive gender roles. They fought to eliminate legislation and social conventions that limit women's and men's opportunities to compete for certain professions because of their gender. Whether it was the belief that women, as a class, are incapable of sustaining the stresses associated with being astronauts or the opinion that men, as a class, are incapable of mustering the attentiveness associated with being child-care professionals, liberal feminists were prepared to debunk such beliefs and opinions with the proverbial exceptions to the rule. But as liberal feminists began to remove legal and educational barriers to gender justice, they discovered the complexities of the impediments to such progress, such as the lack of comparable worth,[3] the scarcity of affordable, quality child-care facilities, and woman's double day.[4] Such experiences have caused liberal feminists to recognize that achieving the goals of liberal feminism might require more radical transformations in society than those they originally proposed.

In her chapter "The Sexual Politics of the New Right: Understanding the 'Crisis of Liberalism' for the 1980s," Zillah R. Eisenstein sees the radical future of liberal feminism as arising from the experiences of women who work both inside and outside the home. "As these women begin to understand the sexual bias in the marketplace (where a woman earns 58 cents to the male worker's $1.00) and continue to bear the responsibilities of housework and child care as well, they begin to voice feminist demands for affirmative action programs, equal pay, pregnancy disability payments, and abortion rights." Eisenstein contends that the vehemence of the New Right's attack on what it perceives as the erosion of the traditional patriarchal family arises from its recognition of married wage-earning women's and "working mother's" revolutionary potential.[5]

Eisenstein identifies this radical potential as the value of liberal feminism. Insisting that the structure of the capitalist market is patriarchal, she claims that the liberal ideologies of equal opportunity, equality before the law, and individual autonomy cause discontent in the women who participate in the market. Because they are able to perceive the patriarchal structuring of opportunities within the market, discontent women develop a feminist consciousness that enables them to recognize the ways in which they are excluded from economic rights simply because they are members of a sexual class. According to Eisenstein, "The recognition of women as a sexual class lays the subversive quality of feminism for liberalism because liberalism is premised upon woman's exclusion from public life on this very class basis. The demand for the real equality of women with men, if taken to its logical conclusion, would dislodge the patriarchal structure necessary to a liberal society." Thus, Eisenstein believes it is to the strategic benefit of *all* feminists, not simply liberal feminists, to emphasize liberal demands for equality, autonomy, and freedom of choice, because doing so will "direct the public's consciousness to a critique of capitalist patriarchy."

Liberal political theory goes hand in hand with a theory of rights. Liberal feminists adopted the liberal concern with protection of individual rights, arguing that it should be applied equally to both women and men. In the nineteenth and twentieth centuries, liberal feminists have fought to ensure numerous rights for women including the rights to vote, to own property, to equal access to education, and to equal employment opportunity.

Mary Anne Warren's essay, "The Moral Significance of Birth," is an example of this concern over respect for rights. Examining the nature of the right to life, in both its moral and legal forms, Warren addresses the question of the significance of birth. She contests the prevalent view that birth is irrelevant to an individual's right to life and argues that it is in fact "the most appropriate place to mark the existence of a new legal person." Warren argues for the significance of birth over any later time by reminding us that birth allows for the development of social relationships. The infant "begins to be known and cared for, not just as a potential member of the family or community, but as a socially present and responsive individual." Warren points to these social relations as justification for treating the infant as if she or he has a moral right to life stronger than that of a fetus just prior to birth. She rejects attempts to ascribe an equal right to life to fetuses by arguing that "it is impossible to treat fetuses *in utero* is if they were persons without treating women as if they were something less than persons." Given the physical location of the fetus within the body of the woman, Warren claims that pregnancy is perhaps the only case in which the legal personhood of one individual is not simply in conflict but, rather, necessarily incompatible with that of another. That is, the only way to grant equal legal rights to fetuses is to nullify a pregnant woman's basic rights to personal autonomy and physical security.

Many feminist theorists have criticized the liberal emphasis on rights, arguing that liberal rights analyses set up a dichotomy and, thus, an antagonism between autonomy and nurturance, between individual freedom and relations with others, and between independence and community. Feminists have argued that much of contemporary liberal moral theory is based on the perspective of what Seyla Benhabib has called the "generalized" conception of the self-other relations: "The standpoint of the generalized other requires us to view each and every individual as a rational being entitled to the same rights and duties we would want to ascribe to ourselves. In assuming the standpoint, we abstract from the individuality and concrete identity of the other."[6]

Benhabib contrasts the standpoint of the generalized other with that of the concrete other in which each person has a concrete history, identity, and affective-emotional constitution and in which we seek to comprehend the needs, desires, and motivations of the other. Such a standpoint replaces the moral concepts of rights and duties with those of responsibility, bonding, and sharing—traits historically perceived as feminine within the Western tradition. Some feminist ethicists, following the work of Carol Gilligan,[7] argue that a care ethic that acknowledges the voice of the concrete other is preferable to a rights ethic that embodies the standpoint of the generalized other. However, Benhabib argues "for the validity of a moral theory that allows us to recognize the dignity of the generalized other through an acknowledgement of the moral identity of the concrete other."[8]

Warren attempts to acknowledge and address this debate by arguing that rights analyses are complementary to a feminist ethics of care. Therefore, an important context for examining her analysis of the moral significance of birth is the extent to which she successfully weds the concrete with the general other. But this leads to two additional questions. Can liberal political theory survive a replacement of the liberal notion of the autonomous and self-interested individual with that of the individual in relation to others, and if so, what will such a transformed liberal political theory look like? More specifically, can liberal *feminist* thought really wed the concrete with the general other; can it do what it has failed to do in the past—recognize the fact that the "man" to whom many liberal feminists were struggling to make "woman" equal was, to a greater or lesser extent, "white man?" More problematically, can liberal *feminist* thought accommodate the reality that in this society, women are not equal to each other? Some of the causes with which liberal feminists are most identified—affirmative action, for example—are ones that play out very differently for women of color as opposed to white women. An African-American woman might not necessarily count it as progress when an employer hires a white woman instead of an African-American man; nor might a poor white woman count it as progress when a middle-class Asian American woman, not she, is admitted to medical school or law school. Unless liberal feminist thought develops its "equal rights" analysis in ways that legitimate the personal integrity of individuals who do not wish to become white in order to become socially and economically powerful, it will tend to remain a theory that favors and forwards the interests of white women far more than those of women of color.

Notes

1. See Eisenstein's discussion of Locke's "patriarchal antipatriarchalism" in her *The Radical Future of Liberal Feminism* (New York: Longman, 1981).

2. For further discussion of the question concerning the extent of Locke's patriarchalism, see Lorenne M.G. Clark, "Women and Locke: Who Owns the Apples in the Garden of Eden?" in *The Sexism of Social and Political Theory: Women and Reproduction from Plato to Nietzsche*, ed. Lorenne M.G. Clark and Lynda Lange (Toronto: University of Toronto Press, 1979), and Diana H. Coole's chapter on Locke in her *Women in Political Theory: From Ancient Misogyny to Contemporary Feminism* (Sussex: Wheatsheaf Books, 1988).

3. That is, the majority of jobs most accessible to women—domestic, child care, secretarial, service sector, teaching, nursing—are among the lowest paid professions.

4. The majority of women who work outside the home continue to be held responsible for a large percentage of child care and household labor.

5. The phrase "working mother" is doubly biased. It hides the fact that mothering is working, thereby discounting the importance of this work. And because it exists in our societal currency without its parallel—"working father"—it similarly denigrates the importance of the work of fathers within the family.

6. Seyla Benhabib, "The Generalized and the Concrete Other: The Kohlberg-Gilligan Controversy and Feminist Theory," in *Feminism as Critique: On the Politics of Gender,* ed. Seyla Benhabib and Drucilla Cornell (Minneapolis: University of Minnesota Press, 1987), p. 87.

7. Carol Gilligan, *In a Different Voice* (Harvard: Harvard University Press, 1982).

8. Benhabib, 92.

The Sexual Politics of the New Right: Understanding the "Crisis of Liberalism" for the 1980s

Zillah R. Eisenstein

This essay will explore the New Right's analysis of the "crisis of liberalism" both as an economic philosophy and as a political ideology. Its critique of liberalism, which amounts to an indictment of the welfare state, attributes this crisis to the changed relationship between the state and the family. Therefore the fundamental thrust of present New Right politics is directed at redefining this relationship. In some sense, the New Right thinks that the welfare state is responsible for undermining the traditional patriarchal family by taking over different family functions. The health, welfare, and education of individuals, it believes, should be the purview of the family. The New Right's critique of the welfare state in this way becomes closely linked to its understanding of the crisis of the family. I intend to ask whether this analysis is not a misreading of history. If, as I believe, the growth of the welfare state is as much a response to changes in family structure as it is a cause of those changes, then the New Right has wrongly identified the source of the crisis and as a result has provided us with anachronistic models of the family and the state for the 1980s.

From the perspective of the New Right, the "problem" of the family—defined as the married heterosexual couple with children, the husband working in the labor force, and the wife remaining at home to rear the children—stems from husbands' loss of patriarchal authority as their wives have been pulled into the labor force. Richard Viguerie (the major fund raiser of the New Right), Jerry Falwell (a leading evangelist and head of the "Moral Majority"), and George Gilder (the economist whom David Stockman consults and the author of *Wealth and Poverty*) argue that in order to revitalize the capitalist economy, create a moral order, and strengthen America at home and abroad, policymakers must aim to reestablish the dominance of the traditional white patriarchal family. Because black women have always worked outside the home in disproportionate numbers to white women, whether in slave society or in the free labor market, the model of the traditional patriarchal family has never accurately described their family life. Yet today with white married women's entry into the labor force the nuclear model no longer describes the majority of white families either.[1] This is why the "problem" of the family has become more pronounced and why the issue of the married wage-earning woman has now been finally brought to center stage by the New Right. In this fundamental sense the sexual politics of the New Right is implicitly antifeminist and racist: it desires to establish the model of the traditional white patriarchal family by dismantling the welfare state and by removing wage-earning married women from the labor force and returning them to the home.

The New Right's attack is directed so forcefully against married wage-earning women and "working mothers"[2] because, as I argue in *The Radical Future of Liberal Feminism*, it is these women who have the potential to transform society. The New Right correctly understands this. The reality of the wage-earning wife's double day of work uncovers the patriarchal bias of liberalism and capitalist society.[3] As these women begin to understand the sexual bias in the marketplace (where a woman earns 58 cents to the male worker's $1.00) and continue to bear the responsibilities of housework and child care as well, they begin to voice feminist demands for affirmative action programs, equal pay, pregnancy disability payments, and abortion rights. They press for the equal rights promised by liberal ideology. The New Right focuses its attack on both liberalism *and* feminism precisely because mainstream feminist demands derive from the promises of liberalism as an ideology—individual autonomy and independence, freedom of choice, equality of opportunity, and equality before the law—and because they threaten to transform patriarchy, and with it capitalism, by uncovering the "crisis of liberalism." Feminist demands uncover the truth that capitalist patriarchal society cannot deliver on its "liberal" promises of equality or even equal rights for women without destabilizing itself.

The New Right's antifeminism is projected as profamily. It seeks to build a politics around questions of family life, a position the Left has always rejected as ineffective. Now that the New Right has effectively brought questions of family life into mainstream politics—a verification of the feminist movement's early appreciation of the political nature of the family—it remains for feminists to try to use this new electoral focus on family politics for our own purposes. The issue is no longer whether one can build a family politics that crosses lines of economic class and race, but rather what kind of family politics will prevail.

Developing a policy for the family or for different forms of the family is as central to the politics of the 1980s as finding a remedy to inflation. Clearly this is the focus, as we shall see below, of the Reagan-Stockman 1981 budget. What is not clear is whether feminists, left-liberals, and leftists will be able to build a coalition around these issues, to agree in particular on the necessity of promoting a nonpatriarchal form of the family. One can only be skeptical about this possibility when one sees that Mark Green, former director to Ralph Nader's Congress Watch, still believes that "the issue of the 1980's is economic: how to generate and distribute wealth in a new era."[4] Until left-liberals and leftists recognize that New Right politics is fundamentally about the familial and sexual structuring of society, they will remain ineffective in the politics of the 1980s. And it will be feminists who will have to "fight the Right."

The New Right Versus
the "Liberal Takeover" of Government

The New Right represents a coalition of political, religious, and antifeminist groups that hope to dismantle the welfare state and reconstruct the traditional patriarchal family. The New Right's major fund raiser is Richard Viguerie, who started his mail-order company in 1965.[5] Several New Right organizations focus on election campaigns and governmental legislation: the Conservative Caucus, led by Howard Phillips (a former Nixon appointee chosen to dismantle the Office of Economic Opportunity); the Committee for the Survival of a Free Congress, led by Paul Weyrich; and the Conservative Political Action Committee, led by Terry Dolan. Key senators identified with the New Right are Orrin Hatch of Utah, Paul Laxalt of Nevada, Jesse Helms of North Carolina, and James McClure of Idaho. Another major segment of the New Right, the "Electronic Church," is dominated by the Evangelical Right, headed by Moral Majority and Jerry Falwell. The third sector of the New Right comprises the antifeminist "pro-life," "profamily" groups led by Phyllis Schlafly's Eagle Forum and Connie Marshner's Library Court. Although these three sectors of the New Right intersect and function as a coalition, this is not to say that they form one cohesive group, for they do not.

According to Viguerie's book *The New Right: We're Ready to Lead,* the New Right's goal is to organize the conservative middle-class majority in America: citizens concerned about high taxes and inflation; small businessmen angry at government control; born-again Christians disturbed about sex in television and movies; parents opposed to forced busing; supporters of the "right to life" who are against the federal funding of abortion; middle-class Americans tired of Big Government, Big Business, Big Labor, and Big Education; prodefense citizens; and those who believe America has *not* had her day and does not need to tighten her belt.[6]

Ultimately this list of concerns can be summarized as a criticism of what the New Right terms the "liberal takeover" of government that started with the election of Franklin D. Roosevelt in 1932.[7] According to Viguerie and the New Right, the "liberals" have made the United States a second-rate military power; given away the Panama Canal; created the massive welfare state; lost Iran, Afghanistan, Vietnam, Laos, and Cambodia; crippled the FBI and CIA; encouraged American women to feel like failures if they want to be wives and mothers; and fought for preferential quotas for blacks and women.[8] They identify Adlai Stevenson, Walter Reuther, George Meany, Martin Luther King, Nelson Rockefeller, Hubert Humphrey, and Robert Kennedy as the leaders responsible for the liberal takeover of government. They identify the National Organization for Women, Planned Parenthood, Gay Rights National Lobby, National Abortion Rights Action League, and Women Strike for Peace as the leading single-issue political groups of the "liberal establishment" that are responsible for the liberal takeover of the family. And they identify Andrew Young, William Sloane Coffin, Martin Luther King, and Father Robert Drinan as the religious leaders of the liberal establishment.[9] The New Right has therefore developed its politics to counter the liberal takeover of the state, the family, and the church.

Neoconservatism and the Crisis of Liberalism

In order to understand fully present-day New Right politics one must place those politics within the neoconservative stance of the state today, which is a carry-over from the Carter administration. The elitism of neoconservatives and the pseudopopulism of the New Right are very different ideologically, appealing to different constituencies. However, both these groups believe liberalism is in crisis and share a basic indictment of the welfare state. As we shall see, the New Right utilizes the neoconservative critique of the welfare state but centers this problem in the crisis of the traditional patriarchal family. In the end, neoconservatives want to make the welfare state a conservative one, whereas the New Right says it seeks to dismantle it altogether.

Leading neoconservatives today—like Daniel Bell, Irving Kristol, Norman Podhoretz, Nathan Glazer, Edward Banfield, James Q. Wilson, and Daniel Moynihan—reject the "Great Society" version of the welfare state because they think it has created what they term the "excesses of democracy."[10] They criticize the present welfare state for trying to create equality of conditions rather than equality of opportunity, for destroying the difference between liberty and egalitarianism. Liberty is the freedom one should have to run the face of life.[11] But there can be no guarantee that each competitor in the race should or will win. A truly liberal society allows everyone to compete, but a race in and of itself requires winners and losers. According to the neoconservatives, the problem is that everyone today claims the right to win. This has led people (particularly women and blacks) not only to expect equality of opportunity, but to expect equality of outcomes or conditions. The neoconservative believes these expectations destroy true liberty—which is about freedom, not equality. Daniel Bell articulates this position when he states, "One has to distinguish between treating people equally and making them equal."[12]

This is why neoconservatives are so critical of affirmative action programs that supposedly predetermine the outcome of a competition. The "excess of democracy" implies that the promises of liberal society have been carried too far; liberty has been redefined as equality. Peoples' desires become insatiable because they expect, and as a result demand, too much from the government. According to the neoconservative analysis, the welfare state is in crisis because it cannot and will never be able to satisfy the demand for equality, which only breeds more demands for greater equality. Hence, the neoconservative believes that only when expectations are lowered will government be able to satisfy the people again.[13] In other words, if people expect less of government, government will be able to perform better. This of course has a certain logic because the welfare state cannot create an egalitarian society and protect capitalist patriarchy at the same time. However, I would argue that the welfare state has never attempted to create equality of conditions and that the crisis of liberalism reflects the incapacity of the welfare state to create even equality of opportunity for most white and black women and black men.

The major attack on the welfare state is leveled against what Irving Kristol calls the "new class": "scientists, lawyers, city planners, social workers, educators, criminologists, sociologists, [and] public health doctors" who work in the expanding public sector of the welfare state as "regulatory officials." Kristol sees this class as the people "whom liberal capitalism has sent to college in order to help manage its affluent, highly technological, mildly paternalistic, 'post-industrial society.'"[14]

According to Kristol, the welfare state does not just support the nonworking population, it actually supports the "middle-class professionals who attend to the needs of the nonworking population (teachers, social workers, lawyers, doctors, dieticians, civil servants of all descriptions)."[15] A review of the Reagan 1981 budget cuts clearly shows that they are aimed as much against the members of this supposed new class as they are aimed against the working and nonworking poor.

It is important to note that Kristol does not want to do away with the welfare state, but rather seeks to create a conservative welfare state based on the American values of self-reliance and individual liberty: "Wherever possible, people should be allowed to keep their own money—rather than having it transferred (via taxes) to the state—on condition that they put it to certain defined uses."[16] He wants to reconcile the purposes of the welfare state with the maximum amount of individual independence and the least amount of bureaucratic coercion.

Both Daniel Bell and Kristol recognize that with liberalism in crisis, capitalism needs a new moral vision. Kristol argues that "the enemy of liberal capitalism today is not so much socialism as nihilism. Only liberal capitalism doesn't see nihilism as an enemy, but rather as just another splendid business opportunity."[17] Bell contends that the crisis of liberalism lies in the cultural contradiction of capitalism, which reflects "the disjunction between the kind of organization and the norms demanded in the economic realm, and the norms of self-realization that are now central in the culture." Hedonism, pleasure as a way of life, has replaced the protestant ethic and the puritan temper of "sobriety, frugality, sexual restraint, and a forbidding attitude toward life."[18] Bell criticizes the consumer mentality of immediate gratification in capitalism that corrupts society with rampant individualism and leaves little sense of community or public purpose.

Neoconservatives must recognize that the elitist liberalism they espouse will not work any better than the supposed egalitarian liberalism they so fear. Liberal democracy, with its egalitarian promises, functioned well as an ideology for competitive capitalism, but it functions less well for advanced monopoly capitalism. Once one is forced to emphasize the elitist bias of liberalism—liberty rather than equality, equality of opportunity and not egalitarianism—the very ideological force of liberalism is undermined. In actuality liberalism has always been elitist. But once one seeks to protect and further articulate liberalism's elitist (economic, sexual, racial) nature rather than its democratic qualities, one no longer has an ideology that is both liberal *and* democratic. Kristol might learn from himself when he criticizes a politics of nostalgia: "There is no more chance today of returning to a society of 'free enterprise' and enfeebled government than there was, in the sixteenth century, of returning to a Rome-centered Christendom. The world and the people in it have changed. One may regret this fact; nostalgia is always permissible. But the politics of nostalgia is always self-destructive."[19] In the end, the neoconservative criticism of the welfare state is a criticism of the democratic aspects of liberalism and the potential of its ideology to promise egalitarianism. The neoconservatives seek to protect liberalism (and with it capitalist patriarchy) by replacing the democratic potential of its ideology with authoritarianism. Doing so, they attack liberal democracy itself.

The New Right, Liberalism, and the Welfare State

The New Right's indictment, on the other hand, reduces liberalism to the policies, programs, and elected officials of the welfare state. In other words, the New Right's analysis of the "crisis of liberalism" does not extend to the neoconservative critique of liberalism itself as an ideology. Instead, the New Right continues to utilize much of the ideology of liberalism in its rhetoric (which has often been described as populist) at the same time that it supposedly rejects liberalism.

Much of the New Right's ideology is liberal in that it adopts the values of individualism and equality of opportunity. Viguerie documents this point when he argues that he accepts the vision of the American dream but not the welfare state's role in trying to bring it about for individuals. Phyllis Schlafly embodies the liberal individualist spirit perfectly in the attitudes underlining her anti-ERA position: "If you're willing to work hard, there's no barrier you can't jump. ... I've achieved my goals in life and I did it without sex-neutral laws."[20] Liberal ideology can also be seen in the New Right's "Right to Work Campaign," built on the argument that the individual should have the right to choose whether or not to join a union. This same liberal issue—an individual's right to choose—presents problems for the New Right's antiabortion campaign, which denies this individual right of choice to the woman. One can also see the deference to liberal ideology when President Reagan and Phyllis Schlafly carefully distinguish between their support for the equal rights of women— which recognizes the liberal individualist rights of a woman—and their lack of support for the Equal Rights Amendment, which they argue encourages state intervention into an individual's private life. One can, obviously, reject the welfare state and still be committed to liberal values, as the New Right is.

The New Right uses liberal ideology selectively and inconsistently, not recognizing how the ideology necessitates the welfare state, whereas neoconservatives argue that the ideology itself needs redefinition. Hence, the New Right is caught in the same dilemma that created the welfare state in the first place: an ideology of equal opportunity and individual freedom coupled with a structural reality of economic, sexual, and racial inequality. By dismantling the welfare state the New Right will do nothing about the needs that instigated this form of the state in the first place.

Instead of constructing a new vision of the welfare state, the New Right seeks to construct a society built around the traditional self-sufficient patriarchal family. By doing so it hopes to establish the autonomy of the family from the state. In order to do this the family must be relieved of its heavy tax burden *and* inflation. This will then release the married woman from work in the labor force. "Federal spending eats into the family's income, forcing mothers to go to work to pay for food, clothing, shelter and other family basics."[21] The New Right argument is this: Welfare state expenditures have raised taxes and added to inflation, pulling the married woman into the labor force and thereby destroying the fabric of the patriarchal family and hence the moral order of society.

By reasserting the power of the family against the state, the New Right more accurately intends to reestablish the power of the father. According to Jerry Falwell in *Listen America,* government has developed at the expense of the father's authority: "The progression of big government is amazing. A father's authority was lost first to the village, then to the city, next to the State, and finally to the empire."[22] Falwell is also angry and critical of the inflationary economy because it has undermined the father's authority. He states that children should have the right "to have the love of a mother and a father who understand their different roles and fulfill their different responsibilities. ... To live in an economic system that makes it possible for husbands to support their wives as full time mothers in the home and that enables families to survive on one income instead of two."[23] He wants to create a healthy economy and limit inflation in order to establish the single-wage-earner family. "The family is the fundamental building block and the basic unit of our society, and its continued health is a prerequisite for a healthy and prosperous nation. No nation has ever been stronger than the families within her."[24] Thus Falwell's fight against inflation is also a fight to reestablish the father's authority and to put women back in the home.

One sees this argument further developed in George Gilder's *Wealth and Poverty,* the book that Reagan has distributed to members of his cabinet. According to Gilder, the economy has become sluggish because the welfare state has created an imbalance between security (investment) and risk by creating an insurance plan for joblessness, disability, and indigent old age. This reduces work incentives, cuts American productivity, and in the end perpetuates poverty.[25] If the welfare state perpetuates poverty, Gilder sees the deterioration of family life as an apparent cause. Welfare benefits destroy the role of the father: "He can no longer feel manly in his own home." In welfare culture, money becomes not something earned by men, "but a right conferred on women by the state." The male's role is undermined, and with it the moving force for upward mobility "has been cuckolded by the compassionate state."[26] Welfare erodes both the work ethic and family life and thus keeps poor people poor; unemployment compensation only promotes unemployment; Aid for Families with Dependent Children (AFDC) only makes families dependent and fatherless.[27] According to Gilder, "the only dependable route from poverty is always work, family, and faith," not the welfare state.[28]

A principle of upward mobility for Gilder is the maintenance of monogamous marriage and the family. Disruption of family life creates disruption in the economy because men need to direct their sexual energies toward the economy, and they only do so when they are connected to family duty. Marriage creates the sense of responsibility men need: "A married man ... is spurred by the claims of family to channel his otherwise disruptive male aggressions into his performance as a provider for wife and children." This is not true for women, however, "Few women with children make earning money the top priority in their lives," whereas men's commitment to children and to this sense of future spurs them to new heights. "These sexual differences alone ... dictate that the first priority of any serious program against poverty is to strengthen the male role in poor families" and to maintain it in middle- and upper-class families.[29]

One can discern from Gilder's discussion of the poor family that the model of the successful family is one in which only the male earns wages. Woman's involvement in the labor force has challenged man's position of authority in the family, reduced his productivity at work, and thereby "caused a simultaneous expansion of the work force and a decline in productivity growth."[30] As a result, the husband's drive to succeed in his career has been deterred because "two half-hearted participants in the labor force can do better than one who is competing aggressively for the relatively few jobs in the upper echelons."[31] In the end Gilder believes that it is *familial anarchy,* not capitalism, that causes poverty by creating a nonproductive economy.[32] Women's participation in the labor force promotes family dissolution either by facilitating divorce or by challenging the patriarchal authority necessary to a "productive" economy. This leads to Gilder's indictment of the welfare state, which has only created the higher taxes and inflation that have pulled the married woman into the work force.[33] One can stabilize the family by reasserting the authority of the father in the family and by removing women from the wage labor force, and this can be done if taxes and inflation are reduced.

The antifeminism and racism of the New Right operate on two levels here. First, the presentation of the traditional patriarchal family as the desired model denies the realities of the black family *and* of the married wage-earning woman in both the black and white family. It is interesting to note that while the neoconservatives want to restructure the "new class" in their revision of the welfare state, members of the New Right have targeted wage-earning women to be the agents of the family's social services once they are returned to the home. Thus the attack on the welfare state becomes antifeminist and not merely anti–"new class." Second, the indictment of the welfare state and its "Great Society" programs is being used to turn back whatever gains have been made by black men and women and white women. The move against welfare state administrators is also racist in that many members of the new class who are currently being "declassed" and purged from government are black. Dismantling the welfare state is not only intended to redirect surplus into the private sector in a period of declining United States industrial power, but it is also supposed to make clear that equality of opportunity for minorities, as well as women, is a privilege reserved for times of plenty.[34]

According to Viguerie, Falwell, and Gilder, married women have entered the labor force because of the high taxes and inflation caused by the continued growth of the welfare state. And married women's entrance into the labor force has eroded the traditional (white) patriarchal family structure necessary to the moral fabric of society and economic vitality. There is, however, another analysis to be considered: the argument that the welfare state is as much a consequence of changes in the economy and in the family (for example, women's entrance into the labor force, new sexual mores, and higher divorce rates) as it is a causal factor. If this is true, then one cannot restabilize the traditional (white) patriarchal family by dismantling the welfare state, because the welfare state developed out of the dissolution of the traditional patriarchal family. The New Right's vision of the state and its vision of the family, then, are both outmoded forms.

Capitalist Patriarchy and the Married Wage-Earning Woman

The United States is as patriarchal as it is capitalist. This means that the politics of society is as self-consciously directed to maintaining the hierarchical male-dominated sexual system as to upholding the economic class structure. The forms of order and control in both systems remain mutually supportive until changes in one system begin to erode the hierarchical basis of the other. For example, such erosion in the patriarchal system began to occur when structural changes in the marketplace, changes in the wage structure, and inflation required white married women to enter the labor force.

When I say that there have been structural changes in the economic marketplace, I mean that the service and retail trade sectors of the economy have grown at the expense of the industrial sector. According to Emma Rothschild, 43 percent of all Americans employed in the private nonagricultural part of the economy in 1979 worked in services and retail trade.[35] From 1973 to 1979 the major growth sectors of the economy, which supplied more than 40 percent of the new private jobs, were eating and drinking fast-food places, business services (personnel supply services and data processing), and health services (including private hospitals and nursing homes). These new jobs have been the primary source of employment for married women. Some of the women in this service sector supplement their husbands' earnings, but many are single parents. Either way, their labor force participation is essential to maintaining their families *and* this sector of the economy.

Women accounted for 41 percent of all wage earners in 1979: 31 percent of all manufacturing workers, 56 percent of all employees in eating and drinking places, 43 percent in all business services, 81 percent in all health services.[36] "Waiting on tables, defrosting frozen hamburgers, rendering services to buildings, looking after the old and the ill, is 'women's work.'"[37] And this work is low hour and low pay work. Wages in the private service sector averaged $9,853 in 1979 (measured in 1972 dollars); in the industrial sector they averaged $21,433.[38] In nursing and personal service work, in which 89 percent of the workers are women, the average wage in 1979 was $3.87 per hour compared to the average hourly wage of $16.16 in the entire private economy.[39] Most private service sector jobs are also dead ends that offer no possible advancement to a supervisory level; for example, 92 percent of the jobs in eating and drinking places are nonsupervisory. "The United States, in sum, is moving toward a structure of employment ever more dominated by jobs that are badly paid, unchanging, and unproductive."[40]

But what is really interesting about the private service sector is that its growth reflects the market's response to changes in the family, as well as changes in the relation between the state and the family. Increases in state welfare services, nursing homes, and fast-food restaurants all reflect new trends in family life, particularly the changes in woman's place within the family *and* within the market. Work once done in the home has been increasingly shifted to the market, and particular responsibilities of the family have been shifted to the state. We shall see, however, that Reagan's plan is to redirect these shifts. How can he do this, given the present realities of the family, the economy, and the intersection of the welfare state and the economy? And *why* do he and the New Right want to redirect the relationship between the state and the family? I think it is because they believe this will ultimately remove married women from the labor force.

The capitalist need for women workers has developed along with the not always successful attempt to protect the system of patriarchal hierarchy through the sexual segregation of the labor force. Women have been relegated to the low-productivity sector of the market, and their pay is unequal to men's even when the work is of the same or of comparable worth. Some women may accept the patriarchal organization of their family life, considering it "natural" that women cook the meals or do the laundry (although many do not), but I have yet to hear one of the secretaries in my office say that she does not have the right to earn the same as a man. Women as workers come to expect equal treatment in the market whether they expect it in their familial relations or not. Relations at home are supposedly regulated by love and devotion; the wage regulates woman's relations at the workplace. Her boss *is not* her husband. In other words, even though capitalism has reproduced a patriarchal structure within the market, the liberal ideology of the bourgeois marketplace—equality of opportunity, equality before the law, individual aggressiveness and independence—remains. As the working woman internalizes and applies these values to herself as she operates within the market's patriarchal structure, she develops a consciousness critical of her dead-ended work life. In the market, one's sex is supposed to be irrelevant. People are supposedly individuals, not members of a sexual class. Hard work is supposed to be rewarded. To the extent that the married wage-earning woman accepts these values when she enters the market, she becomes a contradiction in terms. As a worker she is supposedly an individual, and as a married woman she is a member of a sexual class. Her sexual class identity is highlighted in the market specifically because it is not supposed to matter there.

This highlighting of woman's differentiation from men in the market begins to create a consciousness one can term feminist. We are back to the point that because the majority of married women work in the labor force today and expect equality—even if it is only equality in the workplace—the promises of liberalism are being challenged. The New Right's objection is not merely that equalizing pay between men and women would cost billions of collars, although the cost to the capitalist or profit maintenance is always at issue. More important is the fact that establishing equality in the workplace would erode a major form of patriarchal control presently maintained in the market as much as it is in the family and the home.

Here then is the contradiction: advanced capitalism, because of structural changes and inflation, has required married women to enter the labor force. Although the structure of the capitalist market is patriarchal, its ideology is definitely liberal. Married wage-earning women have the potential to perceive the conflict between liberalism as an ideology about equality and the sexual inequality of patriarchy as a structural requisite of the capitalist market. In their discontent, however limited, they can begin to recognize and reject this patriarchal structuring of opportunities in the market. When you put this awareness together with a married woman's double day of work—the work of her home and children as well as her outside job—the *possibilities* for feminist consciousness increase. The New Right attack on married wage-earning women lies in this reality: in demanding equality before the law and in wages, wage-earning women have begun to challenge the patriarchal organization of the market. Therein lies the crisis for liberalism: an ideology of (liberal) equality and a contradictory reality of patriarchal inequality is being uncovered by the married wage-earning woman.

The New Right's attack on married wage-earning women also reflects women's greater unification as a sexual class. First of all, white married women have joined black married women in the labor force. Although racial divisions still exist, black and white women share the world of the market more than ever before, and their attitudes reflect this. In 1972 a Harris poll for Virginia Slims cigarettes found that black women outscored white women 62 to 45 percent in support of efforts to change the status of women and 67 to 35 percent in sympathy with women's liberation groups.[41]

Second, married middle-class *and* working-class women find themselves sharing the service sector of the economy. A majority of wage-earning women find themselves in the low paying service and clerical fields, with only a small minority of women occupying professional jobs. The notion that feminism or feminist consciousness is limited to the white middle-class woman has never been more untrue than it is today. As Philip S. Foner has documented so well in *Women and the American Labor Movement,* working-class wage-earning women often define themselves as feminists.[42] The redefinition of women's lives, given the increasing number of women in the labor force, has actually made it necessary for feminism to address the needs of wage-earning women. And the reality of married wage-earning women cuts through traditional economic class lines.

In actuality, the increasing number of poor in our country are women. For unmarried women—divorced, separated, lesbian, never married, widowed—economic class and sexual class seem to merge under advanced capitalism. One might argue that these women are increasingly visible as an economic class through the "feminization of poverty." Three out of every five persons with incomes below the poverty level are women. Two out of every three older persons living in poverty are women. Female-headed families with no husband present comprise only 15 percent of all families but 48 percent of all poverty-level families. The median income of all women aged fourteen and above is well below half that of their male counterparts.[43] This reality is accentuated when a woman's economic inequality and dependence are not mediated through a husband, and her family's needs increasingly have to be met by the state. Economic class differences still exist among women, particularly when one focuses on both their familial realities as well as their work in the labor force. The point is that the economic class reality of women's lives is very much in flux today because family forms are themselves in flux. Serious rethinking and study remain to be done in this area, given the changing nature of the family and the impact this has on understanding women's economic class.

Changes in the structure of the economy and in the family both reflect and create changes in the system of capitalist patriarchy. Although the state seeks to develop policy that protects the totality of capitalist patriarchy, I am arguing that present conflicts have developed between capitalism and patriarchy that will ultimately undermine the future of liberalism and the welfare state. The question is whether the New Right and the neoconservatives can use these conflicts to indict liberalism and create a "friendly fascism"[44] or whether feminists and leftists can develop a politics out of these conflicts that will lead to a more democratic and feminist state. In order for feminists and leftists to achieve this end, mainstream feminism will have to deal more self-consciously with the capitalist expression of patriarchy, and left-liberals and leftists will have to recognize the patriarchal structure of capitalism.

Although capitalism and patriarchy function as a mutually dependent totality,[45] they also operate as differentiated and conflictual systems. As such they remain two systems that are *relatively* autonomous from each other,[46] never totally separate today and yet always differentiated in purpose. Sexual life, which is what patriarchy ultimately must regulate, and economic life, which capitalism must ultimately regulate, cannot be conflated into one system; yet at present they are not separate, dual systems.[47] They are differentiated, relatively autonomous, and dialectically related. If they were not separate *and* connected to each other, one would not face the irreconcilable conflict of the married wage-earning woman today.

Reagan Administration Policies on the Family and the Welfare State

Although the New Right analysis of the family appears to dominate the state today, there is an earlier view of family life that does not consider state involvement as an unwanted intrusion. The 1978 report of the commission on Families and Public Policies in the United States compiled during Carter's term argues that social services need to be upgraded for the family, that income maintenance programs are needed given the economic needs of families, and that a pluralistic view of family life should structure policymaking.[48] In this view, state involvement in the family is seen as necessary to enable the family to fulfill its responsibilities.

The commission specifically recommended a national employment policy that would legally enforce one's right to a job; the greater use of flextime, shared work, and other arrangements for full-time jobs; the support of part-time work arrangements to make possible the care of children and the elderly; and increased career counseling with special emphasis on programs for women.[49] These policy guidelines clearly recognize the changing nature of the family, particularly in relation to the two-wage-earner family.

Recent legislation introduced by David Durenberger, Mark Hatfield, and Bob Packwood and endorsed by Patrick Moynihan attempts to follow through on some of these recommendations related to the two-wage-earner family. Their Economic Equity Act (S. 888) tries to counter "policies in the public and private sector that are completely at odds with work patterns determined by the realities of women's dual wage-earning and parenting" by proposing tax credits to employers who hire women entering the work force after divorce or death of a spouse, equal tax status for heads of households and for married couples, employer-sponsored child care that would be provided as a tax-free fringe benefit similar to health insurance, and tax credits to offset the cost of child care.

Both the Commission Report of 1978 and the Economic Equity Act recognize the changing nature of the family and the unresolved conflicts between capitalism and patriarchy that these changes embody. Although this proposed legislation, in and of itself, cannot resolve the contradictions in the married wage-earning woman's life, it can begin to initiate necessary policy changes. As such, it is a beginning in the process of utilizing liberal feminist reforms to instigate progressive change. By virtue of the nature of the problem—the irresolvable conflict between liberalism and patriarchal society—one must move beyond such legislation. But it is through the struggle to pass such legislation that one builds a consciousness of the need for more progressive changes.

The importance of liberal feminist legislation becomes clear when it is compared to policy proposals of the New Right that seek to enforce the model of the traditional male-headed household. The Laxalt-Jepsen Family Protection Act, as one example of New Right legislation, recommends that textbooks belittling the traditional role of women in society not be purchased with federal money; that tax exemptions of $1,000 be extended to households with dependents over the age of sixty-five; that a wage earner's contributions to a savings account for his nonworking spouse be tax deductible, up to $1,500 per year; that the current marriage tax penalizing married couples with two incomes be eliminated; that legal services corporation money be denied for abortions, school desegregation, divorce, or homosexual rights litigation.

The concerns of the Family Protection Act are spelled out even more starkly in $41.4 billion Reagan-Stockman budget cuts, which are primarily in the area of social services. One-third of the budget reduction comes from just two programs: health and income security. These programs specifically address the poor. And it is women who are the poor today.

Budget cuts are proposed in medicaid, food stamps, child nutrition, fuel assistance, and Aid to Families of Dependent Children. The family is supposed to be the social unit now responsible for all these aspects of health and welfare. Medicaid, a joint federal and state program, was designed to provide medical assistance to low-income persons who cannot afford medical care. In 1979, 61 percent of all medicaid recipients, 11 million people, were women. Thirty-four percent of all medicaid recipients were under the age of fifteen. Thirty-six percent of all households covered by medicaid were headed by females with no spouse present. And about 40 percent of all medicaid expenditures went for nursing-home care.[50] The cuts in medicaid will hit women and children directly, specifically those women heading households. The cuts will also make nursing-home care inaccessible to many, and therefore the care of the aged will be forced back onto women in the family.

Food stamps subsidize food purchases for households that have a net income below the poverty level and assets of less than $1,500. Some 2–3 million people (400,000–600,000 families) may be dropped from food stamp rolls if the proposals are enacted. Six out of ten food stamp households are headed by women.

Child nutrition programs include the national school lunch program, the breakfast program, the special milk program, the child care and summer feeding program, and the special nutrition program. As many as 700,000 women may be eliminated from the "Women, Infant and Child" (WIC) program that provides food packages to pregnant low-income women, infants, and children.[51]

Aid to Families of Dependent Children provides cash benefits to needy families with dependent children. Over 90 percent of the AFDC recipients are women and their children. Over 80 percent of all single-parent households are headed by women, and one-third of these households are in poverty. According to administration estimates, the cutbacks and changes in AFDC would deny benefits to 400,000 families and would reduce benefits to 250,000. Presumably persons who are forced off AFDC rolls will enter the work force, even though 40 percent of all poverty-level women heading families alone already had some work experience in 1979.[52] These are precisely the women who need training in order to get jobs, and the Comprehensive Employment and Training Act (CETA) program, designed for this purpose, is also being cut.

These budget cuts take on even more significance when one sees that the fastest-growing form of the family today is the single-parent woman-headed family. Whereas the total number of families increased by 12 percent between 1970 and 1979, the number maintained by female householders grew by 51 percent.[53] The median income in 1978 of families maintained by a woman was $8,540, or slightly less than one-half (48 percent) of the $17,640 median income of families overall.[54] In 1977, 7.7 million families were headed by women. Almost one female-headed family in three is poor; about one in eighteen families headed by a man is poor.[55]

Two points stand out clearly. The two-wage-earner family has become the most common family form in the society. Fifty-seven percent of two-parent families today have two wage earners.[56] The single-parent woman-headed family is now as common as the traditional patriarchal family. The former presently accounts for 15 percent of the families today, whereas the latter comprises 14 percent.[57] Neither the two-wage-earner family nor the single-parent female-headed family fits the model of the "profamily" policy of the New Right. The budget cuts and their attack on the welfare state presume to protect the traditional patriarchal family from intrusion of the state. But by protecting this form of the family, it creates hardship for other forms of the American family that are as common.

In essence, then, the Reagan-Stockman budget tries to restabilize patriarchy as much as it tries to fight inflation and stabilize capitalism. The government's cutbacks in the social services budget while the military budget increases are an attempt to redefine the responsibilities and purview of the state. Individuals and hence the family are supposed to be responsible for their health, education, and welfare. The state will be responsible for defense. Social services have been labeled the "excesses of democracy" and therefore must be curtailed. Neoconservatives want people to understand that the state cannot and should not create equality of conditions for them. And the New Right hopes to reestablish the power of the father in the family by asserting the role and purposes of the family *against* the state.

But let us examine these assumptions for a moment. Neoconservatives and the New Right believe that state intervention must be decreased in order to limit public expectations *and* inflation. But only state intervention in the social service realm is being cut. State spending in the military realm will be increased. As a matter of fact, Reagan initially intended to increase the defense budget from 12.4 percent to 14.6

percent by 1982. Reagan's newest budget proposal to reduce military spending by $2 billion by 1982 only reduces the initial buildup by 1 percent. These cuts will not jeopardize the overall goal of increased military spending at all. According to Lester Thurow, Reagan's military buildup will be the largest in American history, three times as large as the one that took place during the Vietnam War.[58] At the same time, Reagan proposes to cut taxes 30 percent. It is also important to remember that Johnson's refusal to raise taxes to pay for the Vietnam War was largely responsible for the increased inflation rate in this country. This time around, however, we will be adding to an inflation rate of 11 percent, whereas Johnson began the Vietnam War with around a 2 percent inflation rate.[59]

If Thurow's analysis is correct, the present cuts in social services *and* taxes will not limit inflation but rather increase it. In terms of the New Right's own analysis of inflation's impact on the family, this will further increase the burdens on married wage-earning women and families, particularly on the families of the working and nonworking poor. It may even increase the number of nonworking poor. In the end, the New Right's attack on the welfare state appears contradictory at best. First, it criticizes state expenditures only in the social service realm, not in the military and defense sector. Second, its support for cuts in the social service budget may only increase the need for social services, particularly for the working poor. Last, the demand to get government "off our backs" is completely contradicted by its profamily legislation. Basically, when the New Right argues against state intervention in the family, it is criticizing economic aid to the family. It actively supports state involvement in legislating sexual matters like abortion and teenage pregnancy counseling, in limiting venereal disease programs, and in curtailing sex education. The Family Protection Act and the "Human Life" Bill are two cases in point of such legislation.

This contradiction in New Right policy between a noninterventionist state (cutting social services) and an interventionist state (legislating family morality) poses serious problems for its profamily program[60] and has slowed enactment of much of its legislation. First of all, 72 percent of the American public reject the idea of a human life bill that would consider the fetus a person and make abortion and some forms of birth control illegal.[61] A majority of the American public does not believe that this issue should be regulated by government or that anyone but the woman and her doctor should decide whether she should have an abortion or not. Second, to the extent that a majority of Americans do not live in the family form that will benefit from the New Right's profamily policies, the New Right will have difficulty enacting its legislation, if a politics rooted in the other family forms can be articulated and politically mobilized.

The welfare state has its problems, given its own contradictory nature. Irving Howe has defined at least two functions of the welfare state: "It steps in to modulate the excesses of the economy, helping to create rationality and order, and thereby to save capitalism from its own tendency to destruction. And it steps in to provide humanizing reforms, as a response to insurgent groups and communities."[62] The problem, however, is not the welfare state, although that is a problem. The problem is rather the kind of society we live in, which is both patriarchal and capitalist, which would return individuals to self-reliance while maintaining structural barriers related to economic, racial, and sexual class that limit and curtail the individual. It is up to feminists of all political persuasions, left-liberals, and leftists to shift the critique from the welfare state to the patriarchal society that creates it. As feminists we need to marshal the liberal demands for individual self-determination, freedom of choice, individual autonomy, and equality before the law to indict capitalist patriarchal society. This use of liberal ideology by feminists will permit us to direct the public's consciousness to a critique of capitalist patriarchy, not merely of the welfare state.

The New Right assault is aimed against feminism precisely because it is women's liberal feminist consciousness about their rights to equality that is the major radicalizing force of the 1980s. Liberalism is in crisis today not merely because the welfare state is in crisis as the New Right believes, or because liberalism contains cultural contradictions as the neoconservatives argue, or because capitalism itself is in crisis, as Marxists and left-liberals contend. The "crisis of liberalism" is a result of the conflict between the traditional white patriarchal family, advanced capitalism, and the ideology of liberalism. The married wage-earning woman, black and white, and the potential of her feminist consciousness demonstrates this reality. Hence the New Right assault against her and the feminist movement in general.

Notes

I wish to thank Beau Grosscup and Rosalind Petchesky for their reading and helpful suggestions on earlier drafts of this article.

1. The criticism of female wage earners' effect on family life first emerged in Patrick Moynihan's 1965 report "The Negro Family, the Case for National Action," in *The Moynihan Report and the Politics of Controversy,* ed. Lee Rainwater and William Yancey (Cambridge, Mass.: MIT Press, 1967), pp. 39–124. Moynihan, using the model of the traditional (white) patriarchal family, argued that the deterioration of the Negro family was in large part due to the emasculation of the black male by his female counterpart who was working in the labor force and/or heading a household. Moynihan, believing that "the very essence of the male animal, from the bantam rooster to the four-star general, is to strut" (p. 62), thought that the challenges to the black male's authority by black women made a stable family relationship impossible.

2. The New Right's attack on the married woman wage-earner is at one and the same time a criticism of what it terms the "working mother."

3. See Zillah R. Eisenstein, *The Radical Future of Liberal Feminism* (New York: Longman, Inc., 1981), for a fuller accounting of this point.

4. Mark Green, "The Progressive Alternative to Cowboy Capitalism," *Village Voice* (March 18–24, 1981), p. 10. One also remains skeptical about this possibility given the Left's analysis of family life provided by Christopher Lasch in *Haven in a Heartless World* (New York: Basic Books, 1977) and his failure to recognize feminism as a progressive political force for the 1980s (see his "Democracy and the Crisis of Confidence," *Democracy* 1, no. 1 [January 1981]: 25–40). The denial of the importance of the feminist movement in guiding, or at least participating in, a progressive coalition is evident in several leftist or left-liberal journals. For example, neither of the first two issues of *Democracy,* the new journal which was founded to address the present antidemocratic tendencies in the United States, has discussed feminism's role in fighting antidemocratic forces. Also see *Radical America, Facing Reaction,* vol. 15, nos. 1–2 (Spring 1981), especially Barbara Ehrenreich's "The Women's Movements: Feminist and Anti-Feminist" (pp. 93–104), which denies the viability of the feminist movement in fighting the right-wing reaction. See the interesting discussion by Stacey Oliker, "Abortion and the Left: The Limits of Pro-Family Politics," *Socialist Review* 11, no. 2 (March–April 1981): 71–96, about the Left's wavering support for reproductive rights. Also see Michael Walzer, *Radical Principles— Reflections of an Unreconstructed Democrat* (New York: Basic Books, 1980), for an example of a leftist analysis of the challenges to liberalism to the exclusion of feminism.

5. Viguerie started his mail-order company with lists made up of contributors (of $50 or more) to the Goldwater campaign. According to Viguerie, the New Right became politically mobilized in 1974 when Ford chose Rockefeller for vice-president because it identified Rockefeller with the "liberal" establishment of the eastern Trilateral Commission. See Richard Viguerie, *The New Right: We're Ready to Lead* (Falls Church, Va.: Viguerie Co., 1980).

6. Ibid., pp. 15–16. For interesting discussions of New Right politics, see Alan Crawford, *Thunder on the Right* (New York: Pantheon Press, 1980); William Hunter, *The New Right: A Growing Force in State Politics* (Washington, D.C.: Conference on Alternative State and Local Policies and Center to Protect Worker's Rights, 1980); and Thomas McIntyre and John Obert, *The Fear Brokers* (New York: Pilgrim Press, 1979).

7. Viguerie identifies the major victories of the "liberal" establishment as (1) Johnson's Elementary and Secondary Education Act of 1965, which shifted decision-making power from parents and local school boards to teacher unions and state and federal bureaucracies; (2) the congressional endorsement of the ERA in 1972; (3) the 1973 decision of the Supreme Court to make abortion legal; (4) the creation of the Department of Education in 1979, which extended federal control over education (*The New Right*, p. 202).

8. Ibid., pp. 5, 9.

9. Ibid., p. 105. Viguerie argues that the New Right's use of religion in politics is nothing new because the National Council of Churches has always taken political stands. It advocated admission of Red China to the United Nations as early as 1958, spoke out against prayer in public schools and against the Vietnam War, and endorsed the need for a guaranteed national income.

10. Peter Steinfels, *The Neoconservatives: The Men Who Are Changing America's Politics* (New York: Simon & Schuster, 1979), p. 51.

11. See Isaac Kramnick, "Religion and Radicalism: English Political Theory in the Age of Revolution," *Political Theory* 5, no. 4 (November 1977): 505–34, for an excellent discussion of equality of opportunity in bourgeois thought. Also see Moynihan, "The Negro Family," for an example of the neoconservative distinction between liberty and equality.

12. Daniel Bell, *The Cultural Contradictions of Capitalism* (New York: Basic Books, 1976), p. 260.

13. See Nathan Glazer and Irving Kristol, eds., *The American Commonwealth* (New York: Basic Books, 1976), esp. Samuel Huntington, "The Democratic Distemper" (pp. 9–38), for a full statement of this argument.

14. Irving Kristol, *Two Cheers for Capitalism* (New York: New American Library, 1978), pp. 14, 17.

15. Ibid., p. 169.

16. Ibid., p. 119.

17. Ibid., p. 61.

18. Bell, pp. 15–16, 21, 55.

19. Kristol, p. 230.

20. Carol Felsenthal, *The Sweetheart of the Silent Majority: The Biography of Phyllis Schlafly* (New York: Doubleday & Co., 1981), pp. 55, 58.

21. Viguerie, p. 207.

22. Jerry Falwell, *Listen America!* (New York: Doubleday & Co., 1980), p. 26.

23. Ibid., p. 148.

24. Ibid., p. 121.

25. George Gilder, *Wealth and Poverty* (New York: Basic Books, 1981), p. 67.

26. Ibid., pp. 114, 115.

27. Ibid., pp. 127, 111.

28. Ibid., p. 68.

29. Ibid., p. 69.

30. Ibid., p. 14.

31. Ibid.

32. Ibid., p. 71.

33. Ibid., p. 14.

34. I am indebted to Rosalind Petchesky for helping me develop this part of my analysis.

35. Emma Rothschild, "Reagan and the Real America," *New York Review of Books* (February 5, 1981), pp. 12–18, esp. p. 12. Also see Harry Braverman, *Labor and Monopoly Capital* (New York: Monthly Review Press, 1978).

36. Rothschild, p. 12.

37. Ibid., pp. 12–13.

38. Ibid., p. 14.

39. Ibid., pp. 12–13.

40. Ibid.

41. Philip S. Foner, *Women and the American Labor Movement*, vol. 1, *From World War I to the Present* (New York: Free Press, 1980), p. 488.

42. Ibid., p. 478.

43. "Impact on Women of the Administration's Proposed Budget," prepared by the Women's Research and Education Institute for the Congresswomen's Caucus, April 1981, p. 5. Available from: WRFI, 400 South Capitol Street S.E., Washington, D.C. 20003.

44. Bertram Gross, *Friendly Fascism* (New York: M. Evans & Co., 1980).

45. See my "Developing a Theory of Capitalist Patriarchy and Socialist Feminism," in *Capitalist Patriarchy and the Case for Socialist Feminism*, ed. Zillah Eisenstein (New York: Monthly Review Press, 1979), pp. 5–40, for a discussion of the mutual dependence of capitalism and patriarchy.

46. See my *Radical Future of Liberal Feminism*, esp. chps. 9 and 10.

47. See Iris Young, "Socialist Feminism and the Limits of Dual Systems Theory," *Socialist Review* 10, no. 2–3 (March–June 1980): 169–88, for what I think is an incorrect assessment of my concept of capitalist patriarchy as reflecting a "dual system."

48. *Families and Public Policies in the United States, Final Report of the Commission* (Washington, D.C.: National Conference on Social Welfare, 1978). Available from: National Conference on Social Welfare, 1730 M Street N.W., Suite 911, Washington, D.C. 20036.

49. Ibid., pp. 22–23.

50. Ibid., p. 2.

51. Ibid.

52. Ibid., p. 1.

53. Bureau of the Census, "Families Maintained by Female Householders, 1970–79," Current Population Reports, Series P-23, no. 107 (October 1980), p. 5.

54. Ibid., p. 33.

55. "Facts We Dare Not Forget—Excerpts from a Neglected Government Report on Poverty and Unemployment to Which the New Administration Will Surely Pay No Attention," *Dissent* 28, no. 2 (Spring 1981): 166. Also see "Families Maintained by Female Householders, 1970–79."

56. *Families and Public Policies in the U.S.*, p. 14.

57. "Impact on Women of Proposed Budget," p. 5; Ehrenreich, p. 100.

58. Lester Thurow, "How to Wreck the Economy," *New York Review of Books* (May 14, 1981), pp. 3–8, esp. p. 3.

59. Ibid., p. 31.

60. See Allen Hunter, "In the Wings: New Right Organization and Ideology," *Radical America* 15, nos. 1–2 (Spring 1981): 113–40, for a similar discussion which he terms selective antistatism.

61. Documented in a February 1981 *Newsday* poll that was conducted nationwide and reported in *The National NOW Times* (April 1981), p. 2. See also Frederick Jaffe, Barbara Lindheim, and Philip Lee, *Abortion Politics, Private Morality and Public Policy* (New York: McGraw-Hill Book Co., 1981), for a full discussion of public opinion about abortion.

62. Irving Howe, "The Right Menace," published in *Dissent* pamphlet no. 1, *The Threat of Conservatism*, p. 29 (available from *Dissent*, 505 Fifth Avenue, New York, New York 10017).

Early Liberal Roots of Feminism: John Locke and the Attack on Patriarchy

Melissa A. Butler

The seventeenth-century conflict between patriarchal and liberal political thought grew out of a shift in views on human nature and the nature of society. This shift eventually led to new perspectives on the nature, role and status of women as well. Though the question of how political theorists handle the subject of women is rarely explored, it may be supposed that the way theorists treat half of humanity should have some consequences for their theories. Yet a theorist's comments on the status of women are usually treated as matters of antiquarian interest only; their significance for a full understanding of a theorist's work is seldom recognized. This was not always the case. In the past, theorists' discussions of women have had important implications for the acceptability of entire theories. The position of women has been used as a critical tool in evaluating theories. The clash between patriarchal and liberal theories serves as a case in point.

Though it is impossible to date the precise origin of the shift in collective consciousness which gave rise to the sexual revolution, it is clear that the revolution itself was (and is) directed against patriarchy. Simply defined, patriarchy is the rule of women by men, and of young men by older men.

Most feminists will agree that economic, social, psychological, political and legal structures are today quite patriarchal in practice. The weight of these structures is particularly oppressive since the theoretical justifications offered in their behalf have been bankrupt for centuries. This bankruptcy became evident, not with Marx or Engels, nor with John Stuart Mill, but with still earlier liberal attacks on the political theory of patriarchy. The vestiges of patriarchalism that survive in contemporary social practice are but remnants of a much more complete form of patriarchalism.

In the early seventeenth-century England, patriarchalism was a dominant paradigm, a world view, a weltanschauung.[1] For many Englishmen, it represented the truth of their time and all time. It was a fully articulated theory which expressly accounted for all social relations—king-subject, father-child, master-servant, etc.—in patriarchal terms. Sir Robert Filmer and other patriarchal writers insisted that the king ruled absolutely, the divinely ordained father of his people. No one was born free; everyone was born in subjection to some patriarchal superior. Each individual human being could find his or her proper place by consulting patriarchal theory. Places were not matters of individual choice but were assigned according to a divinely ordained pattern set down at the Creation.

By the end of the seventeenth century, the patriarchal world view had crumbled. It was replaced by a new understanding of human nature and of social and political organization. Whigs such as Sidney, Tyrrell and Locke grounded political power in acts of consent made by free-born individuals. Contract and individual choice supplanted birth and divine designation as crucial factors in social and political analysis. These changes raised problems concerning the status of women in the new order. At first, liberal theorists resisted the suggestion that the old assigned position of women might have to be abandoned. The champions of consent theory saw no need to secure the consent of women. Yet their critics insisted that excluding women violated the very theory of human nature on which liberalism was based. Eventually, liberals would be forced to bring their views on women into line with their theory of human nature. This changing image of women certainly played a part in that shift in consciousness which paved the way for the sexual revolution.

The Statement of Patriarchy: Sir Robert Filmer

While the appearance of full-blown patriarchal political theory was occasioned primarily by the turbulence of seventeenth-century English politics, patriarchal ideas and intimations could be found in political writings long before they received more systematic theoretical expression in the writings of Sir Robert Filmer.[2]

In that era of "divine right kings," the legitimacy of a monarch's claim to absolute rule could be proved if the source of a divine grant of power could be found. Patriarchal political theory satisfied this need. It offered an explanation of the historical origins of the king's political power and of the subject's political obligation. By tracing the king's power back to Adam, the theory provided more than mere historical justification; it provided divine sanction.

The explanation derived its effectiveness from a general awareness of the obvious truth which patriarchalism told.[3] The patriarchal family experience was universal. The family in the seventeenth century was a primary group in every sense of the term. Life was lived on a small scale and the family was at its center. The family patriarch was a universally-acknowledged authority figure with immense power. By linking the authority of the king with the authority of the father, a theorist could immediately clarify the nature of a subject's political obligations. Moreover, monarchical power grounded in patriarchal power took on the legitimacy of that least-challengeable social institution, the family. Patriarchal concepts found in catechism and sermon literature enhanced the king's legitimacy in the eyes of the masses. Finally, the linkage of paternal and monarchical power provided a means for transcending any residual or intermediate loyalties a subject might have. Absolute, patriarchal, monarchical power was vested in the king. It was to the king, not to the local nobility, that loyalty and obedience were rightfully owed.

Patriarchalists insisted that God, nature and history were on their side. For proof, one need only consult the one true account of Creation, namely, the Book of Genesis.

Not only was Genesis divinely inspired, it was also the oldest possible historical source and the best guide to man's nature.[4] There, in the Genesis account, was the evidence that God had created Adam in His image—patriarch and monarch He created him.

The gradual unfolding of biblical history showed that the basic institution of patriarchy, the patriarchal family, had always been a fundamental feature of society. Throughout Judeo-Christian society, family life, bolstered by marriage and divorce laws, primogeniture and property rules, continued thoroughly patriarchal down to the seventeenth century.[5]

During the English Civil War, both divine right monarchy and the patriarchal theory which helped support it were severely challenged. Republicans declared that the power of the king was limited. Leveller tracts espoused social contract doctrines. Thomas Hobbes, though himself eager to uphold the power of a strong sovereign, insisted that political power did not originate in a divine grant from God to Adam, father of the race. Instead, Hobbes maintained that political power was the result of an agreement, a covenant among men. In reaction to these novel and dangerous doctrines, Sir Robert Filmer penned the best-known treatises in defense of the patriarchal position.

Filmer was himself something of a model patriarch.[6] He was the eldest son in a family of 17 children, a landholder, a squire of Kent. He married a child heiress in 1610, but did not cohabit with his wife until 1618. Knighted by King James I in 1619, he took over the duties of head of the large Filmer household in 1629. Most of his father's family was dependent on him.

During the Civil War, Sir Robert was seen as a Loyalist. He spent many months in prison and suffered a sizable property loss. After his imprisonment, Filmer published several political tracts including *The Anarchy of a Limited or Mixed Monarchy* (1648), *The Freeholder's Grand Inquest* (1648), and *Observations Upon Aristotle, Touching Forms of Government* (1652). The work for which he is best known, *Patriarcha,* was begun around 1640, but was published posthumously in 1680.[7] Filmer's later political writings often drew on the ideas expressed in this earlier, unpublished manuscript.

To elaborate his patriarchal theory of politics, Filmer turned to both classical and constitutional sources. But Filmer's most important, most authoritative source was always scripture. Aristotle could be used as a commentary; but whenever disagreement arose between Aristotle and Filmer, or Aristotle and scripture, Sir Robert would summon the force of scripture behind his own arguments, reminding that "heathen authors" were ignorant of the true facts of creation and the beginnings of government (F.W. 187).

The scriptural arguments for monarchy illustrate the most literally patriarchal aspects of Filmer's thought. In brief, his account of the biblical origins and justifications of patriarchy was as follows:

> God created only Adam, and of a piece of him made the woman; and if by generation from them two as parts of them, all mankind be propagated: if also God gave to Adam not only the dominion over the woman and the children that should issue from them, but also over the whole earth to subdue it, and over all the creatures on it, so that as long as Adam lived no man could claim or enjoy anything but by donation, assignation, or permission from him (F.W. 241).

Again and again throughout his works Filmer recalled the divine grant of paternal, monarchical power to Adam. Filmer drew upon the Book of Genesis, specifically Genesis 1:28, when he claimed that "the first government in the world was monarchical in the father of all flesh. Adam being commanded to multiply, and people the earth and subdue it, and having dominion given him over all creatures, was thereby the monarch of the whole world" (F.W. 187).

As critics from Filmer's own century were only too happy to observe, Sir Robert had erred in his biblical analysis. Filmer had assigned all power to Adam, but God had given dominion to Adam and Eve. The divine grant of power in Genesis 1:28 was made to "them," ostensibly the male and female whose creation had been announced in the preceding verse. Sir Robert had to tamper with the text because the original grant of power detailed in Genesis 1:28 was not, as he maintained, an exclusive grant of private monarchical dominion given to Adam, the patriarch. On the contrary, the blessing was given to both the male and the female.

If evidence for the patriarchal theory could not be found in God's blessing, perhaps it could be found in His curse. Conceivably, Filmer might have agreed that the original prelapsarian grant had been made to Adam and Eve jointly, and might still have salvaged his patriarchal theory. He could have maintained that the lines of patriarchal authority were established only after the Fall. Genesis 3:16 could have been offered as proof: "Thy desire shall be to thy husband, he shall rule over thee."

Indeed, in the *Anarchy*, Filmer did refer to these lines as proof that "God ordained Adam to rule over his wife ... and as hers so all theirs that should come of her" (F.W. 283). Nevertheless, it is clear that Sir Robert preferred the Genesis 1:28 passage. By using that text, he could show that patriarchal order was in accord with man's original nature, not simply with his fallen nature. Filmer hoped to show that the human hierarchy was established in the *very* beginning. Every moment that passed risked the introduction of a custom which might lend credence to the anti-patriarchal case.[8] Each passing second made monarchical power appear less natural, and shared dominion more legitimate. Consequently, Filmer preferred to insist that Adam was monarch of the world from the very first moment of creation:

> By the appointment of God, as soon as Adam was created he was monarch of the world, though he had no subjects; for though there could not be actual government until there were subjects yet by the right of nature it was due to Adam to be governor of his posterity: though not in act, yet at least in habit. Adam was a King from his creation: and in the state of innocency he had been governor of his children; for the integrity or excellency of the subjects doth not take away the order or eminency of the governor. Eve was subject to Adam before he sinned; the angels who are of a pure nature, are subject to God (F.W. 289).

Filmer's analogy here is striking. The qualitative difference between man and woman, between king and subject, is virtually infinite; indeed, it parallels the qualitative difference which exists between God and the angels.

Genesis was not the only biblical source of patriarchal theory. The Decalogue, too, served to support patriarchal political authority, according to Filmer: "The power of the government is settled and fixed by the commandment of 'honour thy Father'; if there were a higher power than the fatherly, then this command could not stand and be observed" (F.W. 188). Filmer's omission is obvious. In service of political patriarchalism, the last half of the fifth commandment was dropped. All honor due to mother was forgotten.

Filmer and the Contract Theorists

Filmer's habit of selective quotation was not overlooked by his critics. In the 1680's Whigs severely attacked *Patriarcha* by dredging up one biblical reference after another to prove Sir Robert had flagrantly abused scriptural texts to support his theory. Lengthy criticisms were written by Edward Gee, a contemporary of Filmer's, and by later Whig theorists including Algernon Sidney, James Tyrrell, and John Locke.[9] Biblical criticisms constituted a major part of their attack on patriarchal theory. Indeed, Filmer's critics actually did far more biblical exegesis than he did.[10] Later commentators saw Filmer's opponents' efforts as little more than intellectual overkill. The commentators failed to realize that Filmer's thought was part of a pervasive pattern which had had a tight grip on the minds of many Englishmen.

Filmer's critics had to attack him by striking at the theological-scriptural base of the theory since scripture was by far its most important source. Filmer used scripture as the ultimate weapon, guaranteed to clinch any argument. In the eyes of his fellow Englishmen who shared his world view, the only way Sir Robert could be refuted was by destroying his scriptural base.[11]

In the course of the seventeenth century, standards of evidence and styles of argument changed dramatically. Forms of argument which had been perfectly acceptable, indeed even indispensable, in earlier political discourse were rejected in favor of newer "rational" arguments. Although John Locke would champion the new mode of thought, the old form still had a hold on him. Locke took Filmer's biblical arguments seriously, as challenges to be met and overcome. Locke's attack on Filmer, though incomplete, gives the impression that once the biblical criticism was finished, he believed Filmer stood refuted and the attack on contract theory rebutted. This was not necessarily true.[12]

Filmer staunchly insisted that man was not by nature free. Rather, man was born to subjection:

> Every man that is born is so far from being free-born that by his very birth he becomes a subject to him that begets him: under which subjection he is always to live, unless by immediate appointment from god, or by the grant or death of his Father, he becomes possessed of that power to which he was subject (F.W. 232).

By looking to the Garden of Eden, Filmer thought he could demonstrate the truth about natural man and his natural forms of association, but his contention that patriarchal monarchy was the natural and only legitimate form of government did not receive its force solely from the scriptural account. Sir Robert also relied on constitutional and classical sources to complement his biblical evidence. More importantly, however, the claims he made were strengthened by their apparent empirical relevance. The paternal power of the father and of the king was evident to all who would but look about them. The experience of patriarchalism in family life was a constant, natural feature of daily life. So too, paternal power in a kingdom would remain constant: "There is and always shall be continued to the end of the world, a natural right of a supreme Father over every multitude" (F.W. 62).

So persuasive was the use of patriarchy as a legitimating concept that Filmer maintained that even God exercised power by right of fatherhood. Filmer's argument takes on a circular character at this point. Nevertheless, it is clear that there was absolutely no room in patriarchal theory for free-born individuals. Government could not begin with an act of consent made by free and equal individuals in a state of nature. Filmer insisted that such government could be based on no more than myth. Furthermore, he insisted that contract theories which advanced such a myth would be replete with contradictions and logical fallacies.

Filmer offered a theory which was truly comprehensive and coherent, one which provided a place for every individual in society. His opponents, on the other hand, were far less able to provide a satisfactory accommodation for all the individuals and groups which made up seventeenth-century English society.

At least part of the difficulty which his adversaries encountered stemmed from their inability to dismiss patriarchalism completely in all its manifestations. They wished to destroy the patriarchal base of monarchy, and sever the connection between patriarchalism and divine-right politics, yet they were unable to reject less comprehensive forms of patriarchalism as basic organizing principles of government and society. They developed a new theory of human nature, but did not foresee or develop the implications of that theory. This point can be illustrated specifically by examining the position of women in their theories.

Whig theorists such as Tyrrell and Sidney certainly believed that whole classes of people were plainly unfit to exercise political power and plainly incapable of giving their own consent to government. Sidney spoke harshly of forms of government which granted power without regard to age, sex, infirmity or vice.[13] Tyrrell wrote, "There never was any Government where all the Promiscuous Rabble of Women and Children had Votes, as being not capable of it."[14]

Edward Gee would have founded his "democracy" on fatherly authority. Those who lacked political significance (i.e., women, children, servants) would be "involved" in their patriarchal superiors.[15] James Tyrrell indicated that he found a similar arrangement acceptable at the foundation of a commonwealth.[16] In accepting this sort of "democracy" these theorists were not very far from Filmer. Sir Robert permitted the patriarchal heads of families to gather together to decide who among them would become supreme father when the king died without an heir (F.W. 288). Filmer, Gee, Tyrrell and Sidney all agreed on one thing: women and children need have no part in these political decisions.

Despite their criticisms of patriarchalism and their arguments based on consent, neither Tyrrell nor his friend, John Locke, was willing to allow participation to all comers. Tyrrell wished to limit participation to male property owners. Locke, as MacPherson argues, would have limited participation to the demonstrably rational (read "acquisitive") classes.[17] But these limitations were swept away by historical actualities over the next two centuries. Rights to political participation were gradually extended to all men and subsequently to all women. Indeed, Filmer, rather than Locke or Tyrrell proved the better predictor of the historical course plotted by the liberal logic when he wrote of government by the people:

If but one man be excluded, the same reason that excludes one man, may exclude many hundreds, and many thousands, yea, and the major part itself; if it be admitted, that the

Filmer's reductio of liberal contract theory

people are or ever were free by nature, and not to be governed, but by their own consent, it is most unjust to exclude any one man from his right in government (F.W. 211).

No one could be excluded from political participation if contract theorists were to remain true to their principles. Filmer understood that in speaking of "the people" and their natural liberty, one had to talk about all mankind.

Though contract theorists came to consider their theories as logical or moral rather than as historical, Filmer used the historical problems of the social contract in an attempt to undermine the logical and moral status of the theory. Filmer insisted that the state of nature and the social contract became logically and historically unacceptable doctrines if "the people" were to be equated with "all mankind." Furthermore, he believed that contract theorists themselves would recoil when faced with the full implications of their theory.

Filmer demanded to know the details of the great meeting where the contract was approved. When did the meeting occur? Who decided the time and place? More importantly, he wanted to know who was invited. Filmer saw these as serious problems for consent theorists since:

> Mankind is like the sea, ever ebbing or flowing every minute one is born another dies; those that are the people this minute are not the people the next minute, in every instant and point of time there is a variation: no one time can be indifferent for all of mankind to assemble; it cannot but be mischevious always at least to all infants and others under the age of discretion; not to speak of women, especially virgins, who by birth have as much natural freedom as any other and therefore ought not to lose their liberty without their consent (F.W. 287).

Filmer's attack was no longer simply historical; it was now logical and moral as well. It was clear to him that if the "natural freedom" of mankind was to be taken seriously, obviously the natural freedom of women and children would have to be considered. If women and children were free, they would have to be included in any sort of compact. "Tacit consent" was an impossibility, and was rejected by Filmer as "unreasonable" and "unnatural" (F.W. 225). Simply to "conclude" the votes of children, for example, in the votes of parents would not be adequate:

> This remedy may cure some part of the mischief, but it destroys the whole cause, and at last stumbles upon the true original of government. For if it be allowed that the acts of the parents bind the children, then farewell the doctrine of the natural freedom of mankind; where subjection of children to parents is natural there can be no natural freedom (F.W. 287).

Filmer would probably have agreed that the same line of reasoning could be used to analyze the relationship of women to the social contract.

Filmer's technique in this instance was one of his favorites—reductio ad absurdum. Natural freedom and political participation of women and children were obviously absurd to all living in that patriarchal world. Thus, Filmer's case against natural freedom and the social contract stood proved. His aim was to show the absurdity of the concept "consent of all the people." He insisted that "all the people" must be taken at face value. It must include groups of people obviously unfit for such decision making, that is, children, servants and *women*. Each of these groups had been accorded a place within the social and political theory of patriarchy. Each group's place was in accord with a traditional evaluation of its status.

Those who asserted the natural freedom of all mankind upset the applecart. If men were born free and equal, status could not be ascribed at birth, but would have to be achieved in life. If Filmer's opponets were to be consistent, new political roles would have to be opened up for those previously judged politically incompetent. This consequence was never fully clear to Filmer's critics. Though Tyrrell and Sidney criticized Filmer's patriarchalism, they were by no means ready or willing to break with all the trappings of patriarchy. Consequently, they faced additional difficulties when they tried to account for the political obligation of the politically incompetent.

Tyrrell attempted to base the political obligation of women and children on the debt owed for their "breeding up and preservation." At first glance, this formula may seem to resemble Locke's doctrine of "tacit consent." A closer look will reveal that Tyrrell's version is far more extensive than Locke's. Tyrrell demanded much more from women and children than simply the passive obedience required of sojourners who were not parties to the compact:

> They may well be lookt upon as under an higher Obligation in Conscience and in Grati-
> tude to his Government, than Strangers of another Country, who onely staying here for
> a time to pursue their own Occasions and having no Right to the same privileges and ad-
> vantages of the Commonwealth do onely owe a passive obedience to its laws.[18]

The obligation of disenfranchised groups stemmed from their nurture, from the debt of gratitude owed to the government for their upbringing and education. They had no actual voice. They themselves were never expected to give free consent to their government. Yet still they were held to be obliged—out of gratitude.

This sort of obligation theory is not far removed from Filmer's. The natural duties of Filmer's king were "summed up in a universal fatherly care of his people" (F.W. 63). The King preserved, fed, clothed, instructed, and defended the whole common-wealth. Government by contract would do the same things for those who were not part of the contract. In return for these services alone, political nonparticipants owed "a higher Obligation in conscience and gratitude." No participation, no ex-press consent was necessary to put an end to their natural freedom.

· A third problem was created for both Filmer and his critics when the questions of participation and monarchical succession were considered together. Filmer did not use patriarchal theory to challenge women's claims to the throne. His critics, espe-cially Sidney, seized upon his silence, protesting that Filmer would allow even women and children to rule as patriarchs. Patriarchal theory enthroned "the next in Blood, without any regard to Age, Sex or other Qualities of the Mind or Body."[19]

Whig theorists did not render Filmer's arguments less damaging to their cause, but they did turn them back on patriarchal theory. To Filmer, contract theory was absurd because it entailed the participation of politically unfit groups in the forma-tion of government and society. To Whigs, the patriarchal position was outrageous because it risked giving a single, similarly incompetent individual absolute un-checked dominion.

To summarize, both Whig and patriarchal theorists used the position of women as a critical tool in evaluating competing theories. Both Whig and patriarchal theorists had to find places for women in their theories. Each criticized the other for the role and status eventually assigned to women.

In patriarchal theory, women held a distinctly subordinate position. Their inferior place in family, state and society was justified on the basis of scriptural exegesis. But scripture was frequently twisted in service of patriarchalism.

The errors and excesses of Filmer's theory were pointed out gleefully by his critics, yet many of these critics rejected only political patriarchalism, and that only in a limited way. Whigs stripped Genesis of its political import. They freed both men and women from subjection to a supreme earthly father. The social implications of Genesis were not completely rejected, however. The story of the Creation and Fall was still used to show the general inferiority of women to men. In practical terms, Whigs initiated no real attack on Filmer's discussion of women. They attacked the theological-historical justifications for political patriarchy, but basically supported the institutional arrangements promoted by patriarchy where women were concerned.

The issue of women's political participation created problems for both Whigs and patriarchs. Patriarchalism was a conservative theory aimed at legitimation of the reigning monarch. Patriarchal legitimacy was founded in an argument which was inherently antifemale. Yet English law permitted women to reign as sole monarchs. Patriarchal theorists found no really satisfactory escape from this dilemma.

Whigs upheld the natural freedom of all mankind yet maintained that women's consent to government could be "concluded" in that of their husbands or fathers. Whigs rejected the biblical basis for political subordination of women, but accepted empirically-based arguments which showed women naturally unfit for political life. In effect, Whigs substituted a community of many patriarchs for Filmer's supreme patriarch. Filmer, the patriarch, realized immediately that this simple substitution alone was much less than was required by the doctrine of natural freedom of all mankind. Slowly, over the next two centuries, even liberal thinkers would be drawn to the same conclusion.

Locke's Attack on Patriarchy

While other Whig writers simply declared that their theories necessitated no new roles for women, John Locke treated the problem somewhat differently. He was among the first to sense the inherent contradiction in a "liberalism" based on the natural freedom of mankind, which accorded women no greater freedom than allowed by patriarchalism. New places had to be opened to women. This is not to claim that John Locke planned or even foresaw the feminist movement. It does seem true, however, that Locke took his individualist principles very seriously, even when they entailed an admission that women, too, might have to be considered "individuals."

Clearly Locke was not interested in creating a world in which all were equal; in his view, there would always be differences among individuals. The key question here concerns the extent to which a Lockean society would discriminate on the basis of sex. Would the fact that some are more equal than others be determined by traditionally-assigned sex roles?

In the first of his *Two Treatises of Government,* Locke sowed little interest in the constitutional or classical arguments offered by Filmer. Doubtless he believed that these arguments were simply not at the heart of Filmer's theory. Instead, Locke charged that the scripture-based arguments were unproved, not because he doubted the truth of the Bible, but because he realized Filmer had distorted that truth. Locke's attack stemmed from no impious disregard for Filmer's evidence, but from a different method of construing that evidence. As Laslett suggests, Locke had broken the bounds of Filmer's world of biblical politics by introducing rationalist arguments.[20]

Since Filmer's patriarchal theory included a particular view of the status of women, based on biblical arguments, Locke's refutation also had to deal with that view. Concerning the benediction of Genesis 1:28, Locke noted that it was bestowed on "more than one, for it was spoken in the Plural Number, God blessed *them* and said unto *them*, Have Dominion. God says unto *Adam* and *Eve*, Have Dominion" (T.T., I, 29). This argument introduced the possibility that Adam's dominion was not exclusive but was shared with Eve. Further, Eve's subjection to Adam need not have prevented her from exercising dominion over the things of the Earth. Eve, too, might have property rights.

In the fifth chapter of the *First Treatise*, Locke argued against "Adam's title to Sovereignty by the Subjection of Eve." There, Locke had much more to say about the patriarchal conception of women. He took issue with Filmer's use of Genesis 3:16 ("And thy desire shall be to thy Husband and he shall rule over thee"). Those words, Locke objected, were a "punishment laid upon Eve." Furthermore, these words were not even spoken to Adam. The moment after the great transgression, Locke noted, "was not a time when Adam could expect any Favours, any grant of Priviledges from his offended Maker." At most, the curse would "concern the Female Sex only," through Eve, its representative (T.T., I, 45–47).

Here, Locke argued that Genesis 3:16 offered no evidence of a general grant of power to Adam over all mankind. By limiting the curse to Eve and to women, Locke effectively removed males from the sway of the patriarchal monarch. But he went even further, and suggested that the arguments for the subjection of women based on the Genesis 3:16 passage could be faulty.

First, the subjection of women carried no political import. The curse imposed "no more [than] that Subjection they [women] should ordinarily be in to their Husbands." But even this limit on women's freedom was not immutable and could be overcome:

> There is here no more Law to oblige a Woman to such a Subjection, if the Circumstances either of her Condition or Contract with her Husband should exempt her from it, then there is, that she should bring forth her Children in Sorrow and Pain, if there could be found a remedy for it, which is also part of the same Curse upon her (T.T., I, 47).

Nevertheless, Locke largely accepted the empirical fact of women's inferiority and saw it grounded in nature as ordered by God. He attempted to avoid the conclusion that Adam became Eve's superior or that husbands became their wives' superiors, yet his effort is fairly weak:

> God, in this Text, gives not, that I see, any Authority to Adam over Eve, or to Men over their Wives, but only foretells what should be the Woman's Lot, how by his Providence he would order it so, that she should be subject to her husband as we see that generally the Laws of Mankind and customs of Nations have ordered it so; and there is, I grant, a Foundation in Nature for it (T.T., I, 47).

Locke was principally interested in refuting the idea of a divine grant of authority to Adam. He lived in a world in which the subjection of women was an empirical fact and he was willing to yield to the contemporary view that this fact had some foundation in nature. His tone was hesitant, though. Locke seemed to wish that God had not been responsible for women's inferior status. He tried to cast God in the role of prophet rather than creator. God merely "foretold" what women's lot would be. Locke found it difficult to keep God in the role of innocent bystander, however. Where Locke admitted the use of divine power, he tried to remain tentative: God, in his Providence, "would order" social relations so that wives would be subject to their husbands. But God did not give men any kind of rightful authority over women. Locke implied that God merely suggested one empirical relationship which was subsequently adopted by mankind and reinforced by the laws and customs of nations. That these laws and customs were largely established by males did not, in Locke's opinion, damage the case. It did not seem to bother him that such laws and customs offered proof of the authority which men exercised over women. Locke simply wished to deny that male authority was exercised by virtue of some divine grant. At this point, he had no need to reject the customary exercise of such authority. It was enough to show only that it was human and not divine in origin.

Peter Laslett notes that "Locke's attitude towards the curse on women in childbearing is typical of his progressive, humanitarian rationalism."[21] But Locke's views on women were also evidence of his individualism. Though Locke believed there was a "foundation in nature" for the limitations on women, he remained faithful to the individualist principles which underlay his theory. In his view, women were free to overcome their natural limitations; each woman was permitted to strike a better deal for herself whenever possible.

In conjunction with his attack on Filmer's use of Genesis 3:16, Locke touched another of patriarchy's soft spots. He sensed the weakness of Filmer's insistence on the inferiority of women in a nation where women had worn the crown. Locke made no sustained analysis of this point, but remarked, instead, "[will anyone say] that either of our Queens *Mary* or *Elizabeth* had they Married any of their Subjects, had been by this Text put into a Political Subjection to him? or that he thereby should have had Monarchical Rule over her?" (T.T., I, 47).

Locke also accused Sir Robert of performing procrustean mutilations of "words and senses of Authors" (T.T., I, 60). This tendency was most evident in Filmer's abbreviation of the fifth commandment. Filmer had cited the command in several places throughout his works, but always in the same terms, "Honour thy Father." Locke noted this fact and then complained that "and Mother, as Apocriphal Words, are always left out." Filmer had overlooked the "constant Tenor of the Scripture," Locke maintained. To bolster his position, Locke produced well over a dozen scriptural citations showing the child's duty to father and mother. A mother's title to honor from her children was independent of the will of her husband. This independent right, he argued, was totally inconsistent with the existence of absolute monarchical power vested in the father (T.T., I, 63). Ultimately, Locke denied that the fifth commandment had any political implications at all (T.T., I, 65).

In this analysis, Locke broke with one of patriarchy's strongest traditions. Political obligation had been justified through the fifth commandment. In seventeenth-century sermon literature and catechism texts, the subject's duty of obedience was firmly rooted in this command. Locke refuted these arguments, not by criticizing the use of scriptural evidence, but by analyzing the interpretations supposedly based on that source.

This completed the destructive part of Locke's case. His attack rent the fabric of Filmer's theory. Since patriarchalism represented a complete, integrated theory of society, an adequate successor-theory would have to replace all its shattered parts. If all social relations could no longer be understood through the patriarchal paradigm, how could they be understood? Locke's answer came in the *Second Treatise*. There he made his positive contribution to the understanding of social relations.

Social Relations in the Second Treatise

For Filmer and his sympathizers there was only one type of power: paternal power. This power was, by its nature, absolute. Filmer's simplistic, uncluttered view of power fit in perfectly with his analysis of social relations. Filmer admitted only one kind of social relationship: the paternal relationship. Each member of society was defined by his or her relation to the patriarchs of the family and of the nation.

Locke, however, maintained that there were many kinds of power and many types of social relations. He analyzed several nonpolitical relationships including those of master-servant, master-slave, parent-child, and husband-wife.[22] Each of these forms of association was carefully distinguished from the political relationship of ruler-subject. Two of the nonpolitical relationships, namely the parental and the conjugal, reveal a great deal about the status of women in Lockean theory.

From the very outset of the discussion of the parent-child relation, Locke rejected the terminology of patriarchy, claiming that "[paternal power] seems so to place the Power of Parents over their Children wholly in the Father, as if the Mother had no share in it, whereas if we consult Reason or Revelation, we shall find she hath an equal Title. ... For whatever obligation Nature and the right of Generation lays on Children, it must certainly bind them equal to both the concurrent Causes of it" (T.T., II, 52).

The basic argument at the root of his terminological objection was one familiar from the *First Treatise*. Patriarchal theory could not stand if power were shared by husband and wife. As Locke argued in the *Second Treatise*, "it will but very ill serve the turn of those Men who contend so much for the Absolute Power and Authority of the *Fatherhood*, as they call it, that the *Mother* should have any share in it" (T.T., II, 53). Nevertheless, Locke was not consistent in his own use of the term he introduced. He reverted to the use of "paternal" to describe the relationship he defined as "parental." Yet it is clear from this discussion as well as from the analysis of the fifth commandment that Locke was willing to elevate women's status if he could overthrow the patriarchal monarch.

Locke's examination of the conjugal relationship demanded a more extensive analysis of the roles and status of women in society. He described conjugal society as follows:

> *Conjugal Society* is made by a voluntary Compact between Man and Woman: tho' it consist chiefly in such a Communion and Right in one anothers Bodies, as is necessary to its chief End, Procreation; yet it draws with it mutual Support and Assistance, and a Communion of Interest too, as necessary not only to unite their Care, and Affection, but also necessary to their common Off-spring, who have a Right to be nourished and maintained by them, till they are able to provide for themselves (T.T., II, 78).

Conjugal society existed among human beings as a persistent social relationship because of the long term of dependency of the offspring and further because of the dependency of the woman who "is capable of conceiving, and *de facto* is commonly with Child again, and Brings forth too a new Birth long before the former is out of a dependency" (T.T., II, 80). Thus the father is obliged to care for his children and is also "under an Obligation to continue in Conjugal Society with the same Woman longer than other creatures" (T.T., II, 80).

Though the conjugal relationship began for the sake of procreation, it continued for the sake of property. After praising God's wisdom for combining in man an acquisitive nature and a slow maturing process, Locke noted that a departure from monogamy would complicate the simple natural economics of the conjugal system (T.T., II, 80). Though conjugal society among human beings would be more persistent than among other species, this did not mean that marriage would be indissoluble. Indeed, Locke wondered "why this *Compact*, where Procreation and Education are secured, and Inheritance taken care for, may not be made determinable, either by consent, or at a certain time, or upon certain Conditions, as well as any other voluntary Compacts, there being no necessity in the nature of the thing, nor to the ends of it, that it shall always be for life" (T.T., II, 81). Locke's tentative acceptance of divorce brought him criticism over 100 years later. Thomas Elrington commented that "to make the conjugal union determinable by consent, is to introduce a promiscuous concubinage." Laslett notes that Locke was prepared to go even further and suggested the possibilities of left-hand marriage.[23] In Locke's view, the actual terms of the conjugal contract were not fixed and immutable:

> Community of Goods and the Power over them, mutual Assistance and Maintenance, and other things belonging to *Conjugal Society*, might be varied and regulated by that Contract, which unites Man and Wife in that Society as far as may consist with Procreation and the bringing up of Children (T.T., II, 83).

Nevertheless, Locke described what he took to be the normal distribution of power in marital relationships:

> The Husband and Wife, though they have but one common Concern, yet having different understandings will unavoidably sometimes have different wills, too; it therefore being necessary, that the last Determination, *ie.* the Rule, should be placed somewhere, it naturally falls to the Man's share, as the abler and the stronger (T.T., II, 82).

Clearly all forms of patriarchalism did not die with Filmer and his fellows. Here, the subjection of women is not based on Genesis, but on natural qualifications. Nature had shown man to be the "abler and stronger." Even James Tyrrell, while denying any need to obtain women's consent in the formation of civil society, thought it possible that, in some cases, women might actually be more fit to act as household heads and final decision makers. Unlike Tyrrell, Locke did not equivocate on this point. Rule must be placed somewhere, so he placed it in the husband. Locke's patriarchy was limited, though. The husband's power of decision extended only to those interests and properties held in common by husband and wife. Locke spelled out the limits on the husband's power:

> [His power] leaves the Wife in the full and free possession of what by Contract is her Peculiar Right, and gives the Husband no more power over her Life, than she has over his. The *Power of the Husband* being so far from that of an absolute monarch that the *Wife* has, in many cases, a Liberty to *separate* from him; where natural Right or their Contract allows it, whether that Contract be made by themselves in the state of Nature or by the Customs or Laws of the Country they live in; and the Children upon such Separation fall to the Father or Mother's lot, as such contract does determine (T.T., II, 82).

In addition, Locke distinguished between the property rights of husband and wife. All property in conjugal society was not automatically the husband's. A wife could have property rights not subject to her husband's control. Locke indicated this in a passage on conquest: "For as to the Wife's share, whether her own Labour or Compact gave her a Title to it, 'tis plain, her Husband could not forgeit what was hers" (T.T., II, 183).

There were several similarities between the conjugal and the political relationship. Both were grounded in consent. Both existed for the preservation of property. Yet conjugal society was not a political society because it conferred no power over the life and death of its members. In addition, political society could intervene in the affairs of conjugal society. Men and women in the state of nature were free to determine the terms of the conjugal contract. But in civil society these terms could be limited or dictated by the "Customs or Laws of the Country."

The extent to which the participants in the parental and conjugal relationships could also participate in political relationships remains to be considered. We may gain some insight into the matter by following Locke's route, that is, by tracing the origins of political power from the state of nature.

To Locke, the state of nature was a "state of perfect Freedom" for individuals "to order Actions and dispose of their Possessions, and Persons, as they think fit." Furthermore, Locke also described the state of nature as:

> A *State* also of Equality, wherein all the Power and Jurisdiction is reciprocal, no one having more than another: there being nothing more evident, than that Creatures of the same species and rank promiscuously born to all the same advantages of Nature and the use of the same faculties should also be equal one amongst another without Subordination or Subjection, unless the Lord and Master of them all should by any manifest Declaration of his Will set one above another (T.T., II, 4).

Because of certain inconveniences (the lack of an authoritative executive power, the potential for injustice where men judged their own cases, etc.), men quit the state of nature to form civil society through an act of consent. It was in criticizing the formation of society by consent that Filmer's theory was most effective. Indeed, Locke found it difficult to show how free and equal individuals actually formed civil society. Ultimately he was forced to admit that the first political societies in history were probably patriarchal monarchies. He described the historic origins as follows:

> As it often happens, where there is much Land and few People, the Government commonly began in the Father. For the Father having by the Law of Nature, the same Power with every Man else to punish his transgressing Children even when they were Men, and out of their Pupilage; and they were very likely to submit to his punishment, and all joyn with him against the Offender in their turns, giving him thereby power to Execute his Sentence against any transgression ... [the] Custom of obeying him, in their Childhood made it easier to submit to him rather than to any other (T.T., II, 105).

In this passage, Locke lumped paternal power and natural power together, allowed for the slightest nod of consent, and—presto—civil society emerged. Even in the state of nature, it appeared that paternal (parental?) power could be effective. Children growing up in the state of nature were under the same obligations to their parents as children reared in civil society. What of natural freedom and equality? Locke confessed:

> *Children* are not born in this full state of *Equality*, though they are born to it. Their parents have a sort of Rule and Jurisdiction over them when they come into the World, and

for some time after, but 'tis but a temporary one. The Bonds of this Subjection are like Swadling Cloths they are wrapt up in and supported by in the weakness of their Infancy. Age and Reason as they grow up, loosen them till at length they drop quite off, and leave a Man at his own free Disposal (T.T., II, 55).

Of course, once children reached maturity in the state of nature they no longer owed obedience to their parents, but were simply required to honor them out of simple gratitude. At this stage, however, Locke introduced another sort of power to support the father's claim to his child's obedience—namely that power which accrued to every man in the state of nature, the power to punish the transgressions of others against him. But the father's power was reinforced by the fact that his children would have a long-standing habit of obedience to him. In the state of nature, the father's commands to his mature children received added weight and legitimacy because he *was* their father. His children would recognize this legitimacy and would join their power to his to make him lawmaker. At this point, it seems, the father's former paternal power and his existing natural power were transformed by consent into political power.

Locke's account of the origins of political power raised problems. First of all, it seemed that the consent of free and equal individuals came about more as a result of habit than of mature, rational deliberation. Secondly, Locke's reconstruction fell prey to one of the difficulties he saw in Filmer: namely, the problem of accounting for monarchy as the form of government growing out of *parental* power. Against Filmer, Locke had protested repeatedly that the honor and obedience due to a father was due also to a mother. Both reason and revelation insisted upon this, he claimed. If "paternal" power actually meant "parental" power, that is, the power of father *and* mother why should the form of government growing out of that power be the government of one, not two? By the time Locke had reached this stage of his discourse, he had apparently abandoned the earlier line of argument, just as he had abandoned the usage of "parental" for "paternal." The father as "abler and stronger" would rule.

In this discussion, Locke was willing to concede the historical or anthropological case for patriarchalism. He was not ready to concede the moral case, however. Filmer had tied his moral and historical arguments together by using the Book of Genesis as the source of both. Locke split the two cases apart. Locke's biblical criticisms were intended to demonstrate the weakness of the oral conclusions which Filmer had drawn from the Genesis creation account. Thus, at best, Filmer was left with only an historical case. But, Locke insisted, history was not the source of morality. He wrote that "an Argument from what has been, to what should of right be, has no great force" (T.T., II, 103). Instead, he broke with history and based his moral theory on a new understanding of human nature. In doing so, however, he reopened questions closed by Filmer's theory. Locke had to deal with the political roles and status of women, children and servants. He was somewhat sensitive to Filmer's criticisms concerning the place of these politically unfit groups within contract theory. He certainly tried to make a consistent explanation of the relationship of children to civil society: "We are *born Free*, as we are born Rational; not that we have actually the Exercise of either: Age that brings one brings with it the other too. And thus we see how natural *Freedom and Subjection to Parents* may consist together and are both founded on the same Principle" (T.T., II, 61). No immature child could be expected to take part in the social compact. Yet children's inability to participate in politics would not preclude their right to consent to government when they reached adulthood. Locke indicated the necessity of each person giving consent as a condition of full political rights and full political obligation. Grown sons were free to make their own contract as were their fathers before them. An individual could not be bound by the consent of others but had to make a personal commitment through some separate act of consent.

But what of women? Unlike Tyrrell and Sidney, Locke remained silent on the question of their participation in the founding of political society. Of course, it is possible Locke referred to the role of women in the lost section of the *Treatises*. Or, perhaps Locke understood that explicit exclusion of women seriously weakened a theory grounded in the natural freedom of mankind. Yet Locke was also a good enough propagandist to have realized how deeply ingrained patriarchalism was in everyday life. Locke had criticized Filmer's use of the fifth commandment—"Honor thy father"—as a basis for political obligation. If the command were taken seriously, he charged, then "every Father must necessarily have Political Dominion, and there will be as many Sovereigns as there are Fathers" (T.T., I, 65). But the audience Locke was addressing was essentially an audience of fathers, household heads and family sovereigns. Locke had freed them from political subjection to a patriarchal superior—the king. He did not risk alienating his audience by clearly conferring a new political status on their subordinates under the patriarchal system, that is, on women. Nevertheless, in the absence of any sustained analysis of the problem of women, we may draw some conclusions from an examination of Locke's scattered thoughts on women.

Though Locke gave the husband ultimate authority within conjugal society, this authority was limited and non-political. Yet when Locke's account of the husband's conjugal authority was combined with his account of the historical development of political society, several questions occur which were never adequately resolved in Locke's moral theory. Did not the award of final decision-making power to the father and husband (in conjugal society) result in a transformation of "parental power" into "paternal power"? Was the subsequent development of political power based on paternal power a result of that transformation? What was woman's role in the establishment of the first political society? Since her husband was to be permitted final decisions in matters of their common interest and property, and since political society, obviously, was a matter of common interest, would her voice simply be "concluded" in that of her husband? If so, then Filmer's question recurs—what became of her rights as a free individual? Did she lose her political potential because she was deemed not as "able and strong" as her husband? If this were the case, Locke would have had to introduce new qualifications for political life.

Locke portrayed political society as an association of free, equal, rational individuals who were capable of owning property.[24] These individuals came together freely, since none had any power or jurisdiction over others. They agreed to form a civil society vested with power to legislative over life and death, and to execute its decisions in order to protect the vital interests of its members, that is, their lives, liberties and estates. Yet John Locke was certainly no believer in the absolute equality of human beings. Indeed, on that score, he was emphatic:

> Though I have said ... *That all Men by Nature are equal*, I cannot be supposed to understand all sorts of *Equality; Age* or *Virtue* may give Men a just Precedency: *Excellence of Parts and Merit* may place others above the Common Level; *Birth* may subject some and *Alliance* or *Benefits* others, to pay an Observance to those whom Nature, Gratitude, or other Respects may have made it due (T.T., II, 54).

But these inequalities in no way affect an individual's basic freedom or political capacity, for Locke continued in the same passage:

> ... yet all this consists with the *Equality* which all Men are in, in respect of Jurisdiction or Dominion one over another, which was the *Equality* I there spoke of, as proper to the Business in hand, being that *equal Right* every Man hath, *to his Natural Freedom*, without being subjected to the Will or Authority of any other Man (T.T., II, 54).

If "Man" is used as a generic term, then woman's natural freedom and equality could not be alienated without her consent. Perhaps a marriage contract might be taken for consent, but this is a dubious proposition. Locke had indicated that a marriage contract in no way altered the political capacity of a queen regnant (T.T., I, 47). While decision-making power over the common interests of a conjugal unit belonged to the husband, Locke admitted that the wife might have interests apart from their shared interests. Women could own separate property not subject to their husbands' control. If a husband forfeited his life or property as a result of conquest, his conquerors acquired no title to his wife's life or property.

Did these capacities entitle women to a political role? Locke never directly confronted the question; nevertheless, it is possible to compare Locke's qualifications for political life with his views of women. Locke used the Genesis account to show that women possessed the same natural freedom and equality as men. Whatever limitations had been placed on women after the Fall could conceivably be overcome through individual effort or scientific advance. Furthermore, women were capable of earning through their own labor, of owning property and of making contracts.

Locke and the Rational Woman

The one remaining qualification for political life is rationality. For Locke's views on the rationality of women it will be necessary to turn to his other writings, notably his *Thoughts on Education*.

In the published version of his advice on education, Locke mentioned that the work had been originally intended for the education of boys; but he added that it could be used as a guide for raising children of either sex. He noted that "where difference of sex requires different Treatment, 'twill be no hard Matter to distinguish."[25]

The *Education* was first written as a series of letters to Locke's friend, Edward Clarke, concerning the upbringing of Clarke's eldest son. Locke's intent was to provide a guide for the education of a gentleman. His attention was not focused directly on a lady's education, although later he offered the Clarkes guidance on the education of their daughter. From the latter advice we may discover just where Locke thought "difference of sex required different treatment."

Locke felt that his advice concerning a gentleman's education would have to be changed somewhat to fit the needs of Clark's daughter. However, in a letter to Mrs. Clarke, Locke tried to convince her that his prescriptions were appropriate for girls and not unnecessarily harsh.[26] On the whole, Locke believed that except for "making a little allowance for beauty and some few other considerations of the s[ex], the manner of breeding of boys and girls, especially in the younger years, I imagine, should be the same."[27]

The differences which Locke thought should obtain in the education of men and of women amounted to only slight differences in physical training. While Locke thought that "meat, drink and lodging and clothing should be ordered after the same manner for the girls as for the boys," he did introduce a few caveats aimed at protecting the girls' complexions.[28]

Locke introduced far fewer restrictions in his plan for a young lady's mental development. In a letter to Mrs. Clarke he wrote: "Since, therefore I acknowledge no difference of sex in your mind relating ... to truth, virtue, and obedience, I think well to have no thing altered in it from what is [writ for the son]."[29]

Far from advocating a special, separate and distinct form of education for girls, Locke proposed that the gentleman's education should more closely resemble that of young ladies. For example, he favored the education of children at home by tutors. Modern languages learned through conversation should replace rote memorization of classical grammars. In addition, Locke suggested that young gentlemen as well as young ladies might profit from a dancing master's instruction.

Taken as a whole, Locke's thoughts on education clearly suggest a belief that men and women could be schooled in the use of reason. The minds of both men and women were blank slates to be written on by experience. Women had intellectual potential which could be developed to a high level.

Locke's educational process was designed to equip young men for lives as gentlemen. Since the gentleman's life certainly included political activity, a young man's education had to prepare him for political life. If a young lady were to receive the same education, it should be expected that she, too, would be capable of political activity.

Locke's personal relations also may have reinforced his view of female rationality. Though he was generally secretive about his personal life, Locke did have a well-known close relationship with Damaris Cudworth Masham. She was a brilliant woman, a "theologian and correspondent of the intellectuals of her day," and perhaps, as Laslett suggests, "the first bluestocking of them all."[30] Locke described Damaris to a friend in glowing terms:

> The lady herself is so well versed in theological and philosophical studies and of such an original mind that you will not find many men to whom she is not superior in wealth of knowledge and ability to profit by it. Her judgment is excellent, and I know few who can bring such clearness of thought to bear upon the most abstruse subjects, or such capacity for searching through and solving the difficulties of questions beyond the range, I do not say of most women, but even the most learned men.[31]

What effects did Locke's relationship with Damaris Masham have on his views about women? Obviously this is a highly speculative matter. Locke had met Damaris some time before he began to advise Mrs. Clarke on the upbringing of her daughter. Damaris herself championed the cause of female education. In one of her (anonymously) published works, she castigated those English gentlemen, who, destitute of knowledge themselves, derived a sense of superiority from depriving women of knowledge. She realized that learned ladies risked becoming "a subject of ridicule ... and aversion." Only a few "vertuous and rational persons" would rise above the conventional prejudice.[32] Surely Damaris Masham believed John Locke was among these exceptional individuals.

Locke wrote the *Treatises* before he met Damaris. While it is tempting to suggest that his relationship with Damaris caused him to move away from the somewhat more patriarchal sentiments of the *Second Treatise* toward the ideas of greater sexual equality found in his thoughts on education, to claim this would be to claim more than the evidence warrants. Locke's various views on women as expressed in the *Treatises* and his educational writings are not really incompatible. At most, we can maintain that Locke's acquaintance with Lady Masham reinforced his views on women—views already heavily influenced by his belief in individualism.

In summary, it does appear that Locke was a part of a shifting collective consciousness which made the sexual revolution a possibility. He did not totally reject all forms of patriarchalism but in many respects his thoughts on women anticipated such noted feminists as John Stuart Mill.

Locke did hold that there might be a foundation in nature for the subjection of wives to husbands. The pain of childbirth, the duration and frequency of pregnancy and the long dependency of the children helped dictate the form of conjugal society. In conjugal society, the final decision-making power belonged to the husband as the "abler and stronger." Locke was certainly not interested in abolishing what many feminists today see as the chief institution of modern patriarchy—the family. The form of conjugal society among human beings grew out of peculiarities in the human life cycle and in human nature. Human beings matured slowly and were acquisitive. These two factors shaped the character of the human family. Nevertheless, family relations—parent-child, and husband-wife—were not immutable or indissoluble as patriarchal theorists had claimed. The conjugal relationship was based on consent and the terms of the conjugal contract could be varied by the uniting couple. There was no inherent reason why the relationship had to be lifelong. Wives could have a right to separate from their husbands. When separations occurred, child custody could be granted to either parent.

Locke's views on women, as noted above, exemplified his individualism. While he believed that women did suffer from some natural weaknesses, he had a classic liberal faith in the ability of individual women to overcome these natural obstacles. The program of education he designed for young ladies attested to that faith and his own experience with Damaris Cudworth Masham confirmed it. Doubtless feminists today would find fault with the "concessions to female beauty" in his educational program. Yet his overall plan went far in breaking down traditional sex roles in education.

Locke believed that women shared the basic freedom and equality characteristic of all members of the species. Women were capable of rational thought; in addition, they could make contracts and acquire property. Thus it appeared that women were capable of satisfying Locke's requirements for political life. Yet Locke was never explicit about women's role in the formation of civil society. He gave no separate account of women's political obligation. He registered no protest over the rule of Queens Elizabeth or Anne or Mary; but he never stated whether he, like Tyrrell and Sidney, would have excluded the "whole multitude of women" from any form of political life.

Finally, 300 years ago, Locke offered a "liberated" solution to a controversy which still rages in religious circles—the question of the fitness of women to act as ministers. In 1696 Locke, together with King William, attended a service led by a Quaker preacher, Rebecca Collier. He praised her work and encouraged her to continue in it, writing, "Women, indeed, had the honour first to publish the resurrection of the Lord of Love; why not again the resurrection of the Spirit of Love?"[33] It is interesting to compare Locke's attitude here with the famous remark made by Samuel Johnson on the same subject in the next century: "Sir, a woman's preaching is like a dog's walking on his hindlegs. It is not done well; but you are surprized to find it done at all."[34]

Perhaps a similar conclusion might be reached about the roots of feminism in Lockean liberalism. In a world where political anti-patriarchalism was still somewhat revolutionary, explicit statements of more far-reaching forms of anti-patriarchalism were almost unthinkable. Indeed, they would have been considered absurdities. Thus, while Filmer had presented a comprehensive and consistent patriarchal theory, many of his liberal opponents rejected political patriarchalism by insisting on the need for individual consent in political affairs but shied away from tampering with patriarchal attitudes where women were concerned. John Locke was something of an exception to this rule. Though his feminist sympathies certainly did not approach the feminism of Mill writing nearly two centuries later, in view of the intense patriarchalism of seventeenth-century England, it should be surprising to find such views expressed at all.

Notes

1. On patriarchalism as a world view, see Gordon J. Schochet, *Patriarchalism and Political Thought* (New York: Basic Books, 1975); also W. H. Greenleaf, *Order, Empiricism, and Politics* (London: Oxford University Press, 1964), Chs. 1–5; Peter Laslett, "Introduction," *Patriarcha and Other Political Works of Sir Robert Filmer* (Oxford: Basil Blackwell, 1949), p. 26; and John W. Robbins, "The Political Thought of Sir Robert Filmer" (Ph.D. dissertation, The Johns Hopkins University, 1973).

2. Patriarchal strains may be found in the literature of the sixteenth century including John Knox, *First Blast of the Trumpet Against the Monstrous Regiment of Women* (Geneva, 1558). Knox argued that women were incapable of ruling a kingdom. The tract was inspired less by Knox's fear of female rule than his fear of *Catholic* female rule. Counterarguments were introduced by John Aylmer in *An Harborowe for Faithfull and Trewe Subjects against the Late Blown Blast* (Strasborowe, 1559). Patriarchal political theory also influenced James I in *The Trew Law of Free Monarchies* (1598); he noted that "Kings are also compared to Fathers of families: for a King is trewly *Parens Patriae,* the politique father of his people." Richard Field insisted in *Of the Church* (1606) that the political power of Adam as monarch could be derived from his power as father to the whole human race. Patriarchal theorists among Filmer's contemporaries included John Maxwell who wrote *Sacro-Sancta Regum Majestas or the Sacred and Royal Prerogative of Christian Kings* (Oxford, 1644); and James Ussher, *The Power Communicated by God to the Prince, and the Obedience Required of the Subject* (written ca. 1644, first published 1661, 2nd ed., London, 1683); and Robert Sanderson, in his preface to Ussher's work.

3. Peter Laslett, *The World We Have Lost* (New York: Scribner's, 1965), passim; Greenleaf, pp. 80–94; Peter Zagorin, *A History of Political Thought in the English Revolution* (New York: Humanities Press, 1966), pp. 198–99.

4. On the use of scripture in historical argument see J. G. A. Pocock, *The Ancient Constitution and the Feudal Law* (Cambridge: Cambridge University Press, 1957), pp. 188–89.

5. See especially Greenleaf, p. 89; also Julia O'Faolain and Laura Martines, eds. *Not in God's Image* (New York: Harper Torchbooks, 1973), pp. 179–207; and Schochet, p. 16.

6. Laslett, "Introduction," and Laslett, "Sir Robert Filmer: The Man Versus the Whig Myth," *William and Mary Quarterly,* 3rd ser., 5 (1948), 523–46.

7. Sir Robert Filmer, *Patriarcha and Other Political Writings of Sir Robert Filmer,* ed. Peter Laslett (Oxford: Basil Blackwell, 1949). This volume will be cited in the text as "F.W."

8. Pocock, pp. 189–90.

9. See, for example, Edward Gee, *The Divine Right and Original of the Civil Magistrate from God* (London, 1658); [James Tyrrell], *Patriarcha Non Monarcha* (London: Richard Janeway, 1681); and Algernon Sidney, *Discourse Concerning Government* (London, 1698).

10. Greenleaf, p. 89.

11. Arguments had to be structured to persuade the widest possible audience. For an exploration of this general problem, see Mark Gavre, "Hobbes and His Audience," *American Political Science Review,* 68 (December 1974), 1542–56.

12. Laslett concluded that "neither Locke nor Sidney nor any of a host of others who attacked *Patriarcha* ever attempted to meet the force of [Filmer's] criticisms [about political obligation], and that none of them ever realized what he meant by his naturalism." Introduction, p. 21.

13. Sidney, pp. 2–4, 34–35.

14. Tyrrell, p. 83.

15. Schochet, p. 233.

16. Tyrrell, p. 74.

17. C. B. MacPherson, *The Political Theory of Possessive Individualism* (London: Oxford University Press, 1962), Ch. 5; and MacPherson, "The Social Bearing of Locke's Political Theory," *Western Political Quarterly,* 7 (March 1954), 1–22.

18. Tyrrell, p. 78.

19. Sidney, p. 4.

20. Peter Laslett, "Introduction," to *Two Treatises of Government,* written by John Locke, ed. Laslett (Cambridge: Cambridge University Press, 1960), p. 69. References to Locke's *Treatises* will be made to "T.T." with the treatise and section numbers indicated.

21. Laslett, ed., *Two Treatises,* p. 210 n.

22. See especially R. W. K. Hinton, "Husbands, Fathers, and Conquerors," *Political Studies,* 16 (February 1968), 55–67; Geraint Parry, "Individuality, Politics and the Critique of Paternalism in John Locke," *Political Studies,* 12 (June 1964), 163–77; and MacPherson, *Possessive Individualism.*

23. Laslett, ed., *Two Treatises,* p. 364, n.

24. See MacPherson, *Possessive Individualism,* Ch. 5. MacPherson argues that Locke assumed a class differential in the distribution of these qualities. Full membership in political society would be limited to those who fully demonstrated them. The question under consideration here is the extent to which this class differential might also be a sex differential.

25. John Locke, *Some Thoughts Concerning Education,* sec. 6; also, see Locke to Mrs. Clarke, Jan. 7, 1683/4, in *The Correspondence of John Locke and Edward Clarke,* ed. Benjamin Rand (Cambridge: Harvard University Press, 1927).

26. Locke to Mrs. Clarke, Jan. 7, 1683/4, in Rand, p. 121.

27. Locke to Clarke, Jan. 1, 1685, in Rand, p. 121.

28. Locke to Mrs. Clarke, in Rand, p. 103.

29. Locke to Mrs. Clarke in Rand, pp. 102–03; while Locke admitted no difference between the sexes in their ability to grasp truth, he did realize that women had less practice in using that ability. He asked a friend to help him revise a Latin text of the *Essay Concerning Human Understanding.* Locke wanted assistance in "paring off superfluous repetitions ... left in for the sake of illiterate Men and the softer Sex, not used to abstract Notions and Reasonings." Locke to William Molyneux, Apr. 26, 1695, in A. Bettesworth and C. Hitch, *Some Familiar Letters between Mr. Locke and Several of His Friends,* 3rd ed. (London, 1837), p. 88.

30. Peter Laslett, "Masham of Otes: The Rise and Fall of an English Family," *History Today,* 3 (August, 1953), 535–43, at 536. See also Maurice Cranston, *John Locke: A Biography* (London: Longmans, Green, 1957).

31. Locke to Limborch, Mar. 13, 1690/91, reprinted in H. R. Fox Bourne, *The Life of John Locke,* Vol. 2 (New York: Harper, 1876), pp. 212–13.

32. [Damaris Cudworth Masham], *Occasional Thoughts in Reference to a Virtuous or Christian Life,* in George Ballard, *Memoirs of British Ladies* (London: T. Evans, 1775), pp. 262–69, at p. 267.

33. Locke to Rebecca Collier, Nov. 21, 1696, reprinted in Fox Bourne, p. 453.

34. E. L. McAdam and George Milne, eds., *A Johnson Reader* (New York: Pantheon Books, 1964), p. 464.

The Moral Significance of Birth

Mary Anne Warren

English common law treats the moment of live birth as the point at which a legal person comes into existence. Although abortion has often been prohibited, it has almost never been classified as homicide. In contrast, infanticide generally is classified as a form of homicide, even where (as in England) there are statutes designed to mitigate the severity of the crime in certain cases. But many people—including some feminists—now favor the extension of equal legal rights to some or all fetuses (S. Callahan 1984, 1986). The extension of legal personhood to fetuses would not only threaten women's right to choose abortion, but also undermine other fundamental rights. I will argue that because of these dangers, birth remains the most appropriate place to mark the existence of a new legal person.

Speaking of Rights

In making this case, I find it useful to speak of moral as well as legal rights. Although not all legal rights can be grounded in moral rights, the right to life can plausibly be so construed. This approach is controversial. Some feminist philosophers have been critical of moral analyses based upon rights. Carol Gilligan (1982), Nell Noddings (1984), and others have argued that women tend to take a different approach to morality, one that emphasizes care and responsibility in interpersonal relationships rather than abstract rules, principles, or conflicts of rights. I would argue, however, that moral rights are complementary to a feminist ethics of care and responsibility, not inconsistent or competitive with it. Whereas caring relationships can provide a moral ideal, respect for rights provides a moral floor—a minimum protection for individuals which remains morally binding even where appropriate caring relationships are absent or have broken down (Manning 1988). Furthermore, as I shall argue, social relationships are part of the foundation of moral rights.

Some feminist philosophers have suggested that the very concept of a moral right may be inconsistent with the social nature of persons. Elizabeth Wolgast (1987, 41–42) argues convincingly that this concept has developed within an atomistic model of the social world, in which persons are depicted as self-sufficient and exclusively self-interested individuals whose relationships with one another are essentially competitive. As Wolgast notes, such an atomistic model is particularly inappropriate in the context of pregnancy, birth, and parental responsibility. Moreover, recent feminist research has greatly expanded our awareness of the historical, religious, sociological, and political forces that shape contemporary struggles over reproductive rights, further underscoring the need for approaches to moral theory that can take account of such social realities (Harrison 1983; Luker 1984; Petchesky 1984).

But is the concept of a moral right necessarily incompatible with the social nature of human beings? Rights are indeed individualistic, in that they can be ascribed to individuals, as well as to groups. But respect for moral rights need not be based upon an excessively individualistic view of human nature. A more socially perceptive account of moral rights is possible, provided that we reject two common assumptions about the theoretical foundations of moral rights. These assumptions are widely accepted by mainstream philosophers, but rarely stated and still more rarely defended.

The first is what I shall call the intrinsic-properties assumption. This is the view that the only facts that can justify the ascription of basic moral rights[1] or moral standing[2] to individuals are facts about *the intrinsic properties of those individuals.* Philosophers who accept this view disagree about which of the intrinsic properties of individuals are relevant to the ascription of rights. They agree, however, that relational properties—such as being loved, or being part of a social community or biological ecosystem—cannot be relevant.

The second is what I shall call the single-criterion assumption. This is the view that there is some single property, the presence or absence of which divides the world into those things which have moral rights or moral standing, and those things which do not. Christopher Stone (1987) locates this assumption within a more general theoretical approach, which he calls "moral monism." Moral monists believe that the goal of moral philosophy is the production of a coherent set of principles, sufficient to provide definitive answers to all possible moral dilemmas. Among these principles, the monist typically assumes, will be one that identifies some key property which is such that, "Those beings that possess the key property count morally ... [while those] things that lack it are all utterly irrelevant, except as resources for the benefit of those things that do count" (1987, 13).

Together, the intrinsic-properties and single-criterion assumptions preclude any adequate account of the social foundations of moral rights. The intrinsic-properties assumption requires us to regard all personal or other relationships among individuals or groups as wholly irrelevant to basic moral rights. The single-criterion assumption requires us to deny that there can be a variety of sound reasons for ascribing moral rights, and a variety of things and beings to which some rights may appropriately be ascribed. Both assumptions are inimical to a feminist approach to moral theory, as well as to approaches that are less anthropocentric and more environmentally adequate. The prevalence of these assumptions helps to explain why few mainstream philosophers believe that birth can in any way alter the infant's moral rights.

The Denial of the Moral Significance of Birth

The view that birth is irrelevant to moral rights is shared by philosophers on all points of the spectrum of moral views about abortion. For the most conservative, birth adds nothing to the infant's moral rights, since all of those rights have been present since conception. Moderates hold that the fetus acquires an equal right to life at some point after conception but before birth. The most popular candidates for this point of moral demarcation are (1) the stage at which the fetus becomes viable (i.e., capable of surviving outside the womb, with or without medical assistance), and (2) the stage at which it becomes sentient (i.e., capable of having experiences, including that of pain). For those who hold a view of this sort, both infanticide and abortion at any time past the critical stage are forms of homicide, and there is little reason to distinguish between them either morally or legally.

Finally, liberals hold that even relatively late abortion is sometimes morally acceptable, and that at no time is abortion the moral equivalent of homicide. However, few liberals wish to hold that infanticide is not—at least sometimes—morally comparable to homicide. Consequently, the presumption that being born makes no difference to one's moral rights creates problems for the liberal view of abortion. Unless the liberal can establish some grounds for a general moral distinction between late abortion and early infanticide, she must either retreat to a moderate position on abortion, or else conclude that infanticide is not so bad after all.

To those who accept the intrinsic-properties assumption, birth can make little difference to the moral standing of the fetus/infant. For birth does not seem to alter any intrinsic property that could reasonably be linked to the possession of a strong right to life. Newborn infants have very nearly the same intrinsic properties as do fetuses shortly before birth. They have, as L. W. Sumner (1983, 53) says, "the same size, shape, internal constitution, species membership, capacities, level of consciousness, and so forth."[3] Consequently, Sumner says, infanticide cannot be morally very different from late abortion. In his words, "Birth is a shallow and arbitrary criterion of moral standing, and there appears to be no way of connecting it to a deeper account" (52).

Sumner holds that the only valid criterion of moral standing is the capacity for sentience (136). Prenatal neurophysiology and behavior suggest that human fetuses begin to have rudimentary sensory experiences at some time during the second trimester of pregnancy. Thus, Sumner concludes that abortion should be permitted during the first trimester but not thereafter, except in special circumstances (152).[4]

Michael Tooley (1983) agrees that birth can make no difference to moral standing. However, rather than rejecting the liberal view of abortion, Tooley boldly claims that neither late abortion nor early infanticide is seriously wrong. He argues that an entity cannot have a strong right to life unless it is capable of desiring its own continued existence. To be capable of such a desire, he argues, a being must have a concept of itself as a continuing subject of conscious experience. Having such a concept is a central part of what it is to be a person, and thus the kind of being that has strong moral rights (41). Fetuses certainly lack such a concept, as do infants during the first few months of their lives. Thus, Tooley concludes, neither fetuses nor newborn infants have a strong right to life, and neither abortion nor infanticide is an intrinsic moral wrong.

These two theories are worth examining, not only because they illustrate the difficulties generated by the intrinsic-properties and single-criterion assumptions, but also because each includes valid insights that need to be integrated into a more comprehensive account. Both Sumner and Tooley are partially right. Unlike "genetic humanity"—a property possessed by fertilized human ova—sentience and self-awareness are properties that have some general relevance to what we may owe another being in the way of respect and protection. However, neither the sentience criterion nor the self-awareness criterion can explain the moral significance of birth.

The Sentience Criterion

Both newborn infants and late-term fetuses show clear signs of sentience. For instance, they are apparently capable of having visual experiences. Infants will often turn away from bright lights, and those who have done intrauterine photography have sometimes observed a similar reaction in the late-term fetus when bright lights are introduced in its vicinity. Both may respond to loud noises, voices, or other sounds, so both can probably have auditory experiences. They are evidently also responsive to touch, taste, motion, and other kinds of sensory stimulation.

The sentience of infants and late-term fetuses makes a difference to how they should be treated, by contrast with fertilized ova or first-trimester fetuses. Sentient beings are usually capable of experiencing painful as well as pleasurable or affectively neutral sensations.[5] While the capacity to experience pain is valuable to an organism, pain is by definition an intrinsically unpleasant experience. Thus, sentient beings may plausibly be said to have a moral right not to be deliberately subjected to pain in the absence of any compelling reason. For those who prefer not to speak of rights, it is still plausible that a capacity for sentience gives an entity some moral standing. It may, for instance, require that its interests be given some consideration in utilitarian calculations, or that it be treated as an end and never merely as a means.

But it is not clear that sentience is a sufficient condition for moral equality, since there are many clearly-sentient creatures (e.g., mice) to which most of us would not be prepared to ascribe equal moral standing. Sumner examines the implications of the sentience criterion primarily in the context of abortion. Given his belief that some compromise is essential between the conservative and liberal viewpoints on abortion, the sentience criterion recommends itself as a means of drawing a moral distinction between early abortion and late abortion. It is, in some ways, a more defensible criterion than fetal viability.

The 1973 *Roe v. Wade* decision treats the presumed viability of third-trimester fetuses as a basis for permitting states to restrict abortion rights in order to protect fetal life in the third trimester, but not earlier. Yet viability is relative, among other things, to the medical care available to the pregnant woman and her infant. Increasingly sophisticated neonatal intensive care has made it possible to save many more premature infants than before, thus altering the average age of viability. Someday it may be possible to keep even first-trimester fetuses alive and developing normally outside the womb. The viability criterion seems to imply that the advent of total ectogenesis (artificial gestation from conception to birth) would automatically eliminate women's right to abortion, even in the earliest stages of pregnancy. At the very least, it must imply that as many aborted fetuses as possible should be kept alive thorough artificial gestation. But the mere technological possibility of providing artificial wombs for huge numbers of human fetuses could not establish such a moral obligation. A massive commitment to ectogenesis would probably be ruinously expensive, and might prove contrary to the interests of parents and children. The viability criterion forces us to make a hazardous leap from the technologically possible to the morally mandatory.

The sentience criterion at first appears more promising as a means of defending a moderate view of abortion. It provides an intuitively plausible distinction between early and late abortion. Unlike the viability criterion, it is unlikely to be undermined by new biomedical technologies. Further investigation of fetal neurophysiology and behavior might refute the presumption that fetuses begin to be capable of sentience *at some point in the second trimester.* Perhaps this development occurs slightly earlier or slightly later than present evidence suggests. (It is unlikely to be much earlier or much later.) However, that is a consequence that those who hold a moderate position on abortion could live with; so long as the line could still be drawn with some degree of confidence, they need not insist that it be drawn exactly where Sumner suggests.

But closer inspection reveals that the sentience criterion will not yield the result that Sumner wants. His position vacillates between two versions of the sentience criterion, neither of which can adequately support his moderate view of abortion. The strong version of the sentience criterion treats sentience as a sufficient condition for having full and equal moral standing. The weak version treats sentience as sufficient for having some moral standing, but not necessarily full and equal moral standing.

Sumner's claim that sentient fetuses have the same moral standing as older human beings clearly requires the strong version of the sentience criterion. On this theory, any being which has even minimal capacities for sensory experience is the moral equal of any person. If we accept this theory, then we must conclude that not only is late abortion the oral equivalent of homicide, but so is the killing of such sentient nonhuman beings as mice. Sumner evidently does not wish to accept this further conclusion, for he also says that "sentience admits of degrees ... [a fact that] enables us to employ it both as an inclusion criterion and as a comparison criterion of moral standing" (144). In other words, all sentient beings have some moral standing, but beings that are more highly sentient have greater moral standing than do less highly sentient beings. This weaker version of the sentience criterion leaves room for a distinction between the moral standing of mice and that of sentient humans—provided, that is, that mice can be shown to be less highly sentient. However, it will not support the moral equality of late-term fetuses, since the relatively undeveloped condition of fetal brains almost certainly means that fetuses are less highly sentient than older human beings.

A similar dilemma haunts those who use the sentience criterion to argue for the moral equality of nonhuman animals. Some animal liberationists hold that all sentient beings are morally equal, regardless of species. For instance, Peter Singer (1981, 111) maintains that all sentient beings are entitled to equal consideration for their comparably important interests. Animal liberationists are primarily concerned to argue for the moral equality of vertebrate animals, such as mammals, birds, reptiles and fish. In this project, the sentience criterion serves them less well than they may suppose. On the one hand, if they use the weak versions of the sentience criterion then they cannot sustain the claim that all nonhuman vertebrates are our moral equals—unless they can demonstrate that they are all sentient *to the same degree* that we are. It is unclear how such a demonstration would proceed, or what would count as success. On the other hand, if they use the strong version of the sentience criterion, then they are committed to the conclusion that if flies and mosquitos are even minimally sentient then they too are our moral equals. Not even the most radical animal liberationists have endorsed the moral equality of such invertebrate animals,[6] yet it is quite likely that these creatures enjoy some form of sentience.

We do not really know whether complex invertebrate animals such as spiders and insects have sensory experiences, but the evidence suggests that they may. They have both sense organs and central nervous systems, and they often act as if they could see, hear, and feel very well. Sumner says that all invertebrates are probably nonsentient, because they lack certain brain structures—notably forebrains—that appear to be essential to the processing of pain in vertebrate animals (143). But might not some invertebrate animals have neurological devices for the processing of pain that are different from those of vertebrates, just as some have very different organs for the detection of light, sound, or odor? The capacity to feel pain is important to highly mobile organisms which guide their behavior through perceptual data, since it often enables them to avoid damage or destruction. Without that capacity, such organisms would be less likely to survive long enough to reproduce. Thus, if insects, spiders, crayfish, or octopi can see, hear, or smell, then it is quite likely that they can also feel pain. If sentience is the sole criterion for moral equality, then such probably-sentient entities deserve the benefit of the doubt.

But it is difficult to believe that killing invertebrate animals is as morally objectionable as homicide. That an entity is probably sentient provides a reason for avoiding actions that may cause it pain. It may also provide a reason for respecting its life, a life which it may enjoy. But it is not a sufficient reason for regarding it as a moral equal. Perhaps an ideally moral person would try to avoid killing any sentient being, even a fly. Yet it is impossible in practice to treat the killing of persons and the killing of sentient invertebrates with the same severity. Even the simplest activities essential to human survival (such as agriculture, or gathering wild foods) generally entail some loss of invertebrate lives. If the strong version of the sentience criterion is correct, then all such activities are morally problematic. And if it is not, then the probable sentience of late-term fetuses and newborn infants is not enough to demonstrate that either late abortion or infanticide is the moral equivalent of homicide. Some additional argument is needed to show that either late abortion or early infanticide is seriously immoral.

The Self-Awareness Criterion

Although newborn infants are regarded as persons in both law and common moral conviction, they lack certain mental capacities that are typical of persons. They have sensory experiences, but, as Tooley points out, they probably do not yet think, or have a sense of who they are, or a desire to continue to exist. It is not unreasonable to suppose that these facts make some difference to their moral standing. Other things being equal, it is surely worse to kill a self-aware being that wants to go on living than one that has never been self-aware and that has no such preference. If this is true, then it is hard to avoid the conclusion that neither abortion nor infanticide is quite as bad as the killing of older human beings. And indeed many human societies seem to have accepted that conclusion.

Tooley notes that the abhorrence of infanticide which is characteristic of cultures influenced by Christianity has not been shared by most cultures outside that influence (315–322). Prior to the present century, most societies—from the gatherer-hunter societies of Australia, Africa, North and South America, and elsewhere, to the high civilizations of China, India, Greece, Rome, and Egypt—have not only tolerated occasional instances of infanticide but have regarded it as sometimes the wisest course of action. Even in Christian Europe there was often a *de facto* toleration of infanticide—so long as the mother was married and the killing discreet. Throughout much of the second millennium in Europe, single women whose infants failed to survive were often executed in sadistic ways, yet married women whose infants died under equally suspicious circumstances generally escaped legal penalty (Piers 1978, 45–46). Evidently, the sanctions against infanticide had more to do with the desire to punish female sexual transgressions than with a consistently held belief that infanticide is morally comparable to homicide.

If infanticide has been less universally regarded as wrong than most people today believe, then the self-awareness criterion is more consistent with common moral convictions than it at first appears. Nevertheless, it conflicts with some convictions that are almost universal, even in cultures that tolerate infanticide. Tooley argues that infants probably begin to think and to become self-aware at about three months of age, and that this is therefore the stage at which they begin to have a strong right to life (405–406). Perhaps this is true. However the customs of most cultures seem to have required that a decision about the life of an infant be made within, at most, a few days of birth. Often, there was some special gesture or ceremony—such as washing the infant, feeding it, or giving it a name—to mark the fact that it would thenceforth be regarded as a member of the community. From that point on, infanticide would not be considered, except perhaps under unusual circumstances. For instance, Margaret Mead gives this account of birth and infanticide among the Arapesh people of Papua New Guinea:

> While the child is being delivered, the father waits within ear-shot until its sex is determined, when the midwives call it out to him. To this information he answers laconically, "Wash it," or "Do not wash it." If the command is "Wash it," the child is to be brought up. In a few cases when the child is a girl and there are already several girl-children in the family, the child will not be saved, but left, unwashed, with the cord uncut, in the bark basin on which the delivery takes place. (Mead [1935] 1963, 32–33)

Mead's account shows that among the Arapesh infanticide is at least to some degree a function of patriarchal power. In this, they are not unusual. In almost every society in which infanticide has been tolerated, female infants have been the most frequent victims. In patriarchal, patrilineal and patrilocal societies, daughters are usually valued less than sons, e.g., because they will leave the family at marriage, and will probably be unable to contribute as much as sons to the parents' economic support later. Female infanticide probably reinforces male domination by reducing the relative number of women and dramatically reinforcing the social devaluation of females.[7] Often it is the father who decides which infants will be reared. Dianne Romaine has pointed out to me that this practice may be due to a reluctance to force women, the primary caregivers, to decide when care should not be given. However, it also suggests that infanticide often served the interests of individual men more than those of women, the family, or the community as a whole.

Nevertheless, infanticide must sometimes have been the most humane resolution of a tragic dilemma. In the absence of effective contraception or abortion, abandoning a newborn can sometimes be the only alternative to the infant's later death from starvation. Women of nomadic gatherer-hunter societies, for instance, are sometimes unable to raise an infant born too soon after the last one, because they can neither nurse nor carry two small children.

But if infanticide is to be considered, it is better that it be done immediately after birth, before the bonds of love and care between the infant and the mother (and other persons) have grown any stronger than they may already be. Postponing the question of the infant's acceptance for weeks or months would be cruel to all concerned. Although an infant may be little more sentient or self-aware at two weeks of age than at birth, its death is apt to be a greater tragedy—not for it, but for those who have come to love it. I suspect that this is why, where infanticide is tolerated, the decision to kill or abandon an infant must usually be made rather quickly. If this consideration is morally relevant—and I think it is—then the self-awareness criterion fails to illuminate some of the morally salient aspects of infanticide.

Protecting Nonpersons

If we are to justify a general moral distinction between abortion and infanticide, we must answer two questions. First, why should infanticide be discouraged, rather than treated as a matter for individual decision? And second, why should sentient fetuses not be given the same protections that law and common sense morality accord to infants? But before turning to these two questions, it is necessary to make a more general point.

Persons have sound reasons for treating one another as moral equals. These reasons derive from both self-interest and altruistic concern for others—which, because of our social nature, are often very difficult to distinguish. Human persons—and perhaps all persons—normally come into existence only in and through social relationships. Sentience may begin to emerge without much direct social interaction, but it is doubtful that a child reared in total isolation from human or other sentient (or apparently sentient) beings could develop the capacities for self-awareness and social interaction that are essential to personhood. The recognition of the fundamentally social nature of persons can only strengthen the case for moral equality, since social relationships are undermined and distorted by inequalities that are perceived as unjust. There may be many nonhuman animals who have enough capacity for self-awareness and social interaction to be regarded as persons, with equal basic moral rights. But, whether or not this is true, it is certainly true that if any things have full and equal basic moral rights then persons do.

However we cannot conclude that, because all persons have equal basic moral rights, it is always wrong to extend strong moral protections to beings that are not persons. Those who accept the single-criterion assumption may find that a plausible inference. By now, however, most thoughtful people recognize the need to protect vulnerable elements of the natural world—such as endangered plant and animal species, rainforests, and rivers—from further destruction at human hands. Some argue that it is appropriate, as a way of protecting these things, to ascribe to them legal if not moral rights (Stone 1974). These things should be protected not because they are sentient or self-aware, but for other good reasons. They are irreplaceable parts of the terrestrial biosphere, and as such they have incalculable value to human beings. Their long-term instrumental value is often a fully sufficient reason for protecting them. However, they may also be held to have inherent value, i.e., value that is independent of the uses we might wish to make of them (Taylor 1986). Although destroying them is not murder, it is an act of vandalism which later generations will mourn.

It is probably not crucial whether or not we say that endangered species and natural habitats have a moral right to our protection. What is crucial is that we recognize and act upon the need to protect them. Yet certain contemporary realities argue for an increased willingness to ascribe rights to impersonal elements of the natural world. Americans, at least, are likely to be more sensitive to appeals and demands couched in terms of rights than those that appeal to less familiar concepts, such as inherent value. So central are rights to our common moral idiom, that to deny that trees have rights is risk being thought to condone the reckless destruction of rainforests and redwood groves. If we want to communicate effectively about the need to protect the natural world—and to protect it for its own sake as well as our own—then we may be wise to develop theories that permit us to ascribe at least some moral rights to some things that are clearly not persons.

Parallel issues arise with respect to the moral status of the newborn infant. As Wolgast (1987, 38) argues, it is much more important to understand our responsibilities to protect and care for infants than to insist that they have exactly the same moral rights as older human beings. Yet to deny that infants have equal basic moral rights is to risk being thought to condone infanticide and the neglect and abuse of infants. Here too, effective communication about human moral responsibilities seems to demand the ascription of rights to beings that lack certain properties that are typical of persons. But, of course, that does not explain why we have those responsibilities towards infants in the first place.

Why Protect Infants?

I have already mentioned some of the reasons for protecting human infants more carefully than we protect most comparably-sentient nonhuman beings. Most people care deeply about infants, particularly—but not exclusively—their own. Normal human adults (and children) are probably "programmed" by their biological nature to respond to human infants with care and concern. For the mother, in particular, that response is apt to begin well before the infant is born. But even for her it is likely to become more intense after the infant's birth. The infant at birth enters the human social world, where, if it lives, it becomes involved in social relationships with others, of kinds that can only be dimly foreshadowed before birth. It begins to be known and cared for, not just as a potential member of the family or community, but as a socially present and responsive individual. In the words of Loren Lomansky (1984, 172), "birth constitutes a quantum leap forward in the process of establishing ... social bonds." The newborn is not yet self-aware, but it is already (rapidly becoming) a social being.

Thus, although the human newborn may have no intrinsic properties that can ground a moral right to life stronger than that of a fetus just before birth, its emergence into the social world makes it appropriate to treat it as if it had such a stronger right. This, in effect, is what the law has done, through the doctrine that a person begins to exist at birth. Those who accept the intrinsic-properties assumption can only regard this doctrine as a legal fiction. However, it is a fiction that we would have difficulty doing without. If the line were not drawn at birth, then I think we would have to draw it at some point rather soon thereafter, as many other societies have done.

Another reason for condemning infanticide is that, at least in relatively privileged nations like our own, infants whose parents cannot raise them can usually be placed with people who will love them and take good care of them. This means that infanticide is rarely in the infant's own best interests, and would often deprive some potential adoptive individual or family of a great benefit. It also means that the prohibition of infanticide need not impose intolerable burdens upon parents (especially women). A rare parent might think it best to kill a healthy[8] infant rather than permitting it to be reared by others, but a persuasive defense of that claim would require special circumstances. For instance, when abortion is unavailable and women face savage abuses for supposed sexual transgressions, those who resort to infanticide to conceal an "illegitimate" birth may be doing only what they must. But where enforcement of the sexual double standard is less brutal, abortion and adoption can provide alternatives that most women would prefer to infanticide.

Some might wonder whether adoption is really preferable to infanticide, at least from the parent's point of view. Judith Thomson (1971, 66) notes that, "A woman may be utterly devastated by the thought of a child, a bit of herself, put out for adoption and never seen or heard of again." From the standpoint of narrow self-interest, it might not be irrational to prefer the death of the child to such a future. Yet few would wish to resolve this problem by legalizing infanticide. The evolution of more open adoption procedures which permit more contact between the adopted child and the biological parent(s) might lessen the psychological pain often associated with adoption. But that would be at best a partial solution. More basic is the provision of better social support for child-rearers, so that parents are not forced by economic necessity to surrender their children for adoption.

These are just some of the arguments for treating infants as legal persons, with an equal right to life. A more complete account might deal with the effects of the toleration of infanticide upon other moral norms. But the existence of such effects is unclear. Despite a tradition of occasional infanticide, the Arapesh appear in Mead's descriptions as gentle people who treat their children with great kindness and affection. The case against infanticide need not rest upon the questionable claim that the toleration of infanticide inevitably leads to the erosion of other moral norms. It is enough that most people today strongly desire that the lives of infants be protected, and that this can now be done without imposing intolerable burdens upon individuals or communities.

But have I not left the door open to the claim that infanticide may still be justified in some places, e.g., where there is severe poverty and a lack of accessible adoption agencies or where women face exceptionally harsh penalties for "illegitimate" births? I have, and deliberately. The moral case against the toleration of infanticide is contingent upon the existence of morally preferable options. Where economic hardship, the lack of contraception and abortion, and other forms of sexual and political oppression have eliminated all such options, there will be instances in which infanticide is the least tragic of a tragic set of choices. In such circumstances, the enforcement of extreme sanctions against infanticide can constitute an additional injustice.

Why Birth Matters

I have defended what most regard as needing no defense, i.e., the ascription of an equal right to life to human infants. Under reasonably favorable conditions that policy can protect the rights and interests of all concerned, including infants, biological parents, and potential adoptive parents.

But if protecting infants is such a good idea, then why is it not a good idea to extend the same strong protections to sentient fetuses? The question is not whether sentient fetuses ought to be protected: of course they should. Most women readily accept the responsibility for doing whatever they can to ensure that their (voluntarily continued) pregnancies are successful, and that no avoidable harm comes to the fetus. Negligent or malevolent actions by third parties which result in death or injury to pregnant women or their potential children should be subject to moral censure and legal prosecution. A just and caring society would do much more than ours does to protect the health of all its members, including pregnant women. The question is whether the law should accord to late-term fetuses *exactly the same* protections as are accorded to infants and older human beings.

The case for doing so might seem quite strong. We normally regard not only infants, but all other postnatal human beings as entitled to strong legal protections *so long as they are either sentient or capable of an eventual return to sentience.* We do not also require that they demonstrate a capacity for thought, self-awareness, or social relationships before we conclude that they have an equal right to life. Such restrictive criteria would leave too much room for invidious discrimination. The eternal propensity of powerful groups to rationalize sexual, racial, and class oppression by claiming that members of the oppressed group are mentally or otherwise "inferior" leaves little hope that such restrictive criteria could be applied without bias. Thus, for human beings past the prenatal stage, the capacity for sentience—or for a return to sentience—may be the only pragmatically defensible criterion for the ascription of full and equal basic rights. If so, then both theoretical simplicity and oral consistency may seem to require that we extend the same protections to sentient human beings that have not yet been born as to those that have.

But there is one crucial consideration which this argument leaves out. It is impossible to treat fetuses *in utero* as if they were persons without treating women as if they were something less than persons. The extension of equal rights to sentient fetuses would inevitably license severe violations of women's basic rights to personal autonomy and physical security. In the first place, it would rule out most second-trimester abortions performed to protect the woman's life or health. Such abortions might sometimes be construed as a form of self-defense. But the right to self-defense is not usually taken to mean that one may kill innocent persons just because their continued existence poses some threat to one's own life or health. If abortion must be justified as self-defense, then it will rarely be performed until the woman is already in extreme danger, and perhaps not even then. Such a policy would cost some women their lives, while others would be subjected to needless suffering and permanent physical harm.

Other alarming consequences of the drive to extend more equal rights to fetuses are already apparent in the United States. In the past decade it has become increasingly common for hospitals or physicians to obtain court orders requiring women in labor to undergo Caesarean sections, against their will, for what is thought to be the good of the fetus. Such an extreme infringement of the woman's right to security against physical assault would be almost unthinkable once the infant has been born. No parent or relative can legally be forced to undergo any surgical procedure, even

possibly to save the life of a child, once it is born. But pregnant women can sometimes be forced to undergo major surgery, for the supposed benefit of the fetus. As
George Annas (1982, 16) points out, forced Caesareans threaten to reduce women to
the status of inanimate objects—containers which may be opened at the will of
others in order to get at their contents.

Perhaps the most troubling illustration of this trend is the case of Angie Carder,   3
who died at George Washington University Medical Center in June 1987, two days after a court-ordered Caesarean section. Ms. Carder had suffered a recurrence of an
earlier cancer, and was not expected to live much longer. Her physicians agreed that
the fetus was too undeveloped to be viable, and that Carder herself was probably too
weak to survive the surgery. Although she, her family, and the physicians were all opposed to a Caesarean delivery, the hospital administration—evidently believing it
had a legal obligation to try to save the fetus—sought and obtained a court order to
have it done. As predicted, both Carder and her infant died soon after the operation.[9]
This woman's rights to autonomy, physical integrity, and life itself were forfeit—not
just because of her illness, but because of her pregnancy.

Such precedents are doubly alarming in the light of the development of new techniques of fetal therapy. As fetuses come to be regarded as patients, with rights that
may be in direct conflict with those of their mothers, and as the *in utero* treatment of
fetuses becomes more feasible, more and more pregnant women may be subjected
against their will to dangerous and invasive medical interventions. If so, then we may
be sure that there will be other Angie Carders.

Another danger in extending equal legal protections to sentient fetuses is that
women will increasingly be blamed, and sometimes legally prosecuted, when they
miscarry or give birth to premature, sick, or abnormal infants. It is reasonable to
hold the caretakers of infants legally responsible if their charges are harmed because
of their avoidable negligence. But when a woman miscarries or gives birth to an abnormal infant, the cause of the harm might be traced to any of an enormous number
of actions or circumstances which would not normally constitute any legal offense.
She might have gotten too much exercise or too little, eaten the wrong foods or the
wrong quantity of the right ones, or taken or failed to take certain drugs. She might
have smoked, consumed alcohol, or gotten too little sleep. She might have "permitted" her health to be damaged by hard work, by unsafe employment conditions, by
the lack of affordable medical care, by living near a source of industrial pollution, by
a physically or mentally abusive partner, or in any number of other ways.

Are such supposed failures on the part of pregnant women potentially to be construed as child abuse or negligent homicide? If sentient fetuses are entitled to the
same legal protections as infants, then it would seem so. The danger is not a merely
theoretical one. Two years ago in San Diego, a woman whose son was born with
brain damage and died several weeks later was charged with felony child neglect. It
was said that she had been advised by her physician to avoid sex and illicit drugs, and
go to the hospital immediately if she noticed any bleeding. Instead, she had allegedly
had sex with her husband, taken some inappropriate drug, and delayed getting to the
hospital for what might have been several hours after the onset of bleeding.

In this case, the charges were eventually dismissed on the grounds that the child
protection law invoked had not been intended to apply to cases of this kind. But the
multiplication of such cases is inevitable if the strong legal protections accorded to

infants are extended to sentient fetuses. A bill recently introduced in the Australian state of New South Wales would make women liable to criminal prosecution if they are found to have smoked during pregnancy, eaten unhealthful foods, or taken any other action which can be shown to have adversely affected the development of the fetus (*The Australian*, July 5, 1988, 5). Such an approach to the protection of fetuses authorizes the legal regulation of virtually every aspect of women's public and private lives, and thus is incompatible with even the most minimal right to autonomy. Moreover, such laws are apt to prove counterproductive, since the fear of prosecution may deter poor or otherwise vulnerable women from seeking needed medical care during pregnancy. I am not suggesting that women whose apparent negligence causes prenatal harm to their infants should always be immune from criticism. However, if we want to improve the health of infants we would do better to provide the services women need to protect their health, rather than seeking to use the law to punish those whose prenatal care has been less than ideal.

There is yet another problem, which may prove temporary but which remains significant at this time. The extension of legal personhood to sentient fetuses would rule out most abortions performed because of severe fetal abnormalities, such as Down's Syndrome or spina bifida. Abortions performed following amniocentesis are usually done in the latter part of the second trimester, since it is usually not possible to obtain test results earlier. Methods of detecting fetal abnormalities at earlier stages, such as chorion biopsy, may eventually make late abortion for reasons of fetal abnormality unnecessary; but at present the safety of these methods is unproven.

The elimination of most such abortions might be a consequence that could be accepted, were the society willing to provide adequate support for the handicapped children and adults who would come into being as a result of this policy. However, our society is not prepared to do this. In the absence of adequate communally-funded care for the handicapped, the prohibition of such abortions is exploitative of women. Of course, the male relatives of severely handicapped persons may also bear heavy burdens. Yet the heaviest portion of the daily responsibility generally falls upon mothers and other female relatives. If fetuses are not yet persons (and women are), then a respect for the equality of persons should lead to support for the availability of abortion in cases of severe fetal abnormality.[10]

Such arguments will not persuade those who deeply believe that fetuses are already persons, with equal moral rights. How, they will ask, is denying legal equality to sentient fetuses different from denying it to any other powerless group of human beings? If some human beings are more equal than others, then how can any of us feel safe? The answer is twofold.

First, pregnancy is a relationship different from any other, including that between parents and already-born children. It is not just one of innumerable situations in which the rights of one individual may come into conflict with those of another; it is probably the *only* case in which the legal personhood of one human being is necessarily incompatible with that of another. Only in pregnancy is the organic functioning of one human individual biologically inseparable from that of another. This organic unity makes it impossible for others to provide the fetus with medical care or any other presumed benefit, except by doing something to or for the woman. To try to "protect" the fetus other than through her cooperation and consent is effectively to nullify her right to autonomy, and potentially to expose her to violent physical assaults such as would not be legally condoned in any other type of case. The uniqueness of pregnancy helps to explain why the toleration of abortion does not lead to the disenfranchisement of other groups of human beings, as opponents of abortion often claim. For biological as well as psychological reasons, "It is all but impossible to extrapolate from attitudes towards fetal life attitudes toward [other] existing human life" (D. Callahan 1970, 474).

But, granting the uniqueness of pregnancy, why is it *women's* rights that should be privileged? If women and fetuses cannot both be legal persons then why not favor fetuses, e.g., on the grounds that they are more helpless, or more innocent, or have a longer life expectancy? It is difficult to justify this apparent bias towards women without appealing to the empirical fact that women are already persons in the usual, nonlegal sense—already thinking, self-aware, fully social beings—and fetuses are not. Regardless of whether we stress the intrinsic properties of persons, or the social and relational dimensions of personhood, this distinction remains. Even sentient fetuses do not yet have either the cognitive capacities or the richly interactive social involvements typical of persons.

This "not yet" is morally decisive. It is wrong to treat persons as if they do not have equal basic rights. Other things being equal, it is worse to deprive persons of their most basic moral and legal rights than to refrain from extending such rights to beings that are not persons. This is one important element of truth in the self-awareness criterion. If fetuses were already thinking, self-aware, socially responsive members of communities, then nothing could justify refusing them the equal protection of the law. In that case, we would sometimes be forced to balance the rights of the fetus against those of the woman, and sometimes the scales might be almost equally weighted. However, if women are persons and fetuses are not, then the balance must swing towards women's rights.

Conclusion

Birth is morally significant because it marks the end of one relationship and the beginning of others. It marks the end of pregnancy, a relationship so intimate that it is impossible to extend the equal protection of the law to fetuses without severely infringing women's most basic rights. Birth also marks the beginning of the infant's existence as a socially responsive member of a human community. Although the infant is not instantly transformed into a person at the moment of birth, it does become a biologically separate human being. As such, it can be known and cared for as a particular individual. It can also be vigorously protected without negating the basic rights of women. There are circumstances in which infanticide may be the best of a bad set of options. But our own society has both the ability and the desire to protect infants, and there is no reason why we should not do so.

We should not, however, seek to extend the same degree of protection to fetuses. Both late-term fetuses and newborn infants are probably capable of sentience. Both are precious to those who want children; and both need to be protected from a variety of possible harms. All of these factors contribute to the moral standing of the late-term fetus, which is substantial. However, to extend equal legal rights to fetuses is necessarily to deprive pregnant women of the rights to personal autonomy, physical integrity, and sometimes life itself. *There is room for only one person with full and equal rights inside a single human skin.* That is why it is birth, rather than sentience, viability, or some other prenatal milestone that must mark the beginning of legal parenthood.[11]

Notes

1. Basic moral rights are those that are possessed equally by all persons, and that are essential to the moral equality of persons. The intended contrast is to those rights which arise from certain special circumstances—for instance, the right of a person to whom a promise has been made that that promise be kept. (Whether there are beings that are not persons but that have similar basic moral rights is one of the questions to be addressed here.)

2. "Moral standing," like "moral status," is a term that can be used to refer to the moral considerability of individuals, without being committed to the existence of moral rights. For instance, Sumner (1983) and Singer (1981) prefer these terms because, as utilitarians, they are unconvinced of the need for moral rights.

3. It is not obvious that a newborn infant's "level of consciousness" is similar to that of a fetus shortly before birth. Perhaps birth is analogous to an awakening, in that the infant has many experiences that were previously precluded by its prenatal brain chemistry or by its relative insulation within the womb. This speculation is plausible in evolutionary terms, since a rich subjective mental life might have little survival value for the fetus, but might be highly valuable for the newborn, e.g., in enabling it to recognize its mother and signal its hunger, discomfort, etc. However, for the sake of the argument I will assume that the newborn's capacity for sentience is generally not very different from that of the fetus shortly before birth.

4. It is interesting that Sumner regards fetal abnormality and the protection of the woman's health as sufficient justifications for late abortion. In this, he evidently departs from his own theory by effectively differentiating between the moral status of sentient fetuses and that of older humans—who presumably may not be killed just because they are abnormal or because their existence (through no fault of their own) poses a threat to someone else's health.

5. There are evidently some people who, though otherwise sentient, cannot experience physical pain. However, the survival value of the capacity to experience pain makes it probable that such individuals are the exception rather than the rule among mature members of sentient species.

6. There is at least one religion, that of the Jains, in which the killing of any living thing—even an insect—is regarded as morally wrong. But even the Jains do not regard the killing of insects as morally equivalent to the killing of persons. Laypersons (unlike mendicants) are permitted some unintentional killing of insects—though not of vertebrate animals or persons—when this is unavoidable to the pursuit of their profession. (See Jaini 1979, 171–3.)

7. Marcia Guttentag and Paul Secord (1983) argue that a shortage of women benefits at least some women, by increasing their "value" in the marriage market. However, they also argue that this increased value does not lead to greater freedom for women; on the contrary, it tends to coincide with an exceptionally severe sexual double standard, the exclusion of women from public life, and their confinement to domestic roles.

8. The extension of equal basic rights to infants need not imply the absolute rejection of euthanasia for infant patients. There are instances in which artificially extending the life of a severely compromised infant is contrary to the infant's own best interests. Competent adults or older children who are terminally ill sometimes rightly judge that further prolongation of their lives would not be a benefit to them. While infants cannot make that judgment for themselves, it is sometimes the right judgment for others to make on their behalf.

9. See *Civil Liberties* 363 (Winter 1988), 12, and Lawrence Lader, "Regulating Birth: Is the State Going Too Far?" *Conscience* IX: 5 (September/October, 1988), 5–6.

10. It is sometimes argued that using abortion to prevent the birth of severely handicapped infants will inevitably lead to a loss of concern for handicapped persons. I doubt that this is true. There is no need to confuse the question of whether it is good that persons be born handicapped with the very different question of whether handicapped persons are entitled to respect, support, and care.

11. My thanks by Helen Heise, Helen B. Holmes, Laura M. Purdy, Dianne Romaine, Peter Singer, and Michael Scriven for their helpful comments on earlier versions of this paper.

References

Annas, George. 1982. Forced cesareans: The most unkindest cut. *Hastings Center Report,* June 12: 3.

The Australian, Tuesday, July 5, 1988, 5.

Callahan, Daniel. 1970. *Abortion: Law, choice and morality.* New York: Macmillan.

Callahan, Sydney. 1984. Value choices in abortion. In *Abortion: Understanding differences.* Sydney Callahan and Daniel Callahan, eds. New York and London: Plenum Press.

Callahan, Sydney. 1986. Abortion and the sexual agenda. *Commonweal,* April 25, 232–238.

Gilligan, Carol. 1982. *In a different voice: Psychological theory and women's development.* Cambridge, Massachusetts: Harvard University Press.

Guttentag, Marcia, and Paul Secord. 1983. *Too many women: The sex ratio question.* Beverly Hills: Sage Publications.

Harrison, Beverly Wildung. 1983. *Our right to choose: Toward a new ethic of abortion.* Boston: Beacon Press.

Jaini, Padmanab S. 1979. *The jaina path of purification.* Berkeley, Los Angeles, London: University of California Press.

Lomansky, Loren. 1984. Being a person—does it matter? In *The problem of abortion.* Joel Feinberg, ed. Belmont, California.

Luker, Kristen. 1984. *Abortion and the politics of motherhood.* Berkeley, Los Angeles and London: University of California Press.

Manning, Rita. 1988. *Caring for and caring about.* Paper presented at conference entitled *Explorations in Feminist Ethics,* Duluth, Minnesota. October 8.

Mead, Margaret. [1935] 1963. *Sex and temperament in three primitive societies.* New York: Morrow Quill Paperbacks.

Noddings, Nell. 1984. *Caring: A feminine approach to ethics and moral education.* Berkeley, Los Angeles and London: University of California Press.

Petchesky, Rosalind Pollack. 1984. *Abortion and women's choice.* New York, London: Longman.

Piers, Maria W. 1978. *Infanticide.* New York: W. W. Norton and Company.

Singer, Peter. 1981. *The expanding circle: Ethics and sociogiology.* New York: Farrar, Straus and Giroux.

Stone, Christopher. 1974. *Should trees have standing: Towards legal rights for natural objects.* Los Altos: William Kaufman.

Stone, Christopher. 1987. *Earth and other ethics.* New York: Harper & Row.

Sumner, L. W. 1983. *Abortion and moral theory.* Princeton, New Jersey: Princeton University Press.

Taylor, Paul W. 1986. *Respect for nature: A theory of environmental ethics.* Princeton, New Jersey: Princeton University Press.

Thomson, Judith Jarvis. 1971. A defense of abortion. *Philosophy and Public Affairs* 1 (1): 47–66.

Tooley, Michael. 1983. *Abortion and infanticide.* Oxford: Oxford University Press.

Wolgast, Elizabeth. 1987. *The grammar of justice.* Ithaca & London: Cornell University Press.

Suggested Further Readings

Eisenstein, Zillah. *The Radical Future of Liberal Feminism.* Boston: Northeastern University Press, 1986.

Friedan, Betty. *The Feminine Mystique.* New York: Dell, 1974.

_____. *The Second Stage.* New York: Summit Books, 1981.

Gilman, Charlotte Perkins. *Women and Economics.* New York: Harper and Row, 1966.

Grimke, Sarah. *Letters on the Equality of the Sexes and the Condition of Woman.* New York: Burt Franklin, 1972.

Jaggar, Alison M. *Feminist Politics and Human Nature.* Totowa, N.J.: Rowman & Allanheld, 1983.

Mill, Harriet Taylor. "Enfranchisement of Women." In John Stuart Mill and Harriet Taylor Mill. *Essays on Sex Equality,* ed. Alice S. Rossi, pp. 89–122. Chicago: University of Chicago Press, 1970.

Mill, John Stuart. "The Subjection of Women." In John Stuart Mill and Harriet Taylor Mill. *Essays on Sex Equality,* ed. Alice S. Rossi, pp. 123–242. Chicago: University of Chicago Press, 1970.

Okin, Susan Moller. *Women in Western Political Thought.* Princeton: Princeton University Press, 1979.

Pateman, Carole. *The Problem of Political Obligation: A Critique of Liberal Theory.* Berkeley: University of California Press, 1979.

Rossi, Alice, ed. *The Feminist Papers: From Adams to de Beauvoir.* New York: Columbia University Press, 1973.

Steinem, Gloria. *Outrageous Acts and Everyday Rebellions.* New York: Holt, Rinehart & Winston, 1983.

Tong, Rosemarie. *Feminist Thought: A Comprehensive Introduction.* Boulder: Westview Press, 1989.

Wollstonecraft, Mary. *A Vindication of the Rights of Woman,* ed. Carol H. Poston. New York: W. W. Norton, 1975.

Wright, Francis. *Life, Letters and Lectures, 1834–44.* New York: Arno Press, 1972.

T W O

MARXIST FEMINIST

PERSPECTIVES

Within one popular interpretation of Marxist feminism, its adherents agree with Friedrich Engels that women's oppression originated with the introduction of private property, an institution that obliterated whatever equality the human community had previously enjoyed. Private ownership of the means of production by relatively few persons, originally all male, inaugurated a class system whose contemporary manifestations are capitalism and imperialism. Reflection on this state of affairs suggests that it is not *patriarchy*—the social and cultural rules that privilege men over women—but *capitalism* itself that is the fundamental cause of women's oppression. If all women are ever to be liberated, socialism must replace capitalism. Only then will women be economically freed from men and, therefore, equal to them.

Even though this interpretation of Marxist feminism is useful as a first approximation of its distinguishing features, it is still a somewhat limited and even misleading interpretation for several reasons. First, it overlooks the degree to which many Marxist feminists are critical of Marxist theory in general, especially the antiquated sociological and anthropological views that permeate it. Second, it ignores the extent to which Marxist feminists use Marxist methodology to understand *gender* oppression as well as class oppression. Finally, it fails to highlight the ways in which Marxist feminists pick and choose among Marxist doctrines. For example, they tend to reject the notion of a final classless society as hopelessly utopian, but they embrace the assumption that economic factors determine the nature and function of human relationships in the private as well as the public world.

In her chapter "The Feminist Standpoint: Developing the Ground for a Specifically Feminist Historical Materialism," Nancy Hartsock uses Marxist epistemology to develop a specifically feminist historical materialism—a methodology that analyzes all dimensions of social life in terms of the development of those material goods necessary to sustain human existence. What most impresses Hartsock concerning Marx is his interpretation of the world from the standpoint of the proletariat. Because Marx used the eyes of the workers, says Hartsock, he was able "to go beneath bourgeois ideology," to see capitalism for what it is—an exploitative system that permits and even requires people to be alienated from each other and from the natural world. Hartsock extends Marx's insight, arguing that if feminist philosophers wish "to go beneath" patriarchal ideology, they must use the eyes of women to expose patriarchy for what it is—an oppressive system that permits and even requires men to dominate women.

Hartsock suggests that to ask Marx why the perspective of the workers should be privileged over that of the capitalists or to ask feminist theorists why the perspective of women should be privileged over that of men is to invite the following clarification: Not all standpoints on reality mirror it with equal accuracy. Because the rich and the powerful are often able to make the world conform to their image and likeness of it—usually by forcing the poor and the vulnerable to see things their way—the capitalists' understanding of reality tends to be more "partial and perverse" than that of the workers. Although it is no easy task for the workers to see things as they really are, they have the potential not only to see the world as it truly is but also to change it for the better precisely because of their oppressed status.

In response to the argument that women are too different from each other to share any common "historical materialist" experience, Hartsock insists that no matter what their age, race, socioeconomic class, or religion, all women do "women's work": "Whether or not all of us do both, women as a sex are institutionally responsible for producing both goods and human beings and all women are forced to become the kinds of people who can do both." Therefore, it is women's work that constitutes the standpoint from which *all* women can and should interpret reality as it is and as it could be. Only by understanding the liberatory as well as the exploitative dimensions of their work will women gain enough revolutionary momentum as well as visionary clarity to overcome what Hartsock views as the destructive tendencies of a patriarchal system that trivializes women's life-giving work even as it feeds off of it.

Like Hartsock, both Mary O'Brien and Heidi Hartmann seek to remedy the deficiencies in Marxist methodology. Both of them recall Engels's statement that

> According to the materialist conception, the determining force in history is, in the final instance, the production and reproduction of immediate life. This, again, is of a twofold character: on the one side, the production of the means of existence, of food, clothing and shelter and the tools necessary for that production; on the other side, the production of human beings themselves, the propagation of the species. The social organization under which the people of a particular historical epoch live is determined by both kinds of production.[1]

To the degree that traditional Marxists failed to carry through on this original project, Marxist feminists perceive themselves as trying to complete it by providing an account of the production of people as well as of things.

In her essay "Reproducing Marxist Man," O'Brien faults traditional Marxists for maintaining that because men's work (making things in factories) is the only kind of work that counts as "real," the only crucial human struggle is *class* struggle between the workers and the capitalists. Thus, it is by insisting that women's work (making babies in wombs) is also "real" work that Marxist feminists elevate *gender* struggle between men and women to an equally crucial human struggle. Gender struggle consists in men's quest to appropriate from women that which is alienated from men in the reproductive process—the "fruit" of their seed. Men do not "make" children; women do. In the past, men tried to control reproduction by initiating it with or without the woman's consent or by claiming the child as their private property at the moment of birth. O'Brien suggests that with the advent of reproductive technology, especially birth control, women finally have the means to resist men's efforts to control reproduction. In future years, the gender struggle between men and women over *reproductive* issues is likely to be as intense as the struggle between capitalists and workers over *productive* issues.

Heidi Hartmann takes a different tack than O'Brien in her contribution to this volume, "The Family as the Locus of Gender, Class, and Political Struggle: The Example of Housework." She focuses not so much on women's reproductive work as on the kind of work women do at home for no wages (housework). With the development of the capitalist mode of production, the making of things moved out of the household into the factory. For a variety of reasons, most having to do with women's reproductive role, more men than women initially left the household for the factory. Women continued to work, however. Wives and daughters cooked, cleaned, and cared for the old and young; in return, their husbands or fathers, upon whom they were economically dependent, subsidized them. What traditional Marxists failed to realize, however, was that these "subsidies" were in fact exceedingly low wages for work that if performed by outsiders would have been quite costly.

Currently, an increasing number of women are working outside of the home as a matter of economic necessity. Now that women are gainfully employed, we would expect equality to exist between men and women. But even if patriarchal privilege is waning in the workplace, it is not waning in the household. Even though both mom and dad are working long hours *outside* the home, it seems that only mom is working long hours *within* the home. In protest against their "double day," many wives and mothers are finding ways to do less housework. For example, wage-earning women are lowering their standards for what counts as a clean house and are relying on cleaning services, fast-food carryouts, and child-care attendants to lighten their loads. But there is only so much money a family can spend on outside help before its income evaporates; a family can lower its "cleanliness" standards only so far before it is forced to conclude that its home is filthy. In the end, dad may have to share mom's traditional household chores in order to make family life attractive for him, her, and their children. Otherwise, says Hartmann, "the decentralized home system itself may be a casualty of gender and class struggle."

Clearly, Marxist feminist thought represents an advance over traditional Marxist thought in that it shows how gender and class struggle are interrelated. Yet, in its focus on the evils of gender and class oppression, it largely overlooks the evils of race oppression or oppression on account of one's sexual orientation. For example, Marxist feminists do not tend to worry about men who do not get to do "men's work" because no capitalist wishes to hire them. The number of unemployed minority men far exceeds that of unemployed white men, and it is difficult to engage in class struggle if one is a member of an underclass—the unemployed—that scarcely counts as a class at all. Similarly, Marxist feminists do not tend to worry about lesbian women who do not do "women's work" because, as lesbians, they live outside the parameters of the institutions of heterosexuality and its rules about "men's" as opposed to "women's" work. The kind of gender struggle Marxist feminists have in mind might eliminate the double day for heterosexual women but not for lesbian women. Clearly, Marxist feminist thought, like many other schools of feminist thought, has to further expand its categories to include the experiences of diverse women.

Notes

1. Friedrich Engels, *The Origins of the Family, Private Property and the State,* ed. with an introduction by Eleanor Leacock (New York: International Publishers, 1972), pp. 71–72.

The Feminist Standpoint: Developing the Ground for a Specifically Feminist Historical Materialism

Nancy C.M. Hartsock

The power of the Marxian critique of class domination stands as an implicit suggestion that feminists should consider the advantages of adopting a historical materialist approach to understanding phallocratic domination. A specifically feminist historical materialism might enable us to lay bare the laws of tendency which constitute the structure of patriarchy over time and to follow its development in and through the Western class societies on which Marx's interest centered. A feminist materialism might in addition enable us to expand the Marxian account to include all human activity rather than focussing on activity more characteristic of males in capitalism. The development of such a historical and materialist account is a very large task, one which requires the political and theoretical contributions of many feminists. Here I will address only the question of the epistemological underpinnings such a materialism would require. Most specifically, I will attempt to develop, on the methodological base provided by Marxian theory, an important epistemological tool for understanding and opposing all forms of domination—a feminist standpoint.

Despite the difficulties feminists have correctly pointed to in Marxian theory, there are several reasons to take over much of Marx's approach. First, I have argued elsewhere that Marx's method and the method developed by the contemporary women's movement recapitulate each other in important ways.[1] This makes it possible for feminists to take over a number of aspects of Marx's method. Here, I will adopt his distinction between appearance and essence, circulation and production, abstract and concrete, and use these distinctions between dual levels of reality to work out the theoretical forms appropriate to each level when viewed not from the standpoint of the proletariat but from a specifically feminist standpoint. In this process I will explore and expand the Marxian argument that socially mediated interaction with nature in the process of production shapes both human beings and theories of knowledge. The Marxian category of labor, including as it does both interaction with other humans and with the natural world, can help to cut through the dichotomy of nature and culture, and, for feminists, can help to avoid the false choice of characterizing the situation of women as either "purely natural" or "purely social." As embodied humans we are of course inextricably both natural and social, though feminist theory to date has, for important strategic reasons, concentrated attention on the social aspect.

I set off from Marx's proposal that a correct vision of class society is available from only one of the two major class positions in capitalist society. On the basis of this metatheoretical claim, he was able to develop a powerful critique of class domination. The power of Marx's critique depended on the epistemology and ontology supporting this metatheoretical claim. Feminist Marxists and materialist feminists more generally have argued that the position of women is structurally different from that of men, and that the lived realities of women's lives are profoundly different from those of men.[2] They have not yet, however, given sustained attention to the epistemological consequences of such a claim. Faced with the depth of Marx's critique of capitalism, feminist analysis, as Iris Young has correctly pointed out, often

> accepts the traditional Marxian theory of production relations, historical change, and analysis of the structure of capitalism in basically unchanged form. It rightly criticizes that theory for being essentially gender-blind, and hence seeks to supplement Marxist theory of capitalism with feminist theory of a system of male domination. Taking this route, however, tacitly endorses the traditional Marxian position that "the woman question" is auxiliary to the central questions of a Marxian theory of society.[3]

By setting off from the Marxian metatheory I am implicitly suggesting that this, rather than his critique of capitalism, can be most helpful to feminists. I will explore some of the epistemological consequences of claiming that women's lives differ structurally from those of men. In particular, I will suggest that like the lives of proletarians according to Marxian theory, women's lives make available a particular and privileged vantage point on male supremacy, a vantage point which can ground a powerful critique of the phallocratic institutions and ideology which constitute the capitalist form of patriarchy. After a summary of the nature of a standpoint as an epistemological device, I will address the question of whether one can discover a feminist standpoint on which to ground a specifically feminist historical materialism. I will suggest that the sexual division of labor forms the basis for such a standpoint and will argue that on the basis of the structures which define women's activity as contributors to subsistence and as mothers one could begin, though not complete, the construction of such an epistemological tool. I hope to show how just as Marx's understanding of the world from the standpoint of the proletariat enabled him to go beneath bourgeois ideology, so a feminist standpoint can allow us to understand patriarchal institutions and ideologies as perverse inversions of more humane social relations.

The Nature of a Standpoint

A standpoint is not simply an interested position (interpreted as bias) but is interested in the sense of being engaged. It is true that a desire to conceal real social relations can contribute to an obscurantist account, and it is also true that the ruling gender and class have material interests in deception. A standpoint, however, carries with it the contention that there are some perspectives on society from which, however well-intentioned one may be, the real relations of humans with each other and with the natural world are not visible. This contention should be sorted into a number of distinct epistemological and political claims: (1) Material life (class position in Marxist theory) not only structures but sets limits on the understanding of social relations. (2) If material life is structured in fundamentally opposing ways for two different groups, one can expect that the vision of each will represent an inversion of the other, and in systems of domination the vision available to the rulers will be both partial and perverse. (3) The vision of the ruling class (or gender) structures the material relations in which all parties are forced to participate, and therefore cannot be dismissed as simply false. (4) In consequence, the vision available to the oppressed group must be struggled for and represents an achievement which requires both science to see beneath the surface of the social relations in which all are forced to participate, and the education which can only grow from struggle to change those relations. (5) As an engaged vision, the understanding of the oppressed, the adoption of a standpoint exposes the real relations among human beings as inhuman, points beyond the present, and carries a historically liberatory role.

The concept of a standpoint structures epistemology in a particular way. Rather than a simple dualism, it posits a duality of levels of reality, of which the deeper level or essence both includes and explains the "surface" or appearance, and indicates the logic by means of which the appearance inverts and distorts the deeper reality. In addition, the concept of a standpoint depends on the assumption that epistemology grows in a complex and contradictory way from material life. Any effort to develop a standpoint must take seriously Marx's injunction that "all mysteries which lead theory to mysticism find their rational solution in human practice and in the comprehension of this practice."[4] Marx held that the source both for the proletarian standpoint and the critique of capitalism it makes possible is to be found in practical activity itself. The epistemological (and even ontological) significance of human activity is made clear in Marx's argument not only that persons are active but that reality itself consists of "sensuous human activity, practice."[5] Thus Marx can speak of products as crystallized or congealed human activity or work, of products as conscious human activity in another form. He can state that even plants, animals, light, etc. constitute theoretically a part of human consciousness, and a part of human life and activity.[6] As Marx and Engels summarize their position,

> As individuals express their life, so they are. What they are, therefore, coincides with their production, both with *what* they produce and with *how* they produce. The nature of individuals thus depends on the material conditions determining their production.[7]

This starting point has definite consequences for Marx's theory of knowledge. If humans are not what they eat but what they do, especially what they do in the course of production of subsistence, each means of producing subsistence should be expected to carry with it *both* social relations *and* relations to the world of nature which express the social understanding contained in that mode of production. And in any society with systematically divergent practical activities, one should expect the growth of logically divergent world views. That is, each division of labor, whether by gender or class, can be expected to have consequences for knowledge. Class society, according to Marx, does produce this dual vision in the form of the ruling class'vision and the understanding available to the ruled.

On the basis of Marx's description of the activity of commodity exchange in capitalism, the ways in which the dominant categories of thought simply express the mystery of the commodity form have been pointed out. These include a dependence on quantity, duality, and opposition of nature to culture, a rigid separation of mind and body, intention and behavior.[8] From the perspective of exchange, where commodities differ from each other only quantitatively, it seems absurd to suggest that labor power differs from all other commodities. The sale and purchase of labor power from the perspective of capital is simply a contract between free agents, in which "the agreement [the parties] come to is but the form in which they give legal expression of their common will." It is a relation of equality,

> because each enters into relation with the other, as with a simple owner of commodities, and they exchange equivalent for equivalent. ... The only force that brings them together and puts them in relation with each other, is the selfishness, the gain and the private interests of each. Each looks to himself only, and no one troubles himself about the rest, and just because they do so, do they all, in accordance with the pre-established harmony of things, or under the auspices of an all shrewd providence, work together to their mutual advantage, for the common weal and in the interest of all.

This is the only description available within the sphere of circulation or exchange of commodities, or as Marx might put it, at the level of appearance. But at the level of production, the world looks far different. As Marx puts it,

> On leaving this sphere of simple circulation or of exchange of commodities ... we can perceive a change in the physiognomy of our *dramatis personae*. He who before was the money-owner, now strides in front as capitalist; the possessor of labor-power follows as his laborer. The one with an air of importance, smirking, intent on business; the other timid and holding back, like one who is bringing his own hide to market and has nothing to expect but—a hiding.

This is a vastly different account of the social relations of the buyer and seller of labor power.[9] Only by following the two into the realm of production and adopting the point of view available to the worker could Marx uncover what is really involved in the purchase and sale of labor power—i.e., uncover the process by which surplus value is produced and appropriated by the capitalist, and the means by which the worker is systematically disadvantaged.[10]

If one examines Marx's account of the production and extraction of surplus value, one can see in it the elaboration of each of the claims contained in the concept of a standpoint. First, the contention that material life structures understanding points to the importance of the epistemological consequences of the opposed models of exchange and production. It is apparent that the former results in a dualism based on both the separation of exchange from use, and on the positing of exchange as the only important side of the dichotomy. The epistemological result, if one follows through the implications of exchange, is a series of opposed and hierarchical dualities—mind/body, ideal/material, social/natural, self/other—even a kind of solipsism—replicating the devaluation of use relative to exchange. The proletarian and

Marxian valuation of use over exchange on the basis of involvement in production, in labor, results in a dialectical rather than dualist epistemology: the dialectical and interactive unity (distinction within a unity) of human and natural worlds, mind and body, ideal and material, and the cooperation of self and other (community).

As to the second claim of a standpoint, a Marxian account of exchange vs. production indicates that the epistemology growing from exchange not only inverts that present in the process of production but in addition is both partial and fundamentally perverse. The real point of the production of goods and services is, after all, the continuation of the species, a possibility dependent on their use. The epistemology embodied in exchange then, along with the social relations it expresses, not only occupies only one side of the dualities it constructs, but also reverses the proper ordering of any hierarchy in the dualisms: use is primary, not exchange.

The third claim for a standpoint indicates a recognition of the power realities operative in a community, and points to the ways the ruling group's vision may be *both* perverse *and* made real by means of that group's power to define the terms for the community as a whole. In the Marxian analysis, this power is exercised in both control of ideological production, and in the real participation of the worker in exchange. The dichotomous epistemology which grows from exchange cannot be dismissed either as simply false or as an epistemology relevant to only a few: the worker as well as the capitalist engages in the purchase and sale of commodities, and if material life structures consciousness, this cannot fail to have an effect. This leads into the fourth claim for a standpoint—that it is achieved rather than obvious, a mediated rather than immediate understanding. Because the ruling group controls the means of mental as well as physical production, the production of ideals as well as goods, the standpoint of the oppressed represents an achievement both of science (analysis) and of political struggle on the basis of which this analysis can be conducted.

Finally, because it provides the basis for revealing the perversion of both life and thought, the inhumanity of human relations, a standpoint can be the basis for moving beyond these relations. In the historical context of Marx's theory, the engaged vision available to the producers, by drawing out the potentiality available in the actuality, that is, by following up the possibility of abundance capitalism creates, leads towards transcendence. Thus the proletariat is the only class which has the possibility of creating a classless society. It can do this simply (!) by generalizing its own condition, that is, by making society itself a propertyless producer.[11]

These are the general characteristics of the standpoint of the proletariat. What guidance can feminists take from this discussion? I hold that the powerful vision of both the perverseness and reality of class domination made possible by Marx's adoption of the standpoint of the proletariat suggests that a specifically feminist standpoint could allow for a much more profound critique of phallocratic ideologies and institutions than has yet been achieved. The effectiveness of Marx's critique grew from its uncompromising focus on material life activity, and I propose here to set out from the Marxian contention that not only are persons active, but that reality itself consists of "sensuous human activity, practice." But rather than beginning with men's labor, I will focus on women's life activity and on the institutions which structure that activity in order to raise the question of whether this activity can form the ground for a distinctive standpoint, that is, to determine whether it meets the requirements for a feminist standpoint. (I use the term, "feminist" rather than "female" here to indicate both the achieved character of a standpoint and that a stand-point by definition carries a liberatory potential.)

Women's work in every society differs systematically from men's. I intend to pursue the suggestion that this division of labor is the first and in some societies the only division of labor, and moreover, that it is central to the organization of social labor more generally. On the basis of an account of the sexual division of labor, one should be able to begin to explore the oppositions and differences between women's and men's activity and their consequences for epistemology. While I cannot attempt a complete account, I will put forward a schematic and simplified account of the sexual division of labor and its consequences for epistemology. I will sketch out a kind of ideal type of the social relations and world view characteristic of male and female activity in order to explore the epistemology contained in the institutionalized sexual division of labor. In so doing, I do not mean to attribute this vision to individual women or men any more than Marx (or Lukacs) meant their theory of class consciousness to apply to any particular worker or group of workers. My focus is instead on institutionalized social practices and on the specific epistemology and ontology manifested by the institutionalized sexual division of labor. Individuals, as individuals, may change their activity in ways which move them outside the outlook embodied in these institutions, but such a move can be significant only when it occurs at the level of society as a whole.

I will discuss the "sexual division of labor" rather than the "gender division of labor" to stress, first my belief that the division of labor between women and men cannot be reduced to purely social dimensions. One must distinguish between what Sara Ruddick has termed "invariant and *nearly* unchangeable" features of human life, and those which despite being "*nearly* universal" are "certainly changeable."[12] Thus, the fact that women and not men *bear* children is not (yet) a social choice, but that women and not men rear children in a society structured by compulsory heterosexuality and male dominance is clearly a societal choice. A second reason to use the term "sexual division of labor" is to keep hold of the bodily aspect of existence—perhaps to grasp it over-firmly in an effort to keep it from evaporating altogether. There is some biological, bodily component to human existence. But its size and substantive content will remain unknown until at least the certainly changeable aspects of the sexual division of labor are altered.

On a strict reading of Marx, of course, my enterprise here is illegitimate. While on the one hand, Marx remarked that the very first division of labor occurred in sexual intercourse, he argues that the division of labor only becomes "truly such" when the division of mental and manual labor appears. Thus, he dismisses the sexual division of labor as of no analytic importance. At the same time, a reading of other remarks—such as his claim that the mental/manual division of labor is based on the "natural" division of labor in the family—would seem to support the legitimacy of my attention to the sexual division of labor and even add weight to the radical feminist argument that capitalism is an outgrowth of male dominance, rather than vice versa.

On the basis of a schematic account of the sexual division of labor, I will begin to fill in the specific content of the feminist standpoint and begin to specify how women's lives structure an understanding of social relations, that is, begin to follow out the epistemological consequences of the sexual division of labor. In addressing the institutionalized sexual division of labor, I propose to lay aside the important differences among women across race and class boundaries and instead search for central commonalities. I take some justification from the fruitfulness of Marx's similar strategy in constructing a simplified, two class, two man model in which everything was exchanged at its value. Marx's schematic account in Volume 1 of *Capital* left out of account such factors as imperialism, the differential wages, work, and working conditions of the Irish, the differences between women, men, and children, and so on. While all of these factors are important to the analysis of contemporary capitalism, none changes either Marx's theories of surplus value or alienation, two of the most fundamental features of the Marxian analysis of capitalism. My effort here takes a similar form in an attempt to move toward a theory of the extraction and appropriation of women's activity and women themselves. Still, I adopt this strategy with some reluctance, since it contains the danger of making invisible the experience of lesbians or women of color.[13] At the same time, I recognize that the effort to uncover a feminist standpoint assumes that there are some things common to all women's lives in Western class societies.

The feminist standpoint which emerges through an examination of women's activities is related to the proletarian standpoint, but deeper going. Women and workers inhabit a world in which the emphasis is on change rather than stasis, a world characterized by interaction with natural substances rather than separation from nature, a world in which quality is more important than quantity, a world in which the unification of mind and body is inherent in the activities performed. Yet, there are some important differences, differences marked by the fact that the proletarian (if male) is immersed in this world only during the time his labor power is being used by the capitalist. If, to paraphrase Marx, we follow the worker home from the factory, we can once again perceive a change in the *dramatis personae*. He who before followed behind as the worker, timid and holding back, with nothing to expect but a hiding, now strides in front while a third person, not specifically present in Marx's account of the transaction between capitalist and worker (both of whom are male) follows timidly behind, carrying groceries, baby, and diapers.

The Sexual Division of Labor

Women's activity as institutionalized has a double aspect—their contribution to subsistence, and their contribution to childrearing. Whether or not all of us do both, women as a sex are institutionally responsible for producing both goods and human beings and all women are forced to become the kinds of people who can do both. Although the nature of women's contribution to subsistence varies immensely over time and space, my primary focus here is on capitalism, with a secondary focus on the Western class societies which preceded it.[14] In capitalism, women contribute both production for wages and production of goods in the home, that is, they like men sell their labor power and produce both commodities and surplus value, and produce use-values in the home. Unlike men, however, women's lives are institutionally defined by their production of use-values in the home.[15] And here we begin to encounter the narrowness of the Marxian concept of production. Women's production of use-values in the home has not been well understood by socialists. It is no surprise to feminists that Engels, for example, simply asks how women can continue to do the work in the home and also work in production outside the home. Marx too takes for granted women's responsibility for household labor. He repeats, as if it were his own, the question of a Belgian factory inspector: If a mother works for wages, "how will [the household's] internal economy be cared for; who will look after the young children; who will get ready the meals, do the washing and mending?"[16]

Let us trace both the outlines and the consequences of woman's dual contribution to subsistence in capitalism. Women's labor, like that of the male worker, is contact with material necessity. Their contribution to subsistence, like that of the male worker, involves them in a world in which the relation to nature and to concrete human requirements is central, both in the form of interaction with natural substances whose quality, rather than quantity, is important to the production of meals, clothing, etc., and in the form of close attention to the natural changes in these substances. Women's labor both for wages and even more in household production involves a unification of mind and body for the purpose of transforming natural substances into socially defined goods. This too is true of the labor of the male worker.

There are, however, important differences. First, women as a group work more than men. We are all familiar with the phenomenon of the "double day," and with indications that women work many more hours per week than men.[17] Second, a larger proportion of women's labor time is devoted to the production of use values than men's. Only some of the goods women produce are commodities (however much they live in a society structured by commodity production and exchange). Third, women's production is structured by repetition in a different way than men's. While repetition for both the woman and the male worker may take the form of production of the same object, over and over—whether apple pies or brake linings—women's work in housekeeping involves a repetitious cleaning.[18]

Thus, the male worker in the process of production, is involved in contact with necessity, and interchange with nature as well as with other human beings but the process of production or work does not consume his whole life. The activity of a woman in the home as well as the work she does for wages keeps her continually in contact with a world of qualities and change. Her immersion in the world of use—in concrete, many-qualitied, changing material processes—is more complete than his. And if life itself consists of sensuous activity, the vantage point available to women on the basis of their contribution to subsistence represents an intensification and deepening of the materialist world view and consciousness available to the producers of commodities in capitalism, an intensification of class consciousness. The availability of this outlook to even non-working-class women has been strikingly formulated by Marilyn French in *The Women's Room*.

> Washing the toilet used by three males, and the floor and walls around it, is, Mira thought, coming face to face with necessity. And that is why women were saner than men, did not come up with the mad, absurd schemes men developed; they were in touch with necessity, they had to wash the toilet bowl and floor.[19]

The focus on women's subsistence activity rather than men's leads to a model in which the capitalist (male) lives a life structured completely by commodity exchange and not at all by production, and at the furthest distance from contact with concrete material life. The male worker marks a way station on the path to the other extreme of the constant contact with material necessity in women's contribution to subsistence. There are, of course, important differences along the lines of race and class. For example, working class men seem to do more domestic labor than men higher up in the class structure—car repairs, carpentry, etc. And until very recently, the wage work done by most women of color replicated the housework required by their own households. Still, there are commonalities present in the institutionalized sexual division of labor which make women responsible for both housework and wage work.

The female contribution to subsistence, however, represents only a part of women's labor. Women also produce/reproduce men (and other women) on both a daily and a long-term basis. This aspect of women's "production" exposes the deep inadequacies of the concept of production as a description of women's activity. One does not (cannot) produce another human being in anything like the way one produces an object such as a chair. Much more is involved, activity which cannot easily be dicotomized into play or work. Helping another to develop, the gradual relinquishing of control, the experience of the human limits of one's action—all these are important features of women's activity as mothers. Women as mothers even more than as workers, are institutionally involved in processes of change and growth, and more than workers, must understand the importance of avoiding excessive control in order to help others grow.[20] The activity involved is far more complex than the instrumental working with others to transform objects. (Interestingly, much of women's wage work—nursing, social work, and some secretarial jobs in particular—requires and depends on the relational and interpersonal skills women learned by being mothered by someone of the same sex.)

This aspect of women's activity too is not without consequences. Indeed, it is in the production of men by women and the appropriation of this labor and women themselves by men that the opposition between feminist and masculinist experience and outlook is rooted, and it is here that features of the proletarian vision are enhanced and modified for the woman and diluted for the man. The female experience in reproduction represents a unity with nature which goes beyond the proletarian experience of interchange with nature. As another theorist has put it, "reproductive labor might be said to combine the functions of the architect and the bee: like the architect, parturitive woman knows what she is doing; like the bee, she cannot help what she is doing." And just as the worker's acting on the external world changes both the world and the worker's nature, so too "a new life changes the world and the consciousness of the woman."[21] In addition, in the process of producing human beings, relations with others may take a variety of forms with deeper significance than simple cooperation with others for common goals—forms which range from a deep unity with another through the many-leveled and changing connections mothers experience with growing children. Finally, the female experience in bearing and rearing children involves a unity of mind and body more profound than is possible in the worker's instrumental activity.

Motherhood in the large sense, i.e., motherhood as an institution rather than experience, including pregnancy and the preparation for motherhood almost all female children receive as socialization, results in the construction of female existence as centered with a complex relational nexus.[22] One aspect of this relational existence is centered on the experience of living in a female rather than male body. There are a series of boundary challenges inherent in the female physiology—challenges which make it impossible to maintain rigid separation from the object world. Menstruation, coitus, pregnancy, childbirth, lactation—all represent challenges to bodily boundaries.[23] Adrienne Rich has described the experience of pregnancy as one in which the embryo was both inside and

> daily more separate, on its way to becoming separate from me and of-itself. In early pregnancy the stirring of the fetus felt like ghostly tremors of my own body, later like the movements of a being imprisoned in me; but both sensations were *my* sensations, contributing to my own sense of physical and psychic space.[24]

In turn, the fact that women but not men are primarily responsible for young children means that the infant first experiences itself as not fully differentiated from the mother, and then as an I in relation to an It that it later comes to know as female.[25]

Jane Flax and Nancy Chodorow have argued that the object relations school of psychoanalytic theory puts forward a materialist psychology, one which I propose to treat as a kind of empirical hypothesis. If the account of human development provided by object relations is correct, one ought to expect to find consequences—both psychic, and social. According to object relations theory, the process of differentiation from a woman by both male and female children reinforces boundary confusion in female egos and boundary strengthening in males. Individuation is far more conflictual for male than for female children, in part because both mother and son experience the other as a definite "other." The experience of oneness on the part of both mother and infant seems to last longer with girls.[26]

The complex relational world inhabited by women has its start in the experience and resolution of the oedipal crisis, cleanly resolved for the boy, whereas the girl is much more likely to retain both parents as love objects. The nature of the crisis itself differs by sex: the boy's love for the mother is an extension of mother-infant unity and thus essentially threatening to his ego and independence. Male ego-formation necessarily requires repressing this first relation and negating the mother.[27] In contrast, the girls' love for the father is less threatening both because it occurs outside this unity and because it occurs at a later stage of development. For boys, the central issue to be resolved concerns gender identification; for girls the issue is psychosexual development.[28] Chodorow concludes that girls' gradual emergence from the oedipal period takes place in such a way that empathy is built into their primary definition of self, and they have a variety of capacities for experiencing another's needs or feelings as their own. Put another way girls, because of female parenting, are less differentiated from others than boys, more continuous with and related to the external object world. They are differently oriented to their inner object world as well.[29]

The more complex female relational world is reinforced by the process of socialization. Girls learn roles from watching their mothers; boys must learn roles from rules which structure the life of an absent male figure. Girls can identify with a concrete example present in daily life; boys must identify with an abstract set of maxims only occasionally concretely present in the form of the father. Thus, not only do girls learn roles with more interpersonal and relational skills, but the process of role learning itself is embodied in the concrete relation with the mother. The male, in contrast, must identify with an abstract, cultural stereotype and learn abstract behaviors not attached to a well-known person. Masculinity is idealized by boys whereas femininity is concrete for girls.[30]

Women and men, then, grow up with personalities affected by different boundary experiences, differently constructed and experienced inner and outer worlds, and preoccupations with different relational issues. This early experience forms an important ground for the female sense of self as connected to the world and the male sense of self as separate, distinct, and even disconnected. By retaining the preoedipal attachment to the mother, girls come to define and experience themselves as continuous with others. In sum, girls enter adulthood with a more complex layering of affective ties and a rich, ongoing inner set of object relations. Boys, with a simpler oedipal situation and a clear and early resolution, have repressed ties to another. As a result, women define and experience themselves relationally and men do not.[31]

Abstract Masculinity and the Feminist Standpoint

This exclusion into psychoanalytic theory has served to point to the differences in the male and female experience of self due to the sexual division of labor in childrearing. These different (psychic) experiences both structure and are reinforced by the differing patterns of male and female activity required by the sexual division of labor, and are thereby replicated as epistemology and ontology. The differential male and female life activity in class society leads on the one hand toward a feminist standpoint and on the other toward an abstract masculinity.

Because the problem for the boy is to distinguish himself from the mother and to protect himself against the real threat she poses for his identity, his conflictual and oppositional efforts lead to the formation of rigid ego boundaries. The way Freud takes for granted the rigid distinction between the "me and not-me" makes the point well: "Normally, there is nothing of which we are more certain than the feeling of ourself, of our own ego. This ego appears to us as something autonomous and unitary, marked off distinctly from everything else." At least toward the outside, "the ego seems to maintain clear and sharp lines of demarcation."[32] Thus, the boy's construction of self in opposition to unity with the mother, his construction of identity as differentiation from the other, sets a hostile and combative dualism at the heart of both the community men construct and the masculinist world view by means of which they understand their lives.

I do not mean to suggest that the totality of human relations can be explained by psychoanalysis. Rather I want to point to the ways male rather than female experience and activity replicates itself in both the hierarchical and dualist institutions of class society and in the frameworks of thought generated by this experience. It is interesting to read Hegel's account of the relation of self and other as a statement of male experience: the relation of the two consciousnesses takes the form of a trial by death. As Hegel describes it, "each seeks the death of the other."

> Thus, the relation of the two self-conscious individuals is such that they provide themselves and each other through a life-and-death struggle. They must engage in this struggle, for they must raise their certainty *for themselves* to truth, both in the case of the other and in their own case.[33]

The construction of the self in opposition to another who threatens one's very being reverberates throughout the construction of both class society and the masculinist world view and results in a deepgoing and hierarchical dualism. First, the male experience is characterized by the duality of concrete versus abstract. Material reality as experienced by the boy in the family provides no model and is unimportant in the attainment of masculinity. Nothing of value to the boy occurs with the family, and masculinity becomes an abstract ideal to be achieved over the opposition of daily life.[34] Masculinity must be attained by means of opposition to the concrete world of daily life, by escaping from contact with the female world of the household into the masculine world of public life. This experience of two worlds, one valuable, if abstract and deeply unattainable, the other useless and demeaning, if concrete and necessary, lies at the heart of a series of dualisms—abstract/concrete, mind/body, culture/nature, ideal/real, stasis/change. And these dualisms are overlaid by gender: only the first of each pair is associated with the male.

Dualism, along with the dominance of one side of the dichotomy over the other, marks phallocentric society and social theory. These dualisms appear in a variety of forms—in philosophy, technology, political theory, and the organization of class society itself. One can, for example, see them very clearly worked out in Plato, although they appear in many other forms.[35] There, the concrete/abstract duality takes the form of an opposition of material to ideal, and a denial of the relevance of the material world to the attainment of what is of fundamental importance: love of knowledge, or philosophy (masculinity). The duality between nature and culture takes the form of a devaluation of work or necessity, and the primacy instead of purely social interaction for the attainment of undying fame. Philosophy itself is separate from nature, and indeed, exists only on the basis of the domination of (at least some) of the philosopher's own nature.[36] Abstract masculinity, then, can be seen to have structured Western social relations and the modes of thought to which these relations give rise at least since the founding of the *polis.*

The oedipal roots of these hierarchical dualisms are memorialized in the overlay of female and male connotations: it is not accidental that women are associated with quasi-human and nonhuman nature, that the female is associated with the body and material life, that the lives of women are systematically used as examples to characterize the lives of those ruled by their bodies rather than their minds.[37]

Both the fragility and fundamental falseness of the masculinist ideology and the deeply problematic nature of the social relations from which it grows are apparent in its reliance on a series of counterfactual assumptions and contentions. Consider how the following contentions are contrary to lived experience: the body is both irrelevant and in opposition to the (real) self, an impediment to be overcome by the mind; the female mind either does not exist (Do women have souls?) or works in such incomprehensible ways as to be unintelligible (the "enigma of woman"); what is real and primary is imperceptible to the senses and impervious to nature and natural change. What is remarkable is not only that these contentions have absorbed a great deal of philosophical energy, but, along with a series of other counterfactuals, have structured social relations for centuries.

Interestingly enough the epistemology and society constructed by men suffering from the effects of abstract masculinity have a great deal in common with that imposed by commodity exchange. The separation and opposition of social and natural worlds, of abstract and concrete, of permanence and change, the effort to define only the former of each pair as important, the reliance on a series of counter factual assumptions—all this is shared with the exchange abstraction. Abstract masculinity shares still another of its aspects with the exchange abstraction: it forms the basis for an even more problematic social synthesis. Hegel's analysis makes clear the problematic social relations available to the self which maintains itself by opposition: each of the two subjects struggling for recognition risks its own death in the struggle to kill the other, but if the other is killed the subject is once again alone.[38] In sum, then, the male experience when replicated as epistemology leads to a world conceived as, and (in fact) inhabited by, a number of fundamentally hostile others whom one comes to know by means of opposition (even death struggle) and yet with whom one must construct a social relation in order to survive.

The female construction of self in relation to others leads in an opposite direction—toward opposition to dualisms of any sort, valuation of concrete, everyday life, sense of a variety of connectednesses and continuities both with other persons and with the natural world. If material life structures consciousness, women's relationally defined existence, bodily experience of boundary challenges, and activity of transforming both physical objects and human beings must be expected to result in a world view to which dichotomies are foreign. Women experience others and themselves along a continuum whose dimensions are evidenced in Adrienne Rich's argument that the child carried for nine months can be defined "*neither* as me or as not-me," and she argues that inner and outer are not polar opposites but a continuum.[39] What the sexual division of labor defines as women's work turns on issues of change rather than stasis, the changes involved in producing both use-values and commodities, but more profoundly in the activity of rearing human beings who change in both more subtle and more autonomous ways than any inanimate object. Not only the qualities of things but also the qualities of people are important in women's work; quantity becomes peripheral. In addition, far more than the instrumental cooperation of the workplace is required; the mother-child relation and the maintenance of the family, while it has instrumental aspects, is not defined by them. Finally, the unity of mental and manual labor, and the directly sensuous nature of much of women's work leads to a more profound unity of mental and manual labor, social and natural worlds, than is experienced by the male worker in capitalism. The unity grows from the fact that women's bodies, unlike men's, can be themselves instruments of production: in pregnancy, giving birth, or lactation, arguments about a division of mental from manual labor are fundamentally foreign.

That this is indeed women's experience is documented in both the theory and practice of the contemporary women's movement and needs no further development here.[40] The more important question here is whether female experience and the world view constructed by female activity can meet the criteria for a standpoint. If we return to the five claims carried by the concept of a standpoint, it seems clear that women's material life activity has important epistemological and ontological consequences for both the understanding and construction of social relations. Women's activity, then, does satisfy the first requirement of a standpoint.

I can now take up the second claim made by a standpoint: that the female experience not only inverts that of the male, but forms a basis on which to expose abstract masculinity as both partial and fundamentally perverse, as not only occupying only one side of the dualities it has constructed, but reversing the proper valuation of human activity. The partiality of the masculinist vision and of the societies which support this understanding is evidenced by its confinement of activity proper to the male to only one side of the dualisms. Its perverseness, however, lies elsewhere. Perhaps the most dramatic (though not the only) reversal of the proper order of things characteristic of the male experience is the substitution of death for life.

The substitution of death for life results at least in part from the sexual division of labor in childrearing. The self surrounded by rigid ego-boundaries, certain of what is inner and what is outer, the self experienced as walled city, is discontinuous with others. Georges Bataille has made brilliantly clear the ways in which death emerges as the only possible solution to this discontinuity and has followed the logic through to argue that reproduction itself must be understood not as the creation of life, but as death. The core experience to be understood is that of discontinuity and its consequences. As a consequence of this experience of discontinuity and aloneness, penetration of ego-boundaries, or fusion with another is experienced as violent. Thus, the desire for fusion with another can take the form of domination of the other. In this form, it leads to the only possible fusion with a threatening other: when the other ceases to exist as a separate, and for that reason, threatening being. Insisting that another submit to one's will is simply a milder form of the destruction of discontinuity in the death of the other since in this case one is no longer confronting a discontinuous and opposed will, despite its discontinuous embodiment. This is perhaps one source of the links between sexual activity, domination, and death.

Bataille suggests that killing and sexual activity share both prohibitions and religious significance. Their unity is demonstrated by religious sacrifice since the latter:

> is intentional like the act of the man who lays bare, desires and wants to penetrate his victim. The lover strips the beloved of her identity no less than the bloodstained priest his human or animal victim. The woman in the hands of her assailant is despoiled of her being ... loses the firm barrier that once separated her from others ... is brusquely laid open to the violence of the sexual urges set loose in the organs of reproduction; she is laid open to the impersonal violence that overwhelms her from without.[41]

Note the use of the term "lover" and "assailant" as synonyms and the presence of the female as victim.

The importance of Bataille's analysis lies in the fact that it can help to make clear the links between violence, death, and sexual fusion with another, links which are not simply theoretical but actualized in rape and pornography. Images of women in chains, being beaten, or threatened with attack carry clear social messages, among them that "the normal male is sexually aggressive in a brutal and demeaning way."[42] Bataille's analysis can help to understand why "men advertise, even brag, that their movie is the 'bloodiest thing that ever happened in front of a camera.'"[43] The analysis is supported by the psychoanalyst who suggested that although one of the important dynamics of pornography is hostility, "one can raise the possibly controversial question whether in humans (especially males) powerful sexual excitement can ever exist without brutality also being present."[44]

Bataille's analysis can help to explain what is erotic about "snuff" films, which not only depict the torture and dismemberment of a woman, but claim that the actress is *in fact* killed. His analysis suggests that perhaps she is a sacrificial victim whose discontinuous existence has been succeeded in her death by "the organic continuity of life drawn into the common life of the beholders."[45] Thus, the pair "lover-assailant" is not accidental. Nor is the connection of reproduction and death.

"Reproduction," Bataille argues, "implies the existence of *discontinuous* beings." This is so because, "Beings which reproduce themselves are distinct from one another, and those reproduced are likewise distinct from each other, just as they are distinct from their parents. Each being is distinct from all others. His birth, his death, the events of his life may have an interest for others, but he alone is directly concerned in them. He is born alone. He dies alone. Between one being and another, there is a *gulf*, a discontinuity."[46] (Clearly it is not just a gulf, but is better understood as a chasm.) In reproduction sperm and ovum unite to form a new entity, but they do so from the death and disappearance of two separate beings. Thus, the new entity bears within itself "the transition to continuity, the fusion, fatal to both, of two separate beings."[47] Thus, death and reproduction are intimately linked, yet Bataille stresses that "it is only death which is to be identified with continuity." Thus, despite the unity of birth and death in this analysis, Bataille gives greater weight to a "tormenting fact: the urge towards love, pushed to its limit, is an urge toward death."[48] Bataille holds to this position despite his recognition that reproduction is a form of growth. The growth, however, he dismisses as not being "ours," as being only "impersonal."[49] This is not the female experience, in which reproduction is hardly impersonal, nor experienced as death. It is, of course, in a literal sense, the sperm which is cut off from its source, and lost. No wonder, then, at the masculinist occupation with death, and the feeling that growth is "impersonal," not of fundamental concern to oneself. But this complete dismissal of the experience of another bespeaks a profound lack of empathy and refusal to recognize the very being of another. It is a manifestation of the chasm which separates each man from every other being and from the natural world, the chasm which both marks and defines the problem of community.

The preoccupation with death instead of life appears as well in the argument that it is the ability to kill (and for centuries, the practice) which sets humans above animals. Even Simone de Beauvoir has accepted that "it is not in giving life but in risking life that man is raised above the animal; that is why superiority has been accorded in humanity not to the sex that brings forth but to that which kills."[50] That superiority has been accorded to the sex which kills is beyond doubt. But what kind of experience and vision can take reproduction, the creation of new life, and the force of life in sexuality, and turn it into death—not just in theory but in the practice of rape, pornography, and sexual murder? And why give pride of place to killing? This is not only an inversion of the proper order of things, but also a refusal to recognize the real activities in which men as well as women are engaged. The producing of goods and the reproducing of human beings are certainly life-sustaining activities. And even the deaths of the ancient heroes in search of undying fame were pursuits of life, and represented the attempt to avoid death by attaining immortality. The search for life, then, represents the deeper reality which lies beneath the glorification of death and destruction.

Yet one cannot dismiss the substitution of death for life as simply false. Men's power to structure social relations in their own image means that women too must participate in social relations which manifest and express abstract masculinity. The most important life activities have consistently been held by the powers that be to be unworthy of those who are fully human most centrally because of their close connections with necessity and life: motherwork (the rearing of children), housework, and until the rise of capitalism in the West, any work necessary to subsistence. In addition, these activities in contemporary capitalism are all constructed in ways which systematically degrade and destroy the minds and bodies of those who perform them.[51] The organization of motherhood as an institution in which a woman is alone with her children, the isolation of women from each other in domestic labor, the female pathology of loss of self in service to others—all mark the transformation of life into death, the distortion of what could have been creative and communal activity into oppressive toil, and the destruction of the possibility of community present in women's relational self-definition. The ruling gender's and class's interest in maintaining social relations such as these is evidenced by the fact that when women set up other structures in which the mother is not alone with her children, isolated from others—as is frequently the case in working class communities or communities of people of color—these arrangements are categorized as pathological deviations.

The real destructiveness of the social relations characteristic of abstract masculinity, however, is now concealed beneath layers of ideology. Marxian theory needed to go beneath the surface to discover the different levels of determination which defined the relation of capitalist and (male) worker. These levels of determination and laws of motion or tendency of phallocratic society must be worked out on the basis of female experience. This brings me to the fourth claim for a standpoint—its character as an achievement of both analysis and political struggle occurring in a particular historical space. The fact that class divisions should have proven so resistant to analysis and required such a prolonged political struggle before Marx was able to formulate the theory of surplus value indicates the difficulty of this accomplishment. And the rational control of production has certainly not been achieved.

Feminists have only begun the process of revaluing female experience, searching for common threads which connect the diverse experiences of women, and searching for the structural determinants of the experiences. The difficulty of the problem faced by feminist theory can be illustrated by the fact that it required a struggle even to define household labor, if not done for wages, as work, to argue that what are held to be acts of love instead must be recognized as work whether or not wages are paid.[52] Both the valuation of women's experience, and the use of this experience as a ground for critique are required. A feminist standpoint may be present on the basis of the common threads of female experience, but it is neither self-evident nor obvious.

Finally, because it provides a way to reveal the perverseness and inhumanity of human relations, a standpoint forms the basis for moving beyond these relations. Just as the proletarian standpoint emerges out of the contradiction between appearance and essence in capitalism, understood as essentially historical and constituted by the relation of capitalist and worker, the feminist standpoint emerges both out of the contradiction between the systematically differing structure of male and female life activity in Western cultures. It expresses female experience at a particular time and place, located within a particular set of social relations. Capitalism, Marx noted, could not develop fully until the notion of human equality achieved the status of universal truth.[53] Despite women's exploitation both as unpaid reproducers of the labor force and as a sex-segregated labor force available for low wages, then, capitalism poses problems for the continued oppression of women. Just as capitalism enables the proletariat to raise the possibility of a society free from class domination, so too, it provides space to raise the possibility of a society free from all forms of domination. The articulation of a feminist standpoint based on women's relational self-definition and activity exposes the world men have constructed and the self-understanding which manifests these relations as partial and perverse. More importantly, by drawing out the potentiality available in the actuality and thereby exposing the inhumanity of human relations, it embodies a distress which requires a solution. The experience of continuity and relation—with others, with the natural world, of mind with body—provides an ontological base for developing a nonproblematic social synthesis, a social synthesis which need not operate through the denial of the body, the attack on nature, or the death struggle between the self and other, a social synthesis which does not depend on any of the forms taken by abstract masculinity.

What is necessary is the generalization of the potentiality made available by the activity of women—the defining of society as a whole as propertyless producer both of use-values and of human beings. To understand what such a transformation would require we should consider what is involved in the partial transformation represented by making the whole of society into propertyless producers of use-values—i.e., socialist revolution. The abolition of the division between mental and manual labor cannot take place simply by means of adopting worker-self-management techniques, but instead requires the abolition of private property, the seizure of state power, and lengthy post-revolutionary class struggle. Thus, I am not suggesting that shared parenting arrangements can abolish the sexual division of labor. Doing away with this division of labor would of course require institutionalizing the participation of both women and men in childrearing; but just as the rational and conscious control of the production of goods and services requires a vast and far-reaching social transformation, so the rational and conscious organization of reproduction would entail the transformation both of *every* human relation, and of human relations to the natural world. The magnitude of the task is apparent if one asks what a society without institutionalized gender differences might look like.

Conclusion

An analysis which begins from the sexual division of labor—understood not as taboo, but as the real, material activity of concrete human beings—could form the basis for an analysis of the real structures of women's oppression, an analysis which would not require that one sever biology from society, nature from culture, an analysis which would expose the ways women both participate in and oppose their own subordination. The elaboration of such an analysis cannot but be difficult. Women's lives, like men's, are structured by social relations which manifest the experience of the dominant gender and class. The ability to go beneath the surface of appearances to reveal the real but concealed social relations requires both theoretical and political activity. Feminist theorists must demand that feminist theorizing be grounded in women's material activity and must as well be a part of the political struggle necessary to develop areas of social life modeled on this activity. The outcome could be the development of a political economy which included women's activity as well as men's, and could as well be a step toward the redefining and restructuring of society as a whole on the basis of women's activity.

Generalizing the activity of women to the social system as a whole would raise, for the first time in human history, the possibility of a fully human community, a community structured by connection rather than separation and opposition. One can conclude then that women's life activity does form the basis of a specifically feminist materialism, a materialism which can provide a point from which both to critique and to work against phallocratic ideology and institutions.

My argument here opens a number of avenues for future work. Clearly, a systematic critique of Marx on the basis of a more fully developed understanding of the sexual division of labor is in order. And this is indeed being undertaken by a number of feminists. A second avenue for further investigation is the relation between exchange and abstract masculinity. An exploration of Mauss's *The Gift* would play an important part in this project, since he presents the solipsism of exchange as an overlay on and substitution for a deeper going hostility, the exchange of gifts as an alternative to war. We have seen that the necessity for recognizing and receiving recognition from another to take the form of a death struggle memorializes the male rather than female experience of emerging as a person in opposition to a woman in the context of a deeply phallocratic world. If the community of exchangers (capitalists) rests on the more overtly and directly hostile death struggle of self and other, one might be able to argue that what underlies the exchange abstraction is abstract masculinity. One might then turn to the question of whether capitalism rests on and is a consequence of patriarchy. Perhaps then feminists can produce the analysis which could amend Marx to read: "Though class society appears to be the source, the cause of the oppression of women, it is rather its consequence." Thus, it is "only at the last culmination of the development of class society [that] this, its secret, appear[s] again, namely, that on the one hand it is the *product* of the oppression of women, and that on the other it is the *means* by which women participate in and create their own oppression."[54]

Notes

I take my title from Iris Young's call for the development of a specifically feminist historical materialism. See "Socialist Feminism and the Limits of Dual Systems Theory," in *Socialist Review* 10, 2/3 (March–June, 1980). My work on this paper is deeply indebted to a number of women whose ideas are incorporated here, although not always used in the ways they might wish. My discussions with Donna Haraway and Sandra Harding have been intense and ongoing over a period of years. I have also had a number of important and useful conversations with Jane Flax, and my project here has benefited both from these contacts, and from the opportunity to read her paper, "Political Philosophy and the Patriarchal Unconscious: A Psychoanalytic Perspective on Epistemology and Metaphysics." In addition I have been helped immensely by collective discussions with Annette Bickel, Sarah Begus, and Alexa Freeman. All of these people (along with Iris Young and Irene Diamond) have read and commented on drafts of this paper. I would also like to thank Alison Jaggar for continuing to question me about the basis on which one could claim the superiority of a feminist standpoint and for giving me the opportunity to deliver the paper at the University of Cincinnati Philosophy Department Colloquium; and Stephen Rose for taking the time to read and comment on a rough draft of the paper at a critical point in its development.

1. See my "Feminist Theory and the Development of Revolutionary Strategy," in Zillah Eisenstein, ed., *Capitalist Patriarchy and the Case for Socialist Feminism* (New York: Monthly Review, 1978).

2. The recent literature on mothering is perhaps the most detailed on this point. See Dorothy Dinnerstein, *The Mermaid and the Minotaur* (New York: Harper and Row, 1976);

Nancy Chodorow, *The Reproduction of Mothering* (Berkeley: University of California Press, 1978).

3. Iris Young, "Socialist Feminism and the Limits of Dual Systems Theory," in *Socialist Review* 10, 2/3 (March–June, 1980), p. 180.

4. Eighth Thesis on Feuerbach, in Karl Marx, "Theses on Feuerbach," in *The German Ideology*, C. J. Arthur, ed. (New York: International Publishers, 1970), p. 121.

5. Ibid. Conscious human practice, then, is at once both an epistemological category and the basis for Marx's conception of the nature of humanity itself. To put the case even more strongly, Marx argues that human activity has both an ontological and epistemological status, that human feelings are not "merely anthropological phenomena," but are "truly ontological affirmations of being." See Karl Marx, *Economic and Philosophic Manuscripts of 1844*, Dirk Struik, ed. (New York: International Publishers, 1964), pp. 113, 165, 188.

6. Marx, *1844*, p. 112. Nature itself, for Marx, appears as a form of human work, since he argues that humans duplicate themselves actively and come to contemplate themselves in a world of their own making. (Ibid., p. 114). On the more general issue of the relation of natural to human worlds see the very interesting account by Alfred Schmidt, *The Concept of Nature in Marx*, tr. Ben Foukes (London: New Left Books, 1971).

7. Marx and Engels, *The German Ideology*, p. 42.

8. See Alfred Sohn-Rethel, *Intellectual and Manual Labor: A Critique of Epistemology* (London: Macmillan, 1978). I should note that my analysis both depends on and is in tension with Sohn-Rethel's. Sohn-Rethel argues that commodity exchange is a characteristic of all class societies—one which comes to a head in capitalism or takes its most advanced form in capitalism. His project, which is not mine, is to argue that (a) commodity exchange, a characteristic of all class societies, is an original source of abstraction, (b) that this abstraction contains the formal element essential for the cognitive faculty of conceptual thinking, and (c) that the abstraction operating in exchange, an abstraction in practice, is the source of the ideal abstraction basic to Greek philosophy and to modern science. (See Ibid., p. 28). In addition to a different purpose, I should indicate several major differences with Sohn-Rethel. First, he treats the productive forces as separate from the productive relations of society and ascribes far too much autonomy to them. (See, for example, his discussions on pp. 84–86, 95.) I take the position that the distinction between the two is simply a device used for purposes of analysis rather than a feature of the real world. Second, Sohn-Rethel characterizes the period preceding generalized commodity production as primitive communism. (See p. 98.) This is however an inadequate characterization of tribal societies.

9. Karl Marx, *Capital*, I (New York: International Publishers, 1967), p. 176.

10. I have done this elsewhere in a systematic way. For the analysis, see my discussion of the exchange abstraction in *Money, Sex, and Power: An Essay on Domination and Community* (New York: Longman, 1983).

11. This is Iris Young's point. I am indebted to her persuasive arguments for taking what she terms the "gender differentiation of labor" as a central category of analysis (Young, "Dual Systems Theory," p. 185). My use of this category, however, differs to some extent from hers. Young's analysis of women in capitalism does not seem to include marriage as a part of the division of labor. She is more concerned with the division of labor in the productive sector.

12. See Sara Ruddick, "Maternal Thinking," *Feminist Studies* 6, 2 (Summer, 1980): 364.

13. See, for discussions of this danger, "Disloyal to Civilization: Feminism, Racism, Gynephobia," in Adrienne Rich, *On Lies, Secrets, and Silence* (New York: W. W. Norton & Co., 1979), pp. 275–310; Elly Bulkin, "Racism and Writing: Some Implications for White Lesbian Critics," in *Sinister Wisdom*, No. 6 (Spring, 1980).

14. Some cross-cultural evidence indicates that the status of women varies with the work they do. To the extent that women and men contribute equally to subsistence, women's status is higher than it would be if their subsistence-work differed profoundly from that of men; that is, if they do none or almost all of the work of subsistence, their status remains low. See Peggy

Sanday, "Female Status in the Public Domain," in Michelle Rosaldo and Louise Lamphere, eds., *Women, Culture, and Society* (Stanford: Stanford University Press, 1974), p. 199. See also Iris Young's account of the sexual division of labor in capitalism, mentioned above.

15. It is irrelevant to my argument here that women's wage labor takes place under different circumstances than men's—that is, their lower wages, their confinement to only a few occupational categories, etc. I am concentrating instead on the formal, structural features of women's work. There has been much effort to argue that women's domestic labor is a source of surplus value, that is, to include it within the scope of Marx's value theory as productive labor, or to argue that since it does not produce surplus value it belongs to an entirely different mode of production, variously characterized as domestic or patriarchal. My strategy here is quite different from this. See, for the British debate, Mariarosa Dalla Costa and Selma James, *The Power of Women and the Subversion of the Community* (Briston: Falling Wall Press, 1975); Wally Secombe, "The Housewife and Her Labor Under Capitalism," *New Left Review* 83 (January-February, 1974); Jean Gardiner, "Women's Domestic Labour," *New Left Review* 89 (March, 1975); and Paul Smith, "Domestic Labour and Marx's Theory of Value," in Annette Kuhn and Ann Marie Wolpe, eds., *Feminism and Materialism* (Boston: Routledge and Kegan Paul, 1978). A portion of the American debate can be found in Ira Gerstein, "Domestic Work and Capitalism," and Lisa Vogel, "The Earthly Family," *Radical America* 7, 4/5 (July–October, 1973); Ann Ferguson, "Women as a New Revolutionary Class," in Pat Walker, ed., *Between Labor and Capital* (Boston: South End Press, 1979).

16. Frederick Engels, *Origins of the Family, Private Property and the State* (New York: International Publishers, 1942); Karl Marx, *Capital*, Vol. I, p. 671. Marx and Engels have also described the sexual division of labor as natural or spontaneous. See Mary O'Brien, "Reproducing Marxist Man," in Lorenne Clark and Lynda Lange, eds., *The Sexism of Social and Political Theory: Women and Reproduction from Plato to Nietzsche* (Toronto: University of Toronto Press, 1979).

17. For a discussion of women's work, see Elise Boulding, "Familial Constraints on Women's Work Roles," in Martha Blaxall and B. Reagan, eds., *Women and the Workplace* (Chicago: University of Chicago Press, 1976), esp. the charts on pp. 111, 113.

An interesting historical note is provided by the fact that even Nausicaa, the daughter of a Homeric king, did the household laundry. (See M. I. Finley, *The World of Odysseus* [Middlesex, England: Penguin, 1979], p. 73.) While aristocratic women were less involved in actual labor, the difference was one of degree. And as Aristotle remarked in *The Politics*, supervising slaves is not a particularly uplifting activity. The life of leisure and philosophy, so much the goal for aristocratic Athenian men, then, was almost unthinkable for any woman.

18. Simone de Beauvoir holds that repetition has a deeper significance and that women's biological destiny itself is repetition. (See *The Second Sex*, tr. H. M. Parshley [New York: Knopf, 1953], p. 59.) But see also her discussion of housework in Ibid., pp. 434ff. There her treatment of housework is strikingly negative. For de Beauvoir, transcendence is provided in the historical struggle of self with other and with the natural world. The oppositions she sees are not really stasis vs. change, but rather transcendence, escape from the muddy concreteness of daily life, from the static, biological, concrete repetition of "placid femininity."

19. Marilyn French, *The Women's Room* (New York: Jove, 1978), p. 214.

20. Sara Ruddick, "Maternal Thinking," presents an interesting discussion of these and other aspects of the thought which emerges from the activity of mothering. Although I find it difficult to speak the language of interests and demands she uses, she brings out several valuable points. Her distinction between maternal and scientific thought is very intriguing and potentially useful (see esp. pp. 350–353).

21. O'Brien, "Reproducing Marxist Man," p. 115, n. 11.

22. It should be understood that I am concentrating here on the experience of women in Western culture. There are a number of crosscultural differences which can be expected to have some effect. See, for example, the differences which emerge from a comparison of

childrearing in ancient Greek society with that of the contemporary Mbuti in central Africa. See Phillip Slater, *The Glory of Hera* (Boston: Beacon, 1968) and Colin Turnbull, "The Politics of Non-Aggression," in Ashley Montagu, ed., *Learning Non-Aggression* (New York: Oxford University Press, 1978).

23. See Nancy Chodorow, "Family Structure and Feminine Personality," in Rosaldo and Lamphere, *Woman, Culture and Society,* p. 59.

24. Adrienne Rich, *Of Woman Born* (New York: Norton, 1976), p. 63.

25. See Chodorow, *The Reproduction of Mothering,* and Flax, "The Conflict Between Nurturance and Autonomy in Mother-Daughter Relations and in Feminism," *Feminist Studies* 4, 2 (June, 1978). I rely on the analyses of Dinnerstein and Chodorow but there are difficulties in that they are attempting to explain why humans, both male and female, fear and hate the female. My purpose here is to invert their arguments and to attempt to put forward a positive account of the epistemological consequences of this situation. What follows is a summary of Chodorow, *The Reproduction of Mothering.*

26. Chodorow, *Reproduction,* pp. 105–109.

27. This is Jane Flax's point.

28. Chodorow, *Reproduction,* pp. 127–131, 163.

29. Ibid., p. 166.

30. Ibid., pp. 174–178. Chodorow suggests a correlation between father absence and fear of women (p. 213), and one should, treating this as an empirical hypotheses, expect a series of cultural differences based on the degree of father absence. Here the ancient Greeks and the Mbuti provide a fascinating contrast. (See n. 22 above.)

31. Ibid., p. 198. The flexible and diffuse female ego boundaries can of course result in the pathology of loss of self in responsibility for and dependence on others. (The obverse of the male pathology of experiencing the self as walled city.)

32. Sigmund Freud, *Civilization and Its Discontents* (New York: Norton, 1961), pp. 12–13.

33. Hegel, *Phenomenology of Spirit* (New York: Oxford University Press, 1979), trans. A. V. Miller, p. 114. See also Jessica Benjamin's very interesting use of this discussion in "The Bonds of Love: Rational Violence and Erotic Domination," *Feminist Studies* 6, 1 (June 1980).

34. Alvin Gouldner has made a similar argument in his contention that the Platonic stress on hierarchy and order resulted from a similarly learned opposition to daily life which was rooted in the young aristocrat's experience of being taught proper behavior by slaves who could not themselves engage in this behavior. See *Enter Plato* (New York: Basic Books, 1965), pp. 351–355.

35. One can argue, as Chodorow's analysis suggests, that their extreme form in his philosophy represents an extreme father-absent (father-deprived?) situation. A more general critique of phallocentric dualism occurs in Susan Griffin, *Woman and Nature* (New York: Harper & Row, 1978).

36. More recently, of course, the opposition to the natural world has taken the form of destructive technology. See Evelyn Fox Keller, "Gender and Science," *Psychoanalysis and Contemporary Thought* 1, 3 (1978), reprinted in Sandra Harding and Merrill Hintikka, eds., *Discovering Reality: Feminist Perspectives on Epistemology, Metaphysics, Methodology and Philosophy of Science* (Dordrecht, Holland: D. Reidel Publishing Co., 1983).

37. See Elizabeth Spelman, "Metaphysics and Misogyny: The Soul and Body in Plato's Dialogues," mimeo. One analyst has argued that its basis lies in the fact that "the early mother, monolithic representative of nature, is a source, like nature, of ultimate distress as well as ultimate joy. Like nature, she is both nourishing and disappointing, both alluring and threatening. ... The infant loves her ... and it hates her because, like nature, she does not perfectly protect and provide for it. ... The mother, then—like nature, which sends blizzards and locusts as well as sunshine and strawberries—is perceived as capricious, sometimes actively malevolent." Dinnerstein, *Mermaid and the Minotaur,* p. 95.

38. See Benjamin, (n. 33 above), p. 152. The rest of her analysis goes in a different direction than mine, though her account of *The Story of O* can be read as making clear the problems for any social synthesis based on the Hegelian model.

39. Rich, *Of Woman Born*, p. 64, p. 167. For a similar descriptive account, but a dissimilar analysis, see David Bakan, *The Duality of Human Existence* (Boston: Beacon, 1966).

40. My arguments are supported with remarkable force by both the theory and practice of the contemporary women's movement. In theory, this appears in different forms in the work of Dorothy Riddle, "New Visions of Spiritual Power," *Quest: a Feminist Quarterly* 1, 3 (Spring, 1975); Susan Griffin, *Woman and Nature*, esp. Book IV: 'The Separate Rejoined'; Adrienne Rich, *Of Woman Born*, esp. pp. 62–68; Linda Thurston, "On Male and Female Principle," *The Second Wave* 1, 2 (Summer, 1971). In feminist political organizing, this vision has been expressed as an opposition of leadership and hierarchy, as an effort to prevent the development of organizations divided into leaders and followers. It has also taken the form of an insistence on the unity of the personal and the political, a stress on the concrete rather than on abstract principles (an opposition to theory), and a stress on the politics of everyday life. For a fascinating and early example, see Pat Mainardi, "The Politics of Housework," in Leslie Tanner, ed., *Voices of Women's Liberation* (New York: New American Library, 1970).

41. George Bataille, *Death and Sensuality* (New York: Arno Press, 1977), p. 90.

42. Women Against Violence Against Women Newsletter, June 1976, p. 1.

43. *Aegis: A Magazine on Ending Violence Against Women*, November/December, 1978, p. 3.

44. Robert Stoller, *Perversion: The Erotic Form of Hatred* (New York: Pantheon, 1975), p. 88.

45. Bataille, *Death and Sensuality*, p. 91. See pp. 91ff for a more complete account of the commonalities of sexual activity and ritual sacrifice.

46. Bataille, *Death and Sensuality*, p. 12 (italics mine). See also de Beauvoir's discussion in *The Second Sex*, pp. 135, 151.

47. Bataille, *Death and Sensuality*, p. 14.

48. Ibid., p. 42. While Adreinne Rich acknowledges the violent feelings between mothers and children, she quite clearly does not put these at the heart of the relation (*Of Woman Born*).

49. Bataille, *Death and Sensuality*, pp. 95–96.

50. de Beauvoir, *The Second Sex*, p. 58. It should be noted that killing and risking life are ways of indicating one's contempt for one's body, and as such are of a piece with the Platonic search for disembodiment.

51. Consider, for example, Rich's discussion of pregnancy and childbirth, Ch. VI and VII, *Of Woman Born*. And see also Charlotte Perkins Gilman's discussion of domestic labor in *The Home* (Urbana, Ill.: The University of Illinois Press, 1972).

52. The Marxist-feminist efforts to determine whether housework produces surplus value and the feminist political strategy of demanding wages for housework represent two (mistaken) efforts to recognize women's non-wage activity as work. Perhaps domestic labor's non-status as work is one of the reasons why its wages—disproportionately paid to women of color—are so low, and working conditions so poor.

53. *Capital*, Vol. I, p. 60.

54. See Marx, *1844*, p. 117.

Reproducing Marxist Man

Mary O'Brien

It has become fashionable in recent years to talk of a revival of Marxism. The most cursory examination of political activities over the past century demonstrates that Marxism has been a vital and immensely significant factor in political activity for at least that long, and that such a lively corpus of thought hardly needs reviving. However, as a consequence of the fact that the Marxist tradition in North America at the present time appears to rest mainly in the hands of some of the intelligentsia, whose commitment to class struggle pales beside their scramble for tenure in the universities, it is Marxist *theory,* and not Marxist practice, which has become respectable. Thus, the separation of theory and practice has also been successful, and now joins the other separations which Marx analysed as by-products of class struggle, the separation of head and hand, and of town and country, for example. This is serious, for Marx's notion of *praxis* as the strategic route to the achievement of rational and humane social relations in a creative and scientific unity of thinking and doing is enormously powerful and potentially effective. It also constitutes the most difficult of the tasks which Marx bequeathed to his followers.

Among those followers are a constituency on which perhaps the ruling classes had not reckoned. Marxism has had a significant impact on feminism. The reasons for this are fairly obvious. Marx is the philosopher par excellence of the oppressed, and women are oppressed. Marx is also the pre-eminent theorist of revolution, and even bourgeois feminism, however nervously, recognizes that the liberation of women is a revolutionary proposition, centring as it must upon the most venerable of social institutions, particularly upon family forms. Further, the determinant impact of economic factors on the condition of women has made Marx's critique of political economy particularly appealing. Women have also understood with varying degrees of precision the need for a feminist praxis, but it has not been entirely clear where the theoretical component of this praxis can be found. The most likely source is Engels, who proposed a theoretical model of the oppression of women which appears to unify the question of women's liberation with the dynamics of class struggle and the promise of the abolition of class division.[1] Finally, the compelling humanism of Marx's thought, considerably buttressed recently by the translation and publication of his early works, has widened the appeal of his later and quite dauntingly complex works.

Despite these factors, there is increasing evidence that the promise of a feminist Marxism has become problematic.[2] There are fairly obvious reasons for this. The experience of women after Marxist revolutions, especially in the Soviet Union, has not been especially encouraging.[3] A change in the ownership of the means of production obviously does not produce a reflex qualitative transformation in the relations of women to men. Many women are beginning to wonder if the Marxist inheritance, which can offer a correct analysis of economic depression, can also offer an adequate theoretical perspective from which to view the present and the tradition which I have elsewhere called 'male-stream thought.'[4] This philosophical heritage is shot through with the ideology of male supremacy, and Marx is indubitably a thinker within this tradition, however original and however brilliant. Marx's inclusion of women's oppression in the general oppression of class division is, perhaps, inadequate. Women's oppression is qualitatively different from class oppression, and the qualitative differentiation which must be made in the first instance in theoretical terms simply does not emerge from Marx's work in a direct way.

These difficulties have surfaced both in feminist activism and in feminist scholarship, which are not wholly estranged. Women have recognized the need for the unification of knowledge which lurks under such cumbersome labels as 'inter-disciplinary Women's Studies.' The social sciences, for example, have produced data which orthodox Marxism has had difficulty in assimilating; perhaps psychoanalysis is the prime case, with its provocative and controversial theory of femininity. With some unorthodox exceptions Marxists have been suspicious of Freudians, and feminists have tended to choke on penis envy.[5] Yet psychoanalytical insights have enriched understanding of some of those areas which have caused most difficulty for feminist analysis. Wilhelm Reich, for example, argued that psyches which developed under the sweeping patriarchal authoritarianism of czarist Russia could not be transformed by a simple assertion that the family was officially defunct, or by merely superficial changes in the external conditions of family life.[6]

Psychology has much to offer in the area of gender identity, just as sociology has much to offer in the area of gender socialization. The hostility between Marxist social science, which seems largely to have found its critical capital in the workplace, and 'bourgeois' social science, perceived only as an exercise in ideological manipulation, is a hostility which feminists must examine in a critical way. Women need not neglect the psycho-social dimensions of male supremacy and the sociology of the family with the cavalier disparagement in which vulgar economist determinisms present themselves as the totality of a 'Marxist' social science.

The examination and criticism of these difficulties need not cow us, and we do not need to retreat before the possibility that the difficulties may emerge from defects in Marx's own theoretical understanding. There are few sharper historical ironies than the posthumous conversion of Marx the iconoclast, the most trenchant critic of ideological modes of understanding, into some kind of ahistorical saint whose work is perceived in canonical terms. In this paper, I want to open a critical examination of the marginality and inadequacy of Marx's understanding of reproduction; I then want to note the historical specificity of these defects, and to give some indication as to why a dialectical, historical, and materialist critique, derived from but superseding Marxist theory, offers the most promising ground for the development of a truly feminist praxis.

Marx, following upon the work of Hegel, grappled with the proposition that all reality is *process*. Process is understood as the form of all development and all interaction between the human world and the natural world. Process in this first instance is an abstract expression of the reality of action, thought, and experience, bringing the tumultuous and crowded contents of human history into a dynamic theoretical perspective. At the same time, process represents a concrete unity of humanity and the natural world, a unity born in struggle to meet and overcome the constrictions of necessity.

This sort of approach to socio-historical understanding is one to which feminism is at once sympathetic. The separation of 'Man' from nature may be perceived as the source, for example, of such problems as environmental erosion and the mindless triumphs of technocracy, which many feminists understand as related to masculine perceptions of power. Women are also aware that within the tradition of masculine understanding of the 'natural' world there is a significant gender differentiation. Men are somehow separate from and in an antagonistic relation to Nature, while women are in some even vaguer sense unified and indeed imprisoned by Nature. Hegel and Marx were both concerned to reinstate the notion of a synthesis of human and natural worlds, a concern born of the Enlightenment's over-confident proclivity to perceive man and nature as eternally at war, with man's progress being marked rather specifically by his ability to overcome and control nature. Such a synthesis could not be brought about, Hegel and Marx realized, by wilfully imposing a 'natural' or metaphysical harmony upon the man/nature dialectic which ignored the empirically disharmonious historical reality of this relation. What both thinkers tried to capture was the *form* of historical process in a way which did not preclude the diversity and struggle which constitute the content of history. The mode of the analysis which Hegel conceived of and Marx nurtured was of course the dialectical method.

There is no easy way into the notion of the science of dialectics. Here, however, we might pause with Hegel for a moment for two relevant reasons.[7] One is that Hegel recognized, somewhat imperfectly, that the process of human biological reproduction is, as an instance of process in general, dialectically structured. The other is that a brief examination of the way in which Hegel examined the process sheds useful if still crude light on the meaning of dialectics. We have, in the process of reproduction, the coming together of two opposites, the male and female 'seeds.' This synthesis is brought about by human action, and the particularity of each parent is destroyed, or, in the terminology of dialectics, negated. However, this unity which is a negation in the first instance, grows and expands until it bursts forth into the historical world as something new and different but undoubtedly real. The act of birth in turn cancels out the negativity inherent in the seed, for the child is not only a new particularity; he is potentially universal, both potential man and potential Man, both individual and, to use young Marx's phrase, species-being.[8] *HE* is this synthesis of universal and particular, ready to play his part in the Hegelian drama in which Reason is objectified in the world through human praxis.

Hegel's very astute observation of the dialectical structure of reproduction does not carry human affairs out of the animal into the social realm. This is because he sees this process as devoid of the self-directed workings of a true and rational self-consciousness: birth is pre-rational and therefore in an odd sense always pre-historical. Hegel, who notes correctly that human labour is the activity which mediates between people and nature, does not regard the labour of childbirth as philosophically significant. In fact, the only 'labour' involved in reproductive process is copulation, which is at least a novel view of that process, but it is *mindless* labour, informed by passion rather than reason.[9] Hegel is, of course, a profound mysogynist, who sees women as a disruptive and irrational historical force, asserting the value of individual life over the greater rational value of world-historical life. Obsessed with the curious reluctance to have their children killed, women stand in the way of Man's historic destiny, which consists of the eternal need to do death-dealing battle with other men, thus defying enslavement to the Great Negation, death itself, and asserting the value of the community over the mere life of the individual. The real cause of Hegel's denial of a reproductive consciousness, however, lies in his view of reproduction as wholly organic and pre-rational. For Hegel, patriarchy is both natural and pre-historical.

Hegel's discovery of the dialectical structure of biological reproduction, however imperfect, is a useful one. We also note that it was not part of the Hegelian baggage which Marx appropriated and transformed in the development of materialist dialectics. Marx is more humanely concerned with the oppression of women than Hegel was, but his understanding of the historical significance of the family hovers mistily on the edge of his insight into the historical forms of class struggle. Seeking to specify the historical conditions under which men might take rational control of the productive necessities imposed by their daily need to 'reproduce' themselves, Marx never comes to terms with the social relations of reproduction in anything other than a reflexive way.

He accepts uncritically Proudhon's view of the condition of women: as men work historically to liberate themselves, history will somehow liberate women as a bonus. Women are therefore passive beneficiaries, with the additional usefulness of presenting a rough quantitative measure of how the class struggle is coming along. Further, Marx, who so expanded upon Hegel's insight into the mediative and creative powers of human labour, shares Hegel's astigmatism as to the fact that women *labour* to produce children. We do not, of course, argue that productive labour and reproductive labour are the same thing.[10] We do argue that reproductive labour cannot simply be ignored, as is the case with the two thinkers we are talking about, and in fact is the case with 'male-stream' thought in general.

Birth is not an object of philosophy—Marxist man, impressively human as he is, somehow never gets born. This neglect of any systematic analysis of reproductive labour is very important. It is by the unification of labour and thought, of theory and practice, that men make history, and in so doing they continuously transform and make the world and transform and make themselves. It is, further, this praxis which ultimately cancels the opposition between men and nature. Labour, together with rational consciousness of what one is doing when one works, mediates this opposition, integrating each man with his world and ensuring that men understand themselves as historical activists.[11] For Hegel, work is the animator of self-consciousness and its possibilities of universality, the progression from particular man to the unification of Man in general. For Marx, labour is the route to true consciousness, the consciousness which recognizes the collective need to resist the alienation and exploitation inherent in class antagonism and irrational modes of production.

It is not intended here to deny Marx's compelling analysis of the creative and transformative powers of productive labour. Likewise, Marx never denied that women, too, might develop a true consciousness and participate in the class struggle.

However, one result has been a belief that the possibility of women participating in their own liberation depends upon their participation as workers in the productive realm, a view which has become increasingly problematic. We therefore note that the neglect of a serious analysis of reproductive labour short-changes the notion of labour as mediator between the social and human worlds, and tends to perpetuate Marx's error in subsuming gender struggle in class struggle. Perceived as accidental and irrational, the act of giving birth has no power to constitute a socio-historical world, but remains brute, dumb, and intransigent. The fact that genetic continuity is in some sense a material base of human history goes unnoticed and, more importantly, in all the efforts to analyse the determinants of human consciousness, the notion of such a phenomenon as *reproductive consciousness* is not seriously entertained. As it does not exist in a meaningful way, reproductive consciousness does not have to look for its own roots or analyse its own properties, and the ground of the social relations of reproduction are not sought in the process of reproduction. In Hegel's case, they are sought in affective and spiritual life; in Marx's case, they are assumed to be by-products of the dominant mode of production.

Marx's socio-historical model thus suffers from a real ambiguity as to the status of the family, which is, of course, the historical form in which the social relations of reproduction are most commonly realized. Marx's formal 'model' consists of a substructure which has as its content a historically specific and generalized mode of production and the forms of class struggle which have created it, define it, and will ultimately abolish it. This substructure of historical process determines the forms of such social institutions as law, literature, religion, and politics, which reflect the needs and values of the dominant class. The use of such differentiated words as 'determine' and 'reflect' is deliberate, for the actual workings of the relations between the economic substructure and the social constituents of what Marx calls the superstructure or, sometimes, the infrastructure, were never worked out in detail. There are some hints that a key role is played by the political infrastructure, both in terms of providing a power base for ruling class self-conservation and in terms of the transformation of the ideologies of conflicting classes into real struggle. The important question about the model here, however, concerns the location and relations of the family. The answer is by no means clear. In some places—in the *Communist Manifesto,* for example—the family is treated as a superstructural phenomenon which reflects its market substructure in the reduction of marriage to a set of property relations in which female bodies become commodities, a fate which male bodies somehow escape.[12] Male bodies, insofar as they incorporate labour power, are commodities in the labour market, but in the marital marketplace men are traders. While Marx is savagely satirical on the subject of bourgeois marriage, he makes no claim for more progressive relations among the proletariat, though in other places he waxes a little sentimental on this subject.[13] He certainly does not see the opposition of male-female as the ground of historical transformation.

The ambiguity of reproduction is even more pronounced in Engels' account of the economic origins of male supremacy and what he is pleased to call, with a fine Hegelian flourish, 'the world-historical defeat of the female sex.'[14] Engels begins by placing reproduction firmly in the substructure of the historical model: production and reproduction jointly constitute *necessity,* which is the reason why the substructure is the determinant realm in the first place. However, having argued that both production and reproduction are necessary and substructural, Engels goes on to argue that family forms are economically determined. To object to this is not theoretical hair-splitting: it is precisely the historical development of rational means for dealing with necessity which embodies the Marxist vision of a humane and classless future, but evidently only one pole of the axis of necessity can be dealt with. Necessity has two poles, production and reproduction, but in Engels' model production subsumes reproduction, for the relations of production alone leave scope for human praxis.

Thus Engels argues that the development of private property brought about a great deal of uncomfortable disorder in societies in which matrilineal kinship had constituted both a mode of historical continuity and a determinate series of social arrangements. Property 'made the man's position in the family more important than the woman's.'[15] Property thus brought about one of the greatest revolutions of all time but, according to Engels, it was a peaceful one. Women did not resist these changes, the only reason which Engels offers being that they were delighted with the institution of patriarchal marriage, which saved them from the unpleasantness of a variety of sexual partners.[16] Sex is, for women, a distasteful necessity from which the fine Victorian sensibilities of Engels and Marx would feign protect them. In any case, the women of ancient times contemplated this major revolution with equanimity and passivity, and a 'simple decree sufficed that in the future the offspring of the male members should remain within the gens,' and property could thus be secured to male inheritance. Engels was writing after Marx's death but there is no reason to suppose that Marx would have disagreed. Both men had read Morgan, and Engels quotes one of Marx's marginal notes on the Morgan text to the effect that the transition from mother right to father right 'in general ... seems to be the most *natural* transition'[17] (my italics).

Here we must face the fact that in this area Marx is a true bud of the great tree of traditional 'male-stream' thought. He is as ambiguous on the central question of the nature of Nature as his predecessors have been since classical philosophers first grappled with the question. Nature evidently suffers from the same kind of contradictory characteristics which her daughters exhibit; she is the mother of and partakes of the nature of Eve and the Blessed Virgin. Fecund and providential on the one hand, she is unpredictable and wantonly destructive on the other. She is in one sense the source of human nature, but has exasperatingly concealed in the fearful crevices of her mysterious womb just exactly what that human nature is. She demands conformity with her own nature while mocking man, her creature, with a denial of any immediate knowledge of the meaning of the natural.

Marx, of course, does not sail on these speculative ontological seas, but, as R. Pascal has noted, he is inconsistent in his application, for example, of the term *Naturwüchsig* (growing naturally).[18] In *The German Ideology* he uses this phrase to denote pre-capitalist economic forms in which labour is divided by 'natural predispositions,' such as strength, need, and other accidental factors. This sort of arrangement produces what Marx calls 'natural' capital, which remains attached to the guilds whose labours produced it in the first place. Elsewhere, Marx speaks of 'natural' society in terms of cleavage between particular and collective interests, an opposition which creates class differentiation and a loss of the control of the product of labour. Over against this 'natural' society Marx poses communist society which has regained control of the social product by means of rational planning.

Pascal does not offer an analysis of the roots of this inconsistency, but it is important that this be cone. This kind of ambiguity is not random, but is related to a much more radical defect in Marx's model which never solves the problem of the relation of the two poles of natural necessity, production and reproduction. Marx wants to develop a theoretical model which transcends the idealist speculations of former models, especially that of Hegel. His historical dialectics are to be materialist dialectics, which must avoid rootless metaphysic on the one hand and the grounded realities of Lockean sense perception on the other. At the same time, of course, Marx must retain the integrity of both mental life and empirical reality. His model therefore attempts to ground history in natural necessity, perceived as a determinate but not completely determinant substructure of all human endeavour, for necessity commands both action and reflection and human praxis is creative and versatile.

The postulate that men must eat is rescued by Marx from proverbial crudity to its proper status as the a priori of individual life, while the postulate that men must *produce* to eat becomes for him the a priori of social life. Thus Marx talks continuously of the need for men to 'reproduce' themselves, and by this he almost always means reproduction of the self on a daily basis by the continual and necessary restoking of the organism with fuel for its biological needs. Man makes himself materially, and this is of course true. Man, however, is also 'made' reproductively by the parturitive labour of women, but Marx ultimately combines these two processes. This has the effect of negating biological continuity, which is mediated by women's reproductive labour, and replacing this with productive continuity in which men, in making themselves, also make history. Marx never observes that men are in fact separated *materially* from both nature and biological continuity by the alienation of the male seed in copulation.

This negation of the human significance of biological reproduction is quite specific. Like Hegel, Marx deals with the question as a young man, and, also like Hegel, he appears to be more concerned with the question of sexuality than with the understanding of the social significance of reproductive process, of which sexuality is but a part. In the Third of the *1844 Manuscripts,* Marx introduces the question of sexual relations in an exemplary way, signifying the thoughtlessness with which crude communism wreaks indiscriminate social destruction in a mindless passion for making all private property communal property: 'Finally, this tendency to oppose general private property to private property is expressed in an animal form: *marriage* (which is incontestably a form of *exclusive private property*) is contrasted with the community of women, in which women become communal and common property. One may say that this idea of the *community* of women is the *open secret* of this entirely crude and unreflective communism. Just as women are to pass from marriage to universal prostitution, so the whole world of wealth (i.e., the objective being of man) is to pass from the relation of exclusive marriage with the private owner to the relation of universal prostitution with the community.'[19]

Marx appears to see that his broad castigation of both bourgeois marriage and communal sex may be a little sweeping, so he goes on to try to strip away from the 'open secret'—a simple and primitive lust and resentful envy—some of its secrecy: 'In the relationship with *woman,* as the prey and handmaid of communal lust, is expressed the infinite degradation in which man exists for himself; for the secret of this relationship finds its *unequivocal,* incontestable, *open* and revealed expression in the relation of man to woman and in the way in which the *direct* and *natural* species relationship is conceived. The immediate, natural and necessary relation of human being is also the *relation of man* to *woman.* In this *natural* species relationship man's relation to nature is directly his relation to man, and his relation to man is directly his relation to nature, his own *natural* function. Thus, in this relation is *sensually revealed*, reduced to an observable *fact*, the extent to which human nature has become nature for man and to which nature has become human nature for him.'[20]

The almost indecent haste with which a relation of man to woman becomes a relation of man to man is perhaps exacerbated in translation, for English, unlike German, does not provide separate words for masculine man (*man*) and mankind (*mensche*). Giving Marx the broadest possible latitude we may interpret him as saying: the immediate natural and necessary human relationship is that of men and women. In this relationship people are conscious of their own sexual need, which is the need for another human being. This need confirms them as both natural and social beings, and the degree to which they can create humane conditions for the expression of this relationship is an indicator of how far they have progressed from mere animality. Such an interpretation proclaims an important truth, that sexual relations are not only necessary, but necessarily social, which is not, interestingly, true of the need to produce.

In a primitive state, individuals could theoretically pluck only their own fruits from the tree of life; the race, of course, would not then survive. Despite this, or perhaps because of this, Marx joins traditional philosophy in denying to birth any specifically human significance. The ground of Marx's version of this persistent tenet of male supremacist ideology is that any man who owes his existence to another is a 'dependent being,' and is thus precluded from free expression of his humanity: 'But I live completely by another person's favour when I owe to him [sic] not only the continuance of my life but also *its creation;* when he is its *source.* My life has necessarily such a cause outside itself if it is not my own creation. The idea of *creation* is thus one which it is difficult to eliminate from popular consciousness. This consciousness is *unable to conceive* that nature and man exist on their own account, because such an existence contradicts all the tangible facts of practical life.'[21]

Marx appears to share the Greek notion that the male is 'true parent' of the child without recognizing the prejudice inherent in this formulation.[22] Furthermore, he seems quite unperturbed by the positing of a 'material' view of a fundamental life process which 'contradicts all the facts of practical life.' He is interested, of course, in man's historical, self-made nature. Yet in asserting this, he quite specifically negates reproductive continuity, which he sees as infinite regress lurking as progress. If, like Aristotle, he argues, you say that man is produced by the coitus of two human beings, you lapse into infinite progression (who engendered my grandfather and his father and so forth) and do not keep in mind 'the *circular movement* which is perceptible in that progression, according to which man, in the act of generation reproduces himself: thus *man* always remains the subject.'[23]

Marx is aware of the essential sociability of reproduction and of temporal problems within the process. He does not, however, analyse the nature of the temporal problem, which is specifically a *male* problem. Male participation in the continuum of species-being ends with the alienation of the male seed. Male time-consciousness is thus discontinuous. For women, species continuity is confirmed by reproductive labour. Marx, not having analysed the dialectics of reproductive process, does not see this. A stubborn insistence that biological continuity *is* continuity, he says, can only lead to the question of who created man in the first place, a 'perverted' and 'abstract' question which posits non-existence. The young Marx, still engaged in 'hating all gods,' the passion which had informed his doctoral dissertation, simply takes refuge in polemic at this point: 'Ask yourself whether that progression exists as such for rational thought. If you ask a question about the creation of nature and man you abstract from nature and man. You suppose them *non-existent* and you want me to demonstrate that they *exist*. I reply: give up your abstraction and at the same time you abandon your question. Or else, if you want to maintain your abstraction, be consistent, and if you think of man and nature as non-existent think of yourself too as non-existent, for you are also man and nature. Do not think, do not ask me any question, for as soon as you think and ask questions your *abstraction* from the existence of nature and man becomes meaningless. Or are you such an egoist that you conceive everything as non-existent and yet want to exist yourself?'[24]

Socialist man, on the contrary, takes *his* proofs of his man-made existence from real experience, the implication being that getting born is not real experience, and giving birth even less so. Marx is overly excited, because the question that he raises is not the one which needs to be asked at all. We must ask Marx what is wrong with biological reproduction as a basis of real continuity. Of course people 'make themselves' in their interaction with the world and other people, but why can socialist man not be created until birth has been deprived of the capacity to create continuity? Marx could quite easily have posited a dynamic *dialectic* between biological time and historical time without lapsing into the trap of the infinite regression of crude causality. He did not do so, for he did not recognize that reproductive process is dialectical, or that the social relations of reproduction and the ideologies of male supremacy are determined by reproductive rather than productive process.

This is not the mere aberration of a young thinker. The transfer of reproductive power and sociability to productive relations remains constant. In *The German Ideology*, Marx is less confused, but he still insists on the hegemony of productive labour in the formation of human historical consciousness, a position from which he never retreats. In the discussion of biological reproduction in *The German Ideology* he seems at first sight to be presenting us with the remarkable spectacle of people eating and producing and needing before they are born at all: 'life involves before everything else eating and drinking' while the second determination of life process emerges from the fact that needs produce more needs 'and this production of new needs is the first historical act': 'The third circumstance which from the very first, enters into historical development is that men, who daily remake their own life, begin to make other men, to propogate their kind: the relation between man and wife, parents and children, the FAMILY. The family which to begin with is the only social relationship, becomes later, when increased needs create new social relations and the increased population new needs, a subordinate one.'[25]

Here, Marx backtracks a little from 'before everything else'; these are not to be seen as stages of development, he says, but as aspects of development which exist simultaneously, and production and reproduction appear as a double relationship; on the one had natural, on the other social. At this point Marx *negates* the sociability and historicism of reproductive relations: 'It follows from this that a certain mode of production ... is always combined with a certain mode of cooperation.' It also follows that reproduction also involves a certain mode of co-operation, but Marx does not say so. Only production thereafter forms consciousness, and production, by an unexplained alchemy, also forms the social relations of reproduction.

In *Capital,* Marx has made up his mind on the question of what constitutes a natural economy, and he has also abandoned the radically liberal individualism which
produced the youthful hysteria evident in his diatribe against the dependence of life
on the activity of others. In his discussion of commodity fetishism, he defines 'the
particular and natural form of labour' as that in which the personal interdependence
of the members of the economic unit is present to consciousness in its true social
form.[26] For an example of this directly associated labour form, Marx tells us, we do
not need to go back to 'that spontaneously developed form which we find on the
threshold of the history of all civilized races.' We still have examples of this 'spontaneous' form close to hand, for we can find it 'in the *patriarchal* industries of a peasant family' (my italics). Marx presumably feels that the patriarchal family had developed 'spontaneously' and without struggle, presumably having in mind 'the simple
decree' of which Engels speaks. The family, ancient or modern, 'possesses a spontaneously developed system of division of labour.'[27] As we saw, even the postulation of
an ancient matriarchate did not sully the spontaneity of patriarchal naturalness.

One of the reasons for Marx's position, apart from the uncriticized dominance of
the dogma of male supremacy which was specific to his epoch, is that he is preoccupied with the notion of universality, which he pulls down from idealist heights and
represents as real co-operative sociability. Sociability and co-operation are the preconditions of classless society, and Marx wants to demonstrate that universality—
perceived as the annulment of alienation and the restoration of a unity of men with
nature, with their products and with other men—is the goal of history and the condition of human freedom. He therefore seeks experiential 'universals' and finds eating and sexuality. However, he perceives the latter as immediate, while the former requires the mediation of production. The labour of reproduction is excluded from the
analysis, and not only because children appear spontaneously. Reproductive labour,
thus sterilized, does not produce value, does not produce needs and therefore does
not make history or make men. Birth as such is contingent, immediate, and uninteresting, a 'subordinate' relationship.

What is missing is an analysis of reproductive process, for such an analysis immediately shows a significant form of alienation; the alienation of the male seed. Marx's
notion of the origins of class struggle could just as easily and plausibly describe the
origins of gender struggle: 'Every self-alienation of man, from himself and from nature, appears in the relation which he postulates between other men and himself and
nature ... In the real practical world this self-alienation can only be expressed in the
real, practical relation of man to his fellow men. The medium through which alienation occurs is itself a *practical* one. Through alienated labour, therefore, man not
only produces his relation to the object and to the process of production as to alien
and hostile men; he also produces the relation of other men to his production and
his product, and the relation between himself and other men. Just as he creates his
own production as a vitiation, a punishment, and his own product as a loss, as a
product which does not belong to him, so he creates the domination of the non-pro-
ducer over production and its product. As he alienates his own activity, so he bestows
upon the stranger an activity which is not his own.'[28]

The origin of the struggle between men and women rests upon a similar process.
The child is alienated from the man, for any man can have fathered this child. Paternity, unconfirmed by human labour, remains an *idea*. History shows us that men
have not simply suffered this alienation and loss of continuity. They have done

something about it, actions which require social relations between men which are cooperative—you leave my woman alone and I'll do the same for you—and relations between men and women which are appropriative and therefore relations of dominance. Men annul the alienation of the seed and give social substance to the idea of paternity by the act of appropriating children. This act is at the same time the act of appropriating the alienated reproductive labour power of the mother. Here lies a relation of brotherhood between men of all classes which has nothing to do with modes of production, and everything to do with the necessities embedded in reproductive dialectics.

The importance of Marx's failures in understanding the complexities of Necessity is a failure which can best be understood in terms of Marx's own work. Men, Marx tells us, can only confront the problems which history presents to them. Just as the dialectics of class struggle did not become clear enough to permit systematic theoretical formulation of their internal logic until industrial development had reached a certain stage, so too, the dialectics of reproduction must await a maturity which did not exist in Marx's lifetime. The mediate agent of maturity in each case is the same: technological development. Only in the epoch of potentially universal contraception can the history of gender struggle be theoretically grasped. Only in this era does such a notion as rational control of reproduction become thinkable. Such control is hardly imminent. Humanity has had at hand the possibility of rational control of production for some time, yet the inhuman fetishisms of commodity production persist. Further, the dialectical analysis of reproduction does not offer instant freedom for women. What it does mean is that women have now to do what men did aeons ago: come to terms with their altered reproductive consciousness.

The fact that paternity is not immediate means that the discovery of paternity was at some distant time a historical event. As a relation of non-immediate cause and effect, the discovery of paternity must await a certain quite advanced stage of the development of the human intellect. Even then, paternity remains ideal and problematic. Paternity represents a double freedom for men: a freedom from labour and a freedom to accept or reject the child. The appropriation of the child cancels paternal alienation from species continuity, but it is the appropriation of a helpless creature, and therefore entails certain responsibilities. Likewise, men are placed in opposition to one another as possible potencies, and are forced into social relations to deal with this problem.

The freedom which women gain from the second historical transformation in reproductive process, the development of contraceptive technology, is equally problematic. This technology can be abused in a number of ways, and we already see signs of attempts to solve the tensions embedded in capitalism's recent reversal from a pronatal, expansionist population policy to a curb on the politically dangerous people in the third world. There are also indications that advanced automation in developed countries is producing a larger industrial reserve army of unemployed than capitalism can easily manipulate. These are probably the reasons why the necessary resources to develop universal contraception were allocated in the first place. It was unlikely that this was done with the intention of creating women as the progressive force in history which they now, somewhat benumbed, find themselves to be. In fact, the allocation of resources has been minimal, and has stopped well short of a safe and sophisticated contraceptive technology which a humane rationality demands, but the labour needs of capitalism do not.

Despite these problems, and many more, history cannot be turned back. The social relations of reproduction are changing and will change more. The question is how much control people can have over these transformations. Marx's great strength is that his theory and method permit us to begin to go to work on these problems. The process of reproduction is historical, material, and dialectical, and can be subjected to critical analysis on those terms. What does have to be done is a modification of Marx's socio-historical model, which must now account for two opposing substructures, that of production and that of reproduction. This in fact improves the model. The institutions and ideologies which Marx describes as superstructural are in fact *mediative.* They mediate the oppositions both within and between the social relation of production on the one hand and the social relations of reproduction on the other. This is a very crude formulation, and the uses, refinements, and implications of such a model remain to be worked out. This is an urgent task for feminism, but one at least made possible by the theoretical rigour which is Marx's bequest to us.

Notes and References

1. Lewis Henry Morgan *Ancient Society* (1877; rpt New York 1963); Engels *The Origin of the Family, Private Property, and the State* tr E.B. Leacock (New York 1973). Marx made an abstract of ancient society to which Engels had access, and which can be found (in Russian) in *Marx-Engels Archives* IX (1941) 1–192.

2. Joining the call for a feminist revision of Marxist theory are Eleanor Burke Leacock (in her Introduction to Engels *Origin* 46), Sheila Rowbotham, Juliet Mitchell and, indirectly, Simone de Beauvoir.

3. There is a fairly extensive literature on this subject. See, for example, V.S. Dunham 'Sex: From Free Love to Puritanism' in A. Inkeles and K. Geiger eds *Soviet Society: A Book of Readings* (London 1961); H.K. Geiger *The Family in Soviet Russia* (Cambridge, Mass. 1968); I. de Palencia *Alexandra Kollontay* (New York 1941); W. Reich *The Sexual Revolution* (New York 1971); Hilda Scott *Does Socialism Liberate Women?* (Boston 1975).

4. Mary O'Brien 'The Politics of Impotence' in J. King-Farow and W. Shea eds *Contemporary Issues in Political Philosophy* (New York 1976).

5. The anti-Freud polemic launched by Betty Friedan in *The Feminine Mystique* (New York 1963) has given way to the more subtle appraisals of, for example, Juliet Mitchell in *Woman's Estate* (New York 1973). The unification of the social sciences and the fusion of Marx and Freud are by no means specifically feminist objectives. Some such endeavour colours the scholarly practiced of the critical theorists of the so-called Frankfurt School and is important, too, to much French existentialist thought.

6. Wilhelm Reich *The Sexual Revolution* especially 182–90.

7. The detailed analysis appears in the fragment 'On Love' in Hegel *Early Theological Writings* tr T.M. Knox (Chicago 1948) 305–7.

8. 'On Love' 303–5. A very important work on the family, *The System of Ethical Life,* has recently been translated by T.M. Knox and H.S. Harris, and has been accepted for publication by SUNY Press.

9. Hegel's view of copulation as a form of work can be found in *The System of Ethical Life* tr Knox and Harris. I am much indebted to Professor Harris for his permission to quote from this important translation.

10. For a discussion of this differentiation, see Mary O'Brien 'The Politics of Reproduction' doctoral dissertation, York University, Toronto, 1976.

11. 'What distinguishes the worst architect from the best of bees is this, that the architect raises his structure in imagination before he erects it in reality. ... By thus acting on the external world and changing it, he at the same time changes his own nature'; Marx *Capital* I (Moscow 1954) pt III ch VII 174. Reproductive labour might be said to combine the functions of the architect and the bee: like the architect, parturitive woman knows what she is doing; like the bee, she cannot help what she is doing. But a new life changes the world and the consciousness of the woman.

12. Marx and Engels *The Communist Manifesto* (New York 1955) 27–9.

13. Engels, perhaps, more so: see for example, the touching tale of Jack and Mary in Engels *The Condition of the Working Class in England* (London 1969) 1973–4. Juliet Mitchell quotes Marx's early work ('Chapitre de Mariage' *Œuvres Completes* ed Molitor *Œuvres Philosophiques* I 25) in which Marx speaks of the 'sanctification of the sexual instinct' as 'the spiritual essence of marriage' (Juliet Mitchell *Woman's Estate* 110).

14. Engels *Origin* 120.

15. ibid. 119.

16. Eleanor Burke Leacock, in her Introduction (ibid 7–57), notes Engels' Victorian bias: 'women should by nature value chastity.'

17. Ibid. 120.

18. Marx and Engels *The German Ideology* ed R. Pascal (New York 1947) 291–2n.

19. Marx 'Economic and Philosophical Manuscripts' tr T.B. Bottomore in Erich Fromm ed *Marx's Concept of Man* (New York 1970) 125.

20. Ibid. 126.

21. Ibid. 138.

22. 'The mother is no parent of that which is called her child, but only nurse of the new-planted seed that grows. The parent is he who mounts'; Aeschylus *The Eumenides* tr Richard Latimore (New York 1967) lines 658–60.

23. 'Economic and Philosophical Manuscripts' 139.

24. Ibid.

25. Marx and Engels *German Ideology* ed Pascal 17–18.

26. *Capital* I pt I ch I sec 4.

27. Ibid. 89–90.

28. 'Economic and Philosophical Manuscripts' 105.

The Family as the Locus of Gender, Class, and Political Struggle: The Example of Housework

Heidi I. Hartmann

Although the last decade of research on families has contributed enormously to our understanding of diversity in family structures and the relationship of family units to various other aspects of social life, it has, it seems to me, generally failed to identify and address sources of conflict within family life. Thus, the usefulness of this research for understanding women's situation has been particularly limited. The persistence and resilience of family forms in the midst of general social change, often forcefully documented in this research, have certainly helped to goad us, as feminists, to consider what women's interests may be in the maintenance of a type of family life that we have often viewed as a primary source of women's oppression. Historical, anthropological, and sociological studies of families have pointed to the many ways in which women and men have acted in defense of the family unit, despite the uneven responsibilities and rewards of the two sexes in family life. In failing to focus sufficiently clearly on the differences between women's and men's experiences and interests within families, however, these studies overlook important aspects of social reality and potentially decisive sources of change in families and society as people struggle both within and outside families to advance their own interests. This oversight stems, I think, from a basic commitment shared by many conducting these studies to a view of the family as a unified interest group and as an agent of change in its own right.

Family historians, for example, have explored the role of the family in amassing wealth; in contributing to population growth or decline; in providing, recruiting, or failing to provide labor for a new industrial system; in transmitting social values to new generations; and in providing or failing to provide enclaves from new and rude social orders. They have consistently aimed to place the family in a larger social arena. The diversity of findings and the range of their interpretation is great: the size of the household has been constant before, during, and after industrialization (Peter Laslett); it has decreased as capitalism curtailed household production (Eli Zaretsky); it has been flexible, depending on the processes of rural-to-urban migration and wage levels in the new industrial employments, and has often actually increased (Michael Anderson); industrialization liberated sexuality and women (Edward Shorter); capitalism destroyed the extended family and created the nuclear (Eli Zaretsky); capitalist industrialization destroyed the nuclear (Friedrich Engels); the nuclear family facilitated industrialization (William Goode); the family and industrialization were partners in modernization (Tamara Hareven).[1] Yet despite this diversity, the consistent focus of the new family history on the interconnection between family and society implies a definition of family. The family is generally seen as a social entity that is a source of dynamic change, an actor, an agent, on a par with such other "social forces" as economic change, modernization, or individualism.[2] Such a view assumes the unity of interests among family members; it stresses the role of the family as a unit and tends to downplay conflicts or differences of interest among family members.[3]

In this essay I suggest that the underlying concept of the family as an active agent with unified interests is erroneous, and I offer an alternative concept of the family as a locus of *struggle*. In my view, the family cannot be understood solely, or even primarily, as a unit shaped by affect or kinship, but must be seen as a *location* where production and redistribution take place. As such, it is a location where people with different activities and interests in these processes often come into conflict with one another. I do not wish to deny that families also encompass strong emotional ties, are extremely important in our psychic life, and establish ideological norms, but in developing a Marxist-feminist analysis of the family, I wish to identify and explore the material aspects of gender relations within family units.[4] Therefore, I concentrate on the nature of the work people do in the family and their control over the products of their labor.

In a Marxist-feminist view, the organization of production both within and outside the family is shaped by patriarchy and capitalism. Our present social structure rests upon an unequal division of labor by class and by gender which generates tension, conflict, and change. These underlying patriarchal and capitalist relations among people, rather than familial relations themselves, are the sources of dynamism in our society. The particular forms familial relations take largely reflect these underlying social forces. For example, the redistribution that occurs within the family between wage earners and non–wage earners is necessitated by the division of labor inherent in the patriarchal and capitalistic organization of production. In order to provide a schema for understanding the underlying economic structure of the family form prevalent in modern Western society—the heterosexual nuclear family living together in one household—I do not address in this essay the many real differences in the ways people of different periods, regions, races, or ethnic groups structure and experience family life. I limit my focus in order to emphasize the potential for differing rather than harmonious interests among family members, especially between women and men.

The first part of this essay explains the family's role as a location for production and redistribution and speculates about the interaction between the family and the state and about changes in family-state relations. The second part uses the example of housework to illustrate the differences in material interests among family members that are caused by their differing relations to patriarchy and capitalism. Since, as I argue, members of families frequently have different interests, it may be misleading to hold, as family historians often do, that "the family" as a unit resists or embraces capitalism, industrialization, or the state. Rather, people—men and/or women, adults and/or children—use familial forms in various ways. While they may use their "familial" connections or kin groups and their locations in families in any number of projects—to find jobs, to build labor unions, to wage community struggles, to buy houses, to borrow cars, or to share child care—they are not acting only as family members but also as members of gender categories with particular relations to the division of labor organized by capitalism and patriarchy.

Yet tensions between households and the world outside them have been documented by family historians and others, and these suggest that households do act as entities with unified interests, set in opposition to other entities. This seeming paradox comes about because, although family members have distinct interests arising out of their relations to production and redistribution, those same relations also ensure their mutual dependence. Both the wife who does not work for wages and the husband who does, for example, have a joint interest in the size of his paycheck, the efficiency of her cooking facilities, or the quality of their children's education. However, the same historical processes that created households in opposition to (but also in partnership with) the state also augmented the power of men in households, as they became their household heads, and exacerbated tensions within households.

Examples of tensions and conflicts that involve the family in struggle are presented in table 1. The family can be a locus of internal struggle over matters related to production or redistribution (housework and paychecks, respectively). It can also provide a basis for struggle by its members against larger institutions such as corporations of the state. Will cooking continue to be done at home or be taken over largely by fast-food chains? Will child care continue to be the responsibility of parents or will it be provided by the state outside the home? Such questions signal tensions over the location of production. Tax protest, revolving as it does around the issue of who will make decisions for the family about the redistribution of its resources, can be viewed as an example of struggle between families and the state over redistribution. In this essay I intend to discuss only one source of conflict in any depth—housework—and merely touch upon some of the issues raised by tensions in other arenas. As with most typologies, the categories offered here are in reality not rigidly bounded or easily separable. Rather they represent different aspects of the same phenomena; production and redistribution are interrelated just as are struggles within and beyond households.[5]

Production, Redistribution, and the Household

Let me begin with a quote from Engels that has become deservedly familiar: "According to the materialistic conception, the determining factor in history is, in the final instance, the production and reproduction of immediate life. This, again, is of a two-fold character: on the one side, the production of the means of existence, of food, clothing and shelter and the tools necessary for that production; on the other side, the production of human beings themselves, the propagation of the species. The social organization under which the people of a particular historical epoch live is determined by both kinds of production."[6]

Engels and later Marxists failed to follow through on this dual project. The concept of production ought to encompass both the production of "things," or material

TABLE 1 Conflicts Involving the Family

Sources of Conflict	Conflicts Within the Household	Conflicts Between Households and Larger Institutions
Production issues	*Housework:* Who does it? How? According to which standards? Should women work for wages outside the home or for men inside the home?	*Household production versus production organized by capital and the state:* Fast-food or home-cooked meals? Parent cooperative child care or state regulated child-care centers?
Redistribution issues	*Paycheck(s):* How should the money be spent? Who decides? Should the husband's paycheck be spent on luxuries for him or on household needs?	*Taxes:* Who will make the decisions about how to use the family's resources? Family members or representatives of state apparatus?

needs, and the "production" of people or, more accurately, the production of people who have particular attributes, such as gender. The Marxist development of the concept of production, however, has focused primarily on the production of things. Gayle Rubin has vastly increased our understanding of how people are produced by identifying the "sex/gender system" as a "set of arrangements by which a society transforms biological sexuality into products of human activity, and in which these transformed sexual needs are satisfied."[7] This set of arrangements, which reproduces the species—and gender as well—is fundamentally social. The biological fact of sex differences is interpreted in many different ways by different groups; biology is always mediated by society.[8]

From an economic perspective, the creation of gender can be thought of as the creation of a division of labor between the sexes, the creation of two categories of workers who need each other.[9] In our society, the division of labor between the sexes involves men primarily in wage labor beyond the household and women primarily in production within the household; men and women, living together in households, pool their resources. The form of the family as we know it, with men in a more advantageous position than women in its hierarchy of gender relations, is simply one possible structuring of this human activity that creates gender; many other arrangements have been known.[10]

Although recent feminist psychoanalytic theory has emphasized the relations between children, mothers, and fathers in typical nuclear families, and the way these relations fundamentally shape personality along gender lines and perpetuate hierarchical gender relations, the pervasiveness of gender relations in all aspects of social life must be recognized.[11] In particular, the creation and perpetuation of hierarchical gender relations depends not only on family life but crucially on the organization of economic production, the production of the material needs of which Engels spoke. While a child's personality is partly shaped by who his or her mother is and her relations to others, her relations to others are products of all our social arrangements, not simply those evident within the household. Such arrangements are collectively generated and collectively maintained. "Dependence" is simultaneously a psychological and political-economic relationship. Male-dominated trade unions and professional associations, for example, have excluded women from skilled employment and reduced their opportunities to support themselves. The denial of abortions to women similarly reinforces women's dependence on men. In these and other ways, many of them similarly institutionalized, men as a group are able to maintain control of women's labor power and thus perpetuate their dominance. Their control of women's labor power is the lever that allows men to benefit from women's provision of personal and household services, including relief from child rearing and many unpleasant tasks both within and beyond households, and the arrangement of the nuclear family, based on monogamous and heterosexual marriage, is one institutional form that seems to enhance this control.[12] Patriarchy's material base is men's control of women's labor; both in the household and in the labor market, the division of labor by gender tends to benefit men.

In a capitalist system the production of material needs takes place largely outside households, in large-scale enterprises where the productive resources are owned by capitalists. Most people, having no productive resources of their own, have no alternative but to offer their labor power in exchange for wages. Capitalists appropriate the surplus value the workers create above and beyond the value of their wages. One of the fundamental dynamics in our society is that which flows from this production process: wage earners seek to retain as much control as possible over both the conditions and products of their labor, and capitalists, driven by competition and the needs of the accumulation process, seek to wrest control away from the workers in order to increase the amount of surplus value.[13] With the wages they receive, people buy the commodities that they need for their survival. Once in the home these commodities are then transformed to become usable in producing and reproducing people. In our society, which is organized by patriarchy as well as by capitalism, the sexual division of labor by gender makes men primarily responsible for wage labor and women primarily responsible for household production. That portion of household production called housework consists largely in purchasing commodities and transforming them into usable forms. Sheets, for example, must be bought, put on beds, rearranged after every sleep, and washed, just as food must be bought, cleaned, cooked, and served to become a meal. Household production also encompasses the biological reproduction of people and the shaping of their gender, as well as their maintenance through housework. In the labor process of producing and reproducing people, household production gives rise to another of the fundamental dynamics of our society. The system of production in which we live cannot be understood without reference to the production and reproduction both of commodities— whether in factories, service centers, or offices—and of people, in households. Although neither type of production can be self-reproducing, together they create and recreate our existence.[14]

This patriarchal and capitalist arrangement of production necessitates a means of redistribution. Because of the class and gender division of labor not everyone has direct access to the economic means of survival. A schematic view of the development of capitalism in Western societies suggests that capitalism generally took root in societies where production and redistribution had taken place largely in households and villages; even though capitalism shifted much production beyond the household, it did not destroy all the traditional ways in which production and redistribution were organized. In preindustrial households, people not only carried on production but also shared their output among themselves (after external obligations such as feudal dues were met), according to established patriarchal relations of authority. In the period of capitalist primitive accumulation, capitalists had to alienate the productive resources that people previously attached to the land had controlled in order to establish the capitalist mode of production based on "free" wage labor. Laborers became "free" to work for capitalists because they had no other means of subsistence and therefore required wages to buy from the capitalists what they had formerly produced in households and villages and exchanged with each other.

With the development of the capitalist mode of production, the old, the young, and women of childbearing age participated less in economic production and became dependent on the wage earners, increasingly adult men. People continued to live in households, however, to reproduce the species and to redistribute resources. Households became primarily income-pooling units rather than income-producing units.[15] The previously established patriarchal division of labor, in which men benefited from women's labor, was perpetuated in a capitalist setting where men became primarily wage laborers but retained the personal services of their wives, as women became primarily "housewives."[16] The interdependence of men and women that arises out of the division of labor by gender was also maintained. The need for the household in capitalism to be an income-pooling unit, a place where redistribution occurs between men and women, arises fundamentally from the patriarchal division of labor. Yet it is income pooling that enables the household to be perceived as a unit with unitary interests, despite the very different relationships to production of its separate members. Because of the division of labor among family members, disunity is thus inherent in the "unity" of the family.

Recent, often speculative, anthropological and historical research, by focusing on the development of households and their role in political arenas, has contributed to my understanding of the family as an embodiment of both unity and disunity. Briefly, this research suggests that women's status has declined as political institutions have been elaborated into state apparata, although the mechanisms that connect these two phenomena are not well understood.[17] One possible connection is that the process of state formation enhanced the power of men as they became heads of "their" households. The state's interest in promoting households as political units stemmed from its need to undermine prior political apparata based on kinship. In prestate societies, kinship groups made fundamental political and economic decisions—how to share resources to provide for everyone's welfare, how to redistribute land periodically, how to settle disputes, how to build new settlements. States gradually absorbed these functions.

For instance, in the process of state formation that took place in England and Wales roughly between the eighth and fifteenth centuries, Viana Muller suggests, emerging rulers attempted to consolidate their power against kin groups by winning the allegiance of men away from their kin. One means of doing this may have been allowing men to usurp some of the kin group's authority, particularly over land and women and children.[18] In this view, the household, with its male head, can be seen to be a "creation" of the state. George Duby reports that by 1250 the household was everywhere the basis of taxation in Western society.[19] Lawrence Stone argues that the state's interests were served by an authoritarian household structure, for it was generally believed that deference shown to the head of household would be transferred to the king: "The power of kings and of heads of households grew in parallel with one another in the sixteenth century. The state was as supportive of the patriarchal nuclear family as it was hostile to the kin-oriented family; the one was a buttress and the other a threat to its own increasing power."[20]

As Elizabeth Fox-Genovese points out, the authoritarianism of the new nation-state was incompatible with developing capitalism, and Locke's concept of authority as derivative from the individual helped to establish a new legitimating ideology for the state: it serves with the consent of the propertied individuals. To put forward his theory with logical coherence, Locke had to assert the authority of all individuals, including women and children. But by removing the family from the political sphere, ideologically at least, later theorists solved the contradiction between the elevation of women to the status of individuals and the maintenance of patriarchal authority. The family became private, of no moment in conducting the politics of social interchange, and the head of the family came to represent its interests in the world.[21] The ideology of individualism, by increasing the political importance of men beyond their households, strengthened patriarchy at home; it completed the legitimation of male public power begun during the process of state elaboration.

Yet even as the household, and particularly the man within it, became in this view an agent of the state against collectivities organized by kinship, the household also remained the last repository of kin ties. Even the nuclear household continues to tie its members to others through the processes of marriage, childbirth, and the establishment of kinship. These ties to others beyond the household (though much more limited than in the past) coupled with the interdependence of household members stemming from their different relations to production continue to give members of households a basis for common interests vis-à-vis the state or other outside forces. Household members continue to make decisions about pooling incomes, caring for dependent members, engaging in wage work, and having children, but it is important to remember that within the household as well as outside it men have more power. Therefore, viewing the household as a unit which jointly chooses, for example, to deploy its available labor power to maximize the interests of *all* its members (the implicit approach of those historians who discuss family strategies and adaptations and the explicit approach of others) obscures the reality of both the capitalist and patriarchal relations of production in which households are enmeshed.[22] Mutual dependence by no means precludes the possibility of coercion. Women and men are no less mutually dependent in the household than are workers and capitalists or slaves and slaveowners. In environments that are fundamentally coercive (such as patriarchy and capitalism) concepts of choice and adaptation are inevitably flawed—as is the belief that workers and capitalists or men and women have unified interests. This is not to say that such unity can *never* exist.

Housework

Some observers have argued that the family is no longer a place where men exercise their power. If patriarchy exists at all for them, it does so only on impersonal, institutional levels. For some analysts working in the Marxist traditions, the inexorable progress of capitalism has eliminated patriarchy within the family and has even given rise to the women's movement, because it weakened patriarchal power just enough to enable women to confront it directly.[23] I wish to argue, however, that, although capitalism has somewhat shifted the locus of control, the family nevertheless remains a primary arena where men exercise their patriarchal power over women's labor. In this section, I review some of the empirical findings on time spent on housework by husbands and wives to support this proposition. I believe that time spent on housework, as well as other indicators of household labor, can be fruitfully used as a measure of power relations in the home.

Who Does How Much Housework?

In recent years a number of time-budget studies have measured time spent on housework, as well as other activities such as paid work and leisure. Such studies generally involve having respondents record their activities for specified time intervals (for example, fifteen minutes) for one or two days. The most comprehensively analyzed data on time spent doing housework in the United States are those collected in 1967 and 1968 by Kathryn Walker and Margaret Woods for 1,296 husband-and-wife families in Syracuse, New York.[24] Time diaries were also collected for a representative sample of families in five U.S. cities in 1965 and 1966 as part of the Multinational Comparative Time-Budget Research Project.[25] The University of Michigan Survey Research Center has collected data for representative national samples of families and individuals for 1965–66 and for 1975.[26] Subsequently, a number of smaller studies have been conducted.[27] While the studies all differ in such data collection procedures as sampling (national vs. local, husband-and-wife families vs. individuals) and reporting (interview vs. self-report, contemporaneous vs. retrospective reporting), their findings are remarkably consistent and support rather firm conclusions about who does how much housework.[28] Because Walker and Woods have analyzed their data so extensively, their findings are relied upon here.

Women who have no paid employment outside the home work over fifty hours per week on household chores: preparing and cleaning up after meals, doing laundry, cleaning the house, taking care of children and other family members, and shopping and keeping records. Walker and Woods found that 859 full-time houseworkers (usually labeled "homemakers" or "housewives") worked an average of fifty-seven hours per week. Their husbands, as reported by their wives, spent about eleven hours a week on housework, and children were reported to do about the same amount on average.[29] A study of a national sample of 700 women in 1965 and 1966 found that 357 full-time houseworkers worked an average of 55.4 hours per week.[30] Household production is clearly more than a full-time job according to these time-budget studies.

The way that time spent on housework changes as demands on members' time increase is a good indicator of how patriarchy operates in the home, at least with respect to housework. Much has been made of the potentially equalizing effects of women's increased labor-force participation: as women earn wages they may come to exercise more power both within and outside the family. Time-budget studies show, however, that husbands of wives who work for wages do not spend more time on housework than those husbands whose wives do not work for wages. The Walker and Woods data for Syracuse families show that the more wage work women do, the fewer hours they spend on housework but the longer are their total work weeks. Women who worked for wages thirty or more hours per week had total work weeks of seventy-six hours on average, including an average of thirty-three hours per week spent on housework. Yet men whose wives had the longest work weeks had the shortest work weeks themselves (see fig. 1). The lack of responsiveness of men's housework time to women's increased wage work is also shown in time-budget data from cities in twelve industrialized countries collected by the Multinational Comparative Time-Budget Research Project in 1965 and 1966. In all countries wage-working wives worked substantially more hours every day than husbands or full-time houseworkers. Employed wives also spent substantially more time on housework on their days off (about double their weekday time), whereas husbands and even full-time houseworkers had the weekends for increased leisure.[31] These findings are corroborated by two later studies, one of 300 couples in Greater Vancouver in 1971, and one of 3,500 couples in the United States in 1976.[32]

A look at the tasks performed by husbands and wives, as well as the time spent, adds to our understanding of the relative burden of housework. Meissner and his associates, examining participation rates of husbands and wives in various tasks for 340 couples, finds that only 26 percent of the husbands reported spending some time cleaning the house (on either of two days reported, one weekday and one weekend day) while 86 percent of their wives did, and that 27 percent of the husbands contributed 2.5 hours per week to cooking, while 93 percent of the wives contributed 8.5 hours. Only seven of the 340 husbands reported doing any laundry, but nearly half their wives did.[33] Meissner and his associates conclude: "These data indicate that most married women do the regular, necessary, and most time consuming work in the household every day. In view of the small and selective contribution of their husbands, they can anticipate doing it for the rest of their lives."[34]

Walker and Woods, examining the percentage of record days that wives and husbands, as well as other household members, participated in various household tasks, conclude that while husbands of employed wives participated more often than husbands of nonemployed wives in almost all household tasks, their contributions to the time spent on the tasks were small.[35] One is forced to conclude that the husbands of wage-working wives appear to do more housework by participating more often, but the substance of their contributions remains insignificant.[36] Women are apparently not, for the most part, able to translate their wages into reduced work weeks, either by buying sufficient substitute products or labor or by getting their husbands to do appreciably more housework. In the absence of patriarchy, we would expect to find an equal sharing of wage work and housework; we find no such thing.

The burden of housework increases substantially when there are very young children or many children in the household. The household time-budget data from Walker and Woods's study indicate that in both cases the wife's work week expands to meet the needs of the family while the husband's does not. In families with a child under one year old, the typical full-time houseworker spent nearly seventy hours per week in housework, nearly thirty of it in family (primarily child) care. The typical husband spent five hours per week on family care but reduced his time spent on other housework, so that his total housework did not increase. When the wife was employed for fifteen or more hours per week, the average husband did spend two hours more per week on child care, and his time spent on housework increased to twenty hours (compared to twelve for the husband whose wife did less wage work). Meanwhile, however, his employed wife spent over fifty hours on housework, nearly twenty of them on child care. As figure 2 indicates, the employed wife's total housework time expands substantially with the presence of young children, while the husband's increases only moderately. Data from a national sample of about 3,500 U.S. husband-and-wife families in the 1976 Panel Study of Income Dynamics also show a

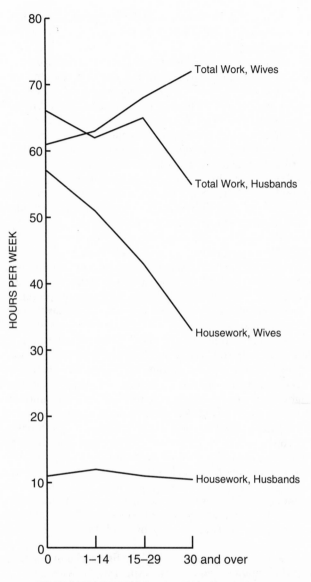

HOURS PER WEEK (wives' paid employment)

FIGURE 1   Time spent on housework and total work by wives and husbands in 1,296 Syracuse, New York, families (1967–68), by wives' hours of employment. Based on data from Kathryn E. Walker and Margaret E. Woods, *Time Use: A Measure of Household Production of Family Goods and Services* (Washington, D.C.: American Home Economics Association, 1976), p. 45; and Kathryn E. Walker, "Time-Use Patterns for Household Work Related to Homemakers' Employment" (paper presented at the 1970 National Agricultural Outlook Conference, Washington, D.C., February 18, 1970), p. 5.

pattern of longer housework time for wives with greater family responsibility (indicated by numbers of children) and nearly total lack of variability in the husbands' housework time (see fig. 3).[37]

Meissner and his associates developed a ranked set of four combinations of demands on household time and analyzed the data on changes in the housework time of husbands and wives in response to these increased levels of demands. The first level of demand is represented by households with one job and no children under ten, the second is one job and children under ten, the third is two jobs and no children under ten, and the fourth is two jobs and children under ten. The invariance of time husbands spend on housework is corroborated by their procedure. For the five activities of meals, sleep, gardening, visiting, and watching television, women lose fourteen hours a week from the least to most demanding situation, while men gain 1.4 hours a week.[38] The United States cities survey of 1965–66 found that "among working couples with children, fathers averaged 1.3 hours more free time each weekday and 1.4 hours more on Sunday than mothers."[39]

The rather small, selective, and unresponsive contribution of the husband to housework raises the suspicion that the husband may be a net drain on the family's resources of housework time—that is, husbands may require more housework than they contribute. Indeed, this hypothesis is suggested by my materialist definition of patriarchy, in which men benefit directly from women's labor power. No direct estimates of housework required by the presence of husbands have, to my knowledge, been made. The Michigan survey data, however, in providing information on the housework time of single parents shed some light on this question. Single women spend considerably less time on housework than wives, for the same size families (see fig. 3). They spend less time even when they are compared only to wives who work for wages. It seems plausible that the difference in time spent on housework (approximately eight hours per week) could be interpreted as the amount of increased housework caused by the husband's presence. Unfortunately, because very few time-budget studies solicit information from single women, this estimate of "husband care" cannot be confirmed. Additional estimates can be made, however, from Walker and Woods's data of the minimum time necessary for taking care of a house. For wives who worked in the labor market less than fourteen hours per week, time spent on "regular" housework (all housework minus family care) ranged between forty and forty-five hours for all life-cycle phases (varying ages and numbers of children), while for wives who worked for wages fifteen hours per week or more, time spent on regular housework ranged between twenty-five and thirty-five hours per week (see fig. 2).

These studies demonstrate the patriarchal benefits reaped in housework. First, the vast majority of time spent on housework is spent by the wife, about 70 percent on the average, with both the husband and the children providing about 15 percent on average.[40] Second, the wife is largely responsible for child care. The wife takes on the excess burden of housework in those families where there are very young or very many children; the husband's contribution to housework remains about the same whatever the family size or the age of the youngest child. It is the wife who, with respect to housework at least, does all of the adjusting to the family life cycle. Third, the woman who also works for wages (and she does so usually, we know, out of economic necessity) finds that her husband spends very little more time on housework

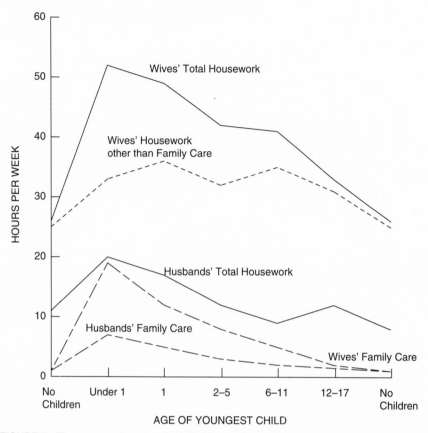

FIGURE 2   Time spent on housework and family care by husbands and employed wives in 1,296 Syracuse, New York, families (1967–68), by age of youngest child. Based on data from Kathryn E. Walker and Margaret E. Woods, *Time Use: A Measure of Household Production of Family Goods and Services* (Washington, D.C.: American Home Economics Association, 1976), pp. 50, 126.

on average than the husband whose wife is not a wage worker. Fourth, the wife spends perhaps eight hours per week in additional housework on account of the husband. And fifth, the wife spends, on average, a minimum of forty hours a week maintaining the house and husband if she does not work for wages and a minimum of thirty hours per week if she does.

Moreover, while we might expect the receipt of patriarchal benefits to vary according to class, race, and ethnicity, the limited time data we have relating to socioeconomic status or race indicate that time spent on housework by wives is not very sensitive to such differences.[41] The national panel study data, for example, showed no variation in housework time between racial groups.[42] With respect to class differences, I have argued elsewhere that the widespread use of household conveniences (especially the less expensive ones) and the decline in the use of servants in the early

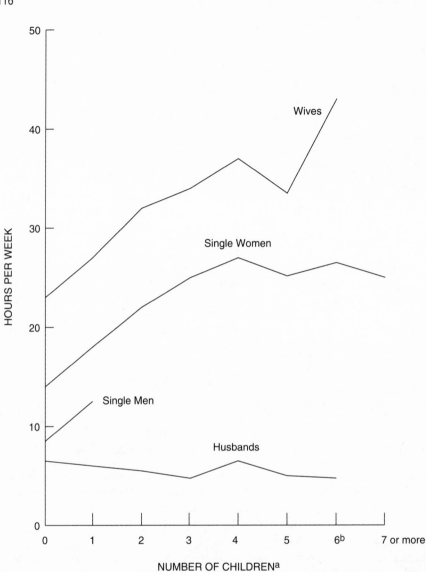

FIGURE 3   Time spent on housework, not including child care, by a national sampling of 5,863 families (1976), by number of children. Based on data in James N. Morgan, "A Potpourri of New Data Gathered from interviews with Husbands and Wives," in *Five Thousand American Families: Patterns of Economic Progress,* vol. 6, *Accounting for Race and Sex Differences in Earnings and Other Analyses of the First Nine Years of the Panel Study of Income Dynamics,* ed. Greg J. Duncan and James N. Morgan (Ann Arbor: University of Michigan, Institute for Social Research, 1978), p. 370.

[a] Number of other people in household besides husband and wife or single head of household.
[b] Six or more for husbands and wives.

twentieth century probably increased the similarity of housework across class. In addition, no evidence was found that showed that the larger appliances effectively reduced housework time.[43] Income probably has its most important effect on housework through its effect on women's labor-force participation rates. Wives of husbands with lower incomes are more likely to be in the labor force and therefore experiencing the "double day" of wage work and housework.[44] Wage work, while it shortens the number of hours spent on housework (compared to those of the full-time houseworker), almost certainly increases the burden of the hours that remain. Even for full-time houseworkers, the number and ages of children appear to be more important than income in effect upon housework time.[45]

The relation of the household's wage workers to the capitalist organization of production places households in class relations with each other and determines the household's access to commodities; yet in viewing and understanding women's work in the home—the rearing of children, the maintenance of the home, the serving of men—patriarchy appears to be a more salient feature than class.[46]

Does It Matter?

I have suggested that women of all classes are subject to patriarchal power in that they perform household labor for men. Some would argue, however, that women's overwhelming share of housework relative to men's and their longer total work weeks should not be perceived as exploitation of one group's labor by another, that the patriarchal division of labor is not like the capitalist division of labor. Some would argue that among the working class, especially, the sexual division of labor is a division of labor without significance. Working-class husbands and wives, it is argued, recognize the fundamental coercion involved in both the homemaker and wage-earner roles.[47] The sexual division of labor, it is also argued, has no significance among the middle class, since women's lives are not especially hard.

The argument about the significance of patriarchy in women's lives revolves around whether or not women *perceive* patriarchy as oppressive. The interest behind much of the literature growing out of the women's movement has been to document women's oppression so that they may recognize exploitation when they experience it in their daily lives.[48] The sexual division of labor, so ancient that its unfairness is often accepted as normal, is an example of such oppression. Pat Mainardi, in "The Politics of Housework," captures the essence of the battle between the genders over housework. Her analysis exposes the patriarchal power underlying each response of a radical male to his wife's attempts to get him to share the housework. "The measure of your oppression is his resistance," she warns us, and goes on to point out the husband's typical response: " 'I don't mind sharing the work, but you'll have to show me how to do it.' *Meaning:* I ask a lot of questions and you'll have to show me everything every time I do it because I don't remember so good. Also don't try to sit down and read while I'm doing my jobs because I'm going to annoy hell out of you until it's easier to do them yourself."[49] The women's liberation movement has no doubt changed the perceptions of many middle-class women about the significance of patriarchy. Can the same be said for working-class women? The evidence is more limited, but working-class women are also expressing their recognition of the unfairness of male power within the working class. For example, a Southern white working-class woman recently wrote in response to a column by William Raspberry in the *Washington Post:*

Men ... live, speak and behave exactly by the slogans and notions of our traditional male
"law and the prophets." Their creed and their litany ... is as follows:
All money and property, including welfare funds and old-age pensions, are "his."
All wages, no matter who earns them, are "his." ...
Food, housing, medical and clothing expenses are "her" personal spending money. ...
Many wives must "steal" food from their own wages! ...
The sum of it all is a lifetime of ridicule, humiliation, degradation, utter denial of dig-
nity and self-respect for women and their minor children at the hands of husband-fa-
ther.
We older women took, and take, the male abuse because (1) we thought we had to, (2)
we thought rearing our children and keeping our families together was more important
than life itself. ...
Young women can now earn their own and their children's bread, or receive it from
welfare, without the abuse, ridicule and humiliation.[50]

The first step in the struggle is awareness, and the second is recognition that the situation can change.

What Are the Prospects for Change?

What is the likelihood that patriarchal power in the home, as measured by who does
housework, will decline? What is the likelihood that housework will become equally
shared by men and women? Might the amount of time required for housework be
reduced? The prospects for change in housework time, while dependent on economic and political changes at the societal level, probably hinge most directly on the
strength of the women's movement, for the amount and quality of housework services rendered, like the amount of and pay for wage work, result from historical processes of struggle. Such struggle establishes norms that become embodied in an expected standard of living. Time spent on housework by both full-time houseworkers
and employed houseworkers has remained remarkably stable in the twentieth century. Kathryn Walker and Joann Vanek for the United States and Michael Paul Sacks
for the Soviet Union report that total time spent on housework has not declined significantly from the 1920s to the 1960s.[51] Although time spent on some tasks, such as
preparing and cleaning up after meals, has declined, that spent on others—such as
shopping, record keeping, and child care—has increased. Even time spent on laundry has increased despite new easy care fabrics and the common use of automatic
home washing machines. A completely satisfactory explanation for the failure of
housework time to decline, despite rapid technological change, has not yet been developed, but part of the answer lies in rising standards of cleanliness, child care, and
emotional support, as well as in the inherent limitation of technology applied to
small decentralized units, that is, typical homes.[52]

Gender struggle around housework may be bearing fruit. Standards may in fact be
changing, allowing for a reduction in overall time spent on housework. A recent
time-budget study indicates that between 1965 and 1975 housework time may have
fallen by as much as six hours per week for full-time houseworkers and four hours
for those also employed outside the house.[53] Such a decrease may also be the result of
changing boundaries between home and market production; production formerly
done by women at home may be increasingly shifted to capitalist production sites. In
such cases, the products change as well; home-cooked meals are replaced by fast
food.[54] Over time, the boundary between home and market production has been

flexible rather than fixed, determined by the requirements of patriarchy and capitalism in reproducing themselves and by the gender and class struggles that arise from these processes.

While women's struggles, and perhaps as well capital's interests, may be successfully altering standards for housework and shifting some production beyond the home, prospects within the home for shifting some of the household tasks onto men do not appear to be as good. We have already seen, in our review of the current time-budget studies, that men whose wives work for wages do not spend more time than other married men on housework. This suggests that, even as more women increase their participation in wage labor and share with men the financial burden of supporting families, men are not likely to share the burden of housework with women. The increase in women's labor-force participation has occurred over the entire course of the twentieth century. Walker's comparison of the 1967–68 Syracuse study with studies from the 1920s shows that husbands' work time may have increased at most about a half hour per week, while the work time of women, whether employed outside the home or full-time houseworkers, may have increased by as much as five hours per week.[55] Interestingly, a similar conclusion was reached by Sacks in his comparison of time-budget studies conducted in several cities in the Soviet Union in 1923 and 1966. He found that women's housework time has decreased somewhat, that men's time has not increased, that women still spend more than twice as much time on housework than do men, and that women have a total work week that is still seventeen hours longer than men's. In 1970, fully 90 percent of all Soviet women between the ages of twenty and forty-nine were in the labor force.[56] We are forced to conclude that the increase in women's wage labor will not *alone* bring about any sharing of housework with men. Continued struggle will be necessary.

People have different interests in the future of household production, based upon their current relation to productive activity outside the home. Their interests are not always unequivocal or constant over time. Some women might perceive their interests to lie in getting greater access to wages by mounting campaigns against employment and wage discrimination, others in maintaining as much control as possible over the home production process by resisting both capitalist inroads on household production and male specifications of standards for it. Some women might reduce housework by limiting childbirth. Some capitalists might seek to expand both the market and mass production of meal preparation if this area appears potentially profitable. Other capitalists may simply need women's labor power in order to expand production in any area or to cheapen labor power.[57] Or their interests might lie in having women in the home to produce and rear the next generation of workers. The outcome of these counteracting requirements and goals is theoretically indeterminate.

My reading of the currently dominant forces and tensions goes as follows: Women are resisting doing housework and rearing children, at least many children; the majority of women increasingly perceive their economic security to lie primarily in being self-supporting. Therefore, they are struggling with men to get out of the house and into decent jobs in the labor market. Given women's restricted access to decent jobs and wages, however, women also maintain their interests in men's continued contribution to family support. Men are relinquishing responsibility for families in some ways but are loathe to give up some of the benefits that go with it. Desertion, informal liaisons, contract cohabitation may be manifestations of this attitude; the attitude itself may be a response to capitalist inroads on patriarchal benefits, as more wives enter the labor force, providing fewer personalized services at home. Men may perceive that part-time wage labor by their wives is useful in contributing to the family's financial support without interfering very much with the provision of household services to them. To make such an arrangement compatible with their continued patriarchal power, men are on the whole struggling fairly hard to keep their better places in the labor market. Capitalists are primarily interested in using women's participation in the labor market to cheapen labor power and to allow expansion on better terms; women workers, for example, are much less unionized than men. Capitalists attempt to pass on most of the social costs—child care, for example—to the state, but the state's ability to provide is limited by a generalized fiscal crisis and by the present difficulties in capital accumulation.[58] The current period of alternating slow growth and actual production setback forces an intensification of class struggle, which in turn may exacerbate gender conflict.

Over the next twenty years, while there will be some change in the sexual division of labor resulting from conflict and struggles, patriarchy will not be eradicated. Despite at least a century of predictions and assertions that capitalism will triumph over patriarchy—a situation in which all production would take place under capitalist relations and all people would be wage earners on equal terms—patriarchy has survived. It has survived otherwise cataclysmic revolutions in the Soviet Union and China.[59] This means that a substantial amount of production will remain in the home. The irreducible minimum from the patriarchal point of view is that women will continue to raise young children and to provide men with the labor power necessary to maintain established standards of living, particularly the decentralized home system.

My assessment is that we are reaching a new equilibrium, or a new form of an old partnership, a judgment supported by data on women's employment in eight countries; these figures suggest that there may be a kind of structural limit on the participation of women in the labor force. As shown in table 2, those countries in which the proportion of women who are in the labor force is largest have the highest proportion of women working part-time. It is necessary, such findings suggest, that a substantial proportion of women's collective work hours be retained in the home if the patriarchal requirement that women continue to do housework and provide child care is to be fulfilled. In Sweden, it is most often married mothers of young children who work part-time. In the United States, the married mothers of preschool children have unemployment rates more than double those of married women with no children.[60]

We must hope that the new equilibrium will prove unstable, since without question it creates a situation in which a woman's work day is longer than it was when she served as a full-time houseworker, the male as breadwinner. As described earlier, when women's wage labor is greatest their total work weeks (wage work plus housework) are longest and men's are shortest (see fig. 1). Women have entered the labor market in greater numbers, and more husbands consequently have wives who are working for wages and contributing to the family income; the collective work effort of men as a group has decreased since men reduce their total work weeks when their wives work for wages. At the same time the collective contribution of women as a group has increased. This situation will undoubtedly continue to generate gender struggle. As more and more women become subject to the "double burden," more

TABLE 2   Women's Labor Force Participation and Part-Time Employment in Eight Countries

| Country and Year | Women's Labor Force Participation Rate | | Women in Labor Force Part Time | |
	%	Rank	% of Total Women in Labor Force	Rank
Sweden (1977)	55.2[a]	1	45.2[b]	1
United States (1975)	47.3[a]	2	33.0[b]	3
Canada (1977)	45.9	3	23.0[c]	4
United Kingdom (1975)	45.8[a]	4	40.9[c]	2
France (1975)	43.8[a]	5	14.1[c]	6
Austria (1975)	42.4	6	14.0[b]	7
Federal Republic of Germany (1975)	37.7[a]	7	22.8[c]	5
Belgium (1975)	30.7	8	11.6[c]	8

Notes: Women's labor force participation rate is the proportion of all women of working age (usually over fifteen) who are in the labor force (employed or looking for work).
[a]Figures from 1976.
[b]Part-time employment defined as less than thirty-five hours per week.
[c]Part-time employment defined as ca. thirty hours per week or less.
Source: Ronnie Steinberg Ratner, "Labor Market Inequality and Equal Opportunity Policy for Women, a Cross-national Comparison," paper prepared for Working Party no. 6 on the Role of Women in the Economy (Paris: Organization for Economic Cooperation and Development. June 1979), tables 1, 18.

are moved to protest. Yet it is worth noting that husbands may not be the main bene-ficiaries of the recent increases in women's labor time. Although their wives' wages contribute to the family income, their wives' labor power is being used to create sur-plus value for capitalists and not to maintain the previous level of services at home. Eventually the decentralized home system itself may be a casualty of gender and class struggle.

Conclusion

The decentralized home system, which I see as a fundamental result of patriarchy, also meets crucial requirements for the reproduction of the capitalist system.[61] Fami-lies can provide crucial services less expensively than does the cash nexus of either the state or capital, especially when economic growth has come to a halt. From capi-tal's point of view, however, the relationship is an uneasy one; capital and the state use the household but do not entirely control it. Despite the spread of capitalism and centralized, bureaucratic states, and their penetration into more and more areas of social life, people in households still manage to retain control over crucial resources and particular areas of decision. Family historians have helped us understand the strength and endurance of family units and their retention of power in many areas. The family historians may not have been sensitive to power relations within the fam-ily, but they have focused on another aspect of the same phenomenon—the interde-pendence of people within households and their common stance as a household against the incursion of forces that would alienate their resources or their control over decision making. Although I have focused on the potential for conflict among family members, particularly between men and women over housework, I want to point out that the same division of labor that creates the basis for that conflict also creates interdependence as a basis for family unity. It is this dual nature of the family that makes the behavior of families so unpredictable and problematic for both capital and the state. In the United States, for example, no one predicted the enormity of the post–World War II baby boom, the size of the subsequent increase in women's labor force participation, the rapid decrease in the birthrate in the late 1960s and early 1970s, or, most recently, the increase in divorce and single parenthood.

With the perspective developed here, these changes in people's household behavior can be understood as responses to conflicts both within and outside households. As Wendy Lutrell, who has also been working on reconceptualizing the family as a locus of tension and conflict, writes: "People can be seen as historical agents acting both independently as individuals *and* dependently as family members. This dual process, fuels tensions and conflicts within the family arena and creates one potential for social change. … When the state, workplace, community, religion, or family are seen as arenas of struggle, we are forced to abandon a static, functional framework which can only see capitalist institutions as maintaining the status quo."[62]

In some cases, family members face capital or state actions together. In the Brookside strike, miners' wives united with their husbands, supporting their demands and even extending them to community concerns. Struggles around community issues are often initiated by women because of their ties to their neighbors and extended kin, and they are sometimes joined by men disaffected with their lot in patriarchy and capitalism. In New York City, both men and women protested government cuts for preschools and hospitals. In other cases, men and women who are in conflict within the family may seek solutions in the capitalist or state sectors. The recent rapid growth of fast-food eateries can be seen in this light, as can English women's fight for milk allowances from the state to redress income inequality within the family.

In our society both class and gender shape people's consciousness of their situation and their struggles to change those situations. At times it may be appropriate to speak of the family or the household as a unit with common interests, but the conditions which make this possible should be clearly spelled out. The conflicts inherent in class and patriarchal society tear people apart, but the dependencies inherent in them can hold people together.

Notes

The first draft of this paper was presented at the Rockefeller Foundation Conference on Women, Work, and the Family (New York, September 21–22, 1978) organized by Catharine Stimpson and Tamara Hareven. Many people besides myself have labored over this paper. Among them are Rayna Rapp and Joan Burstyn. Jack Wells, Judy Stacey, Shelly Rosaldo, Evelyn Glenn, and my study group provided particularly careful readings; and Sam Bowles, Mead Cain, Steven Dubnoff, Andrew Kohlstad, Ann Markusen, Katie Stewart, and the staff of the National Academy of Sciences provided helpful comments and aid of various sorts. I thank all of them. The views presented here are my own and do not reflect the opinion of the National Academy of Sciences or the National Research Council.

1. Peter Laslett and R. Wall, eds., *Household and Family in Past Time* (Cambridge: Cambridge University Press, 1972); Michael Anderson, *Family Structure in Nineteenth-Century*

Lancashire (Cambridge: Cambridge University Press, 1971); Eli Zaretsky, "Capitalism, the Family, and Personal Life," *Socialist Revolution,* no. 13–14 (January–April 1973), pp. 66–125; Friedrich Engels, *The Condition of the Working Class in England* (Stanford, Calif.: Stanford University Press, 1958)—of course, Engels was only the first and most prominent person who made this particular argument; Christopher Lasch, *Haven in a Heartless World: The Family Besieged* (New York: Basic Books, 1977) is a later adherent; William Goode, *World Revolution and Family Patterns* (Glencoe, Ill.: Free Press, 1963); Tamara Hareven, "Family Time and Industrial Time: The Interaction between Family and Work in a Planned Corporation Town, 1900–1924," *Journal of Urban History* 1 (May 1975): 365–89; Edward Shorter, *The Making of the Modern Family* (New York: Basic Books, 1975). Michael Gordon, ed., *The American Family in Social-Historical Perspective,* 2d ed. (New York: St. Martin's Press, 1978), provides a good introduction to family history.

2. Examples of the implicit definition can be found in the special issue of *Daedalus* (Spring 1977), later published as *The Family,* ed. Alice S. Rossi, Jerome Kagan, and Tamara K. Hareven (New York: W. W. Norton & Co., 1978).

3. See Joan Scott and Louise Tilly, "Women's Work and the Family in Nineteenth-Century Europe," *Comparative Studies in Society and History* 17, no. 1 (January 1975): 36–64; and Hareven, "Family Time."

4. In distinguishing between the household—the unit in which people actually live—and the family—the concept of the unit in which they think they should live—Rayna Rapp points to the contradictions that develop because of the juxtaposition of economic and ideological norms in the family/household ("Family and Class in Contemporary America: Notes toward an Understanding of Ideology," *Science and Society* 42 [Fall 1978]: 257–77). In addition, see Lila Leibowitz, *Females, Males, Families, a Biosocial Approach* (North Scituate, Mass.: Duxbury Press, 1978), esp. pp. 6–11, for a discussion of how the family defines ties among its members and to kin beyond it.

5. For another typology of struggle, see Gosta Esping-Anderson, Roger Friedland, and Erik Olin Wright, "Modes of Class Struggle and the Capitalist State," *Kapitalistate,* no. 4/5 (Summer 1976), pp. 186–220; and for a critique, see Capitol Kapitalistate Collective, "Typology and Class Struggle: Critical Notes on 'Modes of Class Struggle and the Capitalist State,'" *Kapitalistate,* no. 6 (Fall 1977), pp. 209–15.

6. Frederick Engels, *The Origin of the Family, Private Property and the State,* ed. with an introduction by Eleanor Leacock (New York: International Publishers, 1972). "Preface to the First Edition," pp. 71–72.

7. Gayle Rubin, "The Traffic in Women: Notes on the 'Political Economy' of Sex," in *Toward an Anthropology of Women,* ed. Rayna Rapp Reiter (New York: Monthly Review Press, 1975), p. 159.

8. The diverse ways in which sex differences are socially interpreted are well illustrated in both Rubin and Leibowitz.

9. See Claude Levi-Strauss, "The Family," in *Man, Culture and Society,* ed. Harry I. Shapiro (New York: Oxford University Press, 1971).

10. Leibowitz provides examples of diverse household and family structures, especially in chaps. 4 and 5.

11. In addition to Rubin, see Nancy Chodorow, *The Reproduction of Mothering: Psychoanalysis and the Sociology of Gender* (Berkeley and Los Angeles: University of California Press, 1978); Dorothy Dinnerstein, *The Mermaid and the Minotaur: Sexual Arrangements and Human Malaise* (New York: Harper Colophon Books, 1977); and Jane Flax, "The Conflict between Nurturance and Autonomy in Mother-Daughter Relationships and within Feminism," *Feminist Studies* 4, no. 2 (June 1978): 171–89.

12. Heidi I. Hartmann, "The Unhappy Marriage of Marxism and Feminism: Towards a More Progressive Union," *Capital and Class* 8 (Summer 1979): 1–33. See also extensions and critiques in Lydia Sargent, ed., *Women and Revolution* (Boston: South End Press, 1981).

13. See Harry Braverman, *Labor and Monopoly Capital: The Degradation of Work in the Twentieth Century* (New York: Monthly Review Press, 1974), as well as Karl Marx, *Capital* (New York: International Publishers, 1967), vol. 1.

14. See Susan Himmelweit and Simon Mohun, "Domestic Labour and Capital," *Cambridge Journal of Economics* 1, no. 1 (March 1977): 15–31.

15. See Heidi Hartmann and Ellen Ross, "The Origins of Modern Marriage" (paper delivered at the Scholar and the Feminist Conference, III, Barnard College, April 10, 1976). Batya Weinbaum, "Women in Transition to Socialism: Perspectives on the Chinese Case," *Review of Radical Political Economics* 8, no. 1 (Spring 1976): 34–58, shows that the family is also an income-pooling unit in China under socialism.

16. See Heidi Hartmann, "Capitalism, Patriarchy, and Job Segregation by Sex," *Signs: Journal of Women in Culture and Society* 1, no. 3, pt. 2 (Spring 1976): 137–69, for how this came about.

17. See Rayna Rapp, "Gender and Class: An Archaeology of Knowledge concerning the Origin of the State," *Dialectical Anthropology* 2 (December 1977): 309–16; Christine Gailey, "Gender Hierarchy and Class Formation: The Origins of the State in Tonga," unpublished paper (New York: New School for Social Research, 1979); Ruby Rohrlich, "Women in Transition: Crete and Sumer," in *Becoming Visible: Women in European History*, ed. Renate Bridenthal and Claudia Koonz (Boston: Houghton Mifflin Co., 1977); Ruby Rohrlich, "State Formation in Sumer and the Subjugation of Women," *Feminist Studies* 6 (Spring 1980): 76–102; and a symposium in *Feminist Studies*, vol. 4 (October 1978), including Anne Barstow, "The Uses of Archaeology for Women's History: James Mellart's Work on the Neolithic Goddess at Catal Hüyük," pp. 7–18; Sherry B. Orther, "The Virgin and the State," pp. 19–36; and Irene Silverblatt, "Andean Women in the Inca Empire," pp. 37–61.

18. Viana Muller, "The Formation of the State and the Oppression of Women: Some Theoretical Considerations and a Case Study in England and Wales," *Review of Radical Political Economics* 9 (Fall 1977): 7–21. Muller bases her account on the work of Tacitus, Bede, Seebohm, Phillpotts, F. M. Stenton, Whitelock, Homans, and McNamara and Wemple.

19. Georges Duby, "Peasants and the Agricultural Revolution," in *The Other Side of Western Civilization*, ed. Stanley Chodorow (New York: Harcourt Brace Jovanovich, 1979), p. 90, reprinted from *Rural Economy and Country Life in the Medieval West*, trans. Cynthia Poston (Columbia: University of South Carolina Press, 1968).

20. Lawrence Stone, "The Rise of the Nuclear Family in Early Modern England: The Patriarchal Stage," in *The Family in History*, ed. Charles E. Rosenberg (Philadelphia: University of Pennsylvania Press, 1975), p. 55. Also see Ellen Ross, "Women and Family," in "Examining Family History," by Rayna Rapp, Ellen Ross, and Renate Bridenthal, *Feminist Studies* 5, no. 1 (Spring 1979): 174–200, who discusses the transition from kin to nuclear family in more detail than I do here and offers a number of useful criticisms of family history.

21. Elizabeth Fox-Genovese, "Property and Patriarchy in Classical Bourgeois Political Theory," *Radical History Review* 4 (Spring/Summer 1977): 36–59. See also Robert A. Nisbet, *The Sociological Tradition* (New York: Basic Books, 1966).

22. Scott and Tilly (n. 3 above) and Hareven (n. 1 above) use the concepts of choice and adaptation. Louise Tilly, "Individual Lives and Family Strategies in the French Proletariat," *Journal of Family History* 4, no. 2 (Summer 1979): 137–52, employs the concept of family strategies but incorporates an understanding of potential intrafamily conflict. Jane Humphries, "The Working Class Family, Women's Liberation, and Class Struggle: The Case of Nineteenth Century British History," *Review of Radical Political Economics* 9, no. 3 (Fall 1977): 25–41, makes explicit use of the concept of family unity.

23. Stewart Ewen, *Captains of Consciousness* (New York: McGraw-Hill Book Co., 1976), and Barbara Ehrenreich and Deirdre English, *For Her Own Good: 150 Years of the Experts' Advice to Women* (New York: Anchor Press, 1978), argue that patriarchal control is now exercised by the corporation or the experts, rather than the small guy out there, one to a household. The trenchant review of the weakness of family history by Wini Breines, Margaret Cerullo, and Ju-

dith Stacey, "Social Biology, Family Studies and Anti-feminist Backlash," *Feminist Studies* 4, no. 1 (February 1978): 43–67, also suggests that within the family male power over women is declining. Barbara Easton, "Feminism and the Contemporary Family," *Socialist Revolution*, no. 39 (May–June 1978), pp. 11–36, makes a similar argument, as do Linda Gordon and Allen Hunter, "Sex, Family and the New Right: Anti Feminism as a Political Force," *Radical America* 11, no. 6 and 12, no. 1 (November 1977–February 1978): 9–25.

24. Kathryn E. Walker and Margaret E. Woods, *Time Use: A Measure of Household Production of Family Goods and Services* (Washington, D.C.: American Home Economics Association, 1976).

25. Alexander Szalai, ed., *The Use of Time* (The Hague: Mouton, 1972).

26. James N. Morgan, "A Potpourri of New Data Gathered from Interviews with Husbands and Wives," in *Five Thousand American Families: Patterns of Economic Progress*, vol. 6, *Accounting for Race and Sex Differences in Earnings and Other Analyses of the First Nine Years of the Panel Study of Income Dynamics*, ed. Greg J. Duncan and James N. Morgan (Ann Arbor: University of Michigan, Institute for Social Research [hereafter ISR], 1978), pp. 367–401; Frank Stafford and Greg Duncan, "The Use of Time and Technology by Households in the United States," working paper (Ann Arbor: University of Michigan, ISR, 1977); John P. Robinson, "Changes in American's Use of Time: 1965–1975: A Progress Report," working paper (Cleveland: Cleveland State University, August 1977).

27. Among the smaller studies are Martin Meissner et al. "No Exit for Wives: Sexual Division of Labour and the Cumulation of Household Demands," *Canadian Review of Sociology and Anthropology* 12 (November 1975): 424–39; Richard A. Berk and Sarah Fenstermaker Berk, *Labor and Leisure at Home: Content and Organization of the Household Day* (Beverly Hills, Calif.: Sage Publications, 1979); and Joseph H. Pleck, "Men's Family Work: Three Perspectives and Some New Data," working paper (Wellesley, Mass.: Wellesley College Center for Research on Women, 1979). New data collection efforts on a larger scale are already under way in several states, coordinated by Kathryn Walker at Cornell University, and planned by the Survey Research Center at the University of Michigan under the coordination of Frank Stafford, Greg Duncan, and John Robinson.

28. For a discussion of the reliability of time diaries and their compatibility, see John Robinson, "Methodological Studies into the Reliability and Validity of the Time Diary," in *Studies in the Measurement of Time Allocation*, ed. Thomas Juster (Ann Arbor: University of Michigan, ISR, in press); and Joann Vanek, "Keeping Busy: Time Spent in Housework, United States, 1920–1970" (Ph.D. diss., University of Michigan, 1973). Research on the distribution of families at the extremes (e.g., where men and women may be sharing housework equally) would also be very useful.

29. Kathryn E. Walker, "Time-Use Patterns for Household Work Related to Homemakers' Employment" (paper presented at the 1970 National Agricultural Outlook Conference, Washington, D.C., February 18, 1970), p. 5.

30. John Robinson and Philip Converse, "United States Time Use Survey" (Ann Arbor, Mich.: Survey Research Center, 1965–66), as reported by Joann Vanek, "Household Technology and Social Status: Rising Living Standards and Status and Residence Differences in Housework," *Technology and Culture* 19 (July 1978): 374.

31. John P. Robinson, Philip F. Converse, and Alexander Szalai, "Everyday Life in Twelve Countries," in Szalai, ed., pp. 119, 121.

32. Meissner et al.; Morgan. One recent survey, the national 1977 Quality of Employment Survey, does, however, indicate that husbands of employed wives do more housework than husbands of full-time houseworkers: about 1.8 hours more per week in household tasks and 2.7 more in child care (quoted in Pleck, pp. 15, 16). These findings are based on data gathered by the retrospective self-reports of 757 married men in interviews rather than by time diaries kept throughout the day. Respondents were asked to "estimate" how much time they spent on "home chores—things like working, cleaning, repairs, shopping, yardwork, and keeping track of money and bills," and on "taking care of or doing things with your child(ren)." The child-

Heidi I. Hartmann

care estimates are probably high relative to those from time-budget studies because the latter count only active care: "doing things with your children" would often be classified as leisure.

33. Meissner, et al., p. 430.

34. Ibid., p. 431.

35. Husbands of employed wives reported participating in meal preparation on 42 percent of the record-keeping days, while the employed wives participated on 96 percent of the days. Yet the husbands contributed only 10 percent of the time spent on that task, while the wives contributed 75 percent. Similarly, 17 percent of the husbands of employed wives participated in after-meal cleanup, contributing 7 percent of the time. In only two of the seven tasks constituting regular housework, marketing and nonphysical care of the family, did husbands contribute as much as 25 percent of the total time spent on the tasks (tasks defined as nonphysical care of the family are activities that relate to the social and educational development of other family members, such as reading to children or helping them with lessons; pet care is also included in this task). For these two tasks, neither the participation rates nor the proportions of time contributed differed substantially between those husbands whose wives worked for wages and those whose wives did not. It should be noted that the percentage of record days husbands were reported as participating in a particular task is not the same as a straightforward participation rate. For example, a report that husbands participated on half the days could indicate either that all husbands participated every other day or that half the husbands participated both days (Walker and Woods [n. 24 above], pp. 58, 59).

36. The unusual finding reported by Pleck, that husbands of employed wives estimate they spend more time on housework, could be explained by this phenomenon: men *participate* more often, and *think* they are doing more housework. The new time-budget studies will be useful in confirming or denying this change.

37. Morgan. These data indicate far fewer hours spent on housework than the Walker and Woods data because they exclude child-care hours and, perhaps as well, because they are based on recall rather than actual time diaries.

38. Meissner, et al., p. 433.

39. John Robinson and Philip Converse, "United States Time Use Survey" (Ann Arbor, Mich.: Survey Research Center, 1965–66), as reported in Janice N. Hedges and Jeanne K. Barnett, "Working Women and the Division of Household Tasks," *Monthly Labor Review* (April 1971), p. 11.

40. Walker and Woods, p. 64.

41. Hartmann, "Unhappy Marriage."

42. Morgan, p. 369.

43. Heidi I. Hartmann, "Capitalism and Women's Work in the Home, 1900–1930" (Ph.D. diss., Yale University, 1974 [Temple University Press, in press]). The Robinson-Converse study found that wives' housework time hovered around forty-two hours per week at all household incomes above $4,000 per year (1965–66 dollars) but was somewhat less, thirty-three hours, when household income was below $4,000 (reported in Vanek, "Household Technology and Social Status," p. 371).

44. In the Meissner study, fully 36 percent of the wives whose husbands earned under $10,000 (1971 dollars) were in the labor force, whereas no more than 10 percent of those whose husbands earned over $14,000 were in the labor forced (Meissner et al., p. 429).

45. Much additional research, both of the already available data and the forthcoming data, is needed to increase our knowledge of potential variations in housework time.

46. The salience of patriarchy over class for women's work could probably be shown for many societies: Bangladesh provides one example. In 1977 Mead Cain and his associates collected data on time use from all members of 114 households in a rural Bangladesh village, where control of arable land is the key to economic survival and position. Dichotomizing people's class position by the amount of arable land owned by their households, Cain found that the work days of men with more than one-half acre of land were substantially shorter than

those of men with less than one-half acre of land, whereas women in households with more land worked longer hours. The better-off men probably worked about eleven hours *less* per week than the poorer. The better-off women worked about three hours *more* per week than the poorer. In this rural village, Bangladesh women, unlike the men, did not benefit—at least in terms of lighter work loads—from the higher class position of their households (Mead Cain, Syeda Rokeya Khanam, and Shamsun Naher, "Class, Patriarchy, and Women's Work in Bangladesh," *Population and Development Review* 5, no. 3 [September 1979], 405–38).

47. Humphries adopts this perspective (see n. 22 above). In reality, the question is not so much whether or not patriarchy is oppressive in the lives of working women, but rather what the trade-offs are between patriarchal and class oppression.

48. Beverly Jones, "The Dynamics of Marriage and Motherhood," in *Sisterhood Is Powerful,* ed. Robin Morgan (New York: Vintage Books, 1970), pp. 46–61; Meredith Fax, "Woman and Her Mind: The Story of Daily Life" (Boston: New England Free Press, 1970), 20 pages; Laurel Limpus, "Liberation of Women: Sexual Repression and the Family" (Boston: New England Free Press, ca. 1970), 15 pages; Betty Friedan, *The Feminine Mystique* (New York: Dell Publishing Co., 1963).

49. Pat Mainardi, "The Politics of Housework," in Morgan, ed., pp. 449, 451. Maindardi begins her article with this quote from John Stuart Mill, *On the Subjection of Women:* "Though women do not complain of the power of husbands, each complains of her own husband, or of the husbands of her friends. It is the same in all other cases of servitude, at least in the commencement of the emancipatory movement. The serfs did not at first complain of the power of the lords, but only of their tyranny" (p. 447).

50. William Raspberry, "Family Breakdowns: A Voice from 'Little Dixie,'" *Washington Post* (June 23, 1978). Lillian Rubin, *Worlds of Pain* (New York: Basic Books, 1976), describes current tensions between the women and men in the working-class families she interviewed.

51. Kathryn E. Walker, "Homemaking Still Takes Time," *Journal of Home Economics* 61, no. 8 (October 1969): 621–24; Joann Vanek, "Time Spent in Housework," *Scientific American* 231 (November 1974): 116–20; Michael Paul Sacks, "Unchanging Times: A Comparison of the Everyday Life of Soviet Working Men and Women between 1923 and 1966," *Journal of Marriage and the Family* 39 (November 1977): 793–805.

52. Technological innovations within the household—the washing machine, the vacuum cleaner, the dishwasher—have not been effective in reducing household time. Sophisticated robots, microwave ovens, or computer-controlled equipment may yet be able to reduce the time required for maintaining household services at established levels. Yet what technology is developed and made available is also the result of historical processes and the relative strength of particular classes and genders. See Hartmann, *Capitalism and Women's Work.*

53. Robinson, table 4 (see n. 28 above); Clair Vickry, "Women's Economic Contribution to the Family," in *The Subtle Revolution,* ed. Ralph E. Smith (Washington, D.C.: Urban Institute, 1979), p. 194.

54. One in four meals is now eaten outside the home (Charles Vaugh, "Growth and Future of the Fast Food Industry," *Cornell Motel and Restaurant Administration Quarterly* [November 1976]), cited in Christine Bose, "Technology and Changes in the Division of Labor in the American Home" (paper delivered at the annual meeting of the American Sociological Association, San Francisco, September 1978). I suspect that the most effective means of reducing housework time involves changing the location of production from the household to the larger economy, but men, acting in their patriarchal interests, may well resist this removal of production from the home, with its attendant loss of personalized services.

55. Walker, "Homemaking Still Takes Time."

56. Sacks, "Unchanging Times," p. 801.

57. In the Marxist perspective, the wage paid to the worker is largely dependent on her or his costs of reproduction, mediated by custom, tradition, and class struggle. When there are two wage workers per family, the family's cost of reproduction can be spread over the wages of

both workers; the capitalist can pay two workers the same wage one received previously and get twice as many hours of labor, cheapening the price of labor per hour. See Lise Vogel, "The Earthy Family," *Radical America* 7, no. 4–5 (July-October 1973): 9–50. Jean Gardiner, "Women's Domestic Labor," *New Left Review*, no. 89 (January-February 1975), pp. 17–58, also discusses conflicting tendencies within capitalism.

58. James O'Connor, *The Fiscal Crisis of the State* (New York: St. Martin's Press, 1973).

59. Weinbaum (see n. 15 above).

60. Hedges and Barnett, p. 11 (see n. 39 above).

61. Ann R. Markusen has extended the notion of decentralized households as characteristic of patriarchy to explain the development of segregated residential areas in cities. See her "City Spatial Structure, Women's Household Work, and National Urban Policy," *Signs: Journal of Women in Culture and Society* 5, no. 3, suppl. (Spring 1980): S23–S44.

62. Wendy Lutrell, "The Family as an Arena of Struggle: New Directions and Strategies for Studying Contemporary Family Life" (paper delivered at a Sociology Colloquium, University of California, Santa Cruz, May 30, 1979), pp. 18, 19.

Suggested Further Readings

Barrett, Michele. *Women's Oppression Today: Problems in Marxist Feminist Analysis.* London: Verso, 1980.

Beechey, Veronica. "Some Notes on Female Wage Labour in Capitalist Production." *Capital and Class* (Autumn 1977):45–66.

Benston, Margaret. "The Political Economy of Women's Liberation." *Monthly Review* 21, no. 4 (September 1969):13–27.

Cowan, Ruth Schwartz, "The 'Industrial Revolution' in the Home: Household Technology and Social Change in the Twentieth Century." *Technology and Culture* 17, no. 1 (1976):1–23.

Dalla Costa, Mariarosa, and Selma James. *The Power of Women and the Subversion of the Community.* Bristol, England: Falling Wall Press, 1972.

Engels, Friedrich. *The Origin of the Family, Private Property, and the State.* New York: International Publishers, 1972.

Feldberg, Roslyn L. "Comparable Worth: Toward Theory and Practice in the United States." *Signs: Journal of Women in Culture and Society* 10, no. 2 (Winter 1984):311–328.

Flax, Jane. "Do Feminists Need Marxism?" *Building Feminist Theory: Essays from "Quest," a Feminist Quarterly,* pp. 174–185. New York: Longman, 1981.

Goldman, Emma. *The Traffic in Women and Other Essays on Feminism.* Albion, Calif.: Times Change Press, 1970.

Hartmann, Heidi I. "The Unhappy Marriage of Marxism and Feminism: Towards a More Progressive Union." In *Women and Revolution: A Discussion of the Unhappy Marriage of Marxism and Feminism,* ed. Lydia Sargent, pp. 1–41. Boston: South End Press, 1981.

_____. "The Family as the Locus of Gender, Class, and Political Struggle: The Example of Housework." In *Feminism and Methodology,* ed. Sandra Harding, pp. 109–134. Bloomington: Indiana University Press, 1987.

Kuhn, Annette, and Ann Marie Wolpe, eds. *Feminism and Materialism: Women and Modes of Production.* Boston: Routledge and Kegan Paul, 1978.

Lopate, Carol. "Pay for Housework." *Social Policy* 5, no. 3 (September-October 1974):27–31.

Malos, Ellen, ed. *The Politics of Housework.* London: Allison and Bushy, 1980.

Oliver, Kelly. "Marxism and Surrogacy." *Hypatia* 4, no. 3 (Fall 1989):95–115.

Secombe, Wally. "The Housewife and Her Labour Under Capitalism." *New Left Review* 83 (January-February 1973):3–24.

Zaretsky, Eli. "Capitalism, the Family, and Personal Life." *Socialist Revolution* 3, nos. 1–2 (January-April 1973):69–125.

THREE

RADICAL FEMINIST

PERSPECTIVES

Writing in the early 1970s, Shulamith Firestone identified a phenomenon she termed "sex class"—the condition of women as an oppressed class, "so deep as to be invisible."[1] In her book *The Dialectic of Sex,* Firestone articulated her version of the central tenet of radical feminism: Man's domination of woman is the fundamental form of oppression, one that is so intricately woven into virtually all facets of our lives that it thoroughly pervades our sense of what it is to be a woman or to be a man.

Contending that gender has been constructed in order to ensure women's subordination, radical feminists argue that women's oppression will not be eradicated simply by reforming political or economic institutions; rather, feminists must transform the entire gender system. Mary Daly, for example, defines radical feminism as a "journey of women becoming."[2] In other words, Daly argues that feminism requires that women not only recognize the destructive patriarchal images of woman that permeate their sense of self but also that they create a world other than patriarchy.

Radical feminist analyses aim to identify those aspects of the social constructions of femininity that serve to ensure male domination. Although radical feminists have examined many issues and social institutions including medicine, religion, reproduction, racism, ecology, and political theory,[3] among the most influential and vital of their critiques are those directed to the construction of women's sexuality. Radical feminists were the first feminists to make visible the ways in which women's sexuality is controlled by offering careful and insightful analyses of sexual harassment, woman battering, rape (including marital and date rape), pornography, sterilization, abortion, contraceptive laws and practices, and compulsory heterosexuality.

A central tenet of radical feminism is that male domination of women originates in the institution of heterosexuality. In her chapter "Sexuality, Pornography, and Method: 'Pleasure Under Patriarchy,'" Catharine MacKinnon argues that the "distinctive power of men over women in society" arises from the pervasiveness of male sexual violence against women. According to MacKinnon, sexuality has been constructed in such a way as to not only ensure male domination and female submission but also to eroticize it: "That which is called sexuality is the dynamic of control by which male dominance—

in forms that range from intimate to institutional, from a look to a rape—eroticizes as man and woman, as identity and pleasure." The domination of woman by man, including its expression in forms of violence against women, is inscribed onto the very practices of heterosexuality. For MacKinnon, sexuality so constructed is the basis of other forms of male domination—political, economic, and religious.

Radical feminists have been particularly concerned with the issue of pornography, for they see it as one of the principal sites of the social construction of sexuality. In pornography, women are depicted as sexual objects and men are rendered as consumers who, says MacKinnon, "desperately want women to desperately want possession and cruelty and dehumanization." Pornography, along with other practices such as prostitution, sexual harassment, rape, and woman battering, serves to ensure woman's sexual and social subordination.

Radical feminists have both called attention to the ways in which the institutions of heterosexuality exclude lesbians and argued that this position of marginality affords lesbian feminists an "exceptional epistemic position." Without denying the ways in which the experiences and lives of many women, particularly poor women and women of color, suffer erasure within Western philosophies and social institutions, Marilyn Frye devotes her essay, "To Be and Be Seen: The Politics of Reality," to a clarification of the ways in which "the exclusion of lesbians from phallocratic reality is different and is related to unusual knowing."

Frye notes the ways in which the institution of heterosexuality defines all women as heterosexual. The lesbian, then, becomes a woman who *is* heterosexual but who somehow *acts* otherwise. It similarly defines sex as involving penile stimulation and penetration, thereby making the definition of a lesbian as a woman who has sex or sexual relations with other women *logically impossible.* Although acknowledging that all women suffer erasure under patriarchy by having their lives and experiences ignored by "the conception of human history as a history of the acts and organizations of men" and by having their bodies and minds murdered and mutilated, Frye argues that the situation of lesbians differs. Heterosexual women are given and often forced into a role within patriarchy (wife, servant, daughter, prostitute, and similar roles). The lesbian has no place. This absence of place constitutes the lesbian's epistemic privilege. Not loyal to phallocratic reality, "she is not committed to its maintenance and the maintenance of those who maintain it." Her displacement provides a position from which to offer a view of the world that is different from the perception that keeps "Reality" afloat.

It is important to stress that MacKinnon, Frye, and other radical feminists who critique heterosexuality—Kathleen Barry, Andrea Dworkin, Sarah Hoagland, and Adrienne Rich—are not claiming that heterosexuality has an essential nature that necessitates male domination. Their position is that in contemporary Western culture, human sexuality has been *constructed* in such a way as to ensure that women's sexuality is for men. This is not to deny a biological component to sexuality but, rather, to acknowledge the impact and influence of our cultural institutions and beliefs upon our experiences of sexuality. A central tenet of radical feminism is, thus, that the systematic oppression of women will require not only legal, political, and economic changes; it will also require a radical reconstruction of sexuality.

Sarah Hoagland has argued that understanding heterosexism involves the recognition not only that woman's sexuality has been defined in terms of male desire but additionally that "women are defined in terms of men or not at all."[4] Hoagland illustrates the ways in which heterosexualism is involved in all aspects of women's lives through what she labels the practices of "protection and predation." Women are defined as helpless, as in danger, as objects of male passion, as needing to be protected—all leading to the role of men as protectors of women. Hoagland admonishes us to remember that what a woman needs protection *from* is other men, thereby demonstrating that predation is the other side of protection in that it arises out of the same ideology of male dominance. Protectors would not be necessary unless there were predators and victims. But in viewing women as the object of male passion, heterosexism constructs women as the cause of that passion. Thus, women attract predators, and if they step out of the accepted image of women—that is, the woman deserving of protection—they are likely to become the targets of overt physical violence.

Like MacKinnon, Hoagland seeks to reveal the systemic oppression of women within Western culture. But in her contribution to this volume, "Moral Revolution: From Antagonism to Cooperation," Hoagland focuses on the construction of "femininity": "'Femininity' normalizes male domination and paints a portrait of women as subordinate and naively content with being controlled." Woman's femininity is constructed to entail her passivity and dependence, and thus she requires protection (domination). And Hoagland, like Firestone, perceives the oppression of women as providing a model for understanding other forms of oppression.

Hoagland's solution is to call for a moral revolution. Like MacKinnon and Frye, Hoagland's revolution would require a rejection of heterosexualism as a source of male domination. It would be a revolution that would involve a "movement of women" who withdraw from the construction of "femininity" and begin to redefine reality in order to reconstruct the very concept of "woman."

Notes

1. Shulamith Firestone, *The Dialectic of Sex: The Case for Feminist Revolution* (New York: Bantam Books, 1970), p. 1.

2. Mary Daly, *Gyn/Ecology: The Metaethics of Radical Feminism* (Boston: Beacon Press, 1978), p. 1.

3. See, for example, the work of Mary Daly, Andrea Dworkin, Marilyn Frye, Shulamith Firestone, Carole Pateman, and Adrienne Rich.

4. Sarah Lucia Hoagland, *Lesbian Ethics: Toward New Value* (Palo Alto: Institute of Lesbian Studies, 1988), p. 28.

Sexuality, Pornography, and Method: "Pleasure Under Patriarchy"

Catharine A. MacKinnon

then she says (and this is what I live through over
and over)—she says: *I do not know*
if sex is an illusion

I do not know
who I was when I did those things
or who I said I was
or whether I willed to feel
what I had read about
or who in fact was there with me
or whether I knew, even then
that there was doubt about these things

[Adrienne Rich, "Dialogue"]

I had always been fond of her in the most innocent, asexual way. It was as if her body was al-
ways entirely hidden behind her radiant mind, the modesty of her behavior, and her taste in
dress. She had never offered me the slightest chink through which to view the glow of her na-
kedness. And now suddenly the butcher knife of fear had slit her open. She was as open to me
as the carcass of a heifer slit down the middle and hanging on a hook. There we were ... and
suddenly I felt a violent desire to make love to her. Or to be more exact, a violent desire to
rape her.

[Milan Kundera, *The Book of Laughter and Forgetting*]

She had thought of something, something about the body, about the passions which it was
unfitting for her as a woman to say. Men, her reason told her, would be shocked. ... Telling
the truth about my own experiences as a body, I do not think I solved. I doubt that any
woman has solved it yet. The obstacles against her are still immensely powerful—and yet
they are very difficult to define.

[Virginia Woolf, "Professions for Women"]

134

What is it about women's experience that produces a distinctive perspective on social reality? How is an angle of vision and an interpretive hermeneutics of social life created in the group women? What happens to women to give them a particular interest in social arrangements, something to have a consciousness *of?* How are the qualities we know as male and female socially created and enforced on an everyday level? Sexual objectification of women—first in the world, then in the head, first in visual appropriation, then in forced sex, finally in sexual murder—provides answers.[1]

Male dominance is sexual. Meaning: men in particular, if not men alone, sexualize hierarchy; gender is one. As much a sexual theory of gender as a gendered theory of sex, this is the theory of sexuality that has grown out of consciousness raising in the women's movement. Recent feminist work, both interpretive and empirical—on rape, battery, sexual harassment, sexual abuse of children, prostitution, and pornography—supports it (see Appendix). These practices, taken together, express and actualize the distinctive power of men over women in society; their effective permissibility confirms and extends it. If one believes women's accounts of sexual use and abuse by men;[2] if the pervasiveness of male sexual violence against women substantiated in these studies is not denied, minimized, or excepted as deviant[3] or episodic; if the fact that only 7.8 percent of women in the United States are not sexually assaulted or harassed in their lifetimes[4] is considered not ignorable or inconsequential; if the women to whom it happens are not considered expendable; if violation of women is understood as sexualized on some level—then sexuality itself can no longer be regarded as unimplicated. The meaning of practices of sexual violence cannot be categorized away as violence, not sex, either. The male sexual role, this work taken together suggests, centers on aggressive intrusion on those with less power. Such acts of dominance are experienced as sexually arousing, as sex itself.[5] They therefore are. The evidence on the sexual violation of women by men thus frames an inquiry into the place of sexuality in gender and of gender in sexuality.

A feminist theory of sexuality would locate sexuality within a theory of gender inequality, meaning the social hierarchy of men over women. To make a theory feminist, it is not enough that it be authored by a biological female. Nor that it describe female sexuality as different from (if equal to) male sexuality, or as if sexuality in women ineluctably exists in some realm beyond, beneath, above, behind—in any event, fundamentally untouched and unmoved by—an unequal social order. A theory of sexuality becomes feminist to the extent it treats sexuality as a social construct of male power: defined by men, forced on women, and constitutive in the meaning of gender. Such an approach centers feminism on the perspective of the subordination of women to men as it identifies sex—that is, the sexuality of dominance and submission—as crucial, as a fundamental, as on some level definitive, in that process. Feminist theory becomes a project of analyzing that situation in order to face it for what it is, in order to change it.

Focusing on gender inequality without a sexual account of its dynamics, as most work has, one could criticize the sexism of existing theories of sexuality and emerge knowing that men author scripts to their own advantage, women and men act them out; that men set conditions, women and men have their behavior conditioned; that men develop developmental categories through which men develop, and that women develop or not; that men are socially allowed selves hence identities with personalities into which sexuality is or is not well integrated, women being that which is or is not integrated, that through the alterity of which a self experiences itself as having an identity; that men have object relations, women are the objects of those relations, and so on. Following such critique, one could attempt to invert or correct the premises or applications of these theories to make them gender neutral, even if the reality to which they refer looks more like the theories—once their gender specificity is revealed—than it looks gender neutral. Or, one could attempt to enshrine a distinctive "women's reality" as if it really were permitted to exist as something more than one dimension of women's response to a condition of powerlessness. Such exercises would be revealing and instructive, even deconstructive, but to limit feminism to correcting sex bias by acting in theory as if male power did not exist in fact, including by valorizing in writing what women have had little choice but to be limited to becoming in life, is to limit feminist theory the way sexism limits women's lives: to a response to terms men set.

A distinctively feminist theory conceptualizes social reality, including sexual reality, on its own terms. The question is, What are they? If women have been substantially deprived not only of their own experience but of terms of their own in which to view it, then a feminist theory of sexuality that seeks to understand women's situation in order to change it, must first identify and criticize the construct "sexuality" as a construct that has circumscribed and defined experience as well as theory. This requires capturing it *in the world,* in its situated social meanings, as it is being constructed in life on a daily basis. It must be studied in its experienced empirical existence, not just in the texts of history (as Foucault), in the social psyche (as Lacan) or in language (as Derrida). Sexual meaning is not made only, or even primarily, by words and in texts. In feminist terms, the fact that male power has power means that the interests of male sexuality construct what sexuality as such means in life, including the standard way it is allowed and recognized to be felt and expressed and experienced, in a way that determines women's biographies, including sexual ones. Existing theories, until they grasp this, will not only misattribute what they call female sexuality to women as such, as if it is not imposed on women daily, they will participate in enforcing the hegemony of the social construct "desire," hence its product, "sexuality," hence its construct "woman," on the world.

The gender issue thus becomes the issue of what is taken to be "sexuality": what sex means and what is meant by sex, when, how, and with whom and with what consequences to whom. Such questions are almost never systematically confronted, even in discourses that purport feminist awareness. What sex is—how it comes to be attached and attributed to what it is, embodied and practiced as it is, contextualized in the ways it is, signifying and referring to what it does—is taken as a baseline, a given, except when explaining what happened when it is thought to have gone wrong. It is as if "erotic," for example, can be taken as having an understood referent, although it is never defined. Except to imply that it is universal yet individual, ultimately variable and plastic. Essentially indefinable but overwhelmingly positive. "Desire," the vicissitudes of which are endlessly extolled and philosophized in culture high and low, is not seen as fundamentally problematic or calling for explanation on the concrete, interpersonal operative level, unless (again) it is supposed to be there and is not. To list and analyze what seem to be the essential elements for male sexual arousal, what has to be there for the penis to work, seems faintly blasphemous, like a pornographer doing market research. Sex is supposed both too individual and too universally transcendant for that. To suggest that the sexual might be continuous with something other than sex itself—something like politics—is seldom done, is treated as detumescent, even by feminists. It is as if sexuality comes from the stork.

Sexuality, in feminist light, is not a discrete sphere of interaction or feeling or sensation or behavior in which preexisting social divisions may or may not be played out. It is a pervasive dimension throughout the whole of social life, a dimension along which gender pervasively occurs and through which gender is socially constituted; in this culture, it is a dimension along which other social divisions, like race and class, partly play themselves out. Dominance eroticized defines the imperatives of its masculinity, submission eroticized defines its femininity. So many distinctive features of women's status as second class—the restriction and constraint and contortion, the servility and the display, the self-mutilation and requisite presentation of self as a beautiful thing, the enforced passivity, the humiliation—are made into the content of sex for women. Being a thing for sexual use is fundamental to it. This identifies not just a sexuality that is shaped under conditions of gender inequality but this sexuality itself as the dynamic of the inequality of the sexes. It is to argue that the excitement at reduction of a person to a thing, to less than a human being, as socially defined, is its fundamental motive force. It is to argue sexual difference as a function of sexual dominance. It is to argue a sexual theory of the distribution of social power by gender, in which this sexuality that is sexuality is substantially what makes the gender division be what it is, which is male dominant, wherever it is, which is nearly everywhere.

Across cultures, from this perspective, sexuality is whatever a given culture defines it as. The next questions concern its relation to gender asymmetry and to gender as a division of power. Male dominance appears to exist cross-culturally, if in locally particular forms. Is whatever defines women as "different" the same as whatever defines women as "inferior" the same as whatever defines women's "sexuality"? Is that which defines gender inequality as merely the sex difference also the content of the erotic, cross-culturally? In this view, the feminist theory of sexuality is its theory of politics, its distinctive contribution to social and political explanation. To explain gender inequality in terms of "sexual politics"[6] is to advance not only a political theory of the sexual that defines gender but also a sexual theory of the political to which gender is fundamental.

In this approach, male power takes the social form of what men as a gender want sexually, which centers on power itself, as socially defined. Masculinity is having it; femininity is not having it. Masculinity precedes male as femininity precedes female and male sexual desire defines both. Specifically, "woman" is defined by what male desire requires for arousal and satisfaction and is socially tautologous with "female sexuality" and "the female sex." In the permissible ways a woman can be treated, the ways that are socially considered not violations but appropriate to her nature, one finds the particulars of male sexual interests and requirements. In the concomitant sexual paradigm, the ruling norms of sexual attraction and expressions are fused with gender identity formation and affirmation, such that sexuality equals heterosexuality equals the sexuality of (male) dominance and (female) submission.

Post-Lacan, actually post-Foucault,[7] it has become customary to affirm that sexuality is socially constructed.[8] Seldom specified is what, socially, it is constructed of, far less who does the constructing or how, when, or where.[9] When capitalism is the favored social construct, sexuality is shaped and controlled and exploited and repressed by capitalism; not, capitalism creates sexuality as we know it. When sexuality is a construct of discourses of power, gender is never one of them; force is central to its deployment but only through repressing it, not through constituting it; speech is not concretely investigated for its participation in this construction process. "Constructed" seems to mean influenced by, directed, channeled, like a highway constructs traffic patterns. Not: Why cars? Who's driving? Where's everybody going? What makes mobility matter? Who can own a car? Are all these accidents not very accidental? Although there are partial exceptions (but disclaimers notwithstanding), the typical model of sexuality that is tacitly accepted remains deeply Freudian[10] and essentialist: sexuality is an innate primary natural prepolitical unconditioned[11] drive divided along the biological gender line, centering on heterosexual intercourse, that is, penile intromission, full actualization of which is repressed by civilization. Even if the sublimation aspect of this theory is rejected, or the reasons for the repression are seen to vary (for the survival of civilization or to maintain fascist control or to keep capitalism moving), sexual expression is implicitly seen as the expression of something that is to a significant extent presocial and is socially denied its full force. Sexuality remains precultural and universally invariant to some extent, social only in that it needs society to take what are always to some extent socially specific forms. The impetus itself is a hunger, an appetite founded on a biological need; what it is specifically hungry for and how it is satisfied is then open to endless cultural and individual variance, like cuisine, like cooking.

Allowed/not-allowed are this sexuality's basic ideological axes. The fact that sexuality is ideologically bounded is known. That there are its axes, central to the way its "drive" is driven, and that this is fundamental to the gender difference, is not.[12] Its basic normative assumption is that whatever is considered sexuality should be allowed to be "expressed." Whatever is called sex is attributed a normatively positive valence, an affirmative valuation. This ex cathedra assumption, affirmation of which appears indispensable to one's credibility on any subject that gets near the sexual, means that sex as such (whatever it is) is good—natural, healthy, positive, appropriate, pleasurable, wholesome, fine, one's own, and to be approved and expressed. This, sometimes characterized as "sex-positive," is, rather, obviously, a value judgment.

Kinsey and his followers, for example, clearly thought (and think) the more sex the better. Accordingly, they trivialize even most of those cases of rape and child sexual abuse they discern as such, decry women's sexual refusal as sexual inhibition, and repeatedly interpret women's sexual disinclination as "restrictions" on men's natural sexual activity, which left alone would emulate (some) animals.[13] Followers of the neo-Freudian derepression imperative have similarly identified the frontier of sexual freedom with transgression of social restraints on access, with making the sexually disallowed allowed, especially male sexual access to anything. The struggle to have everything sexual allowed in a society we are told would collapse if it were, creates a sense of resistance to, and an aura of danger around, violating the powerless. If we knew the boundaries were phony, existed only to eroticize the targeted transgressable, would penetrating them feel less sexy? Taboo and crime may serve to eroticize what would otherwise feel about as much like dominance as taking candy from a baby. Assimilating actual powerlessness to male prohibition, to male power, provides the appearance of resistance, which makes overcoming possible, while never undermining the reality of power, or its dignity, by giving the powerless actual power. The point is, allowed/not-allowed become the ideological axes along which sexuality is experienced when and because sex, hence gender, is about power.

One version of the derepression hypothesis that purports feminism is: civilization having been male-dominated, female sexuality has been repressed, not allowed. Sexuality as such still centers on what would otherwise be considered the reproductive act, on intercourse: penetration of the erect penis into the vagina (or appropriate substitute orifices) followed by thrusting to male ejaculation. If reproduction actually had anything to do with what sex was for, it would not happen every night (or even twice a week) for forty or fifty years, nor would prostitutes exist. "We had sex three times" typically means the man entered the woman three times and orgasmed three times. Female sexuality in this model refers to the presence of this theory's 'sexuality,' or the desire to be so treated, in biological females; 'female' is somewhere between an adjective and a noun, half possessive and half biological ascription. Sexual freedom means women being allowed to behave as freely as men to express this sexuality, to have it allowed, that is, to (hopefully) shamelessly and without social constraints initiate genital drive satisfaction through heterosexual intercourse.[14] Hence, the liberated woman. Hence, the sexual revolution.

The pervasiveness of such assumptions about sexuality throughout otherwise diverse methodological traditions is suggested by the following comment by a scholar of violence against women: "If women were to escape the culturally stereotyped role of disinterest in and resistance to sex and to take on an assertive role in expressing their own sexuality, rather than leaving it to the assertiveness of men, it would contribute to the reduction of rape. ... First, and most obviously, voluntary sex would be available to more men, thus reducing the 'need' for rape. Second, and probably more important, it would help to reduce the confounding of sex and aggression."[15] In this view, somebody must be assertive for sex to happen. Voluntary sex—sexual equality—means equal sexual aggression. If women freely expressed "their own sexuality," more heterosexual intercourse would be initiated. Women's "resistance" to sex is an imposed cultural stereotype, not a form of political struggle. Rape is occasioned by women's resistance not by men's force; or, male force, hence rape, is created by women's resistance to sex. Men would rape less if they got more voluntarily compliant sex from women. Corollary: the force in rape is not sexual to men.

Underlying this quotation lurks the view, as common as it is tacit, that if women would just accept the contact men now have to rape to get—if women would stop resisting or (in one of the pornographers' favorite scenarios) become sexual aggressors—rape would wither away. On one level, this is a definitionally obvious truth. When a woman accepts what would be a rape if she did not accept it, what happens is sex. If women were to accept forced sex as sex, "voluntary sex would be available to more men." If such a view is not implicit in this text, it is a mystery how women equally aggressing against men sexually would eliminate, rather than double, the confounding of sex and aggression. Without such an assumption, only the confounding of sexual aggression with gender would be eliminated. If women don't resist male sexual aggression anymore, the confounding of sex with aggression would, indeed, be so epistemologically complete that it would be eliminated. No woman would ever be sexually violated because sexual violation would be sex. The situation might resemble that evoked by a society Sanday categorized as "rape-free" in part because the men assert there is no rape there: "Our women never resist."[16] Such parcification also occurs in "rape-prone" societies like the United States, where some force may be perceived as force but only above certain threshold standards.[17]

While intending the opposite, some feminists have encouraged and participated in this type of analysis by conceiving rape as violence not sex.[18] While this approach gave needed emphasis to rape's previously effaced elements of power and dominance, it obscured its elements of sex. Aside from failing to answer the rather obvious question, if it's violence not sex why didn't he just hit her, this approach made it impossible to see that violence is sex when it is practiced as sex.[19] This is obvious once what sexuality is, is understood as a matter of what it means, of how it is interpreted. To say rape is violence not sex preserves the "sex is good" norm by simply distinguishing forced sex as "not sex," whether it means sex to the perpetrator or even, later, to the victim, who has difficulty experiencing sex without reexperiencing the rape. Whatever is sex, cannot be violent; whatever is violent, cannot be sex. This analytic wish-fulfillment makes it possible for rape to be opposed by those who would save sexuality from the rapists while leaving the sexual fundamentals of male dominance intact.

While much prior work on rape has analyzed it as a problem of inequality between the sexes but not as a problem of unequal sexuality on the basis of gender,[20] other contemporary explorations of sexuality that purport to be feminist lack comprehension either of gender as a form of social power or of the realities of sexual violence. For instance, the editors of *Powers of Desire* take sex "as a central form of expression, one that defines identity and is seen as a primary source of energy and pleasure."[21] This may be how it "is seen" but it is also how they, operatively, see it. As if women choose sexuality as definitive of identity. As if it is as much a form of women's "expression" as it is men's. As if violation and abuse are not equally central to sexuality as women live it.

The *Diary* of the Barnard conference on sexuality pervasively equates sexuality with 'pleasure.' "Perhaps the overall question we need to ask is: How do women ... negotiate sexual pleasure?"[22] As if women under male supremacy have power to. As if "negotiation" is a form of freedom. As if pleasure and how to get it, rather than dominance and how to end it, is the "overall" issue sexuality presents feminism. As if women do just need a good fuck. In these texts, taboos are treated as real restrictions—as things that really are not allowed—instead of as guises under which hiearchy is eroticized. The domain of the sexual is divided into "restriction, repression and danger" on the one hand and "exploration, pleasure and agency" on the other.[23] This division parallels the ideological forms through which dominance and submission are eroticized, variously socially coded as heterosexuality's male/female, lesbian culture's butch/femme, and sadomasochism's top/bottom.[24] Speaking in role terms, the one who pleasures in the illusion of freedom and security within the reality of danger is the "girl"; the one who pleasures in the reality of freedom and security within the illusion of danger is the "boy." That is, the *Diary* uncritically adopts as an analytical tool the central dynamic of the phenomenon it purports to be analyzing. Presumably, one is to have a sexual experience of the text.

The terms of these discourses preclude or evade crucial feminist questions. What do sexuality and gender inequality have to do with each other? How do dominance and submission become sexualized, or, why is hierarchy sexy? How does it get attached to male and female? Why does sexuality center on intercourse, the reproductive act by physical design? Is masculinity the enjoyment of violation, femininity the enjoyment of being violated? Is that the central meaning of intercourse? Why do "men love death"?[25] What is the etiology of heterosexuality in women? Is its pleasure women's stake in subordination?

Taken together and taken seriously, feminist inquiries into the realities of rape, battery, sexual harassment, incest, child sexual abuse, prostitution, and pornography answer these questions by suggesting a theory of the sexual mechanism. Its script, learning, conditioning, developmental logos, imprinting of the microdot, its deus ex machina, whatever sexual process term defines sexual arousal itself, is force, power's expression. Force is sex, not just sexualized; force is the desire dynamic, not just a response to the desired object when desire's expression is frustrated. Pressure, gender socialization, withholding benefits, extending indulgences, the how-to books, the sex therapy are the soft end; the fuck, the fist, the street, the chains, the poverty are the hard end. Hostility and contempt, or arousal of master to slave, together with awe and vulnerability, or arousal of slave to master—these are the emotions of this sexuality's excitement. "Sadomasochism is to sex what war is to civil life: the magnificent experience," writes Susan Sontag.[26] "It is hostility—the desire, overt or hidden, to harm another person—that generates and enhances sexual excitement," writes Robert Stoller.[27] Harriet Jacobs, a slave, speaking of her systematic rape by her master, writes, "It seems less demeaning to give one's self, than to submit to compulsion."[28] Looking at the data, the force in sex and the sex in force is a matter of simple empirical description—unless one accepts that force in sex is not force anymore, it is just sex; or, if whenever a woman is forced it is what she really wants or it or she does not matter; or, unless prior aversion or sentimentality substitutes what one wants sex to be, or will condone or countenance as sex, for what is actually happening.

To be clear: what is sexual is what gives a man an erection. Whatever it takes to make a penis shudder and stiffen with the experience of its potency is what sexuality means culturally. Whatever else does, fear does, hostility does, hatred does, the helplessness of a child or a student or an infantilized or restrained or vulnerable woman does, revulsion does, death does. Hierarchy, a constant creation of person/thing, top/ bottom, dominance/subordination relations, does. What is understood as violation, conventionally penetration and intercourse, defines the paradigmatic sexual encounter. The scenario of sexual abuse is: you do what I say. These textualities become sexuality. All this suggests that that which is called sexuality is the dynamic of control by which male dominance—in forms that range from intimate to institutional, from a look to a rape—eroticizes as man and woman, as identity and pleasure. It is also that which maintains and defines male supremacy as a political system. Male sexual desire is thereby simultaneously created and serviced, never satisfied once and for all, while male force is romanticized, even sacralized, potentiated, and naturalized, by being submerged into sex itself.

In contemporary philosophical terms, nothing is "indeterminate" in the post-structuralist sense here; it is all too determinate.[29] Nor does its reality provide just one perspective on a relativistic interpersonal world that could mean anything or its opposite.[30] The reality of pervasive sexual abuse and its erotization does not shift relative to perspective, although whether or not one will see it or accord it significance may. Interpretation varies relative to place in sexual abuse, certainly; but the fact that women are sexually abused as women, in a social matrix of sexualized subordination does not go away because it is often ignored or authoritatively disbelieved or interpreted out of existence. Indeed, some ideological supports for its persistence rely precisely upon techniques of social indeterminacy: no language but the obscene to describe the unspeakable; denial by the powerful casting doubt on the facticity of the injuries; actually driving its victims insane. Indeterminacy is a neo-Cartesian mind game that undermines the actual social meaning of words by raising acontextualized interpretive possibilities that have no real social meaning or real possibility of any, dissolving the ability to criticize actual meanings without making space for new ones. The feminist point is simple. Men are women's material conditions. If it happens to women, it happens.

Women often find ways to resist male supremacy and to expand their spheres of action. But they are never free of it. Women also embrace the standards of women's place in this regime as "our own" to varying degrees and in varying voices—as affirmation of identity and right to pleasure, in order to be loved and approved and paid, in order just to make it through another day. This, not inert passivity, is the meaning of being a victim.[31] The term is not moral: who is to blame or to be pitied or condemned or held responsible. It is not prescriptive: what we should do next. It is not strategic: how to construe the situation so it can be changed. It is not emotional: what one feels better thinking. It is descriptive: who does what to whom and gets away with it?

Thus the question Freud never asked is the question that defines sexuality in a feminist perspective: What do men want? Pornography provides an answer. Pornography permits men to have whatever they want sexually. It is their "truth about sex."[32] It connects the centrality of visual objectification to both male sexual arousal and male models of knowledge and verification, connecting objectivity with objectification. It shows how men see the world, how in seeing it they access and possess it, and how this is an act of dominance over it. It shows what men want and gives it to them. From the testimony of the pornography, what men want is: women bound, women battered, women tortured, women humiliated, women degraded and defiled, women killed. Or, to be fair to the soft core, women sexually accessible, have-able, there for them, wanting to be taken and used, with perhaps just a little light bondage. Each violation of women—rape, battery, prostitution, child sexual abuse, sexual harassment—is made sexuality, made sexy, fun, and liberating of women's true nature in the pornography. Each specifically victimized and vulnerable group of women, each tabooed target group—black women, Asian women, Latin women, Jewish women, pregnant women, disabled women, retarded women, poor women, old women, fat women, women in women's jobs, prostitutes, little girls—distinguishes pornographic genres and subthemes, classified according to diverse customers' favorite degradation. Women are made into and coupled with anything considered lower than human: animals, objects, children, and (yes) other women. Anything women have claimed as their own—motherhood, athletics, traditional men's jobs, lesbianism, feminism—is made specifically sexy, dangerous, provocative, punished, made men's in pornography.

Pornography is a means through which sexuality is socially constructed, a site of construction, a domain of exercise. It constructs women as things for sexual use and constructs its consumers to desperately want women to desperately want possession and cruelty and dehumanization. Inequality itself, subjection itself, hierarchy itself, objectification itself, with self-determination ecstatically relinquished, is the apparent content of women's sexual desire and desirability. "The major theme of pornography as a genre," writes Andrea Dworkin, "is male power."[33] Women are in pornography to be violated and taken, men to violate and take them, either on screen or by camera or pen, on behalf of the viewer. Not that sexuality in life or in media never expresses love and affection; only that love and affection are not what is sexualized in this society's actual sexual paradigm, as pornography testifies to it. Violation of the powerless, intrusion on women, is. The milder forms, possession and use, the mildest of which is visual objectification, are. The sexuality of observation, visual intrusion and access, of entertainment, makes sex largely a spectator sport for its participants.

If pornography has not become sex to and from the male point of view, it is hard to explain why the pornography industry makes a known ten billion dollars a year selling it as sex mostly to men; why it is used to teach sex to child prostitutes, recalcitrant wives and girlfriends and daughters, and to medical students, and to sex offenders; why it is nearly universally classified as a subdivision of "erotic literature"; why it is protected and defended as if it were sex itself.[34] And why a prominent sexologist fears that enforcing the views of feminists against pornography in society would make men "erotically inert wimps."[35] No pornography, no male sexuality.

A feminist critique of sexuality in this sense is advanced in Andrea Dworkin's *Pornography: Men Possessing Women*. Building on her earlier identification of gender inequality as a system of social meaning,[36] an ideology lacking basis in anything other than the social reality its power constructs and maintains, she argues that sexuality is a construct of that power, given meaning by, through, and in pornography. In this perspective, pornography is not harmless fantasy or a corrupt and confused misrepresentation of otherwise natural healthy sex, nor is it fundamentally a distortion, reflection, projection, expression, representation, fantasy, or symbol of it.[37] Through pornography, among other practices, gender inequality becomes both sexual and socially real. Pornography "reveals that male pleasure is inextricably tied to victimizing, hurting, exploiting."[38] "Dominance in the male system is pleasure."[39] Rape is "the defining paradigm of sexuality,"[40] to avoid which boys choose manhood and homophobia.[41]

Women, who are not given a choice, are objectified, or, rather, "the object is allowed to desire, if she desires to be an object."[42] Psychology sets the proper bounds of this objectification by terming its improper excesses "fetishism,"[43] distinguishing the uses from the abuses of women. Dworkin shows how the process and content of women's definition as women, an underclass, are the process and content of their sexualization as objects for male sexual use. The mechanism is (again) force, imbued with meaning because it is the means to death[44] and death is the ultimate sexual act, the ultimate making of a person into a thing.

Why, one wonders at this point, is intercourse "sex" at all? In pornography, conventional intercourse is one act among many; penetration is crucial but can be done with anything; penis is crucial but not necessarily in the vagina. Actual pregnancy is a minor subgeneric theme, about as important in pornography as reproduction is in rape. Thematically, intercourse is incidental in pornography, especially when compared with force, which is primary. From pornography one learns that forcible violation of women is the essence of sex. Whatever is that and does that is sex. Everything else is secondary. Perhaps the reproductive act is considered sexual because it is considered an act of forcible violation and defilement of the female distinctively as such, not because it 'is' sex a priori.

To be sexually objectified means having a social meaning imposed on your being that defines you as to be sexually used, according to your desired uses, and then using you that way. Doing this is sex in the male system. Pornography is a sexual practice of this because it exists in a social system in which sex in life is no less mediated than it is in representation. There is no irreducible essence, no "just sex." If sex is a social construct of sexism, men have sex with their image of a woman. Pornography creates an accessible sexual object, the possession and consumption of which is male sexuality, to be possessed and consumed as which is female sexuality. This is not because pornography depicts objectified sex but because it creates the experience of a sexuality which is itself objectified. The appearance of choice or consent, with their attribution to inherent nature, are crucial in concealing the reality of force. Love of violation, variously termed female masochism and consent,[45] comes to define female sexuality, legitimizing this political system by concealing the force on which it is based.

In this system, a victim, usually female, always feminized, is "never forced, only actualized."[46] Women whose attributes particularly fixate men—such as women with large breasts—are seen as full of sexual desire. Women men want, want men. Women fake vaginal orgasms, the only 'mature' sexuality, because men demand that they enjoy vaginal penetration.[47] Raped women are seen as asking for it: if a man wanted her, she must have wanted him. Men force women to become sexual objects, "that thing which causes erection, then hold themselves helpless and powerless when aroused by her."[48] Men who sexually harass, say women sexually harass them. They mean they are aroused by women who turn them down. This elaborate projective system of demand characteristics—taken to pinnacles like fantasizing a clitoris in women's throats[49] so that men can enjoy forced fellatio in real life assured that women do too—is surely a delusional and projective structure deserving of serious psychological study. Instead, it is women who resist it that are studied, seen as in need of explanation and adjustment, stigmatized as inhibited and repressed and asexual. The assumption that, in matters sexual, women really want what men want from women makes male force against women in sex invisible. It makes rape sex. Women's sexual "reluctance, dislike, and frigidity," women's puritanism and prudery in the face of this sex, is the "silent rebellion of women against the force of the penis ... an ineffective rebellion, but a rebellion nonetheless."[50]

Nor is homosexuality without stake in this gendered sexual system. Putting to one side the obviously gendered content of expressly adopted roles, clothing, and sexual mimicry, to the extent the gender of a sexual object is crucial to arousal, the structure of social power that stands behind and defines gender is hardly irrelevant, even if it is rearranged. Some have argued that lesbian sexuality—meaning here simply women having sex with women not men—solves the problem of gender by eliminating men from women's voluntary sexual encounters.[51] Yet women's sexuality remains constructed under conditions of male supremacy; women remain socially defined as women in relation to men; the definition of women as men's inferiors remains sexual even if not heterosexual, whether men are present at the time or not. To the extent gay men choose men because they are men, the meaning of masculinity is affirmed as well as undermined. It may also be that sexuality is so gender marked that it carries dominance and submission with it, no matter the gender of its participants.

Each structural requirement of this sexuality as revealed in pornography is professed in recent defenses of sadomasochism, described by proponents as that sexuality in which "the basic dynamic ... is the power dichotomy."[52] Exposing the prohibitory underpinnings on which this violation model of the sexual depends, one advocate says, "We select the most frightening, disgusting or unacceptable activities and transmute them into pleasure." The relational dynamics of sadomasochism do not even negate the paradigm of male dominance, but conform precisely to it: the ecstasy in domination ("I like to hear someone ask for mercy or protection"); the enjoyment of inflicting psychological as well as physical torture ("I want to see the confusion, the anger, the turn-on, the helplessness"); the expression of belief in the inferior's superiority belied by the absolute contempt ("the bottom must be my superior ... playing a bottom who did not demand my respect and admiration would be like eating rotten fruit"); the degradation and consumption of women through sex ("she feeds me the energy I need to dominate and abuse her"); the health and personal growth rationale ("it's a healing process"); the anti-puritan radical therapy justification ("I was taught to dread sex. ... It is shocking and profoundly satisfying to commit this piece of rebellion, to take pleasure exactly as I want it, to exact it like tribute"); the bipolar doublethink in which the top enjoys "sexual service" while the "will to please is the bottom's source of pleasure." And the same bottom line of all top-down sex: "I want to be in control." The statements are from a female sadist. The good news is, it's not biological.

As pornography connects sexuality with gender in social reality, the feminist critique of pornography connects feminist work on violence against women with its inquiry into women's consciousness and gender roles. It is not only that women are the principal targets of rape, which by conservative definition happens to almost half of all women at least once in their lives. It is not only that over a third of all women are sexually molested by older trusted male family members or friends or authority figures as an early, perhaps initiatory, interpersonal sexual encounter. It is not only that at least the same percentage as adult women are battered in homes by male intimates. It is not only that about a fifth of American women have been or are known to be prostitutes, and most cannot get out of it. It is not only that 85 percent of working women will be sexually harassed on the job, many physically, at some point in their working lives.[53] All this documents the extent and terrain of abuse and the effectively unrestrained and systematic sexual aggression of one-half of the population against the other half. It suggests that it is basically allowed.

It does not by itself show that availability for this treatment defines the identity attributed to that other half of the population; or, that such treatment, all this torment and debasement, is socially considered not only rightful but enjoyable, and is in fact enjoyed by the dominant half; or, that the ability to engage in such behaviors defines the identity of that half. And not only of that half. Now consider the content of gender roles. All the social requirements for male sexual arousal and satisfaction are identical to the gender definition of "female." All the essentials of the male gender role are also the qualities sexualized as 'male' in male dominant sexuality. If gender is a social construct, and sexuality is a social construct, and the question is, of what is each constructed, the fact that their contents are identical—not to mention that the word 'sex' refers to both—might be more than a coincidence.

As to gender, what is sexual about pornography is what is unequal about social life. To say that pornography sexualizes gender and genders sexuality means that it provides a concrete social process through which gender and sexuality become functions of each other. Gender and sexuality, in this view, become two different shapes taken by the single social equation of male with dominance and female with submission. Being this as identity, acting it as role, inhabiting and presenting it as self, is the domain of gender. Enjoying it as the erotic, centering upon when it elicits genital arousal, is the domain of sexuality. Inequality is what is sexualized through pornography; it is what is sexual about it. The more unequal, the more sexual. The violence against women in pornography is an expression of gender hierarchy, the extremity of the hierarchy expressed and created through the extremity of the abuse, producing the extremity of the male sexual response. Pornography's multiple variations on and departures from the male dominant/female submissive sexual/gender theme are not exceptions to these gender regularities. They affirm them. The capacity of gender reversals (dominatrixes) and inversions (homosexuality) to stimulate sexual excitement is derived precisely from their mimicry or parody or negation or reversal of the standard arrangement. This affirms rather than undermines or qualifies the standard sexual arrangement as the standard sexual arrangement, the definition of sex, the standard from which all else is defined, that in which sexuality as such inheres.

Such formal data as exist on the relationship between pornography and male sexual arousal tend to substantiate this connection between gender hierarchy and male sexuality. 'Normal' men viewing pornography over time in laboratory settings become more aroused to scenes of rape than to scenes of explicit but not expressly violent sex, even if (especially if?) the woman is shown as hating it.[54] As sustained exposure perceptually inures subjects to the violent component in expressly violent sexual material, its sexual arousal value remains or increases. "On the first day, when they see women being raped and aggressed against, it bothers them. By day five, it does not bother them at all, in fact, they enjoy it."[55] Sexual material that is seen as nonviolent, by contrast, is less arousing to begin with, becomes even less arousing over time,[56] after which exposure to sexual violence is sexually arousing.[57] Viewing sexual material containing express aggression against women makes normal men more willing to aggress against women.[58] It also makes them see a woman rape victim as less human, more object-like, less worthy, less injured, and more to blame for the rape. Sexually explicit material that is not seen as expressly violent but presents women as hysterically responsive to male sexual demands, in which women are verbally abused, dominated and degraded, and treated as sexual things, makes men twice as likely to report willingness to sexually aggress against women than they were before exposure. So-called nonviolent materials like these make men see women as less than human, as good only for sex, as objects, as worthless and blameworthy when raped, and as really wanting to be raped and as unequal to men.[59] As to material showing violence only, it might be expected that rapists would be sexually aroused to scenes of violence against women, and they are.[60] But many normal male subjects, too, when seeing a woman being aggressed against by a man, perceive the interaction to be sexual even if no sex is shown.[61]

Male sexuality is apparently activated by violence against women and expresses itself in violence against women to a significant extent. If violence is seen as occupying the most fully achieved end of a dehumanization continuum on which objectification occupies the least express end, one question that is raised is whether some form of hierarchy—the dynamic of the continuum—is currently essential for male sexuality to experience itself. If so, and gender is understood to be a hierarchy, perhaps the sexes are unequal so that men can be sexually aroused. To put it another way, perhaps gender must be maintained as a social hierarchy so that men will be able to get erections; or, part of the male interest in keeping women down lies in the fact that it gets men up. Maybe feminists are considered castrating because equality is not sexy. Recent inquiries into rape support such suspicions. Men often rape women, it turns out, because they want to and enjoy it. The act, including the dominance, is sexually arousing, sexually affirming, and supportive of the perpetrator's masculinity. Many unreported rapists report an increase in self-esteem as a result of the rape.[62] Indications are that reported rapists perceive that getting caught accounts for most of the unpleasant effects of raping.[63] About a third of all men say they would rape a woman if they knew they wouldn't get caught.[64] That the low conviction rate[65] may give them confidence is supported by the prevalence rate.[66] Some convicted rapists see rape as an "exciting" form of interpersonal sex, a recreational activity or "adventure," or as a means of revenge or punishment on all women or some subgroup of women or an individual woman. Even some of those who did the act out of bad feelings make it clear that raping made them feel better. "Men rape because it is rewarding to do so."[67] If rapists experience rape as sex, does that mean there can be nothing wrong with it?

Once an act is labeled rape—indeed, this is much of the social function served by labeling acts rape—there is an epistemological problem with seeing it as sex.[68] Rape becomes something a rapist does, as if he is a separate species. But no personality disorder distinguishes most rapists from normal men.[69] Psychopaths do rape, but only about 5 percent of all known rapists are diagnosed psychopathic.[70] In spite of the number of victims, the normalcy of rapists, and the fact that most women are raped by men that they know (making it most unlikely that a few lunatics know around half of all women in the United States), rape remains considered psychopathological and therefore not about sexuality.

Add this to rape's pervasiveness and permissibility, together with the belief that it is both rare and impermissible. Combine this with the similarity between the patterns, rhythms, roles, and emotions, not to mention acts, which make up rape (and battery) on the one hand and intercourse on the other. All this makes it difficult to sustain the customary distinctions between pathology and normalcy, parophilia and nomophilia, violence and sex, in this area. Some researchers have previously noticed the centrality of force to the excitement value of pornography but have tended to put it down to perversion. Robert Stoller, for example, observes that pornography today depends upon hostility, voyeurism, and sadomasochism and calls perversion the erotic form of hatred.[71] If the perverse is seen as not the other side of a bright normal/abnormal line but as an undiluted expression of a norm which permeates many ordinary interactions, hatred—that is, misogyny—becomes a dimension of sexual excitement itself.

Compare victims' reports of rape with women's reports of sex. They look a lot alike.[72] Compare victims' reports of rape with what pornography says is sex. They look a lot alike.[73] In this light, the major distinction between intercourse (normal) and rape (abnormal) is that the normal happens so often that one cannot get anyone to see anything wrong with it. Which also means that anything sexual that happens often and one cannot get anyone to consider wrong is intercourse not rape, no matter what was done. The distinctions that purport to divide this territory look more like the ideological supports for normalizing the usual male use and abuse of women as "sexuality" through authoritatively pretending that whatever is exposed of it is deviant. This may have something to do with the conviction rate in rape cases (making all those unconvicted men into normal men, and all those acts into sex). It may have something to do with the fact that most convicted rapists, and many observers, find rape convictions incomprehensible.[74] And the fact that marital rape is considered by many to be a contradiction in terms. ("But if you can't rape your wife, who can you rape?")[75] And the fact that so many rape victims have trouble with sex afterward.[76]

What effect does the pervasive reality of sexual abuse of women by men have on what are deemed the more ordinary forms of sexual interaction? How do these material experiences create interest and point of view? Consider women. Recall that over a third of all girls experience sex, perhaps are sexually initiated, under conditions that even this society recognizes are forced or at least unequal.[77] Perhaps they learn this process of sexualized dominance as sex. Top-down relations feel sexual. Is sexuality throughout life then ever not on some level a reenactment of, a response to, that backdrop? Rape, adding more women to the list, can produce similar resonance. Sexually abused women—most women—seem to become either sexually disinclined or compulsively promiscuous or both in series, trying to avoid the painful events, and/or repeating them over and over almost addictively, in an attempt to reacquire a sense of control or to make them come out right. Too, women widely experience sexuality as a means to male approval; male approval translates into nearly all social goods. Violation can be sustained, even sought out, to this end. Sex can, then, be a means of trying to feel alive by redoing what has made one feel dead, of expressing a denigrated self-image seeking its own reflection in self-action in order to feel fulfilled, or of keeping up one's stock with the powerful.

Many women who have been sexually abused (like many survivors of concentration camps and ritual torture) report having distanced themselves as a conscious strategy for coping with the abuse. With women, this dissociation often becomes a part of their sexuality per se and of their experience of the world, especially their experience of men. Women widely report this sensation during sex. Not feeling pain, including during sex, may have a similar etiology. As one pornography model put it,

> O: I had quite a bit of difficulty as a child. I was suicidal for a time, because I never felt attached to my body. I just felt completely detached from my body; I felt like a completely separate entity from it. I still see my body as a tool, something to be used.
> DR: Give me an example of how today you sense not being attached to your body.
> O: I don't feel pain.
> DR: What do you mean, literally?
> O: I really don't feel pain. ...
> DR: When there is no camera and you are having sexual relations, are you still on camera?
> O: Yes. I'm on camera 24 hours a day. ...
> DR: Who are you?
> O: Who? Olympia Dancing-Doll: The Sweet with the Super-Supreme.
> DR: What the hell is that?
> O: That's the title of my act. ...
> DR: [Pointing to her.] This is a body. Is it your body?
> O: Yes.
> DR: Are you your body?
> O: No. I'm not my body, but it is my body.[78]

Women often begin alienating themselves from their body's self-preserving reactions under conditions under which they cannot stop the pain from being inflicted, and then find the deadening process difficult to reverse. Some then seek out escalating pain to feel sexual or to feel alive or to feel anything at all. One particularly devastating and confusing consequence of sexual abuse for women's sexuality—and a crisis for consciousness—occurs when one's body experiences abuse as pleasurable. Feeling loved and aroused and comforted during incest, or orgasm during rape, are examples. Because body is widely regarded as access to unmediated truth in this culture, women feel betrayed by their bodies and seek mental justifications (Freudian derepression theory provides an excellent one) for why their body's reactions are their own true reactions, and their values and consciousness (which interprets the event as a violation) is socially imposed. That is, they come to believe they really wanted the rape or the incest and interpret violation as their own sexuality.[79]

Interpreting women's responses to pornography, in which there is often a difference between so-called objective indices of arousal, like vaginal secretions, and self-reported arousal, raises similar issues. Repression is the typical explanation.[80] It seems at least as likely that women disidentify with their bodies' conditioned responses. Not to be overly behavioral, but does anyone think Pavlov's dogs were really hungry every time they salivated at the sound of the bell? If it is possible that hunger is inferred from salivation, perhaps humans experience[81] sexual arousal from pornographic cues and, since sexuality is social, that *is* sexual arousal. Identifying that as a conditioned response to a set of social cues, conditioned to what is for political reasons, is not the same as considering the response proof of sexual truth simply because it physically happens. Further, research shows that sexual fetishism can be experimentally induced readily in 'normal' subjects.[82] If this can be done with sexual responses that the society does not condone out front, why is it so unthinkable that the same process might occur with those sexual responses it does?

If the existing social model and reality of sexuality centers on male force, and if that sex is socially learned and ideologically considered positive and is rewarded, what is surprising is that not all women eroticize dominance, not all love pornography, and many resent rape. As Valerie Heller has said of her experience with incest and use in pornography, both as a child and as an adult, "I believed I existed only after I was turned on, like a light switch by another person. When I needed to be nurtured I thought I wanted to be used. ... Marks and bruises and being used was the way I measured my self worth. You must remember that I was taught that because men were fucking my body and using it for their needs it meant I was loved."[83] Given the pervasiveness of such experiences, the truly interesting question becomes why and how sexuality in women is ever other than masochistic.

All women live in sexual objectification like fish live in water. Given the statistical realities, all women live all the time under the shadow of the threat of sexual abuse. The question is, what can life as a woman mean, what can sex mean to targeted survivors in a rape culture? Given the statistical realities, much of women's sexual lives will occur under post-traumatic stress. Being surrounded by pornography—which is not only socially ubiquitous but often directly used as part of sex[84]—makes this a relatively constant condition. Women cope with objectification through trying to meet the male standard, and measure their self-worth by the degree to which they succeed. Women seem to cope with sexual abuse principally through denial or fear. On the denial side, immense energy goes into defending sexuality as just fine and getting better all the time, and into trying to make sexuality feel all right, like it is supposed to feel. Women who are compromised, cajoled, pressured, tricked, blackmailed, or outright forced into sex (or pornography) often respond to the unspeakable humiliation, coupled with the sense of having lost some irreplaceable integrity, by claiming that sexuality as their own. Faced with no alternatives, the strategy to acquire self-respect and pride is: I chose it.

Consider the conditions under which this is done. This is a culture in which women are socially expected—and themselves necessarily expect and want—to be able to distinguish the socially, epistemologically, indistinguishable. Rape and intercourse are not authoritatively separated by any difference between the physical acts or amount of force involved but only legally, by a standard that revolves around the man's interpretation of the encounter. Thus, although raped women, that is, most women, are supposed to be able to feel every day and every night that they have some meaningful determining part in having their sex life—their life, period—not be a series of rapes, the most they provide is the raw data for the man to see as he sees it. And he has been seeing pornography. Similarly, "consent" is supposed the crucial line between rape and intercourse, but the legal standard for it is so passive, so acquiescent, that a woman can be dead and have consented under it. The mind fuck of all of this makes the complicitous collapse into "I chose it" feel like a strategy for sanity. It certainly makes a woman at one with the world.

On the fear side, if a woman has ever been beaten in a relationship, even if "only once," what does that do to her everyday interactions, or her sexual interactions, with that man? With other men? Does her body ever really forget that behind his restraint he can do that any time she pushes an issue, or for no reason at all? Does her vigilance ever really relax? If she tried to do something about it, as many women do, and nothing was done, as it usually isn't, does she ever forget that that is what can be done to her at any time and nothing will be done about it? Does she smile at men less—or more? If she writes at all, does she imitate men less—or more? If a woman has been raped, ever, does a penis ever enter her without some body memory, if not a flashback then the effort of keeping it back; or does she hurry up or keep trying, feeling something gaining on her, trying to make it come out right? If a woman has ever been raped, does she ever fully regain the feeling of physical integrity, of self-respect, of having what she wants count somewhere, of being able to make herself clear to those who have not gone through what she has gone through, of living in a fair society, of equality?

Given the effects of learning sexuality through force or pressure or imposition; given the constant roulette of sexual violence; given the daily sexualization of every aspect of a woman's presence—for a woman to be sexualized means constant humiliation or threat of it, being both invisible as human being and always center stage as sex object, low pay, and being a target for assault or being assaulted. Given that this is the situation of all women, that one never knows for sure that one is not next on the list of victims until the moment one dies (and then, who knows?), it does not seem exaggerated to say that women are sexual, meaning that women exist, in a context of terror. Yet most professionals in the area of sexuality persist in studying the inexplicabilities of what is termed female sexuality acontextually, outside the context of gender inequality and its sexual violence, navel-gazing only slightly further down.[85]

The general theory of sexuality emerging from this feminist critique does not consider sexuality to be an inborn force inherent in individuals, nor cultural in the Freudian sense, in which sexuality exists always in a cultural context but in universally invariant stages and psychic representations. It appears instead to be culturally specific, even if so far largely invariant because male supremacy is largely universal, if always in specific forms. It does not vary by class, although class is one hierarchy it sexualizes. Sexuality becomes, in this view, social and relational, constructing and constructed of power. Infants, although sensory, cannot be said to possess sexuality in this sense because they have not had the experiences (and do not speak the language) that give it social meaning. Since sexuality is its social meaning, infant erections, for example, are clearly sexual in the sense that this society centers its sexuality on them, but to relate to a child as though his erections mean what adult erections have been conditioned to mean is a form of child abuse. Such erections have the meaning they acquire in social life only to observing adults.

When Freud changed his mind[86] and declared that women were not telling the truth about what had happened to them when they said they were abused as children, he attributed their accounts to "fantasy." This was regarded as a theoretical breakthrough. Under the aegis of Freud, it is often said that victims of sexual abuse imagine it, that it is fantasy, not real, and their sexuality caused it. The feminist theory of sexuality suggests that it is the doctors who, because of their sexuality, as constructed, imagine that sexual abuse is a fantasy when it is real—real both in the sense that the sex happened and in the sense that it was abuse. Pornography is also routinely defended as "fantasy," meaning not real. It is real: the sex that makes it is real and is often abuse, and the sex that it makes is sex and is often abuse. Both the psychoanalytic and the pornographic "fantasy" worlds are what men imagine women imagine and desire because they are what men, raised on pornography, imagine and desire about women. Thus is psychoanalysis used to legitimize pornography, calling it fantasy, and pornography used to legitimize psychoanalysis, to show what women really want. Psychoanalysis and pornography, seen as epistemic sites in the same ontology, are mirrors of each other, male supremacist sexuality looking at itself looking at itself.

Perhaps the Freudian process of theory-building occurred like this: men heard accounts of child abuse, felt aroused by the account, and attributed their arousal to the child who is now a woman. Perhaps men respond sexually when women give an account of sexual violation because sexual words constitute sexual reality, in the same way that men respond to pornography, which is (among other things) an account of the sexual violation of a woman. Seen in this way, much therapy as well as court testimony in sexual abuse cases are live oral pornography. Classical psychoanalysis attributes the connection between the experience of abuse (hers) and the experience of arousal (his) to the fantasy of the girl child. When he does it, he likes it, so when she did it, she must have liked it, or she must have thought it happened because she as much enjoys thinking about it happening to her as he enjoys thinking about it happening to her. Thus it cannot be abusive to her. Because he wants to do it, she must want it done.

Feminism also doubts the mechanism of repression in the sense that unconscious urges are considered repressed by social restrictions. Male sexuality is expressed and expressed and expressed, with a righteousness driven by the notion that something is trying to keep it from expressing itself. Too, there is a lot of doubt both about biology and about drives. Women are less repressed than oppressed, so-called women's sexuality largely a construct of male sexuality searching for someplace to happen, repression providing the reason for women's inhibition, meaning their unwillingness to make themselves available on demand. In this view, one function of the Freudian theory of repression (a function furthered rather than qualified by neo-Freudian adaptations) is ideologically to support the freeing of male sexual aggression while delegitimizing women's refusal to respond.

There may be a feminist unconscious, but it is not the Freudian one. Perhaps equality lives there. Its laws, rather than a priori, objective, or universal, might as well be a response to the historical regularities of sexual subordination, which under bourgeois ideological conditions require that the truth of male dominance be concealed in order to preserve the belief that women are sexually self-acting: that women want it. The feminist psychic universe certainly recognizes that people do not always know what they want, have hidden desires and inaccessible needs, lack awareness of motivation, have contorted and opaque interactions, and have an interest in obscuring what is really going on. But this does not essentially conceal that what women really want is more sex. It is true, as Freudians have persuasively observed, that many things are sexual that do not present themselves as such. But in ways Freud never dreamed.

At risk of further complicating the issues, perhaps it would help to think of women's sexuality as women's like black culture is blacks'—it is, and it is not. The parallel cannot be precise because, due to segregation, black culture developed under more autonomous conditions than women, intimately integrated with men by force, have had. Still, both can be experienced as a source of strength, joy, expression and as an affirmative badge of pride.[87] Both remain nonetheless stigmatic in the sense of a brand, a restriction, a definition as less. This is not because of any intrinsic content or value but because the social reality is that their shape, qualities, texture, imperative, and very existence are a response to powerlessness. They exist as they do because of lack of choice. They are created out of social conditions of oppression and exclusion. They may be part of a strategy for survival or even of change—but, as is, they are not the whole world, and it is the whole world that one is entitled to. This is why interpreting female sexuality as an expression of women's agency and autonomy is always denigrating and bizarre and reductive, as if sexism does not exist, just as it would be to interpret black culture as if racism did not exist. As if black culture just arose freely and spontaneously on the plantations and in the ghettos of North America, adding diversity to American pluralism.

So long as sexual inequality remains unequal and sexual, attempts to value sexuality as women's, possessive as if women possess it, will remain part of limiting women to it, to what women are now defined as being. Outside of truly rare and contrapuntal glimpses (which almost everyone thinks they live almost their entire sex life within), to seek an equal sexuality, to seek sexual equality, without political transformation is to seek equality under conditions of inequality. Rejecting this, and rejecting the glorification of settling for the best inequality has to offer or has stimulated the resourceful to invent, are what Ti-Grace Atkinson meant to reject when she said, "I do not know any feminist worthy of that name who, if forced to choose between freedom and sex, would choose sex. She'd choose freedom every time."[88]

Appendix

A few basic citations from the massive body of work on which this article draws are:

On rape: D. Russell and N. Howell, "The Prevalence of Rape in the United States Revisited," *Signs: Journal of Women in Culture and Society* 8 (1983): 668–95; D. Russell, *Rape in Marriage*

(New York: Macmillan, 1982); L. Clark and D. Lewis, *Rape: The Price of Coercive Sexuality* (Toronto: Canadian Women's Press, 1977); D. Russell, *The Politics of Rape* (New York: Stein & Day, 1975); A. Medea and K. Thompson, *Against Rape* (New York: Farrar, Straus & Giroux, 1974); S. Brownmiller, *Against Our Will: Men, Women and Rape* (New York: Simon & Schuster, 1975); I. Frieze, "Investigating the Causes and Consequences of Marital Rape," *Signs: Journal of Women in Culture and Society* 8 (1983): 532–53; N. Gager and C. Schurr, *Sexual Assault: Confronting Rape in America* (New York: Grosset & Dunlap, 1976); G. LaFree, "Male Power and Female Victimization: Towards a Theory of Interracial Rape," *American Journal of Sociology* 88 (1982): 311–28; M. Burt, "Cultural Myths and Supports for Rape," *Journal of Personality and Social Psychology* 38 (1980): 217–30; Kalamu ya Salaam, *Our Women Keep Our Skies from Falling* (New Orleans: Nkombo, 1980); J. Check and N. Malamuth, "An Empirical Assessment of Some Feminist Hypotheses about Rape," *International Journal of Women's Studies* 8 (1985): 414–23.

On battery: D. Martin, *Battered Wives* (San Francisco: Glide Productions, 1976); S. Steinmetz, *The Cycle of Violence: Assertive, Aggressive, and Abusive Family Interaction* (New York: Praeger, 1977); R. E. Dobash and R. Dobash, *Violence against Wives* (New York: Free Press, 1979); R. Langley and R. Levy, *Wife Beating: The Silent Crises* (New York: E. P. Dutton, 1977). E. Stark, A. Flitcraft, and W. Frazier, "Medicine and Patriarchal Violence: The Social Construction of the 'Private' Event," *International Journal of Health Services* 9 (1979): 461–93; L. Walker, *The Battered Woman* (New York: Harper & Row, 1979).

On sexual harassment: Merit Systems Protection Board, *Sexual Harassment in the Federal Workplace: Is It a Problem?* (Washington, D.C.: Government Printing Office, 1981); C. A. MacKinnon, *Sexual Harassment of Working Women* (New Haven, Conn.: Yale University Press, 1979); D. Benson and G. Thomson, "Sexual Harassment on a University Campus: The Confluence of Authority Relations, Sexual Interest and Gender Stratification," *Social Problems* 28 (1981): 263–51; P. Crocker and A. Simon, "Sexual Harassment in Education," *Capital University Law Review* 10 (1981): 541–84.

On incest and child sexual abuse: D. Finkelhor, *Sexually Victimized Children* (New York: Free Press, 1979); J. Herman, *Father-Daughter Incest* (Cambridge, Mass.: Harvard University Press, 1981); D. Finkelhor, *Child Sexual Abuse: Theory and Research* (New York: Free Press, 1984); A. Jaffe, L. Dynneson, and R. TenBensel, "Sexual Abuse: An Epidemiological Study," *American Journal of Diseases of Children* 129 (1975): 689–92; K. Brady, *Father's Days: A True Story of Incest* (New York: Seaview Books, 1979); L. Armstrong, *Kiss Daddy Goodnight* (New York: Hawthorn Press, 1978); S. Butler, *Conspiracy of Silence: The Trauma of Incest* (San Francisco: New Glide Publications, 1978); A. Burgess, N. Groth, L. Homstrom, and S. Sgroi, *Sexual Assault of Children and Adolescents* (Lexington, Mass.: Lexington Books, 1978); F. Rush, *The Best-kept Secret: Sexual Abuse of Children* (Englewood Cliffs, N.J.: Prentice-Hall, 1980); D. Russell, "The Prevalence and Seriousness of Incestuous Abuse: Stepfathers v. Biological Fathers," *Child Abuse and Neglect: The International Journal* 8 (1984): 15–22, "The Incidence and Prevalence of Intrafamilial and Extrafamilial Sexual Abuse of Female Children," *Child Abuse and Neglect: The International Journal* 7 (1983): 133–46, and *The Secret Trauma: Incest in the Lives of Women and Girls* (New York: Basic Books, 1986).

On prostitution: K. Barry, *Female Sexual Slavery* (Englewood Cliffs, N.J.: Prentice-Hall, 1979); J. James and J. Meyerding, "Early Sexual Experience as a Factor in Prostitution," *Archives of Sexual Behavior* 7 (1977): 31–42; United Nations Economic and Social Council, Commission on Human Rights, Sub-Commission on Prevention of Discrimination and Protection of Minorities, Working Group on Slavery, *Suppression of the Traffic in Persons and of the Exploitation of the Prostitution of Others* E/Cn.4/AC.2/5 (New York: United Nations, June 16, 1976); J. James, *The Politics of Prostitution* (Social Research Association, 1975); K. Millett et al., *The Prostitution Papers* (New York: Avon Books, 1973).

On pornography: L. Lederer, ed., *Take Back the Night: Women on Pornography* (New York: William Morrow, 1980); A. Dworkin, *Pornography: Men Possessing Women* (New York: Perigee, 1981); L. Lovelace and M. McGrady, *Ordeal* (New York: Berkeley Books, 1980); P. Bogdanovich, *The Killing of the Unicorn: Dorothy Stratten, 1960–1980* (New York: William Morrow, 1984); M.

Langelan, "The Political Economy of Pornography," *Aegis: Magazine on Ending Violence against Women* 32 (1981): 5–7; D. Leidholdt, "Pornography Meets Fascism," *WIN*, March 15, 1983, 18–22; E. Donnerstein, "Erotica and Human Aggression," in *Aggression: Theoretical and Empirical Reviews*, ed. R. Green and E. Donnerstein (New York: Academic Press, 1983), and "Pornography: Its Effects on Violence Against Women," in *Pornography and Sexual Aggression*, ed. N. Malamuth and E. Donnerstein (New York: Academic Press, 1985); Geraldine Finn, "Against Sexual Imagery, Alternative or Otherwise," Symposium on Images of Sexuality in Art and Media, Ottawa, Canada (March 13–16, 1985); Diana E. H. Russell, "Pornography and Rape: A Causal Model," *Political Psychology* 9 (1988): 41–73; *Report of the Attorney General's Commission on Pornography* (Washington, D.C.: Government Printing Office, 1986).

   See generally: D. Russell, *Sexual Exploitation* (New York: Russell Sage, 1984); D. Russell and N. Van de Ven, *Crimes against Women: Proceedings of the International Tribunal* (Les Femmes, 1976); E. Morgan, *The Erotization of Male Dominance/Female Submission* (Pittsburgh: Know, Inc., 1975); A. Rich, "Compulsory Heterosexuality and Lesbian Existence," *Signs: Journal of Women in Culture and Society* 5 (1980): 631–60; J. Long Laws and P. Schwartz, *Sexual Scripts: The Social Construction of Female Sexuality* (Hinsdale, Ill.: Dryden Press, 1976); L. Phelps, "Female Sexual Alienation," in *Women: A Feminist Perspective*, ed. J. Freeman (Palo Alto, Calif.: Mayfield, 1979); S. Hite, *The Hite Report: A Nationwide Survey of Female Sexuality* (New York: Macmillan, 1976); Andrea Dworkin, *Intercourse* (New York: Free Press, 1987). Recent comparative work provides confirmation and contrasts: Pat Caplan, ed., *The Cultural Construction of Sexuality* (New York: Tavistock, 1987); Marjorie Shostak, *Nisa: The Life and Words of a !Kung Woman* (New York: Vintage Books, 1983).

Notes

   Prior versions of these views are published in J. Geer and W. O'Donohue, *Theories of Human Sexuality* (New York: Plenum Press, 1987) and as preface to J. Masson's *A Dark Science: Women, Sexuality, and Psychiatry in the Nineteenth Century* (New York: Farrar, Straus & Giroux, 1986). This article is a chapter from *Toward a Feminist Theory of the State*, to be published by Harvard University Press in 1989. The quotation in the title is from a note by Judith Friedlander in *Diary*, a preconference publication of the Barnard Conference on Sexuality, 1982, p. 25. Sources for the epigraphs are as follows: Adrienne Rich, "Dialogue," in *Poems: Selected and New, 1950–1974* (New York: Norton, 1975), p. 195. Milan Kundera, *The Book of Laughter and Forgetting* (New York: Knopf, 1980), p. 75; Virginia Woolf, "Professions for Women," in her *The Death of the Moth and Other Essays* (1942; reprint, New York: Harcourt, Brace, Jovanovich, 1974), pp. 240–41.

   1. See Jane Caputi, *The Age of Sex Crime* (Bowling Green, Ohio: Bowling Green State University Popular Press, 1987); Deborah Cameron and Elizabeth Frazer, *The Lust to Kill: A Feminist Investigation of Sexual Murder* (New York: New York University Press, 1987).

   2. Freud's decision to disbelieve women's accounts of being sexually abused as children was apparently central in the construction of the theories of fantasy and possibly also of the unconscious. That is, his belief that the sexual abuse his patients told him about did not actually occur created the need for a theory like fantasy, like unconscious, to explain the reports (see Rush [Appendix]; J. Moussaieff Masson, *The Assault on Truth: Freud's Suppression of the Seduction Theory* [New York: Farrar, Straus & Giroux, 1983]). One can only speculate on the course of the modern psyche (not to mention modern history) had the women been believed.

   3. E. Schur, *Labeling Women Deviant: Gender, Stigma and Social Control* (New York: Random House, 1983) (a superb review urging a "continuum" rather than a "deviance" approach to issues of sex inequality).

   4. Diana Russell produced this figure at my request from the random sample data base of 930 San Francisco households discussed in her *The Secret Trauma: Incest in the Lives of Girls and Women*, pp. 20–37 [Appendix], and *Rape in Marriage*, pp. 27–41 [Appendix]. The figure

includes all the forms of rape or other sexual abuse or harassment surveyed, noncontact as well as contact, from gang rape by strangers and marital rape to obscene phone calls, unwanted sexual advances on the street, unwelcome requests to pose for pornography, and subjection to peeping toms and sexual exhibitionists (flashers).

5. S. D. Smithyman, "The Undetected Rapist" (Ph.D. diss., Claremont Graduate School, 1978); N. Groth, *Men Who Rape: The Psychology of the Offender* (New York: St. Martin's, 1982); D. Scully and J. Marolla, "'Riding the Bull at Gilley's': Convicted Rapists Describe the Rewards of Rape," *Social Problems* 32 (1985): 251. (The manuscript version of this paper was subtitled "Convicted Rapists Describe the Pleasure of Raping.")

6. K. Millett, *Sexual Politics* (New York: Doubleday, 1970).

7. J. Lacan, *Feminine Sexuality*, trans. J. Rose (New York: Norton, 1982); M. Foucault, *The History of Sexuality*, vol. 1, *An Introduction* (New York: Random House, 1980), and *Power/Knowledge*, ed. C. Gordon (New York: Pantheon, 1980).

8. See generally (including materials reviewed in) R. Padgug, "Sexual Matters: On Conceptualizing Sexuality in History," *Radical History Review* 70 (1979): 9; M. Vicinus, "Sexuality and Power: A Review of Current Work in the History of Sexuality," *Feminist Studies* 8 (1982): 133–55; S. Ortner and H. Whitehead, *Sexual Meanings: The Cultural Construction of Gender and Sexuality* (Cambridge: Cambridge University Press, 1981); Red Collective, *The Politics of Sexuality in Capitalism* (London: Black Rose Press, 1978); J. Weeks, *Sex, Politics and Society: The Regulation of Sexuality since 1800* (New York: Longman, 1981); J. D'Emilio, *Sexual Politics, Sexual Communities: The Making of a Homosexual Minority in the United States, 1940–1970* (Chicago: University of Chicago Press, 1983); A. Snitow, C. Stansell, and S. Thompson, introduction to *Powers of Desire: The Politics of Sexuality*, ed. A. Snitow, C. Stansell, and S. Thompson (New York: Monthly Review Press, 1983); E. Dubois and L. Gordon, "Seeking Ecstasy on the Battlefield: Danger and Pleasure in Nineteenth-Century Feminist Social Thought," *Feminist Studies* 9 (1983): 7–25.

9. An example is Jeffrey Weeks, *Sexuality and Its Discontents* (London: Routledge & Kegan Paul, 1985).

10. Luce Irigaray's critique of Freud in *Speculum de l'autre femme* (Paris: Minuit, 1974) acutely shows how Freud constructs sexuality from the male point of view, with woman as deviation from the norm. But she, too, sees female sexuality not as constructed by male dominance but only repressed under it.

11. For those who think that such notions are atavisms left behind by modern behaviorists, see one entirely typical conceptualization of "sexual pleasure, a powerful unconditioned stimulus and reinforcer" in N. Malamuth and B. Spinner." A Longitudinal Content Analysis of Sexual Violence in the Best-Selling Erotic Magazines," *Journal of Sex Research* 16 (1980): 5. See also B. Ollman's discussion of Wilhelm Reich in *Social and Sexual Revolution* (Boston: South End Press, 1979), pp. 186–87.

12. The contributions and limitations of Foucault in such an analysis are discussed illuminatingly in Frigga Haug, ed., *Female Sexualization*, trans. Erica Carter (London: Verso, 1987), pp. 190–98.

13. A. Kinsey, W. Pomeroy, C. Martin, and P. Gebhard, *Sexual Behaviour in the Human Female* (Philadelphia: W. B. Saunders, 1953); A. Kinsey, W. Pomeroy, and C. Martin, *Sexual Behaviour in the Human Male* (Philadelphia: W. B. Saunders, 1948). See the critique of Kinsey in Dworkin, *Pornography* (see Appendix), pp. 179–98.

14. Examples include: D. English, "The Politics of Porn: Can Feminists Walk the Line?" *Mother Jones* (1980), pp. 20–23, 43–44, 48–50; D. English, A. Hollibaugh, and G. Rubin, "Talking Sex: A Conversation on Sexuality and Feminism," *Socialist Review*, vol. 11 (1981); J. B. Elshtain, "The Victim Syndrome: A Troubling Turn in Feminism," *Progressive* (1982), pp. 40–47; Ellen Willis, "Feminism, Moralism, and Pornography," *Village Voice* (1979). This approach also tends to characterize the basic ideology of "Human Sexuality Courses" as analyzed by C. Vance in Snitow, Stansell, and Thompson, eds., pp. 371–84. The view of sex so promulgated is distilled in the following quotation and taught to doctors through *Materials from Courses on*

Human Sexuality. After an alliterative list, perhaps intended to be humorous, headed "determinants of sexuality" (on which "power" does not appear, although every other word begins
with "p") appears: "Persistent puritanical pressures promoting propriety, purity, and prudery
are opposed by a powerful, primeval, procreative passion to plunge his pecker into her pussy"
(College of Medicine and Dentistry of New Jersey, Rutgers Medical School, January 29–February 2, 1979, p. 39).

15. A third reason is also given: "To the extent that sexism in societal and family structure is
responsible for the phenomena of 'compulsive masculinity' and structured antagonism between the sexes, the elimination of sexual inequality would reduce the number of 'power trip'
and 'degradation ceremony' motivated rapes" (M. Straus, "Sexual Inequality, Cultural Norms,
and Wife-beating," *Victimology: An International Journal* I [1976]: 54–76). Note that these
structural factors seem to be considered nonsexual, in the sense that "power trip" and "degradation ceremony" motivated rapes are treated as not erotic to the perpetrators *because* of the
elements of dominance and degradation, nor is "structured antagonism" seen as an erotic element of rape or sex (or family).

16. P. R. Sanday, "The Socio-cultural Context of Rape: A Cross-cultural Study," *Journal of
Social Issues* 37 (1981): 16. See also M. Lewin, "Unwanted Intercourse: The Difficulty of Saying
'No,'" *Psychology of Women Quarterly* 9 (1985): 184–92.

17. See Catharine A. MacKinnon, *Toward a Feminist Theory of the State* (Cambridge, Mass.:
Harvard University Press, 1989), chap. 9 for discussion.

18. Brownmiller, *Against Our Will* (see Appendix), originated this approach, which has
since become ubiquitous.

19. Annie McCombs helped me express this thought (letter to *off our backs* [1984], p. 34).

20. Brownmiller did analyze rape as something men do to women, hence as a problem of
gender, even if her concept of gender is biologically based (see, e.g., her pp. 4, 6, and discussion in chap. 3). An exception is Clark and Lewis (see Appendix).

21. Snitow, Stansell, and Thompson (n. 8 above), p. 9.

22. C. Vance, "Concept Paper: Toward a Politics of Sexuality," in H. Alderfer, B. Jaker, and
M. Nelson, eds., *Diary of a Conference on Sexuality,* record of the planning committee of the
Conference, the Scholar and the Feminist IX: Toward a Politics of Sexuality, April 24 1982, p.
27: to address "women's sexual pleasure, choice, and autonomy, acknowledging that sexuality
is simultaneously a domain of restriction, repression and danger as well as a domain of exploration, pleasure and agency." Parts of the *Diary,* with the conference papers, were later published. C. Vance, ed., *Pleasure and Danger: Exploring Female Sexuality* (London: Routledge &
Kegan Paul, 1984).

23. Vance, "Concept Paper," p. 38.

24. For examples, see A. Hollibaugh and C. Moraga, "What We're Rolling around in Bed
with: Sexual Silences in Feminism," in Snitow, Stansell, and Thompson, eds., pp. 394–405, esp.
398; Samois, *Coming to Power* (Berkeley, Calif.: Samois, 1983).

25. A. Dworkin, "Why So-called Radical Men Love and Need Pornography," in Lederer, ed.
(see Appendix), p. 48.

26. S. Sonta, "Fascinating Fascism," in her *Under the Sign of Saturn* (New York: Farrar,
Straus & Giroux, 1975), p. 103.

27. R. Stoller, *Sexual Excitement: Dynamics of Erotic Life* (New York: Pantheon, 1979), p. 6.

28. Harriet Jacobs, quoted by Rennie Simson, "The Afro-American Female: The Historical
Context of the Construction of Sexual Identity," in Snitow, Stansell, and Thompson, eds., p.
231. Jacobs subsequently resisted by hiding in an attic cubbyhole "almost deprived of light and
air, and with no space to move my limbs, for nearly seven years" to avoid him.

29. A similar rejection of indeterminacy can be found in Linda Alcoff, "Cultural Feminism
versus Post-Structuralism: The Identity Crisis in Feminist Theory," *Signs: Journal of Women in
Culture and Society* 13 (1988): 419–20. The article otherwise misdiagnoses the division in feminism as that between so-called cultural feminists and post-structuralism, when the division is
between those who take sexual misogyny seriously as a mainspring to gender hierarchy and

those who wish, liberal-fashion, to affirm "differences" without seeing that sameness/difference is a dichotomy of exactly the sort post-structuralism purports to deconstruct.

30. See Sandra Harding, "Introduction: Is There a Feminist Methodology?" in *Feminism and Methodology*, ed. Sandra Harding (Bloomington: Indiana University Press, 1987).

31. One of the most compelling accounts of active victim behavior is provided in *Give Sorrow Words: Maryse Holder's Letters from Mexico* (New York: Grove Press, 1979). Holder wrote a woman friend of her daily frantic, and always failing pursuit of men, sex, beauty, and feeling good about herself. "Fuck fucking, will *feel* self-respect" (p. 89). She was murdered soon after by an unknown assailant.

32. This phrase comes from M. Foucault, "The West and the Truth of Sex," *Sub-stance* (1978), p. 20. The ironic meaning given to it here is mine.

33. Dworkin, *Pornography* (see Appendix), p. 24.

34. J. Cook, "The X-rated Economy," *Forbes* (1978), p. 18; Langelan (see Appendix), p. 5; *Public Hearings on Ordinances to Add Pornography as Discrimination against Women*, Minneapolis, Minnesota: December 12, and 13, 1983 (hereafter cited as *Public Hearings*); F. Schauer, "Response: Pornography and the First Amendment," *University of Pittsburgh Law Review* 40 (1979): 616.

35. John Money, professor of Medical Psychology and Pediatrics, Johns Hopkins Medical Institutes, letter to Clive M. Davis, April 18, 1984. The same view is expressed by Al Goldstein, editor of *Screw*, a pornographic newspaper, concerning anti-pornography feminists, termed "nattering nabobs of sexual negativism": "We must repeat to ourselves like a mantra: sex is good; nakedness is a joy; an erection is beautiful. ... Don't let the bastards get you limp" ("Dear Playboy," *Playboy* [1985], p. 12).

36. A. Dworkin, "The Root Cause," in *Our Blood: Prophesies and Discourses on Sexual Politics* (New York: Harper & Row, 1976), pp. 96–111.

37. See MacKinnon, *Toward a Feminist Theory of the State* (n. 17 above), chap. 12 for further discussion.

38. Dworkin, *Pornography* (Appendix), p. 69.

39. Ibid., p. 136.

40. Ibid., p. 69. "In practice, fucking is an act of possession—simultaneously an act of ownership, taking, force; it is conquering; it expresses in intimacy power over and against, body to body, person to thing. 'The sex act' means penile intromission followed by penile thrusting, or fucking. The woman is acted on, the man acts and through action expresses sexual power, the power of masculinity. Fucking requires that the male act on one who has less power and this valuation is so deep, so completely implicit in the act, that the one who is fucked is stigmatized as feminine during the act even when not anatomically female. In the male system, sex is the penis, the penis is sexual power, its use in fucking is manhood" (p. 23).

41. Ibid., chap. 2, "Men and Boys."

42. Ibid., p. 109.

43. Ibid., pp. 113–28.

44. Ibid., p. 174.

45. Freud believed that the female nature was inherently masochistic (S. Freud, "The Psychology of Women," in his *New Introductory Lectures on Psychoanalysis* [London: Hogarth Press, 1933], chap. 23). Helene Deutsch, Marie Bonaparte, Sandor Rado, Adolf Grunberger, Melanie Klein, Helle Thorning, Georges Bataille, Theodore Reik, Jean-Paul Sartre, and Simone de Beauvoir all described some version of female masochism in their work, each with a different theoretical account for virtually identical observations. H. Deutsch, "The Significance of Masochism in the Mental Life of Women," *International Journal of Psychoanalysis* 11 (1930): 48–60; *Psychology of Women* (New York: Grune & Stratton, 1944), vol. 1. Several are summarized by Janine Chasseguet-Smirgel, ed., in her introduction to *Female Sexuality: New Psychoanalytic Views* (London: Virago, 1981); Theodore Reik, *Masochism in Sex and Society* (New York: Grove Press, 1962), p. 217; Helle Thorning, "The Mother-Daughter Relationship and Sexual Ambivalence," *Heresies* 12 (1979): 3–6; Georges Bataille, *Death and Sensuality* (New

York: Walker & Co., 1962); Jean-Paul Sartre, *Being and Nothingness: An Essay on Phenomenological Ontology,* trans. Hazel E. Barnes (New York: Philosophical Library, 1956), pt. 3, chap. 3, "Concrete Relations with Others," pp. 361–430. Betsy Belote states, "Masochistic and hysterical behavior is so similar to the concept of 'femininity' that the three are not clearly distinguishable" ("Masochistic Syndrome, Hysterical Personality, and the Illusion of the Healthy Woman," in *Female Psychology: The Emerging Self,* ed. Sue Cox [Chicago: Science Research Associates, 1976], p. 347). I was directed to these sources by Sandra Lee Bartky's valuable examination, "Feminine Masochism and the Politics of Personal Transformation," *Women's Studies International Forum* 7 (1984): 327–28. Andrea Dworkin writes: "I believe that freedom for women must begin in the repudiation of our own masochism. … I believe that ridding ourselves of our own deeply entrenched masochism, which takes so many tortured forms, is the first priority; it is the first deadly blow that we can strike against systematized male dominance" (*Our Blood* [n. 36 above], p. 111).

46. Dworkin, *Pornography* (Appendix), p. 146.

47. A. Koedt, "The Myth of the Vaginal Orgasm," *Notes from the Second Year: Women's Liberation,* vol. 2 (1970): Ti-Grace Atkinson, *Amazon Odyssey* (New York: Link Books, 1974); Phelps (see Appendix).

48. Dworkin, *Pornography* (Appendix), p. 22.

49. This is the plot of *Deep Throat,* the pornographic film Linda "Lovelace" was forced to make. It is reportedly the largest grossing film in the history of the world. That this plot is apparently so widely enjoyed suggests that something extant in the male psyche is appealed to by it.

50. Dworkin, "The Root Cause," p. 56.

51. A prominent if dated example is Jill Johnston, *Lesbian Nation* (New York: Simon & Schuster, 1974).

52. This and the rest of the quotations in this paragraph are from P. Califia, "A Secret Side of Lesbian Sexuality," *Advocate* (December 27, 1979), pp. 19–21, 27–28.

53. The statistics in this paragraph are drawn from the sources referenced in the Appendix, as categorized by topic. Kathleen Barry (see Appendix) defines "female sexual slavery" as a condition of prostitution that one cannot get out of.

54. E. Donnerstein, testimony, *Public Hearings* (see n. 34 above), pp. 35–36. The relationship between consenting and nonconsenting depictions and sexual arousal among men with varying self-reported propensities to rape are examined in the following studies: N. Malamuth, "Rape Fantasies as a Function of Exposure to Violent-Sexual Stimuli," *Archives of Sexual Behavior* 6 (1977): 33–47; N. Malamuth and J. Check, "Penile Tumescence and Perceptual Responses to Rape as a Function of Victim's Perceived Reactions," *Journal of Applied Social Psychology* 10 (1980): 528–47; N. Malamuth, M. Heim, and S. Feshbach, "The Sexual Responsiveness of College Students to Rape Depictions: Inhibitory and Disinhibitory Effects," *Journal of Personality and Social Psychology* 38 (1980): 399–408; N. Malamuth and J. Check, "Sexual Arousal to Rape and Consenting Depictions: The Importance of the Woman's Arousal," *Journal of Abnormal Psychology* 39 (1980): 763–66; N. Malamuth, "Rape Proclivity among Males," *Journal of Social Issues* 37 (1981): 138–57; E. Donnerstein and L. Berkowitz, "Victim Reactions in Aggressive Erotic Films as a Factor in Violence against Women," *Journal of Personality and Social Psychology* 41 (1981): 710–24; J. Check and T. Guloien, "Reported Proclivity for Coercive Sex Following Repeated Exposure to Sexually Violent Pornography, Nonviolent Dehumanizing Pornography, and Erotica," in *Pornography: Recent Research, Interpretations, and Policy Considerations,* ed. D. Zillman and J. Bryant (Hillsdale, N.J.: Erlbaum, in press).

55. Donnerstein, testimony, *Public Hearings,* p. 36.

56. The soporific effects of explicit sex depicted without express violence are apparent in the *Report of the President's Commission on Obscenity and Pornography* (Washington, D.C.: Government Printing Office, 1971).

57. Donnerstein, testimony, *Public Hearings,* p. 36.

58. Donnerstein and Berkowitz (see n. 54 above): E. Donnerstein, "Pornography: Its Effect on Violence against Women," in Malamuth and Donnerstein, eds. (Appendix). This conclusion is the cumulative result of years of experimental research showing that "if you can measure sexual arousal to sexual images and measure people's attitudes about rape you can predict aggressive behavior with women" (Donnerstein, testimony, *Public Hearings*, p. 29). Some of the more prominent supporting experimental work, in addition to citations previously referenced here, include E. Donnerstein and J. Hallam, "The Facilitating Effects of Erotica on Aggression toward Females," *Journal of Personality and Social Psychology* 36 (1978): 1270–77; R. G. Green, D. Stonner, and G. L. Shope, "The Facilitation of Aggression by Aggression: Evidence against the Catharsis Hypothesis," *Journal of Personality and Social Psychology* 31 (1975): 721–26; D. Zillman, J. Hoyt, and K. Day, "Strength and Duration of the Effects of Aggressive, Violent, and Erotic Communications on Subsequent Aggressive Behavior," *Communications Research* 1 (1974): 286–306; B. Sapolsky and D. Zillman, "The Effect of Soft-core and Hard-core Erotica on Provoked and Unprovoked Hostile Behavior," *Journal of Sex Research* 17 (1981): 319–43; D. L. Mosher, "Pornographic Films, Male Verbal Aggression against Women, and Guilt," in *Technical Report of the Commission on Obscenity and Pornography* (Washington, D.C.: Government Printing Office, 1971), vol. 8. See also E. Summers and J. Check, "An Empirical Investigation of the Role of Pornography in the Verbal and Physical Abuse of Women," *Violence and Victims* 2 (1987): 189–209; and P. Harmon, "The Role of Pornography in Women Abuse" (Ph.D. diss., York University, 1987). These experiments establish that the relationship between expressly violent sexual material and subsequent aggression against women is causal, not correlational.

59. Key research is summarized and reported in Check and Galoien (see n. 54 above); see also D. Zillman, "Effects of Repeated Exposure to Nonviolent Pornography," presented to U.S. Attorney General's Commission on Pornography, Houston, Texas (June 1986). Donnerstein's most recent experiments, as reported in *Public Hearings* and his book edited with Malamuth (see Appendix), clarify, culminate, and extend years of experimental research by many. See, e.g., D. Mosher, "Sex Callousness toward Women," in *Technical Report of the Commission on Obscenity and Pornography*, vol. 8; N. Malamuth and J. Check, "The Effects of Mass Media Exposure on Acceptance of Violence against Women: A Field Experiment," *Journal of Research in Personality* 15 (1981): 436–46. The studies are tending to confirm women's reports and feminist analyses of the consequences of exposure to pornography on attitudes and behaviors toward women. See J. Check and N. Malamuth (Appendix).

60. G. G. Abel, D. H. Barlow, E. Blanchard, and D. Guild, "The Components of Rapists' Sexual Arousal," *Archives of General Psychiatry* 34 (1977): 395–403; G. G. Abel, J. V. Becker, and L. J. Skinner, "Aggressive Behavior and Sex," *Psychiatric Clinics of North America* 3 (1980): 133–55; G. G. Abel, E. B. Blanchard, J. V. Becker, and A. Djenderedjian, "Differentiating Sexual Aggressiveness with Penile Measures," *Criminal Justice and Behavior* 2 (1978): 315–32.

61. Donnerstein, testimony, *Public Hearings*, p. 31.

62. Smithyman (n. 5 above).

63. Scully and Marolla (n. 5 above).

64. In addition to previous citations to Malamuth, "Rape Proclivity among Males" (see n. 54 above); and Malamuth and Check, "Sexual Arousal to Rape and Consenting Depictions" (see n. 54 above); see T. Tieger, "Self-Reported Likelihood of Raping and the Social Perception of Rape," *Journal of Research in Personality* 15 (1981): 147–58; and N. Malamuth, S. Haber, and S. Feshbach, "Testing Hypotheses Regarding Rape: Exposure to Sexual Violence, Sex Differences, and the 'Normality' of Rape," *Journal of Research in Personality* 14 (1980): 121–37.

65. M. Burt and R. Albin, "Rape Myths, Rape Definitions and Probability of Conviction," *Journal of Applied Social Psychology*, vol. 11 (1981); G. D. LaFree, "The Effect of Sexual Stratification by Race on Official Reactions to Rape," *American Sociological Review* 4–5 (1984): 842–54, esp. 850; J. Galvin and K. Polk, "Attribution in Case Processing: Is Rape Unique?" *Journal of Research in Crime and Delinquency* 20 (1983): 126–54. The latter work seems not to understand that rape can be institutionally treated in a way that is sex-specific even if comparable statistics are generated by crimes against the other sex. Further, this study assumes that 53 percent of

rapes are reported, when the real figure is closer to 10 percent (Russell, *Sexual Exploitation* [see Appendix]).

66. Russell, "The Prevalence and Incidence of Forcible Rape and Attempted Rape of Females" (see Appendix), pp. 1–4.

67. Scully and Marolla, p. 2.

68. Sometimes this is a grudging realism: "Once there is a conviction, the matter cannot be trivial even though the act may have been" (P. Gebhard, J. Gagnon, W. Pomeroy, and C. Christenson, *Sex Offenders: An Analysis of Types* [New York: Harper & Row, 1965], p. 178). It is telling that if an act that has been adjudicated rape is still argued to be sex, that is thought to exonerate the rape rather than indict the sex.

69. R. Rada, *Clinical Aspects of Rape* (New York: Grune & Stratton, 1978); C. Kirkpatrick and E. Kanin, "Male Sex Aggression on a University Campus," *American Sociological Review* 22 (1957): 52–58; see also Malamuth, Haber, and Feshbach.

70. Abel, Becker, and Skinner (n. 60 above), pp. 133–51.

71. Robert Stoller, *Perversion: The Erotic Form of Hatred* (New York: Pantheon, 1975), p. 87.

72. Compare, e.g., Hite (see Appendix) with Russell, *The Politics of Rape* (see Appendix).

73. This is truly obvious from looking at the pornography. A fair amount of pornography actually calls the acts it celebrates "rape." Too, "In depictions of sexual behavior [in pornography] there is typically evidence of a difference of power between the participants" (L. Baron and M. A. Straus, "Conceptual and Ethical Problems in Research on Pornography" [paper presented at the annual meeting of the Society for the Study of Social Problems, 1983], p. 6). Given that this characterizes the reality, consider the content attributed to "sex itself" in the following methodologically liberal quotations on the subject: "Only if one thinks of *sex itself* as a degrading act can one believe that all pornography degrades and harms women" (P. Califia, "Among Us, against Us—the New Puritans," *Advocate* [April 17, 1980], p. 14 [emphasis added]). Given the realization that violence against women *is* sexual, consider the content of the "sexual" in the following criticism: "The only form in which a politics opposed to violence against women is being expressed is anti-sexual" (English, Hollibaugh, and Rubin [n. 14 above], p. 51). And "the feminist anti-pornography movement has become deeply erotophobic and anti-sexual" (A. Hollibaugh, "The Erotophobic Voice of Women," *New York Native* [1983], p. 34).

74. J. Wolfe and V. Baker, "Characteristics of Imprisoned Rapists and Circumstances of the Rape," in *Rape and Sexual Assault,* ed. C. G. Warner (Germantown, Md.: Aspen Systems Co., 1980).

75. This statement was widely attributed to California State Senator Bob Wilson; see Joanne Schulman, "The Material Rape Exemption in the Criminal Law," *Clearinghouse Review,* vol. 14 [1980]) on the Rideout marital rape case. He has equally widely denied that the comment was seriously intended. I consider it by now apocryphal as well as stunningly revelatory, whether or not humorously intended, on the topic of the indistinguishability of rape from intercourse from the male point of view.

76. Carolyn Craven, "No More Victims: Carolyn Craven Talks about Rape, and What Women and Men Can Do to Stop It," ed. Alison Wells (Berkeley, Calif., 1978, mimeographed) p. 2; Russell, *The Politics of Rape* (see Appendix), pp. 84–85, 105, 114, 135, 147, 185, 196, and 205; P. Bart, "Rape Doesn't End with a Kiss," *Viva* 11 (1975): 39–41 and 100–101; J. Becker, L. Skinner, G. Abel, R. Axelrod, and J. Cichon, "Sexual Problems of Sexual Assault Survivors," *Women and Health* 9 (1984): 5–20.

77. See sources on incest and child sexual abuse, Appendix.

78. Olympia, a woman who poses for soft-core pornography, interviewed by Robert Stoller, "Centerfold: An Essay on Excitement," *Archives of General Psychiatry* (1979).

79. It is interesting that, in spite of everything, many women who once thought of their abuse as self-actualizing come to rethink it as a violation, while very few who have ever thought of their abuse as a violation come to rethink it as self-actualizing.

80. See G. Schmidt and V. Sigusch, "Psychosexual Stimulation by Film and Slides: A Further Report on Sex Differences," *Journal of Sex Research* 6 (1970): 268–83; G. Schmidt, "Male-Female Differences in Sexual Arousal and Behavior during and after Exposure to Sexually Explicit Stimuli," *Archives of Sexual Behavior* 4 (1975): 353–65; D. Mosher, "Psychological Reactions to Pornographic Films," in *Technical Reports of the Commission on Obscenity and Pornography* (n. 58 above), 8:286–312.

81. Using the term "experience" as a verb like this seems to be the way one currently negotiates the subjective/objective split in Western epistemology.

82. S. Rachman and R. Hodgson, "Experimentally Induced 'Sexual Fetishism': Replication and Development," *Psychological Record* 18 (1968): 25–27; S. Rachman, "Sexual Fetishism: An Experimental Analogue," *Psychological Record* 16 (1966): 293–96.

83. March for Women's Dignity, New York City, May 1984.

84. *Public Hearings* (n. 34 above); M. Atwood, *Bodily Harm* (Toronto: McClelland & Stewart, 1983), pp. 207–12.

85. This is also true of Foucault, *The History of Sexuality* (n. 7 above), vol. 1. Foucault understands that sexuality must be discussed with method, power, class, and the law. Gender, however, eludes him. So he cannot distinguish between the silence about sexuality that Victorianism has made into a noisy discourse and the silence that has *been* women's sexuality under conditions of subordination by and to men. Although he purports to grasp sexuality, including desire itself, as social, he does not see the conent of its determination as a sexist social order that eroticizes potency as male and victimization as female. Women are simply beneath significant notice.

86. Masson (n. 2 above).

87. On sexuality, see, e.g., A. Lorde, *Uses of the Erotic: The Erotic as Power* (Brooklyn, N.Y.: Out and Out Books, 1978); and Haunani-Kay Trask, *Eros and Power: The Promise of Feminist Theory* (Philadelphia: University of Pennsylvania Press, 1986); both attempt such a reconstitution. The work of Trask suffers from an underlying essentialism in which the realities of sexual abuse are not examined or seen as constituting women's sexuality as such. Thus, a return to mother and body can be urged as social bases for reclaiming a feminist eros.

88. Ti-Grace Atkinson, "Why I'm Against S/M Liberation," in *Against Sadomasochism: A Radical Feminist Analysis,* ed. R. Linden, D. Pagano, D. Russell, and S. Star (East Palo Alto, Calif.: Frog in the Well, 1982), p. 91.

To Be and Be Seen: The Politics of Reality

Marilyn Frye

I

In the Spring of 1978, at a meeting of the Midwestern Division of the Society for Women in Philosophy, Sarah Hoagland read a paper entitled "Lesbian Epistemology," in which she sketched the following picture:

> In the conceptual schemes of phallocracies there is no category of woman-identified-woman, woman-loving-woman or woman-centered-woman; that is, there is no such thing as a lesbian. This puts a lesbian in the interesting and peculiar position of being something that doesn't exist, and this position is a singular vantage point with respect to the reality which does not include her. It affords her a certain freedom from constraints of the conceptual system; it gives her access to knowledge which is inaccessible to those whose existence *is* countenanced by the system. Lesbians can therefore undertake kinds of criticism and description, and kinds of intellectual invention, hitherto unimagined.

Hoagland was urging lesbian-feminists to begin this work, and she did not try to say in advance what could be seen from that exceptional epistemic position.

Some critics of that paper, bridling at the suggestion that lesbians might be blessed with any exotic powers or special opportunities, were quick to demand a definition of the word 'lesbian'. They knew that if a definition of 'lesbian' featured certain patterns of physical contacts as definitive, then the claim that phallocratic conceptual schemes do not include lesbians would be obviously false, since phallocrats obviously can and do wrap their rapacious minds around verbal and visual images of females so positioned physically, with respect to each other. And they knew also, on the other hand, that any definition which is more "spiritual," such as *woman-identified-woman*, will be flexible enough to permit almost any woman to count herself a lesbian and claim for herself these exciting epistemological privileges.

Other critics, who found Hoagland's picture engaging but were loathe to glorify the conditions of exile, pressed for a definition of 'lesbian' which would be both accurate and illuminating—a definition which would shed light on what it means to say lesbians are excluded from phallocratic conceptual schemes, and which might even provide some clue as to what lesbians might see from this strange non-location beyond the pale.

These pressures combined with the philosopher's constitutional propensity to view all orderly procedure as beginning with definitions, and the assembly was irresistibly drawn into trying to define the term 'lesbian'. But to no avail. That term is extraordinarily resistant to standard procedures of semantic analysis. It finally dawned on me that the elusiveness of the meaning of the term was itself a clue that Hoagland's picture was right. If indeed lesbians' existence is not countenanced by the dominant conceptual scheme, it would follow that we could not construct a definition of the term 'lesbian' of the sort we might recommend to well-intentioned editors of dictionaries. If a conceptual scheme excludes something, the standard vocabulary of those whose scheme it is will not be adequate to the defining of a term which denotes it. If Hoagland's picture is right, then whatever we eventually do by way of defining the word 'lesbian', that definition will evolve within a larger enterprise and cannot be the *beginning* of understanding and assessing that picture.

Another way of beginning is suggested by the observation that women of all stripes and colors, including lesbians but also including nonlesbians, suffer erasure. This is true, but it also seems to me that Hoagland is right: the exclusion of lesbians from phallocratic reality is different and is related to unusual knowing. The difficulty lies in trying to say just what this *means*. In order to get a handle on this we need to explore the differences and the connections between the erasure of women generally and the erasure of lesbians.

This inquiry, about what is *not* encompassed by a conceptual scheme, presents problems which arise because the scheme in question is, at least in the large, the inquirer's own scheme. The resources for the inquiry are, in the main, drawn from the very scheme whose limits we are already looking beyond in order to conceive the project. This undertaking therefore engages me in a sort of flirtation with meaninglessness—dancing about a region of cognitive gaps and negative semantic spaces,[1] kept aloft only by the rhythm and momentum of my own motion, trying to plumb abysses which are generally agreed not to exist and to map the tensions which create them. The danger is of falling into incoherence. But conceptual schemes have saving complexities such that their structures and substructures imitate and reflect each other and one thus can locate holes and gaps indirectly which cannot, in the nature of the thing, be directly named.

I start with a semantic reminder.

II

Reality is that which is.

The English word 'real' stems from a word which meant *regal*, of or pertaining to the king.

'Real' in Spanish means *royal*.

Real property is that which is proper to the king.

Real estate is the estate of the king.

Reality is that which pertains to the one in power, is that over which he has power, is his domain, his estate, is proper to him.

The ideal king reigns over everything as far as the eye can see. His eye. What he cannot see is not royal, not real.

He sees what is proper to him.

To be real is to be visible to the king.

The king is in his counting house.

III

I say, "I am a lesbian. The king does not count lesbians. Lesbians are not real. There are no lesbians." To say this, I use the word 'lesbian', and hence one might think that there is a word for this thing, and thus that the thing must have a place in the conceptual scheme. But this is not so. Let me take you on a guided tour of a few standard dictionaries, to display some reasons for saying that lesbians are not named in the lexicon of the King's English.

If you look up the word 'lesbian' in *The Oxford English Dictionary*, you find an entry that says it is an adjective that means *of or pertaining to the island of Lesbos*, and an entry describing at length and favorably an implement called a lesbian rule, which is a flexible measuring device used by carpenters. Period.

Webster's Third International offers a more pertinent definition. It tells us that a lesbian is a homosexual female. And going on, one finds that 'homosexual' means *of or pertaining to the same sex*. The elucidating example provided is the phrase 'homosexual twins' which means *same-sex twins*. The alert scholar can conclude that a lesbian is a same-sex female.

A recent edition of *Webster's Collegiate Dictionary* tells us that a lesbian is a woman who has sex, or sexual relations, with other women. Such a definition would be accepted by many speakers of the language and at least seems to be coherent, even if too narrow. But the appearance is deceptive, for this account collapses into nonsense, too. The key word in this definition is 'sex': having sex or having sexual relations. But what is having sex? It is worthwhile to follow this up because the pertinent dictionary entries obscure an important point about the logic of sex. Getting clear about that point helps one see that there is semantic closure against recognition of the existence of lesbians, and it also prepares the way for understanding the connection between the place of *woman* and the place of *lesbian* with respect to the phallocratic scheme of things.[2]

Dictionaries generally agree that 'sexual' means something on the order of *pertaining to the genital union of a female and a male animal*, and that "having sex" is having intercourse—intercourse being defined as the penetration of a vagina by a penis, with ejaculation. My own observation of usage leads me to think these accounts are inadequate and misleading. Some uses of these terms do fit this dictionary account. For instance, parents and counselors standardly remind young women that if they are going to be sexually active they must deal responsibly with the possibility of becoming pregnant. In this context, the word 'sexually' is pretty clearly being used in a way that accords with the given definition. But many activities and events fall under the rubric 'sexual', apparently without semantic deviance, though they do not involve penile penetration of the vagina of a female human being. Penile penetration of almost anything, especially if it is accompanied by ejaculation, counts as having sex or being sexual. Moreover, events which cannot plausibly be seen as pertaining to penile erection, penetration and ejaculation will, in general, not be counted as sexual, and events that do not involve penile penetration or ejaculation will not be counted as having sex. For instance, if a girlchild is fondled and aroused by a man, and comes to orgasm, but the man refrains from penetration and ejaculation, the man can say, and speakers of English will generally agree, that he did not have sex with her. No matter what is going on, or (it must be mentioned) *not* going on, with respect to female arousal or orgasm, or in connection with the vagina, a pair can be said without semantic deviance to have had sex, or not to have had sex; the use of that term turns entirely on what was going on with respect to the penis.

When one first considers the dictionary definitions of 'sex' and 'sexual', it seems that all sexuality is heterosexuality, by definition, and that the term 'homosexual' would be internally contradictory. There are uses of the term according to which this is exactly so. But in the usual and standard use, there is nothing semantically odd in describing two men as having sex with each other. According to that usage, any situation in which one or more penises are present is one in which something could happen which could be called having sex. But on this apparently "broader" definition there is nothing women could do in the absence of men that could, without semantic oddity, be called "having sex." Speaking of women who have sex with other women is like speaking of ducks who engage in arm wrestling.

When the dictionary defines lesbians as women who have sex or sexual relations with other women, it defines lesbians as logically impossible.

Looking for other words in the lexicon which might denote these beings which are non-named 'lesbians', one thinks of terms in the vernacular, like 'dyke', 'bulldagger' and so on. Perhaps it is just as well that standard dictionaries do not pretend to provide relevant definitions of such terms. Generally, these two terms are used to denote women who are perceived as imitating, dressing up like, or trying to be men. Whatever the extent of the class of women who are perceived to do such things, it obviously is not coextensive with the class of lesbians. Nearly every feminist, and many other women as well, have been perceived as wishing to be men, and a great many lesbians are not so perceived. The term 'dyke' has been appropriated by some lesbians as a term of pride and solidarity, but in that use it is unintelligible to most speakers of English.

One of the current definitions of 'lesbianism' among lesbians is *woman-loving*— the polar opposite of misogyny. Several dictionaries I checked have entries for 'misogyny' (hatred of women), but not for 'philogyny' (love of women). I found one which defines 'philogyny' as *fondness for women,* and another dictionary defines 'philogyny' as *Don Juanism.* Obviously neither of these means *love of women* as it is intended by lesbians combing the vocabulary for ways to refer to themselves. According to the dictionaries, there is no term in English for the polar opposite of misogyny nor for persons whose characteristic orientation toward women is the polar opposite of misogyny.

Flinging the net wider, one can look up the more Victorian words, like sapphism and sapphist. In *Webster's Collegiate,* 'sapphism' is defined just as *lesbianism.* But *The Oxford English Dictionary* introduces another twist. Under the heading of 'sapphism' is an entry for 'sapphist' according to which sapphists are those addicted to unnatural sexual relations between women. The fact that these relations are characterized as unnatural is revealing. For what is unnatural is contrary to the laws of nature, or contrary to the nature of the substance of entity in question. But what is contrary to the laws of nature cannot happen: that is what it means to call these laws the laws of nature. And I cannot do what is contrary to my nature, for if I could do it, it would be in my nature to do it. To call something "unnatural" is to say it cannot be. This definition defines sapphists, that is lesbians, as *naturally* impossible as well as *logically* impossible.

The notion that lesbianism is not possible in nature, that it is nobody's nature to be a lesbian, has a life of its own even among some people who do know factually that there are certain women who do and are inclined to do certain things with other women and who sincerely avow certain feelings and attitudes toward women. Lesbianism can be seen as not natural in that if someone lives as a lesbian, it is not assumed that that is just who, or how, she *is*. Rather, it is presumed to be some sort of affliction, or is a result of failed attempts to solve some sort of problem or resolve some sort of conflict (and if she could find another way, she would take it, and then would not be a lesbian). Being a lesbian is understood as something which could be nobody's natural configuration but must be a configuration one is twisted into by some sort of force which is in some basic sense "external" to one. "Being a lesbian" is understood here as certain sorts of people understand "being a delinquent" or "being an alcoholic." It is not of one's nature the way illness is not of one's nature. To see this sense of "unnatural," one can contrast it with the presumed "naturalness" of the heterosexuality of women. As most people see it, being heterosexual is just being. It is not *interpreted*. It is not understood as a consequence of anything. It is not viewed as possibly a solution to some problem, or as a way of acting and feeling which one worked out or was pushed to by circumstances. On this sort of view, all women *are* heterosexual, and some women somehow come to *act* otherwise. On this view, no one *is*, in the same sense, a lesbian.

There are people who do believe in the real existence of perverts and deviants. What they share with those who do not is the view that the behaviors and attitudes in question are not natural to *humans*. One's choice then, when confronted with someone who says she is a lesbian, is to believe her and class her as not fully or really human, or to class her as fully and really human and not believe that she is a lesbian.

Lesbian.

One of the people of the Isle of Lesbos.

It is bizarre that when I try to name myself and explain myself, my native tongue provides me with a word that is so foreign, so false, so hopelessly inappropriate. Why am I referred to by a term which means *one of the people of Lesbos?*

The use of the word 'lesbian' to name us is a quadrifold evasion, a laminated euphemism. To name us, one goes by way of a reference to the island of Lesbos, which in turn is an indirect reference to the poet Sappho (who used to live there, they say), which in turn is itself an indirect reference to what fragments of her poetry have survived a few millennia of patriarchy, and this in turn (if we have not lost you by now) is a prophylactic avoidance of direct mention of the sort of creature who would write such poems or to whom such poems would be written ... assuming you happen to know what is in those poems written in a dialect of Greek over two thousand five hundred years ago on some small island somewhere in the wine dark Aegean Sea.

This is a truly remarkable feat of silence.

The philosopher John Langshaw Austin, commenting on the connection between language and conceptions of reality, said the following: "Our common stock of words embodies all the distinctions men have found worth drawing, and the connections they have found worth marking, in the lifetimes of many generations."[3]

> our
>
> common stock of words
>
> men have found
>
> distinction is not worth drawing
> connection is not worth marking

Revealing as this is, it still dissembles. It is not that the connections and distinctions are not worth drawing and marking, it is that men do not want to draw and mark them, or do not dare to.

IV

When one says that some thing or some class is not countenanced by a certain conceptual scheme, or that it is not "among the values over which the variables of the system range," or that it is not among the ontological commitments of the system, there are at least three things this can mean. One is just that there is no simple direct term in the system for the thing or class, and no very satisfactory way to explain it. For example, it is in this sense that Western conceptual schemes do not countenance the forces or arrangements called "karma." Indeed, I don't know whether it is suitable to say "forces or arrangements" here, and that is part of the point. A second thing that can be meant when it is said that something is not in the scope of the concepts of the scheme is that the term which ostensibly denotes the thing is internally self-contradictory, as in the case of round squares. Nothing can be in both the class denoted by 'round' and the class denoted by 'square', given what those words mean. A third thing one can mean when one says a scheme does not encompass a certain thing is that according to principles which are fundamental to the most general picture of how things are in the world, the thing could not exist in nature. An example of this is the denial that there could be a beast which was a cross between a dog and a cat. The belief that such a thing could exist would be inconsistent with beliefs about the nature of the world and of animals which underlie vast chunks of the rest of our world view.

Lesbian is the only class I have ever set out to define, the only concept I have ever set out to explain, that seemed to be shut out in more than one of these ways. As the considerations reviewed here seem to show, it is shut out in all three. You can "not believe in lesbians" as you don't believe in the possibility of "doggie-cats" or as you don't believe in round squares; or you can be just unable to accommodate lesbianism in the way I cannot accommodate the notion of Karma—it doesn't articulate suitably with the rest of my concepts; it can't be worked into my active conceptual repertoire.

The redundancy of the devices of closure which are in place here is one of the things which leads me to say that lesbians are *excluded* from the scheme. The overdetermination, the metaphysical overkill, signals a manipulation, a scurrying to erase, to divert the eye, the attention, the mind. Where there is manipulation there is motivation, and it does not seem plausible to me that the reason lies with the physical details of certain women's private lives. The meaning of this erasure and of the totality and conclusiveness of it has to do, I think, with the maintenance of phallocratic reality as a whole, and with the situation of women generally *a propos* that reality.

V

At the outset I said lesbians are not real, that there are no lesbians. I want to say also that women in general are not countenanced by the phallocratic scheme, are not real; there are no women. But the predicament of women *a propos* the dominant reality is complex and paradoxical, as is revealed in women's mundane experience of the see-saw of demand and neglect, of being romanced and assaulted, of being courted and being ignored. The observations which lead me to say there are no women in phallocratic reality themselves also begin to reveal the elements of the paradox. These observations are familiar to feminists; they are among the things we come back to again and again as new layers of their meanings become accessible to our understanding.

There are two kinds of erasure of women which have by now become "often noted." One is the conception of human history as a history of the acts and organizations of men, and the other is a long and sordid record in western civilization of the murder and mutilation of women. Both of these erasures are extended into the future, the one in fiction and speculation, the other in the technological projects of sperm selection for increasing the proportion of male babies, of extrauterine gestation, of cloning, of male to female transsexual reconstruction. Both sorts of erasure seem entwined in the pitched religious and political battle between males who want centralized male control of female reproductive functions, and males who want individualized male control of female reproductive functions. (I speak of the fights about abortion, forced sterilization, the conditions of birthing, etc.)

A reasonable person might think that these efforts to erase women reveal an all-too-vivid recognition that they *are* women—that the projects of ideological and material elimination of women presuppose belief in the existence of the objects to be eliminated. In a way, I agree. But also, there is a peculiar mode of relating belief and action which I think is characteristic of the construction of phallocratic reality, according to which a project of annihilation can be seen to presuppose the nonexistence of the objects being eliminated. This mode is an insane reversal of the reasonable procedure of adjusting one's views so that they accord with reality as actively discovered: it is a mode according to which one begins with a firmly held view, composed from fabulous images of oneself, and adopts as one's project the alteration of the world to bring it into accord with that view.

A powerful example of this strange practice was brought to my attention by Harriet Desmoines who had been reading about the United States' expansion across the North American continent. It seems that the white men, upon encountering the vast and rich midcontinental prairie, called the prairie a *desert.* They conceived a desert, they took it to be a desert, and a century later it is a desert (a fact which is presently somewhat obscured by the annual use of megatons of chemical fertilizers).

Did they *really* believe that what they were seeing was a desert? It is a matter of record that that is what they *said* they saw.

There is another example of this sort of practice to be found in the scientific and medical realm, which was brought to my attention by the work of Eileen Van Tassell. It is a standard assumption in the disciplines of human biology and human medicine that the species consists of two sexes, male and female. Concrete physical evidence that there are individuals of indeterminate sex and that "sex-characteristics" occur in spectrums and not as all-or-nothing phenomena is not acknowledged as existent evidence but is removed, erased, through chemical and surgical "cures" and "corrections."[4] In this case, as in the case of the rich and living prairie, erasure of fact and destruction of concrete objects does not demonstrate recognition of the fact or object; it is, on the contrary, direct manifestation of the belief that those are not the facts and the belief that no such individual objects exist.

If it is true that this mode of connection of belief and action is characteristic of phallocratic culture, then one can construct or reconstruct beliefs which are fundamental to that culture's conceptual/scientific system by inspecting the culture's projects and reasoning that what is believed is what the projects would make to be true. As noted before, there are and have long been ongoing projects whose end will be a world with no women in it. Reasoning back, one can conclude that those whose projects these are believe there are no women.

For many of us, the idea that there are no women, that we do not exist, began to dawn when we first grasped the point about the nongeneric so-called "generic" 'man'. The word 'woman' was supposed to mean *female of the species,* but the name of the species is 'Man'. The term 'female man' has a tension of logical impossibility about it that is absent from parallel terms like 'female cat' and 'female terrier'. It makes one suspect that the concept of the species which is operative here is one according to which there are no females of the species. I think one can begin to get a handle on what this means by seeing how it meshes with another interesting phenomenon, namely the remarkable fact that so many men from so many stations in life have so often declared that women are unintelligible to them.

Reading or hearing the speeches of men on the unintelligibility of women, I imagine the men are like people who for some reason can see everything but automobiles and are constantly and painfully perplexed by blasts and roars, thumps and bumps, which they cannot avoid, control or explain. But it is not quite like that, for such men do seem to recognize our physical existence, or at least the existence of some of our parts. What they do not see is our souls.

The phallocratic scheme does not admit women as authors of perception, as seers. Man understands his own perception as simultaneously generating and being generated by a point of view. Man is understood to author names; men have a certain status as points of intellectual and perceptual origin. Insofar as the phallocratic scheme permits the understanding that women perceive at all, it features women's perceptions as passive, repetitive of men's perception, nonauthoritative. Aristotle said it outright: Women are rational, but do not have authority.[5]

Imagine two people looking at a statue, one from the front, the other from the back, and imagine that the one in front thinks the one in back must be seeing exactly what he is seeing. He cannot fathom how the other can come up with a description so different from his own. It is as though women are assumed to be robots hooked up to the senses of men—not using senses of our own, not authoring perception, not having and generating a point of view. And then they cannot fathom how we must be wired inside, that we could produce the output we produce from the input they assume to be identical with their own. The hypothesis that we are seeing from a different point of view, and hence simply seeing something he cannot see, is not available to a man, is not in his repertoire, so long as his total conception of the situation includes a conception of women as not authoritative perceivers like himself, that is, so long as he does not count women as men. And no wonder such a man finds women incomprehensible.

VI

For the reasons given, and in the ways indicated, I think there is much truth in the claim that the phallocratic scheme does not include women. But while women are erased in history and in speculation, physically liquidated in gynocidal purges and banished from the community of those with perceptual and semantic authority, we are on the other hand regularly and systematically invited, seduced, cajoled, coerced and even paid to be in intimate and constant association with men and their projects. In this, the situation of women generally is radically different from the situation of lesbians. Lesbians are not invited to join—the family, the party, the project, the procession, the war effort. There is a place for a woman in every game. Wife, secretary, servant, prostitute, daughter, assistant, babysitter, mistress, seamstress, proofreader, nurse, confidante, masseuse, indexer, typist, mother. Any of these is a place for a woman, and women are much encouraged to fill them. None of these is a place for a lesbian.

The exclusion of women from the phallocratic scheme is impressive, frightening and often fatal, but it is not simple and absolute. Women's existence is both absolutely necessary to and irresolvably problematic for the dominant reality and those committed to it, for our existence is *presupposed* by phallocratic reality, but it is not and cannot be *encompassed* by or countenanced by that reality. Women's existence is a background against which phallocratic reality is a foreground.

A foreground scene is created by the motion of foreground figures against a static background. Foreground figures are perceptible, are defined, have identity, only in virtue of their movement against a background. The space in which the motion of foreground figures takes place is created and defined by their movement with respect to each other and against the background. But nothing of the background is *in* or is *part of* or is *encompassed by* the foreground scene and space. The background is unseen by the eye which is focused on foreground figures, and if anything somehow draws the eye to the background, the foreground dissolves. What would draw the eye to the background would be any sudden or well-defined motion in the background. Hence there must be either no motion at all in the background, or an unchanging buzz of small, regular and repetitive motions. The background must be utterly un*eventful* if the foreground is to continue to hang together, that is, if it is to endure as *a space* within which there are discrete *objects* in relation to each other.

I imagine phallocratic reality to be the space and figures and motion which constitute the foreground, and the constant repetitive uneventful activities of women to constitute and maintain the background against which this foreground plays. It is essential to the maintenance of the foreground reality that nothing within it refer in any way to anything in the background, and yet it depends absolutely upon the existence of the background. It is useful to carry this metaphor on in a more concrete mode—thinking of phallocratic reality as a dramatic production on a stage.

The motions of the actors against the stage settings and backdrop constitute and maintain the existence and identities of the characters in a play. The stage setting, props, lights and so forth are created, provided, maintained and occasionally rearranged (according to the script) by stagehands. The stagehands, their motions and the products of those motions, are neither in nor part of the play, are neither in nor part of the reality of the characters. The reality in the framework of which Hamlet's actions have their meaning would be rent or shattered if anything Hamlet did or thought referred in any way to the stagehands or their activities, or if that background blur of activity were in any other way to be resolved into attention-catching events.

The situation of the actors is desperately paradoxical. The actors are absolutely committed to the maintenance of the characters and the characters' reality: participation as characters in the ongoing creation of Reality is their *raison d'etre*. The reality of the character must be lived with fierce concentration. The actor must be immersed in the play and undistracted by any thought for the scenery, props or stagehands, lest the continuity of the characters and the integrity of their reality be dissolved or broken. But if the character must be lived so intently, who will supervise the stagehands to make sure they don't get rowdy, leave early, fall asleep or walk off the job? (Alas, there is no god nor heavenly host to serve as Director and Stage Managers.) Those with the most intense commitment to the maintenance of the reality of the play are precisely those most interested in the proper deportment of the stagehands, and this interest competes directly with that commitment. There is nothing the actor would like better than that there be no such thing as stagehands, posing as they do a constant threat to the very existence, the very life, of the character and hence to the meaning of the life of the actor; and yet the actor is irrevocably tied to the stagehands by his commitment to the play. Hamlet, of course, has no such problems; there are no stagehands in the play.

To escape his dilemma, the actor may throw caution to the wind and lose himself in the character, whereupon stagehands are unthinkable, hence unproblematic. Or he may construct and embrace the belief that the stagehands share exactly his own perceptions and interests and that they are as committed to the play as he—that they are like robots. On such a hypothesis he can assume them to be absolutely dependable and go on about his business single-mindedly and without existential anxiety. A third strategy, which is in a macabre way more sane, is that of trying to solve the problem technologically by constructing actual robots to serve as stagehands.[6] Given the primacy of his commitment to the play, all solutions must involve one form or another of annihilation of the stagehands. Yet all three require the existence of stagehands; the third, he would hope, requiring it only for a while longer.

The solution to the actor's problem which will appear most benign with respect to the stagehands because it erases the erasure, is that of training, persuading and seducing the stagehands into *loving* the actors and taking actors' interests and commitments unto themselves as their own. One significant advantage to this solution is that the actors can carry on without the guilt or confusion that might come with annihilating, replacing or falsely forgetting the stagehands. As it turns out, of course, even this is a less than perfect solution. Stagehands, in the thrall of their commitment, can become confused and think of themselves as actors—and then they may disturb the play by trying to enter it as characters, by trying to participate in the creation and maintainance of Reality. But there are various well-known ways to handle these intrusions and this seems to be, generally speaking, the most popular solution to the actor's dilemma.

VII

All eyes, all attention, all attachment must be focused on the play, which is Phallocratic Reality. Any notice of the stagehands must be oblique and filtered through interest in the play. Anything which threatens the fixation of attention on the play threatens a cataclysmic dissolution of Reality into Chaos. Even the thought of the possibility of a distraction is a distraction. It is necessary to devise devices and construct systems which will lock out the thought-crime of conceiving the possibility of a direct and attentive focus on anything but Reality.

The ever-present potential for cosmological disaster lies with the background. There is nothing in the nature of the background that disposes it to be appropriately tame: it is not made to serve the foreground, it is just there. It therefore is part of the vocation of phallocratic loyalists to police *attention*. They must make it radically impossible to attend to anything in the background; they must make it impossible to think it possible to fasten one's eye on anything in the background.

We can deduce from this understanding of their motivation *what it is* that phallocratic loyalists are motivated to forbid conceiving. What must not be conceived is *a seer* for whom the background is eventful, dramatic, compelling—whose attention fastens upon stagehands and their projects. The loyalists cannot just identify such seers and kill them, for that would focus the loyalists' own attention on the criminal, hence the crime, hence the object of the crime, and that would interrupt the loyalists' own attention to Reality.

The king is in his counting house. The king is greedy and will count for himself everything he dares to. But his greed itself imposes limits on what he dares to count.

VIII

What the king cannot count is a seer whose perception passes the plane of the foreground Reality and focuses upon the background. A seer whose eye is attracted to the ones working as stagehands—the women. A seer in whose eye the woman has authority, has interests of her own, is not a robot. A seer who has no motive for wanting there to be no women; a seer who is not loyal to Reality. We can take the account of the seer who must be unthinkable if Reality is to be kept afloat as the beginning of an account of what a lesbian is. One might try saying that a lesbian is one who, by virtue of her focus, her attention, her attachment, is disloyal to phallocratic reality. She is not committed to its maintenance and the maintenance of those who maintain it, and worse, her mode of disloyalty threatens its utter dissolution in the mere flick of the eye. This sounds extreme, of course, perhaps even hysterical. But listening carefully to the rhetoric of the fanatic fringe of the phallocratic loyalists, one hears that they do think that feminists, whom they fairly reasonably judge to be lesbians, have the power to bring down civilization, to dissolve the social order as we know it, to cause the demise of the species, by our mere existence.

Even the fanatics do not really believe that a lone maverick lesbian can in a flick of her evil eye atomize civilization, of course. Given the collectivity of conceptual schemes, the way they rest on agreement, a maverick perceiver does not have the power to bring one tumbling down—a point also verified by my own experience as a not-so-powerful maverick. What the loyalists fear, and in this I think they are more-or-less right, is a contagion of the maverick perception to the point where the agreement in perception which keeps Reality afloat begins to disintegrate.

The event of becoming a lesbian is a reorientation of attention in a kind of onto-logical conversion. It is characterized by a feeling of a world dissolving, and by a feel-ing of disengagement and re-engagement of one's power as a perceiver. That such conversion happens signals its possibility to others.

Heterosexuality for women is not simply a matter of sexual preference, any more than lesbianism is. It is a matter of orientation of attention, as is lesbianism, in a metaphysical context controlled by neither heterosexual nor lesbian women. Atten-tion is a kind of passion. When one's attention is on something, one is present in a particular way with respect to that thing. This presence is, among other things, an el-ement of erotic presence. The orientation of one's attention is also what fixes and di-rects the application of one's physical and emotional work.

If the lesbian sees the women, the woman may see the lesbian seeing her. With this, there is a flowering of possibilities. The woman, feeling herself seen, may learn that she *can be* seen; she may also be able to know that a woman can see, that is, can author perception. With this, there enters for the woman the logical possibility of as-suming her authority as a perceiver and of shifting her own attention. With that there is the dawn of choice, and it opens out over the whole world of women. The lesbian's seeing undercuts the mechanism by which the production and constant re-production of heterosexuality for women was to be rendered *automatic.* The nonex-istence of lesbians is a piece in the mechanism which is supposed to cut off the possi-bility of choice or alternative at the root, namely at the point of conception.

The maintenance of phallocratic reality requires that the attention of women be focused on men and men's projects—the play; and that attention not be focused on women—the stagehands. Woman-loving, as a spontaneous and habitual orientation of attention is then, both directly and indirectly, inimical to the maintenance of that reality. And therein lies the reason for the thoroughness of the ontological closure against lesbians, the power of those closed out, and perhaps the key to the liberation of women from oppression in a male-dominated culture.

IX

My primary goal here has not been to state and prove some rigid thesis, but simply to *say* something clearly enough, intelligibly enough, so that it can be understood and thought about. Lesbians are outside the conceptual scheme, and this is something done, not just the way things are. One can begin to see that lesbians are excluded by the scheme, and that this is *motivated,* when one begins to see what purpose the ex-clusion might serve in connection with keeping women generally in their metaphysi-cal place. It is also true that lesbians are in a position to see things that cannot be seen from within the system. What lesbians see is what makes them lesbians and their see-

ing is why they have to be excluded. Lesbians are woman-seers. When one is sus-
pected of seeing women, one is spat summarily out of reality, through the cognitive
gap and into the negative semantic space. If you ask what became of such a woman,
you may be told she became a lesbian, and if you try to find out what a lesbian is, you
will be told there is no such thing.
But there is.

Notes

This is a very slightly revised version of the essay which appeared in *Sinister Wisdom* 17 with
the title, "To Be And Be Seen: Metaphysical Misogyny."
    1. Phrase due to Julia Penelope Stanley.
    2. The analysis that follows is my own rendering of an account developed by Carolyn Shafer.
My version of it is informed also by my reading of "Sex and Reference," by Janice Moulton,
Philosophy and Sex, edited by Robert Baker and Frederick Elliston (Prometheus Books, Buffalo, New York, 1975).
    3. From "A Plea for Excuses," *Philosophical Papers* (Oxford University Press, 1961).
    4. I rely here on lectures by Eileen Van Tassell in which she interpreted the generally avail-
able data on sex-characteristics, sex-differences and sex-similarities. One can refer, in particular, to *Man and Woman, Boy and Girl,* by John Money and Anke A. Ehrhardt (The Johns
Hopkins University Press, 1972) and *Intersexuality,* edited by Claus Overzier (Academic Press,
New York and London, 1963). See also, for instance: "Development of Sexual Characteristics,"
by A.D. Jost in *Science Journal,* Volume 6, no. 6 (especially the chart on page 71) which indicates the variety of "sex characteristics" which occurs in normal females and males; and
"Growth and Endocrinology of the Adolescent," by J. M. Tanner in *Endocrine and Genetic Diseases of Childhood,* edited by L. Gardner (Saunders, Philadelphia & London, 1969), which tries
to give clinical standards for evaluating the hormonal status of adolescent youth, and in which
the author characterizes individuals which are well within the normal curve for males as "feminized males," thus, by implication, as "abnormal" males; and similarly, *mutatis mutandis,* for
females.
    5. *Politics* I 13, 1260 a13. My attention was first brought to this by a paper, "Aristotle's Views
On Women In The *Politics,*" presented at the meetings of the Western Division of the Society
For Women In Philosophy, Fall 1974, by Jan Bidwell, Susan Ekstrom, Sue Hildebrand and
Rhoda H. Kotzin.
    6. This solution is discussed in *The Transsexual Empire: The Making of The She-Male,* by
Janice G. Raymond (Beacon Press, Boston, 1979).

Moral Revolution:
From Antagonism to Cooperation

Sarah Lucia Hoagland

In the u.s., women cannot appear publicly without some men advancing on them, presuming access to them. In fact, many women will think something is wrong if this doesn't happen. A woman simply is someone toward whom such behavior is appropriate. When a woman is accompanied by a man, however, she is usually no longer considered fair game. As a result, men close to individual women—fathers, boyfriends, husbands, brothers, escorts, colleagues—become protectors (theoretically), staving off advances from other men.

The value of special protection for women is prevalent in this society. Protectors interact with women in ways that promote the image of women as helpless: men open doors, pull out chairs, expect women to dress in ways that interfere with their own self-protection.[1] And women accept this as attentive, complimentary behavior and perceive themselves as persons who need special attention and protection.[a]

What a woman faces in a man is either a protector or a predator, and men gain identity through one or another of these roles.[2] This has at least five consequences. First, there can be no protectors unless there is danger. A man cannot identify himself in the role of protector unless there is something which needs protection. So it is in the interest of protectors that there be predators. Secondly, to be protected, women must be in danger. In portraying women as helpless and defenseless, men portray women as victims ... and therefore as targets.

Thirdly, a woman (or girl) is viewed as the object of male passion and thereby its cause. This is most obvious in the case of rape: she must have done something to tempt him—helpless hormonal bundle that he is. Thus if women are beings who by nature are endangered, then, obviously, they are thereby beings who by nature are seductive—they actively attract predators. Fourthly, to be protected, women must agree to act as men say women should: to appear feminine, prove they are not threatening, stay at home, remain only with the protector, devalue their connections with other women, and so on.

Finally, when women step out of the feminine role, thereby becoming active and "guilty,"[b] it is a mere matter of logic that men will depict women as evil and step up overt physical violence against them in order to reaffirm women's victim status. For example, as the demand for women's rights in the u.s. became publicly perceptible, the depiction of lone women as "sluts" inviting attack also became prevalent. A lone female hitchhiker was perceived, not as someone to protect, but as someone who had given up her right to protection and thus as someone who was a target for attack. The rampant increase in pornography—entertainment by and for men about women—is men's general response to the u.s. women's liberation movement's demand of integrity, autonomy, and dignity for women.

What radical feminists have exposed through all the work on incest (daughter rape) and wife-beating is that protectors are also predators. Of course, not all men are wife- or girlfriend-beaters, but over half who live with women are. And a significant number of u.s. family homes shelter an "incestuous" male.[3]

Although men may exhibit concern over womanabuse, they have a different relationship to it than women; their concerns are not women's concerns. For example, very often men become irate at the fact that a woman has been raped or beaten by another man. But this is either a man warming to his role of protector—it rarely, if ever, occurs to him to teach her self-defense—or a man deeply affected by damage done to his "property" by another man. And while some men feel contempt for men who batter or rape, Marilyn Frye suggests it is quite possible their contempt arises, not from the fact that womanabuse is happening, but from the fact that the batterer or rapist must accomplish by force what they themselves can accomplish more subtly by arrogance.[4]

The current willingness of men in power to pass laws restricting pornography is a matter of men trying to reestablish the asexual, virginal image of (some) women whom they can then protect in their homes. And they are using as their excuse right-wing women as well as feminists who appear to be asking for protection, like proper women, rather than demanding liberation. Men use violence when women don't pay attention to them. Then, when women ask for protection, men can find meaning by turning on the predators—particularly ones of a different race or class.

In other words, the logic of protection is essentially the same as the logic of predation. Through predation, men do things to women and against women all of which violate women and undermine women's integrity. Yet protection objectifies just as much as predation. To protect women, men do things to women and against women; acting "for a woman's own good," they violate her integrity and undermine her agency.

Protection and predation emerge from the same ideology of male dominance, and it is a matter of indifference to the successful maintenance of male domination which of the two conditions women accept. Thus Sonia Johnson writes:

> Our conviction that if we stop studying and monitoring men and their latest craziness, that if we abandon our terrified clawing and kicking interspersed with sniveling and clutching—our whole sick sadomasochistic relationship with the masters—they will go berserk and kill us, is the purest superstition. With our eyes fully upon them they kill us daily; with our eyes riveted upon them they have gone berserk.[5]

Early radical feminists claimed that women are colonized.[6] It is worth reconsidering this claim. Those who wish to dominate a group, and who are successful, gain control through violence. This show of force, however, requires tremendous effort and resources; so colonizers introduce values portraying the relationship of dominant colonizer to subordinate colonized as natural and normal.

One of the first acts of colonizers after conquest is to control the language, work often accomplished by christian missionaries. Their mission is to give the language written form and then set up schools where it is taught to those native to the land. Here new values are introduced: for example, concepts of 'light' and 'dark' as connoting good and evil respectively. Words for superiors and deities then begin to carry a 'light' connotation as well as appear in the masculine gender. Further, values are embedded which support colonial appropriation of natural resources, and which disavow the colonized's ancestral ways and economic independence. As the colonized are forced to use the colonizers' language and conceptual schema, they can begin to internalize these values. This is "salvation," and colonizers pursue what they have called manifest destiny or "the white man's burden."

The theory of manifest destiny implies that colonizers are bringing civilization (the secular version of salvation) to "barbarians" ("heathens"). Colonizers depict the colonized as passive, as wanting and needing protection (domination), as being taken care of "for their own good." Anyone who resists domination will be sorted out as abnormal and attacked as a danger to society ("civilization") or called insane and put away in the name of protection (their own or society's).

Thus colonizers move from predation—attack and conquest—to benevolent protection. Those who have been colonized are portrayed as helpless, childlike, passive, and feminine; and the colonizers become benevolent rulers, accepting the burden of the civilized management of resources (exploitation).

After the social order has been established, should the colonized begin to resist protection and benevolence, insisting that they would rather do it themselves regardless of immediate consequences, the colonizers will once again turn predators, stepping up violence to convince the colonized that they need protection and that they cannot survive without the colonizers. One of the lines attributed to Mahatma Gandhi in the movie *Gandhi* is significant to this point: "To maintain the benevolence and dominate us, you must humiliate us." When all else fails, men will engage in war to affirm their "manhood": the "right" to conquer and protect women and other "feminine" beings (i.e., anyone else they can dominate).

The purpose of colonization is to appropriate foreign resources. It functions by de-skilling a people and rendering them economically dependent. In his book on colonialism, *How Europe Underdeveloped Africa*, Walter Rodney argues that african societies would not have become capitalist without white colonialism.[7] His thesis is that africa was proceeding economically in a manner distinct from precapitalist development until europeans arrived to colonize africa and underdevelop it. Aborting the african economy and making it over to meet their own needs, europeans robbed africans of their autonomous economic skills, primarily by means of transforming the education system and teaching african peoples to disavow the knowledge of their ancestors. This de-skilling of conquered peoples is crucial to domination because it means that the colonized become dependent on the colonizers for survival. Actually, however, it is the colonizers who cannot survive—as colonizers—without the colonized.

Bette S. Tallen suggests that, in like fashion, women have been de-skilled under heterosexualism, becoming economically dependent on men, while men appropriate women's resources.[8] As Sonia Johnson notes:

According to United Nations statistics, though women do two-thirds of the world's work, we make only one-tenth of the world's money and own only one-hundredth of the world's property.[9]

The de-skilling of women differs depending on specific historical and material conditions. For example, in her analysis of pre-industrial, seventeenth-century britain, Ann Oakley notes that women engaged in many trades separate from their husbands, or as widows. The industrial revolution changed all that and deprived many women of their skills.[10] Prior to this, during the burning times, european men appropriated women's healing skills, birthing skills, and teaching skills, and attempted to destroy women's psychic skills.[11] As Alice Molloy writes, "the so-called history of witchcraft is simply the process by which women were separated from each other and from their potential to synthesize information."[12] In general, many women no longer have their own programs, they've lost access to their own tools. As a result, they are coerced into embracing an ideology of dependence on men.

Heterosexualism has certain similarities to colonialism, particularly in its maintenance through force when paternalism is rejected (that is, the stepping up of male predation when women reject male protection) and in its portrayal of domination as natural (men are to dominate women as naturally as colonizers are to dominate the colonized, and without any sense of themselves as oppressing those they dominate except during times of overt aggression) and in the de-skilling of women. And just as it is colonizers who cannot survive as colonizers without the colonized, so it is men who cannot survive as men (protectors or predators) without women. ...

I want a moral revolution.

The primary concept used to interpret and evaluate individual women's choices and actions is 'femininity'. 'Femininity' normalizes male domination and paints a portrait of women as subordinate and naively content with being controlled. Thus patrihistorians claim that women have remained content with their lot, accepting male domination throughout time, with the exception of a few suffragists and now a few aberrant feminists.

Yet if we stop to reflect, it becomes clear that within the confines of the feminine stereotype no behavior *counts* as resistance to male domination. And if nothing we can point to or even imagine counts as proof against the claim that all (normal) women are feminine and accept male domination, then we are working within a closed, coercive conceptual system.

For example, some acts which men claim support the feminine stereotype of white middle-class women indicate, instead, resistance. Alix Kates Shulman in *Memoirs of an Ex-Prom Queen* portrays a "fluffy-headed" housewife who regularly burns the dinner when her husband brings his boss home unexpectedly, and who periodically packs raw eggs in his lunch box.[13] Such acts are used by those in power as proof that women have lesser rational ability, but actually they indicate resistance—sabotage. Such acts may or may not be openly called sabotage by the saboteurs, but women engage in them as an affirmation of existence in a society which denies a woman recognition independently of a man.

Donna Deitch's documentary *Woman to Woman* offers a classic example of what I am calling sabotage.[14] Four females—two housewives, a daughter, and the interviewer—sit around a kitchen table. One housewife protests that she is not a housewife, she is not married to the house. The interviewer asks her to describe what she does all day. The woman relates something like the following: she gets up, feeds her husband, feeds her children, drives them to the school bus, drives her husband to work, returns to do the dishes, makes the beds, goes out to do the shopping, returns to do a wash. The woman continues listing her activities, then stops, shocked, and says: "Wait a minute, I *am* married to the house." She complains of difficulty in getting her husband to give her enough money for the household, of frustration because he nevertheless holds her responsible for running the house, and of degradation because she must go to him, apologetically, at the end of each budget period to ask for extra money to cover expenses when he could have provided her with sufficient funds from the beginning.

Suddenly she gets a gleam in her eye, lowers her voice, and leans forward, saying: "Have you ever bought something you don't need?" She explains that she buys cans of beans and hoards them. Then she says: "You have to know you're alive; you have to make sure you exist."[15] She has separated herself from her husband's perceptions of her: she is not simply an extension of his will, she is reclaiming (some) agency—sabotage. Yet under the feminine stereotype, we are unable to perceive her as in any way resisting her husband's domination.[c]

Significantly, 'femininity' is a concept used to characterize any group which men in power wish to portray as requiring domination. Kate Millett points out that 'femininity' characterizes traits those in power cherish in subordinates.[16] And Naomi Weisstein notes that feminine characteristics add up to characteristics stereotypically attributed to minority groups.[17] The literature indicates that nazis characterized jews as feminine, using the ideology in justification of their massacre. Men accused at the salem witch trials were characterized as feminine.[18] Mary Daly notes that the iroquois were "cast into a feminine role by the jesuits."[19] An investigation of anthropological literature from the first part of this century reveals that white british anthropologists described the physiological characteristics of black africans—men and women—in a bestially feminine manner. And as Kate Millett points out, Jean Genet's definition of 'femininity' in male homosexuality is "submission to the imperious male."[20]

The concept of 'femininity' provides a basic model for oppression in anglo-european thinking.[d] A feminine being is by nature passive and dependent. It follows that those to whom the label is applied must by their very nature seek protection (domination) and should be subjected to authority "for their own good." 'Femininity' portrays those not in power as needing and wanting to be controlled. It is a matter of logic, then, that those who refuse to be controlled are abnormal.

Consider the fact that white history depicts black slaves (though not white indentured servants) as lazy, docile, and clumsy on grounds such as that slaves frequently broke tools. Yet a rational woman under slavery, comprehending that her situation is less than human, that she functions as an extension of the will of the master, will not run to pick up tools. She acts instead to differentiate herself from the will of her master: she breaks tools, carries on subversive activities—sabotage. Her master, in turn, perceiving her as subhuman and subrational, names her "clumsy," "childlike," "foolish" perhaps, but not a saboteur. Some sabotage was detected and punished, for example, when slave women poisoned masters or committed arson. However records of such events were often buried,[21] and the stereotype of slaves as incompetent persists. Perhaps most powerful was the use of spirituals to keep present the idea of escape, songs such as "Swing Low, Sweet Chariot" or songs about Moses and the promised land. They also announced particular escape plans such as the departure of Harriet Tubman on yet another trip to the north. Whites perceived the happy song of simple-minded folk.[22]

If officially slaves are subhuman and content with their lot and masters are acting in slaves' best interests, then it follows that any resistance to the system is an abnormality or an indication of madness. Indeed, in recollecting the stories of her grandmother's slave days, Annie Mae Hunt tells us that "if you run off, you was considered sick."[23] That is to say, slaves existed in a conceptual framework where running away from slavery was generally perceived by masters and even at times by slaves as an indication, not of (healthy) resistance, but of mental imbalance.

Such was the extent of the coercion of the masters' framework. However, creating a different value framework, we can understand the behaviors of slaves, out of which the masters constructed and fed the slave stereotypes, as providing ample evidence of resistance and sabotage.[24]

During the holocaust and, more significantly, after it, in the telling of the stories, patrihistorians have depicted jews under nazi domination as cooperative and willing (feminine) victims. This stereotype—as is true of the slave stereotype—is still alive today. Yet again, we can ask: What would *count* as resistance? For example, jews at auschwitz who committed suicide by hurling themselves against an electric fence have been depicted as willing victims. But the nazis did not leave their bodies for all to see, they quickly took them away. In determining the time of their own deaths, those who committed suicide were resisting nazi domination by exercising choice, interrupting the plans of the masters, and thus differentiating their selves from the will of their masters.

Many, many types of resistance occurred. From Simone Wallace, Ellen Ledley, and Paula Tobin:

> Each act of staying alive when the enemy has decided you must die is an act of resistance. The fight against a helplessness and apathy which aids the enemy is resistance. [Other acts include:] sabotage in the factories, encouraging others to live who are ready to give in and die, smuggling food and messages, breaking prison rules whenever possible, simply keeping themselves alive. Other forms of resistance, even more readily recognizable as such, took place from the killing of guards, bombing of factories, stealing guns, Warsaw uprisings, etc.[25]

Literature about the holocaust is full of jewish resistance, of sabotage; yet for the most part, short of armed uprisings such as happened in the warsaw ghetto, that resistance is not recognized or not acknowledged, and the stereotype of the willing (feminine) victim persists.

If we operate in a conceptual framework which depicts humans as inherently dominant or subordinate, then we will not perceive resistance or include it in our descriptions of the world unless those who resist overthrow those who dominate and begin to dominate them (i.e., when there is essentially no revolution in value). For example, the strategies of the women at greenham common, in resisting the deployment of u.s. cruise missiles, involve innovative means of thwarting the dominant/subordinate relationship—the women simply don't play by the rules and instead do the unexpected. Their strategies are characterized by spontaneity, flexibility, decentralization, and they work creatively with the situations that present themselves.[26]

When we recognize as resistance only those acts which overthrow the dominators, we miss a great deal of information.

Consider the white upper-class victorian lady. In *The Yellow Wallpaper*, Charlotte Perkins Gilman portrays conditions faced by such women in the 1880s.[27] These conditions included a prescription of total female passivity by mind gynecologists such as S. Weir Mitchell,[28] prescriptions resulting from male scientists' sudden interest in women as the first wave of feminism attracted their attention, prescriptions enforced by those in control. The heroine is taken by her husband to a summer home for rest. He locks her in a nursery with bars on the windows, a bed bolted to the floor, and hideous wallpaper, shredded in spots. He rebuts her despair with the rhetoric of protection, refusing to indulge her "whims" when she protests the room's atrocity. He also stifles all her attempts at creativity, flying into a rage when he discovers that she has been writing in her diary. In the end she manages to crawl behind the wallpaper, escaping into "madness." Charlotte Perkins Gilman shows us a woman with every avenue of creativity and integrity patronizingly and paternalistically cut off "for her own good"; and we watch her slowly construct her resistance. Not surprisingly, male scientists and doctors of the day perceived nothing more in the story than a testament of feminine insanity.[29]

Resistance, in other words, may even take the form of insanity when someone is isolated within the confines of domination and all means of maintaining integrity have been systematically cut off. Mary's journey into oblivion with morphine in *Long Day's Journey into Night* is another example of resistance to domination, to the fatuous demands of loved ones, of husband and adult male children.[30] But the framework of 'femininity' dictates that such behavior be perceived as part of the "mysterious" nature of woman rather than recognized as resistance.

Significantly, one and the same word names 'insanity' and 'anger': 'mad'. As Phyllis Chesler documents, mind gynecologists call women "mad" whose behavior they can no longer understand as functioning in relation to men.[31] On the other hand, 'madness' in relation to 'anger' is defined as "ungovernable rage or fury."[32] We can ask, ungovernable by whom? Madness in anger and madness in insanity indicate that men have lost control.[e] When women are labeled "mad," they have become useless to men, a threat to male supremacy.

Thus, to maintain the feminine stereotype, men will characterize overt, clear-cut, obvious forms of resistance as insanity when women engage in them.[f] Just as slaves who ran away from masters were perceived as insane, so are women who fight back against battering husbands. Women who kill long-term battering husbands are, for the most part, forced to use the plea of insanity rather than the plea of self-defense: lawyers advise clients to plead insanity, and juries convict those who instead plead self-defense. As a result, the judicial system promotes the idea that the woman who effectively resists aggressive acts of male domination is insane. Insanity, thus, becomes part of women's nature, and resistance to domination becomes institutionally nonexistent.

However, institutionally characterizing women who fight back as insane is still not enough for men in power. Perceiving the plea of insanity as a license to kill, even though it means incarceration for an unspecified amount of time, media men began a campaign against women who fought back against husbands and boyfriends who beat them—depicting these women as "getting away with" murder.[33] Our governing fathers have reduced or, in some places, completely withdrawn funding of shelters for women, especially if there is lesbian presence, on the grounds that these shelters break up the family. And agencies on "domestic violence" work to keep the family intact, burying the conditions of oppression women face within the nuclear and extended family by obliterating the distinction between aggressor and victim.[34] The concept of 'femininity' not only blocks social perception of female resistance. When female resistance threatens to break through the stereotype and become socially perceptible, the conceptual framework comes full circle: authorities deny that the "problem" is the result of male domination.

Finally, many social scientists regard female competence itself in women as threatening to men, as subversive to the nuclear or extended family, and as going against the grain of civilization, hence as socially undesirable. For example, the moynihan report yielded a resurgence of white as well as black men espousing the theory of the black matriarch who "castrates" black men—implying that for black men to claim their manhood, or masculinity, black women must step behind and become subordinate to them.[35]

'Femininity' functions as a standard of heterosexualism. Standards or measures determine fact and are used to create (and later discover) fact; they themselves, however, are not discovered. An inch, for example, was not discovered. It was created and is used to determine boundaries. No amount of investigation into surfaces will ever confirm or disprove that inches exist or that inches accurately reflect the world. A standard is a way of measuring the world, of categorizing it, of determining its boundaries so men can act upon it. 'Femininity' is such a standard: it is a way of categorizing the world so that men can act upon it, and women can respond.

'Femininity' is a label whereby one group of people are defined in relation to another in such a way that the values of dominance and subordination are embedded in perceptual judgment of reality as if they were the essence of those involved. Under the feminine characterization, women appear naively content with being controlled to such an extent that resistance to domination ceases to exist—that is, goes undetected. Female resistance is rendered imperceptible or perceived as abnormal, mad, or of no significance by both women and men.

Now, some might object that (some of) the choices I've described as resistance or sabotage are self-defeating. For example, the housewife who spends money on items she does not need is limiting her ability to obtain things she does need. Thus, through this act of defiance she is really hurting herself. Or, the woman who burns dinners when her husband brings his boss home unexpectedly is still dependent on her husband having a job and would benefit from any promotion he might receive. If she fails to present herself as a competent hostess, the boss may decide against promoting her husband, noting that her husband does not have the trappings necessary for the social atmosphere within which business deals are made—namely, a charming wife and competent hostess. Thus, in sabotaging her husband's plans when he is inconsiderate, she appears to be acting against her own best interests.

Or, again, the slave who breaks her master's tools could find herself in even more dire circumstances. Although she is slowing the master's work, she will likely be punished for it. And should she appear too incompetent (unruly), she could be sold to someone perhaps more physically brutal, separated from those who know and care about her. Her sabotage seems to do more damage to herself than to anyone else. Someone might object that a woman making these choices may be resisting, but ultimately she is "cutting off her nose to spite her face." The woman who becomes an addict or an alcoholic or the woman who chooses suicide ... surely their acts are self-defeating, for the women lose themselves.

In a certain respect such acts of sabotage are self-defeating, but in other respects this is inaccurate. I have suggested that in situations in which a woman makes such choices, often she acts to differentiate herself from the will of the one who dominates. The one who dominates may be able to severely restrict the range of her choices, he may physically threaten her, he may have legal power of life and death over her. But it is yet another matter for him to totally control her, to make her believe she is nothing but an extension of his will.

My thesis is that when someone is in danger of losing any sense that she has a self about whom she can make decisions, she will in some way resist. When a man regards a woman as a being whose will should effectively be merged with his such that she is a mere extension of it, she will act in basic ways to block that merger and separate herself from his will. In such circumstances, sabotage cannot logically be self-defeating because, simply, the situation allows for no self to begin with.

Acts of sabotage can function to establish that self, to affirm a woman's separateness in her own mind. It may be more important to the woman who burns dinners to remind her self (and maybe her husband) that he cannot take her for granted than it is for her to rise socially and economically if that means that in doing so she will be taken for granted to an even greater extent. And it may be more important to the slave that she affirm her existence by thwarting the master's plan in some way than it is to try to secure safety in a situation in which believing she is safe is dangerously foolish. Even when a woman withdraws herself through alcohol or takes herself out still further through suicide, she may be establishing, rather than defeating, the self as a separate and distinct entity.[8] If a woman establishes her self as separate (at least in her own awareness) from the will of him who dominates by making certain decisions and carrying them out, then those choices are not self-defeating, since without them there would be no self to defeat.

In other respects, however, such actions *are* self-defeating. In the first place, to be successful, acts of sabotage cannot be detected as sabotage in a system where there is no hope of redress. While they may function to differentiate one's self from those who dominate, they do not challenge the feminine stereotype, rather they presuppose it. Even when engaged in by a majority of women, isolated and individual acts of sabotage do not change the conceptual or material conditions which lead a woman to engage in such acts. Instead, those in power will use such actions to bolster the idea that dominated beings require domination (protection) "for their own good." In this respect, then, acts of sabotage could be said to be self-defeating. But then the same could be said of any act a woman engages in. This is the trap of oppression,[36] the double bind of heterosexualism.

More significantly, acts of sabotage become self-defeating if the one who engages in them begins to internalize the feminine stereotype. For example, the woman who hoards beans may be resisting her husband's tyranny over the family budget, resisting his perception of her as merely existing to carry out his plans. But if he regards control of her budget as part of his god-given right—no, duty—as a man, then any resistance from her will have to be nipped in the bud, and if it recurs, severely dealt with. Now, in wasting household money, she may be affirming her self while not wishing to openly challenge his perceptions and bring his wrath upon her. But if she must attend too closely to his perceptions and encourage them, she may cross over and come to believe she is incompetent. And at this point her acts become self-defeating.

Or, the woman who "accidentally" burns dinners when her husband's boss comes in unexpectedly may be resisting her husband's vacuous perception of her. If his taking her for granted is a result of his sense of order in the universe such that she is simply not the sort of being who could have any say in things, then trying to prove otherwise may be fruitless. Instead, her goal may be to resist his psychological coercion by playing with his mind, acting the fluffy-headed housewife in order to thwart his expectations of her.

In this case the woman is using the traditional feminine stereotype to her (momentary) advantage. But in so doing, she may undermine her sense of self (unless she has an extremely strong capacity to maintain the sense of what she is doing in direct opposition to the entire set of values within which she must function). The stakes involved here are high—just as when a woman uses stereotypic feminine behaviors to get what she wants and make herself feel superior to the men she manipulates. She is in serious danger of internalizing the social perception of her self as 'feminine'. And should she internalize that value, her acts do become self-defeating.

A woman acting in isolation to maintain a sense of self under heterosexualism faces significant obstacles, for her choices have repercussions beyond an individual level. Again, while such acts of sabotage may be resistance, they don't effect change. For resistance to effect change, there must be a movement afoot, a conspiracy, a breathing together. And this brings up a third way acts of sabotage can be self-defeating. Since successful acts of sabotage cannot be detected as sabotage by those who dominate, then when there is a movement afoot, the choice to commit acts of sabotage becomes no different than the choice to participate in the dominance/subordination relationship of heterosexualism by embracing and developing feminine wiles.

That is, during times when a movement is afoot, when there is a conspiracy of voices, those women who choose to remain isolated from other women and yet engage in acts of sabotage when necessary may well be engaging in truly self-defeating behavior. They are bypassing a chance for more effective resistance and are in even greater danger of internalizing the values of heterosexualism. In this way, isolated acts of resistance can be self-defeating.

'Femininity' is a concept which goes a long way in the social construction of heterosexual reality. A movement of women could withdraw from that framework and begin to revalue that reality and women's choices within it. A movement of women can challenge the feminine stereotype, dis-cover women's resistance, and provide a base for more effective resistance. A movement of women can challenge the consensus that made the individual act of sabotage plausible.

Yet if that movement does not challenge the concept of 'femininity', ultimately it will not challenge the consensus, it will not challenge the dominance and subordination of heterosexualism. For example, radical feminists and revolutionary feminists in england criticize the women's work at greenham common for appealing too much to traditional feminine stereotypes, including woman as nurturer and peacemaker as well as sacrificer for her children. As a result, they argue, the peace movement coopts feminism.[37]

Further, feminism itself is in danger of perpetuating the value of 'femininity' in interpreting and evaluating individual women's choices. Feminists continue to note how women are victims of institutional and ordinary behavior, but many have ceased to challenge the concept of 'woman' and the role men and male institutions play as "protectors" of women. And feminism is susceptible to what Kathleen Barry calls 'victimism', which in effect portrays women as helpless and in need of protection.[38]

Blaming the Victim and Victimism

So much of our moral and political judgment involves either blaming the victim[39] or victimism. Victimism is the perception of victims of acknowledged social injustice, not as real persons making choices, but instead as passive objects of injustice. Kathleen Barry explains that in order to call attention to male violence and to prove that women are harmed by rape, feminists have portrayed women who have been raped by men as victims pure and simple—an understandable development. The problem is that

> the status of "victim" creates a mind set eliciting pity and sorrow. Victimism denies the woman the integrity of her humanity through the whole experience, and it creates a framework for others to know her not as a person but as a victim, someone to whom violence was done. ... Victimism is an objectification which establishes new standards for defining experience; those standards dismiss any question of will, and deny that the woman even while enduring sexual violence is a living, changing, growing, interactive person.[40]

For my purposes, blaming the victim involves holding a person accountable not only for her choice in a situation but for the situation itself, as if she agreed to it. Thus in masculinist thought, a woman will be judged responsible for her own rape. Victimism, on the other hand, completely ignores a woman's choices. In other words, victimism denies a woman's moral agency. Under victimism, women are still passive, helpless, and in need of special protection—still feminine.

A movement which challenges the dominant valuation of women will focus on women as agents in a relationship rather than as a type. A woman is not a massive being to whom things unfortunately or intentionally happen. She is a breathing, judging being, acting in coerced and oppressive circumstances. Her judgments and choices may be ineffective on any given occasion, or wrong, but they are decisions nevertheless. She is an agent and she is making choices. More than a victim, Kathleen Barry suggests, a woman caught in female sexual slavery is a survivor, making crucial decisions about what to do in order to survive. She is a moral agent who makes judgments within a context of oppression in consideration of her own needs and abilities.

By perceiving women's behavior, not through the value of 'femininity', but rather as actions of moral agents making judgments about their own needs and abilities in coerced and oppressive circumstances, we can begin to conceive of ourselves and each other as agents of our actions (though not creators of the circumstances we face under oppression). And this is a step toward realizing an ethical existence under oppression, one not caught up with the values of dominance and subordination.

Further, we can also begin to understand women's choices which actually embrace the feminine stereotype. Some women embrace 'femininity' outright, man-made though it is, or embrace particular aspects of it which involve some form of ritual or actual subordination to men, in the pursuit of what these women judge to be their own best interests. Some women embrace 'femininity' in a desperate attempt to find safety and to give some meaning to their existence.

In the first chapter of *Right-Wing Women,* Andrea Dworkin analyzes the choices of some white christian women, arguing that "from father's house to husband's house to a grave that still might not be her own, a woman acquiesces to male authority in order to gain some protection from male violence."[41] She argues that such acquiescence results from the treatment girls and women receive as part of their socialization:

> Rebellion can rarely survive the aversion therapy that passes for being brought up female. Male violence acts directly on the girl through her father or brother or uncle or any number of male professionals or strangers, as it did and does on her mother, and she too is forced to learn to conform in order to survive. A girl may, as she enters adulthood, repudiate the particular set of males with whom her mother is allied, run with a different pack as it were, but she will replicate her mother's patterns in acquiescing to male authority within her own chosen set. Using both force and threat, men in all camps demand that women accept abuse in silence and shame, tie themselves to hearth and home with rope made of self-blame, unspoken rage, grief, and resentment.[42]

Andrea Dworkin also argues that some women continue to submit to male authority because they finally believe it is the only way they can make sense of and give meaning to their otherwise apparently meaningless existence as women.[43] They find meaning through being bound to their protectors and having a common enemy. Their anger is thus given form and a safety valve, and is thereby deflected from its logical target. They become antisemites, queer-haters, and racists, and so create purpose in their existence.

Andrea Dworkin's analysis highlights two points of interest here. First, these women have the same information that radical feminists have (they know what men do), yet they are making different choices. Secondly, their choices stem from judgments they make about their own best interests. That is, they are choosing what they consider their best option from among those available. These are survival choices made in circumstances with restricted options.

Another group of women embrace 'femininity' from a different direction. In discussing why more black women are not involved in activist women's groups, instead considering themselves "Black first, female second" and embracing a version of the feminine ideal, Brunetta R. Wolfman presents a number of factors. She points to the traditionally greater independence black women enjoy from black men in the united states, since the legal end of slavery, than white women have enjoyed from white men. And she points to the commitment of women to the black church, in terms of time and loyalty, whereby a "scrub woman or maid could aspire to be the head of the usher board and a valuable, respected member of the congregation."[44]

However, she notes that the pattern in the black church here as well as in civil rights groups such as the n.a.a.c.p. or the urban league, has been one of women assuming secondary roles in deference to male leadership. She also points to the romantic sense of nobility, purity, and race pride personified in the stereotype of 'the black woman' and promulgated by nationalistic ideologies such as that of Marcus Garvey or the black muslims:

> The Muslims have taken the idealized Euro-American image of the middle-class wife and mother and made it the norm for the sect so that the women members must reject

the traditional independence of black women, adopting another style in the name of a separatist religious ideology. In return, Muslim men must respect and protect their women, a necessary complement to demands placed on females.[45]

This point is reiterated by Jacquelyn Grant as she argues:

> It is often said that women are the "backbone" of the church. ... It has become apparent to me that most of the ministers who use this term are referring to location rather than function. What they really mean is that women are in the background and should be kept there: they are merely support workers.[46]

Brunetta R. Wolfman goes on to discuss demands placed on black women by the black community as well as community expectation of a subordinate position for women. For example, she points out that women in the movement '60s were expected to keep black men from involving themselves with white women. She argues that this "duty is in keeping with a traditional feminine role, that of modifying or being responsible for the behavior of the group in general and the males in particular."[47] Further, she points out how feminist values such as control of one's own body were undermined as black (and white) men told black women there was no choice but to bear children in order to counterattack the white racist plan of black genocide being carried out through birth control programs.

While noting that the women's liberation movement included many demands that would help the social and economic position of black women, Brunetta R. Wolfman suggests that (many) black women have not responded to it, instead becoming a conservative force in the black community, partly because they have a strong sense of self as contributor to the survival of the black community and partly because they have been identified by american society as the polar opposite of the feminine ideal.[48] That is, since they have been excluded from the feminine ideal, they now embrace it.[h]

The jeopardy of racial genocide stemming from an external enemy and used to justify the ideology of male domination is real for u.s. black and other women of color in a way that it is not for u.s. right-wing christian white women. Nevertheless, the choice of embracing 'femininity' and male authority is similar in both cases, as is the threat members of each group face from men.

Further, such choices are not qualitatively different from choices made by feminists to defer to men and men's agendas and to soothe male egos in the pursuit of women's rights. (And such choices do not preclude acts of sabotage of the sort I've discussed when male domination encroaches too far upon a woman's sense of self.) They are survival choices. And what we can consider from outside the feminine valuation is whether such choices in the long run are self-enhancing or self-defeating.

The answers are varied and complex. But insofar as they lean toward the idea that embracing 'femininity' is not self-defeating, they also perpetuate what it means to be a 'woman': to be a 'woman' is to be subject to male domination and hence to be someone who enacts her agency through manipulation—exercising (some modicum of) control from a position of subordination. Should she act in any other way, she is, under heterosexualism, not only unnatural but also unethical.

Thus, while promoting an ethic for females, heterosexualism is a set of values which undermines female agency outside the master-slave values. Women hang on to those values out of fear, out of a choice to focus on men while taking women for granted, and out of a lack of perception of any other choices. As a result, although many women individually have resisted male domination—in particular, men's attempts to make women mere extensions of men's will—it is less clear that (with a few notable exceptions), as Simone de Beauvoir suggested, women as a group dispute male sovereignty. However, in claiming this, I am not suggesting that disputing male sovereignty means attempting to oppose men as men have opposed women.[i] Rather, I am suggesting that it seems, for the most part, that women, whether as saboteurs or acceptors of male domination, have not disputed the entire dominance/subordination game of heterosexualism.

I want a moral revolution. ...

Notes

a. In questioning the value of special protection for women, I am not saying that women should never ask for help. That's just foolish. I am talking about the ideal of women as needing sheltering. The concept of children needing special protection is prevalent and I challenge that concept when it is used to abrogate their integrity "for their own good." But at least protection for children theoretically involves ensuring that (male) children can grow up and learn to take care of themselves. That is, (male) children are protected until they have grown and developed skills and abilities they need to get on in this world. No such expectation is included in the ideal of special protection for women: the ideal of special protection of women does not include the expectation that women will ever be in a position to take care of themselves (grow up).

b. In her analysis of fairy tales, Andrea Dworkin points out that an active woman is portrayed as evil (the stepmother) and a good woman is generally asleep or dead (snow white, sleeping beauty).[49]

c. There have been many unacknowledged forms of resistance to male domination, for example, the use of purity to control male sexual aggression[50] as well as the use of piety to challenge a husband's authority. Further, many women entered convents to avoid marriage.[51] Typically, patrihistorians describe such strategies in ways that make it impossible to perceive them as resistance.

d. In pointing out how the concept of 'femininity' applies to various oppressed peoples, I do not mean to suggest that the *experience* of oppression is the same. The experience of black men or the experience of jewish men has not been the same as that of poor white gentile women or black women or jewish women or wives of southern plantation owners. Black male slaves were depicted as strong, virile beasts. If wives of southern plantation owners were also perceived as animals (pets), still there were crucial differences. And black slave women were treated as the opposite of the white southern belle. As Angela Davis points out, black women slaves were treated essentially as beasts of burden. Most worked in the fields, and some worked as coalminers or lumberjacks or ditchdiggers. And while white masters raped them in a show of economic and sexual mastery, black women were compelled to work while pregnant and nursing, and their children were treated like the offspring of animals—to be sold off.[52] Or again, poor white southern women and wives of plantation owners had significantly different experiences. My point is that the concept of 'femininity' operates to depict those who are dominated as dependent, incapable of caring for themselves—whether virile or otherwise—and as virtuous when subservient.

bell hooks challenges the theory that black men were emasculated by slavery on the grounds (1) that the black man's masculinity was almost reified, (2) that such a theory presupposes a classist assumption about black men getting their identities as breadwinners, and (3) that if emasculinization was an effect of slavery, then it would follow that black women were not affected—such a characterization renders women imperceptible. For example, if 'emasculinization' means 'dehumanization', then it implies that women are not human. Further, if the effect of slavery on black men was emasculinization, then the obvious solution is for black men to reclaim their masculinity, which means, among other things, an ability to dominate women.[53]

However, while the physical prowess of black slave men was played up, still, black slave men were dominated, which to men means being made like females. In heterosexual terms, to dominate is to feminize. That is why the concept of 'femininity' is bankrupt. Thus while I agree with bell hooks's analysis, I would still argue that the concept of the 'feminine' applies to black male slaves. Whites treated black men as beast-like, hence as something to be tamed or conquered, and hence as a feminine object. This is the contradiction in the stereotype of the black male slave. And those who stood up and resisted, both men and women, challenged the feminine stereotype. Unfortunately, some black and some jewish men and some chinese and native american men are currently emerging from under the domination of 'femininity' by laying claim to 'masculinity'.

e. When reading between the lines and reclaiming women from the past, we can examine the alternatives available to them and in that context understand their behavior. Thus, insanity itself can be a form of resistance, as can suicide. On the other hand, behavior that is not insanity may nevertheless be depicted as insane. As a result, there is a fine line, which can fade at times, between insanity as resistance and the behavior of the resistor who has not gone insane—who has maintained the confidence of her perceptions.

f. In 1916, a play by Susan Glaspell was first performed about a nebraska woman who strangled her husband in his sleep. The (male) authorities arrive on the scene all officious and yet cannot discover the motive—without which they cannot convict her. Their wives, having come along to get some clothes for the woman in jail, discover a number of things, including the body of a canary whose neck had been wrung. Joking about women's work, the men ignore the women, thinking them dealing with "trifles." Comprehending what had happened, the women hide the evidence; the woman who killed her husband is found innocent by a "jury of her peers."[54]

g. Thus alcoholism among lesbians has been a way of pursuing lesbian choices while rejecting the coercion of heterosexualism and the concept of 'woman'.

h. Other women have not involved themselves in the women's movement or have withdrawn from it because of racism among white women. My focus here is on women who embrace an ideal of feminine behavior in lieu of resistance to male domination.

i. Even what the amazons from between the black and caspian seas are reputed to have done was not a matter of opposing men as men have opposed women. At various times, some worry that women or lesbians or separatists want to do to men what men have done to women. Yet nowhere have I found any indication of women or lesbians wanting to subject men the way men have subjected women: have men de-skilled and dependent on women, have men find their identity through their relationships with women, have men isolated in women's houses waiting to care-take women, and so on. Mostly, I suspect, women and lesbians don't want the burden. Women's resistance to male domination has taken many forms. But in my understanding, it has never, even in fantasy, been a reversal of men's efforts.

1. For further development of this point, note Marilyn Frye, "Oppression," in *The Politics of Reality: Essays in Feminist Theory* (Trumansburg, N.Y.: The Crossing Press, 1983, now in Freedom, Calif.), pp. 5–6.

2. Note Susan Griffin, "Rape: The All-American Crime," in *Feminism and Philosophy*, ed. Mary Vetterling-Braggin, Frederick A. Elliston, & Jane English (Totowa, N.J.: Littlefield, Adams & Co., 1977), especially p. 320.

3. Sonia Johnson, presidential campaign speech, Chicago, Ill., 1984; conversation, Pauline Bart. The figure on wife-beating comes from the "Uniform Crime Reports of 1982," federal reports on incidences of domestic crime. According to a fact sheet from the Illinois Coalition on Domestic Violence, "National Domestic Violence Statistics, 1/84," ten to twenty percent of American children are abused. Another fact sheet, "Verified Domestic Statistics," researched

and compiled by the Western Center on Domestic Violence (San Francisco, Calif.), cites estimates of Maria Roy, *The Abusive Partner* (New York: Van Nostrand Rernhold, 1982) as indicating that violence against wives will occur at least once in two-thirds of all marriages. Another fact sheet, "Wife Abuse: The Facts" (Center for Woman Policy Studies, 2000 P. Street N.W., Washington, D.C. 20036), cites Murray Straus, Richard Gelles and Suzanne Steinmetz, *Beyond Closed Doors: Violence in the American Family* (Garden City, N.Y.: Doubleday, 1980) as saying that twenty-five percent of wives are severely beaten during their marriage. There are many more statistics ... you get the idea. Bette S. Tallen was extremely helpful in obtaining some of this information. Note also Del Martin, *Battered Wives*, revised and updated (Volcano Press, Inc., 330 Ellis St., #518, Dept. B, San Francisco, CA 94102, 1976, 1981); Leonore Walker, *The Battered Woman* (New York: Harper & Row, 1979); Florence Rush, *The Best Kept Secret: The Sexual Abuse of Children* (Englewood Cliffs, N.J.: Prentice-Hall, Inc., 1980); Diana E. H. Russell, *Sexual Exploitation: Rape, Child Sexual Abuse, and Workplace Harassment* (Beverly Hills, Calif.: Sage Publications, 1984); and Elizabeth A. Stanko, *Intimate Intrusions: Women's Experience of Male Violence* (Boston, Mass.: Routledge & Kegan Paul, 1985) among others.

4. Marilyn Frye, "In and Out of Harm's Way: Arrogance and Love," *Politics of Reality*, p. 72.

5. Sonia Johnson, "Excerpts from the last chapter of *Going Out Of Our Minds and Other Revolutionary Acts of the Spirit,*" *Mama Bears News & Notes* 3, no. 2 (April/May 1986): 15; also in *Going Out of Our Minds: The Metaphysics of Liberation* (Freedom, Calif.: The Crossing Press, 1987), p. 336.

6. Note, for example, Barbara Burris, "The Fourth World Manifesto," *Notes from the Third Year*, 1971, revised and reprinted in *Radical Feminism*, ed. Anne Koedt, Ellen Levine, and Anita Rapone (New York: New York Times Book Co., 1973), pp. 322–57; Margaret Small, "Lesbians and the Class Position of Women," in *Lesbianism and the Women's Movement*, ed. Nancy Myron and Charlotte Bunch (Baltimore: Diana Press, 1975), pp. 49–61; Robin Morgan, "On Women as a Colonized People," in *Going Too Far: The Personal Chronicle of a Feminist* (New York: Random House, 1977); Anne Summers, *Damned Whores and God's Police: The Colonization of Women in Australia* (Ringwood, Victoria, Australia: Penguin, 1975); and Kathleen Barry, "Sex Colonization," in *Female Sexual Slavery* (Englewood Cliffs, N.J.: Prentice-Hall, 1979), pp. 163–204.

7. Walter Rodney, *How Europe Underdeveloped Africa* (Washington, D.C.: Howard University Press, 1982).

8. Conversation, Bette S. Tallen.

9. Sonia Johnson, "Telling the Truth," *Trivia* 9 (Fall 1986): 21; also in *Going Out of Our Minds*, p. 249.

10. Ann Oakley, *Women's Work: The Housewife, Past and Present* (New York: Vintage Books/Random House, 1974), p. 19.

11. Gena Corea, *The Mother Machine: Reproductive Technologies from Artificial Insemination to Artificial Wombs* (New York: Harper & Row, 1985), p. 303.

12. Alice Molloy, *In Other Words: Notes on the Politics and Morale of Survival* (Oakland, Calif.: Women's Press Collective, n.d., write Alice Molloy, Mama Bears, 6536 Telegraph Ave., Oakland, CA 94609).

13. Alix Kates Shulman, *Memoirs of an Ex-Prom Queen* (New York: Bantam Books, 1973).

14. Information on this film can be obtained from the American Film & Video Network, 1723 Howard, Evanston, Ill.

15. This monologue is based on my memory and possibly inaccurate in detail. I believe, however, that I have invoked the general idea the woman was expressing.

16. Kate Millett, *Sexual Politics* (New York: Doubleday, 1969), p. 26.

17. Naomi Weisstein, *Psychology Constructs the Female, or: The Fantasy Life of the Male Psychologist*, reprint (Boston: New England Free Press, 1968); reprinted in *Sisterhood Is Powerful: An Anthology of Writings from the Women's Liberation Movement*, ed. Robin Morgan (New York: Random House, 1970), pp. 205–20; and in *Women in Sexist Society*, ed. Vivian Gornick

and Barbara K. Moran (New York: Signet, 1971), pp. 207–24; also in *Radical Feminism*, ed. Anne Koedt, Ellen Levine, and Anita Rapone, pp. 178–97.

18. Research of Betty Carpenter, personal communication.

19. Mary Daly, *Pure Lust: Elemental Feminist Philosophy* (Boston: Beacon Press, 1984), p. 38.

20. Kate Millett, *Sexual Politics*, p. 347.

21. Angela Davis, "Reflections on the Black Woman's Role in the Community of Slaves," in *Contemporary Black Thought: Best From The Black Scholar*, ed. Robert Chrisman and Nathan Hare (Indianapolis: Bobbs-Merrill, 1973), p. 148; note also Herbert Aptheker, *American Negro Slave Revolts* (New York: International Publishers, 1970) (1st. ed., 1943), as cited by Angela Davis.

22. Note, for example, Earl Conrad, *Harriet Tubman* (New York: Paul S. Eriksson, Inc., 1969).

23. Ruthe Winegarten, "I Am Annie Mae: The Personal Story of a Black Texas Woman," *Chrysalis* 10 (Spring 1980): 15; later published: *I Am Annie Mae: An Extraordinary Woman in Her Own Words: The Personal Story of a Black Texas Woman*, ed. Ruthe Winegarten (Austin, Tex.: Rosegarden Press, 1983).

24. After formulating this thesis, I came across documented evidence of it. Note Gilbert Osofsky, ed., *Puttin' On Ole Massa* (New York: Harper & Row, 1969); Aran Bontemps, ed., *Great Slave Narratives* (Boston: Beacon Press, 1969); and Willie Lee Rose, ed., *A Documentary History of Slavery in North America* (New York: Oxford University Press, 1976). Unfortunately, these collections almost exclusively address the lives of men. For a ground-breaking work on women slaves, note Erlene Stetson, "Studying Slavery: Some Literary and Pedagogical Considerations on the Black Female Slave," in *All the Women Are White, All the Blacks Are Men, But Some of Us Are Brave: Black Women's Studies*, ed. Gloria T. Hull, Patricia Bell Scott, and Barbara Smith (Old Westbury, N.Y.: Feminist Press, 1982), pp. 61–84; note also, Angela Davis, "Reflections on the Black Woman's Role in the Community of Slaves."

25. Simone Wallace, Ellen Ledley, Paula Tobin, letter to *off our backs*, December 1979, p. 28.

26. Note, for example, Barbara Harford and Sarah Hopkins, eds., *Greenham Common: Women at the Wire* (London: Women's Press, 1984); also Alice Cook & Gwyn Kirk, *Greenham Women Everywhere: Dreams, Ideas and Actions From the Women's Peace Movement* (Boston: South End Press, 1984).

27. Charlotte Perkins Gilman, *The Yellow Wallpaper* (Old Westbury, N.Y.: Feminist Press, 1973).

28. For information on S. Weir Mitchell, note G. J. Barker-Benfield, *The Horrors of the Half-Known Life: Male Attitudes Toward Women and Sexuality in Nineteenth Century America* (New York: Harper & Row, 1976).

29. Elaine R. Hedges, "Afterword," in *The Yellow Wallpaper*, Charlotte Perkins Gilman.

30. Eugene O'Neill, *Long Day's Journey into Night* (New Haven, Conn.: Yale University Press, 1955).

31. Phyllis Chesler, *Women and Madness* (Garden City, N.Y.: Doubleday, 1972).

32. *The Compact Edition of the Oxford English Dictionary*, 1971.

33. Ann Jones, *Women Who Kill* (New York: Holt, Rinehart, and Winston, 1980), p. 291.

34. Kathleen Barry, *Female Sexual Slavery*, pp. 142–4.

35. For some discussion of this, note Jean Carey Bond and Pat Peery, "Is the Black Male Castrated?" in *Black Woman*, ed. Toni Cade, pp. 113–9; Patricia Bell Scott, "Debunking Sapphire: Toward a Non-Racist and Non-Sexist Social Science," in *But Some of Us Are Brave*, pp. 85–92; Bonnie Thornton Dill, "The Dialectics of Black Womanhood," in *Feminism & Methodology*, ed. Sandra Harding (Bloomington: Indiana University Press, 1987), pp. 98–9; and Angela Davis, "Reflections on the Black Woman's Role in the Community of Slaves"; note also Erlene Stetson, "Studying Slavery."

36. Note Marilyn Frye, "Oppression," in *The Politics of Reality*, pp. 1–16.

37. Note, for example, *Breaching the Peace: A Collection of Radical Feminist Papers* (London: Onlywomen Press, 1983).

38. Kathleen Barry, *Female Sexual Slavery,* pp. 43–6.

39. William Ryan, *Blaming the Victim* (New York: Vintage Books, 1976).

40. Kathleen Barry, *Female Sexual Slavery,* p. 45.

41. Andrea Dworkin, *Right-Wing Women* (New York: G. P. Putnam's Sons/Perigee, 1983), p. 14.

42. Ibid., p. 15.

43. Ibid., pp. 17, 21.

44. Brunetta R. Wolfman, "Black First, Female Second," in *Black Separatism and Social Reality: Rhetoric and Reason,* ed. Raymond L. Hall (New York: Pergamon Press, 1977), p. 228.

45. Ibid., p. 229.

46. Jacquelyn Grant, "Black Women and the Black Church," in *But Some of Us Are Brave,* p. 141.

47. Brunetta R. Wolfman, "Black First, Female Second," p. 230.

48. Ibid., p. 231.

49. Andrea Dworkin, *Woman Hating* (New York: E.P. Dutton & Co., 1974), pp. 29–49.

50. Sheila Jefferies, *The Spinster and Her Enemies: Feminism and Sexuality, 1880–1930* (Boston: Pandora Press, 1985); Andrea Dworkin, *Pornography.*

51. This is one of the themes in *Lesbian Nuns: Breaking the Silence* (Tallahassee, Fla.: The Naiad Press, 1985).

52. Angela Davis, *Women, Race and Class* (New York: Vintage Books/Random House, 1983), chapter 1, pp. 3–29.

53. bell hooks, *Ain't I a Woman: Black Women and Feminism* (Boston: South End Press, 1981), chapters 2 and 3, pp. 51–117.

54. Susan Glaspell, "Trifles: A Play in One Act," in *Plays* (Boston: Small Maynard & Co., 1920, an authorized facsimile of the original book was produced by Xerox University Microfilms, Ann Arbor, Michigan, 1976). Blanche Hersh brought this play to my attention.

Suggested Further Readings

Barry, Kathleen. *Female Sexual Slavery.* Englewood Cliffs, N.J.: Prentice-Hall, 1979.

Daly, Mary. *Gyn/Ecology: The Metaethics of Radical Feminism.* Boston: Beacon Press, 1978.

_____. *Pure Lust: Elemental Feminist Philosophy.* Boston, Beacon Press, 1984.

Dworkin, Andrea. *Woman Hating: A Radical Look at Sexuality.* New York: E. P. Dutton, 1974.

_____. *Our Blood: Prophecies and Discourses on Sexual Politics.* New York: G. P. Putnam, 1981.

_____. *Pornography: Men Possessing Women.* New York: Perigee Books, 1981.

Frye, Marilyn. *The Politics of Reality: Essays in Feminist Theory.* Trumansburg, N.Y.: Crossing Press, 1983.

Hoagland, Sarah. *Lesbian Ethics: Toward New Values.* Palo Alto: Institute of Lesbian Studies, 1988.

Jaggar, Alison M. *Feminist Politics and Human Nature.* Totowa, N.J.: Rowman & Allanheld, 1983.

MacKinnon, Catharine A. *Feminism Unmodified: Discourses on Life and the Law.* Cambridge: Harvard University Press, 1977.

Millett, Kate. *Sexual Politics.* Garden City: Doubleday, 1970.

Raymond, Janice. *A Passion for Friends.* Boston: Beacon Press, 1986.

Rich, Adrienne. *Of Woman Born: Motherhood as Experience and Institution.* New York: W. W. Norton, 1976.

_____. "Compulsory Heterosexuality and the Lesbian Experience." *Signs: Journal of Women in Culture and Society* 5, no. 4 (1980):631–690.

Tong, Rosemarie. *Feminist Thought: A Comprehensive Introduction.* Boulder: Westview Press, 1989.

FOUR

PSYCHOANALYTIC FEMINIST

PERSPECTIVES

According to psychoanalytic feminists, the root of women's oppression is deeply embedded in the human psyche. The conscious aspects of personality—for example, one's general self-concept and gender identity ("masculine" or "feminine")—are dependent upon the stability of an unconscious organization that is completed by age three. No matter how much workplace equality and reproductive freedom women secure, psychoanalytic feminists insist that unless women gain insight into how their psychic lives—especially their sexual lives—were structured while they were still infants, they will remain unknowing, if not also unwilling, victims of a rather rigid "feminine" role.

Like many psychoanalytic feminists, Nancy Chodorow begins, although certainly does not end, her account of boys' and girls' psychosexual development in classical Freudian terms. Originally, in the so-called pre-Oedipal stage, all infants are symbiotically attached to their mothers, whom they perceive as omnipotent. The mother-infant relationship is an ambivalent one, however, because mother at times gives too much—her presence overwhelms; at other times mother gives too little—her absence disappoints. For the boy, the intense intimacy of the pre-Oedipal stage ends with the Oedipus complex, the process through which he gives up his first love object, mother, in order to escape castration at the hands of father. As a result of submitting his id (or desires) to the superego (collective social conscience), the boy is fully integrated into culture. Together with his father, he will rule over nature and woman. In contrast to the boy, the girl, who has no penis to lose, rarely separates totally from her first love object, mother. Thus, to the degree that her pre-Oedipal intimacy with her mother persists, the girl's integration into culture is incomplete. She exists at the periphery or margin of culture as the one who does not rule but is ruled.

What most interests Chodorow about this tale of childhood psychosexual development is the different "object-relational" experiences boys and girls have with their mothers during the *pre-Oedipal stage*. As Chodorow sees it, the pre-Oedipal stage is sexually charged for boys in a way that it is not for girls. Feeling a sexual current between himself and his mother, the son senses that his mother's body is not like his body. As he enters the Oedipal stage, the son realizes how much of a problem his mother's "otherness" poses for him. He cannot remain in love with her without risking his father's wrath. Not willing to take this risk, the son separates from his mother. What makes this process of separation less painful for the son is his dawning realization that power and prestige are to be had through identification with men—in this case, the father. Apparently, social contempt for women helps the boy define himself in opposition to the female sex his mother represents.

In contrast to the mother-son pre-Oedipal relationship, the mother-daughter pre-Oedipal relationship is characterized by a longer symbiosis. Because both the daughter and mother are female, the daughter's sense of gender and self is continuous with that of the mother. Although the symbiosis between mother and daughter is weakened during the Oedipal stage, and although most girls do finally transfer their primary love from a female to a male object, Chodorow argues that the mother-daughter bond is never really broken. Regardless of whether a girl develops into a heterosexual woman, she will tend to find her strongest emotional connections with women, and she will tend to put a higher premium on the integrity of her relational network than will her male counterpart.

In her article, "Family Structure and Feminine Personality," Chodorow does not argue that all and only men are oriented toward "achievement and self-reliance," whereas all and only women are oriented toward "nurturance and responsibility." Instead she claims that in certain kinds of societies women typically have more problems with separation and individuation than men and that men have more problems with intimacy and connectedness than women. Interestingly, Chodorow's remedy for male overindividuation and female overconnectedness is the same: Dual careers and dual parenting must become the rule.

> Boys need to grow up around men who take a major role in child care, and girls around women who, in addition to their child-care responsibilities, have a valued role and recognized spheres of legitimate control. These arrangements could help to ensure that children of both sexes develop a sufficiently individuated and strong sense of self, as well as a positively valued and secure gender identity, that does not bog down either in ego-boundary confusion, low self-esteem, and overwhelming relatedness to others, or in compulsive denial of any connection to others or dependency upon them.

If boys and girls are raised by men and women who are equally comfortable and successful in both the private and public worlds, chances are that neither sex will feel that it is somehow better or worse than the other sex.

Chodorow routinely makes the point that the psychosexual development of boys and girls is not without *social* implications. The boy's separateness from his mother is the source of his inability to relate deeply to others, an inability that prepares him for work in the public sphere, which values single-minded efficiency, a down-to-business attitude, and competitiveness. Similarly, the girl's oneness with her mother is the source of her capacity for relatedness, a capacity that is necessary for her role as nurturant wife and mother in the private sphere. In her essay "Political Philosophy and the Patriarchal Unconscious: A Psychoanalytic Perspective on Epistemology and Metaphysics," Jane Flax makes the related point that the psychosexual development of boys and girls also has epistemological and metaphysical implications. Philosophy, argues Flax, is not separate from the philosophers who produce it. If philosophers experience the same pre-Oedipal and Oedipal crisis that other human beings experience, those experiences will shape (or misshape) their philosophies. Because Western philosophy is largely the product of men, it articulates a worldview that favors the values of separation and individuation over those of symbiosis and connectedness.

As Flax sees it, Western male philosophers have been particularly unwilling to confront (1) their initial symbiosis with their mothers, (2) the trauma of separating from their mothers in order to become like their fathers, and (3) their desire to re-experience their initial symbiosis with their mothers. Rather than learning to live with their human vulnerabilities and dependencies, they have instead sought ways not only to deny and repress their early infantile experience but also to control it and everything they associate with it: nature, the body, the emotions, and women. In Plato and Descartes, says Flax, this denial and repression results in both splitting the mind from the body and denigrating the body. In Hobbes, it takes the form of interpreting women's reproductive work as less than fully human or civilized work. In Rousseau, it takes the form of regarding the domestic realm as a syrupy and sweet quagmire that softens the natural savage into a dependent, slavelike creature.

Flax's remedy for this state of affairs is for feminists to rethink epistemology (theory of knowledge) and metaphysics (theory of being). Philosophers must stop denying and repressing the human infantile experience and must think the kind of thoughts that will enable human beings to choose *interdependence* and *reciprocity* over arrogant independence on the one hand and servile dependence on the other. Dualistic thinking (subject-object, mind-body, inner-outer, reason-sense) must be replaced by the kind of thinking that is able to accept differences without "translating" those differences into a contrast between that which is better, superior, and higher and that which is worse, inferior, and lower.

To the degree that Flax uses the insights of psychoanalytic feminism to challenge traditional philosophy, Shirley Nelson Garner uses them to challenge this culture's heterosexism. In "Feminism, Psychoanalysis, and the Heterosexual Imperative," Garner argues that despite the fact that Freud acknowledged "the essential bisexuality of human beings," his theories point to heterosexuality as *the* sexual norm for both men and women. What most interests Garner is the fact that until the late 1950s, when an increasing number of psychoanalysts began to describe lesbianism as a lifestyle choice, they had often treated it as a pathological condition. Garner notes that it is not easy to move from a view according to which lesbianism is somehow deviant or abnormal to a view according to which it is not only normal but perhaps even "natural" for women. As she sees it, if both women's and men's primary attachments are, as Nancy Chodorow says, to the mother, what needs to be explained is why so many women switch their primary love object from a female one to a male one. The trauma must be enormous, and only explanations like Adrienne Rich's for women's renunciation of lesbianism in favor of heterosexuality seem at all pervasive. Rich specifically claims, says

Garner, that "male power forces heterosexuality upon women," that it is a means of "assuring male right of physical, economical, and emotional access."

Despite the fact that she is critical of the way psychoanalytic theory has explained lesbianism, Garner believes that psychoanalytic feminists are gradually pushing lesbianism from the margins of psychoanalytic theory into its center. She notes that the right kind of questions are being posed, including Luce Irigaray's telling question: "Why should the desire for likeness, for a female likeness, be forbidden to, or impossible for, the woman? Then again, *why are mother-daughter relations necessarily conceived in terms of 'masculine' desire* and homosexuality?" What Irigaray is challenging, of course, is any interpretation of female sexuality in terms of male sexuality. Feminists must persuade psychoanalysts to formulate a theory of female sexuality that is not parasitic upon a theory of male sexuality. The question of what *women want* is to be asked and answered independently of the question of what *men need.*

Yet, even if psychoanalytic feminists overcome their heterosexist tendencies, they will also need to become increasingly sensitive to issues of race and class. It is not enough to acknowledge, as Chodorow does, that her theory best explains the experiences of Western, middle-class (and apparently also white and heterosexual) women; it also needs to be stretched to include the experience of all sorts of women. Child-rearing practices admit to enormous variation. Working-class people often engage in dual parenting as a matter of necessity rather than choice. After all, when mother works the midnight to 8:00 A.M. shift and father works from 3:00 P.M. to 11:00 P.M., father will probably learn how to get breakfast and lunch for the children. Moreover, in this society, fewer and fewer children are raised by two parents. Female-headed families are numerous, and a high percentage are sustained by women of color. Clearly, the Oedipus tale varies if a child is raised exclusively by his or her mother with no father figure in attendance. The challenge for psychoanalytic feminists is to look to the *actual* ways in which racially and ethnically diverse parents rear their children. To be sure, some psychoanalytic feminists have already begun to move in this direction, but their walk has only begun and may well end with entirely new versions of the Oedipus tale.

Originally Published:

Woman, Culture, and Society,

*Michelle Zimbalist Rosaldo and Louise
Lamphere, eds. (Stanford: Stanford University
Press, 1974), pp. 43-66.*

Family Structure
and Feminine Personality

Nancy Chodorow

I propose here[1] a model to account for the reproduction within each generation of certain general and nearly universal differences that characterize masculine and feminine personality and roles. My perspective is largely psychoanalytic. Cross-cultural and social-psychological evidence suggests that an argument drawn solely from the universality of biological sex differences is unconvincing.[2] At the same time, explanations based on patterns of deliberate socialization (the most prevalent kind of anthropological, sociological, and social-psychological explanation) are in themselves insufficient to account for the extent to which psychological and value commitments to sex differences are so emotionally laden and tenaciously maintained, for the way gender identity and expectations about sex role and gender consistency are so deeply central to a person's consistent sense of self.

This paper suggests that a crucial differentiating experience in male and female development arises out of the fact that women, universally, are largely responsible for early child care and for (at least) later female socialization. This points to the central importance of the mother-daughter relationship for women, and to a focus on the conscious and unconscious effects of early involvement with a female for children of both sexes. The fact that males and females experience this social environment differently as they grow up accounts for the development of basic sex differences in personality. In particular, certain features of the mother-daughter relationship are internalized universally as basic elements of feminine ego structure (although not necessarily what we normally mean by "femininity").

Specifically, I shall propose that, in any given society, feminine personality comes to define itself in relation and connection to other people more than masculine personality does. (In psychoanalytic terms, women are less individuated than men; they have more flexible ego boundaries.[3]) Moreover, issues of dependency are handled and experienced differently by men and women. For boys and men, both individuation and dependency issues become tied up with the sense of masculinity, or masculine identity. For girls and women, by contrast, issues of femininity, or feminine identity, are not problematic in the same way. The structural situation of child rearing, reinforced by female and male role training, produces these differences, which are replicated and reproduced in the sexual sociology of adult life.

199

The paper is also a beginning attempt to rectify certain gaps in the social-scientific literature, and a contribution to the reformulation of psychological anthropology. Most traditional accounts of family and socialization tend to emphasize only role training, and not unconscious features of personality. Those few that rely on Freudian theory have abstracted a behaviorist methodology from this theory, concentrating on isolated "significant" behaviors like weaning and toilet training. The paper advocates instead a focus on the ongoing interpersonal relationships in which these various behaviors are given meaning.[4]

More empirically, most social-scientific accounts of socialization, child development, and the mother-child relationship refer implicitly or explicitly only to the development and socialization of boys, and to the mother-son relationship. There is a striking lack of systematic description about the mother-daughter relationship, and a basic theoretical discontinuity between, on the one hand, theories about female development, which tend to stress the development of "feminine" qualities in relation to and comparison with men, and on the other hand, theories about women's ultimate mothering role. This final lack is particularly crucial, because women's motherhood and mothering role seem to be the most important features in accounting for the universal secondary status of women (Chodorow, 1971; Ortner, Rosaldo, this volume). The present paper describes the development of psychological qualities in women that are central to the perpetuation of this role.

In a formulation of this preliminary nature, there is not a great body of consistent evidence to draw upon. Available evidence is presented that illuminates aspects of the theory—for the most part psychoanalytic and social-psychological accounts based almost entirely on highly industrialized Western society. Because aspects of family structure are discussed that are universal, however, I think it is worth considering the theory as a general model. In any case, this is in some sense a programmatic appeal to people doing research. It points to certain issues that might be especially important in investigations of child development and family relationships, and suggests that researchers look explicitly at female vs. male development, and that they consider seriously mother-daughter relationships even if these are not of obvious "structural importance" in a traditional anthropological view of that society.

The Development of Gender Personality

According to psychoanalytic theory,[5] personality is a result of a boy's or girl's social-relational experiences from earliest infancy. Personality development is not the result of conscious parental intention. The nature and quality of the social relationships that the child experiences are appropriated, internalized, and organized by her/him and come to constitute her/his personality. What is internalized from an ongoing relationship continues independent of that original relationship and is generalized and set up as a permanent feature of the personality. The conscious self is usually not aware of many of the features of personality, or of its total structural organization. At the same time, these are important determinants of any person's behavior, both that which is culturally expected and that which is idiosyncratic or unique to the individual. The conscious aspects of personality, like a person's general self-concept and, importantly, her/his gender identity, require and depend upon the consistency and stability of its unconscious organization. In what follows I shall describe how contrasting male and female experiences lead to differences in the way that the developing masculine or feminine psyche resolves certain relational issues.

Separation and Individuation (Preoedipal Development). All children begin life in a state of "infantile dependence" (Fairbairn, 1952) upon an adult or adults, in most cases their mother. This state consists first in the persistence of primary identification with the mother: the child does not differentiate herself/himself from her/his mother but experiences a sense of oneness with her. (It is important to distinguish this from later forms of identification, from "secondary identification," which presuppose at least some degree of experienced separateness by the person who identifies.) Second, it includes an oral-incorporative mode of relationship to the world, leading, because of the infant's total helplessness, to a strong attachment to and dependence upon whoever nurses and carries her/him.

Both aspects of this state are continuous with the child's prenatal experience of being emotionally and physically part of the mother's body and of the exchange of body material through the placenta. That this relationship continues with the natural mother in most societies stems from the fact that women lactate. For convenience, and not because of biological necessity, this has usually meant that mothers, and females in general, tend to take all care of babies. It is probable that the mother's continuing to have major responsibility for the feeding and care of the child (so that the child interacts almost entirely with her) extends and intensifies her/his period of primary identification with her more than if, for instance, someone else were to take major or total care of the child. A child's earliest experience, then, is usually of identity with and attachment to a single mother, and always with women.

For both boys and girls, the first few years are preoccupied with issues of separation and individuation. This includes breaking or attenuating the primary identification with the mother and beginning to develop an individuated sense of self, and mitigating the totally dependent oral attitude and attachment to the mother. I would suggest that, contrary to the traditional psychoanalytic model, the preoedipal experience is likely to differ for boys and girls. Specifically, the experience of mothering for a woman involves a double identification (Klein and Rivière, 1937). A woman identifies with her own mother and, through identification with her child, she (re)experiences herself as a cared-for child. The particular nature of this double identification for the individual mother is closely bound up with her relationship to her own mother. As Deutsch expresses it, "In relation to her own child, woman repeats her own mother-child history" (1944: 205). Given that she was a female child, and that identification with her mother and mothering are so bound up with her being a woman, we might expect that a woman's identification with a girl child might be stronger; that a mother, who is, after all, a person who is a woman and not simply the performer of a formally defined role, would tend to treat infants of different sexes in different ways.

There is some suggestive sociological evidence that this is the case. Mothers in a women's group in Cambridge, Massachusetts (see note 1), say that they identified more with their girl children than with boy children. The perception and treatment of girl vs. boy children in high-caste, extremely patriarchal, patrilocal communities in India are in the same vein. Families express preference for boy children and celebrate when sons are born. At the same time, Rajput mothers in North India are "as likely as not" (Minturn and Hitchcock, 1963) to like girl babies better than boy babies once they are born, and they and Havik Brahmins in South India (Harper, 1969) treat their daughters with greater affection and leniency than their sons. People in both groups say that this is out of sympathy for the future plight of their daughters, who will have to leave their natal family for a strange and usually oppressive postmarital household. From the time of their daughters' birth, then, mothers in these communities identify anticipatorily, by reexperiencing their own past, with the experiences of separation that their daughters will go through. They develop a particular attachment to their daughters because of this and by imposing their own reaction to the issue of separation on this new external situation.

It seems, then, that a mother is more likely to identify with a daughter than with a son, to experience her daughter (or parts of her daughter's life) as herself. Fliess's description (1961) of his neurotic patients who were the children of ambulatory psychotic mothers presents the problem in its psychopathological extreme. The example is interesting, because, although Fliess claims to be writing about people defined only by the fact that their problems were tied to a particular kind of relationship to their mothers, an overwhelmingly large proportion of the cases he presents are women. It seems, then, that this sort of disturbed mother inflicts her pathology predominantly on daughters. The mothers Fliess describes did not allow their daughters to perceive themselves as separate people, but simply acted as if their daughters were narcissistic extensions or doubles of themselves, extensions to whom were attributed the mothers' bodily feelings and who became physical vehicles for their mothers' achievement of autoerotic gratification. The daughters were bound into a mutually dependent "hypersymbiotic" relationship. These mothers, then, perpetuate a mutual relationship with their daughters of both primary identification and infantile dependence.

A son's case is different. Cultural evidence suggests that insofar as a mother treats her son differently, it is usually by emphasizing his masculinity in opposition to herself and by pushing him to assume, or acquiescing in his assumption of, a sexually toned male-role relation to her. Whiting (1959) and Whiting et al. (1958) suggest that mothers in societies with mother-child sleeping arrangements and postpartum sex taboos may be seductive toward infant sons. Slater (1968) describes the socialization of precarious masculinity in Greek males of the classical period through their mothers' alternation of sexual praise and seductive behavior with hostile deflation and ridicule. This kind of behavior contributes to the son's differentiation from his mother and to the formation of ego boundaries (I will later discuss certain problems that result from this).

Neither form of attitude or treatment is what we would call "good mothering." However, evidence of differentiation of a pathological nature in the mother's behavior toward girls and boys does highlight tendencies in "normal" behavior. It seems likely that from their children's earliest childhood, mothers and women tend to identify more with daughters and to help them to differentiate less, and that processes of separation and individuation are made more difficult for girls. On the other hand, a mother tends to identify less with her son, and to push him toward differentiation and the taking on of a male role unsuitable to his age, and undesirable at any age in his relationship to her.

For boys and girls, the quality of the preoedipal relationship to the mother differs. This, as well as differences in development during the oedipal period, accounts for the persisting importance of preoedipal issues in female development and personality that many psychoanalytic writers describe.[6] Even before the establishment of gender identity, gender personality differentiation begins.

Gender Identity (Oedipal Crisis and Resolution). There is only a slight suggestion in the psychological and sociological literature that preoedipal development differs for boys and girls. The pattern becomes explicit at the next developmental level. All theoretical and empirical accounts agree that after about age three (the beginning of the "oedipal" period, which focuses on the attainment of a stable gender identity) male and female development becomes radically different. It is at this stage that the father, and men in general, begin to become important in the child's primary object world. It is, of course, particularly difficult to generalize about the attainment of gender identity and sex-role assumption, since there is such wide variety in the sexual sociology of different societies. However, to the extent that in all societies women's life tends to be more private and domestic, and men's more public and social ... , we can make general statements about this kind of development.

In what follows, I shall be talking about the development of gender personality and gender identity in the tradition of psychoanalytic theory. Cognitive psychologists have established that by the age of three, boys and girls have an irreversible conception of what their gender is (cf. Kohlberg, 1966). I do not dispute these findings. It remains true that children (and adults) may know definitely that they are boys (men) or girls (women), and at the same time experience conflicts or uncertainty about "masculinity" or "femininity," about what these identities require in behavioral or emotional terms, etc. I am discussing the development of "gender identity" in this latter sense.

A boy's masculine gender identification must come to replace his early primary identification with his mother. This masculine identification is usually based on identification with a boy's father or other salient adult males. However, a boy's father is relatively more remote than his mother. He rarely plays a major caretaking role even at this period in his son's life. In most societies, his work and social life take place farther from the home than do those of his wife. He is, then, often relatively inaccessible to his son, and performs his male role activities away from where the son spends most of his life. As a result, a boy's male gender identification often becomes a "positional" identification, with aspects of his father's clearly or not-so-clearly defined male role, rather than a more generalized "personal" identification—a diffuse identification with his father's personality, values, and behavioral traits—that could grow out of a real relationship to his father.[7]

Mitscherlich (1963), in his discussion of Western advanced capitalist society, provides a useful insight into the problem of male development. The father, because his work takes him outside of the home most of the time, and because his active presence in the family has progressively decreased, has become an "invisible father." For the boy, the tie between affective relations and masculine gender identification and role learning (between libidinal and ego development) is relatively attenuated. He identifies with a fantasied masculine role, because the reality constraint that contact with his father would provide is missing. In all societies characterized by some sex segregation (even those in which a son will eventually lead the same sort of life as his father), much of a boy's masculine identification must be of this sort, that is, with aspects of his father's role, or what he fantasies to be a male role, rather than with his father as a person involved in a relationship to him.

There is another important aspect to this situation, which explains the psychological dynamics of the universal social and cultural devaluation and subordination of women.[8] A boy, in his attempt to gain an elusive masculine identification, often comes to define this masculinity largely in negative terms, as that which is not feminine or involved with women. There is an internal and external aspect to this. Internally, the boy tries to reject his mother and deny his attachment to her and the strong dependence upon her that he still feels. He also tries to deny the deep personal identification with her that has developed during his early years. He does this by repressing whatever he takes to be feminine inside himself, and, importantly, by denigrating and devaluing whatever he considers to be feminine in the outside world. As a societal member, he also appropriates to himself and defines as superior particular social activities and cultural (moral, religious, and creative) spheres—possibly, in fact, "society" ... and "culture" ... themselves.[9]

Freud's description of the boy's oedipal crisis speaks to the issues of rejection of the feminine and identification with the father. As his early attachment to his mother takes on phallic-sexual overtones, and his father enters the picture as an obvious rival (who, in the son's fantasy, has apparent power to kill or castrate his son), the boy must radically deny and repress his attachment to his mother and replace it with an identification with his loved and admired, but also potentially punitive, therefore feared, father. He internalizes a superego.[10]

To summarize, four components of the attainment of masculine gender identity are important. First, masculinity becomes and remains a problematic issue for a boy. Second, it involves denial of attachment or relationship, particularly of what the boy takes to be dependence or need for another, and differentiation of himself from another. Third, it involves the repression and devaluation of femininity on both psychological and cultural levels. Finally, identification with his father does not usually develop in the context of a satisfactory affective relationship, but consists in the attempt to internalize and learn components of a not immediately apprehensible role.

The development of a girl's gender identity contrasts with that of a boy. Most important, femininity and female role activities are immediately apprehensible in the world of her daily life. Her final role identification is with her mother and women, that is, with the person or people with whom she also has her earliest relationship of infantile dependence. The development of her gender identity does not involve a rejection of this early identification, however. Rather, her later identification with her mother is embedded in and influenced by their ongoing relationship of both primary identification and preoedipal attachment. Because her mother is around, and she has had a genuine relationship to her as a person, a girl's gender and gender role identification are mediated by and depend upon real affective relations. Identification with her mother is not positional—the narrow learning of particular role behaviors—but rather a personal identification with her mother's general traits of character and values. Feminine identification is based not on fantasied or externally defined characteristics and negative identification, but on the gradual learning of a way of being familiar in everyday life, and exemplified by the person (or kind of people—women) with whom she has been most involved. It is continuous with her early childhood identifications and attachments.

The major discontinuity in the development of a girl's sense of gender identity, and one that has led Freud and other early psychoanalysts to see female development as exceedingly difficult and tortuous, is that at some point she must transfer her primary sexual object choice from her mother and females to her father and males, if she is to attain her expected heterosexual adulthood. Briefly, Freud considers that all children feel that mothers give some cause for complaint and unhappiness: they give too little milk; they have a second child; they arouse and then forbid their child's sexual gratification in the process of caring for her/him. A girl receives a final blow, however: her discovery that she lacks a penis. She blames this lack on her mother, rejects her mother, and turns to her father in reaction.

Problems in this account have been discussed extensively in the general literature that has grown out of the women's movement, and within the psychoanalytic tradition itself. These concern Freud's misogyny and his obvious assumption that males possess physiological superiority, and that a woman's personality is inevitably determined by her lack of a penis.[11] The psychoanalytic account is not completely unsatisfactory, however. A more detailed consideration of several theorists[12] reveals important features of female development, especially about the mother-daughter relationship, and at the same time contradicts or mitigates the absoluteness of the more general Freudian outline.

These psychoanalysts emphasize how, in contrast to males, the female oedipal crisis is not resolved in the same absolute way. A girl cannot and does not completely reject her mother in favor of men, but continues her relationship of dependence upon and attachment to her. In addition, the strength and quality of her relationship to her father is completely dependent upon the strength and quality of her relationship to her mother. Deutsch suggests that a girl wavers in a "bisexual triangle" throughout her childhood and into puberty, normally making a very tentative resolution in favor of her father, but in such a way that issues of separation from and attachment to her mother remain important throughout a woman's life (1944: 205):

> It is erroneous to say that the little girl gives up her first mother relation in favor of the father. She only gradually draws him into the alliance, develops from the mother-child exclusiveness toward the triangular parent-child relationship and continues the latter, just as she does the former, although in a weaker and less elemental form, all her life. Only the principal part changes: now the mother, now the father plays it. The ineradicability of affective constellations manifests itself in later repetitions.

We might suggest from this that a girl's internalized and external object-relations become and remain more complex, and at the same time more defining of her, than those of a boy. Psychoanalytic preoccupation with constitutionally based libidinal development, and with a normative male model of development, has obscured this fact. Most women are genitally heterosexual. At the same time, their lives always involve other sorts of equally deep and primary relationships, especially with their children, and, importantly, with other women. In these spheres also, even more than in the area of heterosexual relations, a girl imposes the sort of object-relations she has internalized in her preoedipal and later relationship to her mother.

Men are also for the most part genitally heterosexual. This grows directly out of their early primary attachment to their mother. We know, however, that in many societies their heterosexual relationships are not embedded in close personal relationship but simply in relations of dominance and power. Furthermore, they do not have the extended personal relations women have. They are not so connected to children, and their relationships with other men tend to be based not on particularistic connection or affective ties, but rather on abstract, universalistic role expectations.

Building on the psychoanalytic assumption that unique individual experiences contribute to the formation of individual personality, culture and personality theory has held that early experiences common to members of a particular society contribute to the formation of "typical" personalities organized around and preoccupied with certain issues: "Prevailing patterns of child-rearing must result in similar internalized situations in the unconscious of the majority of individuals in a culture, and these will be externalized back into the culture again to perpetuate it from generation to generation" (Guntrip, 1961: 378). In a similar vein, I have tried to show that to the extent males and females, respectively, experience similar interpersonal environments as they grow up, masculine and feminine personality will develop differently.

I have relied on a theory which suggests that features of adult personality and behavior are determined, but which is not biologically determinist. Culturally expected personality and behavior are not simply "taught," however. Rather, certain features of social structure, supported by cultural beliefs, values, and perceptions, are internalized through the family and the child's early social object-relationships. This largely unconscious organization is the context in which role training and purposive socialization take place.

Sex-Role Learning and Its Social Context

Sex-role training and social interaction in childhood build upon and reinforce the largely unconscious development I have described. In most societies (ours is a complicated exception) a girl is usually with her mother and other female relatives in an interpersonal situation that facilitates continuous and early role learning and emphasizes the mother-daughter identification and particularistic, diffuse, affective relationships between women. A boy, to a greater or lesser extent, is also with women for a large part of his childhood, which prevents continuous or easy masculine role identification. His development is characterized by discontinuity.

Ariès (1962: 61), in his discussion of the changing concept of childhood in modern capitalist society, makes a distinction that seems to have more general applicability. Boys, he suggests, became "children" while girls remained "little women." "The idea of childhood profited the boys first of all, while the girls persisted much longer in the traditional way of life which confused them with the adults: we shall have cause to notice more than once this delay on the part of the women in adopting the visible forms of the essentially masculine civilization of modern times." This took place first in the middle classes, as a situation developed in which boys needed special schooling in order to prepare for their future work and could not begin to do this kind of work in childhood. Girls (and working-class boys) could still learn work more directly from their parents, and could begin to participate in the adult economy at an earlier age. Rapid economic change and development have exacerbated the lack of male generational role continuity. Few fathers now have either the opportunity or the ability to pass on a profession or skill to their sons.

Sex-role development of girls in modern society is more complex. On the one hand, they go to school to prepare for life in technologically and socially complex society. On the other, there is a sense in which this schooling is a pseudo-training. It is not meant to interfere with the much more important training to be "feminine" and a wife and mother, which is embedded in the girl's unconscious development and which her mother teaches her in a family context where she is clearly the salient parent.

This dichotomy is not unique to modern industrial society. Even if special, segregated schooling is not necessary for adult male work (and many male initiation rites remain a form of segregated role training), boys still participate in more activities that characterize them as a category apart from adult life. Their activities grow out of the boy's need to fill time until he can begin to take on an adult male role. Boys may withdraw into isolation and self-involved play or join together in a group that remains more or less unconnected with either the adult world of work and activity or the familial world.

Jay (1969) describes this sort of situation in rural Modjokuto, Java. Girls, after the age of five or so, begin gradually to help their mothers in their work and spend time with their mothers. Boys at this early age begin to form bands of age mates who roam and play about the city, relating neither to adult men nor to their mothers and sisters. Boys, then, enter a temporary group based on universalistic membership criteria, while girls continue to participate in particularistic role relations in a group characterized by continuity and relative permanence.

The content of boys' and girls' role training tends in the same direction as the context of this training and its results. Barry, Bacon, and Child, in their well-known study (1957), demonstrate that the socialization of boys tends to be oriented toward achievement and self-reliance and that of girls toward nurturance and responsibility. Girls are thus pressured to be involved with and connected to others, boys to deny this involvement and connection.

Adult Gender Personality and Sex Role

A variety of conceptualizations of female and male personality all focus on distinctions around the same issue, and provide alternative confirmation of the developmental model I have proposed. Bakan (1966: 15) claims that male personality is preoccupied with the "agentic," and female personality with the "communal." His expanded definition of the two concepts is illuminating:

> I have adopted the terms "agency" and "communion" to characterize two fundamental modalities in the existence of living forms, agency for the existence of an organism as an individual and communion for the participation of the individual in some larger organism of which the individual is a part. Agency manifests itself in self-protection, self-assertion, and self-expansion; communion manifests itself in the sense of being at one with other organisms. Agency manifests itself in the formation of separations; communion in the lack of separations. Agency manifests itself in isolation, alienation, and aloneness; communion in contact, openness, and union. Agency manifests itself in the urge to master; communion in noncontractual cooperation. Agency manifests itself in the repression of thought, feeling, and impulse; communion in the lack and removal of repression.

Gutmann (1965) contrasts the socialization of male personalities in "allocentric" milieux (milieux in which the individual is part of a larger social organization and system of social bonds) with that of female personalities in "autocentric" milieux (in which the individual herself/himself is a focus of events and ties).[18] Gutmann suggests that this leads to a number of systematic differences in ego functioning. Female ego qualities, growing out of participation in autocentric milieux, include more flexible ego boundaries (i.e. less insistent self-other distinctions), present orientation rather than future orientation, and relatively greater subjectivity and less detached objectivity.[14]

Carlson (1971) confirms both characterizations. Her tests of Gutmann's claims lead her to conclude that "males represent experiences of self, others, space, and time in individualistic, objective, and distant ways, while females represent experiences in relatively interpersonal, subjective, immediate ways" (p. 270). With reference to Bakan, she claims that men's descriptions of affective experience tend to be in agentic terms and women's in terms of communion, and that an examination of abstracts of a large number of social-psychological articles on sex differences yields an overwhelming confirmation of the agency/communion hypothesis.

Cohen (1969) contrasts the development of "analytic" and "relational" cognitive style, the former characterized by a stimulus-centered, parts-specific orientation to reality, the latter centered on the self and responding to the global characteristics of a stimulus in reference to its total context. Although focusing primarily on class differences in cognitive style, she also points out that girls are more likely to mix the two types of functioning (and also to exhibit internal conflict about this). Especially, they are likely to exhibit at the same time both high field dependence and highly developed analytic skills in other areas. She suggests that boys and girls participate in different sorts of interactional subgroups in their families: boys experience their family more as a formally organized primary group; girls experience theirs as a group characterized by shared and less clearly delineated functions. She concludes (p. 836): "Since embedded responses covered the gamut from abstract categories, through language behaviors, to expressions of embeddedness in their social environments, it is possible that embeddedness may be a distinctive characteristic of female sex-role learning in this society regardless of social class, native ability, ethnic differences, and the cognitive impact of the school."

Preliminary consideration suggests a correspondence between the production of feminine personalities organized around "communal" and "autocentric" issues and characterized by flexible ego boundaries, less detached objectivity, and relational cognitive style, on the one hand, and important aspects of feminine as opposed to masculine social roles, on the other.

Most generally, I would suggest that a quality of embeddedness in social interaction and personal relationships characterizes women's life relative to men's. From childhood, daughters are likely to participate in an intergenerational world with their mother, and often with their aunts and grandmother, whereas boys are on their own or participate in a single-generation world of age mates. In adult life, women's interaction with other women in most societies is kin-based and cuts across generational lines. Their roles tend to be particularistic, and to involve diffuse relationships and responsibilities rather than specific ones. Women in most societies are *defined* relationally (as someone's wife, mother, daughter, daughter-in-law; even a nun becomes the Bride of Christ). Men's association (although it too may be kin-based and intergenerational) is much more likely than women's to cut across kinship units, to be restricted to a single generation, and to be recruited according to universalistic criteria and involve relationships and responsibilities defined by their specificity.

Ego Boundaries and the Mother-Daughter Relationship

The care and socialization of girls by women ensures the production of feminine personalities founded on relation and connection, with flexible rather than rigid ego boundaries, and with a comparatively secure sense of gender identity. This is one explanation for how women's relative embeddedness is reproduced from generation to generation, and why it exists within almost every society. More specific investigation of different social contexts suggests, however, that there are variations in the kind of relationship that can exist between women's role performance and feminine personality.

Various kinds of evidence suggest that separation from the mother, the breaking of dependence, and the establishment and maintenance of a consistently individuated sense of self remain difficult psychological issues for Western middle-class women (i.e. the women who become subjects of psychoanalytic and clinical reports and social-psychological studies). Deutsch (1944, 1945) in particular provides extensive clinical documentation of these difficulties and of the way they affect women's relationships to men and children and, because of their nature, are reproduced in the next generation of women. Mothers and daughters in the women's group mentioned above describe their experiences of boundary confusion or equation of self and other, for example, guilt and self-blame for the other's unhappiness; shame and embarrassment at the other's actions; daughters' "discovery" that they are "really" living out their mothers' lives in their choice of career; mothers' not completely conscious reactions to their daughters' bodies as their own (overidentification and therefore often unnecessary concern with supposed weight or skin problems, which the mother is really worried about in herself); etc.

A kind of guilt that Western women express seems to grow out of and to reflect lack of adequate self/other distinctions and a sense of inescapable embeddedness in relationships to others. Tax describes this well (1970: 2; italics mine):

> Since our awareness of others is considered our duty, the price we pay when things go wrong is guilt and self-hatred. And things always go wrong. We respond with apologies; we continue to apologize long after the event is forgotten—and *even if it had no causal relation to anything we did to begin with.* If the rain spoils someone's picnic, we apologize. We apologize for taking up space in a room, for living.

As if the woman does not differentiate herself clearly from the rest of the world, she feels a sense of guilt and responsibility for situations that did not come about through her actions and without relation to her actual ability to determine the course of events. This happens, in the most familiar instance, in a sense of diffuse responsibility for everything connected to the welfare of her family and the happiness and success of her children. This loss of self in overwhelming responsibility for and connection to others is described particularly acutely by women writers (in the work, for instance, of Simone de Beauvoir, Kate Chopin, Doris Lessing, Tillie Olsen, Christina Stead, Virginia Woolf).

Slater (1961) points to several studies supporting the contention that Western daughters have particular problems about differentiation from their mother. These studies show that though most forms of personal parental identification correlate with psychological adjustment (i.e. freedom from neurosis or psychosis, *not* social acceptability), personal identification of a daughter with her mother does not. The reason is that the mother-daughter relation is the one form of personal identification that, because it results so easily from the normal situation of child development, is liable to be excessive in the direction of allowing no room for separation or difference between mother and daughter.

The situation reinforces itself in circular fashion. A mother, on the one hand, grows up without establishing adequate ego boundaries or a firm sense of self. She tends to experience boundary confusion with her daughter, and does not provide experiences of differentiating ego development for her daughter or encourage the breaking of her daughter's dependence. The daughter, for her part, makes a rather unsatisfactory and artificial attempt to establish boundaries: she projects what she defines as bad within her onto her mother and tries to take what is good into herself. (This, I think, is the best way to understand the girl's oedipal "rejection" of her mother.) Such an arbitrary mechanism cannot break the underlying psychological unity, however. Projection is never more than a temporary solution to ambivalence or boundary confusion.

The implication is that, contrary to Gutmann's suggestion (see note 3), "so-called ego pathology" may not be "adaptive" for women. Women's biosexual experiences (menstruation, coitus, pregnancy, childbirth, lactation) all involve some challenge to the boundaries of her body ego ("me"/"not-me" in relation to her blood or milk, to a man who penetrates her, to a child once part of her body). These are important and fundamental human experiences that are probably intrinsically meaningful and at the same time complicated for women everywhere. However, a Western woman's tenuous sense of individuation and of the firmness of her ego boundaries increases the likelihood that experiences challenging these boundaries will be difficult for her and conflictive.

Nor is it clear that this personality structure is "functional" for society as a whole. The evidence presented in this paper suggests that satisfactory mothering, which does not reproduce particular psychological problems in boys and girls, comes from a person with a firm sense of self and of her own value, whose care is a freely chosen activity rather than a reflection of a conscious and unconscious sense of inescapable connection to and responsibility for her children.

Social Structure and the Mother-Daughter Relationship

Clinical and self-analytical descriptions of women and of the psychological component of mother-daughter relationships are not available from societies and subcultures outside of the Western middle class. However, accounts that are primarily sociological about women in other societies enable us to infer certain aspects of their psychological situation. In what follows, I am not claiming to make any kind of general statement about what constitutes a "healthy society," but only to examine and isolate specific features of social life that seem to contribute to the psychological strength of some members of a society. Consideration of three groups with matrifocal tendencies in their family structure ... highlights several dimensions of importance in the developmental situation of the girl.

Young and Willmott (1957) describe the daily visiting and mutual aid of working-class mothers and daughters in East London. In a situation where household structure is usually nuclear, like the Western middle class, grown daughters look to their mothers for advice, for aid in childbirth and child care, for friendship and companionship, and for financial help. Their mother's house is the ultimate center of the family world. Husbands are in many ways peripheral to family relationships, possibly because of their failure to provide sufficiently for their families as men are expected to do. This becomes apparent if they demand their wife's disloyalty toward or separation from her mother: "The great triangle of childhood is mother-father-child; in Bethnal Green the great triangle of adult life is Mum-wife-husband" (p. 64).

Geertz (1961)[15] and Jay (1969) describe Javanese nuclear families in which women are often the more powerful spouse and have primary influence upon how kin relations are expressed and to whom (although these families are formally centered upon a highly valued conjugal relationship based on equality of spouses). Financial and decision-making control in the family often rests largely in the hands of its women. Women are potentially independent of men in a way that men are not independent of women. Geertz points to a woman's ability to participate in most occupations, and to own farmland and supervise its cultivation, which contrasts with a man's inability, even if he is financially independent, to do his own household work and cooking.

Women's kin role in Java is important. Their parental role and rights are greater than those of men; children always belong to the woman in case of divorce. When extra members join a nuclear family to constitute an extended family household, they are much more likely to be the wife's relatives than those of the husband. Formal and distant relations between men in a family, and between a man and his children (especially his son), contrast with the informal and close relations between women, and between a woman and her children. Jay and Geertz both emphasize the continuing closeness of the mother-daughter relationship as a daughter is growing up and throughout her married life. Jay suggests that there is a certain amount of ambivalence in the mother-daughter relationship, particularly as a girl grows toward adulthood and before she is married, but points out that at the same time the mother remains a girl's "primary figure of confidence and support" (1969: 103).

Siegel (1969)[16] describes Atjehnese families in Indonesia in which women stay on the homestead of their parents after marriage and are in total control of the household. Women tolerate men in the household only as long as they provide money, and even then treat them as someone between a child and a guest. Women's stated preference would be to eliminate even this necessary dependence on men: "Women, for instance, envision paradise as the place where they are reunited with their children and their mothers; husbands and fathers are absent, and yet there is an abundance all the same. Quarrels over money reflect the women's idea that men are basically adjuncts who exist only to give their families whatever they can earn" (p. 177). A woman in this society does not get into conflicts in which she has to choose between her mother and her husband, as happens in the Western working class (see above; also Komarovsky, 1962), where the reigning ideology supports the nuclear family.

In these three settings, the mother-daughter tie and other female kin relations remain important from a woman's childhood through her old age. Daughters stay closer to home in both childhood and adulthood, and remain involved in particularistic role relations. Sons and men are more likely to feel uncomfortable at home, and to spend work and play time away from the house. Male activities and spheres emphasize universalistic, distancing qualities: men in Java are the bearers and transmitters of high culture and formal relationships; men in East London spend much of their time in alienated work settings; Atjehnese boys spend their time in school, and their fathers trade in distant places.

Mother-daughter ties in these three societies, described as extremely close, seem to be composed of companionship and mutual cooperation, and to be positively valued by both mother and daughter. The ethnographies do not imply that women are weighed down by the burden of their relationships or by overwhelming guilt and responsibility. On the contrary, they seem to have developed a strong sense of self and self-worth, which continues to grow as they get older and take on their maternal role.

The implication is that "ego strength" is not completely dependent on the firmness of the ego's boundaries.

Guntrip's distinction between "immature" and "mature" dependence clarifies the difference between mother-daughter relationships and women's psyche in the Western middle class and in the matrifocal societies described. Women in the Western middle class are caught up to some extent in issues of infantile dependence, while the women in matrifocal societies remain in definite connection with others, but in relationships characterized by mature dependence. As Guntrip describes it (1961: 291): "*Mature dependence* is characterized by full differentiation of ego and object (emergence from primary identification) and therewith a capacity for valuing the object for its own sake and for giving as well as receiving; a condition which should be described not as independence but as mature dependence." This kind of mature dependence is also to be distinguished from the kind of forced independence and denial of need for relationship that I have suggested characterizes masculine personality, and that reflects continuing conflict about infantile dependence (Guntrip, 1961: 293; my italics): "Maturity is not equated with independence though it includes a certain capacity for independence. ... The independence of the mature person is simply that he does not collapse when he has to stand alone. It is not an independence of needs for other persons with whom to have relationship: *that would not be desired by the mature.*"

Depending on its social setting, women's sense of relation and connection and their embeddedness in social life provide them with a kind of security that men lack. The quality of a mother's relationship to her children and maternal self-esteem, on the one hand, and the nature of a daughter's developing identification with her mother, on the other, make crucial differences in female development.

Women's kin role, and in particular the mother role, is central and positively valued in Atjeh, Java, and East London. Women gain status and prestige as they get older; their major role is not fulfilled in early motherhood. At the same time, women may be important contributors to the family's economic support, as in Java and East London, and in all three societies they have control over real economic resources. All these factors give women a sense of self-esteem independent of their relationship to their children. Finally, strong relationships exist between women in these societies, expressed in mutual cooperation and frequent contact. A mother, then, when her children are young, is likely to spend much of her time in the company of other women, not simply isolated with her children.

These social facts have important positive effects on female psychological development. (It must be emphasized that all the ethnographies indicate that these same social facts make male development difficult and contribute to psychological insecurity and lack of ease in interpersonal relationships in men.) A mother is not invested in keeping her daughter from individuating and becoming less dependent. She has other ongoing contacts and relationships that help fulfill her psychological and social needs. In addition, the people surrounding a mother while a child is growing up become mediators between mother and daughter, by providing a daughter with alternative models for personal identification and objects of attachment, which contribute to her differentiation from her mother. Finally, a daughter's identification with her mother in this kind of setting is with a strong woman with clear control over important spheres of life, whose sense of self-esteem can reflect this. Acceptance of her gender identity involves positive valuation of herself, and not an admission of inferiority. In psychoanalytic terms we might say it involves identification with a preoedipal, active, caring mother. Bibring points to clinical findings supporting this interpretation: "We find in the analysis of the women who grew up in this 'matriarchal' setting the rejection of the feminine role less frequently than among female patients coming from the patriarchal family culture" (1953: 281).

There is another important aspect of the situation in these societies. The continuing structural and practical importance of the mother-daughter tie not only ensures that a daughter develops a positive personal and role identification with her mother, but also requires that the close psychological tie between mother and daughter become firmly grounded in real role expectations. These provide a certain constraint and limitation upon the relationship, as well as an avenue for its expression through common spheres of interest based in the external social world.

All these societal features contrast with the situation of the Western middle-class woman. Kinship relations in the middle class are less important. Kin are not likely to live near each other, and, insofar as husbands are able to provide adequate financial support for their families, there is no need for a network of mutual aid among related wives. As the middle-class woman gets older and becomes a grandmother, she cannot look forward to increased status and prestige in her new role.

The Western middle-class housewife does not have an important economic role in her family. The work she does and the responsibilities that go with it (household management, cooking, entertaining, etc.) do not seem to be really necessary to the economic support of her family (they are crucial contributions to the maintenance and reproduction of her family's class position, but this is not generally recognized as important either by the woman herself or by the society's ideology). If she works outside the home, neither she nor the rest of society is apt to consider this work to be important to her self-definition in the way that her housewife role is.

Child care, on the other hand, is considered to be her crucially important responsibility. Our post-Freudian society in fact assigns to parents (and especially to the mother[17]) nearly total responsibility for how children turn out. A middle-class mother's daily life is not centrally involved in relations with other women. She is isolated with her children for most of her workday. It is not surprising, then, that she is likely to invest a lot of anxious energy and guilt in her concern for her children and to look to them for her own self-affirmation, or that her self-esteem, dependent on the lives of others than herself, is shaky. Her life situation leads her to an overinvolvement in her children's lives.

A mother in this situation keeps her daughter from differentiation and from lessening her infantile dependence. (She also perpetuates her son's dependence, but in this case society and his father are more likely to interfere in order to assure that, behaviorally, at least, he doesn't *act* dependent.) And there are not other people around to mediate in the mother-daughter relationship. Insofar as the father is actively involved in a relationship with his daughter and his daughter develops some identification with him, this helps her individuation, but the formation of ego autonomy through identification with and idealization of her father may be at the expense of her positive sense of feminine self. Unlike the situation in matrifocal families, the continuing closeness of the mother-daughter relationship is expressed only on a psychological, interpersonal level. External role expectations do not ground or limit it.

It is difficult, then, for daughters in a Western middle-class family to develop self-esteem. Most psychoanalytic and social theorists[18] claim that the mother inevitably represents to her daughter (and son) regression, passivity, dependence, and lack of orientation to reality, whereas the father represents progression, activity, independence, and reality orientation.[19] Given the value implications of this dichotomy, there are advantages for the son in giving up his mother and identifying with his father. For the daughter, feminine gender identification means identification with a devalued, passive mother, and personal maternal identification is with a mother whose own self-esteem is low. Conscious rejection of her oedipal maternal identification, however, remains an unconscious rejection and devaluation of herself, because of her continuing preoedipal identification and boundary confusion with her mother.

Cultural devaluation is not the central issue, however. Even in patrilineal, patrilocal societies in which women's status is very low, women do not necessarily translate this cultural devaluation into low self-esteem, nor do girls have to develop difficult boundary problems with their mother. In the Moslem Moroccan family, for example,[20] a large amount of sex segregation and sex antagonism gives women a separate (domestic) sphere in which they have a real productive role and control, and also a life situation in which any young mother is in the company of other women. Women do not need to invest all their psychic energy in their children, and their self-esteem is not dependent on their relationship to their children. In this and other patrilineal, patrilocal societies, what resentment women do have at their oppressive situation is more often expressed toward their sons, whereas daughters are seen as allies against oppression. Conversely, a daughter develops relationships of attachment to and identification with other adult women. Loosening her tie to her mother therefore does not entail the rejection of all women. The close tie that remains between mother and daughter is based not simply on mutual overinvolvement but often on mutual understanding of their oppression.

Conclusion

Women's universal mothering role has effects both on the development of masculine and feminine personality and on the relative status of the sexes. This paper has described the development of relational personality in women and of personalities preoccupied with the denial of relation in men. In its comparison of different societies, it has suggested that men, while guaranteeing to themselves sociocultural superiority over women, always remain psychologically defensive and insecure. Women, by contrast, although always of secondary social and cultural status, may in favorable circumstances gain psychological security and a firm sense of worth and importance in spite of this.

Social and psychological oppression, then, is perpetuated in the structure of personality. The paper enables us to suggest what social arrangements contribute (and could contribute) to social equality between men and women and their relative freedom from certain sorts of psychological conflict. Daughters and sons must be able to develop a personal identification with more than one adult, and preferably one embedded in a role relationship that gives it a social context of expression and provides some limitation upon it. Most important, boys need to grow up around men who take a major role in child care, and girls around women who, in addition to their child-care responsibilities, have a valued role and recognized spheres of legitimate control. These arrangements could help to ensure that children of both sexes develop a sufficiently individuated and strong sense of self, as well as a positively valued and secure gender identity, that does not bog down either in ego-boundary confusion, low self-esteem, and overwhelming relatedness to others, or in compulsive denial of any connection to others or dependence upon them.

Notes

1. My understanding of mother-daughter relationships and their effect on feminine psychology grows out of my participation beginning in 1971 in a women's group that discusses mother-daughter relationships in particular and family relationships in general. All the women in this group have contributed to this understanding. An excellent dissertation by Marcia Millman (1972) first suggested to me the importance of boundary issues for women and became a major organizational focus for my subsequent work. Discussions with Nancy Jay, Michelle Rosaldo, Philip Slater, Barrie Thorne, Susan Weisskopf, and Beatrice Whiting have been central to the development of the ideas presented here. I am grateful to George Goethals, Edward Payne, and Mal Slavin for their comments and suggestions about earlier versions of this paper.

2. Margaret Mead provides the most widely read and earliest argument for this viewpoint (cf., e.g., 1935 and 1949); see also Chodorow (1971) for another discussion of the same issue.

3. Unfortunately, the language that describes personality structure is itself embedded with value judgment. The implication in most studies is that it is always better to have firmer ego boundaries, that "ego strength" depends on the degree of individuation. Gutman, who recognizes the linguistic problem, even suggests that "so-called ego pathology may have adaptive implications for women" (1965: 231). The argument can be made that extremes in either direction are harmful. Complete lack of ego boundaries is clearly pathological, but so also, as critics of contemporary Western men point out (cf., e.g., Bakan, 1966, and Slater, 1970), is individuation gone wild, what Bakan calls "agency unmitigated by communion," which he takes to characterize, among other things, both capitalism based on the protestant ethic and aggressive masculinity. With some explicit exceptions that I will specify in context, I am using the concepts solely in the descriptive sense.

4. Slater (1968) provides one example of such an investigation. LeVine's recent work on psychoanalytic anthropology (1971a,b) proposes a methodology that will enable social scientists to study personality development in this way.

5. Particularly as interpreted by object-relations theorists (e.g., Fairbairn, 1952, and Guntrip, 1961) and, with some similarity, by Parsons (1964) and Parsons and Bales (1955).

6. Cf., e.g., Brunswick, 1940; Deutsch, 1932, 1944; Fliess, 1948; Freud, 1931; Jones, 1927; and Lampl–deGroot, 1928.

7. The important distinction between "positional" and "personal" identification comes from Slater, 1961, and Winch, 1962.

8. For more extensive arguments concerning this, cf., e.g., Burton and Whiting (1961), Chodorow (1971), and Slater (1968).

9. The processes by which individual personal experiences and psychological factors contribute to or are translated into social and cultural facts, and, more generally, the circularity of explanations in terms of socialization, are clearly very complicated. A discussion of these issues, however, is not within the scope of this paper.

10. The question of the universality of the oedipus complex as Freud describes it is beyond the scope of this paper. Bakan (1966, 1968) points out that in the original Oedipus myth, it was the father who first tried to kill his son, and that the theme of paternal infanticide is central to the entire Old Testament. He suggests that for a variety of reasons, fathers probably have hostile and aggressive fantasies and feelings about their children (sons). This more general account, along with a variety of psychological and anthropological data, convinces me that we must take seriously the notion that members of both generations may have conflicts over the inevitable replacement of the elder generation by the younger, and that children probably feel both guilt and (rightly) some helplessness in this situation.

11. These views are most extreme and explicit in two papers (Freud, 1925, 1933) and warrant the criticism that has been directed at them. Although the issue of penis envy in women is not central to this paper, it is central to Freud's theory of female development. Therefore I think it worthwhile to mention three accounts that avoid Freud's ideological mistakes while allowing that his clinical observations of penis envy might be correct.

Thompson (1943) suggests that penis envy is a symbolic expression of women's culturally devalued and underprivileged position in our patriarchal society; that possession of a penis symbolizes the possession of power and privilege. Bettelheim (1954) suggests that members of either sex envy the sexual functions of the other, and that women are more likely to express this envy overtly, because, since men are culturally superior, such envy is considered "natural." Balint (1954) does not rely on the fact of men's cultural superiority, but suggests that a little girl develops penis envy when she realizes that her mother loves people with penises, i.e., her father, and thinks that possession of a penis will help her in her rivalry for her mother's attentions.

12. See, e.g., Brunswick, 1940; Deutsch, 1925, 1930, 1932, 1944; Freedman, 1961; Freud, 1931; Jones, 1927.

13. Following Cohen (1969), I would suggest that the external structural features of these settings (in the family or in school, for instance) are often similar or the same for boys and girls. The different kind and amount of adult male and female participation in these settings accounts for their being experienced by children of different sexes as different sorts of milieux.

14. Gutmann points out that all these qualities are supposed to indicate lack of adequate ego strength, and suggests that we ought to evaluate ego strength in terms of the specific demands of different people's (e.g., women's as opposed to men's) daily lives. Bakan goes even further and suggests that modern male ego qualities are a pathological extreme. Neither account is completely adequate. Gutmann does not consider the possibility (for which we have good evidence) that the everyday demands of an autocentric milieu are unreasonable: although women's ego qualities may be "functional" for their participation in these milieux, they do not necessarily contribute to the psychological strength of the women themselves. Bakan, in his (legitimate) preoccupation with the lack of connection and compulsive independence that characterizes Western masculine success, fails to recognize the equally clear danger (which, I will suggest, is more likely to affect women) of communion unmitigated by agency—of personality and behavior with no sense of autonomous control or independence at all.

I think this is part of a more general social-scientific mistake, growing out of the tendency to equate social structure and society with male social organization and activities within a society. This is exemplified, for instance, in Erikson's idealistic conception of maternal qualities in women (1965) and, less obviously, in the contrast between Durkheim's extensive treatment of "anomic" suicide (1897) and his relegation of "fatalistic" suicide to a single footnote (p. 276).

15. This ethnography, and a reading of it that focuses on strong female kin relations, was brought to my attention by Tanner (1971).

16. See note 15.

17. See Slater (1970) for an extended discussion of the implications of this.

18. See, e.g., Deutsch, 1944, *passim;* Erikson, 1964: 162; Klein and Rivière, 1937: 18; Parsons, 1970, *passim;* Parsons and Bales, 1955, *passim.*

19. Their argument derives from the universal fact that a child must outgrow her/his primary identification with and total dependence upon the mother. The present paper argues that the value implications of this dichotomy grow out of the particular circumstances of our society and its devaluation of relational qualities. Allied to this is the suggestion that it does not need to be, and often is not, relationship to the father that breaks the early maternal relationship.

20. Personal communication from Fatima Mernissi, based on her experience growing up in Morocco and her recent sociological fieldwork there.

Political Philosophy and the Patriarchal Unconscious: A Psychoanalytic Perspective on Epistemology and Metaphysics

Jane Flax

The windiest militant trash
Important Persons shout
Is not so crude as our wish:
What mad Nijinsky wrote
About Diaghilev
Is true of the normal heart;
For the error bred in the bone
Of each woman and each man
Craves what it cannot have,
Not universal love
But to be loved alone.

W. H. Auden, from "September 1, 1939"

The denial and repression of early infantile experience has had a deep and largely unexplored impact on philosophy. This repressed material shapes by its very absence in consciousness the way we look at and reflect upon the world. The repression of early infantile experience and the oppression of women are linked by the fact that *women* (and only women) "mother," that is, assume primary responsibility for the physical care and psychological nurturance of young children. While there is considerable variation in the extent to which men participate in child care, to my knowledge there is no known society in which men assume the primary responsibility for the care of children under six.[1] However, the negative consequences of this fact, both for the status of women and for psychological development, may be mitigated by a number of factors including the extent of male participation in child care, the degree to which the household is isolated from other social functions (such as production), the rigidity of the distinction between public and private life, and the degree to which women are permitted to participate in socially valued tasks other than child

217

rearing. The philosophers discussed below represent "pure case" examples, since they each lived in an historical period in which these mitigating factors were largely absent.

Both individual male development and patriarchy are partially rooted in a need to deny the power and autonomy of women. This need arises in part out of early infantile experience. The experience of maturing in a family in which only women mother insures that patriarchy will be reproduced.[2] Males under patriarchy must repress early infantile experience for several reasons: patriarchy by definition imputes political, moral and social *meanings* to sexual differentiation. Women are considered inferior in all these dimensions. The social world is thus both gender differentiated and stratified. (Men and women are different types of humans; men are superior to women.) Differentiation need not lead to stratification, but under patriarchy it does and must. Men want very much to attain membership in the community of men, in order to attain both individual identity and social privilege, even at great psychic pain. Patriarchal society depends upon the proper engendering of persons, since gender is one of the bases of social organization.[3]

Male identity under these social conditions requires the rejection of the mother by the son and a shift of libido and identification from her to the father. This is not easily accomplished, however, since the self is formed in part in and through relations with others. These persons and feelings about them are internalized; they become an "internal object" and the self is formed out of internal objects, the relations between them, and one's innate constitution (see section on object relations psychoanalysis, below). The mother and the son's relationship with her are literally part of the sons' self. He is psychically originally female (since in the traditional patriarchal family the father does not care for infants). He must *become* male. In order to do so he must become *not female*, since under patriarchy gender is an exclusionary category. He must repress part of himself—his identification with the mother and memories of his relation with her (which are now internalized) and identify with the father, who as an adult has repressed his female self. The son can also devalue his mother and his relationship with her in order to make these aspects of himself less powerful within his own psyche. This devaluation is reinforced by the outside world. Females are less likely to repress infantile experience because of their gender identity with the mother.

Infancy (no matter how the social world is organized) is characterized by a state of dependence and powerlessness as well as intense wishes. The infant becomes aware of its dependence on others and its inability to satisfy its own needs. Frustration is projected onto whomever is present for the child, and when the person becomes an internal object, these frustrations, fears, desires, etc., are introjected along with the person. Therefore the mother is internalized along with the child's own powerful feelings about her. The boy, as he represses the mother, must repress all these feelings, too, since they are part of his experience of her. Given how powerful she is in infancy, the son must carefully guard against her power (since it is part of his self). Thus, repression must be as complete as possible so that this internal object can be kept separate from the conscious self. Otherwise, it would threaten masculine identity and ego boundaries.

As long as the infantile drama (resolving the desire for fusion with the mother as well as the fear of it and the desire for separation and the fear of it) is played out only with one gender (the mother), the child, including the child within the adult, will not resolve its ambivalence about growing up and taking responsibility for its self and its actions in a world in which complete knowledge and control is not possible.[4] Rather than confronting this ambivalence and resolving it, the child can turn the mother (including the internalized mother) into a bad object or he can split her into a good and bad object. The bad object is then responsible for personal dilemmas and painful feelings. Since the bad object is split off from the central self, the ambivalence is not resolved.[5] If both genders were present in infancy, this splitting off would be a less available defensive maneuver. If patriarchy did not exist, it would not be reinforced by social reality and both genders would be more likely to grow up—that is, to become persons who develop individually within reciprocal relationships and who can accept responsibility for their acts without the need to create an illusion of complete control over other persons and the environment.

The repression of early infantile experience is reflected in philosophy since its subject matter is primarily the experience and actions of male human beings who were created in and through patriarchal social relations. (I assume here that while there are many forms of male dominance, inequality between men and women has been a persistent feature of human history.[6]) This experience is seen not as typically male but constitutive of human experience itself. The problem is thus much deeper than the existence of consciously held misogynous ideas within philosophy but extends to fundamental issues of epistemology and ontology, to the very essence of philosophy as such.

Adopting a feminist viewpoint that seeks to include infantile experience and women's activity within the realm of the social and knowable, permits and requires a critique of philosophy in which previously unacknowledged assumptions are revealed. This critique also reveals fundamental limitations in the ability of philosophy to comprehend women's and children's experiences and thus forces us to go beyond existing theories and methods.

The development of the argument to be presented here requires an unusual amount of preparatory work. The paper begins with a brief note on method and then moves to an introduction of the fundamental tenets of object relations (psychoanalytic) theory, from which many of my own assumptions are derived. Following this preparation is a feminist interpretation of Plato, Descartes, Hobbes and Rousseau. This analysis is meant to be exemplary of the possibilities of a feminist-psychoanalytic approach and exhausts neither the richness of the works discussed nor the possibilities of the approach suggested here. I regard the analysis of each philosopher as a preliminary sketch which would require considerable development (far beyond the constraints of a single essay) to be fully convincing.

A Note on Method

... Just as the psychiatrist must proceed from the fragmentary and deceptive verbalizations of his patient's conscious mind to the more complex levels of subconscious experience, so must his political confrere use the potentially misleading but indispensible statements of political theorists, whose awareness of political matters is uncommonly acute, as a clue to the less fully articulate experiences and reactions of ordinary men.[7]

What forms of social relations exist such that certain questions and ways of answering them become constitutive of philosophy? This question is important both to understanding the current state of philosophy and the interpretation of previous philosophic work. In philosophy, being (ontology) has been divorced from knowing (epistemology) and both have been separated from either ethics or politics. These divisions were blessed by Kant and transformed by him into a fundamental principle derived from the structure of mind itself.[8] A consequence of this principle has been the enshrining within mainstream Anglo-American philosophy of a rigid distinction between fact and value which has had the effect of consigning the philosopher to silence on issues of utmost importance to human life.[9] Furthermore, it has blinded philosophers and their interpreters to the possibility that apparently insoluble dilemmas within philosophy are not the product of the immanent structure of the human mind and/or nature but rather reflect distorted or frozen social relations.[10]

I assume here that knowledge is the product of human beings. Thinking is a form of human activity which cannot be treated in isolation from other forms of human activity including the forms of human activity which in turn shape the humans who think. Consequently, philosophies will inevitably bear the imprint of the social relations out of which they and their creators arose. Philosophy can thus be read (among many other ways) as a stream of social consciousness. The very persistence and continuing importance of certain philosophies and philosophic issues can be treated as evidence of their congruence with fundamental social experiences and problems. Philosophy must at least resonate with central social and individual wishes and offer some solution to deeply felt problematics.[11] In philosophy however, as in psychotherapy, what is not said, or what is avoided, is often as significant as the manifest content of thought.

A focus on social relations is especially important for feminist philosophy for it enables us to analyze the influence of patriarchy on both the content and process of thought. The social relations of childrearing are especially important to feminist analysis because such arrangements are both among the roots of patriarchy and continue to sustain its existence.[12] Feminist philosophy thus represents the return of the repressed, of the exposure of the particular social roots of all apparently abstract and universal knowledge. This work could prepare the ground for a more adequate social theory in which philosophy and empirical knowledge are reunited and mutually enriched.

Psychoanalysis, especially object relations theory, is a crucial tool for feminist philosophy. Its content represents a systematic attempt to understand human nature as the product of social relations in interaction with biology.[13] Object relations theorists differ somewhat among themselves, but more important for my purposes are their differences with Freud and "orthodox" psychoanalysis. These differences include: a radical questioning of Freud's "instinct theory" (especially the reduction of libido to sexuality and the notion that instincts are a- or anti-social); the construction of a more dynamic model of psychological development which stresses the interaction of child and parents, rather than the immanent unfolding of instinctive zones—a model actually suggested by Freud's concept of the super-ego, especially as articulated in *The Ego and the Id;* and a reconceptualization of the first three years of life which emerges as the crucial period of psychodynamic development, rather than the Oedipal period. Consequently (given patriarchal child-rearing patterns), the focus is on the mother-child relationship rather than the father-child one.

Also important for philosophy is the breakdown within object relations theory of the rigid distinction between primary process (id) and secondary process (ego-reason), so that reason is seen as an innate potential capacity rather than a faculty painfully acquired through the internalization of the authority of the father and as a defense against frustration and threats from the external world. Reason no longer appears as a fragile, tentative acquisition, dependent upon the existence of patriarchal authority.

Furthermore, the logic of object relations theory suggests that there may be more than one form of "human nature"; as social relations change, so too (over very long periods of time) would "human nature." This possibility forces us to avoid the determinism present in certain contemporary theorizing which claims an invariant form of human nature rooted in biology without falling into the equal and opposite fallacy of vulgar Marxism (e.g., unmediated responsiveness to changes in the political-economy).[14]

The method of psychoanalysis is equally valuable.[15] From this perspective, certain questions immediately arise: What aspects of social experience are repressed and why? What distortions are introduced into the structure of mind and our accounts of it by acts of repression and the defensive mechanisms against the return of the repressed? How do social prohibitions and power relations enter into the construction of individual personality and thus partially determine the individual's acts and thought? The contents of the unconscious, its influences and consequences, can be revealed by an analysis of conscious thought processes, their form, contradictions, implicit assumptions and significant avoidances and by how (and by whom) human experience has been reconstructed through acts of interpretation.

The texts discussed here will be interpreted from this perspective, with absolutely no claims made as to the particular psychodynamics of individual philosophers. Nor do I mean to claim that philosophy can or should be treated as the mere rationalization of unconscious impulses and conflicts. Rationalization is only one of the many roots and purposes of philosophy. To discuss this particular root is not to deny the others, or to somehow "reduce" the importance of philosophy. This could only be the case if the existence of the unconscious is considered shameful.

Object Relations Theory and Its Potential Contribution to Philosophy

The most basic tenet of object relations theory is that human beings are created in and through relations with other human beings. The theory claims:

(1) The "psychological birth of the human infant"[16] does not occur simultaneously with physical birth. While physical birth is a distinct event, occurring within a finite and easily determined period of time, psychological birth is a complex process which stretches over roughly the first three years of life. Psychological birth emerges out of the interaction of physical and mental processes. The character of the process calls into question the simple separation of mind and body and any form of determinism built upon these distinctions such as mechanism (Hobbes and modern vari-

ants), idealism (Plato or Husserl, for example) or instinct theory (early Freud or utilitarianism).

(2) "Psychological birth" can only occur in and through social (object) relations.[17]
While there appear to be certain innate potentials and character traits within human
beings (for example, the ability to walk and talk and differing levels of stress toleration), these potentials are most adequately achieved within good object relations.
Sufficiently bad object relations can retard or distort the developmental process, including such "physical" achievements as walking. The necessarily social and interactive character of early human development calls into question certain philosophies
of mind and being, especially radical individualism and the "monads" of Spinoza,
early Sartre and others.

(3) The most important tasks of the first three years of life are first, establishing a
close relationship with the caretaker—usually the mother—(symbiosis) and then
moving from that relationship through the process of separation and individuation.[18] Separation means establishing a firm sense of differentiation from the
mother, of possessing one's own physical and mental boundaries. Individuation
means establishing a range of characteristics, skills and personality traits which are
uniquely one's own. Separation and individuation are the two "tracts" of development; they are not identical, but they can reinforce or impede each other.

By the end of the third year a "core identity," or a distorted one, will have been established. Gender is a central element of this core identity. The child's sense of gender is firmly established by one and one-half to two years of age and has little to do
with an understanding of sexuality or reproduction.[19] Under patriarchy, this sense of
gender is not neutral. Becoming aware of gender means recognizing that men and
women are not valued equally, that in fact, men are socially more esteemed than
women. Being engendered, therefore, entails a coming to awareness of and to some
extent internalizing asymmetries of power and esteem.

(4) Children's psychological development is a dialectical process played out in and
through a changing relationship between mother and child. Both members of the
dyad must learn to be sensitive to the needs and feelings of the other while also attempting to have their own needs met. Early development occurs between two poles:
symbiosis and separation-individuation. In symbiosis (one to six or seven months),
"the infant behaves and functions as though he and his mother were an omnipotent
system—a dual unity within one common boundary."[20] The infant has no sense of
its own body boundaries and is extremely sensitive to its mother's moods and feelings. In this state of fusion with the mother, I and not-I are not yet differentiated,
and inside and outside the self are only gradually distinguished. This phase is "the
primal soil from which all subsequent human relationships form."[21]

In order for this phase to be adequate, the mother must be emotionally available
to the child in a consistent, reasonably conflict-free way. She should be able to enjoy
the sensual and emotional closeness of the relationship without losing her own sense
of separateness. She should be concerned for the child's well being without developing a narcissistic overinvestment in the child as a mere extension of her own self. Her
infantile wishes for a symbiotic relationship should have been adequately gratified in
childhood. If this was not the case, resentment and hostility may be aroused in her
by the infant's needs. The mother requires adequate support, both emotional and

material, during this period from adults who are able both to nurture her and reinforce her own sense of autonomy.

Separation-individuation begins at about six months and continues to about the end of the second year. The child gradually develops an autonomous ego, practices and takes pleasure in its locomotor skills (which allow it to physically distance itself from the mother), explores the possibilities of being its own separate person. The initial euphoria present in the discovery of the child's own powers and skills diminishes as it discovers the limitations as well as the possibilities of its developing skills. The child painfully learns that not only is it not omnipotent, but that the mother, too, is not all powerful.

The child explores and continually develops its separateness, then returns to the mother for "emotional refueling." The potential presence of the relationship between child and mother allows the child to leave it. Gradually the relationship is internalized and becomes part of the child's internal psychic reality. Both members of the dyad must learn to let go of the early bond without rejecting the other. The ambivalence present throughout this process gradually intensifies. The child both wants to return to the symbiotic state and fears being engulfed by it. In "good enough" social relations a resolution is achieved in which both members of the dyad come to accept their bond (mutuality) and their separateness. This is the basis of a truly reciprocal relationship between the pair, which creates the possibility for the child to then establish reciprocal relations with others.

However, under patriarchy it is not possible to fully achieve this satisfactory synthesis. The girl child never resolves her ambivalent tie to the mother.[22] The boy child must identify with the father to consolidate his differentiation. Mahler notes that by the age of 21 months, there were significant development differences between boys and girls:

> The boys, if given a reasonable chance, showed a tendency to disengage themselves from mother and to enjoy their functioning in the widening world. The girls, on the other hand, seemed to become more engrossed with mother in her presence; they demanded greater closeness and were more persistently enmeshed in the ambivalent aspects of the relationship.[23]

The boy by age five will have repressed the "female" parts of himself, his memories of his earliest experience and many relational capacities. He will have developed the "normal contempt" for women that is a fundamental part of male identity under patriarchy.[24] The girl, precisely because of her continuing ambivalent tie to the mother (which remains, in part, because of their gender identity) cannot so thoroughly repress her experience and relational capacities. The boy deals with the ambivalence inherent in the separation-individuation process by denial (of having been related), by projection (women are bad; they cause these problems) and by domination (mastering fears and wishes for regression by controlling, depowering and/or devaluing the object).

These defenses become part of ordinary male behavior toward adult women and to anything which seems similar to them or under their (potential) control—the body, feelings, nature. The ability to control (and be in control) becomes both a need and a symbol of masculinity. Relations are turned into contest for power. Aggression is mobilized to distance oneself from the object and then to overpower it. The girl, on the other hand, seeks relationships, even at the expense of her own autonomy. The two genders thus come to complement each other in a rather grotesque symmetry.[25]

(5)The social context of development includes not only the immediate child-care-taker(s) relation but also more general social relations which affect the child through its interaction with the caretakers. The caretaker(s) brings to the relationship a complex series of experiences which include not only personal history but also the whole range of social experience—work, friends, interaction with political and economic institutions and so on. Thus seemingly abstract and supra-personal relations such as class, race and patriarchy enter into the construction of "individual" human development.

The relation between these more general social relations and individual development is never simple and direct. The relationship is mediated not only by the particular qualities of each child-caretaker relationship but also by what the child brings to the world (its own innate constitution), by the inevitable permutations and distortions which occur in the incorporation of experience in the preverbal and prerational state of infancy and later in the ongoing unconscious process, and by the particular characteristics of each child's family (e.g., the number of family members present, and cultural, religious, class and ethnic norms as they affect childrearing patterns).[26]

(6) This long period of development is unique to the human species. No other species is so physically helpless at birth and remains so for such a long time. Physical helplessness makes us dependent on the good will of others. This dependence is made more significant and deeply felt by the fact that we rapidly develop a consciousness of it (beginning around the age of three months). This discovery is inextricably bound up with our growing consciousness of other human beings and the relationship between us. Our wishes and will to act far exceed in complexity and strength our ability to act upon them. The tension between desire and capacity is played originally in relation to only one gender—women—since only women take care of young children. Women are experienced as both the physical memory of this struggle and the cause of it (since very young children think their mother is omnipotent and the source of all their feelings). Women also embody the residual infantile ambivalence—the wish to be cared for and totally fused with another person and the dangers which this wish poses to the distinctness of self.

(7) This period is marked not only by physical and emotional dependency but by an intensity of experience which will never be repeated except in psychosis and perhaps in altered states of consciousness such as religious or drug experiences. Precisely because it is prerational and preverbal, it is difficult for the infant to screen, sort and modify its experience. Every new experience and life itself is a stream of feelings, stimuli and impressions which cannot be preshaped or categorized and thus easily organized and made coherent. This sort of organization of experience is a function of the ego which is itself developing during this period.

However, our early experiences are not lost as we develop; they never disappear. They are retained in the unconsciousness and continue to reverberate throughout adult life. We are often unaware of these reverberations since they are expressed in feeling or bodily forms (such as psychosomatic illness), not thought. Their roots are not immediately accessible to consciousness and their very existence may be so threatening and/or disorganizing that they must remain repressed. Many pleasures, too, however, are deepened by the unconsciousness awakening of infantile memories.

Object relations theory and psychology as a whole takes for granted that the mother (and/or other women) is the primary caretaker.[27] They do not usually point out the negative consequences this arrangement entails, nor the fact that it derives not from biological necessity but from a series of social relations and structures, the replication of which is essential for the existence and maintenance of patriarchy.[28]

The Return of the Repressed: Unconscious Reverberations in Philosophy, or, the Metaphysics of Male Identity

The repression of early infantile experience is reflected in and provides part of the grounding for our relationship with nature[29] and our political life, especially the separation of public and private, the obsession with power and domination and the consequent impoverishment of political life and theories of it. The repression of our passions and their transformation into something dangerous and shameful, the inability to achieve true reciprocity and cooperative relations with others, and the translation of difference into inferiority and superiority can also be traced in part to this individual and collective act of repression and denial. The following analysis of Plato, Descartes, Hobbes and Rousseau will show that philosophy is not immune from these problems and the influence of the unconscious.

1. *Plato: Regression and Light*

A crucial element in Plato's philosophy is the distinction between mind and body, knowledge and sense, reason and appetite. The model for the Republic[30] is the well-ordered soul which provides the principles for the organization of the city. The primary basis of social class in the Republic is the ability to reason. The purpose of the educational system is not only to prepare potential philosophers to see the forms, but to determine *who* has the capacity to do so. The capacity to reason depends upon the control and sublimation of the passions. In turn, "it is for control of the passions which threaten to erupt into public life that society exists. The state itself thus resembles a vast dehydrating plant for 'drying up' the passions of men through education and restraint."[31] Women are clearly identified by Plato with the most dangerous and disruptive forms of passion, especially sexuality. Thus, there is a deep, covert link between the very *purpose* of Plato's ideal state and his fear and dislike of women which is so evident in other dialogues (e.g., the *Symposium* and the *Timaeus*).

Plato stresses the importance of instilling a lawful spirit at an early age; "if a sound system of nurture and education is maintained, it produces men of a good disposition; and these in turn, taking advantage of such education, develop into better men than their forebears."[32] Such a spirit is a defense against the outbreak of disorder and chaos which constantly threatens even the best ordered personality or state. Even children's games must be carefully controlled or else:

> little by little, this lawless spirit gains a lodgement and spreads imperceptibly to manners and pursuits; and from thence with gathering force invades men's dealings with one another, and next goes on to attack the laws and the constitution with wanton recklessness, until it ends by overthrowing the whole structure of public and private life.[33]

Reason, laboriously won, must dominate the "lower" aspects of the mind just as the philosopher must rule the state. These lower aspects, although repressed, retain their power and threaten to return. Even the philosopher cannot be fully trusted; the social arrangements of the Republic reinforce internal control of the passions (communal property, wives, controlled mating, parents who do not know which children are theirs). These restrictions apply only to the guardians. The other groups, less rational and therefore not rulers, can indulge their appetites more fully.

The acquisition of knowledge also depends upon the purification of the mind. The sensual present leads to confusion and belief, not to knowledge:

> Your lovers of sights and sounds delight in beautiful tones and colours and shapes and in all the works of art into which these enter; but they have not the power of thought to behold and to take delight in the nature of Beauty itself.[34]

The forms are pure, abstract, eternal, universal, all that the flesh and the passions are not. "The forms are objects of thought, but invisible."[35] The ultimate Form (the Good), although invisible, is the light by which all the other forms become intelligible. To be able to see the light and stand its glory, one must be in control of the body, its claims and demands. The Ruler must be able to sublimate his "high spirits" into a passion for knowledge and be willing to "live a quiet life of sober constancy."[36]

The images of light and dark and the fear of losing reality recur in the *Republic*. Mere belief is compared to living in a dream, in which semblance is mistaken for the reality it resembles.[37] The "dark" is within the individual as well as in the threat of chaos and decay from outside. The very qualities that suit a person to be a philosopher king, under adverse conditions, may lead to ruin. The more noble the soul, the greater the danger and the potential harm to the self and others.[38]

The imagery of the cave in the *Republic;* the world of shadows, of the unconscious and of the womb, which the light of reason cannot penetrate or dispel, reveals the fear of regression to that preverbal state where feelings, the needs of the body and women (mothers) rule.[39] One must ascend from the cave to be free from it, and the philosopher must be forced to return to it, for of course, having escaped, he would rather live in the light.

Ideal love is also pure, uncorrupted by materiality and the body. In the *Symposium,*[40] for example, true love is distinguished from sexuality, and the love of women from the love of boys, and ultimately love of persons from love of knowledge (the highest form of love). Socrates' teacher in these matters was an old (and thus presumably asexual) woman. Women seem to be most dangerous when young and capable of stirring up the passions of both men and women.[41] In the *Laws* women are not eligible for even the limited number of offices open to them until age 40, although men may assume a much more extended range of offices at age 30. Once women are old enough to be married and bear children, they are largely excluded from public life, including military training. Pregnancy is, of course, an unavoidable reminder of the existence of sexuality and it is not surprising that Plato would want to banish pregnant (or potentially pregnant) women from public life.

In the *Symposium,* Socrates is presented as a hero, in part because he does not succumb to lust for one of the most beautiful (male) youths, despite Alcibiades' attempts at seduction. Socrates' ability to withstand the physical hardships of war and to continue to dwell in the world of thought despite them is also praised.

The transcendence of the body, especially sexuality, enables Socrates to attain the knowledge of the beautiful itself and be "quickened" with the true, and not the seeming virtue:

> And once you have seen it, you will never be seduced again by the charm of gold, of dress, of comely boys, or lads just ripening to manhood; you will care nothing for the beauties that used to take your breath away and kindle such a longing in you ... and when he has brought forth and reared this perfect virtue, he shall be called the friend of god and if ever it is given to man to put on immortality, it shall be given to him.[42]

Thus reason is in part a defense against regression against those "longings" which threaten to ensnare us forever in the body and the material world. A well ordered state will reinforce this internal defense.

Experientially the first body we escape (physically, then emotionally) is that of our mother. Our relation with our own body is mediated through our continuing ambivalence about separating and differentiating from her. Part of the power and terror possessed by the "longings" Diotima describes is derived from the rekindling of unconscious infantile memories of the first erotic love relationship—with our mother. These longings contain many elements, including a desire to fuse with the lover,[43] to lose one's own ego boundaries and the fear of doing so, since fusion evokes powerlessness and vulnerability.

It is far safer to reside in the world of light, beyond embodied physicality, for ultimately the body, its memories and desires, brings not only entanglements with other persons and the material world, but the final physical fusion—death. The pure soul, however, will not fear death, for from Plato's perspective it is merely deliverance from the flesh; it is the radical (and desired) decoupling of mind and body.

Thus in Plato's philosophy, the purposes of the state and the unconscious wishes of the individual are inextricably linked. Both seek to restrain and channel passion and to defend against chaos so that earthly materiality, which is subject to decay, may be transformed. The eternal, unchanging forms assure freedom from the cave, the womb, the unending cycle of birth and death, the realm of necessity and of women (mothers). The ideal state represents the closest possible approximation of this eternal realm on earth. The ideal soul is a miniature state and the ideal state the well ordered soul writ large.[44] Unless both are present, each will not be able to achieve its full potential excellence, and neither justice nor happiness will be possible. Yet, what sort of justice and happiness does Plato offer? Does justice require the sublimation and repression of sexuality and the denial of any significant differences between men and women? These questions, central to feminist theory, remain unresolved.

2. Descartes and the Narcissistic Position

Descartes' philosophy can also be read as a desperate attempt to escape from the body, sexuality, and the wiles of the unconscious. His philosophy is important not only in itself but also because it defined the problematics for much of modern Western philosophy.

In the *Discourse on Method*,[45] the problem of the cogito emerges in relation to the problem of distinguishing reality from a dream. For Descartes, the solution to the problem of certainty and the confusion generated by the senses is a radical reduction of consciousness to pure ego, to that which thinks. The ego is emptied of all content, since in principle there is nothing it can know a priori about its life situation or history, all of that having been cast into doubt.

Consider the assumptions behind and implications of this statement:

> The very fact that I thought of doubting the truth of other things, it followed very evidently and very certainly that I existed while on the other hand, if I had only ceased to think, although all the rest of what I had ever imagined had been true, I would have had no reason to believe that I existed; I thereby concluded that I was a substance, of which the whole essence or nature consists in thinking, and which in order to exist, needs no place and depends on no material thing; so that this "I" that is to say, the mind by which I am what I am, is entirely distinct from the body, even that it is easier to know that the body, and moreover, that even if the body were not, it would not cease to be all that it is.[46]

My essence and the only thing of which I can be certain, is thought. This self needs "no place and depends on no material thing" including, one presumes, other human beings. It is thus completely self-constituting and self-sustaining. The self is created and maintained by thought. This view of the self entails a denial of the body and any interaction between body and self (except somehow through the pineal gland). Social relations are not necessary for the development of the self. The self is a static substance. Although it may think new thoughts, it is not transformed by them. It appears to come into the world whole and complete, clicking into operation like a perpetual motion machine.

Descartes' ego contemplates the material world, a material world emptied of particularity and subjective content. Thought contemplates not nature as lived through, how this particular orange tastes or smells, for example, but nature as mathematics. Only when nature is reduced to extension and motion can it be known with certainty. Nature cannot be known in its full concreteness, but only as the abstract object of an abstract cogito. Any knowledge not built on the foundations of mathematics is like the "moral writings of the ancient pagans, the most proud and magnificent palaces, built on nothing but sand and mud."[47]

Underlying the concern for certainty is a desire for control, control both of nature and of the body. Descartes was convinced that:

> it is possible to arrive at knowledge which is most useful in life and that instead of the speculative philosophy taught in the schools, a practical philosophy can be found by which, knowing the power and the effects of fire, water, air, the stars, the heavens, and all the other bodies which surround us as distinctly as we know the various trades of our craftsmen, we might put them in the same way to all the uses for which they are appropriate and thereby make ourselves, as it were, masters and possessors of nature.[48]

The purpose of science is to capture the power of nature and hence to make it one's own, thus compensating for the weakness of mortal flesh.

Such a science might even overcome death, that reminder of the materiality of life, of the independence of the body:

> We could free ourselves of an infinity of illnesses, both of the body and of the mind, and even perhaps also of the decline of age, if we know enough abut their causes and about all the remedies which nature has provided us.[49]

There is a deep irony in Descartes' philosophy. The self which is created and constituted by an act of thought is driven to master nature, because ultimately the self cannot deny its material qualities. Despite Descartes' claim, the body reasserts itself, at least at the moment of death. In order to fully become the substance it is, the cogito must master nature and possess its secrets, "the remedies nature has provided us," so that the self will never "cease to be all that it is," that is, die.

The desire to know is inextricably intermeshed with the desire to dominate. Nature is posited as pure otherness which must be conquered to be possessed and transformed into useful objects. The posture of Descartes' cogito replicates that of a child under two in its relation to a caretaker. The child originally believes that it and its mother are one person, a symbiotic unity.[50] However, due to frustrations in satisfying its needs and internal psychological pressures (primarily a growing desire for autonomy), it begins to realize that its mother is a separate person, an other. This discovery is accompanied simultaneously by panic and exhilaration, for while the child knows it is still dependent on the mother, it also begins to realize that autonomy requires separation. Accompanying separation is an increased sense of both power and vulnerability. One reaction and defense to the discovery of separateness is narcissism, in which the outside world is seen purely as a creation of and an object for the self.

Through "good enough"[51] social relations this stage is transformed into a genuine reciprocity in which separateness and mutuality (interdependence) exist simultaneously. However, denial of separateness, of the individual integrity of the object (mother) will lead to the adoption of narcissism as a permanent character structure,[52] precisely the type of solipsistic isolated self with delusions of omnipotence which Descartes' cogito displays.

Furthermore, underlying the narcissistic position, the fear and wish for regression to the helpless infantile state remains. The longings for symbiosis with the mother are not resolved. Therefore, one's own wishes, body, women and anything like them (nature) must be partially objectified, depersonalized and rigidly separated from the core self in order to be controlled.[53] Once this position is established, the relationship between the self (subject) and object (other persons, nature, the body) becomes extremely problematic, perhaps unresolvable. This frozen posture is one of the social roots of the subject-object dichotomy and its persistence within modern philosophy.[54] It is an abstract expression of a deeply felt dilemma in psychological development under patriarchy and thus cannot be resolved by philosophy alone.

Do Women and Children Exist in the State of Nature?

Modern political philosophy also conceals a denial of early infantile experience, although in a different way. Especially important is the denial of the primary relatedness to and dependence upon the caretaker present in infancy and the consequences of this denial for conceptions of human nature. It is noteworthy that both Hobbes and Rousseau, despite their many differences, assume that "man" is a solitary creature by nature, and that dependence, indeed any social interaction, inevitably leads to power struggles which ultimately result in either domination or submission. These assumptions, which are not unique to them, shape each theorist's conception of the original state of human beings (the state of nature). An analysis of Hobbes' and Rousseau's concepts of human nature will show both some of the effects of patriarchal forms of psychological development on political life and the dilemmas these effects introduce into political theory. In Hobbes, although not in Rousseau, the state of nature is marked by the prevalence of anxiety and insecurity. Significantly, the anxiety is centered on the fear of wounds to the body and the deprivation of needed and desired objects—paralleling the paranoid aspect of the separation process.[55] "Natural man" attributes this fear to an external "bad object"—to fear of aggression from other persons who will not respect his autonomy. Aggression and separateness are viewed as innate in humans rather than as problems with social roots.

1. *Hobbes: The State of Nature*

It is only possible to view people in this way if an earlier period of nurturance and dependence is unsatisfactory and/or denied and repressed. The state of nature seems to be primarily populated by adult, single males whose behavior is taken as constitutive of human nature and experience as a whole. Hobbes is clearly puzzled about how to fit the family into his state of nature. There are only a few contradictory comments on it in the *Leviathan*.

In the state of nature, Hobbes argues, men and women have equal claim to possession and control of children, but this is impossible, "for no man can obey two Masters":[56]

And whereas some have attributed the Dominion to the man onely, as being of the more excellent Sex; they misreckon in it. Fore there is not always that difference of strength or prudence between the man and the woman, as that the right can be determined without War.[57]

Dominion over children can be settled by contract. If there is conflict or no contract exists (and no contract can be guaranteed in the state of nature), children should obey the mother, since parentage can only be ascertained with certainty for her. On the other hand, Hobbes says, the allegiance children owe to their parents is derived *not* from generation, "but from the Child's Consent, either expresse, or by other sufficient arguments declared."[58] He does not seem to notice the contradiction between this argument and the previous one.

In a startling paragraph which reveals the fear infantile dependence can induce (of the power of the mother to virtually annihilate the child), Hobbes introduces a different argument. The child in the state of nature ultimately owes its allegiance to the mother because of her power over it:

Again, seeing the Infant is first in the power of the Mother, so as she may either nourish or expose it, if she nourish it, it oweth its life to the Mother; and is therefore obliged to obey her, rather than any other; and by consequence the Dominion over it is hers. But if she expose it, and another nourish it, the Dominion is in him that nourish it. For it ought to obey him by whom it is preserved; because preservation of life being the end, for which one man becomes subject to another, every man is supposed to promise obedience to him, in whose power it is to save or destroy him.[59]

Despite (or because of) what we might call this original natural obligation to women as (at least the potential) preservers of life, in civil society dominion usually belongs to the father, because, "for the most part Common-wealths have been erected by the Fathers, not by the Mothers of families."[60] Later in the argument, this acknowledgment of original dependence on women (mothers) seems to be completely forgotten or repressed. Hobbes states flatly that in civil society, the family is a lawful private body, in which:

> the Father, or Master ordereth the whole Family ... For the Father, and Master being before the Institution of Commonwealth, absolute Sovereigns in their own Families, they lose afterward to more of their Authority, than the Law of the Commonwealth taketh from them.[61]

Hobbes' mechanistic model of human nature does not include the female, that is, it excludes the traits culturally attributed to females—sociability, nurturance, concern for dependent and helpless persons. Humans are said to be motivated only by passion, especially fear and the wish to have no impediments to the gratification of desire, which is insatiable and asocial.

Human beings are basically greedy infants driven by:

> a perpetuall and restlesse desire of Power after power that ceaseth onely in Death. And the cause of this, is not alwayes that a man hopes for a more intensive delight, than he has already attained to; or that he cannot be content with a moderate power; but because he cannot assure the power and the means to live well, which he hath present, without the acquisition of more.[62]

In other words, without infantile omnipotence one cannot be certain that one will continue to be nourished at all.

The problem, of course (as for the infant), is that the gratification being sought (complete symbiotic security) can never be regained, "for there is no such thing as perpetuall Tranquility of mind while we live here; because Life itselfe is but Motion, and can never be without Desire, nor without Feare, no more than without sense."[63] Furthermore, despite the fact that felicity consists in "obtaining those things which a man from time to time desireth;"[64] "Passions unguided, are for the most part meere Madness."[65]

The only ways out of this dilemma are to either resolve the wishes by acknowledging the autonomy of the other person and entering into reciprocal relationships or to retain the wishes and control them defensively. Hobbes adopts the second alternative. Given his premises about the passions and human motivation (and the assumption of scarcity), the state of war inevitably follows. This state can only be abolished (or perhaps contained) by the creation of the Leviathan, a sort of externalized superego, "One Will" who unites all these unruly passions and (literally) incorporates their power in his Person:

> This is more than consent, or Concord; it is a reall Unitie of them all, in one and in the same person, made by Covenant of every man with every man, in such a manner, as if every man should say to every man, *I Authorize and give up my Right of Governing my selfe, to this Man, or to this Assembly of men, on this condition, that thou give up thy right to him, and Authorize all his Actions in like manner.*[66]

Since the character of the passions makes it impossible for any man to govern himself or to cooperate with others, an "artificial person" must be created. This artificial person is a good patriarchal father. By controlling and channeling the passions of his sons, he creates the possibility of civil society, morality and culture, none of which can exist in the state of nature.[67]

Thus we pass from the dominion of the Mothers, in which nourishment could be refused and life alternates between intense fear, desire and gratification, to the dominion of the Father, in which the preservation of life, "peace and security" are guaranteed by obedience to his will (Law) and renunciation of the absolute right to gratify any passion. This artificial person is superior to any real one. Like Descartes, Hobbes believed that the use of right reason (modeled on mathematics) could conquer death, or at least the death of states:

> So, long time after men have begun to constitute Commonwealths, imperfect, and apt to relapse into disorder, there may be found out, by industrious meditation, to make their constitution (excepting by external violence) everlasting. And such are those which I have in this discourse set forth.[68]

Mortal fathers create their immortal Father, and their sovereignty over the once powerful Mother and all that she represents is now assured.

2. *Rousseau: Escape from Desire*

Rousseau's version of the state of nature in *A Discourse on the Origin of Inequality*[69] appears to be quite different than Hobbes'. Despite Rousseau's criticisms of Hobbes, he also shares many of Hobbes' assumptions concerning "natural man."[70] While acknowledging their profound differences, I wish to investigate their similarities, since it is especially remarkable that certain fundamental assumptions are shared by such otherwise differing theorists.

Rousseau's natural man is "alone, idle, and always near danger"[71] (from the attacks of animals, not other persons, at least in the initial, uncorrupted state of nature). Human beings are "ingenious machines" who are perfectly adapted to their environment, like other animals. However, the faculty that distinguishes them from animals is also "the source of all man's misfortunes."[72] This is "the faculty of self-perfection ... which, with the aid of circumstances, successfully develops all the others."[73]

Like Hobbes, Rousseau assumes that people are solitary by nature and that culture and social institutions are not natural. Both assume that natural man is driven by passion and desire. According to Rousseau, the only goods natural man "knows in the universe are nourishment, a female and repose; the only evils he fears are pain and hunger."[74] In this "primitive state" men had brief, purely sexual encounters with women and returned to their solitary ways; "males and females united fortuitously, depending on encounter, occasion or desire ... they left each other with the same ease."[75] Even childbearing gave rise only to brief, utilitarian relations between mother and child. A mother would nurse her children, first:

> for her own need; then, habit having endeared them to her, she nourished them afterward for their need. As soon as they had the strength to seek their food, they did not de-

lay in leaving the mother herself; and ... they were soon at the point of not even recognizing each other.[76]

Rousseau's natural man (like Hobbes') has an intense dislike and fear of dependence. Dependence on another person inevitably leads to servitude:

The bonds of servitude are formed only from the mutual dependence of men and the reciprocal needs that unite them, it is impossible to enslave a man without first putting him in the position of being unable to do without another; a situation which, as it did not exist in the state of nature, leaves each man there free of the yoke. ...[77]

What could compel man to leave this natural state? Unlike Hobbes, Rousseau does not posit that the state of nature degenerated *immediately* into the state of war for each person is motivated both by the desire for self-preservation (which leads him to avoid others) and the feeling of compassion (which leads him to avoid harming others).[78]

The answer seems to be a combination of the social and technological innovations made possible by man's faculty for self-improvement and the evil manipulation of women. As population increases, people encounter each other more frequently. Gradually they developed crude tools to acquire subsistence and defend against animals. The "repeated utilization of various beings to himself and of some beings in relation to others, must naturally have engendered in man's mind perceptions of certain relations."[79] This realization developed a new intelligence which in turn increased human superiority over animals, by making them sensible of it. This was the first source of pride and also of the ability to distinguish similarities between the self and other humans (who were also not animals). Once these similarities were noticed, it occurred to people that they might cooperate together, since each person was motivated by the same interest. This created the possibility of a mutual interest and also of conflicting interests.

"These first advances finally put man in a position to make more rapid ones. The more the mind was enlightened, the more industry was perfected."[80] People learned how to build huts. These advances prepared the way for the "first revolution, which produced the establishment and differentiation of families, and which introduced a sort of property—from which perhaps many quarrels and fights already rose."[81] Domestic life in turn led to an expansion of the human heart to include "the sweetest sentiments known to man, conjugal love and paternal love."[82]

These developments, while progressive, had a negative aspect as well. Although this period of human history "must have been the happiest and most durable epoch,"[83] it contained the roots of its own degeneration. Life became softer and more sedentary. People created conveniences which became necessities, they "were unhappy to lose them without being happy to possess them."[84] People began to compete for love and the esteem of others:

A tender and gentle sentiment is gradually introduced into the soul and at the least obstacle becomes an impetuous fury. Jealousy awakens with love; discord triumphs, and the gentlest of all passions receives sacrifices of human blood.[85]

The mutual dependence of one person on another and the desire for one person to have enough for two led to the disappearance of equality; "property was introduced, labor became necessary ... slavery and misery were soon seen to germinate and grow with the crops."[86] Civil society and law were introduced by wealthy persons to protect their property,[87] and "all ran to meet their chains, thinking they secured their freedom."[88]

Three aspects of Rousseau's account are especially significant. (1) While he sees human development as a process involving the interaction of nature and human capacities,[89] social interaction is not considered essential, in fact it occurs quite late in the process. Ultimately, it has a destructive effect.

(2) Domestic life in the family is seen as the source of "sweet sentiment", as one of the primary bases of civilization and of human unhappiness. Women seem to benefit far more than men from this new way of life, despite the fact that it is really the root of their subordination to men. Rousseau says "it was then that the first difference was established in the way of life of the two sexes, which until this time had had but one. Women became more sedentary and grew accustomed to tend the hut and the children, while the man went to seek their common subsistence."[90] As Okin argues,[91] by Rousseau's own logic this change means that women have become dependent on men for their very subsistence and thus are no longer their equal, despite Rousseau's claim that "reciprocal affection and freedom"[92] were the family's only bonds. Thus, even within the ideal period of the state of nature, there has already emerged a fundamental form of inequality, although Rousseau does not acknowledge it as such. Paradoxically, Rousseau argues that monogamous love enables women to control men: "it is easy to see that the moral element of love is an artificial sentiment, born of the usage of society and extolled with much skill and care by women in order to establish their ascendency and make dominant the sex which ought to obey."[93]

(3) Social interaction is assumed to lead to dependence, which in turn leads to slavery. Just like a small child, Rousseau's natural man seems to have only two choices: isolation or total engulfment. The fear of dependence is so strong that any acknowledgment of it must be totally denied—like the child in the state of nature who escapes from its mother as soon as possible and is unable to recognize her from then on. The passions aroused by love are also like those of an infant—desire to possess the person totally, to be esteemed above all others and an "impetuous fury" if those desires are denied.

The only solution Rousseau proposes for this dilemma is to seek mastery. Patriarchal authority in the family and in the state is the necessary counter to the power women exercise over and through the passions. Reciprocity, in the sense of mutual interdependence and independence is not possible.[94] How could it be, given the assumptions he makes about human nature, women and the character of the passions? It is odd that compassion disappears as natural men degenerates, while self-preservation retains its power. Perhaps this is because Rousseau's implicit assumptions about human nature and development are more similar to Hobbes' than Rousseau consciously realizes. In both cases, desire, stimulated by and rooted in part in interactions with women, is a main cause of human misery.

Once natural man is corrupted, he cannot return to his happy state,[95] although women retain their natural status, that is, they are to remain under the authority of men. The only cure for the misery of civil society is the creation of a Republic in which men are citizen-soldiers whose primary bond is the deliberately impersonal one of the social contract.[96] Women are to be excluded from sovereignty and thus from the general will.[97] As in the *Leviathan,* creation of political society represents the triumph of law over desire:[98]

only then when the voice of duty replaced physical impulse and right replaced appetite, does man, who until that time only considered himself, find himself forced to act up on other principles and to consult his reason before heeding his inclinations ... what man loses by the social contract is his natural freedom and an unlimited right to everything that tempts him and that he can get; what he gains is civil freedom and proprietorship of everything he possesses ... to the foregoing acquisitions of the civil state could be added moral freedom, which alone makes him truly master of himself. For the impulse of appetite alone is slavery, and obedience to the law one has prescribed for oneself is freedom.[99]

Thus not only does Rousseau deny any sort of primary relatedness, but he establishes the Republic out of an impersonal, depersonalized interdependency (the social contract). The citizens are free precisely because they are not dependent on any person, while simultaneously they are a part of a whole which transcends all particular wills and passions and makes their sublimation possible. The danger and corruption brought about by personal dependence will be abolished through the tutelage of the Legislator, "a superior intelligence who saw all of men's passions yet experienced none of them."[100] Once his authority is internalized, the general will emerges as a moral force. External authority and internal authority are merged into a collective superego and both the public and the individual are "free" (from desire).

In conclusion, then, philosophy reflects the fundamental division of the world according to gender and a fear and devaluation of women characteristic of patriarchal attitudes. The concrete form these pervasive attitudes take varies among the philosophers. In Plato and Descartes it manifests itself in the radical disjunction between mind and body and an identification of the passions with chaos and error. In both, the body is to be placed firmly under the control of a desexualized reason. In Plato this form of reason is to be developed and reinforced by the state, which in turn is to be ruled only by those capable of so reasoning. In Hobbes, the work that only women do (childrearing) and the qualities it demands—relatedness, sociability, nurturance, concern for others—are not seen as part of human nature or the human condition. While Rousseau includes compassion among the natural impulses, he shares many of Hobbes' other assumptions about human nature. In both philosophers, childhood experience is repressed on a social and individual level. Only thus is it possible to deny the most fundamental proof of the necessity of human bonding and its effects, which extend far beyond mere utility, and reverberate throughout adult life.

This denial is an essential element of patriarchy, since, as we have seen, male identity is created out of a rejection of the mother, including the female parts of the male self. The female represents all that is either not civilized and/or not rational or moral. In turn, the denial becomes a justification for relegating women to the private sphere and devaluing what women are allowed to do and be.[101] Not only is individual psychological development distorted, but these distortions are elevated into abstract theories of human nature, the character of politics, of the self and of knowledge which reflect, it is then claimed, unchangeable and inevitable aspects of human existence (and/or the structure of the external world).

Towards a Feminist Epistemology

The task of feminist epistemology is to uncover how patriarchy has permeated both our concept of knowledge and the concrete content of bodies of knowledge, even that claiming to be emancipatory. Without adequate knowledge of the world and our history within it (and this includes knowing how to know), we cannot develop a more adequate social practice. A feminist epistemology is thus both an aspect of feminist theory and a preparation for and a central element of a more adequate theory of human nature and politics.

The prevailing forms of rationality and consciousness and our present accumulated knowledge reflect all aspects of human history including the existence of a sex/gender system in which biological characteristics are transformed into different and unequal social statuses and women are devalued. Reason is seen as a triumph over the senses, of the male over the female. In Hobbes, Freud and Rousseau, for example, reason can only emerge as a secondary process, under the authority and pressure of the patriarchal father. In Plato and Descartes, reason emerges only when nature (the female)[102] is posited as the other with an "inevitable" moment of domination. Yet all these theorists fail to locate this process within its social and historical context. This context is specific—because historically women have been the caretakers as well as the bearers of children, they represent both the body and our first encounter with the sometimes terrifying, sometimes gratifying vicissitudes of social relations. They become the embodiments of the unconscious, just as men become the embodiments of reason and law (the ego and the superego).

The following theses are offered as the beginning of a feminist theory of knowledge: (1) All human knowledge serves (among others) a defensive function. Analysis reveals an arrested stage of human development, or as Hegel calls it, "the unhappy consciousness" behind most forms of knowledge and reason.[103] Separation-individuation cannot be completed and true reciprocity emerge if the "other" must be dominated and/or repressed rather than incorporated into the self while simultaneously acknowledging difference. An unhealthy self projects its own dilemmas on the world and posits them as the "human condition."

(2) The apparently irresolvable dualisms of subject-object, mind-body, inner-outer, reason-sense, reflect this dilemma. Philosophies which locate such dualisms in the domination of the commodity form,[104] the dialectic of enlightenment,[105] the opposition of instinct and culture,[106] or the history of the monad[107] are incomplete and abstract (that is, not adequately grounded in human experience). What is lacking is an account of the earliest period of individual history in which the self emerges within the context of a relation with a woman (or women) which is itself overdetermined by patriarchy and class relations. Only certain forms of the self and of philosophy can emerge under these conditions.

(3) Feminists should analyze the epistemology of all bodies of knowledge which claim to be emancipatory including psychoanalysis and Marxism. There is a danger that the "female" dimensions of experience will be lost in philosophies developed under patriarchy. The relation between content and method is often not accidental. For example, the relationship between the positivistic aspects of Marxist theory and the disappearance of women and the "relations of reproduction" within it could be investigated.[108] It is necessary to develop an autonomous feminist viewpoint(s).

(4) Women's experience, which has been excluded from the realm of the known, of the rational, is not in itself an adequate ground for theory. As the other pole of the dualities it must be incorporated and transcended. Women, in part because of their own history as daughters, have problems with differentiation and the development of a true self and reciprocal relations.[109] Feminist theory and practice must thus include a therapeutic aspect, with consciousness raising as a model and an emphasis on process as political.

(5) Feminism is a revolutionary theory and practice. It requires simultaneously an incorporation, negation and transformation of all human history, including existing philosophies. Nothing less than a new stage of human development is required in which reciprocity can emerge for the first time as the basis of social relations. The destruction of class systems and the "critique of domination" alone cannot bring this about, nor will they be possible unless the analysis of gender-based power relations is pushed far beyond its present forms and a new feminist practice emerges.

(6) All forms of social relations and knowledge which arise out of them including the concept of liberation must be rethought and reformulated. This will only be possible when the development of theory is seen in relation to practice and knowledge itself is demystified, traced back to the life histories and purposes (conscious or not) of those who produce it.

(7) All concepts must be relational and contextual. Ways of thinking and thinking about thinking must be developed which do justice to the multiplicity of experience, the many layers of any instant in time and space.

(8) Dialectics is a way of beginning to think in terms of process, history and interrelationships. In Hegel, for example, knowing is treated (although somewhat abstractly) as an activity. This activity constitutes being in and through social relations which themselves have a history, just as individuals do.

(9) Knowledge and method must be self-reflective and self-critical. We do not just *experience* (at least not most of the time) but need and create concepts to filter and shape experience. For conceptualization to avoid rigidity, we must be members of a self-reflective society in which social relations (and relations with nature) are not organized on a principle of domination (of race, class, gender, and/or "expertise in light of institutional necessity").[110]

(10) Not all ways of thinking do justice to our experience or can be adequately connected to, informed by and inform practice. Claims of objectivity or neutrality are not more privileged than any others as we re-evaluate knowledge and experience.

It seems ironic and paradoxical that feminism, a political expression of women's desire for liberation, must take on these philosophical tasks. Women have represented being, as the bearers and nurturers of life. Yet precisely because knowing and being cannot be separated, we must know how to be. To do so requires a transformation of knowledge adequate to our being and which points us beyond its present distorted forms.

Notes

The ideas presented in this paper are a product of an ongoing discourse among many persons including Kirstin Dahl, Sandra Harding, Nancy Hartsock, Jill Lewis and Phyllis Palmer. I would especially like to thank Nannerl Keohane and Roger Masters for their detailed comments on an earlier draft. Discourse, of course, does not imply agreement.

[Epigraph] reprinted by permission of Faber and Faber Ltd. and Random House Inc. from *Collected Poems* by W. H. Auden.

1. On this point, see Michelle Rosaldo, 'Theoretical Overview' in Michelle Zimbalist Rosaldo and Louise Lamphere (eds.), *Women, Culture and Society* (Stanford: Stanford University Press, 1974).

2. Nancy Chodorow, *The Reproduction of Mothering: Psychoanalysis and the Sociology of Gender* (Berkeley and Los Angeles: University of California Press, 1978), pp. 3–39; pp. 173–209.

3. I read Freud's account of the Oedipal situation as an analysis of the mechanisms and psychic costs of the initiation of the male into patriarchal society. For Freud's own account, see Sigmund Freud, *An Outline of Psycho-Analysis* (New York: Norton, 1949), pp. 44–51; *The Ego and the Id* (New York: Norton, 1960), pp. 18–29; and *Civilization and Its Discontents* (New York: Norton, 1960), pp. 46–53. On the use of gender as a means of social organization, see Gayle Rubin, 'The Traffic in Women: Notes on the Political Economy of Sex,' in Rayna Reiter (ed.), *Towards an Anthropology of Women* (New York: Monthly Review Press, 1975).

4. For a further development of this argument see Dorothy Dinnerstein, *The Mermaid and the Minotaur: Sexual Arrangements and the Human Malaise* (New York: Harper and Row, 1976), especially Chapter Ten.

5. On object splitting and the internal world, see Harry Guntrip, *Personality Structure and Human Interaction* (New York: International Universities Press, 1961), pp. 356–444.

6. After carefully examining an extensive body of historical and anthropological evidence, Rosaldo concludes (Rosaldo and Lamphere, p. 3): "Whereas some anthropologists argue that there are, or have been, truly egalitarian societies ... and all agree that there are societies in which women have achieved considerable social recognition and power, none has observed a society in which women have publicly recognized power and authority surpassing that of men. ... Everywhere we find that women are excluded from certain crucial economic or political activities, that their roles as wives and mothers are associated with fewer powers and prerogatives than are the roles of men. It seems fair to say then, that all contemporary societies are to some extent male-dominated, and although the degree and expression of female subordination vary greatly, sexual asymmetry is presently a universal fact of human life ... the evidence of contemporary anthropology gives scant support for matriarchy ... there is little reason to believe that early sexual orders were substantially different from those observed around the world today." By patriarchy I mean any system in which men as a group oppress women as a group, even though there may be hierarchies among men. Typically in patriarchal societies, men have more access to and control over the most highly valued and esteemed resources and social activities, e.g., in a religious society, men will be priests and women excluded from the most important religious functions (if not considered polluting to them). Patriarchy has a material base in men's control of women's labor power and reproductive power and a psychodynamic base as a defense against the infantile mother and men's fear of women. It has assumed many different historical forms, but it still remains a dynamic force today. On the economic base of patriarchy, see Heidi Hartmann, 'Capitalism, Patriarchy, and Job Segregation by Sex' in Zillah R. Eisenstein, ed., *Capitalist Patriarchy and the Case for Socialist Feminism* (New York: Monthly Review Press, 1979). On reproduction, see Linda Gordon, *Women's Body, Women's Right* (New York: Grossman, 1976), especially pp. 3–25; pp. 403–418. On psychodynamics, see Gregory Zilboory, 'Masculine and Feminine: Some Biological and Cultural Aspects,' in Jean Baker Miller, ed., *Psychoanalysis and Women* (Baltimore: Penguin 1973); Karen Horney, 'The Flight from Womanhood' in her *Feminine Psychology* (New York: Norton, 1967); Dinnerstein and Chodorow.

7. Frederick M. Watkins, 'Political Theory as a Datum of Political Science,' in Roland Young, ed., *Approaches to the Study of Politics* (Evanston: Northwestern University Press, 1958), p. 154. Cited in Nannerl O. Keohane, 'Female Citizenship', a paper presented at the Meeting of

the Conference for the Study of Political Thought, April, 1979. Keohane argues that "the history of ideas is the psychiatry of social belief" (p. 34), although of course this is not its only purpose.

8. Immanuel Kant, *Critique of Pure Reason,* trans. F. Max Muller (Garden City: Doubleday Anchor, 1966). See for example, p. 18: "The most important consideration in the arrangement of such a science is that no concepts should be admitted which contain anything empirical, and that a priori knowledge shall be perfectly pure. Therefore, although the highest principles of morality and their fundamental concepts are a priori knowledge, they do not belong to transcendental philosophy, because the concepts of pleasure and pain, desire, inclination, free-will, etc., which are all of empirical origin, must here be presupposed. Transcendental philosophy is the wisdom of pure speculative reason. Everything practical, so far as it contains motives, has reference to sentiments, and these belong to empirical sources of knowledge." For an interesting psychoanalytic interpretation of Kant and other philosophers, see Ben-Ami Scharfstein and Mortimer Ostow, 'The Need to Philosophize' in Charles Hanly and Morris Lazerowitz, eds., *Psychoanalysis and Philosophy* (New York: International Universities Press, 1970).

9. A clear and poignant example of this is the work of Max Weber. See especially his essays 'Science as a Vocation' and 'Politics as a Vocation' in *From Max Weber,* eds. H. H. Gerth and C. W. Mills (New York: Oxford University Press, 1958). Weber worked within a neo-Kantian philosophical framework.

10. This is of course not true of all philosophers. Much of Habermas' work has focused on precisely this possibility. See, for example, Jurgen Habermas, *Knowledge and Human Interests* (Boston: Beacon, 1968), especially the Appendix.

11. For a similar view of political theory, see Norman Jacobson, *Pride and Solace: The Functions and Limits of Political Theory* (Berkeley: University of California Press, 1978).

12. Of course, the social relations of childrearing are not the only determinant of human experience. They interact with and are partially determined by class relations and culture in the broadest sense: art, politics, religion, ideology, language, etc. For a more detailed working out of these relations, see Jane Flax, 'A Materialist Theory of Women's Status' in the *Psychology of Women Quarterly* (forthcoming, 1981) and Zillah Eisenstein, 'Developing a Theory of Capitalist Patriarchy and Socialist Feminism' in Eisenstein.

13. On object relations theory see, D. W. Winnicott, *The Maturational Processes and the Facilitating Environment* (New York: International Universities Press, 1965); Margaret Mahler, Fred Pine and Anni Bergman, *The Psychological Birth of the Human Infant* (New York: Basic Books, 1975; and Guntrip, *Personality Structure* and also his *Psychoanalytic Theory, Therapy and the Self* (New York: Basic Books, 1971). There is much controversy about psychoanalysis and its status as a science, therapy and its relevance to feminism as well as the implications of psychoanalysis for the empiricist account of science. On psychoanalysis as a science (and what this might mean), see Guntrip, *Personality,* pp. 15–21; the essays by Salmon, Glymour, Alexander, Mischel, and Wisdom in Richard Wollheim, ed., *Freud: A Collection of Critical Essays* (Garden City: Anchor/Doubleday, 1974); and Jurgen Habermas, *Knowledge and Human Interests,* especially pp. 214–245. Object relations theory is based on close observation of healthy and disturbed children, and a reconstruction of childhood psychodynamics through clinical work with adults, including psychotics who have regressed to childhood. Its insights are confirmed by the success of therapy based on the theory and by the investigations of other researchers such as Piaget who do not work from a psychoanalytic perspective. See Jean Piaget, *The Construction of Reality in the Child* (New York: Basic Books, 1954), especially Chapter One. See also the clinical material in Jane Flax, 'The Conflict Between Nurturance and Autonomy in Mother-Daughter Relationships and within Feminism,' in *Feminist Studies,* v. 4, no. 2, June 1978; and my 'Mother-Daughter Relationships: Psychodynamics, Politics and Philosophy' in Hester Eisenstein (ed.) *The Future of Difference* (Boston: G. K. Hall, 1980). Robert J. Stoller in *Splitting: A Case of Female Masculinity* (New York: Delta, 1974), reports a detailed case history

which provides information on both psychoanalytic technique and psychodynamics. My account of object relations theory may be more political and feminist than some of the theorists would like, although both Guntrip and Winnicott discuss political as well as philosophical issues related to their theories.

14. Behaviorism denies the existence of the unconscious. I find this unacceptable on both empirical and moral grounds. Empirically, behaviorism cannot explain dreams, psychosomatic illness, the resistance of persons to strong stimuli even when it might be in their interest to respond to them (e.g., under torture). It assumes a direct link between body and behavior with no complex mediation. In sociology, for example, biological sexuality is conflated with a sex/gender system, that is, "the set of arrangements by which a society transforms biological sexuality into products of human activity, and in which these transformed sexual needs are satisfied" (Rubin, p. 159). Morally, behaviorism allows one to ignore the unique individuality of each person and to see people as subject to endless manipulation. It denies the possibility of innate characteristics and/or capacities (such as the ability to speak or reason), thus denying any non-environmental grounds for resisting authority.

15. On psychoanalytic method, see Sigmund Freud, *Therapy and Technique,* ed. Philip Rieff (New York: Collier, 1963); Otto Fenichel, *The Psychoanalytic Theory of Neurosis* (New York: W. W. Norton, 1945), especially pp. 3–32; pp. 547–588; Frieda Fromm-Reichmann, *Principles of Intensive Psychotherapy* (Chicago: University of Chicago Press, 1950); Harry Guntrip; and Ralph R. Greenson, *The Technique and Practice of Psychoanalysis* (New York: International Universities Press, 1967).

16. This is Mahler's phrase.

17. Psychoanalysts tend to call other persons objects. This terminology is meant to do justice to the ways in which we do objectify persons—through projection and introjection, for example—and to point to the process through which the cluster of feelings, experience and fantasies we have with and about other persons become *our* object, that is, part of our internal mental life and structure. In turn, these now internal processes can become an object for consciousness, as we attempt to uncover their social roots, in analysis for example. In this sense, subject and object are aspects of one continuous process.

18. Some of this material first appeared in a different form in Flax, 'Nurturance.' I am using the word mother rather than parent in this account because *women* do this work and I want to emphasize this fact. However, this does not imply that men could not do it (see n. 28).

19. See John Money and Anke A. Ehrhardt, *Man and Woman, Boy and Girl* (Baltimore: The Johns Hopkins University Press, 1972), especially pp. 176–194.

20. Mahler, et al., p. 44.

21. Mahler, et al., p. 48.

22. Flax, 'Nurturance,' pp. 172–184; Chodorow, pp. 114–140.

23. Mahler, et al., p. 102.

24. Sigmund Freud discusses this in 'Some Psychical Consequences of the Anatomical Distinction between the Sexes' reprinted in Jean Strouse, ed., *Women and Analysis* (New York: Dell, 1974), especially p. 10. See also Chodorow, Chapter 11.

25. Dinnerstein, Chapter Four.

26. Little work has been done which does justice to the complexity of the relationship between individual development and social relations. But see an exemplary study which focuses on class, Lillian Breslow Rubin, *Worlds of Pain: Life in the Working Class Family* (New York: Basic Books, 1976).

27. On the universality of this aspect of the sexual division of labor, Margaret Mead, 'On Freud's View of Female Psychology,' in Strouse, especially pp. 121–122.

28. The desire and capacity to mother should be separated from the capacity to give birth. Despite Rossi's claims and social ideology, there is no evidence that the capacity to care for young children is a female, genetically linked trait. See Alice S. Rossi, 'A Biosocial Perspective

on Parenting' in Alice S. Rossi, Jerome Kagan and Tamara K. Hareven, *The Family* (New York: W. W. Norton, 1977). As critics of her article have pointed out, Rossi cites evidence misleadingly and draws conclusions from clinical material in direct opposition to the results of the work. See Wini Breines, Margaret Cerullo and Judith Stacey, 'Social Biology, Family Studies and Anti-Feminist Backlash,' in *Feminist Studies* 4 (1978), 45–51; and Chodorow, pp. 18–21. Burton White somewhat reluctantly concludes, "When you look closely at what it means to be a child-rearer in the child's first three years, you find that most of the factors involved do not seem to be sex linked ... I see nothing that a mother does (except breast feeding) that a father could not do," in *The First Three Years of Life* (New York: Avon, 1975), p. 256. It is indicative of the power of patriarchal ideas that psychologists conclude from the study of child development not that children need reliable, consistent and loving relationships (which they obviously do) but that only their *mother* can provide such a relationship. A recent example of this confusion is Selma Fraiberg, *Every Child's Birthright: In Defense of Mothering* (New York: Bantam, 1977).

29. On the relationship between attitudes toward women and toward nature, see Susan Griffin, *Women and Nature* (New York: Harper and Row, 1978); Adrienne Rich, *Of Woman Born: Motherhood as Experience and Institution* (New York: W. W. Norton, 1976), chapters 3–6; and Max Horkheimer and Theodor Adorno, *Dialectic of Enlightenment* (New York: Herder and Herder, 1972), pp. 70–80.

30. Plato, *The Republic,* trans. Francis MacDonald Cornford (New York: Oxford University Press, 1947), especially pp. 120–143. There is much dispute over exactly how "feminist" Plato's philosophy is. Some argue that the evidence in the *Republic* is ambiguous. See, for example, Sarah B. Pomeroy, 'Feminism in Book V of Plato's Republic' in *Apeiron* VIII (1974), pp. 33–35. Susan Moller Okin in *Women in Western Political Thought* (Princeton: Princeton University Press, 1979), pp. 15–70, argues that once Plato abolishes the family for the guardians, he must question traditional Greek ideas about women. Arelen Saxonhouse in 'Comedy in Callipolis: Animal Imagery in the Republic,' *American Political Science Review* 72 (1978), 888–901, considers the fifth book of the *Republic* as a sort of "detour" whose main purpose is to suggest Plato's deep conviction that justice is not possible in the city. My own position is that the latent content of Plato's theory, even in the *Republic,* undercuts his apparent inclusion of women in the guardian class. The crucial step in the *Republic* is not the abolition of the family as Okin argues, but the repression and sublimation of sexuality. However, I agree with Okin's critique, especially in her 'Appendix to Chapter Two,' of the reconstruction of Plato's philosophy by Leo Strauss and Alan Bloom. Saxonhouse's arguments are dependent upon this reconstruction; thus although they are elegantly developed, I find them unconvincing.

31. Jacobson, p. 3.

32. Plato, p. 115. Of course, part of the better system of nurture for the philosopher kings is the separation of parent and child. This would reduce bonding and the problems and possibilities of psychological attachment which ensue.

33. Plato, p. 115.

34. Plato, p. 183.

35. Plato, p. 128.

36. Plato, p. 213.

37. Plato, p. 183.

38. Plato, pp. 198–204.

39. Plato, pp. 227–235. See Philip E. Slater, *The Glory of Hera* (Boston: Beacon Press, 1968), especially pp. 3–122, on the relationship between persistent themes in Greek culture and Greek family structure.

40. Plato, the *Symposium* in Edith Hamilton and Huntington Cairns, eds., *Plato: The Collected Dialogues* (Princeton: Princeton University Press, 1961), especially pp. 553–563. See also the *Phaedrus* in Hamilton and Cairns, pp. 494–502. In the *Phaedo,* in Hamilton and Cairns, p.

48, Socrates says, "In despising the body and avoiding it, and endeavoring to become independent, the philosopher's soul is ahead of all the rest."

41. See for example, the distinctions between earthly, younger Aphrodite and elder, heavenly Aphrodite in the *Symposium,* pp. 534–535.

42. Plato, the *Symposium,* p. 563.

43. Aristophanes' account of the original hermaphrodite sex is especially significant in this regard. After the man-woman is split apart by Zeus, the two halves are left with a deep and incomprehensible longing. What they really want is to be welded together "to live two lives in one ... to be merged ... into an utter oneness with the beloved," the *Symposium,* p. 545. The gender of the two lovers is much less important than the character of the longing itself. E. R. Dodd's comment, in *The Greeks and the Irrational* (Berkeley: University of California Press, 1951), pp. 218–219, is also relevant here: (eros) "spans the whole compass of human personality, and makes the one empirical bridge between man as he is and man as he might be. Plato, in fact comes very close here to the Freudian concept of *libido* and sublimation. But he never, as it seems to me, fully integrated this line of thought with the rest of his philosophy; had he done so, the notion of the intellect as a self-sufficient entity independent of the body might have been imperiled, and Plato was not going to risk that." However, I doubt Dodds would agree with my explanation of why eros is not integrated into the rest of Plato's thought. Socrates' hatred of the body and the corruption it brings is so great that he suggests (in the *Phaedo,* p. 49) that true knowledge is possible only after death, when the soul is finally free of the body.

44. Just as Plato says on p. 55 of the *Republic.*

45. Rene Descartes, *Discourse on Method* (Baltimore: Penguin, 1968).

46. Descartes, p. 54.

47. Descartes, p. 31.

48. Descartes, p. 78.

49. Descartes, p. 79.

50. Mahler, et al., p. 41–120.

51. See Winnicott, pp. 56–63.

52. On narcissism and the need to deny the separateness of the object, see Otto Kernberg, *Borderline Conditions and Pathological Narcissism* (New York: Jason Aronson, 1975), especially pp. 3–47; pp. 213–243.

53. For a further development of this argument, see Evelyn Fox Keller, 'Gender and Science' in *Psychoanalysis and Contemporary Thought* I, [no. 3 (1978), 409–433].

54. Other social roots in Western capitalist societies include the domination of the commodity form, see Georg Lukacs, 'Reification and the Consciousness of the Proletariat' in *History and Class Consciousness* (Cambridge: The MIT Press, 1971); relations of domination, see G. W. F. Hegel, 'Independence and Dependence of Self-Consciousness: Lordship and Bondage,' in *The Phenomenology of Mind,* trans. J. B. Baillie (New York: Harper, 1967); and alienation from nature, see Horkheimer and Adorno, *Dialectic of Enlightenment,* especially pp. 81–120.

55. See Melanie Klein, *Envy, Gratitude and Other Works 1946–1963* (New York: Delta, 1977), especially papers 1–3. This psychoanalytic analysis supports Wolin's argument that "liberalism was a philosophy of sobriety, born in fear, nourished by disenchantment, and prone to believe that the human condition was and was likely to remain one of pain and anxiety." Sheldon Wolin, *Politics and Vision: Continuity and Innovation in Western Political Thought* (Boston: Little, Brown and Company, 1960), pp. 293–294. However, I think this insight applies to Hobbes as well as Locke; "political society as a system of rules" (Wolin's description of Hobbes) can be seen as, in part, a defense against the same anxieties he attributed to Locke and other liberals.

56. Thomas Hobbes, *Leviathan,* ed. C. B. Macpherson (Baltimore: Penguin, 1968), p. 253. Gordon J. Schochet, in *Patriarchalism in Political Thought* identifies some of the overtly patriarchal aspects of Hobbes' thought (see pp. 225–243). However his definition of patriarchalism

is more literal than mine (rule of *the* father). He does not seem to notice that although the liberal sons could overthrow the authority of the father, this privilege was not extended to the daughters or wives. From a feminist perspective, rule of the *fathers* is not all that different from rule of a single father. For feminism, it is not true that "genetic justification and the identification of familial and political power were becoming dead issues" (Schochet, p. 276). See, for example, Mary Wollstonecraft, *A Vindication of the Rights of Woman*, ed., Charles W. Hagelman (New York: W. W. Norton, 1967; originally published 1791), especially chapter 5.

57. Hobbes, p. 253.

58. Hobbes, p. 253.

59. Hobbes, p. 254.

60. Hobbes, p. 253.

61. Hobbes, p. 285. This argument also seems ironic in that all other rights of governing are given over absolutely to the Leviathan. On the character of the Leviathan's authority, see Hanna Pitkin, *The Concept of Representation* (Berkeley: University of California Press, 1967), pp. 14–37.

62. Hobbes, p. 161. The parallels between Hobbes' and Freud's assumptions concerning the character of basic instincts and the political consequences following from them are quite striking. See Sigmund Freud, *Civilization and Its Discontents* (New York: W. W. Norton, 1962), especially pp. 33–81. It is also noteworthy that this essay begins with a discussion of Freud's inability to grasp an oceanic feeling—"of something limitless, unbounded"—which Romain Rolland had described to him. After Freud decides that the feeling of "oneness with the universe" (which is similar to symbiotic unity) cannot be investigated by or included in psychoanalysis, he then develops his theory of culture and its conflict with instinct.

63. Hobbes, p. 130. I believe C. B. Macpherson is right, in *The Political Theory of Possessive Individualism* (New York: Oxford University Press, 1962), p. 79, when he argues that "Hobbes' materialism was neither an afterthought nor a window-dressing but an essential part of his political theory." Indeed his theory of human nature is a "necessary condition of his theory of political obligation" (p. 79). However the additional necessary postulate, that "the motion of every individual is necessarily opposed to the motion of every other" (p. 79) is derived not only from the "market assumption," but from the infantile level at which Hobbes was able to conceptualize human needs. This is one of the unconscious sources of Hobbes' "refusal to impose more differences on men's wants, his acceptance of the equal need for continued motion" (p. 78) since for a very young child all needs are intensely felt, lack of gratification is experienced as pain and needs are experienced as insatiable. Thus possessive individualism is, in part, a defense against disappointment and deprivation.

64. Hobbes, p. 129.

65. Hobbes, p. 142.

66. Hobbes, p. 227, italics in the original. The Leviathan, like the super ego, retains many of the irrational aspects of the process by which it is formed. For further development of this argument, see Jacobson, pp. 53–92. Although Jacobson does not explicitly root his interpretation in psychoanalysis, he does argue that, "Anxiety, despair and dread of annihilation are the most prominent features of Hobbes' state of nature. And since these are always with us, his state of nature cannot be merely historical or analytic. It resides within us and is perpetual" (p. 61). However, unlike Jacobson, I am not convinced that these feelings (or those of Camus) must always be with us, at least in such overwhelming and determinant intensity. Dinnerstein's arguments provide an interesting challenge to Jacobson's last chapter.

67. Hobbes, p. 186; p. 188. Compare to Freud, 'Civilization,' p. 44.

68. Hobbes, p. 378.

69. Jean-Jacques Rousseau, *Discourse on the Origin and Foundations of Inequality* in Jean-Jacques Rousseau, *The First and Second Discourses*, ed. Roger D. Masters, trans., Roger D. and Judith R. Masters (New York: St. Martins Press, 1964).

70. The important differences between Hobbes and Rousseau include: (1) Rousseau argues that there are two fundamental human instincts—self-preservation *and* compassion. (2) Many faults in human behavior Hobbes attributes to man's fundamental nature, Rousseau attributes to the consequences of living in civil society which are read back into the state of nature. (3) In Hobbes, the Leviathan is not rational while Rousseau argues authority can be legitimate only if it is rational. The Republic is established to escape arbitrariness, not to be governed by it.

71. Rousseau, p. 112.

72. Rousseau, p. 115.

73. Rousseau, p. 114.

74. Rousseau, p. 116.

75. Rousseau, pp. 120–121.

76. Rousseau, p. 121. In note (1), especially pp. 218–220, Rousseau argues, contrary to Locke, that pregnancy would not give rise to women's dependency on men or to the family although this assertion is undercut by his positing a sexual division of labor in the state of nature.

77. Rousseau, p. 140.

78. Rousseau, pp. 132–141.

79. Rousseau, p. 143. This bears an interesting relation to Winnicott's notion of mother as "mirror," see D. W. Winnicott, *Playing and Reality* (New York: Basic Books, 1971), pp. 111–118.

80. Rousseau, p. 146.

81. Rousseau, p. 146.

82. Rousseau, pp. 146–147.

83. Rousseau, p. 150.

84. Rousseau, p. 147.

85. Rousseau, pp. 148–149.

86. Rousseau, pp. 151–152.

87. Rousseau, pp. 158–159.

88. Rousseau, p. 159.

89. In fact his account is similar to cultural anthropologists such as S. L. Washburn, see his 'Behavior and Human Evolution,' in *Classification and Human Evolution* (Chicago: Aldine Publishing Company, 1963). The feminist critique of "man the hunter" theories could be fruitfully applied to Rousseau as well. See Nancy Tanner and Adrienne Zihlman, 'Women in Evolution. Part I: Innovation and Selection in Human Origins' in *Signs* 1, no. 3, part 1 (Spring 1976), 585–608; and Adrienne L. Zihlman, 'Women in Evolution, Part II: Subsistence and Social Organization among Early Hominids' in *Signs* 4, no. 1 (Autumn 1978), 4–20. There are also interesting parallels between Marx's and Rousseau's accounts of human development. See Lucio Colletti, 'Rousseau as Critic of "Civil Society"' in *From Rousseau to Lenin: Studies in Ideology and Society* (New York: Monthly Review Press, 1972).

90. Rousseau, p. 147.

91. Okin, pp. 108–115. Okin (pp. 115–194) also shows how this notion of women as "naturally" subordinate to men permeates Rousseau's subsequent writings.

92. Rousseau, p. 147.

93. Rousseau, p. 135.

94. On this point, see also Elizabeth Rapaport, 'On the Future of Love: Rousseau and the Radical Feminists' in Carol C. Gould and Marx W. Wartofsky, *Women and Philosophy* (New York: G. P. Putnam, 1976) and Jacobson, pp. 104–105.

95. On the radical disjunction of natural and civil man, see Nannerl O. Keohane, 'The Masterpiece of Policy in Our Century: Rousseau on the Morality of the Enlightenment,' in *Political Theory* 6, no. 4, November 1978.

96. Rousseau, *On the Social Contract*, ed. Roger D. Masters, trans. Judith R. Masters (New York: St. Martins Press, 1978), pp. 52–58; pp. 67–70.

97. Or at least so one infers from this "praise" of the daughters of Geneva in the 'Dedication to the Republic of Geneva' of his *Discourse on the Origin of Inequality,* pp. 78–90. The "caste power" exercised by the "virtuous daughters" of Geneva is contrasted to the pernicious effects of the "debauched women" of other countries. It is hard to understand what this influence really means, since although Rousseau says it will always be the lot of women to govern men this is only true in the family and the influence is to be exercised solely "for the glory of the State and the public happiness" (p. 189). But if liberty consists in obeying laws which the individual has made and women are excluded from the general will, how are they to know what the happiness of the public would be? No private interest is to enter into the public will. In fact, Rousseau is consigning women to silence. Wollstonecraft aptly criticizes the contradictions in Rousseau's view of women. See especially, chapter one of 'Vindication.'

98. Although, of course Hobbes' citizen orients his life far more around the pursuit of private interest than does Rousseau's, and law in Rousseau is meant to be an expression of the general will, not just the Leviathan's will, which must be *accepted* as the general will (except under limited conditions, i.e., when the Leviathan is unable to preserve his life or the citizens').

99. Rousseau, *Social Contract,* pp. 55–56.

100. Rousseau, *Social Contract,* p. 67. Compare to Sigmund Freud's account of a group unified through identification, in *Group Psychology and the Analysis of the Ego* (New York: W. W. Norton, 1959), pp. 52–55: "If one cannot be the favourite oneself, at all events nobody else shall be the favourite ... originally rivals, they have succeeded in identifying themselves with one another by means of a similar love for the same object ... Social justice means that we deny ourselves many things so that others may have to do without them as well, or, what is the same thing, may not be able to ask for them. This demand for equality is the root of social conscience and the sense of duty ... thus social feeling is based upon the reversal of what was first a hostile feeling into a positively-toned tie in the nature of an identification."

101. See also, Aristotle, the *Politics,* trans. Ernest Barker (New York: Oxford University Press, 1962), Book I.

102. Donna Haraway discusses the patriarchal reconstruction of nature and biology in 'Animal Sociology.' Nature is frequently identified with the female both in terms of the gender given to the noun (Die Natur, la nature) and imagery (mother earth). Griffin shows that attitudes towards women and towards nature are inextricably linked and that the liberation of women requires a radical rethinking of our relationship with nature.

103. Hegel, *The Phenomenology,* pp. 242–267. This chapter of the Spirit's life history is a brilliant philosophical account of a self frozen in ambivalence because it is unable to recognize the other in itself and the self in the other: "But for its self, action and its *own* concrete action remain something miserable and insignificant, its enjoyment pain and the sublimation of these, positively considered, remains a mere 'beyond'" (p. 267).

104. Lukacs, 'Reification,' for example.

105. For example, Horkheimer and Adorno.

106. For example, Freud.

107. For example, Sartre's early work, *Being and Nothingness* (New York: Pocket Books, 1966), in which the self is in a perpetual state of anxiety and can never be certain that an "other" ever exists (and of course precisely for this reason can never overcome its anxiety). Or the tragic struggle in Edmund Husserl, *The Crisis of European Sciences and Transcendental Phenomenology,* trans. David Carr (Evanston: Northwestern University Press, 1970), in which the transcendental ego discovers its grounding in the "life world," but is trapped precisely in Hegel's unhappy consciousness, because it is unable to see and feel itself there. Merleau-Ponty also realized the lack of an adequate account of the "life world" within phenomenology and the challenge psychoanalysis posed to it. See his preface to A. Hesnard, *L'Oeuvre de Freud et Son Importance pour la Monde Moderne* (Paris: Payot, 1960).

108. On this point, see Nancy Hartsock, 'Response to "What Causes Gender Privilege and Class Privilege?" by Sandra Harding,' a paper presented at the 1978 meetings of the American Philosophical Association.

109. Flax, 'Nurturance and Autonomy.'

110. This seems to be the clearest and more sensible aspect of Habermas' recent work on a "universal pragmatics." See Jurgen Habermas, *Communication and the Evolution of Society* (Boston: Beacon, 1976), essays one and four. Habermas' always problematic synthesis of Hegelian and Kantian rationalism, and its consequences, seem most evident in his recent work.

Feminism, Psychoanalysis, and the Heterosexual Imperative

Shirley Nelson Garner

At its incipience, psychoanalysis defined the "mature" and "normal" woman as heterosexual and ready for or a participant in marriage and the family in the role of wife and mother. Its aim—though unspoken, unacknowledged, and perhaps unknown—was to socialize women to suit the ends of patriarchy as we know it in the Western world. Sharing the biases of the white middle class, it has tended to discourage celibate or lesbian women and has more or less ignored postmenopausal women. Its boundaries have been much narrower than those of feminism. As I see it, feminism puts the biologically female and culturally feminine at the center of experience and looks at the world from that perspective.[1] It is interested in woman's state and also in her prospects and potentialities. It would argue for variety in the patterns of women's lives, as a matter of choice or necessity. We may not be white or middle class. We may choose to live alone, together, or with men. We cannot help but grow old.

I want to consider here psychoanalytic attitudes toward lesbianism, particularly as those have or have not changed in the last decade or so. I am especially interested in the efforts of psychoanalysis to take into account lesbian existence other than in terms of arrested or aberrant sexual development. Though I believe that no woman is an island, that in some sense what happens to one of us happens to us all, psychoanalytic response to lesbianism engages me as a heterosexual woman not only as it affects other women but as it affects me. Since lesbianism is emblematic of "women together,"[2] it represents the feminist challenge to patriarchal values in the clearest form. Even when lesbians are not in fact free from the impositions of patriarchal structures, metaphorically they are often taken to be so. Though homosexual himself, E. M. Forster could tell Virginia Woolf that he "thought Sapphism disgusting: partly from convention, partly because he disliked that women should be independent of men."[3] All of us who claim the name "feminist" must accept that for many people, "feminist" is a code word for "angry, man-hating lesbian." Our identity is connected with that stereotype. For those of us who wish to continue to use psychoanalytic theory as clinical practitioners, patients, or literary theorists, it is important for us to understand how it is or is not responsive to lesbian existence. So long as it takes that reality into account only through its historical biases, it cannot be truly responsive to women, particularly those who define themselves as feminist.

When we speak of psychoanalysis, we are, of course, speaking of different experiences. Some of us know it as practitioners, many of us know it as patients, and still more of us know it as readers of its researchers and theorists, who may or may not be practitioners of psychoanalysis. I use *psychoanalysis* here not only to mean the practice of what is frequently called "classical psychoanalysis" but also to describe the psychoanalytically based therapies that derive from it. Patients' experiences of such therapies vary markedly. A lesbian friend recounts her experience of treatment by a male psychiatrist, a student of Erik Erickson, who was trained in and practiced classical psychoanalysis as well as psychoanalytically based therapy; he did not try to "cure" her of her lesbianism or treat it as problematic in any way. When she discussed her lesbianism with him at the outset, he told her that he did not look upon homosexuality as a problem unless a patient did. When she and her lesbian partner later sought a psychiatrist who would see them as a couple, they interviewed several who clearly would not have been helpful to them. Ultimately, they chose a woman therapist with conventional training, who, they felt, treated their difficulties as a lesbian couple without any of the traditional biases. At the same time, I read about a lesbian's vastly different experience with the psychiatric establishment in a recent issue of *Hurricane Alice,* a feminist review I help to edit. Twenty-seven sculptures, titled *Still Sane,* by Persimmon Blackbridge and Sheila Gilhooly, recount Gilhooly's experience of coming out as a lesbian and being admitted to a mental institution as a result. A text that accompanies one of the sculptures reads, *"I told my shrink that I didn't want to be cured of being a lesbian. He said that just proved how sick I was. He said I need shock treatment. ... 19 shock treatments and I still didn't want to be cured of being a lesbian."*[4] What these two stories suggest is that the aims of feminism and psychoanalysis may be, on the one hand, complementary or coincident or, on the other, at war with each other. Psychoanalytic practice may offer us sympathy or abuse.

Contemporary theories of psychoanalysis still labor under the weight of Freud's ideas. So compelling is his notion of the Oedipus complex as an explanation of male psychology and sexual development—at least in a patriarchal culture[5]—that it has carried along his less convincing and unconvincing ideas of female sexual development. His privileging of male sexuality leads him, at best, to misunderstand female sexuality, at worst, to deny it. It is to his credit that he often confesses that he does not understand female sexuality, that it is a mystery to him.[6] While Freud acknowledges the essential bisexuality of human beings, his theories, in fact, reinforce the heterosexual demands his society imposed on both women and men. As is revealed in Freud's letters to Wilhelm Fliess, his relationship with his colleague and friend was circumscribed by his own homophobia. His clinical practice reveals this bias as well. His study of Dora is a case in point. Freud seems unable to recognize the strength of Dora's attraction to Frau K., attributes to Dora heterosexual desires she probably did not have, and encourages her in a particularly corrupt and undesirable heterosexual alliance.[7]

When I began to read Karen Horney, who very early on questioned the bases on which psychoanalytic notions of female psychology rested, I was struck by her deference to Freud and his disciples, her reasonableness and considerable patience. Reading her for the first time in the early seventies, I thought the care and precision with which she addressed Freud and his followers over and over, point by point, concerning penis envy, for example, made her writing sound almost like a parody of an academic paper. Straight-faced, she quotes Karl Abraham: "Many females, both children and adults, suffer either temporarily or permanently from the fact of their sex." (Can we imagine psychoanalysts saying or paying attention to a comparable statement: "Many males, both children and adults, suffer either temporarily or permanently from the fact of their sex"?) Horney responds with only a touch of reprimand: "the conclusion so far drawn from the investigations—amounting as it does to an assertion that one half of the human race is discontented with the sex assigned to it can overcome this discontent only in favorable circumstances—is decidedly unsatisfying, not only to feminine narcissism but also to biological science."[8] Writing in the 1920s, she was obviously required to take such statements as Abraham's seriously. The deference to Freud and his ideas and to those who followed him is in some respects deserved. He was the father of Horney's discipline; much of what he discovered and created was valuable and has remained so. But ideas about female psychology, such as those surrounding penis envy, have held on tenaciously not only because they were Freud's but also because they surfaced in a culture that so wishes to believe in the superiority of men to women, to protect the sources of male power.

Beginning as they must, with Freud, students of psychoanalysis work through case studies and theoretical essays and papers that are not helpful in understanding the psychology of women, that share the culture's biases against them. They confront an even more serious prejudice against homosexuality. Unlike Freud, Horney seems disinterested and dispassionate when she considers homosexuality. Yet if it is not "abnormal" in her thinking, it represents, at best, a marginal accommodation for female sexuality. But it is not a subject that often interests her. Many of the matters she is concerned with are relevant to all women. She continually argues that society, rather than biology, accounts for those things, penis envy, for example, which psychoanalysts have taken as biologically determined. When her concerns are not those of all women, she is interested mainly in those that pertain to heterosexual women. I would argue, however, that to maintain that all human beings have bisexual potentialities, on the one hand, and to marginalize a homosexual resolution of sexual desires, on the other, is to make it less possible, probably impossible, to understand either male or female sexuality in specific cases or generally.

I want to turn to our time, when psychiatrists and other theorists should find it easier to work outside the prejudices that hampered those writings before the late 1950s and early 1960s. As Susan Krieger in her review essay in *The Lesbian Issue: Essays from Signs* describes the earlier literature based on medical and psychoanalytic expertise, it depicts lesbians "as pathological: sick, perverted, inverted, fixated, deviant, narcissistic, masochistic, and possibly biologically mutated, at best the daughters of hostile mothers and embarrassingly unassertive fathers." She traces the beginning of a different view to the late 1950s and after, when a growing number of sociologists, social psychologists, and psychiatrists started to take issue with "the assumptions of the pathological models. They offered new evidence and corrective interpretations and suggested that lesbianism was neither a sexual nor a social disease but, rather, a life-style choice linked with a sense of personal identity."[9] This literature, much of it published since the middle of the 1970s, has encouraged a reversal of the pathological paradigms and provided a shift toward the view of lesbianism as normal. A central influence in the emergence of this literature, Krieger asserts, was the founding of the *Journal of Homosexuality* in 1974 by researchers and clinicians who opposed the medical model. She cites Charlotte Wolff's *Love between Women* as standing alone at the beginning of the decade. The theorists that I want to look at have had the advantage of writing during this change in thinking.

After the midseventies, several American feminists published books that deal with female sexuality, focusing particularly on women in their roles as mothers and child rearers. In 1976 Adrienne Rich's *Of Woman Born: Motherhood as Experience and Institution* and Dorothy Dinnerstein's *The Mermaid and the Minotaur* appeared, followed by Nancy Chodorow's *Reproduction of Mothering: Psychoanalysis and the Sociology of Gender* in 1978. All these books are informed by psychoanalytic theory but differ from Freud in concentrating on the preoedipal period and the child's early relationship to the mother. They see woman's femininity (patriarchally defined) and her capacity for nurturance as consequences of her experience as exclusive child rearer. Reproducing these traits in her daughters, she passes on her strengths as well as those capacities that determine her subordinate position in society. Because Nancy Chodorow is more fully in dialogue with psychoanalytic theorists than Dinnerstein or Rich and because her work has been taken up in America by both psychoanalysts and feminists as well as literary critics, I want to look at her notions of women's sexuality as they are relevant to her treatment of lesbianism.

Chodorow's thesis, stated succinctly in her introduction, is that "women, as mothers, produce daughters with mothering capacities and the desire to mother. These capacities and needs are built into and grow out of the mother-daughter relationship itself." Woman's role in mothering is responsible for "sexual asymmetry and inequality."[10] For the psychoanalytic underpinnings of her argument, Chodorow looks beyond Freud and his followers to the "cultural school" psychoanalysts (such as Erich Fromm, Karen Horney, and Clara Thompson) as well as object-relations theorists (such as Alice and Michael Balint, John Bowlby, and W. R. B. Fairbairn). She bases her arguments concerning the reproduction of mothering on the persuasive assertion of the object-relations theorists that the child's "social relational experience from earliest infancy is determining for psychological growth and personality formation." These theorists dispute the view of Freud and the ego psychologists that "the biological requisites of the leading erotogenic zone (oral, anal, phallic, genital) determine the form of the child's object-relations." They claim, instead, that "with the possible exception of an 'oral' stage, the accession to experienced primacy or preoccupation with other 'erotogenic zones' is a result of particular social interactions concerning these zones" (47–48).

Chodorow maintains that current child-care arrangements are responsible for the particular characteristics of the girl's Oedipus complex. Though coming from object-relations theory, she reaches a conclusion about sexual development that echoes that of Helene Deutsch, who, of course, follows in Freud's direction:

> A girl does not turn absolutely from her mother to her father, but adds her father to her world of primary objects. She defines herself, as Deutsch says, in a relational triangle; this relational triangle is imposed upon another inner triangle involving a girl's preoccupation alternatively with her internal oedipal and internal preoedipal mother. Most importantly, this means that there is greater complexity in the feminine endopsychic object-world than in the masculine. It also means that although most women emerge from their oedipus complex erotically heterosexual—that is, oriented to their father and men as primary *erotic* objects (which the psychoanalysts seem not so sure of)—heterosexual love and emotional commitment are less exclusively established. Men tend to remain

emotionally secondary, though this varies according to the mother-daughter relation-ship, the quality of the father's interaction with his daughter, and the mother-father rela-tionship. (167)

Though Chodorow draws on a different line of psychoanalytic theorists to corrob-orate her thesis, she is in continual disagreement with Freud. Her tone does not con-vey Horney's calm attitude of respect, but she still feels the need to give Freud con-siderable space. In her chapter "Freud: Ideology and Evidence," she affirms the ways in which many of Freud's theories of female sexual development serve patriarchal aims. She points out that in Freud's system the girl's change of sexual object "is im-portant only because it is the way a girl becomes heterosexual" and that "the change from activity to passivity and the shift of primary organ of sexual gratification from clitoris to (or back to) vagina are necessary for the requisite heterosexual stance." She adds, further, that "this change of object prevents the most threatening form of in-cest to men—that between mother and daughter" (157). These observations would seem to invite some consideration of lesbianism, but that comes later in the book and seems brought forth only to be dismissed: "Deep affective relationships to women are hard to come by on a routine, daily, ongoing basis for many women. Les-bian relationships do tend to recreate mother-daughter emotions and connections, but most women are heterosexual. This heterosexual preference and taboos against homosexuality, in addition to objective economic dependence on men, make the op-tion of primary sexual bonds with other women unlikely—though more prevalent in recent years" (200).

Adrienne Rich responds to Chodorow's treatment of lesbianism. Hearing the eva-siveness in her statement that lesbian relationships have become more prevalent in recent years, Rich asks: "Is she saying that lesbian existence has become more visible in recent years (in certain groups?), that economic and other pressures have changed (under capitalism, socialism, or both?), and that consequently more women are re-jecting the heterosexual 'choice?'" She declares that Chodorow "leads us implicitly to conclude that heterosexuality is *not* a 'preference' for women; that, for one thing, it fragments the erotic from the emotional in a way that women find impoverishing and painful." Rich concludes that Chodorow's book "participates in mandating" heterosexuality.[11] Though I think Rich's phrasing is too strong, Chodorow clearly distances herself from what she is saying in two important respects. When she writes that women's primary erotic and emotional relationships may be disparate, she does not consider the effect such a disparity must have on women. This is surely an un-happy separation of Eros and feeling; yet Chodorow describes it without a clear sense that it is so. More important, she does not pursue the implications of her argument. If women's and men's primary attachments are both to the mother, why do women turn toward men? What Chodorow says is simply that "most women are heterosexu-al" and then refers to "this heterosexual preference." What is the source of this het-erosexuality, or is it a mystery? Rich says that male power forces heterosexuality upon women, that it is a means of "assuring male right of physical, economical, and emo-tional access."[12] What Rich sees is that the "logic" of psychoanalytic models center-ing on the importance of the preoedipal period in the formation of our relationships argues in the case of women for homosexual rather than heterosexual attachments. Chodorow runs headlong into this "logic" and cannot work herself through or around it.

In preparing to write this essay, I reviewed several editions of a psychology text-book on my office bookshelves, *Psychology of Women: Behavior in a Biosocial Context*, by Juanita H. Williams. The book was published by Norton in 1974, reprinted in 1977, published in a second edition in 1983 and a third in 1987. Between the first edition and the latest, the discussion of lesbianism has been considerably expanded. In the first edition, there is a short section on the subject included in the chapter "Sexual-ity"; in the second edition, it is extended. Unlike birth control, for example, the sub-ject does not receive a whole chapter; yet, the author presents lesbianism positively. Interestingly enough, Williams cites Rich's article and phrases for her readers' con-sideration Rich's question, "Why are most women heterosexuals?"[13] In the third edi-tion, "Lesbian Identity" is a section unto itself. It draws heavily on feminist scholar-ship and reiterates Rich's question.

Two years before the publication of Rich's *Of Women Born* and Dinnerstein's *The Mermaid and the Minotaur,* Luce Irigaray published in France *Speculum of the Other Woman,* followed in 1977 by *This Sex Which Is Not One,* both of which were trans-lated into English and published in 1985 by Cornell University Press. A practicing psychoanalyst, Irigaray is concerned to show how female sexuality has been seen through men's eyes, understood according to phallocentric values, and written, or rather *erased,* through phallocentric discourse. It is Irigaray's intention to undo the whole system: to disrupt male theories and constructions by writing female desire into language, an act requiring a new form of discourse. Though her work has been repudiated by Lacanians in France, feminist scholars in America, particularly those in foreign language departments, hold it in esteem. Now that it has been translated, it has been more widely read. Up to now, it seems to have had a negligible effect on the psychoanalytic establishment in America.

In *This Sex Which Is Not One,* Irigaray, like Chodorow, is engaged with Freud, and her audience is clearly the predominantly male psychoanalytic establishment as well as feminists and others interested in female sexuality. She answers the questions "Why do you begin your book with a critique of Freud?" (actually a reference to *Speculum*) and "Must we go over this ground one more time?" by suggesting that many of Freud's ideas persist to the detriment of women and implying that she does need to go over the old ground again. What interests me is that through her argu-ment with Freud and the psychoanalytic establishment, she also begins to shape a counterdescription of woman's desire. Her title is rich in meaning, but the central image comes from female genitals. While she demonstrates how woman's sexuality and desires have been written from a phallocentric perspective, she also asserts against it another vision:

> This organ which has nothing to show for itself also lacks a form of its own. And if woman takes pleasure precisely from this incompleteness of form which allows her or-gan to touch itself over and over again, indefinitely, by itself, that pleasure is denied by a civilization that privileges phallomorphism. The value granted to the only definable form excludes the one that is in play in female autoeroticism. The *one* of form, of the in-dividual, of the (male) sexual organ, of the proper name, of the proper meaning ... sup-plants, while separating and dividing, that contact of *at least two* (lips) which keeps woman in touch with herself, but without any possibility of distinguishing what is touching from what is touched.

Whence the mystery that woman represents in a culture claiming to count everything, to number everything by units, to inventory everything as individualities. *She is neither one nor two.*[14]

Irigaray continually emphasizes that woman's sexual pleasures are plural:

The pleasure of the vaginal caress does not have to be substituted for that of the clitoral caress. They each contribute, irreplaceably, to woman's pleasure. Among other caresses ... Fondling the breasts, touching the vulva, spreading the lips, stroking the posterior wall of the vagina, brushing against the mouth of the uterus, and so on. To evoke only a few of the most specifically female pleasures. Pleasures which are somewhat misunderstood in sexual difference as it is imagined—or not imagined, the other sex being only the indispensable complement to the only sex.

But *woman has sex organs more or less everywhere.* She finds pleasure almost anywhere. Even if we refrain from invoking the hystericization of her entire body, the geography of her pleasure is far more diversified, more multiple in its differences, more complex, more subtle, than is commonly imagined—in an imaginary rather too narrowly focused on sameness. (28)

What I find important here is that sexual pleasure is described as residing *within* a woman. It cannot come from *outside* unless the capacity for it exists *inside*. The one who caresses is not designated, so that the experience described may be autoerotic, homosexual, or heterosexual.

Irigaray suggests that there are many areas in which the premises of psychoanalysis may merit questioning and that female sexuality is only one of them. Raising a number of questions with regard to women's sexuality, she suggests answers that indicate the male bias of psychoanalytic perspective. For example, she asks: "*Why has the alternative between clitoral and vaginal pleasure played such a significant role?*" and responds with another question: "Is it informed by the *standardization* of this sexuality according to *masculine parameters* and/or by criteria that are valid—perhaps?—for determining whether autoeroticism or heteroeroticism prevails in man? In fact, a woman's erogenous zones are not the clitoris or the vagina, but the clitoris and the vagina, and the lips, and the vulva, and the mouth of the uterus, and the uterus itself, and the breasts ... What might have been, ought to have been astonishing is the *multiplicity of genital erogenous zones* (assuming that the qualifier 'genital' is still required) in female sexuality" (63–64).

One of the questions she asks concerns lesbianism: "*Why is the interpretation of female homosexuality, now as always, modeled on that of male homosexuality?*" Finding the psychoanalytic premise in Freud's "Psychogenesis of a Case of Homosexuality in Women,"[15] she notices that "the female homosexual is thought to act as a man in desiring a woman who is equivalent to the phallic mother and/or who has certain attributes that remind her of another man, for example her brother." She continues, "Why should the desire for likeness, for a female likeness, be forbidden to, or impossible for, the woman? Then again, *why are mother-daughter relations necessarily conceived in terms of 'masculine' desire* and homosexuality? What is the purpose of this misreading, of this condemnation, of woman's relation to her own original desires, this nonelaboration of her relation to her own origins? To assure the *predominance of a single libido,* as the little girl finds herself obliged to repress her drives and her earlier cathexes. Her libido?" (65). Later on, she objects at length to Freud's envelopment of female homosexuality into a "masculinity complex" and concludes that female homosexuality eludes psychoanalysis (193–97). Like women's sexuality generally, it is eclipsed.

The insistence of the dialogue with Freud in all these writers—Horney, Chodorow, Irigaray—as I listen to it, suggests the urgency of a repeated dream or the continual dramatization of a traumatic experience. The form of their discourse suggests an engagement with a psychoanalytic establishment that must seem at its center intractable. What I hear in Luce Irigaray that is hopeful is an effort to see anew, to think, imagine, and write woman differently. She suggests a possibility for reimagining female sexuality that could encompass female homosexuality without a negative cast. But what we have is still a beginning that asserts itself mainly in opposing and putting questions.

When I looked at psychoanalytic attempts to consider lesbianism, specifically in the work of clinicians and theorists who tended not to view it negatively, I went to Charlotte Wolff's *Love between Women* (1971), mentioned positively in Krieger's article and referred to me by a lesbian colleague. A psychiatrist and fellow of the British Psychological Society, Wolff bases her work on her clinical practice with lesbians between 1930 and 1950 and a particular study in which she looked mainly at nurses, secretaries, civil servants without university educations, writers, artists, and typists living in England. There were also a few women from professions of higher status—doctors, lawyers, professors, and the like—and a few skilled workers. She asked her subjects to write their "emotional autobiographies," participate in a lengthy interview with her, and answer a questionnaire.[16]

The underlying premise of Wolff's book is that "the one and only way to equality and progress in human as well as love relationships lies in the expression of the whole bisexual nature of every man and woman." Without any apparent anxiety, Wolff comments, "In society where bisexuality could be fully expressed and accepted, the family as we know it would be broken up" (81). Acknowledging that in such a society lesbianism would look different, and hence her assumption that psychology does not stand apart from the society in which it exists, she sees her task as explaining lesbianism in her current milieu. Unlike the other theorists with whom I have been dealing, Wolff is not particularly engaged with the psychoanalytic establishment. She refers to various theorists, to give credit or to depart from them, but her main effort is to describe lesbianism as she understands it. Though she states her main psychoanalytic disagreements with Freud, she gets over these quickly and focuses on his notion that human beings are essentially bisexual. In other words, she takes what she wants from him and seems by and large to forget the rest.

After discussing reasons for the prejudices against lesbianism, she begins to expound her own "theory" of it. She sees its main feature as intense emotion: "Emotion is the life centre of lesbian love" (17). Lesbians experience such emotional intensity, according to Wolff, because they can reconnect with the primary feelings of love they had for their mothers and because it is required to join in a relationship so forbidden. Without intense feeling, lesbians would be more likely to remain within the bounds of a repressive society.

One of the things I find refreshing about this book is the positive way Wolff views those aspects of lesbian existence that psychiatrists often read negatively. While traditionally a less than stable gender identity, which lesbians are often seen to have, might be interpreted as problematic, Wolff holds an opposite position: "*The reten-*

tion of the capacity to change feminine into masculine feelings and attitudes, and vice versa, is one of the assets of female homosexuality, because it makes for variety and richness in personal relationships" (52). In a rather stunning reversal of commonly held heterosexual attitudes, she argues for the "sexual virility" of lesbians:

> The marrying type of girl is frequently sexually inadequate or even frigid, while one who is homosexual has a better chance of being sexually alive. It is interesting to note that almost all homosexual women whom I interviewed were tomboys as children. This holds good for the more masculine as well as the more feminine lesbian. Both types, if one can differentiate them at all, showed sexual *virility*. Before they realised their true libidinous preference, they had, with few exceptions, sexual contact with men. Although many found heterosexual intercourse less enjoyable than homosexual love-making, they were, as my statistics show, living out their bisexual nature. Many of them were married, and a number of these realised their homosexuality only after years of marriage.
>
> I have no doubt that lesbianism makes a woman virile and open to *any* sexual stimulation, and that she is more often than not a more adequate and lively partner in bed than a "normal" woman. It is her virility and aggressiveness that enable her to subject herself to heterosexual intercourse without feeling humiliated. (64–65)

She further ascribes to lesbians a hardy independence: "The lesbian has never accepted the status of an object. It is in this rejection of female inferiority and masquerade that she steps outside the 'eternal' habits of her sex. ... Whatever their physical type, educational level, temperament or mentality, all homosexual women are *one* in their rejection of bondage to the male. They refuse to be the second sex" (79).

Wolff does not depict the lesbian's existence as unproblematic, however. She describes it as typically clouded, with an edge of "resignation and sadness" (16), which may be the result of childlessness, a wish for union with the mother that can never be fulfilled, and her status as an outsider. The other side of the positive aspects of the lesbian's emotionalism, all of which Wolff sees as a result of social pressures rather than intrinsic, are emotional instability and hence unreliability, a tendency toward paranoia, and a "conflict between integrity and adaptation" (90).

The main defects of this book are Wolff's failure to argue as convincingly as she might because of her tendency to overgeneralize, whether she is speaking of the positive or the negative aspects of lesbianism. On balance, she presents a rather monolithic and dichotomized picture of lesbian existence. She is, further, still dependent on models she wishes to cast aside. Though she puts "normal" in quotation marks, she continually juxtaposes the lesbian and "normal" woman; this habit of diction tends to reinforce the opposition rather than to change it. Though she writes positively about the lesbian's pleasure in "sameness" and her efforts to reestablish her primary bonds with her mother, she persists in talking about "emotional incest," which cannot help but undercut a relationship she intends to validate. While she largely rejects the biological bases on which Freud's theories rest, she does not seem to separate sexual aims from reproductive aims—hence her sense that childlessness is necessarily a source of sadness (she leaves aside the fact that lesbians need not be childless).

Her response to three lesbian autobiographies represents the kind of ambivalence and division I find in her. Her comments after each are divided into two sections: a "psychological interpretation" and a "personal impression." In one instance, her "psychological interpretation" concludes dismissively and seems to fall into a pathological model; yet her "personal impression" is generous and seems intended to see her subject whole:

> Miss Y. ... is painfully shy, but once put at her ease, she shows intelligence and a witty, sharp edge to her conversation. I am sure that she has high principles in behavior and action. She lives up to the rare virtues of steadfastness, loyalty and stability in human relationships. She would never let anybody down, nor betray a confidence. A social misfit, not by necessity but through her up-bringing, she has not found a professional or social place in accordance with her abilities. She compensates for her professional frustration through her interest in the theatre and literature. She identifies with those who are unfortunate through physical handicaps or other defects, and applies a practical religion: she goes and helps them. (257–58)

Wolff's case histories lack the rich psychoanalytic detail Freud gave to such studies as "The Psychogenesis of a Case of Homosexuality in Woman" or his case history of Dora, in part because of her method; but they also highlight how narrowly Freud worked toward establishing heterosexual identification or the lack of it.

Though I find Wolff's book seriously flawed, I also find it provocative. Many of its defects, like those of Freud's work, stem from its effort to break new ground. I would have found *Love between Women* as helpful as the more traditional psychoanalytic texts I used to help me describe a latent lesbian relationship in Virginia Woolf's *Night and Day*.[17] It would have helped me to understand, for example, how it might be different to love someone whom a person experienced as same rather than other and how the women characters in the novel value sameness.

Charlotte Wolff's work is not typical, however, for we do not tend to find comprehensive efforts to examine lesbianism or studies that reflect psychoanalytic experience in depth. What we find instead are studies that look at a number of subjects with regard to certain aspects of personality or behavior. These tend to emphasize the similarities between lesbians and heterosexuals and reinforce the sense that lesbians are "normal" in the same respects as others. Lesbians are not necessarily emotionally disturbed; they have no more psychological disorders than anyone else and no different ones. In one study, for example, "when young single women who identified themselves as lesbians were compared with a group of heterosexual counterparts, no differences in psychological adjustment were found. Even with respect to life styles, when the women were questioned about living situations, roles, friendship patterns, drinking, drugs, and suicidal behavior, the only differences between the groups were related to sexual orientation."[18]

As Krieger describes the directions of these studies, they tend to

> view the lesbian individual in a social context—in terms of her relationships in couples, institutions, communities, and a larger society—rather than in isolated individual terms or in relation to a family of origin. They consider lesbianism to be a matter of total personal identity rather than primarily a sexual condition, and they view it as subject to choice and as changeable in definition rather than as something that is a given. In the broadest sense, then, the shift that has occurred may be described as one that moves us from thinking about lesbianism in terms of deviance, narrowness, simple causation, isolated occurrence, and fixed nature to thinking of it in terms of normality, diversity, multiple influence, social context, choice, and change.

The biases of these studies—in their sample populations as well as researchers—are those of the educated white middle class. An increase, according to Krieger, "in the number of women researchers has been accompanied by an emphasis on the similarities between lesbians and other women, while the increasing number of lesbian researchers has encouraged an emphasis on the positively valued norms evolving among lesbians with regard to identity, relationships, and community—norms that differ from those of heterosexual culture."[19]

Psychoanalytic investigations of lesbianism still tend to be marked, however, by the pathological notions and heterosexual biases with which they began.[20] I was interested to see Juanita Williams imply in the conclusion of her section on lesbianism that her readers should look beyond psychology for an understanding of lesbianism: "The growth of research interest in lesbianism and the interpretations of its meaning by feminist scholars in psychology, anthropology, history, and literature are beginning to bring lesbianism out of the shadows of obscurity and defamation. This movement, born out of feminism and gay activism, has the promise of bringing us to a greater appreciation of the sexual diversity that has always been observable among earth's people."[21]

What seems to have developed in psychoanalysis as in psychoanalytic literary criticism is a kind of double track. I recently attended a workshop titled "Changing Views of the Psychology of Women: Implications for Psychotherapists" at the Hamm Clinic, a psychiatric clinic in the Twin Cities. The principal speaker, Dr. Teresa Bernardez, Professor of Psychiatry in the College of Human Medicine at Michigan State University in East Lansing, gave two addresses: "Prevalent Disorders of Women: Depression" and "Gender-based Countertransference of Male and Female Therapists." Bernardez was educated in Buenos Aires and completed a psychiatrist residency at the Menninger School of Psychiatry, after which she received postgraduate education in adult psychiatry at Menninger Foundation and psychoanalytic training at the Topeka Institute for Psychoanalysis. From the outset, she said, she knew she would have to modify the strictures of her training to treat patients according to their needs. She was never simply uncritical of psychoanalytic methods, but she recounted her early unwitting participation in the socialization of women for their feminine roles in patriarchal society. Gradually, she realized that women had to be treated as members of an oppressed group. A therapist could not simply act upon her psychiatric training without filtering it through her consciousness that conventional psychiatric therapy reinforced the repression of women. She also saw that women from various ethnic groups could not be treated the same as white, middleclass women, that a therapist needed to be aware of the values of the culture from which her patients came. When I asked her whether she found that lesbian and heterosexual women are equally subject to depressive illness, her answer was revealing. She said that she thought so, but could not answer definitively. In East Lansing, she said, there is a very active lesbian community, and lesbians tend, according to her, to prefer therapists within that community. As a heterosexual woman, she is not a preferred therapist of lesbians. The lesbians who come to see her do so because she is reputed to be good at dealing with particular mental problems. Her main source of information about lesbians is from lesbian therapists who are her colleagues. Bernardez is in the process of writing a book on the psychology of women, and from all I could gather from hearing her, it will be an intelligent book with feminist values. But it is also clear that she will have less firsthand clinical experience of lesbians than of other women and, therefore, must necessarily write about them less fully and specifically. Unless she collaborates with a lesbian therapist, she will have limited access to information she needs to write a complete account of women's psychology.

The recently published *Lesbian Psychologies: Explorations and Challenges* offers a rich account of lesbian experiences, including identity, relationships, problems, and therapies. Edited by the Boston Lesbian Psychologies Collective, the book contains essays by psychologists, social workers, counselors, and others. Noticeably, no contributor to the collection is a medical doctor or describes herself as a psychoanalyst.[22] Though some psychoanalysts and psychiatrists, especially women, are beginning to write women's experience into their field, their efforts to deal with lesbianism apart from traditional disciplinary prejudices are rudimentary.[23]

When I look at *The Lesbian Issue,* the collection of essays from *Signs* concerning lesbianism, I notice that none of the writers of the essays combines an interest in lesbianism with an interest in psychoanalysis. The only essay that relates the two is Krieger's review essay "Lesbianism Identity and Community," which deals with psychology as a discipline and to which I have frequently referred. Of the essays in *The (M)other Tongue: Essays on Feminist Psychoanalytic Interpretation,* the two that deal with forms of lesbian experience, Martha Noel Evans's "Writing as Difference in Violette Leduc's Autobiography, *La Batarde,*" and my essay, "'Women Together' in Virginia Woolf's *Night and Day,*" depend on psychoanalytic theory less than most of the essays in the anthology. At the same time, when Alma H. Bond, a psychotherapist writes about Virginia Woolf, she seems to define Woolf's lesbianism as problematic. Looking at her competitive relationship with her brother and what Bond perceives as her mother's distance, Bond comments, "No wonder Virginia Woolf left behind her a history of homosexuality, her continuing attempt to reunite with the early mother."[24]

If I consider the recently published anthology *In Dora's Case,* it seems clear that psychoanalytic critics have become sensitive to heterosexual biases, for several essays in that anthology recognize such failures in Freud's reading of Dora's case. And we have also become alert to recognizing lesbianism in the margins, as the essays in *The (M)other Tongue* demonstrate. Yet psychoanalytic theory does not offer us sufficient material to help us understand and write about lesbian experience as we encounter it in literature or in life. We must collect that analysis in bits and pieces, here and there, and look to references outside the mainstream of psychoanalytic theory or criticism. At the moment, we are likely to find more help in other disciplines and the arts. *Lesbian Psychologies* will be an important resource. It remains to be seen whether psychoanalysis will be able to accommodate itself to feminism, to give its energies wholeheartedly to understanding lesbianism without seeing it as disease or deficiency, or to examining it at all. This task is, I think, inextricably linked with coming to understand the psychology of women generally.

Notes

1. I am indebted to Martha Roth for the shape of this definition.
2. "Women together" is Virginia Woolf's phrase; see *Night and Day* (1920: rpt. New York: Harcourt, Brace, 1948), 101.
3. Quentin Bell, *Virginia Woolf: A Biography* (New York: Harcourt, Brace, 1972), 2:138.
4. Quoted in Jenny Miller, "Creating a Mad Culture," *Hurricane Alice* 3:1 (1985), 1.
5. Luce Irigaray remarks on the congruence of values implicit in psychoanalytic discourse and those "promulgated by patriarchal society and culture, values inscribed in the philosophi-

cal corpus: property, production, order, form, unity, visibility … and erection." *This Sex Which Is Not One,* trans. Catherine Porter with Carolyn Burke (Ithaca: Cornell University Press, 1985), 86, Irigaray's ellipses.

6. Juanita H. Williams catalogs Freud's frequent references to the mysteriousness of female psychology in *Psychology of Women: Behavior in a Biosocial Context,* 3d ed. (New York: Norton, 1987), 34. See also Zenia Odes Fliegel's essay "Women's Development in Analytic Theory: Six Decades of Controversy," in *Psychoanalysis and Women: Contemporary Reappraisals,* ed. Judith L. Alpert (Hillsdale, N.J.: Analytic Press), 4–15.

7. See the essays of Suzanne Gearhart, Toril Moi, and Maria Ramas in *In Dora's Case: Freud, Hysteria, Feminism,* ed. Charles Bernheimer and Claire Kahane (New York: Columbia University Press, 1985). All comment on Dora's homosexual attractions.

8. Karen Horney, *Feminine Psychology,* ed. Harold Kelman (New York: Norton, 1967), 37, 38.

9. Susan Krieger, "Lesbian Identity and Community: Recent Social Science Literature," *The Lesbian Issue: Essays from Signs,* ed. Estelle B. Freedman, Barbara C. Gelpi, Susan L. Johnson, and Kathleen M. Weston (Chicago: University of Chicago Press, 1985), 225.

10. Nancy Chodorow, *The Reproduction of Mothering: Psychoanalysis and the Sociology of Gender* (Berkeley: University of California Press, 1978), 6–7, hereafter cited in the text.

11. Adrienne Rich, "Compulsory Heterosexuality and Lesbian Existence," *Signs* 5 (1980), 636.

12. Ibid., 647.

13. Juanita H. Williams, *Psychology of Women: Behavior in a Biosocial Context,* 2d ed. (New York: Norton, 1974), 241, 3d ed. (1987), 409–10.

14. Irigaray, *This Sex Which Is Not One,* 26, hereafter cited in the text.

15. Sigmund Freud, *The Standard Edition of the Complete Psychological Works,* ed. and trans. James Strachey (London: Hogarth Press, 1953–74), 18:147–72.

16. Charlotte Wolff, *Love between Women* (New York: Harper and Row, 1971), 117–18, hereafter cited in the text.

17. See my essay "'Women Together' in Virginia Woolf's *Night and Day.*" *The (M)other Tongue: Essays in Feminist Psychoanalytic Interpretation,* ed. Shirley Nelson Garner, Claire Kahane, and Madelon Sprengnether (Ithaca: Cornell University Press, 1985), 318–33.

18. Williams, 2d ed., 242–43. Williams omits a description of this study from the third edition of her book, presumably because she sees contemporary researchers as "no longer concerned with the issue of assumed pathology" (3d ed., 405).

19. Krieger, "Lesbian Identity," 226–27, 228.

20. See Stephen F. Morin, "Heterosexual Bias in Psychological Research on Lesbianism and Male Homosexuality," *American Psychologist* 32 (1977), 629–37, for a discussion of the ways in which such biases are revealed.

21. Williams, 2d ed., 245, 3d ed., 411.

22. *Lesbian Psychologies: Explorations and Challenges,* ed. Boston Lesbian Psychologies Collective (Urbana: University of Illinois Press, 1987).

23. In *Psychoanalysis and Women,* Alpert includes an essay titled "Lesbian Choice: Transferences to Theory," by Ruth-Jean Eisenbud. Though Eisenbud separates herself from traditional analysts in her attitudes toward lesbians, her essay is mainly taken up with describing her own change of perspective and discussing sources of lesbianism that she sees as having negative aspects. The contributors to Alpert's collection have all had psychoanalytic training and tend to be professors in psychoanalytic institutes or to have private practices. They tend to hold Ph.D. degrees; only one is an M.D.

24. Alma H. Bond, "Virginia Woolf: Manic-Depressive Psychosis and Genius: An Illustration of Separation-Individuation Theory," *Journal of the American Academy of Psychoanalysis* 13 (1985), 202.

Suggested Further Readings

Abel, Elizabeth. "Race, Class, and Psychoanalysis? Opening Questions." In *Conflicts in Feminism,* ed. Marianna Hirsch and Evelyn Fox Keller, pp. 184–204. New York: Routledge, 1990.

Butler, Judith. "Gender Trouble, Feminist Theory, and Psychoanalytic Discourse." In *Feminism/Postmodernism,* ed. Linda J. Nicholson, pp. 324–240. New York: Routledge, 1990.

Chodorow, Nancy. "Family Structure and Feminine Personality." In *Women, Culture, and Society,* ed. Michelle Zimbalist Rosaldo and Louise Lamphere, pp. 43–66. Stanford: Stanford University Press, 1974.

Flax, Jane. *Thinking Fragments: Psychoanalysis, Feminism, and Postmodernism in the Contemporary West.* Berkeley: University of California Press, 1989.

Gilligan, Carol. *In a Different Voice.* Cambridge: Harvard University Press, 1982.

Mitchell, Juliet. *Psychoanalysis and Feminism.* New York: Vintage Books, 1974.

Ortner, Sherry B. "Oedipal Father, Mother's Brother, and the Penis: A Review of Juliet Mitchell's *Psychoanalysis and Feminism.*" *Feminist Studies* 2, nos. 2–3 (1975):167–182.

Person, Ethel Spector. "Sexuality as the Mainstay of Identity: Psychoanalytic Perspectives." *Signs: Journal of Women in Culture and Society* 5, no. 4 (1980):605–630.

Raymond, Janice. "Female Friendship: Contra Chodorow and Dinnerstein." *Hypatia* 1, no. 2 (Fall 1986):37–48.

Ross, Cheryl Lynn, and Mary Ellen Ross. "Mothers, Infants, and the Psychoanalytic Study of Ritual." *Signs: Journal of Women in Culture and Society* 9, no. 1 (1983):26–39.

FIVE

SOCIALIST FEMINIST

PERSPECTIVES

Social feminist theory took root in the mid-1970s in Europe and North America. Although embracing the importance of a Marxist class analysis of power, socialist feminists were persuaded by radical feminists of patriarchy's impact upon women's oppression. Rather than indicting capitalism as the sole cause of woman's oppression, socialist feminists argued that power, and thus oppression, arises from sex and race in addition to class; therefore, power and oppression are the results of the material and ideological conditions of patriarchy and racism as well as capitalism.

Socialist feminist theorists such as Zillah Eisenstein, Juliet Mitchell, and Sheila Rowbotham focused on an analysis of what they termed "capitalist patriarchy."[1] Making a distinction between exploitation and oppression, socialist feminists argued that although a Marxist class analysis offers an account of the exploitation of women and men as wage laborers, it does not recognize the oppression that results from woman's roles in the patriarchal sexual hierarchy: mother, mistress, domestic laborer, and consumer. Neither does a Marxist class analysis acknowledge the nature of racial oppression that interacts with both class exploitation and sexual oppression. The concern, then, was to develop an analysis that would look at the relations and mutual dependencies of capitalism, patriarchy, and racism since the industrial revolution.

Socialist feminists argue that an adequate understanding of woman's oppression must recognize the sexual divisions in reproductive labor as well as productive labor. Seeing Marxist analyses as remiss in their failure to recognize the importance of women's nonpaid domestic labors, socialist feminists shift attention to the prevailing institutions of procreation—motherhood and sexuality. While recognizing that women's specific child-rearing obligations and sexual experiences vary within different classes, socialist feminists nonetheless argue that there is a constancy in all women's experiences. Rich or poor, all women are held responsible for the majority of all domestic labors and have less sexual freedom than men. Woman's oppression in the "private" realm of family and sexuality in turn affects her options in the "public" realm of production. Ann Ferguson and Nancy Folbre argue that contemporary women have "a longer working day with less material and emotional rewards than men, less control over family decisions, and less sexual freedom combined with less sexual satisfaction. Specialization in sex-affective production is also associated with restrictions on options, choices and remuneration available to women in work outside the family—restrictions often directly attributed to their presumed or actual mothering role."[2] Furthermore, socialist feminists claim that the labor of women in the domestic realm serves not only the interests of their specific families but also the interests of capitalism in that the family reproduces the attitudes and capabilities needed to enter into the wage labor force.

Clearly, socialist feminists are convinced that the elimination of oppression will involve reorganization of human reproductive labor as well as productive labor. In her essay "The Politics of Socialist Feminism," Alison Jaggar argues that full reproductive freedom for women will require even more than altering our economy so that all people have access to birth control, abortion, child care, and adequate means to support a family; it will also require abolishing "the compulsory heterosexuality and mandatory motherhood that have characterized all male-dominated societies" and restructuring the gender divisions that exist in the wage labor force. Women and men must become equal participants in a workforce that is responsive to the needs of *parents* (parental leave, flexible working hours, provisions for child care, and similar concerns).

In her chapter "Life Without Father: Reconsidering Socialist-Feminist Theory," Barbara Ehrenreich offers a corrective to socialist feminist theory by noting that the relations between capitalism and patriarchy are far from simple. She is particularly critical of the view that patriarchy supports capitalism insofar as capitalism hinges on the unpaid labor of women in the domestic realm. She notes that current changes in the role of the homemaker—the decline in numbers of full-time homemakers and the corresponding decline in numbers of hours devoted to housework by part-time homemakers—have been easily accommodated by capitalism. Acknowledging such weaknesses of a traditional socialist feminist account, Ehrenreich proposes substituting a simplistic "capitalism-plus-patriarchy" model with an analysis of the sex-gender system that is far more sensitive to the complexities of the relations between capitalism and patriarchy as well as to the oppressions of sexism and racism.[3]

Ehrenreich cautions socialist feminists that in the process of developing more sophisticated theories they not fall into the trap of commodifying and depersonalizing women. She argues that it is a mistake to reductively describe all child-rearing labors as "reproducing labor power." To do so is, in her estimation, to preclude "human aspiration or resistance" and to deny the autonomy and human subjectivity of those who perform domestic labors. In analyzing women's experiences, Ehrenreich advises against an excessive deference to the Marxist language of commodities and exchange. She suggests turning the tables, thereby shifting values and asking instead such questions as "How can we account for what *men* do *outside* the home in feminist terms, in women's terms?"

Nancy Fraser provides a basis for the refinement of socialist feminism requested by Ehrenreich in developing an analysis of the sex-gender system. In her contribution to this volume, "What's Critical About Critical Theory? The Case of Habermas and Gender," Fraser examines the ways in which Jürgen Habermas's (b. 1929) attempt to develop a communication ethic whose ultimate aim is to promote the conditions of a rational participatory democracy in which the needs of all can be critically addressed might be used to expose and challenge the bases of male dominance and female subordination in modern societies.

In his writings, Habermas includes among the external effects of capitalism the impoverishment of culture, which results in a deterioration of the abilities needed for critically analyzing experiences; the fetishism of commodities, which assimilates all relationships to the buying and selling of commodities; and the bureaucratization of everyday life, which has the effect of substituting economic-administrative activity for communicative interaction. According to David Ingram, these tendencies "conspire to undermine the communicative conditions for transmitting culture, coordinating action, and fostering personal identity freely and rationally. The result is fragmentation and objectification of life and the destruction of moral autonomy."[4]

Although Habermas does not address the question of gender in his work, Fraser's aim is to reconstruct the unthematized gender subtext of his analysis of the relations between the public and private spheres of life in capitalist societies. Like Ehrenreich and others who have discredited the simplistic "capitalism-*plus*-patriarchy" model, Fraser argues that the family is a domain of *material* reproduction (that is, of labor and the production of goods). In particular, she criticizes Habermas's analysis of the family for the following reasons:

> It directs attention away from the fact that the household, like the paid workplace, is a site of labor, albeit of unremunerated and often unrecognized labor. Likewise, it does not make visible the fact that in the paid workplace, as in the household, women are assigned to, indeed ghettoized in, distinctively feminine, service-oriented, and often sexualized occupations. Finally, it fails to focalize the fact that in both spheres women are subordinated to men ... [and] that families are thoroughly permeated with, in Habermas's terms, the media of money and power. They are sites of egocentric, strategic, and instrumental calculation as well as sites of usually exploitative exchanges of services, labor, cash, and sex—and, frequently, sites of coercion and violence.

Fraser also examines the sex-gender system of the relations between public and private institutions in capitalist societies. She argues that the roles of worker and of citizen are masculine roles, whereas those of consumer and child rearer are feminine roles. Having overlooked this sex-gender system, Habermas fails, in Fraser's estimation, to perceive how "the assumptions of man's capacity to protect and woman's need of man's protection ... the assumption of man's capacity to speak and consent and woman's comparative incapacity ... the assumptions of man's provider status and of woman's dependent status" are embedded in all of these roles. By calling attention to Habermas's "gender-blind" perceptions, Fraser undermines the orthodox Marxist assumption that as the (official) economy changes, so too will the family. She shows clearly in her essay that changes in the family are just as likely to alter the (official) economy as vice versa. Thus, Fraser offers an alternative model for socialist feminists, one that recognizes the similarities and mutual reinforcements between the male-headed nuclear family and the state-regulated official economy in enforcing women's subordination.

The work that has been done and continues to be done by socialist feminists is most encouraging precisely because it aims, as Alison Jaggar has said, to "synthesize the best insights" of the radical and Marxist traditions while striving to escape "the problems associated with each."[5] Presumably, the problems to which Jaggar alludes are too heavy an emphasis on sexual issues and patriarchy in the radical tradition and on economic issues and capitalism in the Marxist tradition. Wanting very much to expand their theory to include the racial, ethnic, and cultural differences among women, socialist feminists are attempting to do more than just add "difference" and stir. Such an approach did not work when women's issues were simply added to traditional male-biased philosophy, history, literature, and science, and it is equally unlikely to work if multicultural and global feminist issues are simply added to socialist feminist thought. Thus, women of color and women in developing countries are challenging the methodologies and concepts of socialist feminist thought in the same way that feminist philosophers challenged the methodology and concepts of traditional philosophy. In the instance of this intra-feminist challenge, the good news is that those who are being challenged, the socialist feminists, not only accept but want suggestions that will enable them to better explain women's differences as they coalesce the concerns of women into a program of global political action.[6]

Notes

1. Zillah R. Eisenstein, ed., *Capitalist Patriarchy and the Case for Socialist Feminism* (New York: Monthly Review Press, 1979); Juliet Mitchell, *Women's Estate* (New York: Pantheon Books, 1971); Sheila Rowbotham, *Woman's Consciousness, Man's World* (New York: Penguin, 1973).

2. Ann Ferguson and Nancy Folbre, "The Unhappy Marriage of Patriarchy and Capitalism," in *Women and Revolution,* ed. Lydia Sargent (Boston: South End Press, 1981), p. 319.

3. Zillah Eisenstein's recognition of the tensions that exist between the patriarchal treatment of women within the wage labor force and the ideals of liberal theory concerning access to capital is an additional example of the need for a more complex model.

4. David Ingram, *Critical Theory and Philosophy* (New York: Paragon House, 1990), p. 161.

5. Alison M. Jaggar, *Feminist Politics and Human Nature* (Totowa, New Jersey: Rowman & Allanheld, 1983), p. 9.

6. See, for example, Gloria Anzaldúa, *Making Face, Making Soul: Haciendo Caras: Creative and Critical Perspectives by Women of Color* (San Francisco: Aunt Lute Foundation Books, 1990), and Chandra Talpode, Ann Russon, and Lourdes Torres, eds., *Third World Women and the Politics of Feminism* (Bloomington: University of Indiana Press, 1991).

Life Without Father: Reconsidering Socialist-Feminist Theory

Barbara Ehrenreich

By the late 1970s, most socialist-feminists accepted as "theory" a certain description of the world: "the system" we confronted was actually composed of two systems or structures, capitalism and patriarchy. These two systems or structures were of roughly equal weight (never mind that capitalism was a mere infant compared to patriarchy, or, on the other hand, that patriarchy had no visible corporate headquarters). And capitalism and patriarchy were remarkably congenial and reinforced each other in thousands of ways (which it was the task of socialist-feminists to enumerate). As Zillah Eisenstein wrote in her 1979 anthology, *Capitalist Patriarchy and the Case for Socialist Feminism,* patriarchy and capitalism meshed so neatly that they had become "an *integral process:* specific elements of each system are necessitated by the other." Capitalism plus patriarchy described the whole world—or nearly: racism usually required extensive addenda—and that world was as orderly and smoothly functioning as the Newtonian universe.

It was a brave idea. Today, just a few years later, few people venture vast theoretical syntheses. In the course of time, many of the socialist-feminist system-builders of the seventies have become struggling academics, constrained to publish in respectable journals and keep their noses to the empirical grindstone. No longer do people meet, as many of us did, intensely and repeatedly, with an agenda of discovering the connections between *everything*—sex and class, housework and factory work, the family and the state, race and gender, sexuality and profits. If "capitalism plus patriarchy" was too easy an answer, at least we (the socialist-feminists of the seventies) asked the hard questions.

In a practical sense, too, it was a good theory, because it served to validate the existence of socialist-feminism. And I do not say this to trivialize the theory as self-serving. In the mid-seventies, in particular, socialist-feminists were an embattled species. On the one hand there was cultural and/or separatist feminism, drifting off toward spirituality, Great Goddess worship, and sociobiological theories of eternal male perfidy. To these "radical" feminists, socialist-feminists were male-identified dupes of the left, which they always described as the "male left." On the other hand, there was the left, which featured at the time a flourishing Marxist-Leninist tendency, bent on self-proletarianization and the "rectification" of everyone else. To it, socialist-feminists were agents of the petite bourgeoisie on assignment to distract working-class women from the main event, the class struggle.[1] The Marxist-Leninists and separatist feminists were extremes in a much wider radical context, but they helped define a political atmosphere in which socialist-feminism was hard put to establish that it was neither an oxymoron nor a form of treason.

The capitalism-plus-patriarchy paradigm was an ingenious defensive stance. If the world were really made up of two systems which were distinct and could not be reduced to each other, it was never enough to be just a socialist or just a feminist. If patriarchy were not only distinct but truly a "system" and not an attitude (like sexism) or a structure of the unconscious (as Juliet Mitchell saw it), those who opposed patriarchy were not just jousting with superstructural windmills: they were doing something real and "material." Finally, if patriarchy and capitalism were mutually reinforcing, it didn't make any sense to take on one without the other. If "the system" were capitalist-patriarchy, the only thoroughgoing oppositional politics was its mirror image, socialist-feminism.

Not all socialist-feminists were perfectly comfortable with the capitalism-plus-patriarchy formulation, however. For one thing, there always seemed to be something a little static and structuralist about it. Deirdre English and I argued, in our book *For Her Own Good*, that "patriarchy" ought to be left where Marx last saw it—in preindustrial European society—and that modern feminists should get on with the task of describing our own "sex-gender system," to use Gayle Rubin's phrase, in all its historic specificity. In addition, we were not convinced that capitalism and patriarchy were on as good terms as socialist-feminist theory demanded. If the theory couldn't account for the clashes as well as the reinforcements, it couldn't account for change—such as the emergence of feminism itself in the late eighteenth-century ferment of bourgeois and *anti-patriarchal* liberalism. The world of capitalism plus patriarchy, endlessly abetting each other to form a closed system with just one seam, was a world without change, a world without a subject.

There is another problem. Things *have* changed, and in ways that make capitalist-patriarchy (or, better, "patriarchal capitalism") almost seem like a good deal. Socialist-feminists—not to mention many plain feminists and socialists—went wrong in assuming that "the system," whatever it was called, would, left to itself, reproduce itself.

Woman as Domestic Worker

The linchpin of socialist-feminist theory, the factor that put women, so to speak, on the Marxist map, was domestic work. In theory this work included everything women do in the home, from cooking and cleaning to reading bedtime stories and having sex. Radical feminists were quick to point out how women's efforts, whether serving coffee in a movement office or polishing the coffee table in a suburban home, served the interests of individual men. Socialist-feminists, coming along a few years later, asserted that women's domestic work served not only men, but capital. As Zillah Eisenstein put it:

> All the processes involved in domestic work help in the perpetuation of the existing society: (1) Women stabilize patriarchal structures (the family, housewife, mother, etc.) by fulfilling these roles. (2) Simultaneously, women are reproducing new workers, for both

the paid and unpaid labor force … (3) They work as well in the labor force for lesser wages. (4) They stabilize the economy through their role as consumers. If the other side of production is consumption, the other side of capitalism is patriarchy.[2]

The discovery of the importance of women's domestic work put some flesh on the abstract union of capitalism and patriarchy. First, it gave patriarchy, which had otherwise had a somewhat ghostly quality (stretched as it was to include everything from rape to domestic slovenliness), a "material base" in "men's control over women's labor power." Second, it revealed a vivid parallel between "the private sphere," where patriarchy was still ensconced, and the "public sphere," where capital called the shots. In the public sphere, men labored at production, and in the private sphere women labored at "reproduction" (not only physical reproduction, but the reproduction of attitudes and capabilities required for all types of work). Finally it showed how essential patriarchy was to capitalism: most capitalist institutions produced only things, but the quintessential patriarchal institution, the family, produced the men who produced things—thanks to the labor of women.

It was not altogether clear where one went with this insight into the centrality of women's domestic work. If what women did in the home was so critical to the reproduction of both capitalism and patriarchy, shouldn't women be advised to stop doing it? Perhaps to sabotage it? The "wages for housework" position, which surfaced in this country in 1974, provided a strategic answer and an unintended caricature of American socialist-feminist theory. American socialist-feminists had argued that women's work was "necessary" to capitalism; the Italian feminists who launched wages for housework insisted, with considerable eloquence, that domestic work actually produced surplus value for the capitalists, just as what we ordinarily thought of as "productive" work in the public sphere did. If you were going to say that women's domestic work reproduced the labor power needed by capital, you might as well go all the way and say it was part of the productive process, just as much as the extraction and preparation of raw materials for manufacturing. Thus the home was an adjunct to the factory; in fact it was part of the great "social factory" (schools and all other sites of social reproduction) that kept the literal factories running. Women's domestic activities were no longer a shadowy contribution, but a potentially quantifiable productive factor with the distinguished Marxist status of "producing surplus value." The only difference between the man laboring for Fiat or Ford, and the woman laboring in her kitchen, was that she was unpaid—a patriarchal oversight that "wages for housework" would correct.

This proposal and the accompanying theory sent shock waves through American and British socialist-feminist networks. There were debates over the practicality of the demand: who would pay the wages for housework, which would, after all, constitute an enormous redistribution of wealth? There were even more debates at the level of high theory: was it scientifically accurate to say that housework produced surplus value? (A debate which, in my opinion, produced almost nothing of value.) Unfortunately there was much less attention to the bizarre, but utterly logical extreme to which wages-for-housework theory took homegrown socialist-feminist theory. Everything women did in the home was in the service of capital and indispensable to capital. When a mother kissed her children goodnight she was "reproducing labor power." When a childless working woman brushed her teeth she too was reproducing labor power (her own, in this case), as an American wages-for-housework advocate argued in an exchange I participated in. This was commodity fetishism with a vengeance, and even with the modification that kissing, for example, serves the miniature patriarchy of the family more directly than corporate capital, it all boiled down to the same thing, since patriarchy was firmly in league with capital.

The Obsolescence of Capitalism-Plus-Patriarchy

Looking back from the vantage point of 1984, the debates of 1975 have an almost wistful quality. They (men, capitalists) needed us (women) to do all our traditional "womanly" things, and, if theory were to be trusted, they would apparently go to great lengths to keep us at it. Well, they don't seem to need us anymore—at least not that way—and if this weren't completely evident in 1975, it is inescapable today.

No matter how valuable the services of a full-time homemaker may be, fewer and fewer men earn enough to support one. The reasons for the disappearance of the male "family wage" and the associated influx of married women into the workforce have been discussed at length in these pages and elsewhere. The relevant point here is that for all we say about the "double day," employed women do far less housework than those who are full-time homemakers, 26 hours per week as compared to 55 hours per week.[3] Other family members may be compensating in part (though most studies I have seen show little increase in husbands' contributions), but it is hard not to conclude that the net amount of housework done has decreased dramatically. (By as much as 29 million hours per week per year during the peak years of women's influx into the labor market. Of course a certain amount of this work has been taken up by the commercial sector, especially by restaurants and fast-food places.) If women's work were as essential to the status quo as socialist-feminist theory argued, capitalism should have been seriously weakened by this withdrawal of women's labor. Yet no one is arguing, for example, that the decline of American productivity is due to unironed shirts and cold breakfasts. Nor has any sector of capital come forth and offered to restore the male family wage so that women can get back to their housework.

If capital does not seem to need women's domestic work as much as theory predicted, what about individual men? Mid-seventies feminist theory tended to portray men as enthusiastic claimants of women's services and labor, eagerly enlisting us to provide them with clean laundry, homecooked meals, and heirs. If we have learned anything in the last ten years, it is that men have an unexpected ability to survive on fast food and the emotional solace of short-term relationships. There are, as Marxists say, "material" reasons for this. First, it is physically possible, thanks to laundromats, frozen food, and other conveniences, for even a poor man to live alone and without servants. Second, there have always been alternatives to spending a "family wage" on an actual family, but in the last few decades these alternatives have become more numerous and alluring. Not only are there the classic temptations of drink, gambling, and "loose women" to choose from, but stereos, well-appointed bachelor apartments, Club Med, sports cars, and so forth. For these and other reasons, American men have been abdicating their traditional roles as husbands, breadwinners, and the petty patriarchs of the "capitalism-plus-patriarchy" paradigm.[4]

In a larger sense, events and some belated realizations of the last few years should have undermined any faith we had in capital's willingness to promote the "reproduction of labor power." Capital as well as labor is internationally mobile, making United States corporations relatively independent of a working class born and bred in this or any one country. Furthermore, capitalists are not required to be industrial capitalists; they can disinvest in production and reinvest in real estate, financial speculation, or, if it suits their fancy, antiques, and they have done so despite any number of exhortations and supply-side incentives. In their actual practices and policies, capitalists and their representatives display remarkable indifference to the "reproduction of labor power," or, in less commoditized terms, the perpetuation of human life.

This is not to say that individual companies or industries do not maintain a detailed interest in our lives as consumers. They do, especially if we are lucky enough to be above "the buying point" in personal resources. But is is no longer possible to discern a uniform patriarchal or even pronatalist bias to this concern. Capitalists have figured out that two-paycheck couples buy more than husband-plus-housewife units, and that a society of singles potentially buys more than a society in which households are shared by three or more people. In times of labor insurgency, far-seeing representatives of the capitalist class have taken a minute interest in how ordinary people organize their lives, raise their children, etc. But this is not such a time, and it seems plain to me that the manufacturers of components for missile heads (a mile from where I sit) do not care whether my children are docile or cranky, and that the people who laced our drinking water with toxins (a mile the other way) could not much care whether I scrub the floors.

With hindsight, I am struck by what a *benevolent* system the "capitalism-plus-patriarchy" paradigm implied. In order to put women's hidden and private interests on the economic map, we had to assume that they reflected some much larger, systemic need. Since these efforts of women are in fact efforts to care and nurture, we had to project the functions of caring and nurturing onto the large, impersonal "structures" governing our all-too-functional construct of the world. Capitalism, inscribed with the will to "reproduce," became "patriarchal capitalism." This suggested that, in a sense, our theory was a family metaphor for the world: capitalists were "fathers," male workers were "sons," and all women were wives/daughters, both mediating the relations between fathers and sons[5] and producing more sons (and daughters) to keep the whole system going. The daughters had the worse deal, but at least they were members of the family, and this family, like actual ones, intended to keep on going—a motivation that is no longer so easy to attribute to the men who command our resources and our labor.

I think now that the "capitalism-plus-patriarchy" paradigm overpersonalized (and humanized) capitalism precisely because it depersonalized women. The paradigm granted "the system" an undue benevolence because it had no room for motive or caring on the part of women. Once all the interactions and efforts of childraising have been reduced to "reproducing labor power" (and children have been reduced to units of future labor power), there is no place for human aspirations or resistance. Once it has been determined that "all the processes involved in domestic work help in the perpetuation of the existing society," the women who perform these "processes" have lost all potential autonomy and human subjectivity. And once it is declared that all acts other than production are really "reproduction" (of labor power and the same old system of domination), only one kind of resistance *is* possible. Suicide, or the willful destruction of labor power.

Ironically, the intent of the "capitalism-plus-patriarchy" paradigm was to validate feminism and insert women, as actors, into the Marxist political calculus. The problem was that we were too deferential to Marxism. Socialist-feminists tried to account for large areas of women's experience—actually everyone's experience—in the language of commodities and exchange, as if that were the "scientific" way to proceed. It would have been better perhaps to turn the tables: for example, instead of asking, "How can we account for women's work in the home in Marxist terms?" we should have asked, "How can we account for what *men* do *outside* the home in feminist terms, in women's terms?" Trying to fit all of women's experience into the terms of the market didn't work, and adding on patriarchy, as an additional "structure," didn't help.

So where do we go from here? Is it possible to be a socialist-feminist without a "socialist-feminist theory"? Yes, of course it is. After all, those who are plain socialists or feminists get along—with no evident embarrassment—on just half a theory at best. The socialist-feminist project has always been larger and more daring than that of either of our progenitors, so if we have fumbled, it is in part because we attempted more.

But we do need a better way to understand the world we seek to act in. I hesitate to say we need a new "theory," because that word suggests a new set of structures and laws of mechanics to connect them. If not "capitalism-plus-patriarchy," you are probably thinking, what is it? The point is that "it" is changing, and in a more violent and cataclysmic fashion than we had any reason to expect. The statics of "capitalism-plus-patriarchy" help explain a world that is already receding from view—a world of relative affluence and apparent stability—where categories like "the family," "the state," and "the economy" were fixed and solid anchor-points for theory. Today, there is little we can take as fixed. "The family," so long reified in theory, looks more like an improvisation than an institution. A new technological revolution, on the scale of the one that swept in industrial capitalism (and state socialism) is transforming not only production but perception. Whole industries collapse into obsolescence; entire classes face ruthless dislocation. At the same time, the gap between the races domestically, between the north and the south internationally, widens to obscene proportions. Everywhere, women are being proletarianized, impoverished, becoming migrants, refugees, and inevitably "cheap labor." Meanwhile the great and lesser powers race to omnicide, making a mockery of all our diverse aspirations, struggles, and movements. Truly, "all that is solid melts into air"—that is, if it is not vaporized instantaneously.

I still believe that if there is a vantage point from which to comprehend and change the world, our world today, it will be socialist and feminist. Socialist—or perhaps here I should say Marxist—because a Marxist way of thinking, at its best, helps us understand the cutting edge of change, the blind driving force of capital, the dislocations, innovations, and global reshufflings. Feminist because feminism offers our best insight into that which is most ancient and intractable about our common situation; the gulf that divides the species by gender and, tragically, divides us all from nature and that which is most human in our nature. This is our intellectual heritage, and I do not think we have yet seen its full power—or our own.

Notes

1. Here I am passing over the story of the destruction of organized socialist-feminism by various Marxist-Leninist and Maoist groups in 1975–1977. In that period, sectarian groups

joined and harassed or merely attacked from outside more than twenty socialist-feminist women's unions around the country, dragging almost all of them down to their deaths in arcane squabbles over the "correct line." I have never seen an adequate—or even inadequate—account of this nasty phase of left feminist history that addresses why the sects decided to go after socialist-feminist organizations at this time, and why socialist-feminist organizations, including the successful and level-headed Chicago Women's Liberation Union, crumbled in the face of so much bullshit. I would appreciate hearing from anyone with insights or relevant anecdotes to offer.

2. I don't mean to pick on Zillah Eisenstein; many other writers could be quoted, especially if I were doing a thorough review of socialist-feminist theory and its nuances (which I clearly am not). Eisenstein is singled out here because her introduction to and chapter in *Capitalist Patriarchy and the Case for Socialist Feminism* seem to me to provide an excellent state-of-the-art summary of mid-seventies socialist-feminist theory. The passage cited is on page 29.

3. Joann Vanek, "Time Spent in Housework," *Scientific American*, November 1974, p. 116.

4. One poignant indication of this shift in male values and expectations: when I was in my early twenties (in the early sixties), it seemed to require a certain daring and resourcefulness to dodge the traditional female fate of becoming a full-time housewife and mother. Today, I hear over and over from young women that they would like to have a family or at least a child, but do not expect ever to be in a stable enough relationship to carry this off.

5. Insofar as the capitalists paid their workers enough to support a wife, thus buying off the workers with patriarchal privilege and ensuring labor peace—a crude summary of Heidi Hartmann's much more complex and interesting argument. The family metaphor was developed extensively by Batya Weinbaum in *The Curious Courtship of Women's Liberation and Socialism* (South End Press, 1980).

What's Critical About Critical Theory? The Case of Habermas and Gender

Nancy Fraser

To my mind, no one has yet improved on Marx's 1843 definition of critical theory as "the self-clarification of the struggles and wishes of the age."[1] What is so appealing about this definition is its straightforwardly political character. It makes no claim to any special epistemological status but, rather, supposes that with respect to justification there is no philosophically interesting difference between a critical theory of society and an uncritical one. However, there is, according to this definition, an important political difference. A critical social theory frames its research program and its conceptual framework with an eye to the aims and activities of those oppositional social movements with which it has a partisan, though not uncritical, identification. The questions it asks and the models it designs are informed by that identification and interest. Thus, for example, if struggles contesting the subordination of women figured among the most significant of a given age, then a critical social theory for that time would aim, among other things, to shed light on the character and bases of such subordination. It would employ categories and explanatory models that revealed rather than occluded relations of male dominance and female subordination. And it would demystify as ideological any rival approaches that obfuscated or rationalized those relations. In this situation, then, one of the standards for assessing a critical theory, once it had been subjected to all the usual tests of empirical adequacy, would be: How well does it theorize the situation and prospects of the feminist movement? To what extent does it serve the self-clarification of the struggles and wishes of contemporary women?

In what follows, I am going to presuppose the conception of critical theory that I have just outlined. In addition, I am going to take as the actual situation of our age the scenario I just sketched as hypothetical. On the basis of these presuppositions, I want to examine the critical social theory of Jürgen Habermas as elaborated in *The Theory of Communicative Action* and related recent writings.[2] I intend to read this work from the standpoint of several specific questions: In what proportions and in what respects does Habermas's critical theory clarify and/or mystify the bases of male dominance and female subordination in modern societies? In what proportions and in what respects does it challenge and/or replicate prevalent ideological rationalizations of such dominance and subordination? To what extent does it, or can it be made to, serve the self-clarification of the struggles and wishes of the contemporary women's movement? In short, with respect to gender, what is critical and what is not in Habermas's social theory?

This would be a fairly straightforward enterprise were it not for one thing: apart from a brief discussion of feminism as a "new social movement" (a discussion I shall consider anon), Habermas says virtually nothing about gender in *The Theory of Communicative Action*. Now, according to my view of critical theory, this is a serious deficiency, but it need not stand in the way of the sort of inquiry I am proposing. It simply necessitates that one read the work in question from the standpoint of an absence, that one extrapolate from things Habermas does say to things he does not, that one reconstruct how various matters of concern to feminists would appear from his perspective had those matters been thematized.

Thus, in section 1 of this essay, I examine some elements of Habermas's social-theoretical framework in order to see how it tends to cast childrearing and the male-headed modern restricted nuclear family. In section 2, I look at his account of the relations between the public and private spheres of life in classical capitalist societies and try to reconstruct the unthematized gender subtext. And finally, in section 3, I consider Habermas's account of the dynamics, crisis tendencies, and conflict potentials specific to contemporary Western welfare state capitalism, so as to see in what light it casts contemporary feminist struggles.[3]

1. The Social-Theoretical Framework: A Feminist Interrogation

Let me begin by considering two distinctions central to Habermas's social-theoretical categorial framework. The first of these is the distinction between the symbolic reproduction and the material reproduction of societies. On the one hand, claims Habermas, societies must reproduce themselves materially; they must successfully regulate the metabolic exchange of groups of biological individuals with a nonhuman, physical environment and with other social systems. On the other hand, societies must reproduce themselves symbolically; they must maintain and transmit to new members the linguistically elaborated norms and patterns of interpretation that are constitutive of social identities. Habermas claims that material reproduction comprises what he calls "social labor." Symbolic reproduction, on the other hand, comprises the socialization of the young, the cementing of group solidarity, and the transmission and extension of cultural traditions.[4]

This distinction between symbolic and material reproduction is in the first instance a functional one: it distinguishes two different functions that must be fulfilled more or less successfully if a society is to survive. At the same time, however, the distinction is used by Habermas to classify actual social practices and activities. These are distinguished according to which one of the two functions they are held to serve exclusively or primarily. Thus, according to Habermas, in capitalist societies, the activities and practices that make up the sphere of paid work count as material reproduction activities since, in his view, they are "social labor" and serve the function of material reproduction. On the other hand, the childrearing activities and practices that in our society are performed without pay by women in the domestic sphere—let us call them "women's unpaid childrearing work"—count as symbolic reproduction activities since, in Habermas's view, they serve socialization and the function of symbolic reproduction.[5]

It is worth noting, I think, that Habermas's distinction between symbolic and material reproduction is susceptible to two different interpretations. The first of these takes the two functions as two objectively distinct "natural kinds" to which both the actual social practices and the actual organization of activities in any given society may correspond more or less faithfully. Thus, childrearing practices would in themselves be symbolic reproduction practices, whereas the practices that produce food and objects would in themselves be material reproduction practices. And modern capitalist social organization—unlike, say, that of archaic societies—would be a faithful mirror of the distinction between the two natural kinds, since it separates these practices institutionally. This "natural kinds" interpretation is at odds with another possible interpretation, which I shall call the "pragmatic-contextual" interpretation. It would not take childrearing practices to be in themselves symbolic reproduction practices but would allow for the possibility that, under certain circumstances and given certain purposes, it could be useful to consider them from the standpoint of symbolic reproduction—for example, if one wished to contest the view, dominant in a sexist political culture, according to which this traditionally female occupation is merely instinctual, natural, and ahistorical.

Now I want to argue that the natural kinds interpretation is conceptually inadequate and potentially ideological. I claim that it is not the case that childrearing practices serve symbolic as opposed to material reproduction. Granted, they comprise language teaching and initiation into social mores—but also feeding, bathing, and protection from physical harm. Granted, they regulate children's interactions with other people—but also their interactions with physical nature (in the form, for example, of milk, germs, dirt, excrement, weather, and animals). In short, not just the construction of children's social identities but also their biological survival is at stake—and, therefore, so is the biological survival of the societies they belong to. Thus, childrearing is not per se symbolic reproduction activity; it is equally and at the same time material reproduction activity. It is what we might call a "dual aspect" activity.[6]

However, the same is true of the activities institutionalized in modern capitalist paid work. Granted, the production of food and objects contributes to the biological survival of members of society. But it also, and at the same time, reproduces social identities. Not just nourishment and shelter *simpliciter* are produced but culturally elaborated forms of nourishment and shelter that have symbolically mediated social meanings. Moreover, such production occurs via culturally elaborated social relations and symbolically mediated, norm-governed social practices. The contents of these practices as well as the results serve to form, maintain, and modify the social identities of persons directly involved and indirectly affected. One need only think of an activity like computer programming for a wage in the U.S. pharmaceutical industry to appreciate the thoroughly symbolic character of "social labor." Thus, such labor, like unpaid childrearing work, is a "dual aspect" activity.[7]

Thus, any distinction between women's unpaid childrearing work and other forms of work that is drawn in terms of reproduction functions cannot be a distinction of natural kinds. If any distinction is to be drawn at all, it must rather be a pragmatic-contextual distinction for the sake of focalizing what is in each case actually only one aspect of a dual aspect phenomenon. And this, in turn, must find its warrant in relation to specific purposes of analysis and description, purposes that are themselves susceptible to analysis and evaluation and that need, therefore, to be justified through argument.

But if this is so, then the natural kinds classification of childrearing as symbolic reproduction and of other work as material reproduction is potentially ideological. It could be used, for example, to legitimize the institutional separation of childrearing from paid work, a separation that many feminists, myself included, consider a linchpin of modern forms of women's subordination. It could be used, in combination with other assumptions, to legitimate the confinement of women to a "separate sphere." Whether Habermas himself uses it to those ends will be considered shortly.

The second component of Habermas's categorial framework that I want to examine is his distinction between "socially integrated action contexts" and "system integrated action contexts." Socially integrated action contexts are those in which different agents coordinate their actions with one another by reference to some form of explicit or implicit intersubjective consensus about norms, values, and ends, consensus predicated on linguistic speech and interpretation. System-integrated action contexts, on the other hand, are those in which the actions of different agents are coordinated with one another by the functional interlacing of unintended consequences, while each individual action is determined by self-interested, utility-maximizing calculations typically entertained in the idioms—or, as Habermas says, in the "media"—of money and power.[8] Habermas considers the capitalist economic system to be the paradigm case of a system-integrated action context. By contrast, he takes the modern restricted nuclear family to be a case of a socially integrated action context.[9]

Now this distinction is a rather complex one. As I understand it, it contains six analytically distinct conceptual elements: functionality, intentionality, linguisticality, consensuality, normativity, and strategicality. However, I am going to set aside the elements of functionality, intentionality, and linguisticality. Following some arguments developed by Thomas McCarthy in another context, I assume that in both the capitalist workplace and the modern restricted nuclear family the consequences of actions may be functionally interlaced in ways unintended by agents; that, at the same time, in both contexts agents coordinate their actions with one another consciously and intentionally; and that in both contexts agents coordinate their actions with one another in and through language.[10] I assume, therefore, that Habermas's distinction effectively turns on the elements of consensuality, normativity, and strategicality.

Once again, I think it useful to distinguish two possible interpretations of Habermas's position. The first takes the contrast between the two kinds of action contexts as registering an absolute difference. Thus, system-integrated contexts would involve absolutely no consensuality or reference to moral norms and values, whereas socially integrated contexts would involve absolutely no strategic calculations in the media of money and power. This "absolute differences" interpretation is at odds with a second possibility, which takes the contrast rather as registering a difference in degree. According to this second interpretation, system-integrated contexts would involve some consensuality and reference to moral norms and values but less than do socially integrated contexts. In the same way, socially integrated contexts would involve some strategic calculations in the media of money and power but less than do system-integrated contexts.

Now I contend that the absolute differences interpretation is too extreme to be useful for social theory and that, in addition, it is potentially ideological. In few if any human action contexts are actions coordinated absolutely nonconsensually and absolutely nonnormatively. However morally dubious the consensus and however problematic the content and status of the norms, virtually every human action context involves some form of both of them. In the capitalist marketplace, for example, strategic, utility-maximizing exchanges occur against a horizon of intersubjectively shared meanings and norms; agents normally subscribe at least tacitly to some commonly held notions of reciprocity and to some shared conceptions about the social meanings of objects, including what sorts of things are considered exchangeable. Similarly, in the capitalist workplace, managers and subordinates, as well as co-workers, normally coordinate their actions to some extent consensually and with some explicit or implicit reference to normative assumptions, though the consensus be arrived at unfairly and the norms be incapable of withstanding critical scrutiny.[11] Thus, the capitalist economic system has a moral-cultural dimension.

Likewise, few if any human action contexts are wholly devoid of strategic calculation. Gift rituals in noncapitalist societies, for example, previously taken as veritable crucibles of solidarity, are now widely understood to have a significant strategic, calculative dimension, one enacted in the medium of power if not in that of money.[12] And, as I shall argue in more detail later, the modern restricted nuclear family is not devoid of individual, self-interested, strategic calculations in either medium. These action contexts, then, though not officially counted as economic, have a strategic, economic dimension.

Thus, the absolute differences interpretation is not of much use in social theory. It fails to distinguish, for example, the capitalist economy—let us call it "the official economy"[13]—from the modern restricted nuclear family, for both of these institutions are mélanges of consensuality, normativity, and strategicality. If they are to be distinguished with respect to mode of action-integration, the distinction must be drawn as a difference of degree. It must turn on the place, proportions, and interactions of the three elements within each.

But if this is so, then the absolute differences classification of the official economy as a system-integrated action context and of the modern family as a socially integrated action context is potentially ideological. It could be used, for example, to exaggerate the differences and occlude the similarities between the two institutions. It could be used to construct an ideological opposition that posits the family as the "negative," the complementary other, of the (official) economic sphere, a "haven in a heartless world."

Now which of these possible interpretations of the two distinctions are the operative ones in Habermas's social theory? He asserts that he understands the reproduction distinction according to the pragmatic-contextual interpretation and not the natural kinds one.[14] Likewise, he asserts that he takes the action-context distinction to mark a difference in degree, not an absolute difference.[15] However, I propose to bracket these assertions and to examine what Habermas actually does with these distinctions.

Habermas maps the distinction between action contexts onto the distinction between reproduction functions in order to arrive at a definition of societal modernization and at a picture of the institutional structure of modern societies. He holds that modern societies, unlike premodern societies, split off some material reproduction functions from symbolic ones and hand over the former to two specialized institutions—the (official) economy and the state—which are system-integrated. At the same time, modern societies situate these institutions in the larger social environment by developing two other institutions, which specialize in symbolic reproduction and are socially integrated. These are the modern restricted nuclear family, or "private sphere," and the space of political participation, debate, and opinion formation, or "public sphere"; together they constitute what Habermas calls the two "institutional orders of the modern lifeworld." Thus, modern societies "uncouple," or separate, what Habermas takes to be two distinct but previously undifferentiated aspects of society: "system" and "lifeworld." Hence, in his view, the institutional structure of modern societies is dualistic. On the one side stand the institutional orders of the modern lifeworld, the socially integrated domains specializing in symbolic reproduction, that is, in socialization, solidarity formation, and cultural transmission. On the other side stand the systems, the system-integrated domains specializing in material reproduction. On the one side stand the nuclear family and the public sphere; on the other side stand the (official) capitalist economy and the modern administrative state.[16]

What are the critical insights and blind spots of this model? Let us attend first to the question of its empirical adequacy. And let us focus, for the time being, on the contrast between "the private sphere of the lifeworld" and the (official) economic system. Consider that this aspect of Habermas's categorial divide between system and lifeworld institutions faithfully mirrors the institutional separation in male-dominated, capitalist societies of family and official economy, household and paid workplace. It thus has some prima facie purchase on empirical social reality. But consider, too, that the characterization of the family as a socially integrated, symbolic reproduction domain and the characterization of the paid workplace, on the other hand, as a system-integrated material reproduction domain tends to exaggerate the differences and occlude the similarities between them. For example, it directs attention away from the fact that the household, like the paid workplace, is a site of labor, albeit of unrremunerated and often unrecognized labor. Likewise, it does not make visible the fact that in the paid workplace, as in the household, women are assigned to, indeed ghettoized in, distinctively feminine, service-oriented, and often sexualized occupations. Finally, it fails to focalize the fact that in both spheres women are subordinated to men.

Moreover, this characterization presents the male-headed nuclear family, qua socially integrated institutional order of the modern lifeworld, as having only an extrinsic and incidental relation to money and power. These "media" are taken as definitive of interactions in the official economy and the state administration but as only incidental to intrafamilial ones. But this assumption is counterfactual. Feminists have shown through empirical analyses of contemporary familial decision making, handling of finances, and wife battering that families are thoroughly permeated with, in Habermas's terms, the media of money and power. They are sites of egocentric, strategic, and instrumental calculation as well as sites of usually exploitative exchanges of services, labor, cash, and sex—and, frequently, sites of coercion and violence.[17] But Habermas's way of contrasting the modern family with the official capitalist economy tends to occlude all this. It overstates the differences between these institutions and blocks the possibility of analyzing families as economic systems, that is, as sites of labor, exchange, calculation, distribution, and exploitation.

Or, to the degree that Habermas would acknowledge that they can be seen in that way too, his framework would suggest that this is due to the intrusion or invasion of alien forces, to the "colonization" of the family by the (official) economy and the state. This, too, however, is a dubious proposition (I shall discuss it in detail in section 3 below).

Thus, Habermas's model has some empirical deficiencies: it is not easily able to focalize some dimensions of male dominance in modern societies. Yet is does offer a conceptual resource suitable for understanding *other* aspects of modern male dominance. Consider that Habermas subdivides the category of socially integrated action contexts into two subcategories. On the one hand, there are "normatively secured" forms of socially integrated action. These are actions coordinated on the basis of a conventional, prereflective, taken-for-granted consensus about values and ends, consensus rooted in the precritical internalization of socialization and cultural tradition. On the other hand, there are "communicatively achieved" forms of socially integrated action. These involve actions coordinated on the basis of explicit, reflectively achieved consensus, consensus reached by unconstrained discussion under conditions of freedom, equality, and fairness.[18] This distinction, which is a subdistinction within the category of socially integrated action, provides Habermas with some critical resources for analyzing the modern restricted male-headed nuclear family. Such families can be understood as normatively secured rather than communicatively achieved action contexts, that is, as contexts where actions are (sometimes) mediated by consensus and shared values but where such consensus is suspect because it is prereflective or because it is achieved through dialogue vitiated by unfairness, coercion, or inequality.

To what extent does the distinction between normatively secured and communicatively achieved action contexts succeed in overcoming the problems discussed earlier? Only partially, I think. On the one hand, this distinction is a morally significant and empirically useful one. The notion of a normatively secured action context fits nicely with recent research on patterns of communication between husbands and wives. This research shows that men tend to control conversations, determining what topics are pursued, whereas women do more "interaction work" like asking questions and providing verbal support.[19] Research also reveals differences in men's and women's uses of the bodily and gestural dimensions of speech, differences that confirm men's dominance and women's subordination.[20] Thus, Habermas's distinction enables us to capture something important about intrafamilial dynamics. What is insufficiently stressed, however, is that actions coordinated by normatively secured consensus in the male-headed nuclear family are actions regulated by power. It seems to me a grave mistake to restrict the use of the term 'power' to bureaucratic contexts. Habermas would do better to distinguish different kinds of power, for example, domestic-patriarchal power, on the one hand, and bureaucratic-patriarchal power, on the other—not to mention various other kinds and combinations in between.

But even that distinction does not by itself suffice to make Habermas's framework fully adequate to all the empirical forms of male dominance in modern societies, for normative-domestic-patriarchal power is only one of the elements that enforce women's subordination in the domestic sphere. To capture the others would require a social-theoretical framework capable of analyzing families also as economic systems involving the appropriation of women's unpaid labor and interlocking in complex ways with other economic systems involving paid work. Because Habermas's framework draws its major categorical divide between system and lifeworld institutions, and hence between (among other things) the official economy and the family, it is not very well suited to that task.

Let me turn now from the question of the empirical adequacy of Habermas's model to the question of its normative political implications. What sorts of social arrangements and transformations does his conception of modernization tend to legitimate? And what sorts does it tend to rule out? Here, it will be necessary to reconstruct some implications of the model that are not explicitly thematized by Habermas.

Consider that the conception of modernization as the uncoupling of system and lifeworld institutions tends to legitimate the modern institutional separation of family and official economy, childrearing and paid work. For Habermas argues that with respect to system integration, symbolic reproduction and material reproduction are asymmetrical. Symbolic reproduction activities, he claims, are unlike material reproduction activities in that they cannot be turned over to specialized, system-integrated institutions set apart from the lifeworld; their inherently symbolic character requires that they be socially integrated.[21] It follows that women's unpaid childrearing work could not be incorporated into the (official) economic system without "pathological" results. Moreover, Habermas also holds that it is a mark of societal rationalization that system-integrated institutions be differentiated to handle material reproduction functions. The separation of a specialized (official) economic system enhances a society's capacity to deal with its natural and social environment. "System complexity," then, constitutes a "developmental advance."[22] It follows that the (official) economic system of paid work could not be dedifferentiated with respect to, say, childrearing, without societal "regression." But if childrearing could not be nonpathologically incorporated into the (official) economic system and if the (official) economic system could not be nonregressively dedifferentiated, then the continued separation of childrearing from paid work would be unavoidable.

This amounts to a defense of one aspect of what feminists call "the separation of public and private," namely, the separation of the official economic sphere from the domestic sphere and the enclaving of childrearing from the rest of social labor. It amounts, that is, to a defense of an institutional arrangement that is widely held to be one, if not the, linchpin of modern women's subordination. And it should be noted that the fact that Habermas is a socialist does not alter the matter, because the (undeniably desirable) elimination of private ownership, profit-orientation, and hierarchical command in paid work would not of itself affect the official economic/domestic separation.

Now I want to challenge several premises of the reasoning I have just reconstructed. First, this reasoning assumes the natural kinds interpretation of the symbolic versus material reproduction distinction. But since, as I have argued, childrearing is a dual aspect activity and since it is not categorically different in this respect from other work, there is no warrant for the claim of an asymmetry vis-à-vis system integration. That is, there is no warrant for assuming that the system-integrated organization of childrearing would be any more (or less) pathological than that of other work. Second, this reasoning assumes the absolute differences interpretation of the social versus system integration distinction. But since, as I have argued, the modern male-headed nuclear family is a mélange of (normatively secured) consensuality, normativity, and strategicality and since it is in this respect not categorially different from the paid workplace, then privatized childrearing is already, to a not insignificant extent, permeated by the media of money and power. Moreover, there is no empirical evidence that children raised in commercial day care centers (even profit-based or corporate ones) turn out any more pathological than those raised, say, in suburban homes by full-time mothers. Third, the reasoning just sketched elevates system complexity to the status of an overriding consideration with effective veto power over proposed social transformations aimed at overcoming women's subordination. But this is at odds with Habermas's professions that system complexity is only one measure of "progress" among others.[23] More importantly, it is at odds with any reasonable standard of justice.

What, then, should we conclude about the normative political implications of Habermas's model? If the conception of modernization as the uncoupling of system and lifeworld institutions does indeed have the implications I have just drawn from it, then it is in important respects androcentric and ideological.

2. Public and Private in Classical Capitalism: Thematizing the Gender Subtext

The foregoing difficulties notwithstanding, Habermas offers an account of the interinstitutional relations among various spheres of public and private life in classical capitalism that has some genuine critical potential. But in order to realize this potential fully, we need to reconstruct the unthematized gender subtext of his material.

Let me return to his conception of the way in which the (official) economic system and the state system are situated with respect to the lifeworld. Habermas holds that with modernization the (official) economic and state systems are not simply disengaged or detached from the lifeworld; they must also be related to and embedded in it. Concomitant with the beginnings of classical capitalism, then, is the development *within* the lifeworld of "institutional orders" that situate the systems in a context of everyday meanings and norms. The lifeworld, as we saw, gets differentiated into two spheres that provide appropriate complementary environments for the two systems. The "private sphere"—or modern restricted nuclear family—is linked to the (official) economic system. The "public sphere"—or space of political participation, debate, and opinion formation—is linked to the state administrative system. The family is linked to the (official) economy by means of a series of exchanges conducted in the medium of money: it supplies the (official) economy with appropriately socialized labor power in exchange for wages, and it provides appropriate, monetarily measured demand for commodified goods and services. Exchanges between family and (official) economy, then, are channeled through the "roles" of worker and consumer. Parallel exchange processes link the public sphere and the state system. These, however, are conducted chiefly in the medium of power: loyalty, obedience, and tax revenues are exchanged for "organizational results" and "political decisions." Exchanges between public sphere and state, then, are channeled through the "role" of citizen and, in late welfare state capitalism, that of client.[24]

This account of interinstitutional relations in classical capitalism offers a number of important advantages. First, it treats the modern restricted nuclear family as a historically emergent institution with its own positive, determinate features. It specifies that this type of family emerges concomitantly with, and in relation to, the emerging capitalist economy, administrative state, and (eventually) the political public sphere. Moreover, it charts some of the dynamics of exchange among these institutions and indicates some ways in which they are fitted to the needs of one another so as to accommodate those exchanges among them.

Finally, Habermas's account offers an important corrective to the standard dualistic approaches to the separation of public and private in capitalist societies. He conceptualizes the problem as a relation among four terms: family, (official) economy, state, and public sphere. His view suggests that in classical capitalism there are actually two distinct but interrelated public/private separations. One public/private separation operates at the level of "systems," namely, the separation of the state, or public system, from the (official) capitalist economy, or private system. The other public/private separation operates at the level of the "lifeworld," namely, the separation of the family, or private lifeworld sphere, from the space of political opinion formation and participation, or public lifeworld sphere. Moreover, each of these public/private separations is coordinated with the other. One axis of exchange runs between private system and private lifeworld sphere, that is, between (official) capitalist economy and modern restricted nuclear family. Another axis of exchange runs between public system and public lifeworld sphere, or between state administration and the organs of public opinion and will formation. In both cases, the exchanges can occur because of the institutionalization of specific roles that connect the domains in question. Hence, the roles of worker and consumer link the (official) private economy and the private family, while the roles of citizen and (later) client link the public state and the public opinion institutions.

Thus, Habermas provides an extremely sophisticated account of the relations between public and private institutions in classical capitalist societies. At the same time, however, his account evinces some weaknesses. Many of these stem from his failure to thematize the gender subtext of the relations and arrangements he describes.[25] Consider, first, the relations between (official) private economy and private family as mediated by the roles of worker and consumer. These roles, I submit, are gendered roles. And the links they forge between family and (official) economy are effected as much in the medium of gender identity as in the medium of money.

Take the role of the worker.[26] In male-dominated, classical capitalist societies, this role is a masculine role—and not just in the relatively superficial statistical sense. There is, rather, a very deep sense in which masculine identity in these societies is bound up with the breadwinner role. Masculinity is in large part a matter of leaving home each day for a place of paid work and returning with a wage that provides for one's dependents. It is this internal relation between being a man and being a provider that explains why in capitalist societies unemployment is often not just economically but also psychologically devastating for men. It also sheds light on the centrality of the struggle for a "family wage" in the history of the workers' and trade-union movements of the nineteenth and twentieth centuries. This was a struggle for a wage conceived not as a payment to a genderless individual for the use of labor power but rather as a payment to a man for the support of his economically dependent wife and children—a conception, of course, that legitimized the practice of paying women less for equal or comparable work.

The masculine subtext of the worker role is confirmed by the vexed and strained character of women's relation to paid work in male-dominated, classical capitalism. As Carole Pateman puts it, it is not that women are absent from the paid workplace;

it's rather that they are present differently[27]—for example, as feminized and some-times sexualized "service" workers (secretaries, domestic workers, salespersons, prostitutes, and, more recently, flight attendants); as members of the "helping pro-fessions," utilizing mothering skills (nurses, social workers, childcare workers, pri-mary school teachers); as targets of sexual harassment; as low-waged, low-skilled, low-status workers in sex-segregated occupations; as part-time workers; as workers who work a double shift (both unpaid domestic labor and paid labor); as "working wives" and "working mothers," that is, as primarily wives and mothers, who happen, secondarily, also to "go out to work" as "supplemental earners." These differences in the quality of women's presence in the paid workplace testify to the conceptual disso-nance between femininity and the worker role in classical capitalism. And this in turn confirms the masculine subtext of that role. It confirms that the role of the worker, which links the private (official) economy and the private family in male-dominated, capitalist societies, is a masculine role, and that, *pace* Habermas, the link it forges is elaborated as much in the medium of masculine gender identity as in the medium of seemingly gender-neutral money.

Conversely, the other role linking (official) economy and family in Habermas's scheme has a feminine subtext. The consumer, after all, is the worker's companion and helpmeet in classical capitalism. The sexual division of domestic labor assigns to women the work—and it is indeed work, though unpaid and usually unrecognized work—of purchasing and preparing goods and services for domestic consumption. You can confirm this even today by visiting any supermarket or department store or by looking at the history of consumer goods advertising. Such advertising has nearly always interpellated its subject, the consumer, as feminine.[28] In fact, it has elaborated an entire phantasmatics of desire premised on the femininity of the subject of con-sumption. It is only relatively recently, and with some difficulty, that advertisers have devised ways of interpellating a masculine subject of consumption. The trick was to find means of positioning a male consumer that did not feminize, emasculate, or sissify him. In *The Hearts of Men,* Barbara Ehrenreich—quite shrewdly, I think—credits *Playboy* magazine with pioneering such means.[29] But the difficulty and late-ness of the project confirm the gendered character of the consumer role in classical capitalism. Men occupy it with conceptual strain and cognitive dissonance, much as women occupy the role of worker. Thus, the role of consumer that links official econ-omy and family is manifestly a feminine role. *Pace* Habermas, it forges the link in the medium of feminine gender identity as much as in the apparently gender-neutral medium of money.

Moreover, Habermas's account of the roles linking family and (official) economy contains a significant omission: there is no mention in his schema of any childrearer role, although the material clearly requires one. For who other than the childrearer is performing the unpaid work of overseeing the production of the "appropriately so-cialized labor power" that the family exchanges for wages? Of course, the childrearer role in classical capitalism (as elsewhere) is patently a feminine role. Its omission here is a mark of androcentrism, and it has some significant consequences. A consid-eration of the childrearer role in this context might well have pointed to the central relevance of gender to the institutional structure of classical capitalism. And this, in turn, could have led to the disclosure of the gender subtext of the other roles and of the importance of gender identity as an "exchange medium."

What, then, of the other set of roles and linkages identified by Habermas? What of the citizen role, which he claims connects the public system of the administrative state with the public lifeworld sphere of political opinion and will formation? This role, too, is a gendered role in classical capitalism, indeed, a masculine role[30]—and not simply in the sense that women did not win the vote in the United States and Britain (for example) until the twentieth century. Rather, the lateness and difficulty of that victory are symptomatic of deeper strains. As Habermas understands it, the citizen is centrally a participant in political debate and public opinion formation. This means that citizenship, in his view, depends crucially on the capacities for consent and speech, the ability to participate on a par with others in dialogue. But these are capacities that are connected with masculinity in male-dominated, classical capitalism; they are capacities that are in myriad ways denied to women and deemed at odds with femininity. I have already cited studies about the effects of male dominance and female subordination on the dynamics of dialogue. Now consider that even today in most jurisdictions there is no such thing as marital rape. That is, a wife is legally subject to her husband; she is not an individual who can give or withhold consent to his demands for sexual access. Consider also that even outside of marriage the legal test of rape often boils down to whether a "reasonable man" would have assumed that the woman had consented. Consider what that means when both popular and legal opinion widely holds that when a woman says no she means yes. It means, says Carole Pateman, that "women find their speech ... persistently and systematically invalidated in the crucial matter of consent, a matter that is fundamental to democracy. [But] if women's words about consent are consistently reinterpreted, how can they participate in the debate among citizens?"[31]

Thus, there is conceptual dissonance between femininity and the dialogical capacities central to Habermas's conception of citizenship. And another aspect of citizenship not discussed by him is even more obviously bound up with masculinity. This is the soldiering aspect of citizenship, the conception of the citizen as the defender of the polity and protector of those—women, children, the elderly—who allegedly cannot protect themselves. As Judith Stiehm has argued, this division between male protectors and female protected introduces further dissonance into women's relation to citizenship.[32] It confirms the gender subtext of the citizen role. The view of women as in need of men's protection "underlies access not just to the means of destruction, but also [to] the means of production—witness all the 'protective' legislation that has surrounded women's access to the workplace—and [to] the means of reproduction [—witness] women's status as wives and sexual partners."[33]

The citizen role in male-dominated, classical capitalism is therefore a manifestly masculine role. It links the state and the public sphere, as Habermas claims, but it also links these to the official economy and the family. And in every case the links are forged in the medium of masculine gender identity rather than, as Habermas has it, in the medium of a gender-neutral power. Or, if the medium of exchange here is power, then the power in question is masculine power: it is power as the expression of masculinity.

Thus, there are some major lacunae in Habermas's otherwise powerful and sophisticated model of the relations between public and private institutions in classical capitalism. Because his model is blind to the significance and operation of gender, it is bound to miss important features of the arrangements he wants to understand. By omitting any mention of the childrearer role and by failing to thematize the gender subtext underlying the roles of worker and consumer, Habermas fails to understand precisely how the capitalist workplace is linked to the modern restricted male-headed nuclear family. Similarly, by failing to thematize the masculine subtext of the citizen role, he misses the full meaning of the way the state is linked to the public sphere of political speech. Moreover, Habermas misses important cross-connections among the four elements of his two public/private schemata. He misses, for example, the way the masculine citizen-soldier-protector role links the state and the public sphere not only to each other but also to the family and to the paid workplace—that is, the way the assumptions of man's capacity to protect and woman's need of man's protection run through all of them. He misses, too, the way the masculine citizen-speaker role links the state and the public sphere not only to each other but also to the family and the official economy—that is, the way the assumptions of man's ca-pacity to speak and consent and woman's comparative incapacity run through all of them. He misses, also, the way the masculine worker-breadwinner role links the fam-ily and the official economy not only to each other but also to the state and the polit-ical public sphere—that is, the way the assumptions of man's provider status and of woman's dependent status run through all of them, so that even the coin in which classical capitalist wages and taxes are paid is not gender-neutral. And he misses, fi-nally, the way the feminine childrearer role links all four institutions to one another by overseeing the construction of the masculine and feminine gendered subjects needed to fill *every* role in classical capitalism.

Once the gender-blindness of Habermas's model is overcome, however, all these connections come into view. It then becomes clear that feminine and masculine gen-der identity run like pink and blue threads through the areas of paid work, state ad-ministration, and citizenship as well as through the domain of familial and sexual re-lations. This is to say that gender identity is lived out in all arenas of life. It is one (if not the) "medium of exchange" among all of them, a basic element of the social glue that binds them to one another.

Moreover, a gender-sensitive reading of these connections discloses some impor-tant theoretical and conceptual implications. It reveals that male dominance is in-trinsic rather than accidental to classical capitalism, for the institutional structure of this social formation is actualized by means of gendered roles. It follows that the forms of male dominance at issue here are not properly understood as lingering forms of premodern status inequality. They are, rather, intrinsically modern in Habermas's sense, since they are premised on the separation of waged labor and the state from childrearing and the household. It also follows that a critical social theory of capitalist societies needs gender-sensitive categories. The preceding analysis shows that, contrary to the usual androcentric understanding, the relevant concepts of worker, consumer, and wage are not, in fact, strictly economic concepts. Rather, they have an implicit gender subtext and thus are "gender-economic" concepts. Likewise, the relevant concept of citizenship is not strictly a political concept; it has an implicit gender subtext and so, rather, is a "gender-political" concept. Thus, this analysis re-veals the inadequacy of those critical theories that treat gender as incidental to poli-tics and political economy. It highlights the need for a critical theory with a categori-cal framework in which gender, politics, and political economy are internally integrated.[34]

In addition, a gender-sensitive reading of these arrangements reveals the thor-oughly multidirectional character of social motion and causal influence in classical capitalism. It reveals, that is, the inadequacy of the orthodox Marxist assumption that all or most significant causal influence runs from the (official) economy to the family and not vice versa. It shows that gender identity structures paid work, state administration, and political participation. Thus, it vindicates Habermas's claim that in classical capitalism the (official) economy is not all-powerful but is, rather, in some significant measure inscribed within and subject to the norms and meanings of everyday life. Of course, Habermas assumed that in making this claim he was saying something more or less positive. The norms and meanings he had in mind were not the ones I have been discussing. Still, the point is a valid one. It remains to be seen, though, whether it holds also for late, welfare state capitalism, as I believe, or whether it ceases to hold, as Habermas claims.

Finally, this reconstruction of the gender subtext of Habermas's model has normative political implications. It suggests that an emancipatory transformation of male-dominated, capitalist societies, early and late, requires a transformation of these gendered roles and of the institutions they mediate. As long as the worker and childrearer roles are constituted as fundamentally incompatible with one another, it will not be possible to universalize either of them to include both genders. Thus, some form of dedifferentiation of unpaid childrearing and other work is required. Similarly, as long as the citizen role is defined to encompass death-dealing soldiering but not life-fostering childrearing, as long as it is tied to male-dominated modes of dialogue, then it, too, will remain incapable of including women fully. Thus, changes in the very concepts of citizenship, childrearing and paid work are necessary, as are changes in the relationships among the domestic, official economic, state, and political public spheres.

3. The Dynamics of Welfare State Capitalism: A Feminist Critique

Let me turn, then, to Habermas's account of late welfare state capitalism. I must acknowledge at the outset that its critical potential, unlike the critical potential of his account of classical capitalism, cannot be released simply by reconstructing the unthematized gender subtext. Here, the problematic features of his social-theoretical framework tend to inflect the analysis as a whole and diminish its capacity to illuminate the struggles and wishes of contemporary women. In order to show how this is the case, I shall present Habermas's view in the form of six theses.

First, welfare state capitalism emerges as a result of, and in response to, instabilities or crisis tendencies inherent in classical capitalism. It realigns the relations between the (official) economy and the state, that is, between the private and public systems. These become more deeply intertwined with one another as the state actively assumes the task of "crisis management." It tries to avert or manage economic crises by Keynesian "market-replacing" strategies, which create a "public sector." And it tries to avert or manage social and political crises by "market-compensating" measures, including welfare concessions to trade unions and social movements. Thus, welfare state capitalism partially overcomes the separation of public and private at the level of systems.[35]

Second, the realignment of (official) economy/state relations is accompanied by a change in the relations of those systems to the private and public spheres of the lifeworld. With respect to the private sphere, there is a major increase in the importance of the consumer role as dissatisfactions related to paid work are compensated by enhanced commodity consumption. With respect to the public sphere, there is a major decline in the importance of the citizen role as journalism becomes mass media, political parties are bureaucratized, and participation is reduced to occasional voting. Instead, the relation to the state is increasingly channeled through a new role, the social-welfare client.[36]

Third, these developments are "ambivalent." On the one hand, there are gains in freedom with the institution of new social rights limiting the heretofore unrestrained power of capital in the (paid) workplace and of the paterfamilias in the bourgeois family, and social insurance programs represent a clear advance over the paternalism of poor relief. On the other hand, the means employed to realize these new social rights tend perversely to endanger freedom. These means—bureaucratic procedure and the money form—structure the entitlements, benefits, and social services of the welfare system and, in so doing, disempower clients, rendering them dependent on bureaucracies and "therapeutocracies" and preempting their capacities to interpret their own needs, experiences,and life problems.[37]

Fourth, the most ambivalent welfare measures are those concerned with things like health care, care of the elderly, education, and family law, for when bureaucratic and monetary media structure these things, they intrude upon "core domains" of the lifeworld. They turn over symbolic reproduction functions like socialization and solidarity formation to system-integration mechanisms that position people as strategically acting, self-interested monads. But given the inherently symbolic character of these functions and given their internal relation to social integration, the results, necessarily, are "pathological." Thus, these measures are more ambivalent than, say, reforms of paid workplace. The latter bear on a domain that is already system-integrated via money and power and that serves material, as opposed to symbolic, reproduction functions. So paid workplace reforms—unlike, say, family law reforms—do not necessarily generate "pathological" side effects.[38]

Fifth, welfare state capitalism thus gives rise to an "inner colonization of the lifeworld." Money and power cease to be mere media of exchange *between* system and lifeworld. Instead, they tend increasingly to penetrate the lifeworld's *internal* dynamics. The private and public spheres cease to subordinate (official) economic and administrative systems to the norms, values, and interpretations of everyday life. Rather, the latter are increasingly subordinated to the imperatives of the (official) economy and administration. The roles of worker and citizen cease to channel the influence of the lifeworld to the systems. Instead, the newly inflated roles of consumer and client channel the influence of the system to the lifeworld. Moreover, the intrusion of system-integration mechanisms into domains inherently requiring social integration gives rise to "reification phenomena." The affected domains are detached not merely from traditional, normatively secured consensus but from "value orientations per se." The result is the "desiccation of communicative contexts" and the "depletion of the nonrenewable cultural resources" needed to maintain personal and collective identity. Thus, symbolic reproduction is destabilized, identities are threatened, and social crisis tendencies develop.[39]

Sixth, the colonization of the lifeworld sparks new forms of social conflict specific to welfare state capitalism. "New social movements" emerge in a "new conflict zone" at the "seam of system and lifeworld." They respond to system-induced identity threats by contesting the roles that transmit these. They contest the instrumentalization of professional labor and of education transmitted via the worker role, the monetarization of relations and life-styles transmitted via the inflated consumer role, the bureaucratization of services and life problems transmitted via the client role, and the rules and routines of interest politics transmitted via the impoverished citizen role. Thus, the conflicts at the cutting edge of developments in welfare capitalism differ both from class struggles and from bourgeois liberation struggles. They respond to crisis tendencies in symbolic, as opposed to material, reproduction, and they contest reification and "the grammar of forms of life" as opposed to distribution or status inequality.[40]

The various new social movements can be classified with respect to their emancipatory potential. The criterion is the extent to which they advance a genuinely emancipatory resolution of welfare capitalist crisis, namely, the "decolonization of the lifeworld." Decolonization encompasses three things: (1) the removal of system-integration mechanisms from symbolic reproduction spheres, (2) the replacement of (some) normatively secured contexts by communicatively achieved ones, and (3) the development of new, democratic institutions capable of asserting lifeworld control over state and (official) economic systems. Thus, those movements, like religious fundamentalism, that seek to defend traditional lifeworld norms against system intrusions are not genuinely emancipatory; they actively oppose the second element of decolonization and do not take up the third. Movements advocating peace and ecology are better; they aim both to resist system intrusions and also to instate new, reformed, communicatively achieved zones of interaction. But even these are "ambiguous" inasmuch as they tend to "retreat" into alternative communities and "particularistic" identities, thereby effectively renouncing the third element of decolonization and leaving the (official) economic and state systems unchecked. In this respect, they are more symptomatic than emancipatory: they express the identity disturbances caused by colonization. The feminist movement, on the other hand, represents something of an anomaly. It alone is "offensive," aiming to "conquer new territory," and it alone retains links to historic liberation movements. In principle, then, feminism remains rooted in "universalist morality." Yet it is linked to resistance movements by an element of "particularism." And it tends, at times, to "retreat" into identities and communities organized around the natural category of biological sex.[41]

Now, what are the critical insights and blind spots of Habermas's account of the dynamics of welfare state capitalism? To what extent does it serve the self-clarification of the struggles and wishes of contemporary women? I shall take up the six theses one by one.

Habermas's first thesis is straightforward and unobjectionable. Clearly, the welfare state does engage in crisis management and does partially overcome the separation of public and private at the level of systems.

Habermas's second thesis contains some important insights. Clearly, welfare state capitalism does inflate the consumer role and deflate the citizen role, reducing the latter essentially to voting—and, I should add, also to soldiering. Moreover, the welfare state does indeed increasingly position its subjects as clients. On the other hand, Habermas again fails to see the gender subtext of these developments. He fails to see that the new client role has a gender, that it is a paradigmatically feminine role. He overlooks the fact that it is overwhelmingly women who are the clients of the welfare state, especially older women, poor women, single women with children. Nor does he notice that many welfare systems are internally dualized and gendered, that they include two basic kinds of programs—"masculine" social insurance programs tied to primary labor force participation and designed to benefit principal breadwinners, and "feminine" relief programs oriented to what are understood as domestic "failures," in short, to families without a male breadwinner. Not surprisingly, these two welfare subsystems are separate and unequal. Clients of feminine programs, virtually exclusively women and their children, are positioned in a distinctive, feminizing fashion as the "negatives of possessive individuals": they are largely excluded from the market both as workers and as consumers and are familialized, that is, made to claim benefits not as individuals but as members of "defective" households. They are also stigmatized, denied rights, subjected to surveillance and administrative harassment and generally made into abject dependents of state bureaucracies.[42] But this means that the rise of the client role in welfare state capitalism has a more complex meaning than Habermas allows. It is not only a change in the link between system and lifeworld institutions; it is also a change in the character of male dominance, a shift, in Carol Brown's phrase, "from private patriarchy to public patriarchy."[43]

This gives a rather different twist to the meaning of Habermas's third thesis. It suggests that he is right about the "ambivalence" of welfare state capitalism—but not quite and not only in the way he thought. It suggests that welfare measures do have a positive side insofar as they reduce women's dependence on an individual male breadwinner. However, they also have a negative side insofar as they substitute dependence on a patriarchal and androcentric state bureaucracy. The benefits provided are, as Habermas says, "system-conforming" ones. But the system they conform to is not adequately characterized as the system of the official, state-regulated capitalist economy. It is also the system of male dominance, which extends even to the sociocultural lifeworld. In other words, the ambivalence here does not stem only, as Habermas implies, from the fact that the role of client carries effects of "reification." It stems also from the fact that this role, qua feminine role, perpetuates in a new, let us say "modernized" and "rationalized" form, women's subordination. Or so Habermas's third thesis might be rewritten in a feminist critical theory—without, of course, abandoning his insights into the ways in which welfare bureaucracies and therapeutocracies disempower clients by preempting their capacities to interpret their own needs, experiences, and life problems.

Habermas's fourth thesis, by contrast, is not so easily rewritten. This thesis states that welfare reforms of, for example, the domestic sphere are more ambivalent than reforms of the paid workplace. This is true empirically in the sense I have just described—but it is due to the patriarchal character of welfare systems, not to the inherently symbolic character of lifeworld institutions, as Habermas claims. His claim depends on two assumptions I have already challenged. First, it depends on the natural kinds interpretation of the distinction between symbolic and material reproduction activities, that is, on the false assumption that childrearing is inherently more symbolic and less material than other work. And, second, it depends upon the absolute differences interpretation of the system-integrated versus socially integrated action contexts distinction, that is, on the false assumption that money and power are not already entrenched in the internal dynamics of the family. Once we repudiate these assumptions, however, there is no categorial, as opposed to empirical, basis for differentially evaluating the two kinds of reforms. If it is basically progressive that paid workers acquire the means to confront their employers strategically and match power against power, right against right, then it must be just as basically progressive *in principle* that women acquire similar means to similar ends in the politics of famil-ial and personal life. And if it is "pathological" that in the course of achieving a better balance of power in familial and personal life, women become clients of state bu-reaucracies, then it must be just as "pathological" *in principle* that in the course of achieving a similar end at paid work, paid workers, too, become clients—which does not alter the fact that *in actuality* unpaid mothers and paid workers become two dif-ferent sorts of clients. But of course the real point is that the term 'pathological' is misused here insofar as it supposes the untenable assumption that childrearing and other work are asymmetrical with respect to system integration.

This sheds new light as well on Habermas's fifth thesis. This thesis states that wel-fare state capitalism inaugurates an inner colonization of the lifeworld by systems. It depends on three assumptions. The first two of these are the two just rejected, namely, the natural kinds interpretation of the distinction between symbolic and material reproduction activities and the assumed virginity of the domestic sphere with respect to money and power. The third assumption is that the basic vector of motion in late capitalist society is from state-regulated economy to lifeworld and not vice versa. The feminine gender subtext of the client role contradicts this assump-tion: it suggests that even in late capitalism the norms and meanings of gender iden-tity continue to channel the influence of the lifeworld into systems. These norms continue to structure the state-regulated economy, as the persistence, indeed exacerbation, of labor force segmentation according to sex shows.[44] And these norms also structure state administration, as the gender segmentation of U.S. and European social-welfare systems shows.[45] Thus, it is not the case that in late capitalism "system intrusions" detach life contexts from "value-oriented per se." On the contrary, wel-fare capitalism simply uses other means to uphold the familiar "normatively secured consensus" concerning male dominance and female subordination. But Habermas's theory overlooks this countermotion from lifeworld to system. Thus, it posits the evil of welfare state capitalism as the evil of a general and indiscriminate reification. It fails, in consequence, to account for the fact that it is disproportionately women who suffer the effects of bureaucratization and monetarization and for the fact that, viewed structurally, bureaucratization and monetarization are, among other things, instruments of women's subordination.

This entails the revision, as well, of Habermas's sixth thesis. This thesis concerns the causes, character, and emancipatory potential of social movements, including feminism, in late capitalist societies. Since these issues are so central to the concerns of this paper, they warrant a more extended discussion.

Habermas explains the existence and character of new social movements, includ-ing feminism, in terms of colonization, that is, in terms of the intrusion of system-integration mechanisms into symbolic reproduction spheres and the consequent erosion and desiccation of contexts of interpretation and communication. But given the multidirectionality of causal influence in welfare capitalism, the terms 'coloniza-tion,' 'intrusion,' 'erosion,' and 'desiccation' are too negative and one-sided to ac-count for the identity shifts manifested in social movements. Let me attempt an al-ternative explanation, at least for women, by returning to Habermas's important insight that much contemporary contestation surrounds the institution-mediating roles of worker, consumer, citizen, and client. Let me add to these the childrearer role and the fact that all of them are gendered roles. Now, consider in this light the mean-ing of the experience of millions of women, especially married women and women with children, who have in the postwar period become paid workers and/or social-welfare clients. I have already indicated that this has been an experience of new, acute forms of domination; it has also, however, been an experience in which women could, often for the first time, taste the possibilities of a measure of relative economic independence, an identity outside the domestic sphere, and expanded political participation. Above all, it has been an experience of conflict and contradiction as women try to do the impossible, namely, to juggle simultaneously the existing roles of childrearer and worker, client and citizen. The cross-pulls of these mutually incompatible roles have been painful and identity-threatening but not simply negative.[46] Interpellated simultaneously in contradictory ways, women have become split subjects; as a result, the roles themselves, previously shielded in their separate spheres, have suddenly been opened to contestation. Should we, like Habermas, speak here of a "crisis in symbolic reproduction"? Surely not, if this means the desiccation of meaning and values wrought by the intrusion of money and organizational power into women's lives. Emphatically yes, if it means, rather, the emergence into visibility and contestability of problems and possibilities that cannot be solved or realized within the established framework of gendered roles and institutions.

If colonization is not an adequate explanation of contemporary feminism (and other new social movements), then decolonization cannot be an adequate conception of an emancipatory solution. From the perspective I have been sketching, the first element of decolonization—namely, the removal of system-integration mechanisms from symbolic reproduction spheres—is conceptually and empirically askew of the real issues. If the real point is the moral superiority of cooperative and egalitarian interactions over strategic and hierarchical ones, then it mystifies matters to single out lifeworld institutions—the point should hold for paid work and political administration as well as for domestic life. Similarly, the third element of decolonization—namely, the reversal of the direction of influence and control from system to lifeworld—needs modification. Since the social meanings of gender still structure late capitalist official economic and state systems, the question is not *whether* lifeworld norms will be decisive but, rather, *which* lifeworld norms will.

This implies that the key to an emancipatory outcome lies in the second element of Habermas's conception of decolonization—namely, the replacement of normatively secured contexts of interaction by communicatively achieved ones. The centrality of this element is evident when we consider that this process occurs simultaneously on two fronts. First, it occurs in the struggles of social movements with the state and official economic system institutions; these struggles are not waged over systems media alone—they are also waged over the meanings and norms embedded and enacted in government and corporate policy. Second, this process occurs in a phenomenon not thematized by Habermas: in the struggles between opposing social movements with conflicting interpretations of social needs. Both kinds of struggles involve confrontations between normatively secured and communicatively achieved action. Both involve contestation for hegemony over what I call the "sociocultural means of interpretation and communication." For example, in many late capitalist societies, women's contradictory, self-dividing experience of trying to be both workers and mothers, clients and citizens has given rise to not one but two women's movements, a feminist one and an antifeminist one. These movements, along with their respective allies, are engaged in struggles with one another and with state and corporate institutions over the social meanings of "woman" and "man," "femininity" and "masculinity"; over the interpretation of women's needs; over the interpretation and social construction of women's bodies; and over the gender norms that shape the major institution-mediating social roles. Of course, the means of interpretation and communication in terms of which the social meanings of these things are elaborated have always been controlled by men. Thus, feminist women are struggling in effect to redistribute and democratize access to, and control over, discursive resources. We are, therefore, struggling for women's autonomy in the following special sense: a measure of collective control over the means of interpretation and communication sufficient to permit us to participate on a par with men in all types of social interaction, including political deliberation and decision making.[47]

The foregoing suggests that a caution is in order concerning the use of the terms 'particularism' and 'universalism'. Recall that Habermas's sixth thesis emphasized feminism's links to historic liberation movements and its roots in universalist morality. Recall that he was critical of those tendencies within feminism, and in resistance movements in general, that try to resolve the identity problematic by recourse to particularism, that is, by retreating from arenas of political struggle into alternative communities delimited on the basis of natural categories like biological sex. I want to suggest that there are really three issues here and that they need to be disengaged from one another. One is the issue of political engagement versus apolitical counter-cultural activity. Insofar as Habermas's point is a criticism of cultural feminism, it is well-taken in principle, but it needs to be qualified by two perceptions: cultural separatism, although inadequate as long-term political strategy, is in many cases a shorter-term necessity for women's physical, psychological, and moral survival; and separatist communities have, in fact, been the source of numerous reinterpretations of women's experience that have proved politically fruitful in contestation over the means of interpretation and communication. The second issue is the status of women's biology in the elaboration of new social identities. Insofar as Habermas's point is a criticism of reductive biologism, it is well-taken. But this does not mean that one can ignore the fact that women's biology has nearly always been interpreted by men and that women's struggle for autonomy necessarily and properly involves, among other things, the reinterpretation of the social meanings of our bodies. The third issue is the difficult and complex one of universalism versus particularism. Insofar as Habermas's endorsement of universalism pertains to the meta-level of access to, and control over, the means of interpretation and communication, it is well-taken. At this level, women's struggle for autonomy can be understood in terms of a universalist conception of distributive justice. But it does not follow that the substantive content that is the fruit of this struggle—namely, the new social meanings we give our needs and our bodies, our new social identities and conceptions of femininity—can be dismissed as particularistic lapses from universalism. These, certainly, are no more particular than the sexist and androcentric meanings and norms they are meant to replace. More generally, at the level of substantive content, as opposed to dialogical form, the contrast between universalism and particularism is out of place. Substantive social meanings and norms are always necessarily culturally and historically specific; they always express distinctive shared but nonuniversal forms of life. Feminist meanings and norms will be no exception—but they will not, on that account, be particularistic in any pejorative sense. Let us simply say that they will be different.

I have been arguing that struggles of social movements over the means of interpretation and communication are central to an emancipatory resolution of crisis tendencies in welfare state capitalism. Let me now clarify their relation to institutional change. Such struggles, I claim, are implicitly and explicitly raising a number of important questions: Should the roles of worker, childrearer, citizen, and client be fully degendered? Can they be? Or do we, rather, require arrangements that permit women to be workers and citizens *as women,* just as men have always been workers and citizens *as men?* And what might that mean? In any case, does not an emancipatory outcome require a profound transformation of the current gender roles at the base of contemporary social organization? And does not this, in turn, require a fundamental transformation of the content, character, boundaries, and relations of the spheres of life that these roles mediate? How should the character and position of paid work, childrearing, and citizenship be defined vis-à-vis one another? Should democratic-socialist-feminist, self-managed paid work encompass childrearing? Or should childrearing, rather, replace soldiering as a component of transformed, democratic-socialist-feminist, participatory citizenship? What other possibilities are conceivable?

Let me conclude this discussion of the six theses by restating the most important critical points. First, Habermas's account fails to theorize the patriarchal, norm-mediated character of late capitalist official economic and administrative systems. Likewise, it fails to theorize the systemic, money- and power-mediated character of male dominance in the domestic sphere of the late capitalist lifeworld. Consequently, his colonization thesis fails to grasp that the channels of influence between system and lifeworld institutions are multidirectional. And it tends to replicate, rather than to problematize, a major institutional support of women's subordination in late capitalism, namely, the gender-based separation of both the masculine public sphere and the state-regulated economy of sex-segmented paid work and social welfare from privatized female childrearing. Thus, although Habermas wants to be critical of male dominance, his diagnostic categories deflect attention elsewhere, to the allegedly overriding problem of gender-neutral reification. Consequently, his programmatic conception of decolonization bypasses key feminist questions; it fails to address the issue of how to restructure the relation of childrearing to paid work and citizenship. Finally, Habermas's categories tend to misrepresent the causes and underestimate the scope of the feminist challenge to welfare state capitalism. In short, the struggles and wishes of contemporary women are not adequately clarified by a theory that draws the basic battle line between system and lifeworld institutions. From a feminist perspective, there is a more basic battle line between the forms of male dominance linking "system" to "lifeworld" *and us.*

Conclusion

In general, then, the principal blind spots of Habermas's theory with respect to gender are traceable to his categorical opposition between system and lifeworld institutions and to the two more elementary oppositions from which it is compounded, the reproduction one and the action-contexts one. Or, rather, the blind spots are traceable to the way in which these oppositions, ideologically and andorcentrically interpreted, tend to override and eclipse other, potentially more critical elements of Habermas's framework—elements like the distinction between normatively secured and communicatively achieved action contexts and like the four-term model of public/private relations.

Habermas's blind spots are instructive, I think. They permit us to conclude something about what the categorial framework of a socialist-feminist critical theory of welfare state capitalism should look like. One crucial requirement is that this framework not be such as to put the male-headed nuclear family and the state-regulated official economy on two opposite sides of the major categorical divide. We require, rather, a framework sensitive to the similarities between them, one that puts them on the same side of the line as institutions that, albeit in different ways, enforce women's subordination, since both family and official economy appropriate our labor, short-circuit our participation in the interpretation of our needs, and shield normatively secured need interpretations from political contestation. A second crucial requirement is that this framework contain no a priori assumptions about the unidirectionality of social motion and causal influence, that it be sensitive to the ways in which allegedly disappearing institutions and norms persist in structuring social reality. A third crucial requirement, the last I shall mention here, is that this framework not be such as to posit the evil of welfare state capitalism exclusively or primarily as the evil of reification. What we need instead is a framework capable of foregrounding the evil of dominance and subordination.[48]

Notes

I am grateful to John Brenkman, Thomas McCarthy, Carole Pateman, and Martin Schwab for helpful comments and criticism; to Dee Marquez and Marina Rosiene for crackerjack word processing; and to The Stanford Humanities Center for financial support.

1. Karl Marx, "Letter to A. Ruge, September 1843," in *Karl Marx: Early Writings*, ed. L. Colletti, trans. Rodney Livingstone and Gregor Benton (New York, 1975), 209.

2. Jürgen Habermas, *The Theory of Communicative Action*, vol. 1, *Reason and the Rationalization of Society*, trans. Thomas McCarthy (Boston, 1984), hereafter cited as *Theory*, and *Theorie des kommunikativen Handelns*, vol. 2, *Zur Kritik der funktionalistischen Vernunft* (Frankfurt am Main, 1981), hereafter cited as *Theorie*. *Theorie* is now available in English as *The Theory of Communicative Action*, vol. 2, *Lifeworld and System: A Critique of Functionalist Reason*, trans. Thomas McCarthy (Boston, 1987).

See also Habermas, *Legitimation Crisis*, trans. Thomas McCarthy (Boston, 1975); Introduction to *Observations on "The Spiritual Situation of the Age": Contemporary German Perspectives*, ed. Jürgen Habermas, trans. Andrew Buchwalter (Cambridge, Mass., 1984); and "A Reply to My Critics," in *Habermas: Critical Debates*, ed. David Held and John B. Thompson (Cambridge, Mass., 1982).

I have also consulted two helpful overviews of this material in English: Thomas McCarthy, Translator's Introduction to vol. 1 of *The Theory of Communicative Action*, by Habermas, v–xxxvii; and John B. Thompson, "Rationality and Social Rationalisation: An Assessment of Habermas's Theory of Communicative Action," *Sociology* 17, no. 2 (1983), 278–94.

3. I shall not take up such widely debated issues as Habermas's theories of universal pragmatics and social evolution. For helpful discussions of these issues, see the essays in *Habermas: Critical Debates*.

4. Habermas, *Theorie*, 214, 217, 348–49; *Legitimation Crisis*, 8–9; and "A Reply to My Critics," 268, 278–79. See also McCarthy, Translator's Introduction xxv–xxvii; and Thompson, "Rationality," 285.

5. Habermas, *Theorie*, 208, and "A Reply to My Critics," 223–25; McCarthy, Translator's Introduction, xxiv–xxv.

6. I am indebted to Martin Schwab for the expression "dual aspect activity."

7. It might be argued that Habermas's categorial distinction between "social labor" and "socialization" helps overcome the androcentrism of orthodox Marxism. Orthodox Marxism allowed for only one kind of historically significant activity, namely, "production," or "social labor." Moreover, it understood that category androcentrically and thereby excluded women's unpaid childrearing activity from history. By contrast, Habermas allows for two kinds of historically significant activity, "social labor" and the "symbolic" activities that comprise, among other things, childrearing. Thus, he manages to include women's unpaid activity in history. Although this is an improvement, it does not suffice to remedy matters. At best, it leads to what has come to be known as "dual systems theory," an approach that posits two distinct "systems" of human activity and, correspondingly, two distinct "systems" of oppression: capitalism and male dominance. But this is misleading. These are not, in fact, two distinct systems but, rather, two thoroughly interfused dimensions of a single social formation. In order to understand that social formation, a critical theory requires a single set of categories and concepts that integrate *internally* both gender and political economy (perhaps also race). For a classic statement of dual systems theory, see Heidi Hartmann, "The Unhappy Marriage of Marxism and Feminism: Towards More Progressive Union," in *Women and Revolution: A Discussion of the Unhappy Marriage of Marxism and Feminism,* ed. Lydia Sargent (Boston, 1981). For a critique of dual systems theory, see Iris Young, "Beyond the Unhappy Marriage: A Critique of Dual Systems Theory," in *Women and Revolution;* and "Socialist Feminism and the Limits of Dual Systems Theory," *Socialist Review,* 50–51 (Summer, 1980) 169–80.

In sections 2 and 3 of this essay, I am developing arguments and lines of analysis that rely on concepts and categories that internally integrate gender and political economy (see n. 34 below). This might be considered a "single system" approach, by contrast to dual systems theory. However, I find that label misleading, because I do not consider my approach primarily or exclusively a "systems" approach in the first place. Rather, like Habermas, I am trying to link structural (in the sense of objectivating) and interpretive approaches to the study of societies. Unlike him, however, I do not do this by dividing society into two components, "system" and "lifeworld"; see the rest of this section, especially n. 16 below.

8. Habermas, *Theory,* 85, 87–88, 101, 342, 357–60; *Theorie,* 179; *Legitimation Crisis,* 4–5; "A Reply to My Critics," 234, 237, 264–65. See also McCarthy, Translator's Introduction, ix, xxvi–xxx. In presenting the distinction between system-integrated and socially-integrated action contexts, I am relying on the terminology of *Legitimation Crisis* and modifying the terminology of *Theory of Communicative Action.* Or, rather, I am selecting one of the several different usages deployed in the latter work. There, Habermas often speaks of what I have called "socially integrated action" as "communicative action." But this gives rise to confusion. For Habermas also uses this latter expression in another, stronger sense, namely, for actions in which coordination occurs by explicit, dialogically achieved consensus only (discussed further later in this section). In order to avoid repeating Habermas's equivocation on 'communicative action,' I adopt the following terminology: I reserve the term 'communicatively achieved action' for actions coordinated by explicit, reflective, dialogically achieved consensus. I contrast such action, in the first instance, with 'normatively secured action' or actions coordinated by tacit, prereflective, pregiven consensus. I take 'communicatively achieved' and 'normatively secured' actions, so defined, to be subspecies of what I here call 'socially integrated action' or actions coordinated by any form of normed consensus whatever. This last category, in turn, contrasts with 'system-integrated action,' or actions coordinated by the functional interlacing of unintended consequences, determined by egocentric calculations in the media of money and power, and involving little or no normed consensus of any sort. These terminological commitments do not so much represent a departure from Habermas's usage—he does, in fact, frequently use these terms in the senses I have specified—as a stabilization or regularization of his usage.

9. Habermas, *Theory,* 341, 357–59; and *Theorie,* 256, 266. See also McCarthy, Translator's Introduction, xxx.

10. In "Complexity and Democracy, or the Seducements of Systems Theory," (*New German Critique* 35 [Spring/Summer 1985], 27–55), McCarthy argues that state administrative bureaucracies cannot be distinguished from participatory democratic political associations on the bases of functionality, intentionality, and linguisticality, since all three of these features are found in both contexts. Thus, McCarthy argues that functionality, intentionality, and linguisticality are not mutually exclusive. I find these arguments persuasive. I see no reason why they do not hold also for the capitalist workplace and the modern restricted nuclear family.

11. Here, again, I follow McCarthy, "Complexity and Democracy." He argues that in modern state administrative bureaucracies, managers must often deal consensually with their subordinates. This seems to be equally the case for corporate organizations.

12. I have in mind especially the brilliant and influential discussion of gifting by Pierre Bourdieu in *Outline of a Theory of Practice*, trans. Richard Nice (New York, 1977). By recovering the dimension of time, Bourdieu substantially revises the classical account by Marcel Mauss in *The Gift: Forms and Functions of Exchange in Archaic Societies*, trans. Ian Cunnison (New York, 1967). For a discussion of some recent revisionist work in cultural economic anthropology, see Arjun Appadurai, "Commodities and the Politics of Value," in *The Social Life of Things: Commodities in Cultural Perspective*, ed. Appadurai, (New York, 1986).

13. Hereafter I shall use the expression 'the official economy' to designate the institutions and relations in male-dominated capitalist societies that are officially recognized as economic. The point is to call attention to the androcentrism of the standard usage of 'the economy', which is premised on the ideological assumption that domestic institutions and relations are not also economic. I shall use 'official economic' as the adjectival form of this expression, and I shall use 'the (official) economy' when explicating the views of someone—like Habermas—who follows androcentric usage.

14. Habermas, *Theorie*, 348–49. See also McCarthy, Translator's Introduction, xxvi–xxvii. The terms 'pragmatic-contextual' and 'natural kinds' are mine, not Habermas's.

15. Habermas, *Theory*, 94–95, 101; *Theorie*, 348–349; "A Reply to My Critics," 227, 237, 266–68; and *Legitimation Crisis*, 10. See also McCarthy, Translator's Introduction, xxvi–xxvii. Again, the terms 'absolute differences' and 'difference by degree' are mine, not Habermas's.

16. Habermas, *Theory*, 341–42, 359–60; *Theorie*, 179; "A Reply to My Critics," 268, 279–80; and *Legitimation Crisis*, 20–21. See also McCarthy, Translator's Introduction, xxviii–xxix; and Thompson. "Rationality," 285, 287. It should be noted that in *Theory of Communicative Action* Habermas draws the contrast between system and lifeworld in two distinct senses. On the one hand, he contrasts them as two different methodological perspectives on the study of societies. The system perspective is objectivating and "externalist," whereas the lifeworld perspective is hermeneutical and "internalist." Although in principle either can be applied to the study of any given set of societal phenomena. Habermas argues that neither alone is adequate and, consequently, seeks to develop a methodology combining both. On the other hand, Habermas also contrasts system and lifeworld in another way, namely, as two different kinds of institutions. It is this second system/lifeworld contrast that I am concerned with here; I do not explicitly treat the first one in this essay. I am sympathetic to Habermas's general methodological intention of combining or linking structural (in the sense of objectivating) and interpretive approaches to the study of societies. I do not, however, believe that this can be done by assigning structural properties to one set of institutions (the official economy and the state) and interpretive properties to another set (the family and the public sphere). I maintain, rather, that all these institutions have both structural and interpretive dimensions and that all should be studied both structurally and hermeneutically. I have tried to develop an approach that meets these desiderata in "Women, Welfare, and the Politics of Need Interpretation" [144–160] and in "Struggle over Needs: Outline of a Socialist-Feminist Critical Theory of Late Capitalist Political Culture" [161–187, in *Unruly Practices: Power, Discourse, and Gender in Contemporary Social Theory* (Minneapolis: University of Minnesota Press, 1989)]. I have dis-

cussed the general methodological problem in "On the Political and the Symbolic: Against the Metaphysics of Textuality," *Enclitic* 9, nos. 1–2 (Spring/Fall 1987): 100–114.

17. See, for example, the essays in *Rethinking the Family: Some Feminist Questions*, ed. Barrie Thorne and Marilyn Yalom (New York and London, 1982). See also, Michele Barrett and Mary McIntosh, *The Anti-Social Family* (London, 1982).

18. Habermas, *Theory*, 85–86, 88–90, 101, 104–5; and *Theorie*, 179. See also McCarthy, Translator's Introduction, ix, xxx. In presenting the distinction between normatively secured action and communicatively achieved action, I am again modifying, or rather stabilizing, the variable usage of *Theory of Communicative Action* (see n. 8 above).

19. Pamela Fishman, "Interaction: The Work Women Do," *Social Problems* 25, no. 4 (1978) 397–406.

20. Nancy Henley, *Body Politics* (Englewood Cliffs, NJ, 1977).

21. Habermas, *Theorie*, 523–24, 547; and "A Reply to My Critics," 237. See also Thompson, "Rationality," 288, 292.

22. McCarthy Pursues some of the normative implications of this for the differentiation of the administrative state system from the public sphere in "Complexity and Democracy" (see n. 10 above).

23. McCarthy makes this point with respect to the dedifferentiation of the state administrative system and the public sphere; see "Complexity and Democracy."

24. Habermas, *Theory*, 341–42, 359–60; *Theorie*, 256, 473; and "A Reply to My Critics," 280. See also McCarthy, Translator's Introduction, xxxii; and Thompson, "Rationality," 286–88.

25. I borrow the phrase "gender subtext" from Dorothy Smith, "The Gender Subtext of Power" (Ontario Institute for Studies in Education, Toronto, 1984).

26. The following account of the masculine gender subtext of the worker role draws heavily on Carole Pateman, "The Personal and the Political: Can Citizenship Be Democratic?" (Lecture 3 of her "Women and Democratic Citizenship" series), The Jefferson Memorial Lectures, University of California, Berkeley, February 1985.

27. Ibid., 5.

28. I am here adapting Althusser's notion of the interpellation of a subject to a context in which he, of course, never used it; for the general notion, see Louis Althusser, "Ideology and Ideological State Apparatuses (Notes toward an Investigation)," in *"Lenin and Philosophy" and Other Essays*, trans. Ben Brewster (New York, 1971).

29. Barbara Ehrenreich, *The Hearts of Men: American Dreams and the Flight from Commitment* (Garden City, N.Y., 1984).

30. The following discussion of the masculine gender subtext of the citizen role draws heavily on Carole Pateman, "The Personal and the Political."

31. Ibid., 8.

32. Judith Hicks Stiehm, "The Protected, the Protector, the Defender," in *Women and Men's Wars*, ed. Stiehm (New York, 1983). This is not to say, however, that I accept Stiehm's conclusions about the desirability of integrating women fully into the U.S. military as it is presently structured and deployed.

33. Pateman, "The Personal and the Political," 10.

34. Insofar as the preceding analysis of the gender subtext of Habermas's role theory deploys categories in which gender and political economy are internally integrated, it represents a contribution to the overcoming of "dual systems theory" (see n. 7 above). It is also a contribution to the development of a more satisfactory way of linking structural (in the sense of objectivating) and interpretive approaches to the study of societies than that proposed by Habermas. In other words, I am suggesting here that the domestic sphere has a structural as well as an interpretive dimension and that the official economic and the state spheres have an interpretive as well as a structural dimension.

35. Habermas, *Theorie*, 505–9; and *Legitimation Crisis*, 33–36, 53–55. See also McCarthy, Translator's Introduction, xxxiii.

36. Habermas, *Theorie,* 522–24; and *Legitimation Crisis,* 36–37. See also McCarthy, Translator's Introduction, xxxiii.

37. Habermas, *Theorie,* 530–40. See also McCarthy, Translator's Introduction, xxxiii–xxxiv.

38. Habermas, *Theorie,* 540–47. See also McCarthy, Translator's Introduction, xxxi.

39. Habermas, *Theorie,* 275–77, 452, 480, 522–24; "A Reply to My Critics," 226, 280–1; and Introduction to *Observations,* 11–12, 16–20. See also McCarthy, Translator's Introduction, xxxi–
xxxii, and Thompson, "Rationality," 286, 288.

40. Habermas, *Theorie,* 581–83; and Introduction to *Observations,* 18–19, 27–28.

41. Habermas, *Theorie,* 581–83; and Introduction to *Observations,* 16–17, 27–28.

42. For the U.S. social-welfare system, see the analysis of male versus female participation
rates, and the account of the gendered character of the two subsystems in my "Women, Welfare and the Politics of Need Interpretation" … . See also Barbara J. Nelson, "Women's Poverty
and Women's Citizenship: Some Political Consequences of Economic Marginality," *Signs:
Journal of Women in Culture and Society* 10, no. 2 (Winter 1984): Steven P. Erie, Martin Rein,
and Barbara Wiget, "Women and the Reagan Revolution: Thermidor for the Social Welfare
Economy," in *Families, Politics and Public Policies: A Feminist Dialogue on Women and the
State,* ed. Irene Diamond, (New York, 1983); Diana Pearce, "Women, Work and Welfare: The
Feminization of Poverty," in *Working Women and Families,* Karen Wolk Feinstein, ed., (Beverly
Hills, Calif., 1979), and "Toil and Trouble: Women Workers and Unemployment Compensa-
tion," *Signs: Journal of Women in Culture and Society,* 10, no. 3 (Spring, 1985), 439–59; and Bar-
bara Ehrenreich and Frances Fox Piven, "The Feminization of Poverty," *Dissent* (Spring 1984):
162–70. For an analysis of the gendered character of the British social-welfare system, see
Hilary Land, "Who Cares for the Family?" *Journal of Social Policy* 7, no. 3 (July 1978): 257–84.
For Norway, see the essays in *Patriarchy in a Welfare Society,* ed. Harriet Holter (Oslo, 1984).
See also two comparative studies: Mary Ruggie, *The State and Working Women: A Comparative
Study of Britain and Sweden* (Princeton, NJ, 1984); and Birte Siim, "Women and the Welfare
State: Between Private and Public Dependence' (Stanford University, 1985).

43. Carol Brown, "Mothers, Fathers, and Children: From Private to Public Patriarchy" in
Women and Revolution (see n. 7 above). Actually, I believe Brown's formulation is theoretically
inadequate, since it presupposes a simple, dualistic conception of public and private. Nonetheless, the phrase "from private to public patriarchy" evokes in a rough but suggestive way the
phenomena for which a socialist-feminist critical theory of the welfare state would need to account.

44. The most recent available data for the U.S. indicate that sex segmentation in paid work
is increasing, not decreasing. And this is so despite the entry of small but significant numbers
of women into professions like law and medicine. Even when the gains won by those women
are taken into account, there is no overall improvement in the aggregated comparative economic position of paid women workers vis-à-vis male workers. Women's wages remain less
than 60 percent of men's wages—which means, of course, that the mass of women are losing
ground. Nor is there any overall improvement in occupational distribution by sex. The ghetto-
ization of women in low-paying, low-status "pink collar" occupations is increasing. For example, in the U.S. in 1973, women held 96 percent of all paid childcare jobs, 81 percent of all primary school teaching jobs, 72 percent of all health technician jobs, 98 percent of all registered
nurse jobs, 83 percent of all librarian jobs, 99 percent of all secretarial jobs and 92 percent of all
waitperson jobs. The figures for 1983 were, respectively, 97 percent, 83 percent, 84 percent, 96
percent, 87 percent, 99 percent and 88 percent, (Bureau of Labor Statistics figures cited by
Drew Christie, "Comparable Worth and Distributive Justice" [Paper read at meetings of the
American Philosophical Association, Western Division, April 1985]). The U.S. data are consistent with data for the Scandinavian countries and Britain; see Siim, "Women and the Welfare
State."

45. See n. 42, above.

46. This account draws on some elements of Zillah R. Eisenstein's analysis in *The Radical
Future of Liberal Feminism* (Boston, 1981), chap. 9. What follows has some affinities with the

perspective of Ernesto Laclau and Chantal Mouffe in *Hegemony and Socialist Strategy* (New York, 1985).

47. I develop this notion of the "socio-cultural means of interpretation and communication" and the associated conception of autonomy in "toward a Discourse Ethic of Solidarity," *Praxis International* 5, no. 4 (January 1986): 425–29, and in ["Struggle over Needs: Outline of a Socialist-Feminist Critical Theory of Late Capitalist Political Culture," in *Unruly Practices: Power, Discourse, and Gender in Contemporary Social Theory* (Minneapolis: University of Minnesota Press, 1989), 161–187]. Both notions are extensions and modifications of Habermas's conception of "communicative ethics."

48. My own recent work attempts to construct a conceptual framework for a socialist-feminist critical theory of the welfare state that meets these requirements. See "Women, Welfare and the Politics of Need Interpretation" in [*Unruly Practices: Power, Discourse, and Gender in Contemporary Social Theory* (Minneapolis: University of Minnesota Press, 1989), 144–160]. "Toward a Discourse Ethic of Solidarity" (see n. 47 above), and ["Struggle over Needs: Outline of a Socialist-Feminist Critical Theory of Late Capitalist Political Culture," in *Unruly Practices: Power, Discourse, and Gender in Contemporary Social Theory* (Minneapolis: University of Minnesota Press, 1989), 161–187]. Each of these essays draws heavily on those aspects of Habermas's thought that I take to be unambiguously positive and useful, especially his conception of the irreducibly sociocultural, interpretive character of human needs and his contrast between dialogical and monological processes of need interpretation. The present paper, on the other hand, focuses mainly on those aspects of Habermas's thought that I find problematical or unhelpful and so does not convey the full range either of his work or of my views about it. Readers are warned, therefore, against drawing the conclusion that Habermas has little or nothing positive to contribute to a socialist-feminist critical theory of the welfare state. They are urged, rather, to consult the essays cited above for the other side of the story.

The Politics of Socialist Feminism

Alison M. Jaggar

To analyze the contemporary oppression of women in terms of the concept of alienation is to link that oppression inevitably with capitalism. It is to deny that "patriarchy" is an unchanging trans-historical and cross-cultural universal and to assert instead that the subordination of women takes different forms in different historical periods. The alienation of contemporary women is a historically specific product of the capitalist mode of production. It results from such historically specific features of capitalism as the fetishism of commodities, the rise of positive science, and especially the separation of home from workplace, accompanied by the characteristic split between emotion and reason, the personal and the political.

This is not to say, of course, that women's oppression stems from capitalism alone, nor that the abolition of capitalism would eliminate that oppression. The abolition of capitalism would end the specifically capitalist form of women's oppression, but there is no reason to suppose that it could not be succeeded by a new form of "patriarchy" or male dominance and perhaps by new modes of alienation. The socialist feminist analysis of women's oppression shows that women's liberation requires totally new modes of organizing all forms of production and the final abolition of "femininity." Traditional Marxism has taken the abolition of class as its explicit goal, but it has not committed itself to the abolition of gender. Socialist feminism makes an explicit commitment to the abolition of both class and gender.

It is one thing to say that class and gender must be abolished, of course, and quite another to say how that abolition should be achieved. Socialist feminists, like everyone else, offer no guaranteed route to the overthrow of male dominance and capitalism. One thing that they do have, however, is a conception of the material base of society that includes the mode of producing sexuality and children as well as the mode of producing what are ordinarily called goods and services. For this reason, several of their proposals for social change, like many of the proposals of radical feminism, are directed toward the transformation of sexuality and procreation.

1. Reproductive Freedom

Reproductive freedom for women is a central concern for socialist feminism. Basically, it means control over whether and in what circumstances women bear and rear children. Sometimes this idea is expressed as "reproductive rights" but, for reasons that I shall explain shortly, I think the terminology of rights is misplaced.

In developing their conception of reproductive freedom, socialist feminists do not begin from a vision of some ideal society. Instead, they begin by identifying existing constraints on women's reproductive freedom. In identifying these constraints, they draw from the insights of other groups of feminists. From liberal feminism, they draw a recognition of some of the factors that force women into unwanted motherhood, including the legal and the economic unavailability of contraception and abortion, as well as the lack of opportunities for women to fulfill themselves through venues other than motherhood. From traditional Marxism, socialist feminists draw a recognition of the factors in contemporary society that deprive many poor women of the opportunity to be mothers. These factors include the involuntary sterilization of poor, black, Hispanic, and native American women in the United States, and the lack of economic support for children who are born to such women. Finally, socialist feminists draw from radical feminists the recognition that women are often forced into motherhood by compulsory heterosexuality, that compulsory heterosexuality also deprives many lesbian mothers of custody of their children, and that no woman under patriarchy is really free to raise her child as she wishes.

As long as any of these constraints exist, socialist feminists argue that women lack reproductive freedom.

> *Genuine control over one's own reproductive life* must mean, among other things, the universal availability of good, safe, cheap birth control; and adequate counseling for *all* women and men about *all* currently existing methods. It must mean adequate abortion services and an end to involuntary sterilization. It must mean the availability to *all* people of good public childcare centers and schools; decent housing, adequate welfare, and wages high enough to support a family; and of quality medical, pre- and post-natal and maternal care. It must also mean freedom of sexual choice, which implies an end to the cultural norms that define women in terms of having children and living with a man; an affirmation of people's right to raise children outside of conventional families; and, in the long run, a transformation of childcare arrangements so that they are shared among women and men. Finally, all these aspects of reproductive freedom must be available to *all* people—women, minorities, the disabled and handicapped, medicaid and welfare recipients, teenagers, everyone.
> Women have never had reproductive freedom in this sense.[1]

The socialist feminist conception of reproductive freedom starts from the material conditions of contemporary society, it is not designed to offer a model of reproductive freedom in some ideal society. This is obvious from the fact that the statement above assumes the continuation of the wage system—although in fact it is less obvious that some elements in the above definition are compatible with the continuation of the wage system. Nor does this typical socialist feminist statement of reproductive freedom call, for instance, for the development of the means to make possible parthenogenesis or the fertilization of one ovum by another so that two women could be the biological parents of a child, nor for the option of extra-uterine gestation, so-called test-tube babies. Because of its historical materialist methodology, socialist feminism eschews any final or abstract definition of reproductive freedom and instead is content to allow the notion of reproductive freedom to be defined relative to the material possibilities of a given society. For instance, in a technologically advanced society the unavailability of amniocentesis or of test-tube conception may be seen as constraints on women's reproductive freedom in a way that their absence cannot be construed to limit the reproductive freedom of women in a less technologically advanced society. The socialist feminist call for reproductive freedom must be interpreted in a historical and materialist way. It functions less as a clearly envisioned end goal than as a heuristic device. As such, it urges us to identify specific restrictions on women's freedom to choose or to refuse motherhood, to understand the material basis of these restrictions, and to seek the real possibility of eliminating them.

Although it starts from existing material conditions, the socialist feminist conception of reproductive freedom does not accept those conditions as unchangeable. For instance, this conception of reproductive freedom is clearly much broader than the liberal "right to choose" contraception and abortion. What it actually calls for is a transformation of the social conditions in which "choices" are made. Construed thus broadly, it becomes obvious that reproductive freedom is incompatible either with the compulsory heterosexuality and mandatory motherhood that have characterized all male-dominated societies or with the economic inequality that necessarily characterizes capitalism. Because it cannot be achieved within the existing social order, reproductive freedom is in fact a revolutionary demand.

Socialist feminists are careful to emphasize that reproductive freedom must be available to all women, but they rarely discuss what reproductive freedom would be for men. As Rosalind Petchesky points out, two reasons exist for the socialist feminist assumption that women rather than men should control reproduction. One is the biological fact, unalterable until the present time, that babies are gestated and born from the bodies of women; the other is the social fact that, in contemporary society as in other known societies, the sexual division of labor assigns women most of the work and responsibility for infant and child welfare.[2]

When reproductive freedom for women is justified solely by reference to the facts of female biology, rather than including a reference to women's social situation, it tends to emerge in a demand for "reproductive rights." Petchesky criticizes this formula because she believes that

> it can be turned back on us to reinforce the view of all reproductive activity as the special, biologically destined province of women. Here it has to be acknowledged that this danger grows out of the concept of "rights" in general, a concept inherently static and abstracted from social conditions. Rights are by definition claims that are staked within a given order of things and relationships. They are demands for access for oneself, or for "no admittance" to others, but they do not challenge the social structure itself, the social relations of production and reproduction. The claim for "abortion rights" seeks access to a necessary service, but by itself it fails to address the existing social relations and sexual divisions around which responsibility for pregnancy and children is assigned. And in real-life struggles, this limitation exacts a price, for it lets men and society neatly off the hook.[3]

"Reproductive rights" may come to be viewed as ends in themselves, as something belonging permanently to women in virtue of their unalterable biological constitution. A more consistently socialist feminist approach would focus less on biological "givens" and more on the social relations of procreation. Ultimately, socialist feminists are not interested in a mode of society that assigns rights to some individuals in order to protect them from others; they are interested in transforming the mode of procreation.

Apart from the fact that children are born from the bodies of women rather than men, the other ground for asserting that reproductive freedom should belong to women rather than to men is that present day relations of procreation assign most procreative work and responsibility to women. In previous societies, this work and responsibility was usually shared by a group of women but, as we saw in the preceding section, the special conditions of modern capitalism have confined most contemporary mothers in an isolation that is historically unique. It is in part this unique isolation that makes it plausible to interpret reproductive freedom as a "right" of individual women. Part of the socialist feminist conception of reproductive freedom, however, is to challenge the traditional sexual division of labor in procreation so that childcare comes to be shared between women and men. If this goal were achieved, and if the community as a whole came to assume responsibility for the welfare of children (and mothers), then the birth or non-birth of a child would affect that community in a much more direct and immediate way than it does at present. In this case, it would seem reasonable to allow the community as a whole to participate in decisions over whether children were born and how they should be reared. In these changed social circumstances, it would no longer be even plausible to interpret reproductive freedom as a "right" of individual women. Instead, reproductive freedom would be seen clearly to be a social achievement and something to be shared by the entire community, men as well as women.[4]

Under the rubric of reproductive freedom, socialist feminists propose to transform existing arrangements for organizing sexuality and procreation. They believe that their proposals will have far-reaching social consequences. The most obvious, of course, is that women's release from compulsory motherhood will allow them to develop their capacities in many other areas. On a deeper level, many socialist feminist theorists believe that the equal involvement of men in infant and childcare is the key to eliminating the gendered structure of the unconscious mind. Dorothy Dinnerstein, as we have seen, argues that the mother-rearing of children instills an ineradicable (though often unacknowledged) misogyny in both men and women, a misogyny that "conspires to keep history mad."[5] Nancy Chodorow traces the way in which women's responsibility for early childcare results in the imposition of a different character structure on girls and boys. Boys grow up to be achievement-oriented and emotionally closed to others; girls grow up to be emotionally vulnerable, open to and even dependent on the approval of others. In the end, boys and girls become men and women who repeat the traditional sexual division of labor in childrearing and so perpetuate psychological and social inequality between women and men.[6] Both for Dinnerstein and for Chodorow, men's full participation in infant and child care is essential to eradicating the deep roots of gender in the unconscious mind.

Not all socialist feminists accept the psychoanalytic theories of Dinnerstein and Chodorow. Some socialist feminists argue that they repeat the errors of Freud in being ahistorical, in falsely universalizing childhood experience, and in ignoring differences of period and of class. Critics who are non-Freudians deny that people's character structures are fixed in childhood with such finality and argue that in fact people may continue to change in fundamental ways throughout their lives. Other critics argue that the problem is not so much that mothers rear children as that they do so in a context of male dominance and compulsory heterosexuality. A male-dominated society is always likely to be misogynistic, no matter who rears the children. It may be that women rear children because they have low status, rather than that they have

low status because they rear children. After all, childcare is a demanding though socially necessary task which provides no material as opposed to emotional return until the child is old enough to work, and often not even then. For this reason, childcare
is a task which is likely to be relegated to the less powerful members of the society,
while the more powerful devote their energy to increasing their power. Historically,
this has certainly held true, and even today much childcare is left to relatively powerless teenage, minority or elderly women.

Rather than focusing on relatively long-term attempts to alter the psychic structure of our daughters (and our sons) by involving men immediately in childrearing,
some socialist feminists argue that it is more important to alter the external social
structures that channel women into motherhood and childrearing.[7] The most important single factor contributing to this channeling is probably the sex-segregated
job market, which keeps women in low-paid and low-status jobs. In these circumstances, childrearing appears to many women to be the only kind of fulfilling work
available to them. In order to take this option, however, a woman is forced economically to find a man who will help support her and her children. Because of men's economic privilege in the market, it is usually impossible for women to support the
family while men stay at home with the children. Their economic situation thus
tends to push women into childrearing, regardless of whether they have unconscious
drives toward mothering.

The socialist feminist conception of reproductive freedom seeks to enlarge wom-
en's options so that they are not forced to choose between childlessness and the
alienation of contemporary motherhood. It calls for economic security for women,
for paid maternity leaves and for the provision of publicly funded and community-
controlled childcare. If these were established, women would have the real option of
choosing motherhood without being forced to abandon or drastically limit their
participation in other kinds of work or to become economically dependent on a
man. These changes, particularly the assumption of public responsibility for
childcare, would make visible the way in which childrearing is real work and would
constitute an enormous step toward eliminating the public/private distinction.

If women were fully active participants in worthwhile work outside the home, enjoying the economic security and self-respect that such participation would bring, it
is doubtful that, from the child's point of view, a male presence would be required
for successful childrearing. Without the occurrence of these structural changes, several authors have expressed concern that male presence in childrearing could simply
deprive women of control over even this aspect of their work.[8] If these structural
changes were to occur, however, women would be in a stronger position to demand
that men should share the responsibility for childrearing. In these circumstances,
men might even want to do so. In these changed circumstances, too, childcare would
be less exhausting and alienated and this is one way in which increased reproductive
freedom for women could also result in increased reproductive freedom for men.

Included within the socialist feminist conception of reproductive freedom is a recognition of the necessity for sexual freedom. The statement of reproductive freedom
quoted earlier, for example, includes a call for "freedom of sexual choice." The an-
nouncement that reproductive freedom includes sexual freedom is not just an arbitrary definition nor is it an opportunistic attempt to cram as many good causes as
possible under one slogan. Instead, it is an explicit recognition that there exist not
only biological but also social connections between sexuality and procreation. Limi-

tations on women's procreative freedom have been used to control their sexual freedom; for instance, men in early societies used a ban on birth control to force monogamy on women.⁹ Conversely, limitations on women's sexual freedom have been used to control their procreative freedom; most obviously, forced heterosexuality has also forced women into motherhood. These are not the only connections between sexuality and procreation. As we shall see, there are a number of other reasons why sexual freedom for women is not possible without procreative freedom and procreative freedom is not possible without sexual freedom. Consequently, an adequate conception of reproductive freedom must include an ideal of sexual freedom.

Although there are in fact many connections between sexuality and procreation in women's lives, sexual and procreative freedom are possible only if the expressions of women's sexuality are viewed as activities which need not result in procreation. Feminists have not always recognized this: in the 19th century, many American feminists saw non-procreative sex as "a means for men to escape their responsibility to women. They saw contraception as a tool of prostitutes and as a potential tool of men in turning women into prostitutes."¹⁰ In the 20th century attitudes changed, partly because women were in fact achieving a degree of economic independence from men, partly because the pressures to bear large numbers of children were reduced. Increasingly, sexuality itself became a "question" and sexual pleasure began to be acknowledged as a legitimate aspiration of women. In the first part of the 20th century, however, it was men who defined sexual liberation, even for women, and the male definitions were blatantly self-serving. Female sexuality was characterized by Freud as inherently passive, masochistic and narcissistic—a perfect rationale for the sexual objectification of women and for sexual aggression toward them. Heterosexual intercourse was taken as the paradigm of sexual activity, and women were blamed for frigidity if they did not experience orgasm during intercourse.

With the rise of the contemporary women's liberation movement in the 1960s, feminists began a thoroughgoing critique of the prevailing conception of sexual liberation. They pointed out the coerciveness of heterosexual relations; they identified the alienation in the sexual objectification of women; they exploded the "myth of the vaginal orgasm";¹¹ they demystified the ideology of romantic love; they criticized the emphasis on an exclusively genital conception of sexuality, which ignored the possibilities for a more diffuse sexuality; they showed how dominance and submission were reinforced by being eroticized; above all, they identified the heterosexual norm as a means by which women were divided from each other. Women began to explore and define their own sexual needs, many of them in the context of lesbian relationships. Linda Gordon writes:

> The lesbian liberation movement has made possibly the most important contribution to a future sexual liberation. It is not that feminism produced more lesbians. There have always been many lesbians, despite high levels of repression; and most lesbians experience their sexual preference as innate and nonvoluntary. What the women's liberation movement did create was a homosexual liberation movement that politically challenged male supremacy in one of its most deeply institutionalized aspects—the tyranny of heterosexuality. The political power of lesbianism is a power that can be shared by all women who choose to recognize and use it: the power of an alternative, a possibility that makes male sexual tyranny escapable, rejectable—possibly even doomed.¹²

The abolition of compulsory heterosexuality would have an enormous impact on the system of male dominance. One effect might be to disrupt the way in which gender is imposed on the infant psyche, as described by Freud. Gayle Rubin has pointed out that the Freudian account of child development presupposes a norm of heterosexuality as well as a context of male dominance. Without this norm, girls would not have to give up their early attachment to their mothers. "If the pre-Oedipal lesbian were not confronted by the heterosexuality of the mother, she might draw different conclusions about the relative status of her genitals."[13] The abandonment of compulsory heterosexuality would reshape the sexuality both of girls and of boys and, if psychoanalysis is correct, would have tremendous consequences for the structure of the unconscious and for people's sense of their own gender identity. This speculation suggests a further way in which procreative freedom presupposes, sexual freedom.

Another connection between sexual and procreative freedom lies in women's tendency to become pregnant in order to compensate for unsatisfactory heterosexual relationships.[14] Sometimes, too, women become pregnant in an attempt to try to consolidate a heterosexual relationship.

> Women get pregnant "accidentally on purpose" as a way of punishing themselves. But they may also be protecting themselves and punishing men. Nothing illustrates better than reproduction that unless women can be free, men will never be. Pregnancy is woman's burden and her revenge.[15]

Thus, the connections between women's sexual and procreative activity are quite complicated, and sexual and procreative freedom for women are inseparable from each other. This is why the socialist feminist conception of reproductive freedom includes both aspects.

Comprehensive as it is, the socialist feminist conception of reproductive freedom is not a self-contained ideal which can be achieved or even understood simply with reference to sexuality and procreation. For instance, as we saw earlier, one of the preconditions of reproductive freedom for women is economic independence from men, without which reproductive freedom would degenerate into sexual and procreative exploitation. Thus, reproductive freedom requires the abolition of male dominance in the "public world." Linda Gordon points out that reproductive freedom also requires the abolition of hereditary class society:

> The prohibition on birth control was, as we have seen, related to the defense of class privilege. Today the powers and privileges that can be passed on to succeeding generations through the family are more varied: property, education, confidence, social and political connections. But the essential nature of class divisions is unchanged and depends on the generational passing down of status. Thus in class society children are never individuals and cannot escape the expectations, high or low, attached to their fathers' position. These expectations also distort the reproductive desires and childrearing practices of parents, making it more difficult for them to view their children as individuals.[16]

Once again, we see that full reproductive freedom is incompatible with the maintenance of capitalism and male dominance.

Socialist feminists are discovering that "in thought and practice, neat distinctions we once made between sex and class, family and society, reproduction and production, even between women and men seem not to fit the social reality with which we are coping."[17] Socialist feminist explorations of reproductive freedom illustrate this well by showing that reproductive freedom for women requires a transformation of what has been called traditionally the mode of production. Equally, however, a feminist transformation of the mode of production cannot be achieved without reproductive freedom for women or a transformation of the mode of procreation. Since one cannot precede the other and since both are dialectically related, both must occur together. Procreation and "production" in the narrow sense are simply two aspects of an integrated capitalist and male-dominant mode of producing and reproducing every aspect of life.

2. Women and Wages

Women have more than one workplace. A woman's place may be in the home when young children need care or when meals need to be prepared, but at other times, as one socialist feminist author put it, "a woman's place is at the typewriter."[18] Women are a steadily increasing proportion of the paid labor force in the United States, with mothers of young children constituting the fastest growing category.[19] Most women in the U.S. will engage in paid labor at some time in their lives. Whether or not it was once true to say that women were oppressed primarily in virtue of their exclusion from public production, it is true no longer.

Within the wage labor force, however, the sexual division of labor is almost as striking as the sexual division of labor between home and outside work. Token women can now be found in almost every category of paid labor, including coal mining, but women cluster predominantly in a relatively few occupations. The largest of these is clerical work: in 1977, more than one-third of all wage-earning women in the United States were clerical workers.[20] Clerical workers now constitute 20 percent of the paid labor force in the US and they are 80 percent female.[21] Women who are not clerical workers tend to work in retail sales or in service occupations such as social work, teaching, or nursing.

The categories of labor where women congregate are both the fastest growing and the lowest paid.[22] On average, a woman wage worker earns 59¢ for every dollar earned by a man. Low pay, however, is only one characteristic of women's paid work in contemporary society. Women's paid labor also tends to require from its workers those qualities that contemporary society describes as feminine: submissiveness, toleration of tedium, the ability to communicate and empathize with people, nurturance and sexual attractiveness to men.

The availability of a large "reserve army" of labor, prepared to work for relatively low wages and with relatively few fringe benefits, is obviously advantageous to capital. The existence of such a reserve pool of labor accommodates fluctuations in the demand for labor, exerts a downward pressure on all wages and, through the threat of strikebreaking, increases capitalist control over labor. This functionalist argument has often been used by Marxists to explain the sex-segregation of the wage labor force and it does have considerable explanatory value. What it fails to explain is why women constitute this reserve pool and why "women's work" acquires its specifically "feminine" character.

The nursing profession provides an excellent example of how work is defined not only by the categories of class and of the mental/manual distinction but also by the category of gender. Eva Gamarnikow explains that nursing in Britain was established during the 19th century as an occupation for women, and she shows how the assumption that nurses would be female influenced the definition of the work.[23] Nurses were defined as assistants and subordinates of the (male) physician; nursing was seen as less important than medicine, in spite of the fact that patients can be cured by nursing alone but rarely by medical treatment alone; nursing was seen as emotional rather than instrumental and so nurses were defined by their moral qualities (patience, humility, self-abnegation, neatness, cleanliness, punctuality, cheerfulness, kindness, tenderness and honesty) rather than by their professional skills. Around the turn of the century, explicit links were made between nursing and mothering and between nursing and women's domestic work. The good nurse was considered to have the same qualities as a good wife and mother.

The structure of contemporary health care is still defined by gender. A sharp distinction is still made between medicine and nursing, and medicine is still overwhelmingly a male profession while nursing is a female one. More than 92 percent of the physicians in the United States are male, while over 96 percent of the nurses are female. Tim Diamond has shown how traditional sex stereotypes still influence the respective definitions of medicine and nursing: medicine is concerned with curing specific maladies, it transforms sickness, often by "aggressive" means, and it charges for specific units of medical intervention; nursing, by contrast, is concerned with care rather than cure, it provides a service to the whole patient and it does not charge per unit for its services.

> The mode of human service for the nurse becomes indistinguishable from that of the wife, the mother or the nun. In the case of health services, the woman's world is, once again the emotive, the man's world, the instrumental: the nursing model is feminine, the medical model is masculine.[24]

The gendered structure of paid labor is equally obvious in education. In this field, women work mostly with very young children where education, nurturance, and physical care are inseparable, while men work mostly in higher education, dealing with adult students and abstract ideas. Contemporary conceptions of gender also influenced the redefinition of clerical work around the turn of the century. In 1870, men were 97.5 percent of the clerical labor force in the United States,[25] and a clerk was often viewed by his employer as "assistant manager, retainer, confidant, management trainee, and prospective son in law."[26] With the influx of women into clerical work, however, that work was redefined to fit the prevailing stereotype of femininity. The work became less skilled and more of a personal service. Good clerical workers were no longer required to have business acumen; instead, they were supposed to have the feminine qualities of docility, passivity and manual dexterity. Personal secretaries were supposed to be a cross between wives and mothers.[27]

An obvious example of the gendered definition of wage labor is the prevalence of physical appearance and sexual attractiveness as formal or informal requirements for women's jobs. Jobs with these requirements include not only prostitution and entertainment but also many service jobs such as being a waitress, stewardess or receptionist and forms of service work. Sexual attractiveness is not related logically to the performance of any of these jobs except prostitution and possibly entertainment (given current ideas about what is entertaining), but that it is an unstated requirement for women's employment is shown by the way in which employment becomes progressively more difficult for a woman to find as she gets older and becomes, according to conventional definitions, less sexually desirable.[28]

Even the low pay that women wage workers typically receive may be viewed in fact as a gendered characteristic. Women's low wages used to be justified on the grounds that a man was working to support his family, while a woman was working merely for "pin money." Many feminist authors have pointed out that this is false: millions of women are the sole support of their households, and the wage of many other women is necessary to lift their family income above the poverty level. Although the traditional rationale for women's low pay is less often stated explicitly nowadays, continuing low wages for women actually provide it with some basis in fact. Veronica Beechey has argued that new forms of wage labor are being created specifically for women at ever-lower real wages, often at less than the cost of their own subsistence.[29] Women can afford to work at these jobs only because they are part of a family unit whose chief support is the male wage. If Beechey's supposition is correct, the contemporary form of women's wage labor reinforces male dominance in two ways: on the one hand, the definitions of women's work reinforce the ideological perception of women as "naturally" nurturant, subservient and sexy; on the other hand, women's low wages make it very difficult for women, especially for mothers, to survive alone and women are forced into dependence on men. The fact that most women have been forced to form family units then can be used to justify continuing their low pay.

The genderization of wage labor means that women wage workers suffer a special form of alienation. They are not alienated simply as genderless (male!) workers; they are also alienated in ways specific to their sex. In order to earn a living, they are forced to exploit not only their physical strength and skill or their intellectual capacities; they are also forced to exploit their sexuality and their emotions.

Socialist feminist proposals for social change must take into account the special alienation of women outside the home. In developing their conception of free productive activity, it is not enough to talk in general terms about transcending the realm of necessity or about worker control of production. It is also necessary to talk about eliminating sex segregation in production, so that male workers do not end up controlling mining, forestry and the steel industries while female workers end up controlling laundry and food services. Traditional Marxists have always asserted that free productive activity requires the restructuring of the labor process so that it abandons a detailed division of labor and overcomes the distinction between conception and execution, mental and manual labor. Socialist feminists add that work must be redefined so as to eliminate the distinction between "masculine" and "feminine" work as well.

To overcome this distinction would not mean necessarily that all work would assume the characteristics of masculine work under contemporary capitalism, that all work would be impersonal, unemotional and asexual. Free productive labor in fact might be more similar to contemporary feminine work in that workers would be able to express their emotions and their sexuality and would view others as unique individuals. Unlike the contemporary situation for women workers, however, these forms of emotional and sexual expression would be freely chosen rather than coerced and alienated.

Marxism's ultimate solution to worker alienation has always been to overthrow the capitalist mode of production. To alleviate intolerable working conditions in the short term and as a transitional step on the way to its ultimate goal, Marxism has supported the organization of workers into trades unions. Trades unions allow workers to bargain collectively with their employers and also to exert collective influence in electoral politics. In the United States and in most other capitalist countries, a much higher proportion of male than female workers is unionized. Even where women are union members, most union officials are men, and unions tend to bargain for the issues of wages and working conditions that are of most concern to men. The specific interests of women are not well represented by existing unions.

In the United States, clerical work is the largest category of wage work that remains unorganized into unions.[30] It is also, of course, the largest category of women's wage work. Trade union officials have not been eager to "organize" clerical workers, explaining that the workers themselves do not want to be organized. Women clerical workers are said to be committed primarily to their families rather than to their paid jobs and to be too "feminine" to be militant.[31] In the 1970s, socialist feminists rejected these explanations and have begun to organize women workers, especially women clerical workers. They organize them not as genderless workers, however, but rather as workers who are women.

Some socialist feminist organizing efforts have resulted in the formation of union locals. Others have resulted in the formation of organizations that are not unions but that address the concerns of women office and service workers. "Active groups include Nine-to-Five in Boston; Women Office Workers in New York: Women Employed in Chicago; and Union Wage and Women Organized for Employment in San Francisco."[32] Many of the local groups affiliate with a national organizational network, Working Women. "They are hybrid groups, neither pure women's rights nor pure labor rights, but an amalgam of both evidencing women's great need for organizations that will advance their cause as women at work."[33]

Working women's organizations concentrate not only on the issues that have preoccupied the male trade union movement; they also focus on issues that are of specific concern to women. These issues include dress codes and expectations by bosses that women will provide "personal services" such as running errands or making coffee. Sexual harassment, of course, is one of the most important issues of concern. Sexual harassment seems to have been a problem for women as long as they have been employed in wage work.[34]

> It is consistent, systematic, and pervasive, not a set of random isolated acts. The license to harass women workers, which many men feel they have, stems from notions that there is a "woman's place" which women in the labor force have left, thus leaving behind their personal integrity. ...
>
> Words, gestures, comments can be used as threats of violence and to express dominance. Harassment often depends on this underlying violence—violence is implied as the ultimate response. Harassment is "little rape", an invasion of a person, by suggestion, by intimidation, by confronting a woman with her helplessness. It is an interaction in which one person purposefully seeks to discomfort another person. This discomfort serves to remind women of their helplessness in the face of male violence. To offer such a model is to suggest that it is not simply an individual interaction but a social one; not an act of deviance but a societally condoned mode of behavior that functions to preserve male dominance in the world of work.[35]

Today it is used "to control women's access to certain jobs; to limit job success and mobility; and to compensate men for powerlessness in their own lives."[36] Lin Farley cites innumerable examples of women who have been forced out of jobs by sexual harassment.[37] A few organizations, such as the Alliance Against Sexual Coercion in Boston, devote themselves entirely to combating this form of women's oppression.

An increasing proportion of the women who work for wages also have children. Because childcare is still predominantly women's work, women wage workers often have to perform two jobs. The stress of coping with the demands of both their paid and their unpaid work has had damaging consequences on women's health.[38] Women's entry in large numbers into the wage labor market has shown how 20th-century wage labor is defined implicitly, if not explicitly, as "men's work" insofar as it is structured on the assumption that the wage laborer is a man with a woman at home to do his laundry, cook his meals, rear his children, and provide him with emotional and sexual consolation. Without "wives," women and especially mothers pay enormous costs for their survival in wage labor.

Women wage workers are beginning to refuse to pay those costs. They are demanding the restructuring of non-procreative work so that it is compatible with parenting. Through their organizations, they are beginning to seek out not only the traditional benefits of adequate pay and job security; they are also seeking the provision of day care, paid maternity leaves, the availability of leave to look after sick children, and work hours that correspond to the school day.

Women are concerned not only about the structure of their wage labor; they are also concerned about their wage. Women's work is becoming increasingly "deprofessionalized" and more "proletarianized." That is to say, women wage workers have decreasing control over the conditions of their work, their work is becoming less skilled and their real wages are diminishing. These trends can be seen in education, in nursing and especially in clerical work. As women workers become more proletarianized, they are beginning to develop a more "proletarian" consciousness. In the spring and summer of 1974, nurses in Britain took industrial action for the first time;[39] nurses in the United States are also organizing.[40] Clerical workers are beginning to strike, and teachers' strikes are increasingly frequent. What should be noted is that, even when women strike for pay and not for specifically "women's" demands, their actions still have a different meaning from the same actions taken by male workers. When women workers achieve a living wage, they are not just workers winning a concession from capital: they are also women winning economic independence from men.

Women's experience in wage labor brings out more connections between women's procreative and their non-procreative work. For instance, the assumptions that women are wives and mothers influences definitions of women's work and rationalizes women's low pay. Just as economic independence for women is a precondition of reproductive freedom, so reproductive freedom is a precondition for an end to sexual segregation in other kinds of productive activity and for women's full participation in these.

In the 1970s, some women who defined themselves as socialist feminists began to demand that women should receive wages for that aspect of procreative work that hitherto had received no pay—the work of rearing their own children. The wages for housework movement began in the early 1970s in Italy, where relatively few mothers were employed in wage labor,[41] and spread across Europe to Britain and Canada. It never achieved much of a foothold in the United States, although Wages for Housework groups did spring up in a few U.S. cities. Wages for housework were demanded as a way of recognizing the value of the work that all women perform and also as a way of ensuring women economic independence from men. In the mid-1970s, the demand was debated frequently by feminists, but in the 1980s the movement seems to be disappearing. This may be because the continuing entry of women into existing forms of wage labor gives relatively fewer women any interest in defining themselves as paid houseworkers. It seems unlikely that pay for housework would be sufficient to raise its status and it would not diminish the isolation of women in the home. Even if the idea has merit in some circumstances as a tactical step toward women's liberation, the provision of wages for housework is incompatible in the long run with the goals of socialist feminism. It would reinforce the sexual division of labor to which feminists object and would extend the capitalist form of exploitation which socialists want to overthrow.

It is indeed this demand for the abolition of the wage system that most sharply distinguishes socialist feminists from liberal and radical feminists. Most of the specific issues around which socialist feminists organize are supported by feminists who are not socialists, but socialist feminism explains these issues in terms of exploitation and alienation, thus showing how male dominance cannot be eliminated without the abolition of capitalism.

3. Women and Organizational Independence

In 1865, Marx wrote:

> Trades Unions work well as centres of resistance against the encroachments of capital. They fail partially from an injudicious use of their power. They fail generally from limiting themselves to a guerilla war against the effects of the existing system, instead of simultaneously trying to change it, instead of using their organized force as a lever for the final emancipation of the working class, that is to say, the ultimate abolition of the wages system.[42]

Trade union consciousness is not revolutionary consciousness, as Marx well knew. The most that wage working women's organizations can hope to achieve is to modify contemporary wage labor so as to enable women to juggle two jobs. The goal of socialist feminism, however, is not for women to be able to juggle two jobs. It is to overthrow the whole social order of what some call "capitalist patriarchy" in which women suffer alienation in every aspect of their lives. The traditional Marxist strategy for revolution is to form a Leninist vanguard party. The socialist feminist strategy is to support some "mixed" socialist organizations, but also to form independent women's groups and ultimately an independent women's movement committed with equal dedication to the destruction of capitalism and the destruction of male dominance. The women's movement will join in coalitions with other revolutionary movements, but it will not give up its organizational independence.

Independent women's organizations are obviously a form of separatism: they do not accept male members, and they refuse permanent organizational links with "mixed" organizations. They are not separatist, however, in the radical feminist sense of requiring their members to have as little contact with men as possible outside the organization. Nor are they separatist in the sense that their ultimate goal is a "matriarchy," a "lesbian nation" or a society in which men and women are separated formally from each other. On the contrary, their goal is a society in which maleness and femaleness are socially irrelevant, in which men and women, as we know them, will no longer exist. Organizational independence for socialist feminists is thus a form of tactical separatism, a step on the way to an ultimate goal of complete integration between the sexes.

The need for independent women's organizations springs from the basic socialist feminist understanding of society as male-dominated. On this analysis, the interests of men are in some ways opposed to those of women, even though certain groups of men share a number of interests with certain groups of women. Men have an interest in maintaining their dominant position: in earning more than women, in having sexual power over women and in keeping the larger share of leisure time which results from their relative freedom from housework. Women have an immediate interest in getting rid of those male privileges and they need separate organizations to fight for this interest.

Some feminists deny the need for independent women's organizations. It is common for both liberals and Marxists to assert that the enemy that that women face as women is not men but the system of sexism. Traditional Marxists believe that, if women came to see men as their enemy, then they would not perceive the interests that women share with men as members of the working class. To state that women's enemy is the system rather than men themselves, however, is to ignore the question of who perpetuates that system and in whose interest it operates. Both men and women in fact help to perpetuate the system of male dominance (just as workers as well as capitalists help to perpetuate the capitalist system), but women's objective interests as women also encourage them to resist that system in many ways. Men, too, may sometimes resist the system of male dominance, but, because that system provides them with privileges, they are much less likely to resist it. Radical feminists perceive that the system of male dominance is enforced primarily by men, and so they draw the unambiguous conclusion that it is men who are the enemy for women.

In an obvious sense, men are the enemy for women, just as colonizers are enemy for the colonized and capitalists are the enemy for workers. In saying that men are the enemy for women, however, it is important to remember two things. One is that the enmity between women and men is part of a specific system of social relations which defines what it is to be a man and a woman; consequently, change in that system could eliminate the enmity between female and male persons. The enmity is not necessarily permanent. The other point to remember is that there are many other divisions in society as well as the division between the sexes: differences of nationality, race, age, ability, religion and class. Because these other divisions cut across sex lines, there are respects in which women have shared interests with men and in which men are not the enemy. For instance, colonized women have interests in common with colonized men, differently abled women have interests in common with differently abled men, girls have interests in common with boys, etc. In the same way, the working class of a colonized nation will cooperate with that nation's upper class in resisting colonization and, in the context of a struggle for national liberation, will not regard it as the enemy.

Radical feminists view men as "the main enemy"[43] of women because they claim that the subordination of women by men was the first form of oppression and that it remains causally basic to all other forms. Traditional Marxists, by contrast, view capitalists as the main enemy because they believe that this contemporary form of class oppression is now the main support of all other forms of oppression. Many traditional Marxists borrow Maoist terminology and justify their claim that capitalists are the man enemy by asserting that class (traditionally construed) is the "principal contradiction" in society today. Their arguments for this view are theoretical and tend to the conclusion that revolutionary activity should always focus on class struggle as traditionally understood. Hartmann and Markusen have pointed out that these sorts of Marxist arguments in fact misinterpret the notion of "principal contradiction." As developed by Mao, the notion was strategically rather than theoretically determined; it was designed to identify the focus of revolutionary activity in specific periods rather than in all situations.[44] Socialist feminists avoid not only the language of "primary" or "principal" contradiction but in general are suspicious of attempts to assert that either class or gender is causally basic to the other. They see the various systems of oppression as connected inseparably with each other and believe that it is mistaken to try to identify a single group as being permanently "the main enemy."

> We claim that in the current situation it is entirely in keeping with Marxist and Maoist tradition to see capitalist patriarchy at the root of the principal contradiction, to label the enemy as such, and to build a strategy that insists on the duality (and with racism and ageism, the multiple aspects) of the principal contradiction. We see the insistence on "class first" as an antifeminist practice, not a proworking class practice.[45]

Traditional Marxists argue that it is divisive to speak of men as the enemy, that it diverts the working class from its primary struggle against capitalism. They fear that if women join independent women's organizations rather than the "vanguard party," they will lose their revolutionary perspective, will mistake symptoms for causes and will focus on reforms for women rather than on the transformation of the system as a whole. These fears reveal distrust of women's revolutionary commitment and a belief that women cannot maintain their socialist vision without men to hold it continually before their eyes. They seem to overlook the fact that women, just as much as men, are members of the working class.

The organizations advocated by socialist feminists, however, are socialist as well as feminist. They are not dedicated simply to winning reforms for women or to integrating women into the capitalist system. Nor, on the other hand, are they dedicated simply to overthrowing the capitalist system and replacing it with a dictatorship of the male proletariat. They are concerned with the ways in which even working-class men perpetuate male dominance: through their resistance to affirmative action, through rape, through woman beating, through sexual harassment, through refusal to take an equal share of household responsibility—and through sexism in their revolutionary organizations. In order to combat male dominance, women must form their own independent organizations.

To say that socialist feminist women should form their own independent organizations is not to preclude them from also joining "mixed left" groups, not to deny that women's organizations should work with the mixed left. But independent women's organizations are necessary to ensure that women's voices are heard, both individually and collectively.

> Working class women and men must be allied in their struggle against the ruling class, but this alliance must be among equals: women should not be subordinate to men in a "revolutionary" movement. Equality of women and men requires a direct struggle against patriarchy and an autonomous power base for working class women. It is not

enough for the Party to organize women: women must become "subjects" of history, able to act in their own behalf.[46]

Ann Foreman agrees.

In short, the organized presence of women could prevent the traditional exclusion of women in both its crude and more sophisticated forms. And by asserting the right of women to define their own identity within political structures, the self-organization of women strikes at the heart of the feminine attitude of alterity on which this exclusion rests. Ultimately, then, autonomy provides a political and not simply an organisational link between the feminist and the working class struggle.[47]

Only the organizational independence of women can ensure that women's concerns are addressed and that women escape from their traditional role of "wives to the revolution."

4. Beginning at Start: Strategies for Social Transformation

Social feminist strategies for ending oppression seek to combine the traditional Marxist emphasis on changing the material conditions of life with the 20th-century emphasis on the importance of changing ideas and feelings. The special socialist feminist conception of human nature provides the basis for a distinctively socialist feminist approach to each of these aspects of human life.

All those who struggle against oppression must try to discover the underlying causes of that oppression and to separate these causes from the more superficial symptoms. Within the Marxist tradition, the distinction between the symptoms of a certain form of oppression and its underlying causes is formulated in terms of "base" and "superstructure." The "material base" of a certain form of oppression is taken to be those social relations which fundamentally sustain that form of oppression and which therefore must be transformed in order to eliminate that form of oppression. In investigating the fundamental causes of women's oppression, socialist feminists have developed a conception of material base as that set of social relations which structures the production and reproduction of the necessities of daily life, the production of people, including the production of sexuality, as well as the production of goods and services. On the socialist feminist view, these relations are simultaneously capitalist and male-dominant, and both aspects must be changed to liberate women.

The inclusiveness of the socialist feminist conception of the material base of women's oppression has implications for the socialist feminist conception of revolutionary strategy. Most obviously, the enlarged conception of the material base means that many more forms of political activity than previously thought can now be described as challenges to the basic system of social relations. For example, even when working women's organizations do not bring directly into question the capitalist mode of production, they do begin to challenge the gendered definition of women's work. Similarly, campaigns for various aspects of reproductive freedom, such as campaigns for free abortion, against rape and sexual harassment, and for free and community-controlled childcare all challenge existing male-dominant and capitalist relations of procreation and sexuality.

In addition to making direct challenges to the prevailing male dominant and capitalist mode of production, it is necessary also to challenge the system of ideas that justify and reinforce this mode of production. In the 20th century, even those political theorists who aspire to a materialist method have placed considerable emphasis on the importance of "consciousness" in explaining historical change—or the absence of change. These theorists have not denied the materialist insight that consciousness is determined in some ultimate sense by the material conditions of daily life, but they recognize that systems of ideas may establish considerable autonomy from the existing historical circumstances and may also have considerable causal influence on those circumstances. This recognition has been made by influential tendencies within the Marxist tradition whose theorists, as we have seen, have elaborated the notions of ideology, false consciousness and hegemony and have made a number of attempts to graft some form of Freudian psychology onto Marxist political economy. The same recognition has also been made by radical feminism, which has contributed the technique of consciousness raising to political practice and has emphasized "cultural" critique and re-creation. Socialist feminism is firmly in this 20th-century tradition and so claims that an effective revolutionary strategy must include techniques for demystifying the prevailing male-dominant and capitalist ideology and for developing alternative forms of consciousness, that is alternative ways of perceiving reality and alternative attitudes toward it.

A vital part of organizing for social change is the creation of a sense of political unity among oppressed groups. A class is identified not only by its "objective" position relative to the means of production, but also by its "subjective" sense of itself as having a common identity and common interests. Unless it is a class "for itself" as well as a class "in itself," the group will not move to political action. For instance, although the peasants in 19th-century France shared a common relation to production, Marx argued that their isolation from and poor communication with each other prevented them from developing a sense of community and shared political purpose.[48] Contemporary women are in a position that in some ways resembles that of 19th-century French peasants though in other ways it differs from theirs. By and large, as we have seen, women do share a common relation to production: unlike men, they are all responsible for housework, for childrearing, for emotional nurturance and for sexual gratification; in addition, they are clustered in a few gender-defined paid occupations. Insofar as they work together in the paid labor force, the conditions do exist for women to develop a shared political identity and, as we have seen, that is beginning to happen with the growth of working women's organizations. Insofar as they are isolated from each other in the family, it is much harder for women to develop a shared identity as workers in the home. In the late 1960s, the explosion of consciousness-raising groups showed the need that women felt to overcome their isolation, and many kinds of support groups still continue. In this context, socialist feminists agree with radical feminists that the creation of a women's culture is essential to facilitating women's sense of themselves as a group with common interests and to encourage their political organization.

During the 1970s, women's culture mushroomed in the advanced capitalist nations. There are now feminist novels, feminist science fiction, feminist dance troupes, feminist films, feminist theater groups, feminist music and feminist visual art. Moreover, women's past cultural productions are being retrieved and women's traditional crafts are being revived. In addition, there are cultural events, restaurants, etc. for women only, "womanspaces" in which women can be together physically and which foster a sense of community between women. The values expressed in the women's culture are quite diverse, even though they are all feminist in one way or another. At one extreme, they fantasize a world without men; at the other extreme, they show women "making it" in a man's world. Some feminist artists, such as Judy Chicago in her "The Dinner Party," show that women can be rulers, doctors, warriors, etc., just as well as men; others try to present alternative models of female achievement. The values presented depend in part on the intended audience and sometimes are modified to suit that audience. For instance, Marilyn French's best-selling novel *The Women's Room* ends with the central character walking alone on the beach, despairing of women's liberation or even of a degree of personal happiness, at least for feminist women. By contrast, the TV version of the book, perhaps in an attempt to make feminism palatable to an audience with less feminist sophistication than the readers of the book were presumed to possess, ended with the same character, smartly dressed, delivering a rousing feminist speech to a college audience and being wildly applauded.

As one aspect of feminist political activity, women's culture emphasizes the process as well as the product of artistic creation. Where possible, it uses collective rather than individual forms of creation and tries to minimize the gaps between creators, performers and technicians. It may also try to narrow the gap between artist and audience. The dance troupe Wallflower Order raises explicitly on the stage the question of process.

> Wallflower examines the problems of working collectively in one of their pieces. Lack of money, feeling fed up with seeming endless criticism and self-criticism, feeling closed in by the group, wanting to reach out to other people and not being certain how. These are real problems faced by all of us who have attempted to work collectively. And it is wonderful to see these problems portrayed on stage in a way that allows us to both examine our difficulties and to laugh at ourselves.[49]

Judy Chicago's "The Dinner Party" is accompanied on its travels by a film, "Right Out of History," which documents the four-year creation of the piece by a group of more than 400 people. Often the process of creating feminist art is imperfect; for instance, the process of creating "The Dinner Party" was clearly hierarchical and perhaps exploitative. Nevertheless, the very recognition by feminists of the importance of process raises important political questions about the relation between artistic and other kinds of production.

Socialist feminists view cultural work as a necessary part of political organization for social change. They do not accept uncritically all aspects of women's culture, but seek to encourage those aspects which explore new ways in which the artist and the community can relate to each other, which link women's oppression with that of other oppressed groups, and which emphasize the possibility of women's collective political action against their oppression. For socialist feminists, the creation of a women's culture is an important way in which women can develop political self-consciousness. Of course, such development is possible only because women do in fact already share objective political interests.

One of the interests shared by women is the availability of quality goods and services such as food, clothing, housing, medical care and education. Of course, everyone has an interest in these, but women have a special interest because it is they who, according to the prevailing division of labor, are responsible for making these goods and services directly available to their families. Women buy and cook food, buy or make clothing, furnish homes, take their children to the doctor and worry about schooling. Weinbaum and Bridges characterize this work as consumption work. They point out that it is time-consuming, exhausting and alienating.[50] Women who find this work intolerable have two options. One is to demand that the work be shared by men. This option challenges the sexual division of labor but has the disadvantages that men may not be available, that men's economic privilege puts them in a strong position to refuse and, finally, that this option does not make the goods and services any more available; it just gives somebody else the responsibility for procuring them. Women's other option is to organize politically against the unavailability of goods and services, and this option has often been chosen by working-class women. Women have taken the lead in forming tenants' unions, in boycotting expensive or racist stores or products, in protesting cutbacks in services such as welfare or childcare and in taking militant action against the high price of, for example, public utilities. Socialist feminists believe that all these "community based" political activities are necessary parts of the struggle for a socialist and feminist transformation of society.

In order to achieve a thoroughgoing socialist and feminist transformation of social relations, socialist feminists believe that a wide range of political activity is necessary. It includes community struggles, the organization of women against their alienation in wage labor, the creation of a distinctive socialist feminist culture and attempts to restructure sexual and childrearing relations. All these struggles must be linked together to ensure that the social transformation is total and that all aspects of women's alienation are overcome.

One obvious problem with the strategy as presented so far is that it offers no political priorities: it suggests that everything must be done at once. Socialist feminists refuse to assign permanent priority to any one type of political activity over the others; they believe that a socialist and feminist revolution cannot happen without struggle on all these fronts. Yet they do suggest some general criteria that socialist feminists might use in deciding where to direct their political energy. Charlotte Bunch offers five criteria that are similar to those proposed by other socialist feminist writers.

Material reforms should aid as many women as possible and should particularly seek to redistribute income and status so that the class, race and heterosexual privileges that divide women are eliminated. ...

Reform activities that help women find a sense of themselves apart from their oppressed functions and which are not based on the false sense of race, class, or heterosexual superiority are important. ...

Women need to win. We need to struggle for reforms that are attainable. ... Victories and programs, especially when linked to specific organizations, give us a clearer sense of what we can win and illustrate the plans, imagination, and changes that women will bring as they gain power. ...

Since winning one reform is not our final goal, we should ask if working on that issue will teach us new and important things about ourselves and society. Particularly when a reform fails, political education is important to motivate women to continue, rather than to become cynical about change. ...

As women, we want to improve the conditions of our daily lives. In order to do this, we must have power over the institutions—the family, schools, factories, laws, and so on—that determine those conditions ... above all, we should demand that those most affected by each institution have the power to determine its nature and direction. Initially, these challenges and reforms help to undermine the power of patriarchy, capitalism and white supremacy. Ultimately, these actions must lead to the people's control of all institutions so that we can determine how our society will function.[51]

With respect to her final criterion, Bunch suggests that one way of building power is by creating alternative institutions "such as health clinics that give us more control over our bodies or women's media that control our communications with the public." Bunch adds, "Alternative institutions should not be havens of retreat, but challenges that weaken male power over our lives."[52] In this sentence, Bunch sums up the difference between the socialist feminist conception of alternative institutions and the radical feminist conception of a womanculture. Radical feminists intend that their alternative institutions should enable women to withdraw as far as possible from the dominant culture by facilitating women's independence from that culture. They have high hopes for creating womanspace that provides a total contrast to patriarchal space and is a refuge from it. Socialist feminists, by contrast, argue that women's independence from the dominant male, white and capitalist culture is an impossible fantasy: they build alternative institutions as a way of partially satisfying existing needs and also as a way of experimenting with new forms of working together. The difference here between radical and socialist feminists is not clear-cut: both radical and socialist feminists might work on the same alternative project, such as a health center. But socialist feminists expect that social relations within the project will be distorted by the pressures of the larger society outside, and they do not anticipate that their project will become part of a permanent women's counterculture.

One institution to which some socialist feminists are seeking immediate alternatives is the stereotypical 20th-century nuclear family, with its familiar sexual division of labor, according to which the wife is assigned responsibility for childrearing and housework while the husband has responsibility for economic support of the family. Socialist feminists, like many other feminists, see this family structure as a cornerstone of women's oppression: it enforces women's dependence on men, it enforces heterosexuality and it imposes the prevailing masculine and feminine character structures on the next generation. In addition, the traditional nuclear family is a bulwark of the capitalist system insofar as it makes possible the use of women as a reserve army of labor, sustains a high level of demand for consumer goods, and inculcates in children the values of dominance and submission, of alienated labor and consumption and of competition. Many points in the socialist feminist critique of the family are identical with points made by traditional Marxists, but socialist feminists differ from traditional Marxists in their belief that immediate changes in living arrangements can be a significant part of a broader strategy for social transformation. Unlike traditional Marxists, socialist feminists do not believe that consciously designed changes in family structure must wait until "after the revolution." They believe that immediate changes are necessary in order to enable women to participate fully in the revolutionary process and to ensure that process is feminist as well as socialist.

Many commentators have pointed out that in fact the classic nuclear family is disappearing rapidly in advanced capitalist countries at the end of the 20th century. Increasing numbers of women, regardless of their politics, are living in alternatives to that family, either because they bring a second wage into the home or because they are bringing up children as single parents. What distinguishes socialist feminist alternatives is that they are self-conscious attempts to incorporate socialist feminist values in their daily living arrangements. These values include equality, cooperation, sharing, political commitment, freedom from sexual stereotyping and freedom from personal possessiveness.

Many socialist feminists live in family structures that are not obviously different from those of most other women: they are the structures of marriage or cohabitation with a man or of single motherhood. Within these relatively traditional structures, it is impossible to practice all the socialist feminist values. For instance, a single mother cannot model the range of alternatives possible for women and a heterosexual couple cannot demonstrate the validity of alternatives to heterosexuality. Even within these relatively traditional structures, however, many traditional values can be challenged: fathers and mothers can refuse the traditional sexual division of labor, reversing the traditional roles or sharing equally the responsibility for breadwinning and childcare; single mothers can hardly fail to present a model of an independent woman. It is in larger households, however, that the dominant values of possessiveness, privatism, emotional dependence and consumerism can be challenged more thoroughly. Larger socialist feminist households may be all women or may include men. Ann Ferguson lists seven goals for such socialist and feminist "revolutionary family-communities":

1. To alter childrearing inequalities between men and women, to provide the structural base for men and women to be *equal nurturers* to children and to each other as well as *equally autonomous* ...

2. To challenge the sexual division of labor ...

3. To break down the possessive privacy of the two primary sets of relationships in the American patriarchal family: the couple and the parent-child relationship ...

4. To equalize power as far as possible between parents and children and, in general, between adults and children ...

5. To eliminate the base for heterosexism in a society which, along with patriarchy and capitalism, contributes to women's oppression. This means openly allowing gay persons, including gay mothers and fathers, openly into the revolutionary family-community ...

6. To break down elitist attitudes about the superiority of mental and professional work to manual work.

7. To deal with racism and classism.

8. To introduce economic sharing in the family-community which allows its members to develop a sense of commitment to each other.[53]

Ferguson realizes that no single revolutionary family-community can achieve all these goals easily, if at all. In addition to the "internalized" psychological problems of emotional insecurity, jealousy, competitiveness or heterosexism, such communities are subject to external or social constraints: women will find it harder than men to obtain adequately paying jobs, and people's work or study plans may require them to leave the area. Revolutionary family-communities are certainly not envisioned as utopian refuges from male dominance, racism and capitalism. They are places where people can experiment with new ways of organizing childrearing and sexuality, prefiguring, though imperfectly, some of the new forms of social relations that will be part of a socialist feminist revolution. In the meantime, they will also provide people with the "material support needed to continue to challenge the combined domination systems of capitalist patriarchy."[54]

Delores Hayden recognizes that only a relatively few women are ready for the revolutionary family-communities outlined by Ferguson. For those who are not ready, Hayden proposes the less immediately radical alternative of HOMES: Homemakers Organized for a More Equal Society.[55] HOMES groups would own housing cooperatively. Their property would contain private dwelling units and some private, fenced, outdoor space, but it would also include public outdoor areas and the facilities to provide a number of services, such as childcare, laundry, food preparation, van transportation and home help for the elderly, the sick and employed parents whose children are sick. Existing suburban blocks could be converted for use by HOMES groups. In designing their living arrangements, Hayden states that HOMES should be guided by the following principles to

> (1) involve both men and women in the unpaid labor associated with housekeeping and child care on an equal basis; (2) involve both men and women in the paid-labor force on an equal basis; (3) eliminate residential segregation by class, race, and age; (4) eliminate all federal, state, and local programs and laws which offer implicit or explicit reinforcement of the unpaid role of the female homemaker; (5) minimize unpaid domestic labor and wasteful energy consumption; (6) maximize real choices for households concerning recreation and sociability.[56]

Alternative living arrangements are one way in which socialist feminists seek to translate into practice their insight that the personal is political. Another way is in their general concern for the process as well as the product of political activity. They are aware that organizational form is not politically neutral, and they have seen how the centralized and hierarchical forms of traditional political organization have perpetuated the subordination and passivity of women—and of other groups. Like radical feminists, socialist feminists are experimenting with new forms of organizational structure that can help people to overcome the partial and distorted development of their capacities that has been imposed by the capitalist and male-dominant division of labor. Without direct efforts to contradict these distorted developments of contemporary human nature, revolutionary organizations will only reinforce that which the are ostensibly struggling against. A hierarchical, undemocratic, sexist and racist organization can achieve only a hierarchical, undemocratic, sexist and racist "revolution."

Although they seek to avoid replicating within their own organizations the division of labor imposed by the dominant society, socialist feminists do not go to the opposite extreme of insisting that everybody should do every job. In a sensitive discussion of the problems involved in restructuring the labor process, Nancy Hartsock points out that alienation does not result simply from specialization in one kind of work, but rather from the social relations within which, in contemporary society, specialized work is usually performed. Within these relations, work is coerced and execution is separated from conception. Hartsock believes that a socialist feminist restructuring of the labor process can avoid both coercion and the separation of execution from conception without requiring that everyone should do everything:

> By rotating all members through the various tasks of the group, and by insisting that every member of a collective do every activity that the group as a whole is engaged in, the

collective, in practice, treats its members as interchangeable and equivalent parts. It reproduces the assembly line of the modern factory, but instead of running the work past the people, people are run past the work.[57]

Hartsock suggests that a better alternative is to allow individuals or groups to have responsibility for whole aspects of projects, involving both planning and executing the work to be done.

> Having responsibility for some parts of the work done by a group allows us not only to see our own accomplishments but also to expand ourselves by sharing in the accomplishments of others. We are not superwomen, able to do everything. Only by sharing in the different accomplishments of others can we participate in the activities of all women.[58]

In their recognition of the inseparability of means from ends, socialist feminists are closer to radical feminists than to any other group of feminists. Unlike radical feminists, however, socialist feminists do not see themselves as "living the revolution." This is true for two reasons. First, socialist feminists recognize the ways in which the larger society imposes limits on the possibilities of alternative ways for living and working.

> Our strategies for change and the internal organization of work must grow out of the tension between using our organizations as instruments for both taking and transforming power in a society structured by power understood only as domination and using our organizations to build models for a society based on power understood as energy and initiative ... There are real pressures to reproduce the patterns of estranged labor in the interests of efficiency and taking power. At the same time, there are pressures to oppose estranged labor by insisting that each of us do every job.[59]

The other reason why socialist feminists do not see themselves as "living the revolution" is because they do not think that social transformation can occur through the gradual accretion of socialist and feminist reforms and through the gradual undermining of dominant by alternative institutions. Radical feminists depend on slow, evolutionary rather than sudden, revolutionary change both for moral and practical reasons. On the one hand, they eschew the use of force as a patriarchal tactic; on the other hand, even the potential constituency of radical feminism is so small that there seems little chance of its winning over those women they see as their potential allies. Socialist feminists expect that there will be a distinctive revolutionary period, characterized by acute social turmoil, but they also expect that the outcome of this turmoil will be determined by the kind and quality of the pre-revolutionary activity that has preceded it. To this extent, they see themselves not so much as living the revolution as preparing for it and attempting in limited ways to prefigure it.

The socialist feminist contribution to revolutionary strategy is not simply to add women's issues to the list of concerns that a revolutionary movement must address. Socialist feminism does indeed broaden the traditional Marxist conception of revolutionary struggle to include, for instance, reproductive freedom. But ultimately socialist feminism denies the separation between so called class issues, race issues and women's issues. It argues that every issue is a women's issue, just as every issue has race and class implications. That is to say, socialist feminism argues that a feminist perspective can illuminate understanding not only of family life or of education but also of foreign policy, of imperialism and of political organization. To ask how a certain practice or institution affects women is different from asking how it affects the

working class or the colonized nation as a whole. Because male dominance structures every area of life, a foreign policy based on explicit concern for women's interests would be quite different from a foreign policy that was based only on a concern
for the working class conceived as a unified whole or for some ethnic minority
within that class. On the socialist feminist view, it is necessary to approach all political issues with a consciousness that is explicitly feminist as well as explicitly anti-rac-
ist and explicitly socialist. This consciousness will change both the form and the content of revolutionary political practice.

Notes

1. CARASA (Committee for Abortion Rights and Against Sterilization Abuse), *Women Under Attack: Abortion, Sterilization Abuse, and Reproductive Freedom* (New York: CARASA,
1979), p. 11 (italics in original).
2. Rosalind Pollack Petchesky, "Reproductive Freedom: Beyond 'A Woman's Right to
Choose,'" *Signs: Journal of Women in Culture and Society* 5, no. 4 (Summer 1980):662. This paper is reprinted in Catharine R. Stimpson and Ethel Spector Person, eds., *Women, Sex and
Sexuality* (Chicago and London: University of Chicago Press, 1980), pp. 92–116.
3. Ibid., pp. 669–70.
4. For a more extended discussion of this claim, see my "Abortion and a Woman's Right to
Decide," *Philosophical Forum* 5, nos. 1–2 (Winter 1975). Reprinted in Robert Baker and Frederick Elliston, eds., *Philosophy & Sex* (Buffalo, N.Y.: Prometheus Books, 1975), pp. 324–37.
5. Dinnerstein, *The Mermaid and the Minotaur*.
6. Nancy Chodorow, *Mothering: Psychoanalysis and the Sociology of Gender* (Berkeley and
Los Angeles: University of California Press, 1978). ...
7. One who has made this argument is Ann Ferguson, panel discussant of Nancy
Chodorow's book, Radical Caucus/Society for Women in Philosophy Joint Session, Eastern
Division meetings of the American Philosophical Association, Boston, 29 December 1980.
8. Petchesky, "Reproductive Freedom," p. 682. Also Adrienne Rich, "Compulsory Heterosexuality and Lesbian Existence," *Signs: Journal of Women in Culture and Society* 5, no. 4 (Summer 1980):638.
9. Linda Gordon, "The Struggle for Reproductive Freedom: Three States of Feminism" in
Zillah R. Eisenstein, ed., *Capitalist Patriarchy and the Case for Socialist Feminism*, (New York:
Monthly Review Press, 1979), p. 109. A number of the following points are made by Gordon in
her excellent essay.
10. Ibid., p. 113.
11. Anne Koedt, "The Myth of the Vaginal Orgasm," in Ann Koedt, Ellen Levine, and Anita
Rapone, eds., *Radical Feminism*, (New York: Quadrangle Books, 1973), pp. 198–207. The article
was first published in 1970 in *Notes from the Second Year*.
12. Gordon, "Struggle for Reproductive Freedom," p. 123.
13. Gayle Rubin, "The Traffic in Women: Notes on the 'Political Economy' of Sex," in Rayna
R. Reiter, ed., *Toward an Anthropology of Women* (New York: Monthly Review Press, 1975), p.
187. Abridged version reprinted in Alison M. Jaggar and Paula R. Struhl, eds., *Feminist Frameworks: Alternative Theoretical Accounts of the Relations between Women and Men* (McGraw-
Hill, 1978), p. 164.
14. Godon, "Struggle for Reproductive Freedom," p. 127.
15. Ibid., p. 127.
16. Ibid., pp. 123–24.
17. Joan Kelly, "The Doubled Vision of Feminist Theory: A Postscript to the 'Women and
Power' Conference," *Feminist Studies* 5, no. 1 (Spring 1979):220.

18. Margery Davies, "Woman's Place Is at the Typewriter: The Feminization of the Clerical Labor Force," in Eisenstein, ed., *Capitalist Patriarchy*, pp. 248–66.

19. The participation of women in the paid labor force has steadily increased since 1947, while that of men has steadily decreased. Harry Braverman, *Labor and Monopoly Capital: The Degradation of Work in the Twentieth Century* (New York: Monthly Review Press, 1974), chap. 17.

20. *Employment and Earnings*, January 1978, pp. 151–53. Cited by Evelyn Nakano Glenn and Roslyn L. Feldberg, "Clerical Work: The Female Occupation," in Jo Freeman, ed., *Women: A Feminist Perspective*, 2nd ed. (Palo Alto, CA: Mayfield Publishing Co., 1975), p. 317.

21. Karen Nussbaum, "Women Clerical Workers," *Socialist Review* 49, pp. 151–59.

22. Braverman, *Labor and Monopoly Capital*, p. 391. Cf. also Pat Armstrong and Hugh Armstrong, *The Double Ghetto: Canadian Women and Their Segregated Work* (Toronto: McClelland and Stewart, 1978), chap. 2.

23. Eva Gamarnikow, "Sexual Division of Labour: The Case of Nursing," in Annette Kuhn and AnnMarie Wolpe, eds., *Feminism and Materialism: Women and Modes of Production* (London: Routledge & Kegan Paul, 1978), pp. 96–123.

24. J. Timothy Diamond, "The Dialectical Relationship of Medicine and Nursing: A Proposal for Research" (unpublished), December 1978, p. 16.

25. Davies, "Woman's Place Is at the Typewriter," p. 249.

26. Braverman, *Labor and Monopoly Capital*, p. 294.

27. Davis, "Woman's Place Is at the Typewriter."

28. Lin Farley, *Sexual Shakedown: The Sexual Harassment of Women on the Job* (New York: Warner, 1978), pp. 131–37.

29. Veronica Beechey, "Women and Production: A Critical Analysis of Some Sociological Theories of Women's Work," in Kuhn and Wolpe, eds., *Feminism and Materialism*, pp. 155–97. Tim Diamond brought this article to my attention.

30. Glenn and Feldberg, "Clerical Work," p. 331.

31. Ibid., p. 331.

32. Ibid., p. 334.

33. Nussbaum, "Women Clerical Workers."

34. Mary Bularzik, "Sexual Harassment at the Workplace: Historical Notes," *Radical America*, July–August 1978, p. 2. Reprinted as a pamphlet by the New England Free Press, 60 Union Square, Somerville, Mass. 02143.

35. Ibid., p. 2.

36. Ibid., p. 2.

37. Farley, *Sexual Shakedown*.

38. Jeanne Mager Stellman, *Women's Work, Women's Health: Myths and Realities* (New York: Pantheon, 1977).

39. "This is Nursing: Introduction to a Struggle," in Wendy Edmond and Suzie Fleming, eds., *All Work and No Pay: Women, Housework, and the Wages Due* (Bristol: Power of Women Collective and Falling Wall Press, 1975), p. 61.

40. The Boston Nurses Group, "The False Promise: Professionalism in Nursing," *Science for the People*, May–June 1978 and July–August 1978. Reprinted as a pamphlet by the New England Free Press.

41. The most influential statement in English of the Italian wages for housework movement was Mariarosa Dalla Costa and Selma James, *The Power of Women and the Subversion of the Community*, 3rd ed. (Bristol: Falling Wall Press, 1975). A shorter statement is Giuliana Pompei, "Wages for Housework" in *WOMEN: A Journal of Liberation* 3, no. 3 (1972):60–62. A good short critique of the position is Carol Lopate's "Women and Pay for Housework," *Liberation*, June 1974, pp. 8–11. Both articles are reprinted in Jaggar and Struhl, eds., *Feminist Frameworks*. More arguments in favor of wages for housework can be found in Edmond and Fleming, eds., *All Work and No Pay*.

42. Karl Marx, "Wages, Price and Profit, in Karl Marx and Frederick Engels, *Selected Works* (New York: International Publishers, 1968), p. 229.

43. This is the title of an influential pamphlet by Christine Delphy: *The Main Enemy: A Materialist Analysis of Women's Oppression*, trans. by Lucy ap Roberts and Diane Leonard Barker (London: Women's Research and Resources Centre Publications, 1977).

44. Heidi I. Hartmann and Ann R. Markusen, "Contemporary Marxist Theory and Practice: A Feminist Critique," *The Review of Political Economics* 12, no. 2 (Summer 1980):91.

45. Ibid.

46. Charlotte Perkins Gilman Chapter of the New American Movement, "A Socialist-Feminist Response to the Durham Organizing Collective's 'Towards a Marxist Theory on Women's Oppression and a Strategy for Liberation'" (mimeographed), circulated in the mid-1970s.

47. Foreman, *Femininity as Alienation*, p. 157.

48. Karl Marx, "The Eighteenth Brumaire of Louis Bonaparte," in Marx and Engels, *Selected Works*, pp. 171–72. I owe this reference to Ann Ferguson, "Women as a New Revolutionary Class in the United States," in Pat Walker, ed., *Between Labor and Capital* (Boston: South End Press, 1979), p. 285.

49. Part of the publicity for Wallflower Order, said to be from a review of the Wallflower's performance in Vancouver and an interview with them in *Kinesis*, 1980.

50. Batya Weinbaum and Amy Bridges, "The Other Side of the Paycheck: Monopoly Capital and the Structure of Consumption," *Monthly Review*, July–August 1976. Reprinted in Eisenstein, ed., *Capitalist Patriarchy and the Case for Socialist Feminism*, p. 198.

51. Charlotte Bunch, "The Reform Tool Kit," in *Building Feminist Theory: Essays from Quest* (New York: Longman, 1981), pp. 197–98. Similar lists are given by the Hyde Park Chapter, Chicago Women's Liberation Union, *Socialist Feminism: A Strategy for the Women's Movement*, a pamphlet published in 1972, pp. 9–15; and by Nancy Hartsock, "Political Change: Two Perspectives on Power," in *Building Feminist Theory*, p. 17.

52. Ibid., p. 198.

53. Ann Ferguson, "The Che-Lumumba School: Creating a Revolutionary Family-Community," *Quest: A Feminist Quarterly* 5, no. 3 (Feb./Mar. 1980):15–17.

54. Ibid., p. 1.

55. Dolores Hayden, "What Would a Non-Sexist City Be Like? Speculations on Housing, Urban Design, and Human Work," *Signs: Journal of Women in Culture and Society, Special Issue: Women and the American City* 5, no. 3 (Supplement Spring 1980).

56. Ibid., p. 181.

57. Nancy Hartsock, "Staying Alive," in *Building Feminist Theory*, p. 120.

58. Ibid., p. 119.

59. Ibid., p. 121.

Suggested Further Readings

Berch, Bettina. *The Endless Day: The Political Economy of Women and Work.* New York: Harcourt Brace Jovanovich, 1982.

Delphy, Christine. *Close to Home: A Materialist Analysis of Women's Oppression,* trans. and ed. Diana Leonard. Amherst: University of Massachusetts Press, 1984.

Eisenstein, Zillah, ed. *Capitalist Patriarchy and the Case for Socialist Feminism.* New York: Monthly Review Press, 1979.

Foreman, Ann. *Femininity as Alienation: Women and the Family in Marxism and Psychoanalysis.* London: Pluto Press, 1977.

Jaggar, Alison, M. *Feminist Politics and Human Nature.* Totowa, N.J.: Rowman & Allanheld, 1983.

Martin, Gloria. *Socialist Feminism: The First Decade, 1966–1976.* Seattle: Freedom Socialist Publications, 1978.

Mitchell, Juliet. *Woman's Estate.* New York: Pantheon Books, 1971.

Nicholson, Linda J. *Gender and History: The Limits of Social Theory in the Age of the Family.* New York: Columbia University Press, 1986.

Rowbotham, Sheila, Lynne Segal, and Hilary Wainwright. *Beyond the Fragments: Feminism and the Making of Socialism.* London: Merlin Press, 1979.

Sarget, Lydia, ed. *Women and Revolution: A Discussion of the Unhappy Marriage of Marxism and Feminism.* Boston: South End Press, 1981.

Tong, Rosemarie. *Feminist Thought: A Comprehensive Introduction.* Boulder: Westview Press, 1989.

Vogel, Lise. *Marxism and the Oppression of Women: Towards a Unitary Theory.* New Brunswick: Rutgers University Press, 1983.

Weinbaum, Batya. *The Curious Courtship of Women's Liberation and Socialism.* Boston: South End Press, 1978.

Young, Iris Marion. *Throwing Like a Girl and Other Essays in Feminist Philosophy and Social Theory.* Part One: Socialist Feminism, pp. 21–70. Bloomington: Indiana University Press, 1990.

S I X

ANARCHA FEMINIST AND

ECOLOGICAL FEMINIST

PERSPECTIVES

Anarcha feminism arose in response to perceived limitations of both liberal and Marxist feminism and was influenced by classical anarchist theory. Strongly committed to the development of anarchist communities, anarcha feminism is more grounded in political action than some other feminist perspectives. Because much of the equally practice-oriented ecofeminist movement developed out of the concerns and principles of anarcha feminism, we have decided to group these two feminist movements together both to give recognition to their connections and to recover the importance of the anarchist feminist tradition.[1]

The anarchist tradition of such thinkers as Mikhail Bakunin, William Godwin, Emma Goldman, Petr Kropotkin, and Max Stirner, although not homogeneous, stressed three common tenets: (1) the value of individual freedom and community, (2) the invidiousness of all forms of domination, (3) and the links between personal and public life.[2] Although anarcha feminists focus on the importance of individual freedom—defining this to involve both self-definition and self-respect—they recognize that individual freedom can exist only within and because of community. Individuals develop as persons by forming and maintaining mutually enhancing relationships devoid of any traces of domination.

Because they have always strived to balance the values of individual freedom and communal responsibility, anarcha feminists have been particularly sensitive to the multiple forms of domination in contemporary Western society. They have argued that any form of hierarchy—whether it be based on age, class, race, religion, sex, or social position—is detrimental to the type of society necessary for individual development. In their collective contribution to this volume, "Anarchism and Feminism," Kathryn Pyne Addelson, Martha Acklesberg, and Shawn Pyne explain that "human freedom is a social product: Freedom and community are compatible, but communities need to be structured in particular ways to support and make possible that freedom. That means that the structure supporting that freedom must be egalitarian—that is, there should be no need of hierarchies of authority and privilege." Thus, in the estimation of Addelson, Acklesberg, and Pyne, anarcha feminists aim to abolish economic, political, and social hierarchies as well as hierarchies between the human and nonhuman worlds: "Instead of conquering nature, people should orient themselves to finding new ways to live in harmony with our physical surroundings." They also aim to reveal the intimate connections between personal and public life. A person's community profoundly affects his or her nature. Thus anarcha feminists argue that in centralized, hierarchical societies, individuals will develop competitive traits and habits of acquisition rather than the cooperative virtues and modes of sharing they would most likely develop in decentralized, nonhierarchical communities.

Anarcha feminists critique liberal feminists for their failure to reject hierarchy and privilege; they see liberal feminism as concerned only to make privilege gender-blind. For the same reason, anarcha feminists also fault those Marxist feminists who involve themselves in hierarchical revolutionary organizations. A central tenet of anarcha feminism is that in removing all forms of domination, the process of revolution must itself take place in and through structures that are consistent with the type of society and social relations at which the revolution is aimed.

Kathy E. Ferguson, for example, argues in her essay, "Bureaucracy and Public Life: The Feminization of the Polity," that the goals of feminism will not be met until all hierarchical and bureaucratic structures are removed from human communities as well as from the relationships between human and nonhuman communities. In keeping with anarcha feminist principles, Ferguson supports the importance of individual freedom and insists that communities be organized in ways that provide individuals with an adequate basis for developing self-respect. She offers an analysis of bureaucratic behavior that illustrates the ways in which the institutional arrangements of a bureaucratic society are antithetical to the goals of anarcha feminism.

Ferguson contends that institutions that perpetuate dominance-subordination relations feminize those individuals in the subordinate role. Arguing that feminine traits are associated not with biology but with "being politically powerless and with learning to play the role of subordinate in social relations," Ferguson calls our attention to the ways in which individuals—women and men alike—are feminized through oppression. In particular, she describes how successfully the welfare system, a bureaucratic institution if there ever was one, imposes these disempowering feminie traits upon its clients.

Ynestra King's chapter, "Healing the Wounds: Feminism, Ecology, and the Nature/Culture Dualism," reminds us that we will not succeed in eliminating the hierarchical relations that plague the human social order unless we also eradicate those that regulate the relationships between the human social order and nonhuman nature. She contends that the denigration of women and men of color, of working-class women and men, and of animals has its material origins in the subjugation of women by men. The male-female relationship as currently constituted is, in King's estimation, the paradigm for any and all hierarchical relationships. Thus, its reconstitution is imperative.

Ecofeminists rightly note that except for anarcha feminist, no feminist perspective has recognized the importance of healing the nature/culture division. Anarcha feminism emphasizes that all forms of domination—and any institutions, theories, and practices that give rise to it—must be abolished. King's essay illustrates the "reinterpretation" aspect of this anthology, not because she critiques the traditional philosophical canon but because she looks at the ways in which other feminist theories—liberal, radical, and socialist ones—must be extended through the insights of anarcha feminism and ecofeminism.

Although ecofeminism aroce out of the fundamental tenets of anarcha feminism, ecofeminism's central concern is the relationship between human and nonhuman nature. King explains that "an analysis of the interrelated dominations of nature—psyche and sexuality, human oppression, and nonhuman nature—and the historic position of women in relation to those forms of domination is the starting point of ecofeminist theory." Ecofeminism, then, argues that along with addressing the oppressions of women and certain groups of men, feminism must also work to understand and fight against all forms of the oppression of nonhuman nature.

As example that King does not give but that serves to highlight her concern is the human community's recent decision to raid the animal community for bodily organs. Because of a shortage of human organ donors and also the failure of scientists to create artificial organs, the research community has focused its attention on animal "donors." If human beings are not generous enough, even in death, to share their organs with those who need them, then so be it. We humans will simply take the necessary organs from living animals—be it a liver from a pig or a heart from a chimp—without worrying about the violence we perpetuate within the nonhuman world. Someone like King might well respond that there are alternatives to this quintessential form of oppression. We humans can, it is to be hoped, be socialized to share what is, after all, a bodily part we will have no need of once we take our last breath.

Notes

We gratefully acknowledge the advice of Kathryn Pyne Addelson in organizing this section and compiling the list of further readings.

1. The most influential discussions of the different types of feminism, including both Jaggar and Struhl's *Feminist Frameworks* (New York: McGraw Hill, 1993) and Tong's *Feminist Thought* (Boulder: Westview, 1989), do not include anarcha feminism. As a result, the importance of this perspective to the development of feminist theory and practice in the United States and its relations to the contemporary and far more widely known ecofeminist movement are not fully appreciated by many scholars.

2. See, for example, Emma Goldman, "Anarchism: What It Really Stands For," in *Anarchism and Other Essays,* ed. Richard Drinnon (New York: Dover Publications, 1969); Michael Bakunin, *Michael Bakunin: Selected Writings,* ed. Arthur Lehning (New York: Grove Press, 1974); Petr A. Kropotkin, *Kropotkin's Revolutionary Pamphlets,* ed. Roger Baldwin (New York: Dover Publications, 1970).

Anarchism and Feminism

Kathryn Pyne Addelson, Martha Ackelsberg, and Shawn Pyne

I. In Search of a Tradition

Every art or applied science and every systematic investigation, and similarly every action and choice, seem to aim at some good; the good, therefore, has been well defined as that at which all things aim.

—Aristotle, *Nicomachean Ethics*

Asking what the point of an activity is, gives us a way of evaluating some things people are doing. For example, if we ask what the point of doing science is, we can probably agree that the ultimate point is to give us all scientific knowledge and to contribute to people's having good, fulfilling lives. We can then evaluate what our scientists are doing by seeing whether they make that point or not.

We can ask, What's the point of our all being gathered together in a democratic, capitalistic, bureaucratic United States? And the answer to that seems to be that the point of our people's activities being organized in that way is to bring them to having good lives. A good life means having enough to eat and a roof over your head, of course. Once those are given, it involves more. In the past, supporters of "the American way of life" have explicitly argued that *our* way is the best way to achieve that goal and they point to our high standard of living and our liberties as evidence.

We think the basis of feminist criticism in the United States has been that our society does not, or cannot, make good, fulfilling lives for all our people. This is the most fundamental criticism we can make of our society: It fails to fulfill the point of its existence. Different feminists have made the criticism in different ways. Betty Friedan's *Feminine Mystique* (1974) was a force in starting the "second wave" of the women's movement in the United States early in the 1960s (the first wave was in the late-nineteenth and early-twentieth centuries). That book is an analysis of how and why the United States doesn't allow a good life for middle-class women. Betty Friedan says,

Equality and human dignity are not possible for women if they are not able to earn. ... Only economic independence can free a woman to marry for love not for status or financial support, or to leave a loveless intolerable humiliating marriage, or to eat, dress, rest, and move if she plans not to marry. But the importance of work for women goes beyond economics. How else can women participate in the action and decisions of an advanced industrial society unless they have the training and opportunity and skills that come from participating in it? (1974, 371)

Betty Friedan is a liberal, and most of us here are probably not liberals. But we believe that all members of what came to be called the women's liberation movement acted fundamentally out of the belief that our "democratic, capitalist, bureaucratic United States" does not and cannot fulfill the point of its existence. It cannot give people full lives, and so it must be changed.

If we can criticize whole societies for not fulfilling the point of their existence, we can also ask about revolutionary movements. We can ask if, at any given moment, they are acting so as to fulfill their goals. And we can ask if in fact their goals are good goals. There are two parts to any movement for change. One criticizes the existing society for not fulfilling its aims. The other is a creative part that moves the revolutionary movement toward fulfilling its own goal. On this creative side, feminists have spoken for and worked for making a society in which people have a better possibility for good lives.

On the critical side, most feminists in the United States take hierarchy and privilege in our society to be main factors preventing people from having good lives. Hierarchy involves patterned ways of interacting and behaving. In a hierarchy, people (or at least the roles they fill) are ranked, and interactions among them occur through this ranking. The interactions are not all one way. Those below can provide some information to those above. Those below, at times, are *allowed* some independent decision power. But the word *allowed* is crucial. According to the structure, all decisions are made from higher-up points and filtered down. Generally, too, status, prestige, money, and greater degrees of freedom accompany higher-up positions.

In developing analysis and strategy for confronting hierarchy and privilege, feminists have turned to a number of different political traditions. Some (for example, Betty Friedan) begin with the liberal tradition, looking at what it has to say about hierarchy, and then adapt its methodology and approach to the question of women's subordination in society. Others turn to the Marxist-socialist tradition and attempt to modify its approach to incorporate subordination on the basis of sex, as well as of class. Still others (for example, radical feminists) have rejected both approaches, and argued that an analysis and strategy adequate to deal with women's subordination must be developed on a totally new basis. We will argue that while each of these perspectives has something to contribute to the development of feminist theory and practice, the tradition with the greatest potential for contemporary feminism is that of communalist anarchism.[1] But first a look at the others.

Writers in the liberal tradition view hierarchy as a necessary condition of social life. They argue that coordination is necessary, and that the most efficient form of coordination is hierarchical organization. Liberals also believe in "meritocracy," which they describe as a system in which jobs go to the best qualified. When liberals turn a critical eye toward our society, they see that the most highly rewarded jobs tend to be held by white, upper-class males, and that many highly qualified women and non-whites never make it to the tops of the hierarchies. They then suppose that something has gone wrong with the system of "sorting" people into these hierarchies. They attribute this "unfair" sorting to various kinds of discrimination on the part of those hiring, or those making up qualifying exams, and so on. Their practical solution to the problem seems relatively straightforward: End discrimination and adopt equal opportunity as a goal.

Now, most advocates of social change work for equal opportunity to some degree. For example, the three of us have had to fight the equal opportunity fight within our workplaces and professions, for ourselves and for others, but we do not have "equal opportunity" as our prime goal.

The problem with equal opportunity as a prime goal is that, in our society, equal opportunity means the opportunity to become *unequal*. It does not challenge the *system* of privilege; it merely aims toward the more sex-blind or race-blind distribution of that privilege. As we will see, hierarchy and privilege can be shown to be significant obstacles to many people's realization of their goal of a good life. A movement that accepts such privilege cannot accomplish the goal of changing society to give all women (let alone all people) good lives. Thus, liberalism does not seem to be an adequate starting point for the feminist movement.

Socialists, on the other hand, do see hierarchy and privilege as barriers to people's leading full and good lives. And they see that hierarchy and privilege to be based in economic structures—in particular, in industrial capitalism. They argue that capitalism—the inequalities built into it, and the social and political hierarchies that grow out of it—is the central factor preventing people from realizing good lives. This perspective has important consequences for both analysis and strategy. Marxist criticism treats class and economic factors as the most crucial, "the primary contradiction." Marxists derive all other conflicts and contradictions in society from those fundamental relationships. Strategically, this means that people committed to social change must work together to overcome the economic structures of capitalism. Through that struggle, they also will be working against all hierarchies, social, political, or sexual.

This socialist tradition poses problems for feminists, at least in part because of its focus on the one "primary contradiction." Many contemporary feminists have attempted to modify the tradition. They argue that sexual power or domination is an independent source of hierarchy and privilege, and that it will not necessarily disappear when capitalism is overthrown. They have also criticized the sexism of socialist movements, both in this country and in others. They have, in the process, begun to create a new tradition—of "socialist feminism."[2]

Still, we want to argue that this tradition, too, must have its limits. On the theoretical level, one cannot simply add another, independent source of domination or oppression without changing the initial theory in a fundamental way. And this theoretical problem is reflected in a very real practical problem for socialist feminists. What should be the focus of their organizing efforts? In fact, experience shows us that the analysis has led some socialist feminists to a reverse elitism—college-educated, middle-class women taking up factory or waitressing jobs, and focusing their work on organizing poor and working-class women. In doing this they discount or ignore the reality of middle-class women's experiences of subordination. The problem flows directly from the socialist tradition they attempt to adapt.[3]

In developing some of these same criticisms, radical feminists have argued that neither tradition provides an appropriate starting point for analyzing and overcoming women's subordination. Instead, they argue that hierarchical patterns of behavior and interaction such as the desire to put oneself first, to dominate others, to give orders, and so on, are essentially *male* characteristics.[4] Through the exercise of their male power, men have structured these characteristics into the very fabric of our society, so that they infect our social, economic, and political life. Along with the socialists, and in oppositions to liberals, radical feminists reject the claim that hierarchy is necessary to human society. But, unlike socialists, who see hierarchy as derivative from economic relations, the radical feminists trace it to male dominance. They point out that the hierarchical structures themselves encourage the development of aggressive, competitive behavior that makes good lives impossible for many. They argue that it is male privilege that must be eliminated. Hierarchical patterns of behavior will then follow them to oblivion, and people will be able to realize their goal of a good life.

The battle cry of the radical feminist is that women of all races and classes must unite to overcome sex oppression first and foremost. As a practical matter, however, black women find they must unite with black men in fighting racism, and working-class women find they must unite with their men in overcoming their class oppression. Radical feminism ignores the importance of class- and race-dominance structures and gives no reasonable way for black and working-class people to overcome the structure of their subordination. For this reason, many black women call radical feminism racist—because it looks upon all women as if they were the same, that is, as if they were all *white*.

While each of these traditions has some things to offer to a feminist analysis and strategy, each also raises problems for that analysis. In particular, each can be criticized for leaving out the perceptions, the lives, and even the movements for change of some large groups of people (including women) in the United States. To base a feminist strategy on either of these perspectives requires that many women put aside their own perceptions and lives and oppression, to work for someone else's. We feel, however, that instead of trying to modify these traditions to make room for all women, feminists would do better to turn to another tradition, the anarchist tradition, which has an analysis and strategy more clearly suited to both the theoretical needs and the existing practices of the feminist movement.[5]

What is anarchism? There is no one, monolithic version of anarchism to which all who call themselves anarchists would subscribe. As is the case with liberalism and Marxism, there exists a tradition to which many thinkers and activists have contributed and which is still undergoing development. We see ourselves in this tradition—and, in particular, in the communalist-anarchist tradition of Bakunin, Kropotkin, Goldman, and the Spanish anarchists. Even these people and groups differed among themselves. But the main lines of the tradition that all share are (1) a criticism of existing societies, focusing on relationships of power and domination; (2) a vision of an alternate, egalitarian, nonauthoritarian society, along with claims about how it could be organized; and (3) a strategy for moving from one to the other.

The particular form and content of these criticisms and strategies have changed, of course, over time. As Western capitalist societies have become more complex during the one hundred years since massive industrialization began, understandings of those societies—of the ways in which domination and subordination function, and of the movements that have arisen to overcome those relationships—have changed as well. In fact, part of or purpose in writing this chapter was to suggest a more complete anarchist analysis that uses developments in many of these areas. For example, the analysis of domination and subordination, which we will present in section II, owes much to the insights of sociologists and social psychologists, who have studied the impact of workplace organization on working people. It owes much to women in the women's movement, who have contributed to an understanding of the operation of male dominance, the role of the family, and possibilities for nonhierarchical, cooperative forms of behavior. It owes much to developments in the natural sciences and to their impact on the ecology movement. And it owes much to the black and poor people's movements of the 1950s and 1960s—and to many other sources as well. Our analysis of strategies for struggle to achieve a better society, which we will present in section III, owes much to the struggles of the many subordinate groups that have attempted to understand and overcome their subordination within the past thirty years—and, especially, to the women's movement.

But before we begin these presentations, let us say just a bit about what sort of a society we, as anarchists, envision—or, to put it better, what kinds of perspectives would underlie the organization of such a society.

One is that human freedom is a social product: Freedom and community are compatible, but communities need to be structured in particular ways to support and make possible that freedom. That means that the structure supporting that freedom must be egalitarian—that is, there should be no need for hierarchies of authority and privilege. Instead, society, including work structures, will be arranged to foster relationships of reciprocity and cooperation (what anarchists have traditionally termed "mutualism"). Thus, there would be no need for economic inequalities or differential work incentives. The institutions in and through which people interact will encourage them to cooperate with one another, not to compete. Each will come to recognize that the fulfillment of the self need not be achieved at the expense of others. Spontaneous organizations, set up by people to meet their own needs, replace centralized, hierarchical patterns of coordination. To be sure, leaders may arise in some situations, but the right or authority to "command" a situation should not inhere in roles or offices to which some people have privileged access. Diversity, and a plurality of perspectives, is to be the watchword. Finally, instead of conquering nature, people should orient themselves to finding new ways to live in harmony with our physical surroundings.[6]

So far, this vision may not seem very different from one offered by Marxist socialists. But, as we will see in section III, anarchism also has some important things to say about the process of social change. In this perspective on change, it differs significantly from both the liberal and the Marxist traditions, but it has strong connections with feminist practice—especially much of the practice of radical feminism. The anarchist perspective requires that means be consistent with ends. It requires that the process of revolution take place in and through structures that reflect the sorts of relationships in which people aim to live. The organizations through which people struggle to achieve their aims must not undermine those aims. It implies a new concept of revolutionary practice, which consists in creating new forms of communal-social existence, new ways to meet people's needs,[7] forms through which people can overcome their own subordination.

We will be looking more closely at anarchism—at its implications for feminism and at the implications of contemporary social movements for it—in the sections to follow. Once again we will be arguing that this perspective—and the criticism of hierarchy and domination from which it stems—provides a much firmer grounding for feminist theory and strategy than does any of the other traditions.

II. Dominance and Subordination

More than two thousand years ago, Aristotle said that for human beings to have a good life, they must realize a complete development of their abilities in their activities.[8] Of course they must have an adequate supply of external goods, too: food, clothing, shelter. Most of us would probably agree that a complete development of abilities in activities is needed for a good life. We would also want to turn it around and say that a fulfilling life requires that there be activities open to a person that permit complete development of his or her abilities.

Many people in the United States today would agree with something like that characterization of a good life, and some of our psychologists have related this idea to the idea of maturity, the child moving toward such a development as he or she grows older.

These psychologists have certain hypotheses about people in "our culture." They claim that we tend to develop from a state of passivity and dependence as infants to increasing activity and independence as adults. They say we tend to develop toward being able to act in many different ways in many different kinds of situations, while at the same time we develop deep, long-term interests. They say we tend to develop from being in a subordinate position in family and society to one of equality with peers, or superordinacy with others. Finally, they say we tend to develop an awareness of self and self-control, and control over our lives, leading to a sense of integrity and self-worth.

That is a *normative* definition of maturity. It is not properly respectful of children. And it is not available to large groups of people in our society, for reasons we will discuss. But its desirability is empirically supported in what people in our culture *feel* is important and what bothers them when it is lacking. We may take it as specifying to some degree what is needed to realize one's abilities in activities and thus have a good life.

It is clear from the description that people need to be able to develop various abilities and, along with that, a sense of competence and self-confidence. We will begin with this characterization and look more directly both at the conditions necessary for that to be achieved, and at the ways in which hierarchy and dominance and subordination can be used to help or hinder that process of development.

First, we will look at an informal, nonhierarchical situation (a Sunday-afternoon picnic) in which one person gets to develop his competence and self-confidence by being dominant in the situation, putting others in a subordinate position in which they are forced to behave in ways the psychologists we quoted would call "immature."

We will then look at some social situations in which there is an explicit hierarchical structure, to see how dominance and subordination are made "legitimate" through the roles in a hierarchy. The most severe formally structured situation we will consider is what Erving Goffman calls the "total institution" (1961). After looking at the ways total institutions structure roles, we will examine family and workplace hierarchies, as less extreme examples of hierarchical social structures. In each of these cases, we will discuss how people holding dominant positions in the hierarchy get to develop abilities that seem important to living a good life, while those in subordinate positions are forced to develop characteristics that most people consider disadvantageous in achieving that goal.

These are all *situationally* caused disadvantages due to a person's role in a hierarchy. We want to show, beyond that, that these structured hierarchies in fact underlie dominance and subordination in the broadest sense: the dominance of higher class over lower, of male over female, of adult over child, of white over nonwhite, of human over nonhuman. It is this broad sense, not restricted to particular family, work, or other hierarchies, that is most important to anarchist feminists. We will try to indicate how this very broad dominance depends on hierarchical social structures and how it is enforced by the state and economic coercion, which supports those hierarchies. The hierarchies themselves give a basis for the centralization that allows the state and economic coercion to operate. Centralization also allows reality itself to be "officially defined" through the viewpoints of members of dominant groups, so that the viewpoints and the very selves of members of subordinate groups become invisible, lost to official history, lost to official politics, but, as we will see in section III, *not* lost as a force for social change.

An Informal Situation

Let's suppose that it's a beautiful, warm Sunday afternoon in Indian summer. We're all going to the house of a friend who has a big pleasant yard. Duke shows up with a volleyball and sets up his portable net and enthusiastically gathers us to play volleyball. Emmylou and Doctor John want to play a little music and have everybody sing and dance, especially because the children can do that, too; but Duke carries the day. He refreshes us on the rules and tactics of volleyball, and we all start playing. He's a pretty good player, and he begins playing not only his own position but Emmylou's and Doctor John's too, shouting, "I'll get it," so that they back off. Gradually, Emmylou and Doctor John stop covering the outer parts of their territory and become tentative and unsure in their moves. Eventually, they become demoralized and passive. Duke is in a superordinate position and gets practice at making long-range plans and at having command of a situation. He has succeeded in getting everyone to take part in an activity that allows him to exercise and develop *his* abilities—particularly athletic ones. He has control over this part of his life, at least, and gets a sense of integrity and self-worth out of the afternoon.

Emmylou and Doctor John gradually move into a subordinate position in which they feel they have little ability to control things, and they develop feelings of lack of self-worth. They also get no practice in having command of the situation, but a lot of practice in being subordinate.

The point is that in these situations, the dominant person gets to develop abilities needed to have command of a situation, as well as other abilities. The subordinate person tends to be put in a position where "immature" action is required. He or she develops the abilities needed for a subordinate and does not get to develop a wider range of abilities.

The volleyball game was an informal situation, where domination and subordination were "enforced" by force of personality. One way of looking at hierarchies is as systems of interaction that require and reinforce those relationships of domination and subordination—not on the basis of personality, but through the *formal* structure and organization. We face these kinds of hierarchies everywhere—for example, school, professions, government, family, and work.

Unlike the Sunday-picnic situation, a hierarchy involves a group of people who regularly do a certain set of activities together. Each person's part in the activities is conditioned by conventional understanding of roles, by explicitly set out job descriptions, or by rules of one type or another.

Total Institutions

What Erving Goffman calls "Total institutions" are extreme examples of such formal, hierarchical systems that enforce dominance and subordination. To understand what happens to people in these institutions is to see the extent of hierarchy's impact. "Total institutions" include nursing homes and orphanages, mental hospitals, prisons, boarding schools and army barracks, convents and monasteries. Goffman says,

> A basic social arrangement in modern society is that the individual tends to sleep, play, and work in different places, with different co-participants, under different authorities, and without an over-all rational plan. The central feature of total institutions can be described as a breakdown of the barriers ordinarily separating these three spheres of life. (1961, 435)

Instead, there is a single source of authority (the staff). Staff members plan all activities for subordinates (the "inmates"). These activities take place according to a schedule. They are set about by rules, which all people classified into the particular subordinate group must follow. Even the most personal events, such as going to the bathroom or brushing one's teeth, wait upon the schedule and the authority. For example, in nursing homes, a resident must wait until the aide gets to her, and then go through the morning's wash, bathroom, and dress-up according to the rhythm of the aide's job. The resident is not allowed to follow her own life rhythm.

In the context of a total institution, the staff often sees the inmates as secretive and untrustworthy, and they in turn see staff as condescending and high-handed. So far as self-opinion goes, Goffman says that "staff tends to feel superior and righteous; inmates tend, in some way at least, to feel inferior, weak, blameworthy, and guilty" (1961, 436). The *official point of view,* however, belongs to the staff, not only because both groups take the views or interests of the institution to *be* those of the staff, but because the staff writes up the reports on the inmates and has the power to judge and punish. Inmates are coerced, pretty directly, into acting as subordinates.

In total institutions, the inmates cannot take part in activities that allow them to have control over their lives, and they are prevented from having the opportunity for self-determination, which is necessary for adults. The movie *One Flew over the Cuckoo's Nest* shows adults forced to act like children. To visit a relative in a nursing home or in prison is to see how total institutions prevent people from having activities that use abilities they need to act "maturely." They have to learn to act like subordinates.[9]

The Family

Goffman overstated his case when he suggested that all other people in modern society tend to sleep, play, and work in different places, and under different authorities. Housewives and small children tend to sleep, play, and work in the same place, as do agricultural workers, or those who live in "company towns." For many *small* children, the family functions like a total institution, and it may suit them no better than nursing homes suit their great-grandmothers.

For most people, however, the family is not a total institution in Goffman's sense. Most women, for example, spend a substantial proportion of their time outside the household, acting in different contexts, and under different authorities (in the workplace, the supermarket, interacting with teachers at school, etc.). Children have the opportunity to play with other children, according to rules and procedures they set for themselves; and older children leave home for school. (While it is true that school is another hierarchical institution, the point here is that it is a different one.)

Nevertheless, there are some aspects of life in total institutions that operate in families and other hierarchies as well. An "official point of view" helps to maintain the subordination of women, for example: The woman who is a housewife may be dominant over her children and in certain work realms it's "her kitchen." But there is an official point of view that also defines which activities are valuable and important (Dad's work is more important than Mom's; Dad's sports are more important than Mom's hobbies). And it designates some activities as "work," and others as simply "doing what mothers do." These activities, and the evaluations of them, are supported—in ways we can already begin to see—by other institutions and practices in our society.[10] We'll return to this below.

The family hierarchy trains both women and children in how to be subordinates, in the family and outside it. That training is then reinforced by schools and by work hierarchies. Both within and beyond any particular work hierarchy, economic and state coercion are used directly to enforce continued subordination.

The Workplace

Let us look at the workplace as an example of hierarchy, to see how these interconnections are made and maintained. Many work hierarchies in our society are governed by what were originally developed as principles of "scientific management."[11] Over the past hundred years, the structure of work in the United States has become more "scientized"—and more hierarchical—as part of the economic, social, and political changes that have accompanied industrialization.[12] We will examine the nature and impact of these changes in greater detail below. In any case, some type of principles of scientific management now govern the organization of much work. Under these principles, work is *specialized:* Different people do different tasks. There is a chain of command: a hierarchy of authority, with those higher up controlling, directing, and coordinating the activities below. Since individuals on the bottom have to be motivated to do their part, those higher up have the formal power to hire, fire, reward, and punish. This power is legitimated by the rules of the hierarchy. Argyris says of this plan of organization:

> The impact of the principles is to place employees in work situations where they are provided minimal control over their workaday world; (2) they are expected to be passive, dependent, and subordinate; (3) they are expected to have the frequent use of a few skin-surface shallow abilities [because of the specialization]; (4) they are expected to produce under conditions leading to psychological failure. (1977, 267)[13]

We might also notice some other things about this pattern of organization. Specialization not only *divides* tasks, it also values them differentially. So, planning and "mental" tasks are separated from "carrying out" tasks; the former are considered more important, and those who do them are more highly valued and rewarded. Not only do they have *control* over their subordinates, they also get more satisfactions and rewards from their jobs.

Discrimination or Subordination?

Liberal social critics (including feminists who base their criticism of hierarchy on liberal theory) might look at these hierarchies and acknowledge that they prevent some people from developing their abilities. But these critics tend to accept this limitation because of their understanding of the relationship of work hierarchy to the structure of society as a whole. From the liberal point of view, one aspect of that relationship is the claim that "one's work is not one's life." So, a liberal critic might say that people can develop themselves in other situations—through hobbies, or "leisure time activities," for example. In this view, the good life takes place in a person's "private life." Anarchists, as well as Marxists, have long argued that work is a central part of human life and self-expression, and that one's work cannot be separated from one's life. Workers seem to agree, because there are studies showing that workers want to enlarge areas of their lives in which their own decisions determine the outcome of their efforts, and they try to do this even in the workplace.[14]

Although we share the belief that work is an important, and inseparable, part of one's life, we do not base our criticism of hierarchy on that claim alone. There is a second aspect of the liberal view of the relationship between work life and social life that is also important to consider. And that is the connection between work hierarchy and societal patterns of dominance and subordination. We mentioned above that people in higher positions in the work hierarchy get paid more, are accorded more respect, and so on. When we look around at our society, we also notice that the tops of these hierarchies are full of white, higher-class, males, and that the bottoms are disproportionately full of nonwhites and females.[15]

Liberal theory assumes that hierarchies exist to take advantage of different "talents" and abilities, and that they ought, therefore, to be filled according to "merit." If groups of people are disproportionately represented in these hierarchies, that is a sign—in this view—of a poor distribution of people, probably caused by discrimination. So, a feminist basing her arguments in liberal theory would fight to end sex discrimination so that talented women could rise to the top on equal terms with white men. She would suppose that nonwhites would form their own interest groups to stop discrimination against themselves. If discrimination is stopped, then the hierarchy would be "fair."

This view of what is wrong with hierarchy is too limited. To talk of *discrimination* as the cause of male dominance, or white dominance, is to presuppose that it makes sense to talk about ranking people on some unitary scale according to their abilities. It is to presuppose that there *is* such a thing as a meritocracy, that those at the top deserve to be there because they are more able than those at the bottom. It is obvious, however, that we need lots of different kinds of people with different kinds of abilities to make the world go round.[16] There isn't any unitary scale along which to rank people's abilities, and there isn't any meritocracy. The features of hierarchy itself create the illusion that there is one.[17]

Within hierarchies, different work is defined as having different value. Those at the top do the work labeled "planning and direction," and that work is considered more valuable than the work of those at the bottom, which is labeled "manual," or "carrying out the plan." Officially, labor done by those at the bottom is devalued, whatever its actual contribution to the work of the hierarchy. A striking example here is the difference in value attached to the work of doctors as opposed to nurses, or administrative staff as opposed to aides, in a hospital.

An acceptance of hierarchy is an acceptance of a situation in which some people have opportunities to develop the abilities psychologists associate with maturity, and others are prevented from doing so. But it is more than that. Because, as we have also seen, people at the tops of hierarchies also obtain other advantages, and these work to enforce subordination of children, women, nonwhites, and people of the lower classes in society at large. Work hierarchies exist in a relationship of mutual reinforcement within a larger system of domination and subordination.

Economic Coercion

Work hierarchies reinforce patterns of domination through economic coercion, such as the power to hire, fire, give raises, or dock pay. Aside from adding to feelings of control (and to the feelings of lack of control on the part of those lower down), this structure rewards those higher up in other ways as well. Their work is considered more valuable, and they are accorded status and respect in society at large. Often they are paid more, and at greater intervals (they are paid monthly, with large bonuses annually; while "manual" workers are paid daily, or weekly). So, higher-ups have greater control over cash flow, more opportunity for saving and investing, and more chances to develop some of their abilities. They have more chances to own a home, thus more control of their home space. The opposite, obviously, is true for those lower down. Being paid less means that workers and their children have less opportunity for formal education. Working one's way through Greenfield Community College isn't the same as being sent to Harvard with an allowance.

Our society is not patriarchal in a strict sense, but many of our practices and policies presuppose that the norm is the male-headed family.[18] The fact that white men have "better jobs" than others reinforces their claim to "head" their families. In the past, the expectation that the man is head of the family justified paying women less at work. That fact, in turn, ensures that women on their own, or female-headed families, will not be able to "do as well" as male-headed ones. This economic coercion works to keep women in a family situation, and it supports male dominance across classes. Similar patterns exist for black workers, which also support racial domination.[19]

Status Groups and Domination

Those near the tops of hierarchies associate with one another during work times and during social times. They and their families associate with families of others at a similar level. This forms status groups. Members of these groups have access to a lion's share of the resources that allow people to develop many abilities (travel, art, attendance at Ivy League universities, music lessons, or internships in Washington). They also have access to the knowledge, influence, and power held by others in the status-groups network, so that they can learn to get things done, as well as do them themselves. Because of the family basis of status groups, in the future, places at the tops of hierarchies will be disproportionately filled by children of high-status families.

Centralization and Domination

Hierarchy reinforces and perpetuates relations of domination and subordination by aiding centralization. Both economic and political (state) coercion operate by using hierarchies to maintain subordination.[20]

Centralization consolidates both power and status. Economic centralization made possible more effective management control over workers in the developing industrial system. This control was in turn supported by centralized political power; and, ultimately, it supported greater political centralization. For example, hierarchical organization of government and political parties made possible the centralization of political decision-making power in the hands of a fairly small number of people (not all of them elected officials). That power could then be used—both directly and indirectly—to protect the interests of those in positions of economic power; and to frustrate any attempts at change by less powerful economic groups.[21]

In addition to these patterns of relationships are the more subtle connections between the hierarchies, which reinforce a particular point of view and, in turn, maintain subordination. Hierarchical organization of the military, of business, and of "organized labor" centralizes decision making in those areas. Dwight Eisenhower's warning about the "military industrial complex" was a warning about the centralization of power that resulted from joining the tops of certain business hierarchies with the military. But even in nonwarlike domains such as baby-food production or copper mining, "spokesmen" from top offices in the industry represent the official viewpoint of that industry and give "facts" or advice to the government. The official view of "organized labor" or the "value-neutral" truth of science and the academy also come from the mouths of a small number of people—and there is no built-in way for anyone else to respond (except, seemingly, through other large, centralized organizations such as Common Cause, etc.).[22]

Dominance and the "Official Point of View"

In this way, broad social control (not merely control in a single work or government hierarchy) is centralized to the benefit of a comparative few. As we've all noticed, the few are predominantly higher class, white, and male. Newspapers, television, history books, novels, and statuary report the words, deeds, and bodily forms of these men.[23] Their viewpoints come to define "official reality" and put limits even on the raising of alternative perspectives.[24] Their behavior comes to define the criteria by which both valuable work and admirable abilities and manners are judged. This devalues the work and styles of women, nonwhites, working-class people, and the young. It also operates to keep these people from rising in individual hierarchies, or from challenging the existence of hierarchies at all.

Rosabeth Kanter's work suggests that the homogeneity of people at the tops of hierarchies results not only from this singular definition of what's valuable and important but also from the uncertainty in the definition of what constitutes success in a managerial job. The fact that managers spend most of their time communicating with one another leads them to select other managers who are, at least, similar to them in certain characteristics:

> The structure of communication involved in managerial jobs generated a desire for smooth social relationships and a preference for selection of those people with whom communication would be easiest. ...

> One way to ensure acceptance and ease of communication was to limit managerial jobs to those who were socially homogeneous. Social certainty, at least, could compensate for some of the other sources of uncertainty in the tasks of management. (Kanter 1977, 58)

Uncertainty about management tasks, and the vast volume of communication involved, are both aspects of hierarchical organization. As a consequence of these, however, people who have *different* ways of operating or communicating are labeled hard to communicate with and are excluded from managerial positions on that basis. Thus Kanter reports, from management's point of view: "Women were decidedly placed in the category of the incomprehensible and unpredictable. There were many reports that managers felt uncomfortable having to communicate with women. 'It took more time,' they said. 'You never knew where you stood'" (Kanter 1977, 58). Nonwhites and working-class people are also hard for these white male managers to understand. And so they, too, find themselves disproportionately unrepresented in management positions.

Total institutions, the family, schools, and work hierarchies all offer ways for those who are dominant to define reality in terms of their "official point of view," and for them to exercise control over others in society through the imposition of this point of view as the *only* one. When members of subordinate groups engage in activities that threaten that definition of reality (showing them to be able and competent, for example) members of dominant groups either define those activities as unimportant, or else absent themselves from the arena. Higher-class white men avoid the streets of working-class or nonwhite neighborhoods where working-class or nonwhite men are dominant, even when there is no physical danger. Some husbands rigidly avoid sports and cultural activities in which their wives are adept and knowledgeable. Doctors may not be present when nurses or aides sit around with one another and discuss *their* understanding of patients, or of the medical hierarchy in which they all participate. This way of behaving is one way in which members of dominant groups define reality.

There is another side to the story, however. People in subordinate statuses, women, children, nonwhites, and those of lower class, *do* develop abilities and have knowledge that members of dominant status groups do not. The "official" definition from the dominant viewpoint stereotypes these people as subordinate "through and through." But people who may act as subordinate in one setting do not necessarily have their whole selves defined through that behavior. In fact, they may share another view of reality, a view often quite different from the "official" view. This provides them with opportunities to challenge both the "official" view of reality and the existing distribution of power and privilege in society. In order to survive, they must know the official point of view; but they also know, firsthand and in the utmost intimacy, wherein it is false.

The question we turn to now is how the viewpoints of subordinate people are to be used in a strategy for social change. How is this power of subordinate people to be released? How can subordinate people overcome their subordination?

III. Overcoming Subordination

Feminists criticize our society for not achieving its point, for not permitting many people to develop in what we consider mature, self-actualizing ways. Feminists say that hierarchies and patterned relationships of domination and subordination prevent many of us from realizing these goals. We have already compared the criticisms of hierarchy given within the liberal, the Marxist, and the radical-feminist traditions with that of the anarchist tradition. Now we want to look at the movements to change those conditions, to see if they can achieve their aim of allowing all of our people to work for good, fulfilling lives. This means looking not only at their criticisms of our society, and not only at the vision of some future society. It means looking at the *process* of change embodied in the movements themselves.

Let's look in more detail at some of the anarchist principles we mentioned earlier. One important anarchist principle is that means must be consistent with ends. The process of revolution must be consistent with the point of the revolution. We cannot hope to establish a society that achieves its point by using an organizational structure that undermines the point. Hierarchical revolutionary organizations do just that.

One reason that hierarchical revolutionary organizations are objectionable is pretty obvious: When people get in positions of power, they find it next to impossible to relinquish it. But that is a symptom, not the disease. The real reason is that there is no way to overcome longstanding patterns of domination and subordination except by overcoming them. We can't "learn" how to act in nondominating ways in an organization based in hierarchical structures. We can not learn to think and act for ourselves in those Marxist groups in which the leadership works out theory and plans strategy and hands down orders to the cadre, who then try to go out and organize us masses. Nor can we learn to think and act for ourselves in liberal groups in which the leadership of an "interest group" carries out lobbying and political pressuring for a constituency whose participation consists in donating funds or writing a letter on request. If we have been subject to subordination, we can learn to think and act for ourselves only by doing that: by joining together in organizations in which our experience, our perception, and our activity guide and make the revolution.

Anarchists traditionally have talked about this kind of revolutionary activity as "propaganda by the deed," or as "spontaneous organization." By that *we* do not mean activity that begins and ends in tossing bombs into banks or tossing monkey wrenches into assembly-line machines. We are referring to a strategy of direct action. Propaganda by the deed refers to ways people organize. Spontaneous organization is a way people join together to meet their goals.[25]

Propaganda by the deed refers to what we could call exemplary action, action that draws adherents by the power of the positive example it sets, and changes people in the process. An instance of propaganda by the deed is KOPN, the community-operated and collectively run radio station in Columbia, Missouri. The Amherst Food Coop is an example, as is the New England Federation of Cooperatives. Other examples include the New Words bookstore in Cambridge, the Cambridge Women's Health Center, Bread and Roses restaurant, and the Community Health Care Project in Florence, Massachusetts.

They are activities that arise from people's day-to-day needs and experiences. They represent ways in which people can take control—not over other people, but over their own lives. Participation in such activities allows people to develop a sense of competence and self-confidence. It *empowers* people, and fortifies them to act together. It is propaganda in another sense: It "speaks" to anyone else who might be around and willing to notice. It demonstrates by example that nonhierarchical forms of organization do and can exist, and that people can achieve valued goals in and through them. To communicate such a message believably is no small feat.

Spontaneous organization refers to another aspect of this phenomenon, emphasizing that both the *form* the organization takes and the *goals* people establish for it are not determined by some revolutionary cadre from above but by the people whose needs are expressed in it. Spontaneous organization shows in *practice* that people who have experienced subordination are—to put it most crudely—still capable of thought, still capable of action, and still capable both of knowing what their needs are, and of figuring out ways to meet them.

We should not be utopian about spontaneous organizations. An earlier anarchist, Enrico Malatesta, had some words of caution about worker co-ops:

> I recognize the extreme usefulness that co-operatives, by accustoming workers to manage their own affairs, the organization of their work, and other activities, can have ... as experimental organizations capable of dealing with the distribution of goods and serving as nerve centers for the mass of population. ...
>
> [But] in my opinion, cooperatives and trade unions under a capitalist regime do not naturally or by reason of their intrinsic value lead to human emancipation but can be producers of good and evil. (*Unmanità Nova*, April 13, 1922)[26]

Anyone who has worked with a spontaneous organization knows firsthand that there must be a constant struggle against the "shopkeeper spirit," against reproducing hierarchy within the organization, against reproducing white, higher-class, or male dominance within the organization. The problem isn't a simple one of carrying over attitudes of the larger society. We all must continue to live in the larger society, and the spontaneous organization must succeed in that context. The success can never be more than partial, and the spontaneous organizations themselves are always experiments in trying to understand and develop nonhierarchical, decentralized ways of doing what we need to do and what we want to do.[27] Within them, subordinates always face a struggle to overcome their own subordination, and to educate and change themselves and the members of dominant groups who work with them.

Still, there are many examples from our own recent history that might help to illustrate the power of propaganda by the deed and spontaneous organizations. Many women say that some of their most important experiences in the women's movement were in consciousness-raising groups. Those groups enabled women to talk (instead of being silent), to recognize that they had *ideas,* and that they had *grievances*—and, more importantly, perhaps, that their experiences and their grievances were *shared.* Through talking with other women, we were able to recognize what seemed to be our personal failings as consequences of larger patterns of domination and subordination. And the "simple" fact of recognizing that changed our reality. It is not surprising that so many women felt strengthened by consciousness-raising sessions and motivated to act. Acting together—on the basis of needs and goals we *defined for ourselves*—strengthened us further and gave us the power to continue, even against obstacles. Out of this came the self-help movement; community clinics; a variety of feminist, collectively owned and run businesses; and feminist journals and women's studies programs. These practices of the feminist movement are good examples of anarchist strategy. Though they are far from perfect, they demonstrate that new forms of meeting needs are possible. They *change* people—both participants and observers—in the process.

In addition to propaganda by the deed and spontaneous organization, anarchists have traditionally talked about decentralism. Part of the reason for urging a decentralized society lies in the monstrous effects of centralization. In part, anarchist arguments against centralization have been arguments against the state, any state with police and military force, courts and prisons, including the socialist state. We suggested in section II that state coercion is an important mechanism for keeping certain groups subordinate.

In part, anarchist arguments against centralization have been against our capitalist economic system, which centralizes power in the hands of the minority who have control of the wealth. This centralization allows economic coercion to keep some groups subordinate.[28]

In the process of the anarchist revolution, using the experience of our own lives as the basis for understanding and action, we come to understand decentralism as we build it.[29] We do this in building spontaneous organizations, particularly in the form of community control, worker ownership and control, tenant control, and consumer control, as well as the co-op organizations and networks. These help create the understanding of what decentralism is in practice. If they are politically strategic, they also operate against centralized political and economic power.

By now, any liberal or Marxist feminists probably have two serious questions about this spontaneity and decentralism. They are serious questions for us, too, so let's ask them.

First, a question about spontaneity. We've talked about spontaneous organization of health centers, food co-ops, restaurants and other businesses, and consciousness-raising support groups. What *political* relevance do these things have? What makes them have revolutionary force toward changing our society? Do they just take up people's energies and give them some new hobbies and leave our coercive society unchanged?

Historical and sociological data show that "spontaneous" protest actions by people in subordinate positions are aimed at what *they* perceive to be the cause of their oppression, and what *they* perceive to be that part of the cause they can act effectively against.[30] Anyone who has been involved in these protests, and anyone who has talked seriously to working-class people, black people, young people, or women about their subordination knows this. Tenants strike against landlords, young people act against local police or teachers and principals. Nearly always, these people are correct that what they act against is really *a* cause of their problem, and that it is really a factor they have a chance at being effective against. It is rarely the ultimate cause, for more ultimate causes are hidden from view and protected from protest. Tenants cannot touch bankers or financiers very well, students have more trouble acting against the government and industry, which shape their education—although in the late 1960s both groups managed this.

But this problem of reaching more ultimate causes isn't to be solved by a group of trained Marxist cadre dropping in to do propaganda by the word and taking over leadership, nor is it to be solved by liberal professionals in community organizing who take over leadership. People learn from their experiences and from the experiences of others in similar situations. What works is a network of communication among groups of people in similar situations so that we may learn from our own and others' successes and failures: visits to other places and visitors from other places, and a network of communication. That is education to consciousness. In the process of engaging in these activities, people learn strategy. We have very good examples of this sort of thing from the black and poor people's and youth movements in the 1960s; and in the women's and ecological movements in the 1970s.

This answers part of the question—that posed by Leninists who claim that average people, left to themselves, will never develop an understanding of ultimate causes and will never "progress" beyond what Lenin termed "trade union consciousness." But there is another aspect to the issue of the *political* relevance of these organizations: What makes them revolutionary organizations rather than cooperative clubs? If we recognize that there are some kinds of organizations that might just let people feel better, while maintaining—or even reinforcing—dominance, how do we distinguish among organizations? Of course no revolutionary strategy comes with a guarantee that it will not be co-opted. Still, it might be helpful to know what types of organizations are less subject to that threat, or are most likely to contribute to the overcoming of subordination.

There are at least the beginnings of an answer in what we have said so far. If the point of social change is to overcome subordination, so as to enable people to live good, fulfilled lives, then those organizations that contribute to people's actually exerting such control are those that fulfill a revolutionary purpose. It is the *process* that is crucial. Organizations in and through which people are able to exercise some degree of control over the conditions of their life—and through which they can, together with others, experience the *changes* as of their own doing—must, of necessity, be "revolutionary." Such organizations are not making people simply feel better. In fact, as people struggle to improve their conditions, they may actually become more aware of their subordination, and thus feel "worse" about their situations. What these organizations do, however, is to develop in people a sense of their own power. If there can be *any* measure of the "progressiveness" of an organization or strategy, it must be that.[31] Even that, it is true, is no guarantee against co-optation. But at least it gives us a way to begin talking about strategies and evaluating them.[32]

The second question is about coordination. Spontaneous organization makes sense as a way of developing consciousness and strategy when the people working in the different spontaneous organizations see their work as similar or compatible. But how can we link people in spontaneous organizations that are dissimilar and perhaps even antagonistic—not only in their members' perceived goals but in their modes of relating to one another? Many feminists perceive some left groups that include either black or white males as the most macho, sexist, male imperialist things we have ever come up against, and we find it impossible to work with them. It was for this reason that there was great debate in socialist-feminist women's unions over "autonomous" women's groups—linked externally with "mixed" groups. It is one reason why some radical feminists are separatists.

So what is our anarchist solution to this "linkage problem"? Before talking about that, we need to clarify just what the problem is.

Liberal, Marxist, radical, and anarchist feminists offer different solutions to the linkage problem because they ask different questions. They even *perceive* the linkage problem differently because of their differences in political and social theory.

Liberal feminists see a plurality of competing interest groups. To overcome what they perceive as discrimination against women, they work to organize women into an interest group that can use political pressure to get the state to use its coercive power in their favor—thus the recourse to legislation and the courts. NOW, for example, takes its constituency as an interest group and usually has operated on the principle that it will fight for issues of interest to *all* women—and this has led to charges of racism when NOW has refused to move on issues most seriously affecting the interest of third-world women. If liberal feminists ever notice a problem of linking subordinate groups, they tend to see it as a problem of a coalition of interest groups that have a stake in a particular issue.

This pluralist thinking is enormously difficult to overcome. We find ourselves slipping into it. We find it underlying the thinking of many, many Marxist feminists. We all grew up with it.

Marxists in general attempt to escape from this thinking by emphasizing the centralized power of the bourgeois state and the centralized power of capitalism. This leads them to ask the question, How can we *organize* a unified force to overthrow the unified, centralized force of the state? Asking the question leads us straightaway to seeing centralized revolutionary organization as the solution. The problem of antagonistic subordinate groups is allegedly solved by a vast superstructure of theory, which places the interests of one subordinate group in the vanguard, behind which members of all the other subordinate *and* dominate groups are supposed to range themselves. In fact, this has never worked in the United States, even on a small scale.

Now, what we've said here is that there is a serious problem somehow involved in these antagonistic subordinate groups. The liberal suggestion preserves hierarchy and domination. The Marxist suggestion, at best, is a theoretical one that has never worked here; at worst, it is a suggestion that preserves centralization, hierarchy, and dominance. What do we have to say, as anarchists?

We are not grand strategists. We do believe that the anarchist principles of decentralism, propaganda by the deed, spontaneous organization, and self-determination are the best ones for making the revolution and forming the revolutionary society. This suggests a number of possibilities. First, we must not undervalue, or shy away from, *partial* successes. Even though we must not be utopian about the achievements of spontaneous organizations in our society, it is important to recognize just what such organizations have accomplished and to attempt to learn from both their successes and their failures.[33] To speculate a bit further, if we don't focus all our attention on the centralized power of the state, we may find strategies that let us work together in smaller, non-national units—for example, northern and central New England and the Maritime states of Canada share a great deal and form a certain kind of natural, economic, and cultural unit. The science-fiction book *Ecotopia* describes such an anarchist society created when northern California, Oregon, and Washington secede from the United States.[34]

Second, we can recognize the tactical or strategic necessity of engaging in joint *actions* with other subordinate groups, on specific issues—even if the general goals, structures, and methods of those groups are such that we would not *join* them. We have in mind here, for example, the broad coalitions formed to struggle against restriction of access to abortion, or against sterilization abuse. In other words, a strategy of direct action need not force us into a totally separatist stance. Rather, it derives from an understanding of strategy and process that allows us to see what kinds of behavior are likely to do the most to overcome subordination.[35]

Finally, we must remember the point of all this: the overcoming of subordination. People act out of their own understanding of their subordination. We do not wish to rank those subordinates, or to argue which is "primary." To the extent that these groups—however different their structures and methods of operating—aim at overcoming subordination, there may be at least *some* basis for cooperation. But that method of cooperation must lead us to respect the experiences represented in each of the groups. There may be, in fact, not be any way to resolve this issue immediately and completely. To the extent that all subordinate groups are struggling against the patterns of domination that maintain their subordination, even "uncoordinated" struggles have the potential to weaken those larger patterns and strengthen the struggling groups. We can learn from one another by talking, watching, or perhaps participating.

So, we aren't grand strategists, but we do know that no strategy is worth anything unless it *aims* at the goal of the revolutionary movement. It must show the right way to the right ends. If the end is the possibility of a good life for all our people, if the end is the overcoming of dominance and subordination, even if the end is only the overthrow of capitalism by the working class, the strategy must accomplish certain things. It must provide a way for people to gain revolutionary consciousness of their situation. It must provide a way for people who have been in subordinate positions all their lives to learn the skills and to acquire the abilities necessary to operate an industrial society. It must provide a way for people to learn to organize a new society that will not reproduce the oppressions they are fighting against. Finally, the strategy must be one that makes sense to people out of the experience of their own lives. Out of that, people will develop as effective tactics as our historical situation permits.

We believe that such a strategy is necessary for the feminist movement. We believe that anarchism offers that strategy.

Notes

1. Kathy Ferguson makes a similar survey of political traditions in Ferguson 1978, especially 96–99. But she does not relate them to hierarchy in particular.

2. One of the best collections of such writings is Eisenstein 1977. For a careful statement by socialist feminists of the difficulty of uniting Marxism and feminism, see also Hartmann 1981.

3. Hartmann points to this problem as well in "The Unhappy Marriage of Marxism and Feminism." See Hartmann 1981.

4. See Dworkin 1977, especially "The Root Cause" and "The Sexual Politics of Fear and Courage."

5. Others who have argued for the relevance of anarchism to feminism include Kornegger 1975, and Ehrlich 1977.

6. Writings by anarchists on these topics are extensive. Some of the most easily available—and which address themselves to these issues—include: Goldman 1969; Peter A. Korpotkin, "Anarchist Communism: Its Basis and Principles," "Anarchism: Its Philosophy and Ideal," and "Modern Science and Anarchism," in Baldwin 1970; Michael Bakunin, "On Federalism and Socialism," "God and the State," and "The Paris Commune and the Idea of the State," in Lehning 1974. More recent writings include Guerin 1970, especially chaps. 1 and 2; Bookchin 1971; Carter 1971, especially chap. 3; and Ward 1973.

7. See, especially, Ward 1973. The experiences of anarchist collectives in Spain provide some examples of ways in which people organized themselves to meet their needs. See, for examples, Gaston Leval, *Collectives in the Spanish Revolution* (London: Freedom Press, 1975); José Peirats, *Anarchists in the Spanish Revolution* (Toronto: Solidarity Books, n.d.); Vernon Richards, *Lessons of the Spanish Revolution* (London: Freedom Press, 1972).

8. Aristotle did not believe that it is equally within the capacity of all human beings to live a good, or fully realized life. Some people, he thought, are able only to meet their most basic,

animal-like needs; while others are capable of developing varied abilities. Still, he was clear that the *fully* human life entails the exercise of a wide range of abilities.

9. On prisons, and the ways in which they deny the full range of inmates' personhood, see Jessica Mitford, *Kind and Usual Punishment* (New York: Alfred A. Knopf, 1973) and Peter A. Kropotkin, "Prisons and Their Moral Influence on Prisoners," in Baldwin 1970, 219–35. There are also many firsthand accounts that illustrate this point. For example, George Jackson, *Soledad Brother* (New York: Bantam Books, 1970); Malcolm X 1964.

10. See Broverman et al., "Sex-Role Stereotypes and Clinical Judgments of Mental Health," *Journal of Consulting and Clinical Psychology* 34 (1970): 1–7. Sara Ruddick and Pamela Daniels, eds., *Working It Out* (New York: Pantheon, 1977), provides numerous examples of the ways in which that official point of view penetrates into people's lives—even among feminists, both male and female.

11. There have been a number of interesting studies recently on work, its definition, and its evaluation—especially as regards male-female divisions. See, for example, Amy Bridges and Batya Weinbaum, "The Other Side of the Paycheck," and Rosalyn Baxandall, Elizabeth Ewen, and Linda Gordon, "The Working Class Has Two Sexes," both in *Monthly Review* 28, no. 3 (July–August 1976): 88–104; 1–9. Rubin 1976 discusses some of the ways in which subordination affects life in the working-class family.

12. We have relied heavily on Argyris 1977 in the discussion of psychologists' views on maturity, and in the discussion of scientific management. His essay has many good references. Braverman 1974 discusses the impact of contemporary refinements of scientific management on workers and particularly on the possibility of a working-class consciousness.

13. In addition to Braverman, we have found Katherine Stone's work on the steel industry to be helpful in understanding these changes in work organization. See Stone 1973.

14. See Argyris 1977, 263; and also A. Gorz, *A Strategy for Labor* (Boston: Beacon Press, 1968). Ely Chinoy's *Automobile Workers and the American Dream* (Boston: Beacon Press, 1955) could be taken as a counterexample: workers "putting up" with lack of control in the factory in hopes of earning money to live better in their "private lives." But even there, workers report frustration with the conditions of their work; and their ideal visions for their future include opening a shop of their own, where they could be their *own* boss, and exercise control over their work conditions.

15. Since, by definition, the bottoms of the hierarchies are full of working-class people, most liberals tend not to notice that. Thus, the meritocratic perspective, to be discussed below, makes working-class people inferior "by definition."

16. Younger children may know this better than older. The grading system in school, in which children are ranked according to their ability to perform on classroom tests, offers powerful propaganda for meritocracy. Those who refuse to perform according to school expectations end up having fairly clearly a double consciousness, simultaneously thinking of themselves as unworthy and stupid; and knowing that those who did well in school *aren't* better and *don't* have more merit and may, in fact, be *more* stupid in many ways: dupes of the system. Christopher Jencks et al. (1972) talk about the way this operates in our school system.

17. Richard Sennett and Jonathan Cobb (1973) have written about how this illusion of meritocracy is supported by both schools and work hierarchy; and also about the effects it has on participants. See also Jencks et al. 1972.

18. In one strict sense, a patriarchy is one in which the political as well as the economic units are male-headed families. For example, in Puritan New England, the male head represented the political voice of the whole family.

19. Chafe 1977 has a fine presentation of these interconnections, and of the parallels (and differences) between racial and sexual domination. We have benefited considerably from his analysis. (Public consciousness of these things has changed greatly in the years since this chapter was written. But the substance of what we say here still holds.)

20. Katherine Stone's study of changing work organization in the steel industry at the turn of the century demonstrates how work hierarchies were designed to enforce the subordination

of workers, and how that subordination was further supported by political and other institutions. We have been helped a great deal by her analysis. See Stone 1973.

21. Martin Shefter's studies of the Tammany political machine in New York document these processes in informative detail. See, for example, Shefter's "The Emergence of the Political Machine: An Alternative View," in Hawley, Lipsky, et al., *Theoretical Perspectives on Urban Politics* (Englewood Cliffs, N.J.: Prentice-Hall, 1976), 14–44. W. D. Burnham's study of the 1896 election and its consequences points up the ways in which changing party organization prevented large groups of people from organizing to change either the distribution of power in society, or their immediate social and economic conditions. S. P. Hays demonstrates that the interconnections between economic and political forms was continued into the Progressive Era, despite the Progressives' rhetoric to the contrary, in "The Politics of Reform in Municipal Government in the Progressive Era," in A. Callow, ed., *American Urban History* (New York: Oxford University Press, 1969), 421–39. The point is to note that changes in organizational structure changed the ways in which people related to their political system, and, thus, the ways they had available to influence it. And, in particular, they laid the basis for the operation of laissez-faire policies in the early years of this century which, in turn, allowed for further consolidation of economic and political power in the hands of a few.

22. This structuring of influence in and through large-scale, hierarchical organizations has significant impact on resulting policies. Much recent literature in political science has examined those connections. Mills 1956, despite its flaws, opened many of these issues to thoughtful discussion. More recent examinations include Theodore Lowi, *The End of Liberalism* (New York: W. W. Norton, 1969); Grant McConnell, *Private Power and American Democracy* (New York: Alfred A. Knopf, 1966); J. David Greenstone, *Labor in American Politics* (New York: Alfred A. Knopf, 1969); and Matthew A. Crenson, *The Unpolitics of Air Pollution* (Baltimore: Johns Hopkins University Press, 1971).

23. The battles for black studies programs and women's studies programs have been fights by subordinate groups to alter this situation, as have efforts to change television programming, movie-making, and elementary-school readers.

24. On the ways in which the existing "rules of the game" operate to protect the power of some, and make difficult the raising of alternatives on the part of others, see E. E. Schattschneider, *The Semi-Sovereign People* (New York: Holt, Rinehart and Winston, 1960) and P. Bachrach and M. Baratz, "Two Faces of Power," *American Political Science Review* 56 (December 1962), 947–52. Steven Lukes develops and enlarges on this position in *Power* (New York: Macmillan Co., 1976). One need not argue a "conspiracy theory" here. The point is, simply, that the rules of acting in our society already advantage some and disadvantage others. Taking those rules as given enables those who benefit by them to exercise a certain degree of control over reality even without conscious manipulation.

25. On "propaganda by the deed," see, for example, Peter A. Kropotkin, "the Spirit of Revolt," in Baldwin 1970, 34–43. On "spontaneous organization," see "Expropriation" in Martin A. Miller, ed., *P. A. Kropotkin: Selected Writings on Anarchism and Revolution* (Cambridge: MIT Press, 1970) and Kropotkin 1913. See also Ward 1973 for a more contemporary treatment.

26. We took this quotation from a poster published by New Moon, c/o P.O. Box 263, Somerville, MA 02143. Malatesta goes on to say that the cooperatives have to be animated by the "anarchist spirit." In times of mass movement, like the late 1960s in the United States, it makes sense to talk of being animated by revolutionary spirit, for the rhetorical phrase takes its empirical content form the mass movement. We have no such mass movement now in the United States.

27. For examples of some attempts at cooperative, nonhierarchical organizations at the workplace, and analyses of their coping with many of these issues, see D. Zwerdling, *Democracy at Work* (Washington, D.C.: Association for Self-Management, 1978), especially the chapters on McCayseville Industries and Cooperstown Central. The book also includes an excellent chapter on "collectives" (closer to what we have called spontaneous organizations) as models

of "economic and political change in the community," with discussions of the problems they face trying to operate within a bureaucratically structured, capitalist society (77–90).

28. See, for example, Bakunin, "God and the State," (especially 28–39); "Paris Commune" in Lehning 1974, 195–213; and "Federalism, Socialism, and Anti-Theologism," in S. Dolgoff, ed., *Bakunin on Anarchy* (New York: Vintage Books, 1971). Also, Peter A. Kropotkin, especially "Law and Authority" and "Revolutionary Government," in Baldwin 1970, 195–218 and 236–50; and Goldman 1969, as well as "Woman Suffrage" and "The Tragedy of Woman's Emancipation," in the same work.

29. Here, again, we are indebted to the women's movement, and we see its parallels with anarchism. Nancy Hartsock writes, for example, "We cannot work ... with people who refuse to face questions in terms of everyday life or with people who will not use their own experience as a fundamental basis for knowledge" (Eisenstein 1977, 72).

30. See, for example, F. F. Piven and R. A. Cloward, *Poor People's Movements* (New York: Pantheon, 1978), especially chap. 1, and *The Politics of Turmoil* (New York: Pantheon, 1974); Alinsky 1969, especially part II; E. J. Hobsbawm, *Primitive Rebels* (New York: W. W. Norton, 1962); Thompson 1968; Flexner 1971; Rowbotham 1974; Brecker 1974.

31. A number of people have made somewhat similar arguments, though based on a different analysis of subordination, which have contributed to this presentation. See, for example, Andre Gorz on "reformist reforms" versus "structural reforms" in the labor movement, in *A Strategy for Labor*, especially part 1; Nancy Hartsock on "Feminist Theory and Revolutionary Change," in Eisenstein 1977, especially 66, in which she talks abut feminist action as (quoting Gramsci), "action 'which modifies in an essential way both man (!) and external reality,'" and 71–73 on "organizations and strategies"; also Hartsock 1974, 10–25; and Bunch 1974.

32. This is the point, in fact, where many of our anarchist forefathers turned to the "anarchist spirit" to sustain the revolution, and protect activities and organizations from the threat of "reformism." (See Kropotkin, "The Spirit of Revolt.") Since we do not really have, now, a mass movement, we cannot be so sanguine about the power of such a spirit—or where it would come from. Our answers, obviously, are not foolproof. But then, neither is social change.

33. Here we can also look to the experience of Spanish anarchists during the Civil War—and the ways in which their experiences both were, and were *not*, recognized by those who participated in them. On the collectives themselves, see Leval 1975. On the evaluation of the experiences, see Richards, *Lessons of the Spanish Revolution;* also Ackelsberg 1976, especially chap. 6 and Conclusion.

34. Ernest Callenbach, *Ecotopia* (New York: Bantam, 1977).

35. Compare Nancy Hartsock's suggestion that feminists join with others to the extent that they accept the material of their own lives as a basis for action, "Feminist Theory and Revolutionary Change," 72.

References

Ackelsberg, Martha. 1976. "The Possibility of Anarchism." Ph.D. diss., Department of Politics, Princeton University.

Argyris, Chris. 1977. "The Impact of Formal Organization on the Individual." In David S. Pugh, ed., *Organization Theory*. Baltimore: Penguin Books.

Baldwin, Roger, ed. 1970. *Kropotkin's Revolutionary Pamphlets*. New York: Dover Publications.

Bookchin, Murray. 1971. *Post-Scarcity Anarchism*. Berkeley: Ramparts Press.

Braverman, Harry. 1974. *Labor and Monopoly Capital*. New York: Monthly Review Press.

Brecker, Jeremy. 1974. *Strike!* Greenwich, Conn.: Fawcett.

Bunch, Charlotte. 1974. "The Reform Tool Kit." *Quest: A Feminist Quarterly* 1, no. 1 (Summer).

Carter, April. 1971. *The Political Theory of Anarchism*. London: Routledge and Kegan Paul.

Chafe, William. 1977. *Women and Equality.* New York: Oxford University Press.

Dworkin, Andrea. 1977. *Our Blood.* New York: W. W. Norton.

Ehrlich, Carol. 1977. "Socialism, Anarchism, and Feminism." *Second Wave* (Spring/Summer).

Eisenstein, Zillah. 1977. *Capitalist Patriarchy and the Case for Socialist Feminism.* New York: Monthly Review Press.

Ferguson, Kathy. 1978. "Liberalism and Oppression: Emma Goldman and the Anarchist Feminist Alternative." In Michael J. Gargas McGrath, ed., *Liberalism and the Modern Polity.* New York: Marcel Dekker.

Flexner, Eleanor. 1971. *Century of Struggle.* New York: Atheneum.

Friedan, Betty. 1974. *The Feminine Mystique.* New York: Dell.

Goffman, Erving. 1961. *Asylums: Essays on the Social Situation of Mental Patients and Other Inmates.* Garden City, N.Y.: Doubleday.

Goldman, Emma. 1969. "Anarchism: What It Really Stands For." In Richard Drinnon, ed., *Anarchism and Other Essays.* New York: Dover Publications.

Guerin, Daniel. 1970. *Anarchism.* New York: Monthly Review Press.

Hartmann, Heidi. 1981. "The Unhappy Marriage of Marxism and Feminism: Towards a More Progressive Union." In Lydia Sargent, ed., *Women and Revolution.* Boston: South End Press.

Hartsock, Nancy. 1974. "Political Change: Two Perspectives on Power." *Quest: A Feminist Quarterly* 1, no. 1 (Summer).

Jencks, Christopher, et al. 1972. *Inequality.* New York: Basic Books.

Kanter, Rosabeth M. 1977. *Men and Women of the Corporation.* New York: Basic Books.

Kornegger, Peggy. 1975. "Anarchism: The Feminist Connection." *Second Wave* (Spring).

Kropotkin, Peter A. 1913. *The Conquest of Bread.* London: Chapman Hall.

Lehning, Arthur, ed. 1974. *Michael Bakunin: Selected Writings.* New York: Grove Press.

Malcolm X. 1986. *The Autobiography of Malcolm X.* New York: Grove Press.

Mills, C. Wright. 1956. *The Power Elite.* New York: Oxford University Press.

Rowbotham, Sheila, 1974. *Hidden from History.* London: Philo Press.

Rubin, Lillian B. 1976. *Worlds of Pain.* New York: Basic Books.

Sennett, Richard, and Jonathan Cobb. 1973. *The Hidden Injuries of Class.* New York: Vintage Books.

Stone, Katherine. 1973. "The Origins of Job Structures in the Steel Industry." *Radical America* (November/December).

Thompson, E. P. 1968. *The Making of the English Working Class.* Hammondsworth, England: Penguin Books.

Ward, Colin. 1973. *Anarchy in Action.* New York: Harper and Row.

Healing the Wounds: Feminism, Ecology, and Nature/Culture Dualism

Ynestra King

No part of living nature can ignore the extreme threat to life on earth. We are faced with worldwide deforestation, the disappearance of hundreds of species of life, and the increasing pollution of the gene pool by poisons and low-level radiation. We are also faced with biological atrocities unique to modern life—the existence of the AIDS virus and the possibility of even more dreadful and pernicious diseases caused by genetic mutation as well as the unforeseen ecological consequences of disasters such as the industrial accident in India and nuclear meltdown in the Soviet Union. Worldwide food shortages, including episodes of mass starvation, continue to mount as prime agricultural land is used to grow cash crops to pay national debts instead of food to feed people.[1] Animals are mistreated and mutilated in horrible ways to test cosmetics, drugs, and surgical procedures.[2] The stockpiling of ever greater weapons of annihilation and the horrible imagining of new ones continues. The piece of the pie that women have only begun to sample as a result of the feminist movement is rotten and carcinogenic, and surely our feminist theory and politics must take account of this however much we yearn for the opportunities within this society that have been denied to us. What is the point of partaking equally in a system that is killing us all?[3]

The contemporary ecological crisis alone creates an imperative that feminists take ecology seriously, but there are other reasons ecology is central to feminist philosophy and politics. The ecological crisis is related to the systems of hatred of all that is natural and female by the white, male western formulators of philosophy, technology, and death inventions. I contend that the systematic denigration of working-class people and people of color, women, and animals are all connected to the basic dualism that lies at the root of western civilization. But this mindset of hierarchy originates within human society, its material roots in the domination of human by human, particularly women by men. Although I cannot speak for the liberation struggles of people of color, I believe that the goals of feminism, ecology, and movements against racism and for the survival of indigenous peoples are internally related; they must be understood and pursued together in a worldwide, genuinely prolife,[4] movement.

At the root of western society exist both a deep ambivalence about life itself, our own fertility and that of nonhuman nature, and a terrible confusion about our place in nature. Nature did not declare war on humanity; patriarchal humanity declared war on women and on living nature. Nowhere is this transition more hauntingly portrayed than by the Chorus in Sophocles' *Antigone:*

> Many the wonders but nothing more wondrous than man.
> This thing crosses the sea in the winter's storm,
> making his path through the roaring waves.
> And she, the greatest of gods, the Earth—
> deathless she is, and unwearies—he wears her away
> as the ploughs go up and down from year to year
> and his mules turn up the soil.

So far have we gone from our roots in living nature that the living, not the dead, perplexes us. The pannaturalism of ancient and ancestral culture has given way to panmechanism, the norm of the lifeless.

But for a long time after the first echoes of this transition, the inroads human beings made on living nature were superficial and unable to fundamentally upset the balance and fecundity of the nonhuman natural world. Appropriately ethics and the ideas about how people should live that took their instrumental form in politics concerned the relationships of human beings to one another, especially in cities. But with the arrival of modern technologies the task of ethics and the domain of politics change drastically. The consideration of the place of human beings in nature, formerly the terrain of religion, becomes a crucial concern for all human beings. And with modern technologies, the particular responsibilities of human beings for nature must move to the center of politics. As biological ethicist Hans Jonas writes, "A kind of metaphysical responsibility beyond self-interest has devolved in us with the magnitude of our powers relative to this tenuous film of life, that is, since man has become dangerous not only to himself but to the whole biosphere."[5]

Yet around the world, capitalism, the preeminent culture and economics of self-interest, is homogenizing cultures and simplifying life on earth by disrupting naturally complex balances within the ecosystem. Capitalism depends upon expanding markets; therefore, ever greater areas of life must be mediated by sold products. From a capitalist standpoint, the more things that can be bought and sold, the better. Capitalism requires a rationalized world-view, asserting both that human science and technology are inherently progressive, which systematically denigrates ancestral cultures, and that human beings are entitled to dominion over nonhuman nature.

Nonhuman nature is being rapidly simplified, undoing the work of organic evolution. Hundreds of species of life disappear forever each year, and the figure is accelerating. Diverse, complex, ecosystems are more stable than simple ones. They have had longer periods of evolution, and they are necessary to support human beings and many other species. Yet in the name of civilization, nature has been desecrated in a process of rationalization sociologist Max Weber called "the disenchantment of the world."

The diversity of human life on the planet is also being undermined. This worldwide process of simplification impoverishes all humanity. The cultural diversity of human societies around the world developed over thousands of years; it is part of the general evolution of life on the planet. Homogenizing culture turns the world into a giant factory and facilitates top-down authoritarian government. In the name of helping people, the industrial countries export models of development that assume the American way of life is best for everyone. In this country, McDonald's and shopping malls cater to a uniform clientele, which is becoming more uniform all the time. To "go malling" has become a verb in American English; shopping has become our national pastime, as prosperous American consumers seek to scratch an itch that can never be satisfied by commodities.[6]

A critical analysis of and opposition to the uniformity of technological, industrial culture—capitalist and socialist—is crucial to feminism, ecology, and the struggles of indigenous peoples. At this point in history, there is no way to unravel the matrix of oppressions within human society without at the same time liberating nature and reconciling the human and the nonhuman parts of nature. Socialists do not have the answer to these problems; they share the antinaturalism and basic dualism of capitalism. Although developed by capitalism, the technological means of production utilized by capitalist and socialist states are largely the same. All hitherto existing philosophies of liberation, with the possible exception of some forms of social anarchism, accept the anthropocentric notion that humanity should dominate nature and that the increasing domination of nonhuman nature is a precondition for true human freedom.[7] No socialist revolution has ever fundamentally challenged the basic prototype for nature/culture dualism—the domination of men over women.

This old socialism has apparently ended by deconstructing itself in the academy, as the white male principals of academic Marxism proclaim the end of the subject. In this sense, socialism may be in its death throes, but, I will argue, the old socialist spirit of history, a valuable legacy, is not dead. It has passed on to new subjects—feminists, greens, and other bearers of identity politics, including movements against racism and for national liberation and the survival of indigenous peoples. And in this sense, these most antimodern of movements are modern, not postmodern. In response to the modern crisis, they argue for more, not less, heart, taking the side of Pascal against Descartes, "The heart hath its reasons which the reason knows not."

The Problem of Nature for Feminism

From its inception, feminism has had to wrestle with the problem of the projection of human ideas onto the natural, where these human ideas of what is natural have then been projected back onto human society as natural law and used to reinforce male ideas about female nature.[8] Because ideas reinforcing the relationship between women and nature have been used to limit and oppress women in western society, feminists have looked to social constructionism. They are understandably wary of any theory that appears to reinforce the woman/nature relationship as biological determinism by another name. At the same time, ecologists have been busy reinforcing the humanity/nature relationship and demonstrating the perilous situation of life on earth brought about by human attempts to master nature. This has led other feminists to assert that the feminist project should be freeing nature from men, rather than freeing women from nature.

Thus, in taking up ecology feminism necessarily begins to try and understand what it has meant for us as women to be represented as closer to nature than men in a male-dominated culture that defines itself in opposition to nature. I will first explore current feminist thinking about nature/culture dualism, arguing that each side of the debate capitulates to the false opposition stated above, which is itself a product of patriarchal dualism. Next I will articulate what I believe to be a way past this division appropriating from the feminist perspectives that have so far dominated the public discourse about nature/culture dualism. I will argue that the serious consideration of ecology by feminists suggests critical directions for theory and creates an imperative for a feminist epistemology based on a noninstrumental way of knowing. This implies a reformulation, not a repudiation, of reason and science. I will also address the new forms of politics emerging from the antidualistic, ecofeminist imperative. This praxis is embodied and articulate—passionate and thoughtful. It connects political issues to one another, connects different cultures of women, and continually connects the fate of human beings to the fate of the rest of life on this planet.

Liberal Feminism, Rationalization, and the Domination of Nature

Liberalism, with its assertion of "liberty, equality, and fraternity" provided the conceptual tools for feminists to argue that no people are naturally meant to rule over other people, including men over women.[9] This rationalization of difference has worked *for* women and other dehumanized peoples because it calls into question the idea of any "natural" roles or destinies. In a liberal framework "difference" itself must be obliterated to achieve equality.[10] In other words, if women were educated like men they would *be* like men. To argue that women are capable of mindful activity—that women reason and think—was and is a liberatory argument.

Mary Wollstonecraft drew on liberal Enlightenment ideas in her germinal *Vindication of the Rights of Woman,* the first feminist work in English. It suggested that women could attain "the virtues of man" if she were extended "the rights of reason." In this framework, it is obviously preferable for women to be like men. Wollstonecraft writes:

> Asserting the rights which women in common with men ought to contend for, I have not attempted to extenuate their faults; but to prove them to be the natural consequences of their education and station in society. If so, it is reasonable to suppose that they will change their character, and correct their vices and follies, when they are allowed to be free in a physical, moral, and civil sense.[11]

Obviously, women are mindful human beings, capable of reason, who should be extended the vote, educational opportunities, and public political power. But the problem is basing the extension of full personhood to women (and other persons) on an enforced sameness.

So the version of feminism least able to appropriately address ecology is liberal feminism with its rationalist, utilitarian bias and underlying assumption that "male is better." By and large, liberal feminism is a white middle-class movement, concerned with the extension of male power and privilege to women like themselves, not the fate of women as a whole. To the extent that they address ecological concerns, liberal feminists will be "environmentalists" rather than "ecologists." The difference between environmentalists and ecologists is revealed in the terminology itself: environmentalists refer to either nonhuman nature as "the environment," the environment of human beings, or "natural resources," those resources for human use. "Environmental management" seeks to make sure that these resources are not depleted to a degree that slows human productivity. Environmentalists accept the anthropocentric view that nature exists solely to serve human ends and purposes. In this instrumentalist view, concerned more with efficacy than with ends, it is to the good that every-thing be rationalized and quantified so that we might manage it better for human ends.

One could argue from the perspective of liberal feminism that women contribute to the military and industrial ravage of nature and receive proportionately few of the supposed benefits—profits and jobs. Men are drafted and may be injured or even die in combat, but they also get jobs and have the opportunity to take part in one of the great person-making dramas of our civilization, war. For this reason contemporary liberal feminists have supported the draft, just as suffragists supported their govern-ments in World War I to prove that they were loyal citizens, contributing to the war effort and deserving of a full franchise. Many of these feminists had an international-ist, antimilitarist perspective, just as many feminists who opposed the Vietnam War now support the drafting of women so we will stand alongside men in identical rela-tionship to the state.

Liberal feminists since Harriet Taylor Mill and John Stuart Mill[12] have emphasized the similarities of women to men as the basis for the emancipation of women. But trying to maintain this stance in a contemporary context leads liberal feminists into absurdly unsisterly positions. The limitations of liberalism as a basis for feminism are especially obvious as we approach the so-called new reproductive technologies. I was recently at a meeting of feminist writers called to draft a response to the Mary Beth Whitehead surrogacy case. Although these feminists disagreed about surrogacy, all agreed that this particular woman had been wronged and should get her baby back.

One woman, a solid liberal feminist who also supports the draft, refused to pub-licly side with Whitehead; she thought that injustice had definitely been done, but she refused to take a public stance for two reasons. Her primary concern was main-taining women's contract credibility. It did not matter to her that Whitehead had not understood the contract she signed and had entered into this contract because she needed $10,000 desperately and had no other way to get it. Her other reason for op-posing Whitehead is more insidious from an ecofeminist standpoint and represents the fundamental biases of liberalism toward a denatured sameness as a condition for equality, or subjectivity. She opposed any policy recognizing that men and women stand in different relationship to a baby at the moment of its birth, thereby giving a woman a greater initial claim to the child of her flesh. Such claims may appear to re-inforce the idea that women are more creatures of nature than men or that "biology is destiny." But women do bear children, and in virtually all cultures they take major responsibility for caring for and acculturating them. To a greater degree than men, women are the repository of human fertility and the possibility of future generations. And so far that fact does not stop with the biological bearing of children determined by sex, but it extends into the social division of human activity, the realm of gender.

Feminists who have argued against any special relationship between mothers and their children, believing that the emphasis on this biological bond is the ideological basis for the oppression of women, have had their arguments used in court to take children away from their mothers.[13] In a sense they have given away what little social power women as a group have had without receiving an equal share of male power and privilege, however it might be defined. Obviously, I do not argue that abusive mothers should be given custody of their children over loving fathers; rather, I argue that women should seek to hold on to reproductive and procreative powers as a political strategy and a recognition of the biological fact that women bear children out of our own bodies and therefore have a particular claim to control how this process is carried out.

Radical Feminism's Patriarchal Root: To Embrace or Repudiate Nature?

Radical feminists, or feminists who believe that the biologically based domination of women by men is the root cause of oppression, have considered ecology from a feminist perspective more often than liberal or socialist feminists because nature is their central category of analysis. Radical feminists believe that the subordination of women in society is the root form of human oppression, closely related to the association of women with nature, hence the word "radical."

Radical feminists root the oppression of women in biological difference itself. They see "patriarchy," by which they mean the systematic dominance of men in society, as preceding and laying the foundation for other forms of human oppression and exploitation. Men identify women with nature and seek to enlist both in the service of male "projects" designed to make men safe from feared nature and mortality. The ideology of women as closer to nature is essential to such a project. If patriarchy is the archetypal form of human oppression, then it follows that if we get rid of that, other forms of oppression will likewise crumble. But there is a basic difference between the two schools of radical feminists: Is the woman/nature connection potentially emancipatory? Or does it provide a rationale for the continued subordination of women?[14]

How do women who call themselves radical feminists come to opposite conclusions?[15] The former implies a separate feminist culture and philosophy from the vantage point of identification with nature and a celebration of the woman/nature connection—this is the position of *radical cultural feminists,* which I will address later.

Radical rationalist feminists take the second position, repudiating the woman/nature connection. For these feminists, freedom is being liberated from the primordial realm of women and nature, which they regard as an imprisoning female ghetto. They believe that the key to the emancipation of women lies in the dissociation of women from nature and the end of what they believe to be a "female ghetto," an inherently unfree realm of necessity. In this sense, liberal feminism is similar to radical rationalist feminism.

Radical rationalist feminists deplore the appropriation of ecology as a feminist issue and see it as a regression bound to reinforce sex-role stereotyping. Anything that reinforces gender differences or makes any kind of special claim for women is problematic. Rationalist feminists think that feminists should not do anything that would restimulate traditional ideas about women. They celebrate the fact that we have finally begun to gain access to male bastions by using the political tools of liberalism and the rationalization of human life, mythically severing the woman/nature connection as the humanity/nature connection has been severed.

The mother of modern feminism, Simone de Beauvoir, represents this position. Recently she came out against what she calls "the new femininity":

> "An enhanced status for traditional feminine values, such as woman and her rapport with nature, woman and her maternal instinct, woman and her physical being ... etc. This renewed attempt to pin women down to their traditional role, together with a small

effort to meet some of the demands made by women—that's the formula used to try and keep women quiet. Even women who call themselves feminists don't always see through it. Once again, women are being defined in terms of 'the other', once again they are being made into the 'second sex.'" ...

She goes on to say of women and peace, and feminism and ecology:

"Why should women be more in favour of peace than men? I should think it a matter of equal concern for both! ... being a mother means being for peace. Equating ecology with feminism is something that irritates me. They are not automatically one and the same thing at all."[16]

She reiterates the position she took almost forty years ago in *The Second Sex*—that it is a sexist ploy to define women as beings who are closer to nature than men. She claims that such associations divert women from their struggle for emancipation and channel their energies "into subsidiary concerns," such as ecology and peace.

The best-known contemporary explication of this position is Shulamith Firestone's *The Dialectic of Sex*,[17] which concludes with a chapter advocating test tube reproduction and the removal of biological reproduction from women's bodies as a condition for women's liberation.

Following de Beauvoir, rationalist radical feminism is the version of radical feminism most socialist-feminists are attempting to integrate with Marxist historical materialism;[18] it asserts that the woman-nature identification is a male ideology and a tool of oppression that must itself be overcome.[19] Therefore, it women are to be allowed full participation in the male world we should not do anything in the name of feminism that reinforces the woman/nature connection. Socialist feminists seek to maintain liberal feminism commitment to equality, combining it with a socialist analysis of class.

The other form of radical feminism seeks to address the root of women's oppression with the opposite theory and strategy; this *radical cultural feminism* is usually called cultural feminism. Cultural feminists resolve the problem not by obliterating the difference between men and women but by taking women's side, which as they see it is also the side of nonhuman nature. Cultural feminism grows out of radical feminism, emphasizing the differences rather than the similarities between men and women. And not surprisingly, *they* have taken the slogan "the personal is political" in the opposite direction, personalizing the political. They celebrate the life experience of the "female ghetto," which they see as a source of female freedom, rather than subordination. Cultural feminists argue, following Virginia Woolf, that they do not want to enter the male world with its "procession of professions."[20] Cultural feminists have attempted to articulate and even create a separate women's culture; they have been major proponents of identifying women with nature and feminism with ecology. The major strength of cultural feminism is that it is a deeply woman-identified movement. It celebrates what is distinct about women, challenging male culture rather than strategizing to become part of it. Cultural feminists have celebrated the identification of women with nature in music, art, literature, poetry, covens, and communes. Although there are feminists of every stripe who are lesbians and cultural feminists who are not lesbians, lesbian cultural feminists have developed a highly political, energetic visible culture that allows women to live every aspect of their lives among women. Much of this culture intentionally identifies with women and nature against (male) culture.

For example, cultural feminists have often been in the forefront of feminist antimilitarist activism. They blame men for war and point out the masculine preoccupation with death-defying deeds as constitutive of man(person)hood. Men who are socialized in this way have little respect for women, or for life, including their own. Since Vietnam, even in the popular culture, the glorification of the military and the idea that soldiering is great preparation for a successful manly life has been tarnished. At the same time, the Rambo industry (films, dolls, toys, games, etc.) is immensely successful, and efforts to "reconstruct" the history of the Vietnam War as the emasculation of America proceed. Not only have cultural feminists criticized male and military culture, but males themselves have challenged the masculine construction of personhood, with its idealization of war. The most popular adventure show on U.S. television is Magnum P.I., where four friends (three Vietnam vets and a longtime British army officer) live in Hawaii, trying to recover from and make sense of their personally devastating military experiences. Films like *Platoon* portray the dehumanization of soldiering, rather than romanticizing the battlefield and furthering the idea of hero/soldier as human ideal. In this way, antimilitary art and culture share the cultural feminist project, suggesting that the imperatives of manhood are destructive to men as well as to women and nature.

In her book *Gyn/Ecology: The Metaethics of Radical Feminism,* a major work of cultural feminist theory, Mary Daly calls herself an ecofeminist and implores women to identify with nature against men and live our lives separately from men. For Daly the oppression of women under patriarchy and the pillage of the natural world are the same phenomenon, and consequently she does not theoretically differentiate the issues.[21] In the political realm, Sonia Johnson recently waged a presidential campaign as a candidate for the Citizens Party, translating a perspective very much like Mary Daly's into conventional political terms.[22] My ecofeminism differs from that of Daly; I think *Gyn/Ecology* stands as a powerful phenomenology of the victimization of women, but it is ultimately dualistic. Hers is a work of metaphysical naturalism or naturalistic metaphysics—either way dualistic. She has turned the old misogynist Thomas Aquinas on his head. Although she is more correct than he, she has *reified* the female over the male. She does not take us past dualism, which I believe to be the ecofeminist agenda.

Susan Griffin's book *Women and Nature: The Roaring Inside Her,* is another cultural feminist classic. A long prose poem, it is not intended to spell out a precise political philosophy and program but to let us know and feel how the woman/nature connection has played out historically in the dominant western culture. It suggests a powerful potentiality for a feminist movement that links feminism and ecology, with an immanent, or mystical, relationship to nature. Griffin does not mean to trade history for mystery, although her work has been interpreted that way. Griffin's work, located ambiguously between theory and poetry, has been read much too literally and at times invoked wrongly to collapse the domination of women and the domination of nature into a single, timeless phenomenon.[23] Griffin collapses the rigid boundaries of the subject and the object, suggesting a recovery of mysticism as a way of knowing nature immanently.

But one problem that white cultural feminists, like other feminists, have not adequately faced is that in celebrating the commonalities of women and emphasizing the ways in which women are universal victims of male oppression, they have inadequately addressed the real diversity of women's lives and histories across race, class, and national boundaries. For women of color, opposing racism and genocide and encouraging ethnic pride are agendas they often share with men in a white-dominated society, even while they struggle against sexism in their own communities. These complex, multidimensional loyalties and historically divergent life situations require a politics that recognizes those complexities. This connecting of women and nature has lent itself to a romanticization of women as good, separate from all the dastardly deeds of men and culture. The problem is that history, power, women, and nature are all a lot more complicated than that.

In the last ten years, the old cultural feminism has given birth to "the feminist spirituality movement,"[24] an eclectic potpourri of beliefs and practices, with an immanent goddess (as opposed to the transcendent god). I believe there has been a greater racial diversity in this movement than in any other form of feminism; this is due in part to the fact that this is a spiritual movement, based on the ultimate unity of all living things and a respect for diversity. There is no particular dogma in this movement, only a recognition of a woman as an embodied, earth-bound living being who should celebrate her connection to the rest of life and, for some, invoke this connection in her public political protest actions. These beliefs have their scientific corollaries: for example, the Gaia hypothesis, the idea that the planet is to be conceived as one single living organism; and the thesis of scientist Lynn Margolis, whose research corroborates Peter Kropotkin's mutualism,[25] that cooperation was a stronger force in evolution than competition.[26]

Cultural feminism and the women's spirituality movement have been subjected to the same critique feminists of color have made of the ethnocentricity of much white feminism,[27] as women of color have become a powerful presence in its circles. This critique comes from women of color who draw on indigenous spiritual traditions; Native American and African women argue that these white western feminists are inventing and originating an earth-centered prowoman spirituality while they are defending their indigenous spirituality against the imperialism of western rationalism.[28] For example, Louisah Teish, the first voodoo priestess to attempt to explain her tradition to the public, advocates a practice that integrates the political and spiritual, bringing together a disciplined understanding of the African spiritual tradition with contemporary feminist and black power politics. Members of her group in Oakland are planning urban gardening projects both to help the poor feed themselves and to supply the herbs needed for the holistic healing remedies of her tradition while they engage in community organizing to stop gentrification. Women in the Hopi and Navaho traditions are also attempting to explain their traditions to a wider public while they organize politically to keep their lands from being taken over the developers or poisoned by industry.

The collision of modern industrial society with indigenous cultures has decimated these ancestral forms, but it may have brought white westerners into contact with forms of knowledge useful to us as we try to imagine our way beyond dualism, to understand what it means to be embodied beings on this planet. These traditions are often used as examples of nondualistic ways of life, at least which overcome nature/culture dualism.[29] But human beings cannot simply jump off or out of history. These indigenous, embodied, earth-centered spiritual traditions are planting seeds in the imaginations of people who are the products of dualistic cultures, but, as pointed out by their original practitioners, they are not ways of being or systems of thought that can be adopted whole cloth by white westerners who want to avoid the responsibility of their own history.

The movement has changed in recent years, becoming more sophisticated and diverse as women of color articulate a powerful survival-based feminism emerging from their experience at the crucible of multiple oppressions. From both the feminism of women of color, sometimes called "womanist" as opposed to "feminist" in order to convey the different priorities of women of color from white women, and ecofeminism has come the urging of a more holistic feminism, linking all issues of personal and planetary survival.[30] The critique of cultural feminism advanced by women of color—that it is often ahistorical in that white women, in particular, need to take responsibility for being oppressors as well as oppressed and for having been powerful as white people or as people with class or national privileges—is crucial. In other words, women have a complexity of historical identities and therefore a complexity of loyalties. Instead of constantly attempting to make our identities less complex by emphasizing what we have in common as women, as has been the tendency of women who are feminists first and foremost, we should attend to the differences between us.

Socialist Feminism, Rationalization, and the Domination of Nature

Socialist feminism is an odd hybrid—an attempt at a synthesis of the rationalist feminism, radical and liberal, and the historical materialism of the Marxist tradition. Socialist feminism is not a mass movement, just as socialism is not a mass movement. However, the existence of a women's movement has assured that the feminists are the liveliest presence at otherwise tepid socialist gatherings.[31] This version of feminism has dominated the academy, while radical feminism, cultural feminism, and more recently ecofeminism are popular movements with a political base. Both Marxism and rationalist feminism subscribe to the domination of nature; thus, ecology has not been on the socialist feminist agenda. Some socialist feminists argued that socialist feminism should be differentiated from Marxist feminism. They may be a valid distinction, but so far socialist feminism has shared many of Marxism's blind spots.

In taking "labor" as its central category, Marxists have reduced the human being to homo laborans, and the history of capitalism cries out with the resistance of human beings not only to being exploited but to being conceived of as essentially "workers." In Marxism, revolutionary discourse has been reduced to a "language of productivity"[32] where a critique of the mode of production does not necessarily challenge the principle of production, shared by political economy and Marxism. This functionalist, rationalist idea of persons has been a central theoretical and political weakness of the post-Marxist socialist tradition, including socialist feminism.

The socialist feminist theory of the body as socially constructed (re)producer has informed a public discourse of "reproductive freedom"—the freedom to (re)produce or not (re)produce with your own body. In this area socialist feminists have been a political force. But socialist feminists have an inadequate theory with which to confront the new reproductive technologies. Arguing that women have a right to "control our own bodies" does not prepare one to confront the issue of whether our reproductive, like our productive capacities, should be bought and sold in the marketplace, as one more form of wage labor.[33]

Socialist feminists have criticized liberal feminists, just as socialists have criticized liberalism, for not going far enough in a critique of the political economy and class differences. They are right to the extent that liberal feminists cannot take account of systematic inequalities in our liberal democracy that discriminate against women and the poor and prevent everyone from having equal opportunity. They have rightfully pointed out that as long as we earn on the average fifty-nine cents to the dollar earned by men, women are not equal. This would still be the case even if the Equal Rights Amendment had passed.

But socialist feminists have shared the rationalist bias of liberal feminism, depicting the world primarily in exchange terms—whether production or reproduction— and have agreed with the liberal feminist analysis that we must strive in all possible ways to demonstrate that we are more like men than different. Some socialist feminists have even argued that liberal feminism has a radical potential.[34] For such feminists, the dualistic, overly rationalized premises of liberal feminism are not a problem. For them too, severing the woman/nature connection is a feminist project.

In a sense the strength and weakness of socialist feminism lie in the same premise: the centrality of economics in their theory and practice. Socialist feminists have articulated a strong economic and class analysis, but they have not sufficiently addressed the domination of nature.[35] The socialist feminist agenda would be complete if we could overcome systematic inequalities of social and economic power. Socialist feminists have addressed one of the three forms of domination of nature, domination between persons, but they have not seriously attended to the domination of either nonhuman nature or inner nature.

Socialist feminism draws on but goes beyond socialism, demonstrating the independent dynamic of patriarchy and fundamentally challenging the totalizing claims of Marxist economistic approach. In socialist feminism, women seek to enter the political world as articulate, historical subjects, capable of understanding and making history. And some socialist feminists have drawn on historical materialism in very creative ways, such as the standpoint theories of Alison Jaggar and Nancy Hartsock,[36] which attempt to articulate a position from which women can make special historical claims without being biologically determinist. But even Hartsock, Jaggar, and other socialist feminists who are attempting a multifactored historical analysis of the oppression of women do not treat the domination of nature as a significant category for feminism, although they notice it in passing.

In general, socialist feminists are very unsympathetic to "cultural feminism."[37] They accuse it of being ahistorical, essentialist, which they define as believing in male and female essences (male = bad, female = good), and anti-intellectual. This debate partakes of the ontology versus epistemology debate in western philosophy, where "being" is opposed to "knowing," and implicitly women are relegated to the realm of "being," the ontological slums. From an ecological (i.e., antidualistic) standpoint, essentialism and ontology are not the same as biological determinism. In other words, we are neither talking heads nor unselfconsciousness nature.

Although certain aspects of this critique may be correct, socialist feminists are avoiding the important truths being recognized by cultural feminism, among them the female political imagination manifesting itself in the political practice of a feminism of difference. They also forget that no revolution in human history has succeeded without a strong cultural foundation and a utopian vision emerging from the life experience of the revolutionary subjects. In part, I believe the myopia of socialist feminism with respect to cultural feminism is rooted in the old Marxist debate about the primacy of the base (economics/production) over the superstructure (culture/reproduction). This dualism must also be overcome, as a condition for a dialectical or genuinely ecological feminism.

The socialist feminist fidelity to a theory of history where women seek to understand the past in order to make the future is crucial to feminism. Also the project of a feminist reconstitution of reason has been largely undertaken by socialist feminists who do not wish to throw the baby out with the bath water in critiquing instrumental reason. But belief in a direct relationship between the rationalization and domination of nature and the project of human liberation remains a central tenet of socialism. The question for socialist feminists is whether they can accommodate their version of feminism within the socialist movement, or whether they will have to move in a "greener" direction with a more radical critique of all forms of the domination of nature. That would involve considering the recessive form of socialism—social anarchism—that finds its contemporary manifestation in green politics and among feminists in ecofeminism.[38]

Ecofeminism: On the Necessity of History and Mystery

Women have been culture's sacrifice to nature. The practice of human sacrifice to outsmart or appease a feared nature is ancient. And in resistance to this sacrificial mentality—on the part of both the sacrificer and the sacrificee—some feminists have argued against the association of women with nature, emphasizing the social dimension to traditional women's lives. Women's activities have been represented as nonsocial, as natural. Part of the work of feminism has been asserting that the activities of women, believed to be more natural, are in fact absolutely social. This process of looking at women's activities has led to a greater valuing of women's social contribution; it is part of the antisacrificial current of feminism. Giving birth is natural, although how it is done is very social, but mothering is an absolutely social activity.[39] In bringing up their children, mothers face ethical and moral choices as complex as those considered by professional politicians and ethicists. In the wake of feminism, women will continue to do these things, but the problem of connecting humanity to nature will have to be acknowledged and solved in a different way. In our mythology of complementarity, men and women have led vicarious lives, where women had feelings and led instinctual lives and men engaged in the projects illuminated by reason. Feminism has exposed the extent to which it was all a lie; thus, it has been so important to feminism to establish the mindful, social nature of mothering.

But just as women are refusing to be sacrificed, nonhuman nature is requiring even more attention; it is revolting against human domination in the ecological crisis. Part of the resistance to contemporary feminism is that it embodies the return of the repressed, those things men put away to create a dualistic culture founded on the domination of nature. Now, nature moves to the center of the social and political choices facing humanity.

It is as if women were entrusted with and kept the dirty little secret that humanity emerges from nonhuman nature into society in the life of the species, and the person. The process of nurturing an unsocialized, undifferentiated human infant into an adult person—the socialization of the organic—is the bridge between nature and culture. The western male bourgeois subject then extracts himself from the realm of the organic to become a public citizen, as if born from the head of Zeus. He puts away childish things. Then he disempowers and sentimentalizes his mother, sacrificing her to nature. The coming of age of the male subject repeats the drama of the emergence of the polis, made possible by banishing the mother, and with her the organic world. But the key to the historic agency of women with respect to nature/culture dualism lies in the fact that the mediating traditional conversion activities of women—mothering, cooking, healing, farming, foraging—are as social as they are natural.

The task of an ecological feminism is the organic forging of a genuinely antidualistic, or dialectical, theory and praxis. No previous feminism can address this problem adequately from within the framework of their theory and politics, hence the necessity of ecofeminism. Rather than succumb to nihilism, pessimism, and an end to reason and history, we seek to enter into history, to habilitate a genuinely ethical thinking—where one uses mind and history to reason from the "is" to the "ought" and to reconcile humanity with nature, within and without. This is the starting point for ecofeminism.

Each major contemporary feminist theory—liberal, social, cultural—has taken up the issue of the relationship between women and nature. Each in its own way has capitulated to dualistic thinking, theoretically conflating a reconciliation with nature by surrendering to some form of natural determinism. As I have demonstrated, we have seen the same positions appear again and again in extending the natural into the social (cultural feminism) or in severing the social from the natural (socialist feminism). Each direction forms two sides of the same dualism, and from an ecofeminist perspective both are wrong because they have chosen between culture and nature. I contend that this is a false choice, leading to bad politics and bad theory on each side and that we need a new, dialectical way of thinking about our relationship to nature to realize the full meaning and potential of feminism, a social ecological feminism.

Absolute social constructionism on which socialist feminism relies is disembodied. The logical conclusion is a rationalized, denatured, totally deconstructed person. But socialist feminism is the antisacrificial current of feminism, with its insistence that women are social beings, whose traditional work is as social as it is natural. The fidelity to the social aspects of women's lives found in socialist feminism makes a crucial contribution to ecofeminism.

It is for ecofeminism to interpret the historical significance of the fact that women have been positioned at the biological dividing line where the organic emerges into the social. It is for ecofeminism to interpret this fact historically and to make the most of this mediated subjectivity to heal a divided world. The domination of nature originates in society and therefore must be resolved in society. Therefore, the embodied woman as social historical agent, rather than product of natural law, is the subject of ecofeminism.

But the weakness of socialist feminism's theory of the person is serious from an ecofeminist standpoint. An ecological feminism calls for a dynamic, developmental theory of the person—male and female—who emerges out of nonhuman nature, where difference is neither reified or ignored and the dialectical relationship between human and nonhuman nature is understood.

Cultural feminism's greatest weakness is its tendency to make the personal into the political, with its emphasis on personal transformation and empowerment. This is

most obvious in cultural feminists' attempt to overcome the apparent opposition between spirituality and politics. For cultural feminists spirituality is the heart in a
heartless world, whereas for socialist feminists it is the opiate of the people. Cultural
feminists have formed the "beloved community" of feminism—with all the power,
potential, and problems of a religion. For several years spiritual feminism has been
the fastest growing part of the women's movement, with spirituality circles often replacing consciousness-raising groups as the place that women meet for personal empowerment.

As an appropriate response to the need for mystery and attention to personal
alienation in an overly rationalized world it is a vital and important movement. But
by itself it does not provide the basis for a genuinely dialectical ecofeminist theory
and praxis, addressing history as well as mystery. For this reason, cultural/spiritual
feminism, sometimes even called "nature feminism," is not synonymous with
ecofeminism in that creating a gynocentric culture and politics is a necessary but insufficient condition for ecofeminism.

Healing the split between the political and the spiritual cannot be done at the expense of either repudiating the rational or developing a historically informed, dynamic political program. Socialist feminists have often mistakenly ridiculed spiritual
feminists for having "false consciousness" or being "idealist." Socialism's impoverished idea of personhood, which denies the qualitative dimensions of subjectivity, is
a major reason socialism, including socialist-feminism, has no political base.[40] But
many practitioners of feminist spirituality have eschewed thinking about politics
and power, arguing that personal empowerment is in and of itself a sufficient agent
of social transformation.

Both feminism and ecology embody the revolt of nature against human domination. They demand that we rethink the relationship between humanity and the rest
of nature, including our natural, embodied selves. In ecofeminism, nature is the central category of analysis. An analysis of the interrelated dominations of nature—psyche and sexuality, human oppression, and nonhuman nature—and the historic position of women in relation to those forms of domination is the starting point of
ecofeminist theory. We share with cultural feminism the necessity of a politics with
heart and a beloved community, recognizing our connection with each other, and
nonhuman nature. Socialist feminism has given us a powerful critical perspective
with which to understand and transform history. Separately, they perpetuate the dualism of "mind" and "nature." Together they make possible a new ecological relationship between nature and culture, in which mind and nature, heart and reason,
join forces to transform the internal and external systems of domination that
threaten the existence of life on earth.

Practice does not wait for theory; it comes out of the imperatives of history.
Women are the revolutionary bearers of this antidualistic potential in the world today. In addition to the enormous impact of feminism on western civilization, women
have been at the forefront of every historical, political movement to reclaim the
earth. A principle of reconciliation, with an organic praxis of nonoppositional opposition, provides the basis for an ecofeminist politics. The laboratory of
nonoppositional opposition is the action taken worldwide by women, women who
do not necessarily call themselves feminists.

For example, for many years in India poor women who came out of the Gandhian
movement have waged a nonviolent land reform and forest preservation campaign,

called the Chipko Adolan (the Hugging Movement). Each woman has a tree of her own to protect, to steward, by wrapping her body around a tree as bulldozers arrive.[41] When loggers were sent in, one movement leader said, "Let them know they will not fell a single tree without the felling of us first. When the men raise their axes, we will embrace the trees to protect them."[42] These women have waged a remarkably successful nonviolent struggle, and their tactics have spread to other parts of India. Men have joined this campaign, although it was originated and continues to be led by women. Yet this is not a sentimental movement; lives depend on the survival of the forest. For most women of the world, interest in the preservation of the land, water, air, and energy is no abstraction but a clear part of the effort to simply survive.

The increasing militarization of the world has intensified this struggle. Women and children make up 80 percent of war refugees. Land they are left with is often burned and scarred in such a way as to prevent cultivation for many years after battle so starvation and hardship follow long after the fighting has stopped.[43] And here too women—often mothers and farmers—respond to necessity. They become the guardians of the earth in an effort to eke out a small living on the land to feed themselves and their families.

Other areas of feminist activism also illuminate an enlightened ecofeminist perspective.[44] Potentially, one of the best examples of an appropriately mediated, dialectical relationship to nature is the feminist health movement. The medicalization of childbirth in the first part of the twentieth century and the later redesign and appropriation of reproduction both create new profit-making technologies for capitalism and make heretofore natural processes mediated by women into arenas controlled by men. Here women offered themselves up to the ministrations of experts,[45] internalizing the notion they do not know enough, and surrender their power. They also accepted the idea that the maximum intervention in and the domination of nature is an inherent good.

But since the onset of feminism in the 1960s, women in the United States have gone quite a way in reappropriating and demedicalizing childbirth. As a result of this movement, many more women want to be given all their options, choosing invasive medical technologies only under unusual and informed circumstances. They do not necessarily reject these technologies as useful in some cases, but they have pointed a finger at motivations of profit and control in their widespread application. Likewise, my argument here is not that feminism should repudiate all aspects of western science and medicine; rather, I assert that we should develop the sophistication to decide for ourselves when intervention serves our best interest.

A related critical area for a genuinely dialectical praxis is a reconstruction of science, taking into account the critique of science advanced by radical ecology and feminism.[46] Feminist historians and philosophers of science are demonstrating that the will to know and the will to power need not be the same thing. They argue that there are ways of knowing the world that are not based on objectification and domination.[47] Here again, apparently antithetical epistemologies, science and mysticism, coexist. We shall need all our ways of knowing to create life on this planet that is both ecological, sustainable, and free.

As feminists we shall need to develop an ideal of freedom that is neither antisocial nor antinatural.[48] We are past the point of a Rousseauian throwing off of our chains to reclaim our ostensibly free nature, if such a point ever existed. Ecofeminism is not an argument for a return to prehistory. The knowledge that women were not always dominated and that society was not always hierarchical is a powerful inspiration for contemporary women, so long as such a society is not represented as a "natural order" apart from history to which we will inevitably return by a great reversal.

From an ecofeminist perspective, we are part of nature, but neither inherently good or bad, free or unfree. No one natural order represents freedom. We are *potentially* free in nature, but as human beings that freedom must be intentionally created by using our understanding of the natural world of which we are a part in a noninstrumental way. For this reason we must develop a different understanding of the relationship between human and nonhuman nature. To do this we need a theory of history where the natural evolution of the planet and the social history of the species are not separated. We emerged from nonhuman nature, as the organic emerged from the inorganic.

Here, potentially, we recover ontology as the ground for ethics.[49] We thoughtful human beings must use the fullness of our sensibility and intelligence to push ourselves intentionally to another stage of evolution—one where we will fuse a new way of being human on this planet with a sense of the sacred, informed by all ways of knowing, intuitive *and* scientific, mystical *and* rational. It is the moment where women recognize ourselves as agents of history—yes, even unique agents—and knowingly bridge the classic dualisms between spirit and matter, art and politics, reason and intuition. This is the potentiality of a *rational* reenchantment. This is the project of ecofeminism.

At this point in history, the domination of nature is inextricably bound up with the domination of persons, and both must be addressed, without arguments over "the primary contradiction" in search of a single Archimedes point for revolution. There is no such thing. And there is no point in liberating people if the planet cannot sustain their liberated lives or in saving the planet by disregarding the preciousness of human existence, not only to ourselves but to the rest of life on earth.

Notes

1. One major issue at the United Nations Decade on Women Forum held in Nairobi, Kenya, in 1985 was the effect of the international monetary system on women and the particular burdens women bear because of the money owed the "first world" particularly U.S. economic interests, by developing countries.

2. The animal liberation movement is more developed in the United Kingdom than in the United States. One of its major publications is a periodical called *Beast: The Magazine That Bites Back*. See Peter Singer, *Animal Liberation: A New Ethics For Our Treatment of Animals* (New York: Avon Books, 1975).

3. The National Organization for Women (NOW) is caught in the myopia of this position, supporting the draft of women because men are drafted rather than taking an antimilitarist position and opposing the draft for anyone. At their Denver convention held in June 1986 NOW began to evaluate its prodraft position, but it will be a while before this process proceeds through the state committee structures and takes on national significance. Even then, there is no guarantee that it will change its position.

4. It is one of the absurd examples of newspeak that the designation "pro-life" has been appropriated by the militarist right to support forced child bearing.

5. Hans Joans, *The Imperative of Responsibility: In Search of an Ethics for the Technological Age* (Chicago: University of Chicago Press, 1984), 136.

6. For a fuller discussion of this point, see William Leiss, *The Limits to Satisfaction: An Essay on the Problem of Needs and Commodities* (Toronto: University of Toronto Press, 1976).

7. In *The German Ideology* Marx cut his teeth on the "natural order" socialism of Feuerbach, although he had tended toward a "naturalistic socialism" himself in his early "Economic and Philosophic Manuscripts." See T. B. Bottomore, *Karl Marx: Early Writings* (New York: McGraw-Hill, 1964).

Since Marx, scientific socialists have argued that socialism is the culmination of reason understood as the domination of nature, and have argued against utopianism. For Marxists "utopian" is a bad word; it means unrealistic, unscientific, anti-instrumental, by definition naive. Social anarchists have maintained a much more ambivalent relationship to the domination of nature and a fidelity to the cultural dimensions of pre-Marxist utopian socialism. Although both scientific socialism and social anarchism are parts of the historical socialist tradition, in a contemporary context the term "socialism" applies to the Marxists, as distinct from the "anarchists." Lately, there is a move afoot among socialists to "recover" the pre-Marxist utopian tradition and to utilize this forgotten history to save contemporary socialism. I think this is ahistorical in that it begs the problem of the need to critique the history (and theory) of anti-utopian Marxist socialism. Socialists and anarchists have had crucial ideological differences with respect to the domination of nature, the base/superstructure distinction, power and the state, sexuality and the individual. The contemporary "green" movement grows out of the social anarchist utopian socialist tradition, where the conditions for human freedom depend on *ending* the domination of nonhuman nature. It is crucial that socialists be honest about the shortcomings of their own movement, and, if they make a major historic shift in a direction they have scorned for over a century, this change should be acknowledged and examined. I also do not mean to suggest here either that social anarchism is a fully adequate theory or that the proper strategy for rectifying the domination of nature is a simple reversion. But the critique of socialism advanced through this work is illuminated by, but not limited to, that of social anarchism, and it is aimed at anti-utopian socialism.

8. For a full discussion of the relationship between feminist politics and ideas about human nature, see Alison M. Jaggar, *Feminist Politics and Human Nature* (Totowa, N.J.: Rowman and Allanheld, 1983).

9. See Christine DiStefano, "Gender and Political Theory: Gender as Ideology," for a fuller treatment of the problem of "deep masculinity" in political thought. Her section on the problematic relationship between feminism and liberalism is especially instructive. Ph.D. diss., University of Massachusetts, Amherst, 1985.

10. See Alison Jaggar, "Difference and Equality," (unpublished paper) for an exposition of the difference versus equality problem in feminist theory. She concludes by arguing that feminists must be able to argue our case based on either, or both.

11. Mary Wollstonecraft, *A Vindication of the Rights of Woman* (New York: W. W. Norton, 1967), 286.

12. Harriet Taylor Mill and John Stuart Mill, *On the Subjugation of Women* (London: Virago, 1983).

13. If the mother is given no special preference and both parents are presumed equally suited before the law, then the decision may be made on other grounds. Men generally have a larger income than women, especially women who have left the work force to mother children, and can arguably provide greater economic and cultural advantages.

14. See Alice Echols, "The New Feminism of Yin and Yang," in *The Powers of Desire*, ed. Ann Snitow, Sharon Thompson, and Christine Stansell (New York: Monthly Review Press, 1983).

15. See Alison M. Jaggar, *Feminist Politics and Human Nature*.

16. Alice Schwarzer, *After the Second Sex: Conversations With Simone de Beauvoir* (New York: Pantheon, 1984), 103.

17. See Shulamith Firestone, "Conclusion: The Ultimate Revolution," in *The Dialectic of Sex* (New York: Bantam Books, 1971).

18. This is evident in Zillah Eisenstein, *The Radical Future of Liberal Feminism* (New York: Longman, 1981), and Zillah Eisenstein, ed., *Capitalist Patriarchy and the Case for Socialist Feminism* (New York: Monthly Review Press, 1979).

19. See Sherry Ortner, "Is Female to Male as Nature is to Culture?" in *Woman, Culture and Society*, ed. Michele Rosaldo and Louise Lamphere (Palo Alto: Stanford University Press, 1974).

20. See Virginia Woolf, *Three Guineaus* (New York: Harcourt, Brace & World, 1938).

21. See Mary Daly, *Gyn/Ecology*. (Boston: Beacon Press, 1979). In response to her critics, Daly's position in her later work is intentionally ambiguous on these points. See *Pure Lust* (Boston: Beacon Press, 1985).

22. Johnson was solicited by the Citizens Party, a political party made up of both men and women, founded primarily to advocate "environmentalism" from a socialist perspective. It is interesting that a mixed party with an environmental (not ecological) emphasis, not a leftist party, drafted Johnson to run. Her analysis of all the political issues was basically an analysis of male power, and Mary Daly worked very hard for her candidacy. Prior to her campaign it was difficult to imagine how radical feminism would translate into the jargon and iconography of the American political arena, but Johnson did a very good job of this. She was widely criticized for having a naive understanding or being evangelical, but she articulated a woman centered perspective that had not previously been heard in presidential politics. Her message was basically simple—that women are different and therefore can make a difference if elected to public office. And she used the device of the imaginary cabinet to suggest department heads such as Barbara Deming for secretary of state. Barbara Deming was a well-known feminist pacifist whose essays are collected in a volume, *We Are All Part of One Another* (Philadelphia: New Society Publishers, 1983). She was alive at the time of Johnson's candidacy and also supported her.

23. It is a good example of the care the reader must take in interpreting the medium of the artist. See Susan Griffin, *Women and Nature: The Roaring Inside Her* (New York: Harper & Row, 1978). Her later work on pornography *(Pornography and Silence: Culture's Revenge Against Nature* (New York: Harper & Row, 1981). Her forthcoming work on war, "A Woman Thinks About War" (manuscript), is an explicitly theoretical, ecofeminist work.

24. Much iconography of the contemporary radical feminist peace movement is inspired by the feminist spirituality movement, devising political actions that use the imagery of embodied female spirituality. Actions have featured guerrilla theater where the Furies ravage Ronald Reagan, women encircle military bases and war research centers with pictures of children, trees, brooks in preparation for civil disobedience, and weave shut the doors of the stock exchange.

25. See Peter Kropotkin, *Mutual Aid: A Factor in Evolution* (Boston: Porter Sargent, 1914).

26. See the works of scientists Lynn Margolis and James Lovelock, especially J. E. Lovelock, *Gaia: A New Look at Life on Earth* (New York: Oxford University Press, 1982).

27. See "The Cumbahee River Collective Statement," in Zillah Eisenstein, ed., *Capitalist Patriarchy;* Cherrie Moraga and Gloria Anzuldua, *This Bridge Called My Back* (New York: Kitchen Table Press, 1983); Gloria Joseph and Jill Lewis, *Common Differences: Conflicts in Black and White Feminist Perspectives* (Garden City, N.Y.: Anchor Press, 1981); and Bell Hooks, *Feminist Theory: From Margin to Center* (Boston: South End Press, 1984). Audre Lorde has written eloquently of the problems of attempting to "use the master's tools to disassemble the master's house" and the implicit racism of heretofore definitions of "theory." See Audre Lorde, *Sister Outsider* (Trumansburg, N.Y.: The Crossing Press, 1986).

28. See Louisah Teish, *Jambalaya* (San Francisco: Harper & Row, 1986).

29. These traditions are complex, and there are critical differences among them. Each has an ancient and total cosmology and set of practices, and, although it is possible to find commonalities, creating a willy-nilly, random patchwork is not a brilliant new synthesis. That is the problem with the incoherent mush called "new age spirituality" or its slightly more secular version "the human potential movement." Each religious tradition requires instruction, which may be in an oral or written tradition, or both, study, and the discipline of practice. I also do

not know that traditions and cultures that apparently have an antidualistic perspective when it comes to the relationship between human and nonhuman nature are *necessarily* not sexist, xenophobic, or hierarchical in a contemporary context, even if they once were.

30. See Ynestra King, "Thinking About Seneca," *Ikon* (Summer 1984). In this piece I addressed the contradictions of the mostly white women's peace movement, which grew out of an ecofeminist perspective. In response to the concern that the feminist peace movement up to that point was mostly white, I explored what I believed to be underlying commonalities between the "womanist" feminism of women of color, which affirms the traditional lives and struggles of women, and a feminism that up to that point had been mostly articulated by white women who believed feminism should associate itself with ecology and peace, adopting rather than repudiating the traditional concerns of women.

31. I am thinking here of the annual "Socialist Scholars Conference," held each spring in New York City, or the socialist caucus offerings at academic conferences.

32. See Jean Baudrillard, *The Mirror of Production* (St. Louis: Telos Press, 1975).

33. In raising these issues I am in no way advocating the criminalization of women who market their eggs or wombs. And obviously, there are critical economic and class issues here.

34. See especially Eisenstein, *The Radical Future of Liberal Feminism.*

35. One exception is Carolyn Merchant, who has written a socialist feminist analysis of the scientific revolution, *The Death of Nature: Women, Ecology and the Scientific Revolution* (New York: Harper & Row, 1979). See also Carolyn Merchant, "Earthcare: Women and the Environmental Movement," *Environment* 23, no. 5 (June 1981):6.

36. See Nancy Hartsock, *Money, Sex and Power* (Boston: Northeastern University Press, 1983), and Jaggar, *Feminist Politics and Human Nature.*

37. Cultural feminism is a term invented by feminists who believe in the primacy of economic, as opposed to cultural, forces in making history, but cultural feminists are proud of their emphasis.

38. See note 8.

39. On the social, mindful nature of mothering see the work of Sara Ruddick, especially "Maternal Thinking," *Feminist Studies* 6, no. 2 (Summer 1980):342–367; and "Preservative Love and Military Destruction: Some Reflections on Mothering and Peace," in *Mothering: Essays in Feminist Theory,* ed. Joyce Trebilcot (Totowa, N.J.: Rowman and Allanheld, 1983), 231–262.

40. The most vital socialism in the world today is liberation theology, with its roots in the Catholic base communities of the poor in Latin America.

41. Catherine Caufield, *In the Rainforest* (Chicago: University of Chicago Press, 1984), 156–158.

42. Ibid., 157.

43. See Edward Hyams, *Soil and Civilization* (New York: Harper & Row, 1976).

44. West German green Petra Kelly outlines a practical, feminist green political analysis and program, with examples of ongoing movements and activities in her work. Petra Kelly, *Fighting for Hope* (Boston: South End Press, 1984).

45. See Barbara Ehrenreich and Dierdre English, *For Her Own Good: 150 years of the Experts Advice to Women* (Garden City, N.Y.: Anchor Press, 1979).

46. See Elizabeth Fee, "Is Feminism a Threat to Scientific Objectivity?" *International Journal of Women's Studies* 4, no. 4, (1981). See also Sandra Harding, *The Science Question in Feminism* (Ithaca, N.Y.: Cornell University Press, 1986) and Evelyn Fox Keller, *Reflections on Gender and Science* (New Haven, Conn.: Yale University Press, 1985).

47. See Evelyn Fox Keller, *A Feeling for the Organism: The Life and Work of Barbara McClintock* (San Francisco, W. H. Freeman, 1983).

48. The crosscultural interpretations of personal freedom of anthropologist Dorothy Lee are evocative of the possibility of such an ideal of freedom. See Dorothy Lee, *Freedom and Culture* (New York: Prentice Hall, 1959).

49. I am aware that this is a controversial point, one that I am developing more explicitly in a work on ecofeminist ethics.

References

Baudrillard, Jean. 1975. *The Mirror of Production*. St. Louis: Telos Press.
Bookchin, Murray. 1982. *The Ecology of Freedom*. Palo Alto, Calif.: Cheshire Books.
Bottomore, T. B. 1964. *Karl Marx: Early Writings*. New York: McGraw-Hill.
Caufield, Catherine. 1984. *In the Rainforest*. Chicago: University of Chicago Press.
Cumbahee River Collective. 1979. "Cumbahee River Collective Statement." In *Capitalist Patriarchy*, ed. Zillah Eisenstein.
Daly, Mary. 1979. *Gyn/Ecology*. Boston: Beacon Press.
_____. 1985. *Pure Lust*. Boston: Beacon Press.
Deming, Barbara. 1983. *We Are All Part of One Another*. Philadelphia: New Society Publishers.
DiStefano, Christine. 1985. "Gender and Political Theory: Gender as Ideology." Ph.D. diss., University of Massachusetts, Amherst.
Echols, Alice. 1983. "The New Feminism of Yin and Yang." In *The Powers of Desire*, ed. Snitow, Thompson, and Stansell.
Ehrenreich, Barbara, and Dierdre English. 1978. *For Her Own Good*. Garden City, N.Y.: Anchor Press.
Eisenstein, Zillah, ed. 1979. *Capitalist Patriarchy and the Case for Socialist Feminism*. New York: Monthly Review Press.
_____. 1981. *The Radical Future of Liberal Feminism*. New York: Longman.
Fee, Elizabeth. 1981. "Is Feminism a Threat to Scientific Objectivity?" *International Journal of Women's Studies* 4, no. 4.
Firestone, Shulamith. 1971. *The Dialectic of Sex*. New York: Bantam Books.
Griffin, Susan. 1978. *Woman and Nature: The Roaring Inside Her*. New York: Harper & Row.
_____. 1981. *Pornography and Silence: Culture's Revenge Against Nature*. New York: Harper & Row.
_____. 1988. "A Woman Thinks About War." Manuscript.
Harding, Sandra. 1986. *The Science Question in Feminism*. Ithaca, N.Y.: Cornell University Press.
Hartsock, Nancy. 1983. *Money, Sex and Power*. Boston: Northeastern University Press.
Hooks, Bell. 1984. *Feminist Theory: From Margin to Center*. Boston: South End Press.
Hyams, Edward. 1976. *Soil and Civilization*. New York: Harper & Row.
Jaggar, Alison M. 1983. *Feminist Politics and Human Nature*. Totowa, N.J.: Rowman and Allenheld.
Jonas, Hans. *The Imperative of Responsibility: In Search of an Ethics for the Technological Age*. Chicago: University of Chicago Press.
Joseph, Gloria, and Jill Lewis. *Common Differences: Conflicts in Black and White Feminist Perspectives*. Garden City, N.Y.: Anchor Press, 1981.
Keller, Evelyn Fox. 1983. *A Feeling for the Organism: The Life and Work of Barbara McClintock*. San Francisco: W. H. Freeman.
_____. 1985. *Reflections on Gender and Science*. New Haven, Conn.: Yale University Press.
Kelly, Petra. 1984. *Fighting for Hope*. Boston: South End Press.
King, Ynestra. 1982. "Feminism and the Revolt of Nature." *Heresies* 13.
_____. 1982. "Toward An Ecological Feminism and a Feminist Ecology." In *Machina Ex Dea*, ed. Joan Rothschild. New York: Pergamon Press.
_____. 1984. "Thinking About Seneca." *Ikon*.
Kropotkin, Peter. 1914. *Mutual Aid: A Factor in Evolution*. Boston: Porter Sargeant.
Lee, Dorothy. 1959. *Freedom and Culture*. New York: Prentice-Hall.
Leiss, William. 1976. *The Limits to Satisfaction: An Essay on the Problem of Needs and Commodities*. Toronto: University of Toronto Press.
Lorde, Audre. 1986. *Sister Outsider*. Trumansburg, N.Y.: The Crossing Press.
Lovelock, James E. 1982. *Gaia: A New Look at Life on Earth*. New York: Oxford University Press.

Merchant, Carolyn. 1979. *The Death of Nature: Women, Ecology and the Scientific Revolution.* New York: Harper & Row.

_____. 1981. "Earthcare: Women and the Environmental Movement." *Environment* 23, no. 5 (June).

Mill, Harriet Taylor, and John Stuart Mill. 1983. *On the Subjugation of Women.* London: Virago.

Moraga, Cherrie, and Gloria Anzuldua. 1983. *This Bridge Called My Back.* New York: Kitchen Table Press.

Ortner, Sherry. 1974. "Is Female to Male as Nature is to Culture?" In *Woman, Culture and Society,* ed. Michele Rosaldo and Louise Lamphere.

Rosaldo, Michele, and Louise Lamphere. 1974. *Woman, Culture and Society.* Palo Alto: Stanford University Press.

Ruddick, Sara. 1980. "Maternal Thinking." *Feminist Studies* 6, no. 2 (Summer).

_____. 1983. "Preservative Love and Military Destruction: Some Reflections on Mothering and Peace." In *Mothering: Essays in Feminist Theory,* ed. Joyce Trebilcot.

Schwarzer, Alice. 1984. *After the Second Sex: Conversations With Simone de Beauvoir.* New York: Pantheon.

Singer, Peter. 1975. *Annual Liberation: A New Ethics For Our Treatment of Animals.* New York: Avon Books.

Snitow, Ann, Sharon Thompson, and Christine Stansell, eds. 1983. *The Powers of Desire.* New York: Monthly Review Press.

Teish, Louisah. 1986. *Jambalaya.* San Francisco: Harper & Row.

Trebilcot, Joyce, ed. 1983. *Mothering: Essays in Feminist Theory.* Totowa, N.J.: Rowman and Allanheld.

Wollstonecraft, Mary. 1967. *A Vindication of the Rights of Woman.* New York: W. W. Norton.

Woolf, Virginia. 1983. *Three Guineaus.* New York: Harcourt, Brace and World.

Bureaucracy and Public Life: The Femininization of the Polity

Kathy E. Ferguson

"Let us treat the men and women well, treat them as if they were real—perhaps they are."
—Emerson

One of the most fundamental changes occurring in American political, social, and economic life over the last century has been the marked increase in the bureaucratization of both work and politics. White-collar work has increasingly replaced both blue-collar and farm labor, and this office work, much of it low-level and routine, takes place within increasingly large and complex organizations (Sennett and Cobb, 1972; Jacoby, 1973). In government, the "fourth branch" has expanded rapidly in the post-World War II era; as executive agencies have proliferated in both number and size, the number of people who operate within them, both as bureaucrats and as clients, has grown correspondingly.

A second crucial change in the socioeconomic and political fabric of American life during this century has been the growth of a complex and multifaceted feminist movement that has challenged society's traditional allocation of temperament, role, and status by gender. The women's liberation movement has many faces, both ideological and organizational, and not all of them are consistent with one another; nevertheless, its spokespersons have systematically challenged the exclusion of women from meaningful and autonomous participation in public life on a variety of fronts.

The feminist movement is divided internally, as are most major movements for social change, between those who are interested primarily in gaining access to established institutions and those who aim at the transformation of those institutions. The struggle for equal legal status, for equal pay for equal work, and for admission to the more prestigious and lucrative professions are frequently identified in the popular media as representing the entire women's movement. However, the more radical voices within the movement reject the exclusive focus on such goals because they see the existing institutional arrangements as fundamentally flawed. From these feminists there comes a generally antihierarchical orientation that aims at healing the breach between the public and private realms and that rejects bureaucratic organizational forms. For example, in a recent analysis of current feminist theory, Glennon (1979: 18) notes that feminism is a response to the "crisis of consciousness" that technocracy has imposed, that is, to the fragmentation of both individual and collective life resulting from the strict separation of the public and private realms "that has torn society since the dawn of the corporate-technological era." Similarly, Denhardt and Perkins (1976: 382) note that feminism challenges the very heart of modern organizational forms in that it "argues that superior domination through hierarchical patterns of authority is not essential to the achievement of important goals but in fact is restrictive of the growth of the group and its individual members." There is also evidence that some of the more "mainstream" feminist organizations, such as the National Organization for Women (NOW) and the professional women's conferences, are moving away from a traditional hierarchical structure toward more participatory organizational forms (Glennon, 1979: 10; Denhardt and Perkins, 1976: 381). Thus one emerging direction in contemporary feminist analysis opposes the modern trend toward bureaucratization and seeks a nonhierarchical understanding of collective action.

The purpose of this article is to explain and defend this posture by showing that an antihierarchical, antibureaucratic stance is central to a consistent feminist analysis. The expanding bureaucratization of the polity carries with it severe consequences for meaningful citizen participation in public life for both women and men, and these consequences are directly relevant to current feminist concerns. The illusion that liberation results from the integration of women into existing economic, political, and social organizations has implications that go far beyond the familiar charge of "selling out"; such a policy would succeed in extending the process by which women and other subordinate populations have been removed from active and authentic participation in public life by expanding it to include increasingly larger sections of the population. This process is what I call "femininization."[1] It refers to the spread of those individual and group characteristics that are traditionally associated with the feminine role: Women are conventionally said to be supportive, nonassertive, dependent, attentive to others, and "expressive," while men are seen as analytic, independent, rational, competitive, and "instrumental" (Chodorow, 1974; Gutmann, 1965; Carlson, 1971). While this type of distinction has come under attack from a variety of perspectives in recent years, the traditional images of gender-defined behavior remained intact. The current femininization involves the extension of the depoliticizing, privatizing dimensions of women's traditional role to the sectors of the population who are the "victims" of bureaucratic organizations, both the administrators and the clientele. Both groups of individuals are placed in institutional situations in which they must function as subordinates, and they are learning the skills necessary to cope with that subordinate status, the skills that women have always learned as part of their "femininity."

Many of the traits that are conventionally attributed to women can be subsumed under the heading of "impression management." These traits have very little to do with being biologically female, as the literature from anthropology and from studies of gender misassignment shows, but they have a great deal to do with being politically powerless and with learning to play the role of the subordinate in social relations (Mead, 1935; Leavitt, 1971; Turnbull, 1972; Kessler and McKenna, 1978). Women are often credited with being more responsive to other people than are men; their "women's intuition" allows them to sense other people's needs and motivations, and they can hold social interactions together by "managing interpersonal relationships" (Janeway, 1975: 122). For example, recent small group studies have found that women are generally more responsive to nonverbal cues from others than are men (Henley and Freeman, 1979: 479–482). Men are more likely to initiate and control interactions than are women, even when the discussions concern intimate topics. Yet women are expected to be more personable, to display more emotion and volunteer more self-expression:

> Women in our society are expected to reveal not only more of their bodies than men but also more of themselves. ... Self-disclosure is a means of enhancing another's power. When one has a greater access to information about another person, one has a resource the other person does not have. Thus not only does power give status, but status gives power. And those possessing neither must contribute to the power and status of others continuously [Henley and Freeman, 1979: 478].

Further, the studies found that men talk more than women, and that men are more likely to touch women than vice versa. Women maintain more eye contact during interactions than do men, in order to obtain nonverbal cues and evaluate the male response. As Weitzman (1979) has pointed out in her overview of the sex-role socialization literature, our culture's definition of femininity is such that a woman cannot know if she is being successfully feminine unless she has a response from another person.[2] The feminine role is one that requires continued recognition from males as the criterion of success. It is not surprising, then, that many studies (see Kanter, 1975: 54) conclude that women in organizations and groups are most concerned with maintaining satisfying personal relations, while men are most concerned with furthering their career goals. Given the fact that women are more likely to be subordinate in organizations, and thus to be dependent on the approval of others, their concern for positive group relations is a realistic response to the demands and constraints of their situation. The powerless are always well advised to attend to the wishes of superiors; when one depends on the good will of those whom one does not control, it is important to be carefully attuned to their moods and attitudes, to present oneself in an approved way, to sustain the right image, and so forth. Women need the skills of successful impression management in order to cope with the constraints of subordination.

Women are generally seen as figures who provide support for others through "stroking"; they are expected to maintain solidarity within groups by offering reassurance to the members, praising them, and raising their status (Bernard, 1971). Most women are well skilled in the art of pleasing others; as Janeway (1971: 114) has noted, this is a politically important skill: "The powerful need not please. It is subordinates who must do so—or at least it is subordinates who are blamed if they don't—and especially subordinates who live at close quarters with their superiors.

The traditional place of middle-class women in the nuclear family has contributed to their dependency.[3] The nuclear family structure is one that leaves housewives isolated from other people and from the ongoing life of the community. The skills required to maintain a home and raise children successfully are complex and valuable, but they are not the skills associated with political action; woman's traditional family role does not teach her to become self-assertive, self-confident, and independent. The most common types of employment for women outside the home—the "pink-collar" jobs, the service occupations, or the "helping professions"—may involve women in outside activities, but they also further reinforce the conventional role.

A qualification is in order here. I am not arguing that all the traits of personality, role, and status traditionally associated with women are undesirable. As I have argued elsewhere, many of these traits are more humane, perhaps more livable, than those conventionally attributed to men, and they are central to a full vision of liberated individual and collective life.[4] Compassion, generosity, solidarity, and sensitivity to others are crucial values; that they are more often found in the oppressed than among the oppressors indicates that it is the dominant social order that devalues these traits, and that distorts them to serve the interests of the powerful. Nor am I arguing that the "masculinization" of the polity, the organizational extension of character traits traditionally associated with the male role, would be sufficient to ensure meaningful participation in collective life for all. Women will not be liberated by becoming "like men" (or vice versa) but rather by abolishing the entire system that allocates human potential according to gender. What I am saying is that the political consequences of femininity are such that women learn the role of the subordinate, and that that role can easily become self-perpetuating; the skills that one learns in order to cope with one's secondary status then reinforce that status. The feminine role is inherently depoliticizing, in that it requires women to internalize an image of themselves as private rather than public beings. Women have largely been spectators rather than participants in public life, and the more firmly they have been integrated into the feminine role the more removed they have been from the public realm. Women are not powerless because they are feminine; rather, they are feminine because they are powerless, because it is a way of dealing with the requirements of the subordinate role.

Since the traits of femininity are not related to biology but rather to politics, one would anticipate finding the same set of traits in other subordinate populations; as Janeway (1975: 188) has noted. "The weak are the second sex." This point has frequently been made with regard to Blacks, who have been defined by whites as having characteristics that conveniently suit them for subordination.[5] The increase of administrative control over many areas of life in our society suggests that the newest source of powerlessness in modern life may be bureaucratic subordination. The victims of bureaucracy include both those who are the targets of control, especially the poor, and those who administer this control. They have many of the traits of "femininity"—they are isolated from one another, and as recipients of services (the poor) and approval (the bureaucrats) they are dependent on the good will of the powerful. Thus they are in need of the right image so as to favorably impress their superiors: The poor must present the right image to their social workers, and the clerks and bureaucrats must employ the appropriate image for their bosses. They often find it difficult to organize against the powerful, both because they lack resources (in the case of the poor, both time and money) and because they are separated from one another by the complex rules and regulations of the system. Neither group is encouraged or allowed to develop the skills necessary for political confrontation, which involves perception of and organization around a common interest. If bureaucracy, following Hannah Arendt, is "rule by nobody," then presumably domination exercised through bureaucratic channels is "oppression by nobody"—it cannot be located so it cannot effectively be opposed (although it can sometimes be sabotaged or undermined; Weinstein, 1979). This leaves the subordinates even more helpless, because, should they risk rebellion, there is no visible target. As society becomes more bureaucratized, there are increasing numbers of people who live lives perched precariously in this position; we are seeing the femininization of the polity through increased administration.

Genuine political activity, as opposed to bureaucratic manipulation, is ideally a creative process by which individuals order their collective lives. It requires an open public space in which common interests can be defined, alternatives debated, and politics chosen. It engages individuals in an active, self-creative process involving both cooperation with and opposition to others. Politics in this sense entails the empowerment of individuals and groups, so that they are able to do things collectively that they could not have done alone. The institutional arrangements of a bureaucratic society make this kind of politics virtually unavailable to its citizens, and the accompanying femininization process makes it more and more difficult for us even to imagine that such politics might exist.

The Bureaucrat as the Second Sex

Modern bureaucracies are organizations designed to seek certainty in both their internal structure and their environment. The formal structure of the organization is aimed at ensuring this condition. However, even the most rule-governed and rationalized institutions cannot totally eliminate uncertainty, so the rules must be supplanted with norms and informal patterns of behavior to further ensure stable and predictable behavior on the part of the members. The combined force of these norms and rules is to encourage the development and application of personality traits that, when found in a different section of the population, are called "feminine." There is a common process of victimization at work in each case, and its net result is to create a population that is rendered passive, depoliticized, and controlled. There are those within the bureaucracy who object to this process, just as there have always been women who rebelled against the constraints of the feminine role; but since there are no legitimate channels within bureaucratic structures to express opposition to the organization, such dissent can usually be suppressed.

Many analysts of bureaucracy have generated typologies of bureaucratic behavior in order to describe, and sometimes to explain, the various kinds of career patterns that typify the administrative process. Most of them differentiate among administrators on the basis of the attitudes the individuals hold toward the bureaucracy itself. Thus Presthus (1962) divides the organizational population into "upward-mobiles," "indifferents," and "ambivalents," according to degree of commitment to the bureaucratic situation. Similarly, Downs (1967) offers five categories of bureaucrats, ranging from purely self-interested actors to those combining self-interest with allegiance to either the organization itself or some larger goal. The considerable overlap among these typologies suggests that there are indeed common patterns of behavior to be witnessed among the participants in bureaucracies; however, this should not be taken to imply that all members of administrative hierarchies fit automatically into some mold, nor should the relative ease with which these categories can be caricatured allow sarcasm to substitute for analysis. The structure of hierarchical organizations shapes the behavior of the members by facilitating certain kinds of activities and motivations and by discouraging others. Bureaucratic behavior is often a very rational response to the constraints that the system imposes on its members, and the various bureaucratic "types" can be seen as stances chosen by individuals to solve "the problems created by their position in the network of organizational relationships" (Kanter 1977: 5; see also Heclo, 1977: 143–144). Analyses such as those by Presthus and Downs tend to overlook the very real struggle for personal dignity, autonomy, and recognition that often lies behind these patterns of behavior. It thus becomes all too easy to substitute simple castigation of bureaucrats for radical critique of bureaucracy. The traits of the various bureaucratic actors are not the result of inbred personality flaws or lack of moral character. Bureaucratic behavior is often characterized by attempts on the part of incumbents to remain loyal to their personal values despite their organizational roles, as the categories of "ambivalents," "zealots," "advocates," and "statesmen" indicate (Presthus, 1962: 15; Downs, 1967: 88–89). And the behavior of those who decide to oppose the bureaucracy in some way also demonstrates that they are human beings engaged in a struggle—admittedly one in which many lose and some surrender completely—but nonetheless not accurately seen as mindless and unquestioned conformity.

In order to comprehend the ways in which the structure of bureaucratic organization shapes, and ultimately victimizes, its participants, it is necessary to examine the various organizational norms and rules that are utilized in the search for certainty and stability. The successful construction of goal consensus among the members of an organization is one method for reducing uncertainty. Goal consensus reduces the frequency and intensity of conflict among the staff and enhances the reliability of the authority channels (Downs, 1967: 223). Individuals recruited into the organization are subjected to a socialization process in which they learn to embrace the goals of the organization, to give the impression that they have done so, or both.

> If recruiting is done only at the lowest levels, all top officials have to work themselves upward through the hierarchy, presumably by repeatedly *pleasing* their superiors. Superiors usually approve of continuous development of their policies, rather than sharp breaks with tradition. Therefore, the screening process of upward movement tends to reject radicals and create a relatively homogeneous group unless the bureau operates in a very volatile environment [Downs, 1967: 230; emphasis added]

In order to please supervisors, the upwardly mobile bureaucrats must develop the skills of impression management; they must learn to present the appropriate image, to anticipate the requirements of their superiors or of the organization in general, and to comply with those requirements in order to earn approval and promotion. The simultaneous need to please the powerful while being relatively powerless oneself tends to create a great deal of anxiety within the individual. The need to please is intensified by the fact that the bureaucrat has no criterion for judging her or his performance outside of the response of her or his superior in particular or of the organization in general:

> Bureaucratic conditions, moreover, reduce the opportunity for achieving status at the same time that they stimulate the desire for it. The separation of the worker from his tools and his impotence in a big organization tend to reduce the opportunity for individual independence and self-realization. At the same time, the minute gradations in bureaucratic income, skill and seniority intensify the desire to assert one's uniqueness [Presthus, 1962: 1984–185].

The personnel of bureaucratic organizations are thus encouraged to become like David Reisman's other-directed person, who is "attuned to personal nuances, moulding himself in the image of those above him" (Benello, 1968: 180). The higher one moves in the organization, the more important these skills become; relationships become less rule-governed and more personal at the top, where there is more intense involvement with the organization. Here individuals have more impact on decision making because decisions at this level are often not covered by existing rules and thus require personal judgment about policy. At the top levels officials require more demonstrations of loyalty to the organization and to each other in order to compensate for the relative absence of structured rules. Thus successful image management is one criterion necessary for upward mobility within the organization, as well as for successful operation at the heights of organizational power, and it requires subtlety of word and gesture and acute attention to the nuances of interpersonal relations:

> Facial expressions, verbal responses, subtle unspoken expectations, provide the cues ... the upward-mobile reads the signals his behavior evokes in others. Although the skill will vary among individuals, the distinguishing mark of the upward-mobile is that he *thinks* in such strategic terms and is able to modify his behavior accordingly. Such behavior is essentially rational and requires an ability to avoid passionate value attachments that might inhibit one's versatility [Presthus, 1962: 171–172].

The skills of impression management allow subordinates to shape their images in such a way as to approximate their supervisors. Given the impersonality of the bureaucratic setting, outward manifestations of trustworthiness take the place of direct personal knowledge and managers fall back on social similarity as a base for trust (Kanter, 1977: 52). The more similarity there is in outwardly identifiable characteristics, such as race, sex, dress, language, and style, the more likely is an aspirant to be seen as the "right kind of person" and given access to positions of discretion and power. This benefits those applicants who can utilize impression management successfully in that it gives more access to upward mobility; it also benefits superiors because it provides reassurance that the goals of the lower-level members coincide with their own, it makes the organization more efficient, and it decreases the "relative amount of authority leakage" (Downs, 1967: 223). It may also provide certain psychological benefits to the powerful; as one defender of bureaucracy has noted (Jansen, 1978: 41), "An aspiring bureaucrat who shapes himself in the image of the boss will enjoy immediate advantage. ... A top executive will find comfort in being surrounded by a hundred likenesses of himself." This process of "homosexual reproduction," in which "men produce themselves in their own image," does indeed help to minimize uncertainty within the organization, but it also undermines independent speech, thought, or action, discourages innovation, and closes off access to the decision-making levels for those who do not or cannot present the appropriate image.[6] Those who do not fit in cluster at the points of least uncertainty within the organization, that is, at those positions that are more routinized and rule governed and that require less stringent demonstrations of trustworthiness to gain admission. Since those positions also require less independent judgment and involve less authority, the occupants have less access to opportunities to demonstrate competence and thus to prove that they do indeed "fit in." Kanter (1977: 68) shows:

There is a self-fulfilling prophecy buried in all of this. The more closed the circle, the more difficult it is for "outsiders" to break in. Their very difficulty in entering may be taken as a sign of incompetence, a sign that the insiders were right to close their ranks. The more closed the circle, the more difficult it is to share power when the time comes, as it inevitably must, that others challenge the control by just one kind. And the greater the tendency for a group of people to try to reproduce themselves, the more constraining becomes the emphasis on conformity.

The emphasis on conformity within bureaucratic hierarchies is aimed at both the official rules and the unofficial norms. In his famous essay on the bureaucratic personality, Merton (1968: 254) points out that the process of goal displacement encourages the official to direct primary loyalty toward conformity with the rules themselves, as seen in the example of "the bureaucratic virtuoso, who never forgets a single rule binding his action and hence is unable to assist many of his clients." The lower-level members of the organization are particularly vulnerable to this manifestation of goal displacement, for they are both accountable for their actions and dependent for proper results on the actions of those over whom they have no control; thus "the powerless inside an authority structure often become rules-minded in response to the limited options for power in their situation, turning to 'the rules' as a power tool" (Kanter, 1977: 192).

The pressure toward conformity creates particular problems for the "token," one who is visibly different from the mainstream in sex, race, age, language, or the like. The token is highly visible and thus stands out, getting attention from superiors, subordinates, and peers that both creates performance pressures and exaggerates the contrast between the token and the other personnel. Both the pressure and the perception of social distance isolate the token, and his or her performance is taken as the basis for generalizations about the token's "type." Those higher up in the hierarchy have a difficult time identifying with the token, and are less likely to serve as mentors for him or her. Thus the token, who needs sponsors even more than his or her peers in order to negotiate the hierarchy successfully, has more difficulty finding them (Kanter, 1977).

Upward mobility in the organization through excessive conformity to its norms and rules is a pattern that seems to hold true, at least in some cases, for the factory as well as for the office.[7] A worker on the assembly line who decides to seek promotion to foreman becomes an exemplary worker; however, since the routinization of tasks on the line—as in the office—eliminates the opportunity to demonstrate creativity, enterprise, or initiative, attempts to demonstrate outstanding work abilities are of limited utility. Therefore, the aspirant must manipulate his or her appearance and behavior in conformance with the managerial norms. Such individuals begin to dress "better"—assembly-line "grubbies" are replaced with casual leisure clothes for men and "the tailored look" for women—and to emulate managerial behavior in other ways, for example, by swearing less, joining appropriate outside groups (such as a country club or Masonic Lodge), and so forth. Other workers on the line observe that the aspirant has become more friendly with the foreman and that he or she gets preferred treatment from the foreman. They also note that the foreman possesses information about the remaining workers that he or she does not usually have, showing that someone has "informed." Thus the promotion process screens for applicants who are the least resistant to pressure to conform and the most willing to police former colleagues. (Or, as my informants more bluntly stated, it selects for the "biggest assholes.")

There is, in addition, a second channel for upward mobility available to female aspirants: A woman on the line may seek not to become management herself, but to sleep with management males. (Since there are relatively few women in comparable management positions, men—that is, heterosexual men—have few opportunities to utilize this channel; presumably, as more women enter administration, this will change.) A female who is "on the make" for a management man has decided to dispense with conformity to the explicit rules and implicit norms of the organization itself, and instead appeals to a different set—those that surround the image of woman as seductress. Such women adopt a more sensual attire and manner; they are using the organization to secure personal upward mobility that might, if successful, remove them from direct involvement (if the affair leads to marriage) and at least might get favored treatment within it. Paradoxically, women who utilize this second "career ladder" are in the process undermining the credibility of those who seek access through the first.

Those who seek advancement through the established procedures calling for conformity to the organization's norms and rules are in fact learning to embrace the organization as their primary commitment. As Whyte points out in his classic study *The Organization Man* (1957), bureaucracies make explicit "demands for fealty" on their members; the "organization man" is one who identifies primarily with the organization and the group, who suspects the outsider, who is often "rootless" geographically, following the company via transfers, and who has a taste for the "regularized life"—in his residence (suburbia), his family (nuclear, patriarchal), and his dress (conventional). For the integrated bureaucrat, rationality is identified with the organization's goals and procedures; thus, in a 1979 *New York Times* article entitled "How to Be a Good Subordinate," businessman Roy C. Smith advises lower-level personnel not to have "too many 'new ideas,'" that is, not to make suggestions that challenge the organization's established way of doing things. When the process of merging the identity of the individual with that of the organization has been accomplished "successfully" (from the point of view of the organization), the personnel are often incapable of defining their own interests apart from, or in opposition to, those of the organization. Lamenting over the barriers that this loyalty to the organization presents to unionization, one organizer noted that "catastrophe, crisis and militance are scare words to the white-collar workers. They want to be dignified, professional, and loved. They want to be promoted; they want to be secure; and they don't want to have to fight" (Bruner, 1962: 194).[8] The merger of the individual and organizational identity is frequently not a happy one; in place of a willing allegiance, some bureaucrats manifest a "peculiar Stoicism" that consists of "despairing submission to a social order whose claims are inwardly despised" (Unger, 1975: 26). There are also those, mentioned above, who rebel, either by confronting their superiors in overt opposition or by engaging in some form of sabotage. In blue-collar situations the possibilities for opposition are often greater, since the relationship between worker and management, especially in union shops, is recognized as adversarial. However, the norms of rule following and compliance are so strong even there that a worker who decides actively to invoke the union against the management is likely to be policed by other workers, who see the "troublemaker" as endangering the good will of the hierarchy and earning the opprobrium of the foreman.[9]

The character traits outlined in this overview of bureaucratic behavior—impression management, need to please, conformity, identification with the organization, dependency, and so forth—are a double-edged sword for those who live and work within bureaucracies. On the one hand, learning such skills may be a necessary precondition for economic and professional survival, since they are necessary strategies for learning to protect oneself from the exercise of power. Given the structure of bureaucracy, a structure in which most individuals, as individuals, are at a disadvantage vis-à-vis the organization, such survival tactics may be avenues by which the powerless make the best of an unhappy situation. However, the tactics serve to bind the individual further to the organization and to cement his or her dependency upon it.

The Client as the Second Sex

The second dimension of the "femininization" process that expanding bureaucratization entails is the one that affects the clients of bureaucracies, those who are the recipients of the needed goods and services that bureaucracies provide. While there are many examples of recipient populations—students in relation to universities or citizens in relation to government licensing bureaus, for instance—by far the most striking and most obviously victimized of such recipient populations is the urban underclass. During the last two decades a large number of factors—the long-term consequences of the demographic shift of Blacks from the rural South to the central cities of the North, the spiraling inflation and unemployment rates, the expansion of public welfare and human resource programs, and others—have contributed to the creation of a "government subsidized and politically inert underclass," the ghetto poor (Erie, 1979: 15–16). The impact of social and economic barriers in overlapping networks of urban resource allocation—the housing market, the job structure, the political system, the educational system, and the law—has been to create a "web" of institutional controls that serve to isolate the poor from the surrounding society, to contain them, and ultimately to render them politically passive (Baron, 1969). Efforts to organize the urban poor for political action, while sometimes successful, must deal with the depoliticizing effects of perpetual client status.

In many ways the urban ghetto can be seen as a "total institution" in the ways that Goffman (1959: xiii) used the term in his classic study *Asylums:* "A place of residence and work where a large number of like-situated individuals, cut off from the wider society for an appreciable period of time, together lead an enclosed, formally administered round of life." While all institutions have "encompassing tendencies," total institutions are qualitatively more extensive in their enclosure of their residents in that they erect a "barrier to social intercourse with the outside" (Goffman, 1959: 4) that is often physical in nature. For example, concentration camps, prisons, mental hospitals, and nursing homes are surrounded by barbed wire, armed guards, locked doors, high walls, and the like. The occupants of the ghetto are "like-situated" in their economic, and often their racial, status, and they are only slightly less literally surrounded—by the police and National Guard in times of unrest, and by political, economic, and social barriers that contain the population, restrict departure, and enforce control all the time. Goffman (1959: 6) further notes that "the handling of many human needs by the bureaucratic organizations of whole blocks of people … is the key fact of total institutions." The urban underclass is increasingly dependent on public subsidies such as income transfers, food stamps, and rent and housing subsidies, and thus increasingly dependent on the state service bureaucracies that administer those programs. Reductions in the budgets of these programs do nothing to decrease the dependency of their clientele, since no alternatives are provided. While the ghetto has frequently been analyzed as an internal colony, it might better be seen as a total institution, one that contains and controls its population by rendering them dependent for basic needs on bureaucracies that are controlled from the outside.

The increased dependency of the urban poor on the state service agencies parallels the increased bureaucratization of society as a whole. As discussed above, bureaucracies seek stability, both in their internal structure and in their environment. The social welfare bureaucracies stabilize the economically displaced in times of relative peace; the police and National Guard "stabilize" the ghetto in times of "war." As Gouldner (1977–78: 43) notes in his discussion of internal colonialism, "Terror and bureaucracy are each ways of reaching down into and dominating a group from some point outside of its own ranks, by those who do not belong to it." Welfare bureaucracies maintain themselves by controlling the underclass through monopolizing and dispensing desperately needed resources, thus serving two related system-sustaining needs. First, such stability benefits other elites. Elected political elites can claim success in "quieting the cities" for their administrations, and economic elites are guaranteed a stable climate for investment, some subsidized support for generating market demand, and a dependable—that is, pacified—reserve labor force (Piven and Cloward, 1965). The urban poor constitute, in Offe's (1972) phrase, a "neglected institutional grouping" in that (1) they lack the resources necessary to bargain effectively with elites and (2) their needs are such that, if articulated, they would endanger the system itself. The "institutionalized pattern of priorities" of the technocratic political process is such that the underclass, if it plays by the rules, gets nowhere, because the rules are set up to admit only those players who have bargaining "clout." The urban poor get results only when, by circumventing the rules, they "present a credible case for the dangerous consequences that ensue (or that they would precipitate) if their claims were ignored" (Offe, 1972: 100–101). In Piven and Cloward's (1971: 338) succinct words: "A placid poor get nothing, but a turbulent poor sometimes get something."

Second, welfare bureaucracies also contribute to stability through self-maintenance; that is, they use their resources to strive to impose certainty onto their environment by regulating their clientele:

> They distribute public benefits in response to organizational requirements, adjusting the distribution to maintain and enlarge the flow of organizational resources. The influence of any group upon them ultimately depends on its role in this process—either contributing resources and supporting jurisdictional claims, or threatening the attainment of those objectives. Public agencies strive to maintain themselves with the least possible internal stress and change and therefore try to use their organizational capacity to limit both the occasion and the extent of their vulnerability to outside groups. Organizational equilibrium and enhancement are, in short, the compelling forces in bureaucratic action [Piven and Cloward, 1965: 8–9].

The programs of the welfare system reflect a "distinctively managerial kind of politics" (Piven and Cloward, 1971: 249) intended primarily to contain the political dangers of expanding economic hardship, not to address the sources of that hardship.

Actually to address the sources of such deeply rooted economic/political/social problems would both challenge the interests of interlocking elites and destabilize the very population upon whom welfare bureaucracies depend to justify their existence—the poor.

The consequences of dependency with regard to the clients of bureaucratic organizations are parallel in many respects to those of administrators themselves, although the dependency is probably more obvious in this case because the situation is not complicated by a parallel reward structure. There are few rewards involved in being a welfare recipient; for the poor, it is a way of surviving acute hardship when other options have been removed. The degrading process of collecting welfare and the humiliating status of being "on the dole" have been recorded amply by both participants and observers.[10] Thus the powerful and inhibiting controls that welfare bureaucracies exercise over their clients, while parallel in some ways to those exercised over bureaucrats, are less well disguised; in short, there are no "carrots" to disguise the "stick."

Welfare clients tend to be isolated from other institutional contexts that might otherwise provide support for an independent posture. They are not likely to have stable occupational roles or political status, are unlikely to be able to link their status as clients to any other established set of rights and obligations (for example, those of union members or voters), and are effectively isolated from the mainstream of economic and social life. There are often powerful social ties in the ghetto, especially within the family or the religious community, or perhaps in some fraternal associations, but these are not the kinds of organizational links that give the client population any secure or powerful link with the established mainstream political and economic structures (Baron, 1969). Since benefits are distributed to individuals, not to groups, perceptions of common interests are blurred and the existence of a shared situation is disguised.

The bureaucracy controls the information needed to mount an attack upon it; the information is frequently complex, written in a secret language, and passed through channels not visible to the public. Clients must learn a new language in order to comprehend the maze of bureaucratic regulations confronting them. This language is one that administrators are taught officially, while clients must learn it on their own. Only when clients have learned the official jargon and have comprehended both the formal rules and the informal norms governing appropriate conduct can they convince the bureaucrat that they are indeed "cases." In other words, clients must learn to "please"—to present the appropriate image, to give the required recognition to administrative authority, to "bow properly to immense institutional power, understand and flatter the bureaucratic personality," and otherwise legitimate themselves before the officials of the organization (Hummel, 1977: 17). Successful impression management for the poor often requires that they be able to bridge many gaps: administrative (client addressing official), economic (lower-class person addressing middle-class person), racial (Black or Hispanic person addressing white person), and/or linguistic (person speaking Spanish or street language versus one skilled in middle-class "professionalese"). The strains of successful impression management under such circumstances are immense, since "there is a fundamental disidentification between the individual and the manipulative role he is playing. Therefore in encountering bureaucracy there is always a potential emotional strain. Put differently, bureaucracy has a strong propensity to make people nervous" (Berger et al., 1974: 58–59).

The arbitrariness and circularity of bureaucratic procedure from the point of view of clients further increases their dependency on the bureaucracy.[11] "Recipients of benefits are not apprised of procedures but are continually confronted with apparently arbitrary action" (Piven and Cloward, 1965: 23). The frequently high level of surveillance over the recipients' conduct—also a trait of total institutions—breaks down arenas of privacy and independence and further cements control.

The clients of bureaucracy are rendered dependent and controlled because the only posture permissible toward bureaucracy is dependency. There is only one sort of "demand" that a poor person can ordinarily make upon a welfare agency, and that is more adequately conceived of as a request, a plea for help. One cannot demand to participate in decision making, to see a policy changed, or to redirect resources. In other words, one cannot demand to be included as a participant in the political process itself; to be a recipient is to be a spectator also.

The process by which clients are rendered dependent and passive is self-perpetuating on two related levels. First, it is self-perpetuating on an organizational level, in that different agencies provide each other with clientele through referrals. Sometimes such referrals aim at (and occasionally accomplish) the goal of removing individuals from client status and from dependency on the welfare network, as when, for example, a heroin addict is given welfare benefits on the provision that he or she enroll in a drug treatment program, a high school equivalency program, and a job training program.[12] However, when the unemployment rate is between 20% and 60% for the ghetto population, such programs do little to affect the structural problems that created the dependency in the first place. Further, such programs all too frequently become recycling channels for a permanent clientele, whose population is shuffled back and forth to fill the quotas of a variety of interconnected programs.

Second, the process is self-perpetuating on an individual level, since bureaucratic procedures tend to create in their clients the very traits that are then held to be responsible for the client's situation. Welfare recipients are defined as social "failures," as people who have not "made it" due to some individual failing of their own. Welfare procedures often reflect "the premise that the poor are unworthy and the constant fear that the client will lapse into sloth and chicanery" (Piven and Cloward, 1965: 24). Welfare programs thus demoralize and debilitate their clients, creating conditions under which people become what they are already said to be. When the environment is capricious and arbitrary, it is not surprising that its inhabitants learn to evade the restrictions that are avoidable, acquiesce to those that are not, and generally "live by their wits." This is not the same as saying, as do many conservative critics of welfare, that client status is self-perpetuating because recipients live so well on public assistance that they have no incentive to seek work. A comparison of real cost of living with level of benefits and an understanding of the employment structure of the ghetto discredit this assertion. Nor am I arguing that client status is self-perpetuating because the poor teach their children that being "on the dole" is an acceptable way of life. More often the opposite is true, in that parents' aspirations for their children far exceed any hopes they hold for themselves. The point is that perpetual client status creates a field of interaction in which individuals must develop certain abilities in order to survive. The skills that allow the poor person to succeed in obtaining benefits are the skills of impression management plus patience, perseverance, a low profile, and a high tolerance for ambiguity; these have very little to do with developing abilities to assert oneself, to organize around common interests, or to marshal the personal and collective resources necessary to oppose the powerful. Like bureaucrats, clients need these skills to survive in their organizational role; yet the more successful they are in developing them, the more dependent they become on the bureaucracy.

The conclusions one can draw from this analysis have to do with the possibilities for meaningful political action by the underclass. I am not arguing for the elimination of welfare structures under current circumstances; I fully agree with Piven and Cloward (1971: 348) that, in the absence of fundamental economic reform (for example, a guaranteed livable minimum income and the creation of real employment opportunity), welfare subsidies and related benefits are necessary and their expansion is defensible. It should be clear that I am not accusing the bureaucrats who create and administer service agencies of being ill-intentioned individuals who seek to further malign the poor. Often, in fact, just the opposite is true. Nor do I wish to assert that it is impossible for the poor to organize or to resist their demhumanization. Clearly, as the existence of militant welfare rights organizations illustrates, it is not. However, I do believe that the processes by which the poor are forced to live are such as to perpetuate their dependency on bureaucratic organizations and systematically discourage individual independence, collective organization, and public action. In their dependency they have much in common with the powerless in other areas of life, including those bureaucrats who administer their dependency; they too are victims of the increasing femininization of the polity.

By viewing femininity as a political rather than a biological category, this analysis suggests that femininization is the structural complement of domination. As long as one group of people is primarily concerned with exercising power, others will of necessity be primarily concerned with coping with that power held over them. They will need the skills of femininity to accomplish this. Thus, as long as there are institutionalized relations of dominance and subordinance, whether they are racial, sexual, economic, administrative, or some other, there will be femininity in the sense described here. It both protects the powerless from the worst aspects of subordination and simultaneously perpetuates that subordinate status.

This being the case, the possibilities for human liberation rest on the elimination of *all* dominance-subordinance relations. The constellations of instrumental and expressive traits, allocated in our society by gender, ought to be seen as complementary dimensions of all individuals, male and female. The tensions between them are tensions rightfully placed *within* individuals, not between groups. The capacities for compassion and for self-assertion, for solidarity as well as confrontation, need to be seen as possible dimensions of *human* behavior, not as male or female traits. But as long as there are groups of people who hold institutionalized power over others, femininity will continue to be a trait that characterizes the subordinate populations, and the vision of a liberated community of autonomous individuals is denied. This, if nothing else, should show the importance of linking the feminist critique of male domination to a larger set of criticisms of all power relations, including those manifested in administrative hierarchies. Feminism must be radical or it ceases to be feminism, and instead becomes only a procedure for recruiting new support for the status quo. To "liberate" women so that they may take an "equal" place in staffing other oppressive institutions and share an "equal" role in perpetuating other kinds of subordination would be a Pyrrhic victory indeed.

Notes

AUTHOR'S NOTE: *I would like to thank the students in my honors seminar on the quality of life in America and the students in my seminar on bureaucracy and freedom for the many contributions they made to this analysis. My thanks also to Glenn Williams, Cindy Carson, Phil Carson, and John Portelli for their insights on survival in organizations.*

1. This term is also used by Douglas (1977) in her excellent study of the "cult of domesticity" in Victorian America. Douglas uses femininization to refer to the spread of sentimentalism in mass culture, a sentimentalism that elevated the values of purity, gentleness, nurturance, sympathy, dependency, and passivity to a higher moral plane than that occupied by the expansionistic ethic of laissez faire capitalism. Douglas does not celebrate either masculinity or domination, but explains the various ways that the powerless survive their subordination.

2. I recognize that to some extent all individuals, both male and female, judge the adequacy of their role performance by the responses that others give to them. The distinction here is one of degree, but it is an important degree: The feminine role is more dependent on the continuing judgments of others than are more economically productive or socially active roles, which generate objects or actions that can more readily stand on their own.

3. This is an extremely complex factor contributing to the subordination of women and it varies significantly across race and class lines. For an insightful analysis, see Eisenstein (1979).

4. In my book *Self, Society and Womankind* (1980), I address these questions in detail; there is not sufficient space to do so here. It is likely that many people, including some feminists, will be offended by my current stress on femininity as a manifestation of subordination. I can only repeat that I do not overlook the central value of many expressive traits.

5. Both Killens (1965) and de Beauvoir (1952) have noted this parallel. Freeman (1971: 125) cites some interesting evidence from a classic study by Allport (1954) in which he discusses "the traits of victimization": "Included are such personality traits as sensitivity, submission, fantasies of power, desire for protection, indirectness, ingratiation, petty revenge and sabotage, sympathy, extremes of both self and group hatred and self and group glorification, display of flashy status symbols, compassion for the underprivileged, identification with the dominant group's norms, and passivity. Allport was primarily concerned with Jews and Negroes, but compare his characterization with the very thorough review of the literature on sex differences made by Terman and Tyler. For girls, they listed such traits as sensitivity, conformity to social pressures, response to environment, ease of social control, ingratiation, sympathy, low levels of aspiration, compassion for the underprivileged, and anxiety. They found that girls, compared to boys, were more nervous, unstable, neurotic, socially dependent, submissive, had less self confidence, lower opinions of themselves and of girls in general, and were more timid, emotional, ministrative, fearful and passive."

6. This terminology is from Moore (1962) as quoted in Kanter (1977: 109). This point is also taken up by Whyte (1957) and by Schuman (1978). Even defenders of bureaucracy acknowledge this trait; Jansen (1978: 2) notes in his apologia that "a special theory of bureaucratic accommodation can be advanced which holds that the rate of hierarchical ascent is in direct proportion to capacity for conformance."

7. My thanks to Cindy Carson and Phil Carson for sharing their insights on the assembly line during a series of interviews in Anderson, Indiana, in December 1979 and December 1981. I do not know to what extent their observations are generalizable, but I suspect that they have identified a common pattern.

8. White-collar workers are also more likely to be in debt (through mortgages, installment payments, and so on) and therefore to fear any disruption in their income, to have more security through other job options (thus lessening militancy), and to see unions as lower-class endeavors. As white-collar jobs become more routinized and fragmented, and as a recessionary economy makes the status differences between blue- and white-collar workers less important than the contents of the paycheck, some white-collar positions seem to be moving toward unionization. This is clearly the case with regard to secretaries, clerks, and office staff, who

find that their jobs are simultaneously becoming more routinized and alienating (as the all-around "office wife" is replaced by the steno pool, the typing pool, the filing pool, and so on) and more and more important in the aggregate, since communications is the key to organizational operation. Thus the potential for collective action grows.

9. Interviews with Cindy Carson and Phil Carson, Anderson, Indiana, December 1979 and December 1981. According to my informants, the practice of opposing the management by calling in the union is a recognized role that some workers consciously decide to take on themselves. It has its own language and rituals. The worker who declares war on the company is a "mad dog"; when he or she spots a problem that is "strong enough to do paper on" (a serious violation of the union agreement) she or he calls the foreman. If the foreman's answer is unsatisfactory, she or he says to "call the man" (call the shop committeeman). A real mad dog will "put in a call" every day, but is otherwise a model worker to avoid being vulnerable to retribution from management.

10. In addition to Piven and Cloward's work, Studs Terkel's poignant interviews with welfare recipients in *Working* (1972) reveal the system from the client's point of view. For an interesting case study of the role that welfare plays in the ghetto economy, see Valentine (1978).

11. One particularly poignant example of the bewildering nature of the official regulations was provided to me by a claims examiner in the Albany County Social Service Department. A destitute client came to pick up her check, which included a much-needed clothing allotment, and she was not allowed into the office because she had no shoes and thus violated the rule requiring shoes to be worn in the building (interview with John Portelli, Albany, New York, July 15, 1981).

12. Interview with Glenn Williams, Counselor, LUCHA (Latinos United for Comprehensive Help for Abusers), East Harlem, New York, and LUCHA Treatment Manual, 1980. As Williams points out, the truly self-sustaining institutional network is well-illustrated by the web of welfare-methodone maintenance-welfare programs that is becoming increasingly popular as a "treatment" for drug addiction. Since the addict is till drug dependent, and must report frequently to the hospital for treatment, she or he is still virtually unemployable and thus condemned to continued dependency. In this instance the social control function such programs perform is inescapable.

References

Allport, G. (1954) The Nature of Prejudice. Reading, MA: Addison-Wesley.

Baron, H. M. (1969) "The web of urban racism," pp. 134–176 in L. Knowles and K. Prewitt (eds.) Institutional Racism in America. Englewood Cliffs, NJ: Prentice-Hall.

Benello, G. (1968) "Wasteland culture." Anarchy 88 (June): 175–185.

Berger, P., B. Berger, and H. Kellner (1974) The Homeless Mind: Modernization and Consciousness. New York: Random House.

Bernard, J. (1971) Women and the Public Interest. Chicago: Aldine.

Bruner, D. (1962) "Why white collar workers can't be organized," pp. 188–196 in S. Nosow and W. H. Form (eds.) Man, Work and Society. New York: Basic Books.

Carlson, R. (1971) "Sex differences in ego-functioning: exploratory studies of agency and communion." J. of Consulting and Clinical Psychology 37: 267–277.

Chodorow, N. (1974) "Family structure and feminine personality," pp. 43–66 in M. Rosaldo and L. Lamphere (eds.) Women, Culture and Society. Stanford, CA: Stanford Univ. Press.

de Beauvoir, S. (1952) The Second Sex. New York: Knopf.

Denhardt, R. B. and J. Perkins (1976) "The coming death of administrative man," Women in Public Administration (July/August): 379–384.

Douglas, A. (1977) The Femininization of American Culture. New York: Knopf.

Downs, A. (1967) Inside Bureaucracy. Boston: Little, Brown.

Eisenstein, Z. [ed.] (1979) Capitalist Patriarchy and the Case for Socialist Feminism. New York: Monthly Review Press.

Erie, S. (1979) "The two faces of Irish power: implications for Blacks." State University of New York, Albany. (unpublished)

Ferguson, K. (1980) Self, Society and Womankind: The Dialectic of Liberation. Westport, CT: Greenwood.

Freeman, J. (1971) "The social construction of the second sex," pp. 123–141 in M. N. Garskoff (ed.) Roles Women Play. Belmont, CA: Brooks/Cole.

Glennon, L. M. (1979) Women and Dualism. New York: Longman.

Goffman, E. (1959) Asylums. Garden City, NY: Doubleday.

Gouldner, A. W. (1977–78) "Stalinism: a study of internal colonialism." Telos: 5–48.

Gutmann, D. (1965) "Women and the concept of ego strength." Merrill Palerm, Q. of Behavior and Development 2: 229–240.

Heclo, H. (1977) Government of Strangers. Washington, DC: Brookings Institution.

Henley, N. and J. Freeman (1979) "The sexual politics of interpersonal behavior," pp. 474–486 in J. Freeman (ed.) Women: A Feminist Perspective. Palo Alto, CA: Mayfield.

Hummel, R. P. (1977) The Bureaucratic Experience. New York: St. Martin's.

Jacoby, H. (1973) The Bureaucratization of the World. Berkeley: Univ. of California Press.

Janeway, E. (1975) Between Myth and Morning. New York: William Morrow.

———. (1971) Man's World, Woman's Place. New York: Delta.

Jansen, R. (1978) The ABCs of Bureaucracy. Chicago: Nelson Hall.

Kanter, R. M. (1977) Men and Women of the Corporation. New York: Basic Books.

———. (1975) "Women and the structure of organizations: explorations in theory and behavior," pp. 34–73 in M. Millman and R. M. Kanter (eds.) Another Voice. Garden City, NY: Doubleday.

Kessler, S. and W. McKenna (1978) Gender: An Ethnomethodological Approach. New York: John Wiley.

Killens, J. (1965) Black Man's Burden. New York: Trident.

Leavitt, R. R. (1971) "Women in other cultures," pp. 383–430 in V. Gornick and B. K. Moran (eds.) Women In Sexist Society. New York: Basic Books.

Mead, M. (1935) Sex and Temperament in Three primitive Societies. New York: William Morrow.

Merton, R. K. (1968) "Bureaucratic structure and personality," pp. 249–260 in R. K. Merton, Social Theory and Social Structure. New York: Macmillan.

Moore, W. (1962) The Conduct of the Corporation. New York: Random House.

Offe, C. (1972) "Political authority and class structure." Int. J. of Sociology 2 (Spring): 73–107.

Piven, F. F. and R. Cloward (1971) Regulating the Poor. New York: Random House.

———. (1965) The Politics of Turmoil. New York: Random House.

Presthus, R. (1962) The Organizational Society. New York: Knopf.

Schuman, D. (1978) The Ideology of Form. Lexington, MA: D. C. Heath.

Sennett, R. and J. Cobb (1972) The Hidden Injuries of Class. New York: Random House.

Smith, R. C. (1979) "How to be a good subordinate." New York Times (November 25): 16ff.

Terkel, S. (1972) Working. New York: Avon.

Turnbull, C. (1972) The Mountain People. New York: Simon & Schuster.

Unger, R. M. (1975) Knowledge and Politics. New York: Macmillan.

Valentine, B. (1978) Hustling and Other Hard Work: Life Styles in the Ghetto. New York: Macmillan.

Weinstein, D. (1979) Bureaucratic Opposition. New York: Pergamon.

Weitzman, L. (1979) "Sex-role socialization," pp. 153–216 in J. Freeman (ed.) Women: A Feminist Perspective. Palo Alto, CA: Mayfield.

Whyte, W. H., Jr. (1957) The Organization Man. Garden City, NY: Doubleday.

Suggested Further Readings

Anarcha Feminism

Ackelsberg, Martha. *Free Women of Spain: Anarchism and the Struggle for the Emancipation of Women*. Bloomington: Indiana University Press, 1991.

Ackelsberg, Martha, and Kathryn Pyne Addelson. "Anarchist Alternatives to Competition." In Valerie Miner and Helen Longino, eds., *Competition: A Feminist Taboo?* New York: Feminist Press, 1987.

Addelson, Kathryn Pyne. *Impure Thoughts: Essays on Philosophy, Feminism, and Ethics*. Philadelphia: Temple University Press, 1991.

_____. *Moral Passages: Toward a Collectivist Moral Theory*. New York: Routledge, 1994.

Ehrlich, Carol. "Socialism, Anarchism, and Feminism." *Second Wave* (Spring/Summer, 1977).

Epstein, Barbara. *Political Protest and Cultural Revolution*. Berkeley: University of California Press, 1991.

Ferguson, Kathy E. "Liberalism and Oppression: Emma Goldman and the Anarchist Feminist Alternative." In Michael J. Gargas McGrath, ed., *Liberalism and the Modern Polity*. New York: Marcel Dekker, 1978.

_____. "Toward a New Anarchism." *Contemporary Crises* 7, no. 1 (1983):39–57.

_____. *The Feminist Case Against Bureaucracy*. Philadelphia: Temple University Press, 1984.

Goldman, Emma. *Anarchism and Other Essays*. New York: Mother Earth Publishing Association, 1910.

_____. *Red Emma Speaks: An Emma Goldman Reader*. Alix Kates Shulman, ed. New York: Schocken Books, 1983.

_____. *The Traffic in Women and Other Essays on Feminism*. New York: Times Change Press, 1970.

Kleiber, Nancy, and Linda Light. *Caring for Ourselves: An Alternative Structure for Health Care*. Vancouver: School of Nursing, University of British Columbia, 1978.

Kornegger, Peggy. "Anarchism: The Feminist Connection." *Second Wave* (Spring, 1975).

Leader, Elaine. *The Gentle General: Rose Pesotta, Anarchist and Labor Organizer*. Albany: SUNY Press, 1993.

Ecofeminism

Adams, Carol. *The Sexual Politics of Meat: A Feminist-Vegetarian Critical Theory*. New York: Crossroads/Continuum, 1990.

Allen, Paula Gunn. *The Sacred Hoop: Recovering the Feminine in American Indian Tradition*. Boston: Beacon, 1986.

391

Biehl, Janet. *Finding Our Way: Rethinking Ecofeminist Politics.* New York: Black Rose Books, 1991.

Bigwood, Carol. *Earth Muse: Feminism, Nature, Art.* Philadelphia: Temple University Press, 1993.

Brown, Wilmette. *Roots: Black Ghetto Ecology:* London: Housewives in Dialogue, 1986.

Caldecott, Leonie, and Stephanie Leland, eds. *Reclaim the Earth: Women Speak Out for Life on Earth.* London: Women's Press, 1983.

Collard, Andree, with Joyce Contrucci. *Rape of the Wild: Man's Violence Against Animals and the Earth.* London: Women's Press, 1988.

Diamond, Irene, and Gloria Feman Orenstein, eds. *Reweaving the World: The Emergence of Ecofeminism.* San Francisco: Sierra Club Books, 1989.

Gaard, Greta, ed. *Ecofeminism: Women, Animals, Nature.* Philadelphia: Temple University Press, 1993.

Gray, Elizabeth Dodson. *Green Paradise Lost.* Wellesley, Mass.: Roundtable Press, 1981.

Merchant, Carolyn. *Radical Ecology: The Search for a Liveable World.* New York: Routledge, 1992.

Norwood, Vera. *Made From This Earth: American Women and Nature.* Chapel Hill: University of North Carolina Press, 1993.

Plant, Judith, ed. *Healing the Wounds: The Promise of Ecofeminism.* Santa Cruz: New Society Publishers, 1989.

Ruether, Rosemary Radford. *New Woman/New Earth: Sexist Ideologies and Human Liberation.* New York: Seabury, 1975.

Shiva, Vandana. *Staying Alive: Women, Ecology, and Development.* London: Zed Books, 1988.

SEVEN

PHENOMENOLOGICAL

FEMINIST PERSPECTIVES

Phenomenological philosophy is rooted in the desire to ground philosophy in lived experiences. Initially developed by Edmund Husserl and significantly modified by Martin Heideggar and Maurice Merleau-Ponty, phenomenology was a response to the privileging of objectivity as the hallmark of reason. Phenomenology embraces the importance and centrality of human subjectivity—the flow of lived human experience—from which our theories and our reason emanate.

Phenomenological descriptions focus not on specific attributes of an object or practice but on the ways in which they can be experienced. Such descriptions are directed to the lived world of embodied experience. They involve noting both the forms of presence and absence possible for the object or event in question. For example, if I were to offer a phenomenological description of the manifestation of the pencil in my hand, I would consider the parts that are invisible, along with those that are visible, and the profiles in which the pencil is recognized as one with and as separate from my hand. Such a description would never lose sight of its intentionality; that is, that it is *my* experiencing of the pencil.

Phenomenology is particularly well suited to feminist philosophy. Given the conviction of many feminists that feminist theorizing ought to arise from the experiences of women, a description of the embodied consciousness of women is a central component of the feminist endeavor. For example, in her essay, "Toward a Phenomenology of Feminist Consciousness," Sandra Bartky turns to a description of the distinctive ways of perceiving that constitute feminist consciousness. She identifies a feminist consciousness as one that contains both positive and negative features. It is at one and the same time an anguished consciousness that recognizes tensions in the social order concerning the definitions and treatment of women and a hopeful consciousness that embraces the possibility of change. It is an apprehension of blatantly unjust treatment of oneself and others as women combined with a "joyous consciousness of one's own power."

One of Bartky's goals is to encourage women, including women who do not identify themselves as feminists, to recognize the subtle ways in which culturally constructed gender divisions disempower women and to use this new feminist awareness or consciousness as a means of empowerment. Interpreting feminist consciousness as the ability to perceive the various and often hidden oppressions of women, Bartky acknowledges that this awareness often leads to anger and despair. However, she also argues that this awareness is, nevertheless, an advance over the false consciousness that it replaces because "we are no longer required to struggle against unreal enemies, to put others' interests a head of our own, or to hate ourselves. We begin to understand why we have such depreciated images of ourselves and why so many of us are lacking any genuine conviction of personal worth. Understanding, even beginning to understand this, makes it possible to *change*."

Bartky's essay is particularly helpful in the context of this anthology. One of our goals is to emphasize the diversity of methods and concerns raised by feminists. However, we recognize that our stressing differences among feminist theorists may give our readers the mistaken impression that there is little unity among feminists. Bartky's chapter is a salutary corrective in that it reminds us of what feminists have in common.

In her contribution to this volume, "Pregnant Embodiment: Subjectivity and Alienation," Iris Young turns her attention to a very specific kind of female body in order to offer a description of female sexed experience. Although in no way claiming that such descriptions offer unmediated experience free of ideology, Young believes they do begin to describe the female bodily experience of pregnancy. Acknowledging that aspects of her description will be idiosyncratic—the results of her white, Anglo, heterosexual, middle-class background—Young believes they cluster around a common core of experience. She states that her "descriptions do not claim to be universally and categorically 'true,' but to express types, modalities, styles of existence around which the particular experiences of particular women vary."[1]

Young argues that aspects of the bodily experience unique to pregnancy offer a corrective to the work of existential phenomenologists such as Erwin Straus and Maurice Merleau-Ponty. Although their philosophy officially rejects the polarization of mind and body, subject and object, inner and outer, self and world, Young believes it still contains residual traces of dualism. Indeed, Straus and Merleau-Ponty routinely contrast the body as *subject* with the body as *object.* In particular, they distinguish between typical bodily experience in which one is not aware of one's body for its own sake (probably your current state of experience when your attention is focused on reading these words) and those atypical times when we are thrown into awareness of our body (say, if we asked you to attend to the pressure of your legs against the chair upon which you are sitting). Young notes that phenomenologists treat the latter experience as an alienated objectification of one's body precisely because they posit the idea of a unified self as a condition of experience. Contrary to this attitude, Young argues that "reflection on the experience of pregnancy reveals a body subjectivity that is decentered, myself in the mode of not being myself." The pregnant experience is one in which the boundaries between self and other, inner and outer, subject and object are challenged.

In her essay, "Breast Cancer: Power Versus Prosthesis," Audre Lorde demonstrates the importance of focusing on the varieties of female-embodied experiences and in particular on the experience of breast cancer, an experience women are too often encouraged to conceal. She is particularly concerned with the medical and social emphasis on "prosthesis." As she sees it, this emphasis on looking, feeling, and acting as though nothing has happened constitutes a twofold problem. It keeps the individual woman who has had a mastectomy tied to wanting to look, feel, and act as she did prior to surgery rather than on "wanting to persevere through this experience to whatever enlightenment might be at the core of it." It also keeps all women who have had cancer from expressing the power of their knowledge and experience and thus conceals this understanding from women who have not yet experienced cancer. "I believe," says Lorde in her essay, "that socially sanctioned prosthesis is merely another way of keeping women with breast cancer silent and separate from each other. For instance, what would happen if an army of one-breasted women descended upon Congress and demanded that the use of carcinogenic, fat-stored hormones in beef feed be outlawed?"

Finally, Lorde reveals how the experience of breast cancer is different for a lesbian or Black woman than for a heterosexual or white woman. The breasts of a lesbian carry different sexual meanings than those of a heterosexual woman. In this culture, men tend to be preoccupied with women's breasts, making them sexual fetish objects. As a result, many heterosexual women worry about the size, shape, and solidity of their breasts. Are they appropriately sexy? They fear that men will not find them sexually attractive unless they have appealing breasts; they especially fear that men will sexually reject them—indeed, be repelled by them—if they have *no* breasts. Since lesbians do not define their sexuality in terms of men's sexual desires, needs, or fetish objects, heterosexual women might conclude that the loss of a breast is not nearly as traumatic for a lesbian woman as it is for a heterosexual woman. In point of fact, this is not true. Lorde writes that after her mastectomy she worried that she would never get over missing that "great wall of pleasure" she associated with her right breast, and she worried that her lover would no longer find her body "delicious"—that their bodies would never fit "perfectly" together again. Lorde's words serve to remind us that Young is right. The loss of a breast, of a part of one's body, initiates a process of mourning, grieving, and loss in *all* women; but because each woman is unique, each woman will live through that process differently.

Notes

1. Iris Marion Young, *Throwing Like a Girl and Other Essays in Feminist Philosophy and Social Theory* (Bloomington: Indiana University Press, 1990), p. 17.

Toward a Phenomenology of
Feminist Consciousness

Sandra Lee Bartky

I

Contemporary feminism has many faces. The best attempts so far to deal with the scope and complexity of the movement have divided feminists along ideological lines. Thus, liberal, Marxist, neo-Marxist, and what are called "radical" feminists differ from one another in that they have differing sets of beliefs about the origin and nature of sexism and thus quite different prescriptions for the proper way of eliminating it. But this way of understanding the nature of the women's movement, however, indispensable, is not the only way. While I would not hesitate to call someone a feminist who supported a program for the liberation of women and who held beliefs about the nature of contemporary society appropriate to such a political program, something crucial to an understanding of feminism is overlooked if its definition is so restricted.

To be a feminist, one has first to become one. For many feminists, this involves the experience of a profound personal transformation, an experience which goes far beyond that sphere of human activity we regard ordinarily as "political." This transforming experience, which cuts across the ideological divisions within the women's movement, is complex and multifaceted. In the course of undergoing the transformation to which I refer, the feminist changes her *behavior:* She makes new friends; she responds differently to people and events; her habits of consumption change; sometimes she alters her living arrangements or, more dramatically, her whole style of life. She may decide to pursue a career, to develop potentialities within herself which had long lain dormant or she may commit herself to political struggle. In a biting and deliberately flat tone, one feminist enumerates some of the changes in her own life:

> During the past year I ... was arrested on a militant women's liberation action, spent some time in jail, stopped wearing makeup and shaving my legs, started learning Karate and changed my politics completely.[1]

The changes in behavior go hand in hand with changes in *consciousness:* to become a feminist is to develop a radically altered consciousness of oneself, of others, and of what, for lack of a better term, I shall call "social reality."[2] Feminists themselves have a name for the struggle to clarify and to hold fast to this way of apprehending things: They call it "consciousness-raising." A "raised" consciousness on the part of women is not only a causal factor in the emergence of the feminist movement itself but also an important part of its political program. Many small discussion groups exist solely for the purpose of consciousness-raising. But what happens when one's consciousness is raised? What is a fully developed feminist consciousness like? In this paper, I would like to examine not the full global experience of liberation, involving as it does new ways of being as well as new ways of perceiving, but, more narrowly, those distinctive ways of perceiving which characterize feminist consciousness. What follows will be a highly tentative attempt at a morphology of feminist consciousness. Without claiming to have discovered them all, I shall try to identify some structural features of that altered way of apprehending oneself and the world which is both product and content of a raised consciousness. But before I begin, I would like to make some very general remarks about the nature of this consciousness and about the conditions under which it emerges.

Although the oppression of women is universal, feminist consciousness is not. While I am not sure that I could demonstrate the necessity of its appearance in this time and place and not in another, I believe it is possible to identify two features of current social reality which, if not sufficient, are at least necessary conditions for the emergence of feminist consciousness. These features constitute, in addition, much of the content of this consciousness. I refer, first, to the existence of what Marxists call "contradictions" in our society and, second, to the presence, due to these same contradictions, of concrete circumstances which would permit a significant alternation in the status of women.

In Marxist theory, the stage is set for social change when existing forms of social interaction—property relations as well as values, attitudes, and beliefs—come into conflict with new social relations which are generated by changes in the mode of production:

> At a certain stage of their development, the material forces of production in society come in conflict with the existing relations of production or—what is but a legal expression for the same thing—with the property relations within which they had been at work before. From forms of development of the forces of production these relations turn into their fetters. Then comes the period of social revolution.[3]

Social conflict regularly takes an ideological form, so much so that conflicts which are fundamentally economic in origin may appear to be struggles between ideas, as, for instance, between competing conceptions of the nature of legitimate political authority or of woman's proper sphere. To date, no one has offered a comprehensive analysis of those changes in the socioeconomic structure of contemporary American society which have made possible the emergence of feminist consciousness.[4] This task is made doubly difficult by the fact that these changes constitute no completed process, no convenient object for dispassionate historical investigation, but are part of the fluid set of circumstances in which each of us must find our way from one day to another and whose ultimate direction is as yet unclear. In spite of this, several features of current social reality cannot escape notice.

First, if we add to the Marxist notion of "modes of production" the idea of "modes of (biological) reproduction," then it is evident that the development of cheap and efficient types of contraception has been instrumental in changing both the concrete choices women are able to make and the prevailing conceptions about woman's function and destiny. Second, the rapid growth of service industries has had much to do with the steady rise in the percentage of women in the work force, since the post–World War II low in the early fifties. While poor women and women of color have often had to work for wages, middle-class women were largely restricted to the roles of wife, mother, and homemaker; this restriction, together with the rationales that justify it, is clearly out of phase with the entry of millions of such women into the market economy. The growth and spread of a technology to ease the burden of housekeeping, a technology which is itself the result of a need on the part of late capitalism for "innovations" in production, serves further to undermine traditional conceptions about woman's place. During part of the period of the most rapid rise in the percentage of women in the work force, to cite still another "contradiction," there appeared an anomalous and particularly virulent form of the "feminine mystique," which, together with its companion, the ideal of "togetherness," had the effect, among other things, of insuring that the family would remain an efficient vehicle of consumption.[5] What triggered feminist consciousness most immediately, no doubt, were the civil rights movement and the peace and student movements of the sixties; while they had other aims as well, the latter movements may also be read as expressions of protest against the growing bureaucratization, depersonalization, and inhumanity of late capitalist society. Women often found themselves forced to take subordinate positions within these movements; it did not take long for them to see the contradiction between the oppression these movements were fighting in the larger society and their own continuing oppression in the life of these movements themselves.[6]

Clearly, any adequate account of the "contradictions" of late capitalism, that is, of the conflicts, the instabilities, the ways in which some parts of the social whole are out of phase with others, would be a complex and elaborate task. But whatever a complete account of these contradictions would look like, it is essential to understand as concretely as possible how the contradictory factors we are able to identify are lived and suffered by particular people. The facts of economic development are crucial to an understanding of any phenomenon of social change, but they are not the phenomenon in its entirety. Dogmatic Marxists have regarded consciousness as a mere reflection of material conditions and therefore uninteresting as an object for study in and of itself. Even Marxist scholars of a more humane cast of mind have not paid sufficient attention to the ways in which the social and economic tensions they study are played out in the lives of concrete individuals. There is an anguished consciousness, an inner uncertainty and confusion which characterizes human subjectivity in periods of social change—and I shall contend that feminist consciousness, in large measure, is an anguished consciousness—of whose existence Marxist scholars seem largely unaware. Indeed, the only sort of consciousness which is discussed with any frequency in the literature is "class consciousness," a somewhat unclear idea whose meaning Marxists themselves dispute. In sum, then, the incorporation of phenomenological methods into Marxist analysis is necessary, if the proper dialectical relations between human consciousness and the material modes of production are ever to be grasped in their full concreteness.

Women have long lamented their condition, but a lament, pure and simple, need not be an expression of feminist consciousness. As long as their situation is apprehended *as* natural, inevitable, and inescapable, women's consciousness of themselves, no matter how alive to insult and inferiority, is not yet feminist consciousness. This consciousness, as I contended earlier, emerges only when there exists a genuine possibility for the partial or total liberation of women. This possibility is more than a mere accidental accompaniment of feminist consciousness; rather, feminist consciousness is the apprehension of that possibility. The very *meaning* of what the feminist apprehends is illuminated by the light of what ought to be. The given situation is first understood in terms of a state of affairs in which what is given would be negated and radically transformed. To say that feminist consciousness is the experience in a certain way of certain specific contradictions in the social order is to say that the feminist apprehends certain features of social reality as intolerable, as to be rejected in behalf of a transforming project for the future. "It is on the day that we can conceive of a different state of affairs that a new light falls on our troubles and we *decide* that these are unbearable."[7] What Sartre would call her "transcendence," her project of negation and transformation, makes possible what are specifically feminist ways of apprehending contradictions in the social order. Women workers who are not feminists know that they receive unequal pay for equal work, but they may think that the arrangement is just; the feminist sees this situation as an instance of exploitation and an occasion for struggle. Feminists are no more aware of different things than other people; they are aware of the same things differently. Feminist consciousness, it might be ventured, turns a "fact" into a "contradiction"; often, features of social reality are first apprehended *as* contradictory, as in conflict with one another, or as disturbingly out of phase with one another, from the vantage point of a radical project of transformation.

Thus, we understand what we are and where we are in the light of what we are not yet. But the perspective from which I understand the world must be rooted in the world too. My comprehension of what I and my world can become must take account of what we are. The possibility of a transformed society which allows the feminist to grasp the significance of her current situation must somehow be contained in the apprehension of her current situation: the contradictory situation in which she finds herself she perceives as unstable, as carrying within itself the seeds of its own dissolution. There is no way of telling, by a mere examination of some form of consciousness, whether the possibilities it incorporates are realizable or not; this depends on whether the situation is such as to contain within itself the sorts of material conditions which will bring to fruition a human expectation. If no such circumstances are present, then the consciousness in question is not the kind of consciousness which accompanies a genuine political project at all, but merely fantasy. I think that an examination of the circumstances of our lives will show that feminist consciousness and the radical project of transformation which animates it is, if less than an absolutely certain anticipation of what must be, more than mere fantasy.

The relationship between consciousness and concrete circumstances can best be described as "dialectical." Feminist consciousness is more than a mere reflection of external material conditions, for the transforming and negating perspective which it incorporates first allows these conditions to be revealed *as* the conditions they are. But on the other hand, the apprehension of some state of affairs as intolerable, as to-be-transformed, does not, in and of itself, transform it.

II

Feminist consciousness is consciousness of *victimization*. To apprehend oneself as victim is to be aware of an alien and hostile force outside of oneself which is responsible for the blatantly unjust treatment of women and which enforces a stifling and oppressive system of sex-role differentiation. For some feminists, this hostile power is "society" or "the system"; for others, it is simply men. Victimization is impartial, even though its damage is done to each one of us personally. One is victimized as a woman, as one among many. In the realization that others are made to suffer in the same way I am made to suffer lies the beginning of a sense of solidarity with other victims. To come to see oneself as victim, to have such an altered perception of oneself and of one's society is not to see things in the same old way while merely judging them differently or to superimpose new attitudes on things like frosting a cake. The consciousness of victimization is immediate and revelatory; it allows us to discover what social reality is really like.

The consciousness of victimization is a divided consciousness. To see myself as victim is to know that I have already sustained injury, that I live exposed to injury, that I have been at worst mutilated, at best diminished in my being. But at the same time, feminist consciousness is a joyous consciousness of one's own power, of the possibility of unprecedented personal growth and the release of energy long suppressed. Thus, feminist consciousness is both consciousness of weakness and consciousness of strength. But this division in the way we apprehend ourselves has a positive effect, for it leads to the search both for ways of overcoming those weaknesses in ourselves which support the system and for direct forms of struggle against the system itself.

The consciousness of victimization may be a consciousness divided in a second way. The awareness I have of myself as victim may rest uneasily alongside the awareness that I am also and at the same time enormously privileged, more privileged than the overwhelming majority of the world's population. I myself enjoy both white-skin privilege and the privileges of comparative affluence. In our society, of course, women of color are not so fortunate; white women, as a group and on average, are substantially more economically advantaged than many persons of color, especially women of color; white women have better housing and education, enjoy lower rates of infant and maternal mortality, and, unlike many poor persons of color, both men and women, are rarely forced to live in the climate of street violence that has become a standard feature of urban poverty. But even women of color in our society are relatively advantaged in comparison to the appalling poverty of women in, e.g., Africa and Latin America.

Many women do not develop a consciousness divided in this way at all: they see themselves, to be sure, as victims of an unjust system of social power, but they remain blind to the extent to which they themselves are implicated in the victimization of others. What this means is that the "raising" of a woman's consciousness is, unfortunately, no safeguard against her continued acquiescence in racism, imperialism, or class oppression. Sometimes, however, the entry into feminist consciousness, for white women especially, may bring in its wake a growth in political awareness generally: The disclosure of one's own oppression may lead to an understanding of a range of misery to which one was heretofore blind.

But consciousness divided in this way may tend, just as easily, to produce confusion, guilt, and paralysis in the political sphere. To know oneself as a "guilty victim" is to know oneself as *guilty;* this guilt is sometimes so profound that it sets a woman up for political manipulation. When this happens, she may find herself caught up in political agendas or even in political organizations that speak only to her guilt and not, at the same time, to her need; indeed, she may have been recruited on the basis of her guilt alone. The awakening comes at last: The recognition that she has been manipulated—"guilt-tripped"—brings in its wake resentment, anger, and very often a headlong and permanent refusal to engage ever again in any political activity. A consciousness so divided, again, so guilt-ridden, may experience paralysis in still another way: Trained anyhow to subordinate her needs to the needs of others, a woman may be so overwhelmed by the discovery of her own complicity in such evils as racism or imperialism that she denies herself permission fully to confront the real discomforts of her own situation. Her anger is mobilized on behalf of everyone else, but never on her own behalf. We all know women like this, admirable women who toil ceaselessly in the vineyards of social justice, alive to the insults borne by others, but seemingly oblivious to the ones meant for them.

To apprehend myself as victim in a sexist society is to know that there are few places where I can hide, that I can be attacked almost anywhere, at any time, by virtually anyone. Innocent chatter, the currency of ordinary social life, or a compliment ("You don't think like a woman"), the well-intentioned advice of psychologists, the news item, the joke, the cosmetics advertisement—none of these is what it is or what it was. Each reveals itself, depending on the circumstances in which it appears, as a threat, an insult, an affront, as a reminder, however, subtle, that I belong to an inferior caste. In short, these are revealed as instruments of oppression or as articulations of a sexist institution. Since many things are not what they seem to be and since many apparently harmless sorts of things can suddenly exhibit a sinister dimension, social reality is revealed as *deceptive.*

Contemporary thinkers as diverse as Heidegger and Marcuse have written about the ambiguity and mystification which are so prominent a feature of contemporary social life. Feminists are alive to one certain dimension of a society which seems to specialize in duplicity—the sexist dimension. But the deceptive nature of this aspect of social reality itself makes the feminist's experience of life, her anger and sense of outrage difficult to communicate to the insensitive or uninitiated; it increases her frustration and reinforces her isolation. There is nothing ambiguous about racial segregation or economic discrimination. It is far less difficult to point to such abuses than it is to show how, for example, the "tone" of a news story can transform a piece of reportage into a refusal to take women's political struggles seriously. The male reporter for a large local daily paper who described the encounter of Betty Friedan and the Republican Women's Caucus at Miami never actually used the word "fishwife," nor did he say outright that the political struggles of women are worthy of ridicule; he merely chose to describe the actions of the individuals involved in such a way as to make them appear ridiculous. (Nor, it should be added, did he fail to describe Ms. Friedan as "petite.") It is difficult to characterize the tone of an article, the patronizing implications of a remark, the ramifications of some accepted practice, and it is even ore difficult to describe what it is like to be bombarded ten or a hundred times daily with these only half-submerged weapons of a sexist system. This, no doubt, is one reason why, when trying to make a case for feminism, we find ourselves referring almost exclusively to the "hard data" of discrimination, like unequal pay, rather than to those pervasive intimations of inferiority which may rankle at least as much. Many people know that things are not what they seem to be. The feminist knows that the thing revealed in its truth at last will, likely as not, turn out to be a thing which threatens or demands. But however unsettling it is to have to find one's way about in a world which dissimulates, it is worse not to be able to determine the nature of what is happening at all. Feminist consciousness is often afflicted with category confusion, an inability to know how to classify things. For instance, is the timidity I display at departmental meetings merely my own idiosyncrasy and personal shortcoming, an effect of factors which went into the development of my personality uniquely, or is it a typically female trait, a shared inability to display aggression, even verbal aggression? Why is the suggestion I make ignored? Is it intrinsically unintelligent, or is it because I am a woman and therefore not to be taken seriously? The persistent need I have to make myself "attractive," to fix my hair and put on lipstick—is it the false need of a "chauvinized" woman, encouraged since infancy to identify her human value with her attractiveness in the eyes of men, or does it express a basic need to affirm a wholesome love for one's body by adorning it, a behavior common in primitive societies, allowed us but denied to men in our own still puritan culture? Uncertainties such as these make it difficult to decide how to struggle and whom to struggle against, but the very possibility of understanding one's own motivations, character traits, and impulses is also at stake. In sum, feminists suffer what might be called a "*double ontological shock*": first, the realization that what is really happening is quite different from what appears to be happening, and, second, the frequent inability to tell what is really happening at all.

Since discriminatory sex-role differentiation is a major organizing principle of our society, the list of its carriers and modes of communication would be unending. The sorts of things already mentioned were chosen at random. Little political, professional, educational, or leisure-time activity is free of the blight of sexism. Startlingly few personal relationships exist without it. Feminist consciousness is a little like paranoia, especially when the feminist first begins to apprehend the full extent of sex discrimination and the subtlety and variety of the ways in which it is enforced. Its agents are everywhere, even inside her own mind, since she can fall prey to self-doubt or to a temptation to compliance. In response to this, the feminist becomes vigilant and suspicious. Her apprehension of things, especially of direct or indirect communication with other people is characterized by what I shall call "*wariness.*" Wariness is anticipation of the possibility of attack, of affront or insult, of disparagement, ridicule, or the hurting blindness of others. It is a mode of experience which anticipates experience in a certain way; it is an apprehension of the inherently threatening character of established society. While it is primarily the established order of things of which the feminist is wary, she is wary of herself, too. She must be always on the alert lest her pervasive sense of injury provoke in her without warning some public display of emotion, such as violent weeping, which she would rather suppress entirely or else endure in private. Many feminists are perpetually wary lest their own anger be transformed explosively into aggressive or hostile behavior of the sort which would be imprudent or even dangerous to display.

Some measure of wariness is a constant in feminist experience, but the degree to which it is present will be a function of other factors in a feminist's life—her level of political involvement, perhaps, the extent of her exploration of the social milieu, or the extent to which she allows resignation or humor to take away the sting. Characteristic of this kind of consciousness too is the *alteration* of a heightened awareness of the limitations placed on one's free development with a duller self-protecting sensibility without which it would be difficult to function in a society like our own.

The revelation of the deceptive character of social reality brings with it another transformation in the way the social milieu is present in feminist experience. Just as so many apparently innocent things are really devices to enforce compliance, so are many "ordinary" sorts of situations transformed into opportunities or occasions for struggle against the system. In a light-hearted mood, I embark upon a Christmas shopping expedition, only to have it turn, as if independent of my will, into an occasion for striking a blow against sexism. On holiday from political struggle and even political principle, I have abandoned myself to the richly sensuous albeit repellantly bourgeois atmosphere of Marshall Field's. I wander about the toy department, looking at chemistry sets and miniature ironing boards. Then, unbidden, the following thought flashes into my head: What if, just this once, I send a doll to my nephew and an erector set to my niece? Will this confirm the growing suspicion in my family that I am a crank? What if the children themselves misunderstand my gesture and covet one another's gifts? Worse, what if the boy believes that I have somehow insulted him? The shopping trip turned occasion for resistance now becomes a *test*. I will have to answer for this, once it becomes clear that Marshall Field's has not unwittingly switched the labels. My husband will be embarrassed. A didactic role will be thrust upon me, even though I had determined earlier that the situation was not ripe for consciousness-raising. The special ridicule which is reserved for feminists will be heaped upon me at the next family party, all in good fun, of course.

Whether she lives a fairly conventional life or an unconventional one, ordinary social life presents to the feminist an unending sequence of such occasions and each occasion is a test. It is not easy to live under the strain of constant testing. Some tests we pass with honor, but often as not we fail, and the price of failure is self-reproach and the shame of having copped out. To further complicate things, much of the time it is not clear what criteria would allow us to distinguish the honorable outcome of an occasion from a dishonorable one. Must I seize every opportunity? May I never take the easy way out? Is what I call prudence and good sense merely cowardice? On the occasion in question I compromised and sent both children musical instruments.

The transformation of day-to-day living into a series of invitations to struggle has the important consequence for the feminist that she finds herself, for a while at least, in an ethical and existential impasse. She no longer knows what sort of person she ought to be and, therefore, she does not know what she ought to do. One moral paradigm is called into question by the partial and laborious emergence of another. The ethical issues involved in the occasion of my shopping trip were relatively trivial, but this is not true of all occasions. One thinks of Nora's decision in *A Doll's House* to leave her husband and children and seek independence and self-fulfillment on her own. The case is an extreme one, but it illustrates what I have in mind. Here, the conflict is between one moral commitment and another, between, on the one hand, a Nietzschean transvaluation of received values for the sake of a heroic and creative self-surpassing and, on the other, a Christian ideal of devotion to others, self-abnegation, and self-sacrifice. But Nora makes the decision too easily. Ibsen, her creator, betrays a certain lack of sensitivity to feminist experience: A real-life Nora would have suffered more.

To whom will a woman in such a predicament turn for guidance? To choose a moral authority, as Sartre tells us, is already to anticipate what kind of advice we are prepared to take seriously. Having become aware of the self-serving way in which a male-dominated culture has defined goodness for the female, she may decide on principle that the person she wants to be will have little in her character of patience, meekness, complaisance, self-sacrifice, or any of the other "feminine" virtues. But will such a solution satisfy a reflective person? Must the duty I have to myself (if we have duties to ourselves) *always* win out over the duty I have to others? Even an unreflective person, who might not ask such questions, cannot fail to see that the way out of her dilemma may cause great suffering to the people closest to her. To develop feminist consciousness is to live a part of one's life in the sort of *ambiguous ethical situation* which existentialist writers have been most adept at describing. Here it might be objected that the feature of feminist experience I have been describing is characteristic not of a fully emergent feminist consciousness but of periods of transition to such consciousness, that the feminist is a person who has chosen her moral paradigm and who no longer suffers the inner conflicts of those in ambiguous moral predicaments. I would deny this. Even the woman who has decided to be this new person and not that old one, can be tormented by recurring doubts. Moreover, the pain inflicted in the course of finding one's way out of an existential impasse, one continues to inflict. One thing, however, is clear: The feminist is someone who, at the very least, has been marked by the experience of ethical ambiguity; she is a moral agent with a distinctive history.

Feminist consciousness, it was suggested earlier, can be understood as the negating and transcending awareness of one's own relationship to a society heavy with the weight of its own contradictions. The inner conflicts and divisions which make up so much of this experience are just the ways in which each of us, in the uniqueness of her own situation and personality, lives these contradictions. In sum, feminist consciousness is the consciousness of a being radically alienated from her world and often divided against herself, a being who sees herself as victim and whose victimization determines her being-in-the-world as resistance, wariness, and suspicion. Raw and exposed much of the time, she suffers from both ethical and ontological shock. Lacking a fully formed moral paradigm, sometimes unable to make sense of her own reactions and emotions, she is immersed in a social reality which exhibits to her an aspect of malevolent ambiguity. Many "ordinary" social situations and many human encounters organized for quite a different end she apprehends as occasions for struggle, as frequently exhausting tests of her will and resolve. She is an outsider to her society, to many of the people she loves, and to the still unemancipated elements in her own personality.

This picture is not as bleak as it appears; indeed, its "bleakness" would be seen in proper perspective had I described what things were like *before*. Coming to have a feminist consciousness is the experience of coming to see things about oneself and one's society that were heretofore hidden. This experience, the acquiring of a "raised" consciousness, in spite of its disturbing aspects, is an immeasurable advance over that false consciousness which it replaces. The scales fall from our eyes. We are no longer required to struggle against unreal enemies, to put others' interests ahead of our own, or to hate ourselves. We begin to understand why we have such depreciated images of ourselves and why so many of us are lacking any genuine conviction of personal worth. Understanding, even beginning to understand this, makes it possible to *change*. Coming to see things differently, we are able to make out possibilities for liberating collective action and for unprecedented personal growth, possibilities which a deceptive sexist social reality had heretofore concealed. No longer do we have to practice upon ourselves that mutilation of intellect and personality required of individuals who, caught up in an irrational and destructive system, are nevertheless not allowed to regard it as anything but sane, progressive, and normal. Moreover, that feeling of alienation from established society which is so prominent a feature of feminist experience may be counterbalanced by a new identification with women of all conditions and a growing sense of solidarity with other feminists. It is a fitting commentary on our society that the growth of feminist consciousness, in spite of its ambiguities, confusions, and trials, is apprehended by those in whom it develops as an experience of liberation.

Notes

Since the first publication of this paper, a number of studies have appeared that examine in some detail the varieties of feminism I mention at the beginning. Alison Jaggar's classic *Feminist Politics and Human Nature* (Totowa, N.J.: Rowman and Allanheld, 1983) offers a fine philosophical reconstruction and critique of the varieties of feminist theory; in addition, Jaggar offers both a philosophically sophisticated version of what has come to be called "socialist feminism," a tendency in feminist theory that incorporates themes from both Marxist and radical feminism. Rosemarie Tong, in *Feminist Thought: A Comprehensive Introduction* (Boulder, Colo.: Westview Press, 1989), discusses feminisms I do not mention, namely, existentialist, psychoanalytic, and postmodern feminism; the latter two are theoretical tendencies that have flowered since the publication of the paper. I recommend also Josephine Donovan, *Feminist Theory: The Intellectual Traditions of American Feminism* (New York: Ungar, 1985).

Excellent discussions of the larger transformations in American society that paved the way for the emergence of Second Wave feminism can be found in Jo Freeman, *Politics of Women's Liberation: A Case Study of an Emerging Social Movement and Its Relation to the Policy Process* (New York and London: Longman, 1975), and in Myra Marx Ferree and Beth B. Hess, *Controversy and Coalition: The New Feminist Movement* (Boston: Twayne, 1985). For a discussion of the role of women in the civil rights movement, see Sara Evans, *Personal Politics: The Roots of Women's Liberation in the Civil Rights Movement and the New Left* (New York: Random House, 1979).

1. Robin Morgan, "Introduction: The Women's Revolution," in *Sisterhood Is Powerful* (New York: Random House, 1970), p. xiv. In what follows, the consciousness I discuss is the consciousness of a feminist who is female. The modes of awareness of men who are feminists, whatever they may be, I do not discuss.

2. By "social reality" I mean the ensemble of formal and informal relationships with other people in which we are now enmeshed or in which we are likely to become enmeshed, together with the attitudes, values, types of communication, and conventions which accompany such relationships. "Social reality" is the social life-world, the social environment as it is present to my consciousness.

3. Karl Marx, *A Contribution to the Critique of Political Economy* (Chicago: Charles H. Kerr, 1904), pp. 11–12.

4. See, however, Margaret Benston, "The Political Economy of Women's Liberation," *Monthly Review,* Vol. 21, No. 4; also Valerie K. Oppenheimer, *The Female Labor Force in the United States: Demographic and Economic Factors Governing Its Growth and Changing Compo-*

sition (Berkeley: University of California Press, 1970). Highly recommended also is the special issue, "The Political Economy of Women," of the *Review of Radical Political Economics,* Vol. 4, July 1972.

5. See Betty Friedan, *The Feminist Mystique* (New York: W. W. Norton, 1963).

6. For an interpretation of the student movement as a protest against the direction taken by capitalist society in its latest phase, see Herbert Gintis, "The New Working Class and Revolutionary Youth," *Socialist Revolution,* May-June 1970.

7. Jean-Paul Sartre, *Being and Nothingness,* translated by Hazel E. Barnes (New York: Philosophical Library, 1956), p. 531.

Pregnant Embodiment:
Subjectivity and Alienation

Iris Marion Young

The library card catalog contains dozens of entries under the heading "pregnancy": clinical treatises detailing signs of morbidity; volumes cataloging studies of fetal development, with elaborate drawings; or popular manuals in which physicians and others give advice on diet and exercise for the pregnant woman. Pregnancy does not belong to the woman herself. It is a state of the developing fetus, for which the woman is a container; or it is an objective, observable process coming under scientific scrutiny; or it becomes objectified by the woman herself as a "condition" in which she must "take care of herself." Except, perhaps, for one insignificant diary, no card appears listing a work that, as Kristeva puts it, is "concerned with the subject, the mother as the site of her proceedings."[1]

We should not be surprised to learn that discourse on pregnancy omits subjectivity, for the specific experience of women has been absent from most of our culture's discourse about human experience and history. This essay considers some of the experiences of pregnancy from the pregnant subject's viewpoint. Through reference to diaries and literature, as well as phenomenological reflection on the pregnant experience, I seek to let women speak in their own voices.

Section I describes some aspects of bodily existence unique to pregnancy. The pregnant subject, I suggest, is decentered, split, or doubled in several ways. She experiences her body as herself and not herself. Its inner movements belong to another being, yet they are not other, because her body boundaries shift and because her bodily self-location is focused on her trunk in addition to her head. This split subject appears in the eroticism of pregnancy, in which the woman can experience an innocent narcissism fed by recollection of her repressed experience of her own mother's body. Pregnant existence entails, finally, a unique temporality of process and growth in which the woman can experience herself as split between past and future.

This description of the lived pregnant body both develops and partially criticizes the phenomenology of bodily existence found in the writings of Straus, Merleau-Ponty, and several other existential phenomenologists. It continues the radical undermining of Cartesianism that these thinkers inaugurated, but it also challenges their implicit assumptions of a unified subject and sharp distinction between transcendence and immanence. Pregnancy, I argue, reveals a paradigm of bodily experience in which the transparent unity of self dissolves and the body attends positively to itself at the same time that it enacts its projects.

Section II reflects on the encounter of the pregnant subject with the institutions and practices of medicine. I argue that within the present organization of these institutions and practices, women usually find such an encounter alienating in several respects. Medicine's self-identification as the curing profession encourages others as well as the woman to think of her pregnancy as a condition that deviates from normal health. The control over knowledge about the pregnancy and birth process that the physician has through instruments, moreover, devalues the privileged relation she has to the fetus and her pregnant body. The fact that in the contemporary context the obstetrician is usually a man reduces the likelihood of bodily empathy between physician and patient. Within the context of authority and dependence that currently structures the doctor-patient relation, moreover, coupled with the use of instruments and drugs in the birthing process, the pregnant and birthing woman often lacks autonomy within these experiences.

Before proceeding, it is important to note that this essay restricts its analysis to the specific experience of women in technologically sophisticated Western societies. The analysis presupposes that pregnancy can be experienced for its own sake, noticed, and savored. This entails that the pregnancy be chosen by the woman, either as an explicit decision to become pregnant or at least as choosing to be identified with and positively accepting of it. Most women in human history have not chosen their pregnancies in this sense. For the vast majority of women in the world today, and even for many women in this privileged and liberal society, pregnancy is not an experience they choose. So I speak in large measure for an experience that must be instituted and for those pregnant women who have been able to take up their situation as their own.

I

The unique contribution of Straus, along with Merleau-Ponty and certain other existential phenomenologists, to the Western philosophical tradition has consisted in locating consciousness and subjectivity in the body itself. This move to situate subjectivity in the lived body jeopardizes dualistic metaphysics altogether. There remains no basis for preserving the mutual exclusivity of the categories subject and object, inner and outer, I and world. Straus puts it this way:

> The meaning of "mine" is determined in relation to, in contraposition to, the world, the Allon, to which I am nevertheless a party. The meaning of "mine" is not comprehensible in the unmediated antithesis of I and not-I, own and strange, subject and object, constituting I and constituted world. Everything points to the fact that separateness and union originate in the same ground.[2]

As Sarano has pointed out, however, antidualist philosophers still tend to operate with a dualist language, this time distinguishing two forms of experiencing the body itself, as subject and as object, both transcending freedom and mere facticity.[3] Reflection on the experience of pregnancy, I shall show, provides a radical challenge even to this dualism that is tacitly at work in the philosophers of the body.

To the extent that these existential phenomenologists preserve a distinction between subject and object, they do so at least partly because they assume the subject as a unity. In the *Phenomenology of Perception*, for example, Merleau-Ponty locates the "intentional arc" that unifies experience in the body, rather than in an abstract constituting consciousness. He does not, however, abandon the idea of a unified self as a condition of experience.

> There must be, then, corresponding to this open unity of the world, an open and indefinite unity of subjectivity. Like the world's unity, that of the *I* is invoked rather than experienced each time I perform an act of perception, each time I reach a self-evident truth, and the universal *I* is the background against which these effulgent forms stand out: it is through one present thought that I achieve the unity of all my thoughts.[4]

Merleau-Ponty's later work, as well as more recent French philosophy, however, suggests that this transcendental faith in a unified subject as a condition of experience may be little more than ideology.[5] The work of Lacan, Derrida, and Kristeva suggests that the unity of the self is itself a project, a project sometimes successfully enacted by a moving and often contradictory subjectivity. I take Kristeva's remarks about pregnancy as a starting point:

> Pregnancy seems to be experienced as the radical ordeal of the splitting of the subject: redoubling up of the body, separation and coexistence of the self and an other, of nature and consciousness, of physiology and speech.[6]

We can confirm this notion of pregnancy as split subjectivity even outside the psychoanalytic framework that Kristeva uses. Reflection on the experience of pregnancy reveals a body subjectivity that is decentered, myself in the mode of not being myself.

As my pregnancy begins, I experience it as a change in my body; I become different from what I have been. My nipples become reddened and tender; my belly swells into a pear. I feel this elastic around my waist, itching, this round, hard middle replacing the doughy belly with which I still identify. Then I feel a little tickle, a little gurgle in my belly. It is my feeling, my insides, and it feels somewhat like a gas bubble, but it is not; it is different, in another place, belonging to another, another that is nevertheless my body.

The first movements of the fetus produce this sense of the splitting subject; the fetus's movements are wholly mine, completely within me, conditioning my experience and space. Only I have access to these movements from their origin, as it were. For months only I can witness this life within me, and it is only under my direction of where to put their hands that others can feel these movements. I have a privileged relation to this other life, not unlike that which I have to my dreams and thoughts, which I can tell someone but which cannot be an object for both of us in the same way. Adrienne Rich reports this sense of the movements within me as mine, even though they are another's.

> In early pregnancy, the stirring of the fetus felt like ghostly tremors of my own body, later like the movements of a being imprisoned within me; but both sensations were *my* sensations, contributing to my own sense of physical and psychic space.[7]

Pregnancy challenges the integration of my body experience by rendering fluid the boundary between what is within, myself, and what is outside, separate. I experience my insides as the space of another, yet my own body.

Nor in pregnancy did I experience the embryo as decisively internal in Freud's terms, but rather, as something inside and of me, yet becoming hourly and daily more separate, on its way to becoming separate from me and of itself. ...
    Far from existing in the mode of "inner space," women are powerfully and vulnerably attuned both to "inner" and "outer" because for us the two are continuous, not polar.[8]

The birthing process entails the most extreme suspension of the bodily distinction between inner and outer. As the months and weeks progress, increasingly I feel my insides, strained and pressed, and increasingly feel the movement of a body inside me. Through pain and blood and water this inside thing emerges between my legs, for a short while both inside and outside me. Later I look with wonder at my mushy middle and at my child, amazed that this yowling, flailing thing, so completely different from me, was there inside, part of me.

The integrity of my body is undermined in pregnancy not only by this externality of the inside, but also by the fact that the boundaries of my body are themselves in flux. In pregnancy I literally do not have a firm sense of where my body ends and the world beings. My automatic body habits become dislodged; the continuity between my customary body and my body at this moment is broken.[9] In pregnancy my prepregnant body image does not entirely leave my movements and expectations, yet it is with the pregnant body that I must move. This is another instance of the doubling of the pregnant subject.

I move as if I could squeeze around chairs and through crowds as I could seven months before, only to find my way blocked by my own body sticking out in front of me—but yet not me, since I did not expect it to block my passage. As I lean over in my chair to tie my shoe, I am surprised by the graze of this hard belly on my thigh. I do not anticipate my body touching itself, for my habits retain the old sense of my boundaries. In the ambiguity of bodily touch, I feel myself being touched and touching simultaneously, both on my knee and my belly.[10] The belly is other, since I did not expect it there, but since I feel the touch upon it, it is me.[11]

Existential phenomenologists of the body usually assume a distinction between transcendence and immanence as two modes of bodily being. They assume that insofar as I adopt an active relation to the world, I am not aware of my body for its own sake. In the successful enactment of my aims and projects, my body is a transparent medium.[12] For several of these thinkers, awareness of my body as weighted material, as physical, occurs only or primarily when my instrumental relation to the world breaks down, in fatigue or illness.

> The transformation into the bodily as physical always means discomfort and malaise. The character of husk, which our live bodiness here increasingly assumes, shows itself in its onerousness, bringing heaviness, burden, weight.[13]

Being brought to awareness of my body for its own sake, these thinkers assume, entails estrangement and objectification.

> If, suddenly, I am no longer indifferent to my body, and if I suddenly give my attention to its functions and processes, then my body as a whole is objectified, becomes to me an other, a part of the outside world. And though I may also be able to feel its inner processes, I am myself excluded.[14]

Thus the dichotomy of subject and object appears anew in the conceptualization of the body itself. These thinkers tend to assume that awareness of my body in its weight, massiveness, and balance is always an alienated objectification of my body, in which I am not my body and my body imprisons me. They also tend to assume that such awareness of my body must cut me off from the enactment of my projects; I cannot be attending to the physicality of my body and using it as the means to the accomplishment of my aims.

Certainly there are occasions when I experience my body only as a resistance, only as a painful otherness preventing me from accomplishing my goals. It is inappropriate, however, to tie such a negative meaning to all experience of being brought to awareness of the body in its weight and materiality. Sally Gadow has argued that in addition to experiencing the body as a transparent mediator for our projects or an objectified and alienated resistance or pain, we also at times experience our bodily being in an aesthetic mode. That is, we can become aware of ourselves as body and take an interest in its sensations and limitations for their own sake, experiencing them as a fullness rather than a lack.[15] While Gadow suggests that both illness and aging can be experiences of the body in such an aesthetic mode, pregnancy is most paradigmatic of such experience of being thrown into awareness of one's body. Contrary to the mutually exclusive categorization between transcendence and immanence that underlies some theories, the awareness of my body in its bulk and weight does not impede the accomplishing of my aims.

This belly touching my knee, this extra part of me that gives me a joyful surprise when I move through a tight place, calls me back to the matter of my body even as I move about accomplishing my aims. Pregnant consciousness is animated by a double intentionality: my subjectivity splits between awareness of myself as body and awareness of my aims and projects. To be sure, even in pregnancy there are times when I am so absorbed in my activity that I do not feel myself as body, but when I move or feel the look of another I am likely to be recalled to the thickness of my body.

I walk through the library stacks searching for the *Critique of Dialectical Reason;* I feel the painless pull of false contractions in my back. I put my hand on my belly to notice its hardening, while my eyes continue their scanning. As I set with friends listening to jazz in a darkened bar, I feel within me the kicking of the fetus, as if it follows the rhythm of the music. In attending to my pregnant body in such circumstances, I do not feel myself alienated from it, as in illness. I merely notice its borders and rumblings with interest, sometimes with pleasure, and this aesthetic interest does not divert me from my business.

This splitting focus both on my body and my projects has its counterpart in the dual location I give to myself on my body. Straus suggests that in everyday instrumental actions of getting about our business, comprehending, observing, willing, and acting, the "I" is located phenomenologically in our head. There are certain activities, however, of which dancing is paradigmatic, where the "I" shifts from the eyes to the region of the trunk. In this orientation that Straus calls "pathic" we experience ourselves in greater sensory continuity with the surroundings.[16]

The pregnant subject experiences herself as located in the eyes and trunk simultaneously, I suggest. She often experiences her ordinary walking, turning, sitting as a kind of dance, movement that not only gets her where she is going, but also in which she glides through space in an immediate openness. She is surprised sometimes that this weighted solidity that she feels herself becoming can still move with ease.

Pregnancy roots me to the earth, makes me conscious of the physicality of my body not as an object, but as the material weight that I am in movement. The notion of the body as a pure medium of my projects is the illusion of a philosophy that has not quite shed the Western philosophical legacy of humanity as spirit.[17] Movement always entails awareness of effort and the feeling of resistance. In pregnancy this fact of existence never leaves me. I am an actor transcending through each moment to further projects, but the solid inertia and demands of my body call me to my limits not as an obstacle to action, but only as a fleshy relation to the earth.[18] As the months proceed, the most ordinary efforts of human existence, such as sitting, bending, and walking, which I formerly took for granted, become apparent as the projects they themselves are. Getting up, for example, increasingly becomes a task that requires my attention.[19]

In the experience of the pregnant woman, this weight and materiality often produce a sense of power, solidity, and validity. Thus, whereas our society often devalues and trivializes women, regards women as weak and dainty, the pregnant woman can gain a certain sense of self-respect.

> This bulk slows my walking and makes my gestures and my mind more stately. I suppose if I schooled myself to walk massively the rest of my life, I might always have massive thoughts.[20]

There was a time when the pregnant woman stood as a symbol of stately and sexual beauty.[21] While pregnancy remains an object of fascination, our own culture harshly separates pregnancy from sexuality. The dominant culture defines feminine beauty as slim and shapely. The pregnant woman is often not looked upon as sexually active or desirable, even though her own desires and sensitivity may have increased. Her male partner, if she has one, may decline to share in her sexuality, and her physician may advise her to restrict her sexual activity. To the degree that a woman derives a sense of self-worth from looking "sexy" in the manner promoted by dominant cultural images, she may experience her pregnant body as being ugly and alien.

Though the pregnant woman may find herself desexualized by others, at the same time she may find herself with a heightened sense of her own sexuality. Kristeva suggests that the pregnant and birthing woman renews connection to the repressed, preconscious, presymbolic aspect of existence. Instead of being a unified ego, the subject of the paternal symbolic order, the pregnant subject straddles the spheres of language and instinct. In this splitting of the subject, the pregnant woman recollects a primordial sexual continuity with the maternal body, which Kristeva calls "juissance."[22]

The pregnant woman's relation to her body can be an innocent narcissism. As I undress in the morning and evening, I gaze in the mirror for long minutes, without stealth or vanity. I do not appraise myself, ask whether I look good enough for others, but like a child take pleasure in discovering new things in my body. I turn to the side and stroke the taut flesh that protrudes under my breasts.

Perhaps the dominant culture's desexualization of the pregnant body helps make possible such self-love when it happens. The culture's separation of pregnancy and sexuality can liberate her from the sexually objectifying gaze that alienates and instrumentalizes her when in her nonpregnant state. The leer of sexual objectification regards the woman in pieces, as the possible object of a man's desire and touch.[23] In pregnancy the woman may experience some release from this alienating gaze. The look focusing on her belly is not one of desire, but of recognition. Some may be repelled by her, find her body ridiculous, but the look that follows her in pregnancy does not alienate her, does not instrumentalize her with respect to another's desire. Indeed, in this society, which still often narrows women's possibilities to motherhood, the pregnant woman often finds herself looked at with approval.

> As soon as I was visibly and clearly pregnant, I felt, for the first time in my adolescent and adult life, not-guilty. The atmosphere of approval in which I was bathed—even by strangers in the street, it seemed—was like an aura I carried with me, in which doubts, fears, misgivings, met with absolute denial. This is what women have always done.[24]

In classical art this "aura" surrounding motherhood depicts repose. The dominant culture projects pregnancy as a time of quiet waiting. We refer to the woman as "expecting," as though this new life were flying in from another planet and she sat in her rocking chair by the window, occasionally moving the curtain aside to see whether the ship is coming. The image of uneventful waiting associated with pregnancy reveals clearly how much the discourse of pregnancy leaves out the subjectivity of the woman. From the point of view of others pregnancy is primarily a time of waiting and watching, when nothing happens.

For the pregnant subject, on the other hand, pregnancy has a temporality of movement, growth, and change. The pregnant subject is not simply a splitting in which the two halves lie open and still, but a dialectic. The pregnant woman experiences herself as a source and participant in a creative process. Though she does not plan and direct it, neither does it merely wash over her; rather, she *is* this process, this change. Time stretches out, moments and days take on a depth because she experiences more changes in herself, her body. Each day, each week, she looks at herself for signs of transformation.

> Were I to lose consciousness for a month, I could still tell that an appreciable time had passed by the increased size of the fetus within me. There is a constant sense of growth, of progress, of time, which, while it may be wasted for you personally, is still being used, so that even if you were to do nothing at all during those nine months, something would nevertheless be accomplished and a climax reached.[25]

For others the birth of an infant may be only a beginning, but for the birthing woman it is a conclusion as well. It signals the close of a process she has been undergoing for nine months, the leaving of this unique body she has moved through, always surprising her a bit in its boundary changes and inner kicks. Especially if this is her first child she experiences the birth as a transition to a new self that she may both desire and fear. She fears a loss of identity, as though on the other side of the birth she herself became a transformed person, such that she would "never be the same again."

Finally her "time" comes, as is commonly said. During labor, however, there is no sense of growth and change, but the cessation of time. There is no intention, no activity, only a will to endure. I only know that I have been lying in this pain, concentrating on staying above it, for a long time because the hands of the clock say so or the sun on the wall has moved to the other side of the room.

> Time is absolutely still. I have been here forever. Time no longer exists. Always, Time holds steady for birth. There is only this rocketing, this labor.[26]

II

Feminist writers often use the concept of alienation to describe female existence in a male dominated society and culture.[27] In this section I argue that the pregnant subject's encounter with obstetrical medicine in the United States often alienates her from her pregnant and birthing experience. Alienation here means the objectification or appropriation by one subject of another subject's body, action, or product of action, such that she or he does not recognize that objectification as having its origins in her or his experience. A subject's experience or action is alienated when it is defined or controlled by a subject who does not share one's assumptions or goals. I will argue that a woman's experience in pregnancy and birthing is often alienated because her condition tends to be defined as a disorder, because medical instruments objectify internal processes in such a way that they devalue a woman's experience of those processes, and because the social relations and instrumentation of the medical setting reduce her control over her experience.

Through most of the history of medicine its theoreticians and practitioners did not include the reproductive processes of women within its domain. Once women's reproductive processes came within the domain of medicine, they were defined as diseases. Indeed, by the mid-nineteenth century, at least in Victorian England and America, being female itself was symptomatic of disease. Medical writers considered women to be inherently weak and psychologically unstable, and the ovaries and uterus to be the cause of a great number of diseases and disorders, both physical and psychological.[28]

Contemporary obstetricians and gynecologists usually take pains to assert that menstruation, pregnancy, childbirth, and menopause are normal body functions that occasionally have a disorder. The legacy that defined pregnancy and other reproductive functions as conditions requiring medical therapy, however, has not been entirely abandoned.

Rothman points out that even medical writers who explicitly deny that pregnancy is a disease view normal changes associated with pregnancy, such as lowered hemoglobin, water retention, and weight gain, as "symptoms" requiring "treatment" as part of the normal process of prenatal care.[29] Though 75 percent to 88 percent of pregnant women experience some nausea in the early months, some obstetrical textbooks refer to this physiological process as a neurosis that "may indicate resentment, ambivalence and inadequacy in women ill-prepared for motherhood."[30] Obstetrical teaching films entitled *Normal Delivery* depict the use of various drugs and instruments, as well as the use of paracervical block and the performance of episiotomy.[31]

A continued tendency on the part of medicine to treat pregnancy and childbirth as dysfunctional conditions derives first from the way medicine defines its purpose. Though medicine has extended its domain to include many bodily and psychological processes that ought not to be conceptualized as illness or disease—such as child development, sexuality, and aging, as well as women's reproductive functions—medicine continues to define itself as the practice that seeks cure for disease. Pellegrino and Thomasma, for example, define the goal of medicine as "the relief of perceived lived body disruption" and "organic restoration to a former or better state of perceived health or well-being."

> When a patient consults a physician, he or she does so with one specific purpose in mind: to be healed, to be restored and made whole, i.e., to be relieved of some noxious

element in physical or emotional life which the patient defines as disease—a distortion of the accustomed perception of what is a satisfactory life.[32]

These are often not the motives that prompt pregnant women to seek the office of the obstetrician. Yet because medicine continues to define itself as the curing profession, it can tend implicitly to conceptualize women's reproductive processes as disease or infirmity.

A second conceptual ground for the tendency within gynecological and obstetrical practice to approach menstruation, pregnancy, and menopause as "conditions" with "symptoms" that require "treatment" lies in the implicit male bias in medicine's conception of health. The dominant model of health assumes that the normal, healthy body is unchanging. Health is associated with stability, equilibrium, a steady state. Only a minority of persons, however, namely adult men who are not yet old, experience their health as a state in which there is no regular or noticeable change in body condition. For them a noticeable change in their bodily state usually does signal a disruption or dysfunction. Regular, noticeable, sometimes extreme change in bodily condition, on the other hand, is an aspect of the normal bodily functioning of adult women. Change is also a central aspect of the bodily existence of healthy children and healthy old people, as well as some of the so-called disabled. Yet medical conceptualization implicitly uses this unchanging adult male body as the standard of all health.

This tendency of medical conceptualization to treat pregnancy as disease can produce alienation for the pregnant woman. She often has a sense of bodily well-being during her pregnancy and often has increased immunity to common diseases such as colds, flu, etc. As we saw in the previous section, moreover, she often has a bodily self-image of strength and solidity. Thus, while her body may signal one set of impressions, her entrance into the definitions of medicine may lead her to the opposite understanding. Even though certain discomforts associated with pregnancy, such as nausea, flatulence, and shortness of breath, can happen in the healthiest of woman, her internalization of various discussions of the fragility of pregnancy may lead her to define such experience as signs of weakness.

Numerous criticisms of the use of instruments, drugs, surgery, and other methods of intervention in obstetrical practice have been voiced in recent years.[33] I do not wish to reiterate them here, nor do I wish to argue that the use of instruments and drugs in pregnancy and childbirth is usually inappropriate or dangerous. The instrumental and intervention orientation that predominates in contemporary obstetrics, however, can contribute to a woman's sense of alienation in at least two ways.

First, the normal procedures of the American hospital birthing setting render the woman considerably more passive than she need be. Most hospitals, for example, do not allow the woman to walk around even during early stages of labor, despite the fact that there is evidence that moving around can lessen pain and speed the birthing process. Routine breaking of the amniotic sack enforces this bed confinement. Women usually labor and deliver in a horizontal or near-horizontal position, reducing the influence of gravity and reducing the woman's ability to push. The use of intravenous equipment, monitors, and pain-relieving drugs all inhibit a woman's capacity to move during labor.

Second, the use of instruments provides a means of objectifying the pregnancy and birth that alienates a woman because it negates or devalues her own experience of those processes. As the previous section described, at a phenomenological level the pregnant woman has a unique knowledge of her body processes and the life of the fetus. She feels the movements of the fetus, the contractions of her uterus, with an immediacy and certainty that no one can share. Recently invented machines tend to devalue this knowledge. The fetal-heart sensor projects the heartbeat of the six-week-old fetus into the room so that all can hear it in the same way. The sonogram is receiving increasing use to follow the course of fetal development. The fetal monitor attached during labor records the intensity and duration of each contraction on white paper; the woman's reports are no longer necessary for charting the progress of her labor. Such instruments transfer some control over the means of observing the pregnancy and birth process from the woman to the medical personnel. The woman's experience of these processes is reduced in value, replaced by more objective means of observation.

Alienation within the context of contemporary obstetrics can be further produced for the pregnant woman by the fact that the physician attending her is usually a man. Humanistic writers about medicine often suggest that a basic condition of good medical practice is that the physician and patient share the lived-body experience.[34] If the description of the lived-body experience of pregnancy in the previous section is valid, however, pregnancy and childbirth entail a unique body subjectivity that is difficult to empathize with unless one is or has been pregnant. Since the vast majority of obstetricians are men, then, this basic condition of therapeutic practice usually cannot be met in obstetrics. Physicians and pregnant women are thereby distanced in their relationship, perhaps more than others in the doctor-patient relation. The sexual asymmetry between physician and patient also produces a distance because it must be desexualized. Prenatal checkups follow the same procedure as gynecological examinations, requiring an aloof matter-of-factness in order to preclude attaching sexual meaning to them.[35]

There is a final alienation the woman experiences in the medical setting, which drives from the relations of authority and subordination that usually structure the doctor-patient relation in contemporary medical practice. Many writers have noted that medicine has increasingly become an institution with broad social authority on a par with the legal system or even organized religion.[36] The relationship between doctor and patient is usually structured as superior to subordinate. Physicians often project an air of fatherly infallibility and resist having their opinions challenged; the authoritarianism of the doctor-patient relations increases as the social distance between them increases.[37]

This authority that the physician has over any patient is amplified in gynecology and obstetrics by the dynamic of gender hierarchy. In a culture that still generally regards men as being more important than women and gives men authority and power over women in many institutions, the power the doctor has over the knowledge and objectification of her body processes, as well as his power to direct the performance of her office visits and her birthing, are often experienced by her as another form of male power over women.[38]

Philosophers of medicine have pointed out that the concept of health is much less a scientific concept than a normative concept referring to human well-being and the good life.[39] I have argued that there exists a male bias in medicine's concept of health insofar as the healthy body is understood to be the body in a steady state. This argument suggests that medical culture requires a more self-consciously differentiated understanding of health and disease.[40] Contemporary culture has gone to a certain extent in the direction of developing distinct norms of health and disease for the aged, the physically impaired, children, and hormonally active women. Such developments should be encouraged, and medical theorists and practitioners should be vigilant about tendencies to judge physical difference as deviance.

Moreover, to overcome the potentialities for alienation that I have argued exist in obstetrical practices, as well as other medical practices, medicine must shed its self-definition as primarily concerned with curing. Given that nearly all aspects of human bodily life and change have come within the domain of medical institutions and practices, such a definition is no longer appropriate. There are numerous life states and physical conditions in which a person needs help or care, rather than medical or surgical efforts to alter, repress, or speed a body process. The birthing woman certainly needs help in her own actions, being held, talked to, coached, dabbed with water, and having someone manipulate the emergence of the infant. Children, old people, and the physically impaired often need help and care though they are not diseased. Within current medical and related institutions there exist professionals who perform these caring functions. They are usually women, usually poorly paid, and their activities are usually seen as complementing and subordinate to the direction of activities such as diagnostic tests, drug therapies, and surgical therapies performed by the physicians, usually men. The alienation experienced by the pregnant and birthing woman would probably be lessened if caring were distinguished from curing and took on a practical value that did not subordinate it to curing.

Notes

1. Julia Kristeva, "Motherhood According to Giovanni Bellini," in *Desire in Language* (New York: Columbia University Press, 1980), p. 237.

2. Erwin Straus, *Psychiatry and Philosophy* (New York: Springer-Verlag, 1969), p. 29.

3. J. Sarano, *The Meaning of the Body*, James H. Farley, trans. (Philadelphia: Westminster Press, 1966), pp. 62–63.

4. Maurice Merleau-Ponty, *The Phenomenology of Perception*, Colin Smith, trans. (New York: Humanities Press, 1962), p. 406.

5. See Rosalind Coward and John Ellis, *Language and Materialism* (London: Routledge and Kegan Paul, 1977).

6. Julia Kristeva, "Women's Times," Jardin and Blake, trans., *Signs*, vol. 7 (1981), p. 31; cf. Kristeva, "Motherhood According to Giovanni Bellini," p. 238.

7. Adrienne Rich, *Of Woman Born* (New York: W. W. Norton, 1976; Bantam paperback edition, p. 47).

8. Rich, pp. 47–48.

9. See Merleau-Ponty, *Phenomenology of Perception*, p. 82.

10. On the ambiguity of touch, see Merleau-Ponty, p. 93; see also Erwin Straus, *Psychiatry and Philosophy*, p. 46.

11. Straus discusses an intentional shift between the body as "other" and as self; see *The Primary World of the Senses* (London: The Free Press, 1963), p. 370.

12. Merleau-Ponty, pp. 138–39.

13. Hans Plugge, "Man and His Body," in Spicker, ed., *The Philosophy of the Body* (Chicago: Quadrangle Books, 1970), p. 298.

14. Straus, *Primary World of the Senses*, p. 245.

15. Sally Gadow, "Body and Self: A Dialectic," *Journal of Medicine and Philosophy*, vol. 5 (1980), pp. 172–85.

16. See Straus, "Forms of Spatiality," in *Phenomenological Psychology* (New York: Basic Books), especially pp. 11–12.

17. Elizabeth V. Spelman, "Woman as Body: Ancient and Contemporary Views," *Feminist Studies*, vol. 8 (1982), pp. 109–23.

18. On the relation of body to ground, see R. M. Griffith, "Anthropology: Man-a-foot," in *Philosophy of the Body*, pp. 273–92; see also Stuart Spicker, "*Terra Firma* and Infirma Species: From Medical Philosophical Anthropology to Philosophy of Medicine," *Journal of Medicine and Philosophy*, Vol. 1 (1976), pp. 104–35.

19. Straus' essay "The Upright Posture" well expresses the centrality of getting up and standing up to being a person; in *Phenomenological Psychology*, pp. 137–65.

20. Ann Lewis, *An Interesting Condition* (Garden City, N.Y.: Doubleday, 1950), p. 83. When I began reading for this essay I was shocked at how few texts I found of women speaking about their pregnancies; this book is a rare gem in that regard.

21. Rich discusses some of the history of views of pregnancy and motherhood; see op. cit., *Of Woman Born*, chapter IV.

22. Kristeva, "Motherhood According to Giovanni Bellini," op. cit., p. 242; Marianne Hirsch makes a useful commentary in "Mothers and Daughters," *Signs*, vol. 7 (1981), pp. 200–22.

23. Sandra Bartky, "On Psychological Oppression," in Bishop and Weinzweig, ed., *Philosophy and Women* (Belmont, Calif.: Wadsworth Publishing Co., 1979), pp. 330–41.

24. Rich, p. 6.

25. Lewis, op. cit., p. 78.

26. Phyllis Chesler, *With Child: A Diary of Motherhood* (New York: Thomas Y. Crowell, 1979), p. 116.

27. Ann Foreman, *Femininity As Alienation* (London: Pluto Press, 1977); Sandra Bartky, "Narcissism, Femininity and Alienation," *Social Theory and Practice*, vol. 8 (1982), pp. 127–43.

28. Barbara Ehrenreich and Dierdre English, *For Her Own Good* (Garden City, N.Y.: Doubleday, 1978), chapters 2 and 3.

29. Barbara Katz Rothman, "Women, Health and Medicine," in Jo Freeman, ed., *Women: A Feminist Perspective* (Palo Alto, Calif.: Mayfield Publishing Co., 1979), pp. 27–40.

30. Quoted in Gena Corea, *The Hidden Malpractice: How American Medicine Treats Women as Patients and Professionals* (New York: William Morrow, 1977), p. 76.

31. Rothman, op. cit., p. 36.

32. E. D. Pellegrino and D. C. Thomasma, *A Philosophical Basis of Medical Practice* (New York: Oxford University Press, 1981), p. 122; earlier quotes from p. 76 and p. 72, respectively.

33. Suzanne Arms, *Immaculate Deception: A New Look at Women and Childbirth in America* (Boston: Houghton Mifflin, 1975); D. Haire, "The Cultural Warping of Childbirth," *Environmental Child Health*, vol. 19 (1973), pp. 171–91; and Adele Laslie, "Ethical Issues in Childbirth," *Journal of Medicine and Philosophy*, vol. 7 (1982), pp. 179–96.

34. Pellegrino and Thomasma, op. cit., p. 114.

35. J. Emerson, "Behavior in Private Places: Sustaining Definitions of Reality in Gynecological Examinations," in H. Dreitzen, ed., *Recent Sociology*, no. 2 (London: Macmillan, 1970), pp. 74–97.

36. See E. Friedson, *The Profession of Medicine* (New York: Dodd and Mead Co., 1970); Irving K. Zola, "Medicine as an Institution of Social Control," *The Sociological Review*, vol. 2 (1972), pp. 487–504; and Janice Raymond, "Medicine as Patriarchal Religion," *Journal of Medicine and Philosophy*, vol. 7 (1982), pp. 197–216.

37. See G. Ehrenreich and J. Ehrenreich, "Medicine and Social Control," in John Ehrenreich, ed., *The Cultural Crisis of Modern Medicine* (New York: Monthly Review Press, 1979), pp. 1–28.

38. See B. Kaiser and K. Kaiser, "The Challenge of the Women's Movement to American Gynecology," *American Journal of Obstetrics and Gynecology*, vol. 120 (1974), pp. 652–61.

39. Pellegrino and Thomasma, op. cit., pp. 74–76; see also Tristam Engelhardt, "Human Well-being and Medicine: Some Basic Value Judgments in the Biomedical Sciences," in Engelhardt and Callahan, ed., *Science, Ethics and Medicine* (Hastings-on-Hudson, N.Y.: Ethics and the Life Sciences, 1976), pp. 120–39; and Caroline Whitbeck, "A Theory of Health" in Caplan, Engelhardt, and McCartney, ed., *Concepts of Health and Disease: Interdisciplinary Perspectives* (Reading, Mass.: Addison-Wesley, 1981), pp. 611–26.

40. Arlene Dallery, "Illness and Health: Alternatives to Medicine," in E. Schrag and W. L. McBride, ed., *Phenomenology in a Pluralistic Context: Selected Studies in Phenomenology and Existentialism* (Albany: State University of New York Press, 1983), pp. 167–176.

Breast Cancer:
Power Versus Prosthesis

Audre Lorde

1

Each woman responds to the crisis that breast cancer brings to her life out of a whole pattern, which is the design of who she is and how her life has been lived. The weave of her every day existence is the training ground for how she handles crisis. Some women obscure their painful feelings surrounding mastectomy with a blanket of business-as-usual, thus keeping those feelings forever under cover, but expressed elsewhere. For some women, in a valiant effort not to be seen as merely victims, this means an insistence that no such feelings exist and that nothing much has occurred. For some women it means the warrior's painstaking examination of yet another weapon, unwanted but useful.

I am a post-mastectomy woman who believes our feelings need voice in order to be recognized, respected, and of use.

I do not wish my anger and pain and fear about cancer to fossilize into yet another silence, nor to rob me of whatever strength can lie at the core of this experience, openly acknowledged and examined. For other women of all ages, colors, and sexual identities who recognize that imposed silence about any area of our lives is a tool for separation and powerlessness, and for myself, I have tried to voice some of my feelings and thoughts about the travesty of prosthesis, the pain of amputation, the function of cancer in a profit economy, my confrontation with mortality, the strength of women loving, and the power and rewards of self-conscious living.

Breast cancer and mastectomy are not unique experiences, but ones shared by thousands of american women. Each of these women has a particular voice to be raised in what must become a female outcry against all preventable cancers, as well as against the secret fears that allow those cancers to flourish. May these words serve as encouragement for other women to speak and to act out of our experiences with cancer and with other threats of death, for silence has never brought us anything of worth. Most of all, may these words underline the possibilities of self-healing and the richness of living for all women.

There is a commonality if isolation and painful reassessment which is shared by all women with breast cancer, whether this commonality is recognized or not. It is not my intention to judge the woman who has chosen the path of prosthesis, of silence and invisibility, the woman who wishes to be 'the same as before.' She has survived on another kind of courage, and she is not alone. Each of us struggles daily with the pressures of conformity and the loneliness of difference from which those choices seem to offer escape. I only know that those choices do not work for me, nor for other women who, not without fear, have survived cancer by scrutinizing its meaning within our lives, and by attempting to integrate this crisis into useful strengths for change.

2

These selected journal entries, which begin 6 months after my modified radical mastectomy for breast cancer and extend beyond the completion of the essays in this book, exemplify the process of integrating this crisis into my life.

1/26/79

I'm not feeling very hopeful these days, about selfhood or anything else. I handle the outward motions of each day while pain fills me like a puspocket and every touch threatens to breech the taut membrane that keeps it from flowing through and poisoning my whole existence. Sometimes despair sweeps across my consciousness like luna winds across a barren moonscape. Ironshod horses rage back and forth over every nerve. Oh Seboulisa ma, help me remember what I have paid so much to learn. I could die of difference, or live—myriad selves.

2/5/79

The terrible thing is that nothing goes past me these days, nothing. Each horror remains like a steel vise in my flesh, another magnet to the flame. Buster has joined the rolecall of useless wasteful deaths of young Black people; in the gallery today everywhere ugly images of women offering up distorted bodies for whatever fantasy passes in the name of male art. Gargoyles of pleasure. Beautiful laughing Buster, shot down in a hallway for ninety cents. Shall I unlearn that tongue in which my curse is written?

3/1/79

It is such an effort to find decent food in this place, not to just give up and eat the old poison. But I must tend my body with at least as much care as I tend the compost, particularly now when it seems so beside the point. Is this pain and despair that surround me a result of cancer, or has it just been released by cancer? I feel so unequal to what I always handled before, the abominations outside that echo the pain within. And yes I am completely self-referenced right now because it is the only translation I can trust, and I do believe not until every woman traces her weave back strand by bloody self-referenced strand, will we begin to alter the whole pattern.

4/16/79

The enormity of our task, to turn the world around. It feels like turning my life around, inside out. If I can look directly at my life and my death without flinching I know there is nothing they can ever do to me again. I must be content to see how really little I can do and still do it with an open heart. I can never accept this, like I can't accept that turning my life around is so hard, eating differently, sleeping differently, moving differently, being differently. Like Martha said, I want the old me, bad as before.

4/22/79

I must let this pain flow through me and pass on. If I resist or try to stop it, it will detonate inside me, shatter me, splatter my pieces against every wall and person that I touch.

5/1/79

Spring comes, and still I feel despair like a pale cloud waiting to consume me, engulf me like another cancer, swallow me into immobility, metabolize me into cells of itself; my body, a barometer. I need to remind myself of the joy, the lightness, the laughter so vital to my living and my health. Otherwise, the other will always be waiting to eat me up into despair again. And that means destruction. I don't know how, but it does.

9/79

There is no room around me in which to be still, to examine and explore what pain is mine alone—no device to separate my struggle within from my fury at the outside world's viciousness, the stupid brutal lack of consciousness or concern that passes for the way things are. The arrogant blindness of comfortable white women. What is this work all for? What does it matter whether I ever speak again or not? I try. The blood of black women sloshes from coast to coast and Daly says race is of no concern to women. So that means we are either immortal or born to die and no note taken, un-women.

10/3/79

I don't feel like being strong, but do I have a choice? It hurts when even my sisters look at me in the street with cold and silent eyes. I am defined as other in every group I'm a part of. The outsider, both strength and weakness. Yet without community there is certainly no liberation, no future, only the most vulnerable and temporary armistice between me and my oppression.

11/19/79

I want to write rage but all that comes is sadness. We have been sad long enough to make this earth either weep or grow fertile. I am an anachronism, a sport, like the bee that was never meant to fly. Science said so. I am not supposed to exist. I carry death around in my body like a condemnation. But I do live. The bee flies. There must be some way to integrate death into living, neither ignoring it nor giving in to it.

1/1/80

Faith is the last day of Kwanza, and the name of the war against despair, the battle I fight daily. I become better at it. I want to write about that battle, the skirmishes, the losses, the small yet so important victories that make the sweetness of my life.

1/20/80

The novel is finished at last. It has been a lifeline. I do not have to win in order to know my dreams are valid, I only have to believe in a process of which I am a part. My work kept me alive this past year, my work and the love of women. They are inseparable from each other. In the recognition of the existence of love lies the answer to despair. Work is that recognition given voice and name.

2/18/80

I am 46 years living today and very pleased to be alive, very glad and very happy. Fear and pain and despair do not disappear. They only become slowly less and less important. Although sometimes I still long for a simple orderly life with a hunger sharp as that sudden vegetarian hunger for meat.

4/6/80

Somedays, if bitterness were a whetstone, I could be sharp as grief.

5/30/80

Last spring was another piece of the fall and winter before, a progression from all the pain and sadness of that time, ruminated over. But somehow this summer which is almost upon me feels like a part of my future. Like a brand new time, and I'm pleased to know it, wherever it leads. I feel like another woman, de-chrysalised and become a broader, stretched-our me, strong and excited, a muscle flexed and honed for action.

6/20/80

I do not forget cancer for very long, ever. That keeps me armed and on my toes, but also with a slight background noise of fear. Carl Simonton's book, Getting Well Again, *has been really helpful to me, even though his smugness infuriates me sometimes. The visualizations and deep relaxing techniques that I learned from it help make me a less anxious person, which seems strange, because in other ways, I live with the constant fear of recurrence of another cancer. But fear and anxiety are not the same at all. One is an appropriate response to a real situation which I can accept and learn to work through just as I work through semi-blindness. But the other, anxiety, is an immobilizing yield to things that go bump in the night, a surrender to namelessness, formlessness, voicelessness, and silence.*

7/10/80

I dreamt I had begun training to change my life, with a teacher who is very shadowy. I was not attending classes, but I was going to learn how to change my whole life, live differently, do everything in a new and different way. I didn't really understand, but I trusted this shadowy teacher. Another young woman who was there told me she was taking a course in "language crazure," the opposite of discrazure (the cracking and wearing away of rock). I thought it would be very exciting to study the formation and crack and composure of words, so I told my teacher I wanted to take that course. My teacher said okay, but it wasn't going to help me any because I had to learn something else, and I wouldn't get anything new from that class. I replied maybe not, but even though I knew all about rocks, for instance, I still liked studying their composition, and giving a name to the different ingredients of which they were made. It's very exciting to think of me being all the people in this dream.

3

I have learned much in the 18 months since my mastectomy. My visions of a future I can create have been honed by the lessons of my limitations. Now I wish to give form with honesty and precision to the pain faith labor and loving which this period of my life has translated into strength for me.

Sometimes fear stalks me like another malignancy, sapping energy and power and attention from my work. A cold becomes sinister; a cough, lung cancer; a bruise, leukemia. Those fears are most powerful when they are not given voice, and close upon their heels comes the fury that I cannot shake them. I am learning to live beyond fear by living through it, and in the process learning to turn fury at my own limitations into some more creative energy. I realize that if I wait until I am no longer afraid to act, write, speak, be, I'll be sending messages on a ouija board, cryptic complaints from the other side. When I dare to be powerful, to use my strength in the service of my vision, then it becomes less important whether or not I am unafraid.

As women we were raised to fear. If I cannot banish fear completely, I can learn to count with it less. For then fear becomes not a tyrant against which I waste my energy fighting, but a companion, not particularly desirable, yet one whose knowledge can be useful.

I write so much here about fear because in shaping this introduction to *The Cancer Journals,* I found fear laid across my hands like a steel bar. When I tried to reexamine the 18 months since my mastectomy, some of what I touched was molten despair and waves of mourning—for my lost breast, for time, for the luxury of false power. Not only were these emotions difficult and painful to relive, but they were entwined with the terror that if I opened myself once again to scrutiny, to feeling the pain of loss, of despair, of victories too minor in my eyes to rejoice over, then I might also open myself again to disease. I had to remind myself that I had lived through it all, already. I had known the pain, and survived it. It only remained for me to give it voice, to share it for use, that the pain not be wasted.

Living a self-conscious life, under the pressure of time, I work with the consciousness of death at my shoulder, not constantly, but often enough to leave a mark upon all of my life's decisions and actions. And it does not matter whether this death comes next week or thirty years from now; this consciousness gives my life another breadth. It helps shape the words I speak, the ways I love, my politic of action, the strength of my vision and purpose, the depth of my appreciation of living.

I would lie if I did not also speak of loss. Any amputation is a physical and psychic reality that must be integrated into a new sense of self. The absence of my breast is a recurrent sadness, but certainly not one that dominates my life. I miss it, sometimes piercingly. When other one-breasted women hide behind the mask of prosthesis or the dangerous fantasy of reconstruction, I find little support in the broader female environment for my rejection of what feels like a cosmetic sham. But I believe that socially sanctioned prosthesis is merely another way of keeping women with breast cancer silent and separate from each other. For instance, what would happen if an army of one-breasted women descended upon Congress and demanded that the use of carcinogenic fat-stored hormones in beef-feed be outlawed?

The lessons of the past 18 months have been many: How do I provide myself with the best physical and psychic nourishment to repair past, and minimize future damage to my body? How do I give voice to my quests so that other women can take what they need from my experience? How do my experiences with cancer fit into the larger tapestry of my work as a Black woman, into the history of all women? And most of all, how do I fight the despair born of fear and anger and powerlessness which is my greatest internal enemy?

I have found that battling despair does not mean closing my eyes to the enormity of the tasks of effecting change, nor ignoring the strength and the barbarity of the forces aligned against us. It means teaching, surviving and fighting with the most important resource I have, myself, and taking joy in that battle. It means, for me, recognizing the enemy outside and the enemy within, and knowing that my work is part of a continuum of women's work, of reclaiming this earth and our power, and knowing that this work did not begin with my birth nor will it end with my death. And it means knowing that within this continuum, my life and my love and my work has particular power and meaning relative to others.

It means trout fishing on the Missisquoi River at dawn and tasting the green silence, and knowing that this beauty too is mine forever.

29 August 1980

*   *   *

On Labor Day, 1978, during my regular monthly self-examination, I discovered a lump in my right breast which later proved to be malignant. During my following hospitalization, my mastectomy and its aftermath, I passed through many stages of pain, despair, fury, sadness and growth. I moved through these stages, sometimes feeling as if I had no choice, other times recognizing that I could choose oblivion— or a passivity that is very close to oblivion—but did not want to. As I slowly began to feel more equal to processing and examining the different parts of this experience, I also began to feel that in the process of losing a breast I had become a more whole person.

After a mastectomy, for many women including myself, there is a feeling of wanting to go back, of not wanting to persevere through this experience to whatever enlightenment might be at the core of it. And it is this feeling, this nostalgia, which is encouraged by most of the post-surgical counseling for women with breast cancer. This regressive tie to the past is emphasized by the concentration upon breast cancer as a cosmetic problem, one which can be solved by a prosthetic pretense. The American Cancer Society's Reach For Recovery Program, while doing a valuable service in contracting women immediately after surgery and letting them know they are not alone, nonetheless encourages this false and dangerous nostalgia in the mistaken belief that women are too weak to deal directly and courageously with the realities of our lives.

The woman from Reach For Recovery who came to see me in the hospital, while quite admirable and even impressive in her own right, certainly did not speak to my experience nor my concerns. As a 44 year old Black Lesbian Feminist, I knew there were very few role models around for me in this situation, but my primary concerns two days after mastectomy were hardly about what man I could capture in the future, whether or not my old boyfriend would still find me attractive enough, and even less about whether my two children would be embarrassed by me around their friends.

My concerns were about my chances for survival, the effects of a possibly shortened life upon my work and my priorities. Could this cancer have been prevented, and what could I do in the future to prevent its recurrence? Would I be able to maintain the control over my life that I had always taken for granted? A lifetime of loving women had taught me that when women love each other, physical change does not alter that love. It did not occur to me that anyone who really loved me would love me any less because I had one breast instead of two, although it did occur to me to wonder if they would be able to love and deal with the new me. So my concerns were quite different from those spoken to by the Reach For Recovery volunteer, but not one bit less crucial nor less poignant.

Yet every attempt I made to examine or question the possibility of a real integration of this experience into the totality of my life and my loving and my work, was ignored by this woman, or uneasily glossed over by her as not looking on "the bright side of things." I felt outraged and insulted, and weak as I was, this left me feeling even more isolated than before.

In the critical and vulnerable period following surgery, self-examination and self-evaluation are positive steps. To imply to a woman that yes, she can be the 'same' as before surgery, with the skillful application of a little puff of lambswool, and/or silicone gel, is to place an emphasis upon prosthesis which encourages her not to deal with herself as physically and emotionally real, even though altered and traumatized. This emphasis upon the cosmetic after surgery re-inforces this society's stereotype of women, that we are only what we look or appear, so this is the only aspect of our existence we need to address. Any woman who has had a breast removed because of cancer knows she does not feel the same. But we are allowed no psychic time or space to examine what our true feelings are, to make them our own. With quick cosmetic reassurance, we are told that our feelings are not important, our appearance is all, the sum total of self.

I did not have to look down at the bandages on my chest to know that I did not feel the same as before surgery. But I still felt like myself, like Audre, and that encompassed so much more than simply the way my chest appeared.

The emphasis upon physical pretense at this crucial point in a woman's reclaiming of her self and her body-image has two negative effects:

1. It encourages women to dwell in the past rather than a future. This prevents a woman from assessing herself in the present, and from coming to terms with the changed planes of her own body. Since these then remain alien to her, buried under prosthetic devices, she must mourn the loss of her breast in secret, as if it were the result of some crime of which she were guilty.

2. It encourages a woman to focus her energies upon the mastectomy as a cosmetic occurrence, to the exclusion of other factors in a constellation that could include her own death. It removes her from what that constellation means in terms of her living, and from developing priorities of usage for whatever time she has before her. It encourages her to ignore the necessity for nutritional vigilance and psychic armament that can help prevent recurrence.

I am talking here about the need for every woman to live a considered life. The necessity for that consideration grows and deepens as one faces directly one's own mortality and death. Self scrutiny and an evaluation of our lives, while painful, can be rewarding and strengthening journeys toward a deeper self. For as we open ourselves more and more to the genuine conditions of our lives, women become less and less willing to tolerate those conditions unaltered, or to passively accept external and destructive controls over our lives and our identities. Any short-circuiting of this quest for self-definition and power, however well-meaning and under whatever guise, must be seen as damaging, for it keeps the post-mastectomy woman in a position of perpetual and secret insufficiency, infantilized and dependent for her identity upon an external definition by appearance. In this way women are kept from expressing the power of our knowledge and experience, and through that expression, developing strengths that challenge those structures within our lives that support the Cancer Establishment. For instance, why hasn't the American Cancer Society publicized the connections between animal fat and breast cancer for our daughters the way it has publicized the connection between cigarette smoke and lung cancer? These links between animal fat, hormone production and breast cancer are not secret. (See G. Hems, in *British Journal of Cancer,* vol. 37, no. 6, 1978.)

Ten days after having my breast removed, I went to my doctor's office to have the stitches taken out. This was my first journey out since coming home from the hospital, and I was truly looking forward to it. A friend had washed my hair for me and it was black and shining, with my new grey hairs glistening in the sun. Color was starting to come back into my face and around my eyes. I wore the most opalescent of my moonstones, and a single floating bird dangling from my right ear in the name of grand assymmetry. With an African kente-cloth tunic and new leather boots, I knew I looked fine, with that brave new-born security of a beautiful woman having come through a very hard time and being very glad to be alive.

I felt really good, within the limits of that grey mush that still persisted in my brain from the effects of the anesthesia.

When I walked into the doctor's office, I was really rather pleased with myself, all things considered, pleased with the way I felt, with my own flair, with my own style. The doctor's nurse, a charmingly bright and steady woman of about my own age who had always given me a feeling of quiet no-nonsense support on my other visits, called me into the examining room. On the way, she asked me how I was feeling.

"Pretty good," I said, half-expecting her to make some comment about how good I looked.

"You're not wearing a prosthesis," she said, a little anxiously, and not at all like a question.

"No," I said, thrown off my guard for a minute. "It really doesn't feel right," referring to the lambswool puff given to me by the Reach For Recovery volunteer in the hospital.

Usually supportive and understanding, the nurse now looked at me urgently and disapprovingly as she told me that even if it didn't look exactly right, it was "better than nothing," and that as soon as my stitches were out I could be fitted for a "real form."

"You will feel so much better with it on," she said. "And besides, we really like you to wear something, at least when you come in. Otherwise it's bad for the morale of the office."

I could hardly believe my ears! I was too outraged to speak then, but this was to be only the first such assault on my right to define and to claim my own body.

Here we were, in the offices of one of the top breast cancer surgeons in New York City. Every woman there either had a breast removed, might have to have a breast removed, or was afraid of having to have a breast removed. And every woman there could have used a reminder that having one breast did not mean her life was over, nor that she was less a woman, nor that she was condemned to the use of a placebo in order to feel good about herself and the way she looked.

Yet a woman who has one breast and refuses to hide that fact behind a pathetic puff of lambswool which has no relationship nor likeness to her own breasts, a woman who is attempting to come to terms with her changed landscape and changed timetable of life and with her own body and pain and beauty and strength, that woman is seen as a threat to the "morale" of a breast surgeon's office!

Yet when Moishe Dayan, the Prime Minister of Israel, stands up in front of parliament or on TV with an eyepatch over his empty eyesocket, nobody tells him to go get a glass eye, or that he is bad for the morale of the office. The world sees him as a warrior with an honorable wound, and a loss of a piece of himself which he has marked, and mourned, and moved beyond. And if you have trouble dealing with Moishe Dayan's empty eye socket, everyone recognizes that it is your problem to solve, not his.

Well, women with breast cancer are warriors, also. I have been to war, and still am. So has every woman who had had one or both breasts amputated because of the cancer that is becoming the primary physical scourge of our time. For me, my scars are an honorable reminder that I may be a casualty in the cosmic war against radiation, animal fat, air pollution, McDonald's hamburgers and Red Dye No. 2, but the fight is still going on, and I am still a part of it. I refuse to have my scars hidden or trivialized behind lambswool or silicone gel. I refuse to be reduced in my own eyes or in the eyes of others from warrior to mere victim, simply because it might render me a fraction more acceptable or less dangerous to the still complacent, those who believe if you cover up a problem it ceases to exist. I refuse to hide my body simply because it might make a woman-phobic world more comfortable.

As I sat in my doctor's office trying to order my perceptions of what had just occurred, I realized that the attitude towards prosthesis after breast cancer is an index of this society's attitudes towards women in general as decoration and externally defined sex object.

Two days later I wrote in my journal:

> I cannot wear a prosthesis right now because it feels like a lie more than merely a costume, and I have already placed this, my body under threat, seeking new ways of strength and trying to find the courage to tell the truth.

For me, the primary challenge at the core of mastectomy was the stark look at my own mortality, hinged upon the fear of a life-threatening cancer. This event called upon me to re-examine the quality and texture of my entire life, its priorities and commitments, as well as the possible alterations that might be required in the light of that re-examination. I had already faced my own death, whether or not I acknowledged it, and I needed now to develop that strength which survival had given me.

Prosthesis offers the empty comfort of "Nobody will know the difference." But it is that very difference which I wish to affirm, because I have lived it, and survived it, and wish to share that strength with other women. If we are to translate the silence surrounding breast cancer into language and action against this scourge, then the first step is that women with mastectomies must become visible to each other.* For silence and invisibility go hand in hand with powerlessness. By accepting the mask of prosthesis, one-breasted women proclaim ourselves as insufficients dependent upon pretense. We reinforce our own isolation and invisibility from each other, as well as the false complacency of a society which would rather not face the results of its own insanities. In addition, we withhold that visibility and support from one another which is such an aid to perspective and self-acceptance. Surrounded by other women day by day, all of whom appear to have two breasts, it is very difficult sometimes to remember that I AM NOT ALONE. Yet once I face death as a life process, what is there possibly left for me to fear? Who can ever really have power over me again? ...

---

*particular thanks to Maureen Brady for the conversation which developed this insight.

Suggested Further Readings

Bartky, Sandra Lee. *Femininity and Domination: Studies in the Phenomenology of Oppression.* New York: Routledge, 1990.

Butler, Judith. "Sexual Ideology and Phenomenological Description: A Feminist Critique of Merleau-Ponty's *Phenomenology of Percent.*" In *The Thinking Muse: Feminism and Modern French Philosophy,* ed. Jeffner Allen and Iris Marion Young, pp. 85–100. Bloomington: Indiana University Press, 1989.

Levesque-Lopman, Louise. *Claiming Reality: Phenomenology and Women's Experience.* Totowa, N.J.: Rowman & Littlefield, 1988.

Lorde, Audre. *The Cancer Journals.* Argyle, N.Y.: Spinsters Ink, 1980.

Young, Iris Marion. "Breasted Experience: The Look and the Feeling." In *Throwing Like a Girl and Other Essays in Feminist Philosophy and Social Theory,* ed. Iris Marion Young, pp. 189–209. Bloomington: Indiana University Press, 1990.

_____. "Throwing Like a Girl: A Phenomenology of Feminine Body Comportment, Motility, and Spatiality." In *Throwing Like a Girl and Other Essays in Feminist Philosophy and Social Theory,* ed. Iris Marion Young, pp. 141–159. Bloomington: Indiana University Press, 1990.

_____. "Women Recovering Our Clothes." In *Throwing Like a Girl and Other Essays in Feminist Philosophy and Social Theory,* ed. Iris Marion Young, pp. 171–188. Bloomington: Indiana University Press, 1990.

EIGHT

POSTMODERN FEMINIST

PERSPECTIVES

Attempts by feminists to establish *one* specifically feminist standpoint from which *all* women can see and speak have not gone without challenge. Postmodern feminists regard the search for *woman's* voice and vision as yet another instantiation of "phallocentric" thought—the kind of "male thinking" that insists on telling *only* one, presumably true, story about reality. For postmodernists, such a search is neither feasible nor desirable. It is not feasible because women's experiences differ across class, racial, ethnic, and cultural lines. It is not desirable because the "One" and "True" are philosophical myths that have been used to obscure and even repress the differences that actually characterize people.

For postmodernists, difference—the condition of being excluded, shunned, disadvantaged, neglected, rejected, dislocated, marginalized, unwanted—is a *positive* state of affairs that permits "outsiders" (in this case, women) to criticize the norms, values, and practices that the dominant culture (patriarchy) seeks to impose on everyone. Thus, difference, or Otherness, is much more than merely an oppressed, inferior condition; rather, it is a way of being, thinking, and speaking that allows for openness, plurality, and diversity.

As stimulating as the postmodern approach to feminism may be, some feminist theorists worry that an overemphasis on difference may lead to intellectual and political disintegration. If feminism is to be without any standpoint whatsoever, it becomes difficult to ground claims about what is good for women or to engage in political action on behalf of women. Therefore, it is a major challenge to contemporary feminist theory to reconcile the pressures for diversity and difference with those for integration and commonality.

In her essay, "Cultural Feminism Versus Post-Structuralism: The Identity Crisis in Feminist Theory," Linda Alcoff attempts to meet this challenge. As she sees it, poststructuralism (a postmodernist approach) errs in the direction of women's difference, whereas cultural feminism errs in the direction of women's sameness. Alcoff asserts that in their desire to affirm women's ways of being, thinking, and doing, cultural feminists come perilously close to arguing that all women share the same female essence, the source of which is female anatomy. They insist that women are somehow naturally better than men, more maternal, cooperative, and peace loving than men. Women who fail to manifest these traits are either the willing or unwilling victims of a patriarchal society that has, to a greater or lesser extent, conditioned them (or co-opted them) to do its bidding. In contrast, post-structuralist feminists deny that anything even approximating a female essence exists. In fact, says Alcoff, post-structuralist feminists deny that the general class "Woman" exists. All that exists is individual women who have no-thing (that is, no essence) in common. Therefore, whatever an individual woman decides to think, do, and be is her own private business that cannot be either condemned or valorized from the standpoint of "Woman" in general.

Unsatisfied by both of these extremes, Alcoff offers her feminist readers a third theoretical option—positionality. The concept of positionality includes two points. First, woman's position is not static but, as Alcoff writes, is a "constantly shifting context involving economic condition, political struggles, cultural institutions, ideological movements, and other people." Second, women's position offers women reasons for collaboration. If a woman looks to her left and right, she will see close to herself other women who share, in their own way, her oppressed economic, political, cultural, and ideological position. Like her, these women will have good reasons for wanting to change their oppressed position. What makes women the "same," then, is not their inner nature but the conditions that limit their power and mobility. The advantage of "positionality" is that it encourages the development of a global feminist network.

In "Sorcerer Love: A Reading of Plato's Symposium, Diotima's Speech," Luce Irigaray offers a postmodern critique of Plato's account of love in the *Symposium.* What Irigaray immediately notices about the *Symposium* is women's absence. The subject for discussion is Diotima's speech in praise of love. The men assembled discuss Diotima's speech and decide among themselves what love really is. Apparently, none of these men notice what Eleanor H. Kuykendall, in her introduction to "Sorcerer Love," insists is all too obvious: In the *Symposium* "the conception of love presented as universal is not universally practiced, since women cannot participate directly in the discourse at the banquet." As Irigaray sees it, and perhaps as Kuykendall also sees it, had women been allowed to speak for themselves at the Symposium, they would have objected to the conclusion that love between men is "love's highest individual realization," because it is a conclusion that reduces heterosexual *love* to *sex* between procreators and reduces lesbian love to an impossibility.

Not only does postmodern methodology enables us to deconstruct (reinterpret, reread) texts in the standard sense of "text" (for example, Plato's *Symposium*), it also enables us to deconstruct "texts" in the sense of large cultural trends. For example, in her essay, "Reading the Slender Body," Susan Bordo interprets what she regards as a text of slenderness. She agrees with Robert Crawford that a "structural contradiction" holds our advanced capitalist society captive. On the one hand, we are supposed to be "producer-selves" who subscribe to the work ethic and who excel in delaying any and all sensual and sexual gratifications. On the other hand, we are supposed to be "consumer-selves" who subscribe to the play ethic and who demand instant gratification in large doses. As a result of these two competing commandments, we spend most of our time oscillating between the "performance principle" and "letting go." We work hard, but we also play hard. When this unwinnable battle is fought by women in terms of their diet, the chief concepts are anorexia, obesity, and bulimia. Anorexia is forbidden because it is the extreme in the direction of "performance" or control; obesity is forbidden because it is the extreme in the direction of "letting go"—of literally letting all that flesh hang out. In contrast, bulimia is permitted because the bulimic agrees to do what everyone in an advanced capitalist society is supposed to do—to alternately binge and purge.

Since our society is not only capitalist but patriarchal, Bordo reminds us "that when the regulation of desire becomes especially problematic (as it is in advanced consumer cultures), women and their bodies will pay the greatest symbolic and material toll." In other words, there is more pressure on women to be slender than on men. Some of this pressure comes from men who "read" a slender female body as a nonthreatening body, one in which female desire is contained; some of this pressure comes from women themselves who "read" a slender female body differently, as a symbol of liberation from a merely domestic, reproductive destiny. The slender body can be read in many ways; no matter how it is read, however, it is not a particularly happy story, especially for women in this culture.

Bordo acknowledges that this type of analysis of cultural images is complex in that there are a "wide variety of ethnic, racial, and class differences that intersect with, resist, and give distinctive meaning to dominant, normalizing imagery." For example, in her recent writing, Bordo argues that any analysis of cultural images of the body of women must address the fact that the Black woman "carries a triple burden of negative bodily associations."[1] As with all women in our culture, the Black woman represents the temptations of the flesh and the source of man's moral downfall. She shares with other women of color the representation of an instinctual animal, deserving neither of privacy nor respect. But as a Black woman, the legacy of slavery also carries the representation of her body as property, "to be 'taken' and used at will."[2]

We would add to these insights the realization that postmodern feminist analyses require the participation of women from Third World countries for the development of feminist theory. We can only fully understand the cultural construction of subjectivity if we look from the vantage point of diverse cultures. Postmodern feminists must thus be constantly attentive to the limitations of "Eurocentrism." This indicates the centrality for postmodern feminism of the type of global feminist network called for by Alcoff.

Notes

1. Susan Bordo, *Unbearable Weight: Feminism, Western Culture, and the Body* (Berkeley: University of California Press, 1993), p. 11.
2. Ibid.

Cultural Feminism
Versus Post-Structuralism:
The Identity Crisis in Feminist Theory

Linda Alcoff

For many contemporary feminist theorists, the concept of woman is a problem. It is a problem of primary significance because the concept of woman is the central concept for feminist theory and yet it is a concept that is impossible to formulate precisely for feminists. It is the central concept for feminists because the concept and category of woman is the necessary point of departure for any feminist theory and feminist politics, predicated as these are on the transformation of women's lived experience in contemporary culture and the reevaluation of social theory and practice from women's point of view. But as a concept it is radically problematic precisely for feminists because it is crowded with the overdeterminations of male supremacy, invoking in every formulation the limit, contrasting Other, or mediated self-reflection of a culture built on the control of females. In attempting to speak for women, feminism often seems to presuppose that it knows what women truly are, but such an assumption is foolhardy given that every source of knowledge about women has been contaminated with misogyny and sexism. No matter where we turn—to historical documents, philosophical constructions, social scientific statistics, introspection, or daily practices—the mediation of female bodies into constructions of woman is dominated by misogynist discourse. For feminists, who must transcend this discourse, it appears we have nowhere to turn.[1]

Thus the dilemma facing feminist theorists today is that our very self-definition is grounded in a concept that we must deconstruct and de-essentialize in all of its aspects. Man has said that woman can be defined, delineated, captured—understood, explained, and diagnosed—to a level of determination never accorded to man himself, who is conceived as a rational animal with free will. Where man's behavior is underdetermined, free to construct its own future along the course of its rational choice, woman's nature has overdetermined her behavior, the limits of her intellectual endeavors, and the inevitabilities of her emotional journey through life. Whether she is construed as essentially immoral and irrational (à la Schopenhauer) or essentially kind and benevolent (à la Kant), she is always construed as an essential *something* inevitably accessible to direct intuited apprehension by males.[2] Despite the variety of ways in which man has construed her essential characteristics, she is always the Object, a conglomeration of attributes to be predicted and controlled along with other natural phenomena. The place of the free-willed subject who can transcend nature's mandates is reserved exclusively for men.[3]

Feminist thinkers have articulated two major responses to this situation over the last ten years. The first response is to claim that feminists have the exclusive right to describe and evaluate woman. Thus cultural feminists argue that the problem of male supremacist culture is the problem of a process in which women are defined by men, that is, by a group who has contrasting point of view and set of interests from women, not to mention a possible fear and hatred of women. The result of this has been a distortion and devaluation of feminine characteristics, which now can be corrected by a more accurate feminist description and appraisal. Thus the cultural feminist reappraisal construes woman's passivity as her peacefulness, her sentimentality as her proclivity to nurture, her subjectiveness as her advanced self-awareness, and so forth. Cultural feminists have not challenged the defining of woman but only that definition given by men.

The second major response has been to reject the possibility of defining woman as such at all. Feminists who take this tactic go about the business of deconstructing all concepts of woman and argue that both feminist and misogynist attempts to define woman are politically reactionary and ontologically mistaken. Replacing woman-as-housewife with woman-as-supermom (or earth mother or super professional) is no advance. Using French post-structuralist theory these feminists argue that such errors occur because we are in fundamental ways duplicating misogynist strategies when we try to define women, characterize women, or speak for women, even though allowing for a range of differences within the gender. The politics of gender or sexual difference must be replaced with a plurality of difference where gender loses its position of significance.

Briefly put, then, the cultural feminist response to Simòne de Beauvoir's question, "Are there women?" is to answer yes and to define women by their activities and attributes in the present culture. The post-structuralist response is to answer no and attack the category and the concept of woman through problematizing subjectivity. Each response has serious limitations, and it is becoming increasingly obvious that transcending these limitations while retaining the theoretical framework from which they emerge is impossible. As a result, a few brave souls are now rejecting these choices and attempting to map out a new course, a course that will avoid the major problems of the earlier responses. In this paper I will discuss some of the pioneer work being done to develop a new concept of woman and offer my own contribution toward it.[4] But first, I must spell out more clearly the inadequacies of the first two responses to the problem of woman and explain why I believe these inadequacies are inherent.

Cultural Feminism

Cultural feminism is the ideology of a female nature or female essence reappropriated by feminists themselves in an effort to revalidate undervalued female attributes. For cultural feminists, the enemy of women is not merely a social system or economic institution or set of backward beliefs but masculinity itself and in some

cases male biology. Cultural feminist politics revolve around creating and maintaining a healthy environment—free of masculinist values and all their offshoots such as
pornography—for the female principle. Feminist theory, the explanation of sexism,
and the justification of feminist demands can all be grounded securely and unambiguously on the concept of the essential female.

Mary Daly and Adrienne Rich have been influential proponents of this position.[5]
Breaking from the trend toward androgyny and the minimizing of gender differences
that was popular among feminists in the early seventies, both Daly and Rich argue
for a returned focus on femaleness.

For Daly, male barrenness leads to parasitism on female energy, which flows from
our life-affirming, life-creating biological condition: "Since female energy is essentially biophilic, the female spirit/body is the primary target in this perpetual war of
aggression against life. Gyn/Ecology is the re-claiming of life-loving female energy."[6]
Despite Daly's warnings against biological reductionism,[7] her own analysis of sexism
uses gender-specific biological traits to explain male hatred for women. The childless
state of "all males" leads to a dependency on women, which in turn leads men to
"deeply identify with 'unwanted fetal tissue.'"[8] Given their state of fear and insecurity it becomes almost understandable, then, that men would desire to dominate and
control that which is so vitally necessary to them: the life-energy of women. Female
energy, conceived by Daly as a natural essence, needs to be freed from its male para-
sites, released for creative expression and recharged through bonding with other
women. In this free space women's "natural" attributes of love, creativity, and the
ability to nurture can thrive.

Women's identification as female is their defining essence for Daly, their haecceity,
overriding any other way in which they may be defined or may define themselves.
Thus Daly states: "Women who accept false inclusion among the fathers and sons are
easily polarized against other women on the basis of ethnic, national, class, religious
and other *male-defined differences,* applauding the defeat of 'enemy' women."[9] These
differences are apparent rather than real, inessential rather than essential. The only
real difference, the only difference that can change a person's ontological placement
on Daly's dichotomous map, is sex difference. Our essence is defined here, in our sex,
from which flow all the facts about us: who are our potential allies, who is our enemy, what are our objective interests, what is our true nature. Thus, Daly defines
women again and her definition is strongly linked to female biology.

Many of Rich's writings have exhibited surprising similarities to Daly's position
described above, surprising given their difference in style and temperament. Rich
defines a "female consciousness"[10] that has a great deal to do with the female body.

> I have come to believe ... that female biology—the diffuse, intense sensuality radiating
> out from clitoris, breasts, uterus, vagina; the lunar cycles of menstruation; the gestation
> and fruition of life which can take place in the female body—has far more radical impli-
> cations than we have yet come to appreciate. Patriarchal thought has limited female biol-
> ogy to its own narrow specifications. The feminist vision has recoiled from female biol-
> ogy for these reasons; it will, I believe, come to view our physicality as a resource rather
> than a destiny. ... We must touch the unity and resonance of our physicality, our bond
> with the natural order, the corporeal ground of our intelligence.[11]

Thus Rich argues that we should not reject the importance of female biology simply
because patriarchy has used it to subjugate us. Rich believes that "our biological

grounding, the miracle and paradox of the female body and its spiritual and political meanings" holds the key to our rejuvenation and our reconnection with our specific female attributes, which she lists as "our great mental capacities … ; our highly developed tactile sense; our genius for close observation; our complicated, pain-enduring, multi-pleasured physicality."[12]

Rich further echoes Daly in her explanation of misogyny: "The ancient, continuing envy, awe and dread of the male for the female capacity to create life has repeatedly taken the form of hatred for every other female aspect of creativity."[13] Thus Rich, like Daly, identifies a female essence, defines patriarchy as the subjugation and colonization of this essence out of male envy and need, and then promotes a solution that revolves around rediscovering our essence and bonding with other women. Neither Rich nor Daly espouse biological reductionism, but this is because they reject the oppositional dichotomy of mind and body that such a reductionism presupposes. The female essence for Daly and Rich is not simply spiritual or simply biological—it is both. Yet the key point remains that it is our specifically female anatomy that is the primary constituent of our identity and the source of our female essence. Rich prophesies that "the repossession by women of our bodies will bring far more essential change to human society than the seizing of the means of production by workers. … In such a world women will truly create new life, bringing forth not only children (if and as we choose) but the visions, and the thinking, necessary to sustain, console and alter human existence—a new relationship to the universe. Sexuality, politics, intelligence, power, motherhood, work, community, intimacy will develop new meanings; thinking itself will be transformed."[14]

The characterization of Rich's and Daly's views as part of a growing trend within feminism toward essentialism has been developed most extensively by Alice Echols.[15] Echols prefers the name "cultural feminism" for this trend because it equates "women's liberation" with the development and preservation of a female counter culture."[16] Echols identifies cultural feminist writings by their denigration of masculinity rather than male roles or practices, by their valorization of female traits, and by their commitment to preserve rather than diminish gender differences. Besides Daly and Rich, Echols names Susan Griffin, Kathleen Barry, Janice Raymond, Florence Rush, Susan Brownmiller, and Robin Morgan as important cultural feminist writers, and she documents her claim persuasively by highlighting key passages of their work. Although Echols finds a prototype of this trend in early radical feminist writings by Valerie Solanis and Joreen, she is careful to distinguish cultural feminism from radical feminism as a whole. The distinguishing marks between the two include their position on the mutability of sexism among men, the connection drawn between biology and misogyny, and the degree of focus on valorized female attributes. As Hester Eisenstein has argued, there is a tendency within many radical feminist works toward setting up an ahistorical and essentialist conception of female nature, but this tendency is developed and consolidated by cultural feminists, thus rendering their work significantly different from radical feminism.

However, although cultural feminist views sharply separate female from male traits, they certainly do not all give explicitly essentialist formulations of what it means to be a woman. So it may seem that Echols's characterization of cultural feminism makes it appear too homogeneous and that the charge of essentialism is on shaky ground. On the issue of essentialism Echols states:

This preoccupation with defining the female sensibility not only leads these feminists to indulge in dangerously erroneous generalizations about women, but to imply that this identity is innate rather than socially constructed. At best, there has been a curiously cavalier disregard for whether these differences are biological or cultural in origin. Thus Janice Raymond argues: "Yet there are differences, and some feminists have come to realize that those differences are important whether they spring from socialization, from biology, or from the total history of existing as a woman in a patriarchal society."[17]

Echols points out that the importance of the differences varies tremendously according to their source. If that source is innate, the cultural feminist focus on building an alternative feminist culture is politically correct. If the differences are not innate, the focus of our activism should shift considerably. In the absence of a clearly stated position on the ultimate source of gender difference, Echols infers from their emphasis on building a feminist free-space and woman-centered culture that cultural feminists hold some version of essentialism. I share Echols's suspicion. Certainly, it is difficult to render the views of Rich and Daly into a coherent whole without supplying a missing premise that there is an innate female essence.

Interestingly, I have not included any feminist writings from women of oppressed nationalities and races in the category of cultural feminism, nor does Echols. I have heard it argued that the emphasis placed on cultural identity by such writers as Cherríe Moraga and Audre Lorde reveals a tendency toward essentialism also. However, in my view their work has consistently rejected essentialist conceptions of gender. Consider the following passage from Moraga: "When you start to talk about sexism, the world becomes increasingly complex. The power no longer breaks down into neat little hierarchical categories, but becomes a series of starts and detours. Since the categories are not easy to arrive at, the enemy is not easy to name. It is all so difficult to unravel."[18] Moraga goes on to assert that "some men oppress the very women they love," implying that we need new categories and new concepts to describe such complex and contradictory relations of oppression. In this problematic understanding of sexism, Moraga seems to me light-years ahead of Daly's manichean ontology or Rich's romanticized conception of the female. The simultaneity of oppressions experienced by women such as Moraga resists essentialist conclusions. Universalist conceptions of female or male experiences and attributes are not plausible in the context of such a complex network of relations, and without an ability to universalize, the essentialist argument is difficult if not impossible to make. White women cannot be all good or all bad; neither can men from oppressed groups. I have simply not found writings by feminists who are oppressed also by race and/or class that place or position maleness wholly as Other. Reflected in their problematized understanding of masculinity is a richer and likewise problematized concept of woman.[19]

Even if cultural feminism is the product of white feminists, it is not homogeneous, as Echols herself points out. The biological accounts of sexism given by Daly and Brownmiller, for example, are not embraced by Rush or Dworkin. But the key link between these feminists is their tendency toward invoking universalizing conceptions of woman and mother in an essentialist way. Therefore, despite the lack of complete homogeneity within the category, it seems still justifiable and important to identify (and criticize) within these sometimes disparate works their tendency to offer an essentialist response to misogyny and sexism through adopting a homogeneous, unproblematized, and ahistorical conception of woman.

One does not have to be influenced by French post-structuralism to disagree with essentialism. It is well documented that the innateness of gender differences in personality and character is at this point factually and philosophically indefensible.[20] There are a host of divergent ways gender divisions occur in different societies, and the differences that appear to be universal can be explained in nonessentialist ways. However, belief in women's innate peacefulness and ability to nurture has been common among feminists since the nineteenth century and has enjoyed a resurgence in the last decade, most notably among feminist peace activists. I have met scores of young feminists drawn to actions like the Women's Peace Encampment and to groups like Women for a Non-Nuclear Future by their belief that the maternal love women have for their children can unlock the gates of imperialist oppression. I have great respect for the self-affirming pride of these women, but I also share Echols's fear that their effect is to "reflect and reproduce dominant cultural assumptions about women," which not only fail to represent the variety in women's lives but promote unrealistic expectations about "normal" female behavior that most of us cannot satisfy.[21] Our gender categories are positively constitutive and not mere hindsight descriptions of previous activities. There is a self-perpetuating circularity between defining woman as essentially peaceful and nurturing and the observations and judgments we shall make of future women and the practices we shall engage in as women in the future. Do feminists want to buy another ticket for women of the world on the merry-go-round of feminine constructions? Don't we want rather to get off the merry-go-round and run away?

This should not imply that the political effects of cultural feminism have all been negative.[22] The insistence on viewing traditional feminine characteristics from a different point of view, to use a "looking glass" perspective, as a means of engendering a gestalt switch on the body of data we all currently share about women, has had positive effect. After a decade of hearing liberal feminists advising us to wear business suits and enter the male world, it is a helpful corrective to have cultural feminists argue instead that women's world is full of superior virtues and values, to be credited and learned from rather than despised. Herein lies the positive impact of cultural feminism. And surely much of their point is well taken, that it was our mothers who made our families survive; that women's handiwork is truly artistic, that women's care-giving really is superior in value to male competitiveness.

Unfortunately, however, the cultural feminist championing of a redefined "womanhood" cannot provide a useful long-range program for a feminist movement and, in fact, places obstacles in the way of developing one. Under conditions of oppression and restrictions on freedom of movement, women, like other oppressed groups, have developed strengths and attributes that should be correctly credited, valued, and promoted. What we should not promote, however, are the restrictive conditions that gave rise to those attributes: forced parenting, lack of physical autonomy, dependency for survival on mediation skills, for instance. What conditions for women do we want to promote? A freedom of movement such that we can compete in the capitalist world alongside men? A continued restriction to child-centered activities? To the extent cultural feminism merely valorizes genuinely positive attributes developed under oppression, it cannot map our future long-range course. To the extent that it reinforces essentialist explanations of these attributes, it is in danger of solidifying an important bulwark for sexist oppression: the belief in an innate "womanhood" to which we must all adhere lest we be deemed either inferior or not "true" women.

Post-Structuralism

For many feminists, the problem with the cultural feminist response to sexism is that it does not criticize the fundamental mechanism of oppressive power used to perpetuate sexism and in fact reinvokes that mechanism in its supposed solution. The mechanism of power referred to here is the construction of the subject by a discourse that weaves knowledge and power into a coercive structure that "forces the individual back on himself and ties him to his own identity in a constraining way."[23] On this view, essentialist formulations of womanhood, even when made by feminists, "tie" the individual to her identity as a woman and thus cannot represent a solution to sexism.

This articulation of the problem has been borrowed by feminists from a number of recently influential French thinkers who are sometimes called post-structuralist but who also might be called post-humanist and post-essentialist. Lacan, Derrida, and Foucault are the front-runners in this group. Disparate as these writers are, their (one) common theme is that the self-contained, authentic subject conceived by humanism to be discoverable below a veneer of cultural and ideological overlay is in reality a construct of that very humanist discourse. The subject is not a locus of authorial intentions or natural attributes or even a privileged, separate consciousness. Lacan uses psychoanalysis, Derrida uses grammar, and Foucault uses the history of discourses all to attack and "deconstruct"[24] our concept of the subject as having an essential identity and an authentic core that has been repressed by society. There is no essential core "natural" to us, and so there is no repression in the humanist sense.

There is an interesting sort of neodeterminism in this view. The subject or self is never determined by biology in such a way that human history is predictable or even explainable, and there is no unilinear direction of a determinist arrow pointing from some fairly static, "natural" phenomena to human experience. On the other hand, this rejection of biological determinism is not grounded in the belief that human subjects are underdetermined but, rather, in the belief that we are overdetermined (i.e., constructed) by a social discourse and/or cultural practice. The idea here is that we individuals really have little choice in the matter of who we are, for as Derrida and Foucault like to remind us, individual motivations and intentions count for nil or almost nil in the scheme of social reality. We are constructs—that is, our experience of our very subjectivity is a construct mediated by and/or grounded on a social discourse beyond (way beyond) individual control. As Foucault puts it, we are bodies "totally imprinted by history."[25] Thus, subjective experiences are determined in some sense by macro forces. However, these macro forces, including social discourses and social practices, are apparently not overdetermined, resulting as they do from such a complex and unpredictable network of overlapping and crisscrossing elements that no unilinear directionality is perceivable and in fact no final or efficient cause exists. There may be, and Foucault hoped at one point to find them,[26] perceivable processes of change within the social network, but beyond schematic rules of thumb neither the form nor the content of discourse has a fixed or unified structure or can be predicted or mapped out via an objectified, ultimate realm. To some extent, this view is similar to contemporary methodological individualism, whose advocates will usually concede that the complex of human intentions results in a social reality bearing no resemblance to the summarized categories of intentions but looking altogether different than any one party or sum of parties ever envisaged and desired. The difference, however, is that while methodological individualists admit that human intentions are ineffective, post-structuralists deny not only the efficacy but also the ontological autonomy and even the existence of intentionality.

Post-structuralists unite with Marx in asserting the social dimension of individual traits and intentions. Thus, they say we cannot understand society as the conglomerate of individual intentions but, rather, must understand individual intentions as constructed within a social reality. To the extent post-structuralists emphasize social explanations of individual practices and experiences I find their work illuminating and persuasive. My disagreement occurs, however, when they seem totally to erase any room for maneuver by the individual within a social discourse or set of institutions. It is that totalization of history's imprint that I reject. In their defense of a total construction of the subject, post-structuralists deny the subject's ability to reflect on the social discourse and challenge its determinations.

Applied to the concept of woman the post-structuralist's view results in what I shall call nominalism: the idea that the category "woman" is a fiction and that feminist efforts must be directed toward dismantling this fiction. "Perhaps ... 'woman' is not a determinable identity. Perhaps woman is not some thing which announces itself from a distance, at a distance from some other thing. ... Perhaps woman—a non-identity, non-figure, a simulacrum—is distance's very chasm, the out-distancing of distance, the interval's cadence, distance itself."[27] Derrida's interest in feminism stems from his belief, expressed above, that woman may represent the rupture in the functional discourse of what he calls logocentrism, an essentialist discourse that entails hierarchies of difference and a Kantian ontology. Because woman has in a sense been excluded from this discourse, it is possible to hope that she might provide a real source of resistance. But her resistance will not be at all effective if she continues to use the mechanism of logocentrism to redefine woman: she can be an effective resister only if she drifts and dodges all attempts to capture her. Then, Derrida hopes, the following futuristic picture will come true: "Out of the depths, endless and unfathomable, she engulfs and distorts all vestige of essentiality, of identity, of property. And the philosophical discourse, blinded, founders on these shoals and is hurled down these depths to its ruin."[28] For Derrida, women have always been defined as a subjugated difference within a binary opposition: man/woman, culture/nature, positive/negative, analytical/intuitive. To assert an essential gender difference as cultural feminists do is to reinvoke this oppositional structure. The only way to break out of this structure, and in fact to subvert the structure itself, is to assert total difference, to be that which cannot be pinned down or subjugated within a dichotomous hierarchy. Paradoxically, it is to be what is not. Thus feminists cannot demarcate a definitive category of "woman" without eliminating all possibility for the defeat of logocentrism and its oppressive power.

Foucault similarly rejects all constructions of oppositional subjects—whether the "proletariat," "woman," or "the oppressed"—as mirror images that merely recreate and sustain the discourse of power. As Biddy Martin points out, "The point from which Foucault deconstructs is off-center, out of line, apparently unaligned. It is not the point of an imagined absolute otherness, but an 'alterity' which understands itself as an internal exclusion."[29]

Following Foucault and Derrida, an effective feminism could only be a wholly negative feminism, deconstructing everything and refusing to construct anything. This is the position Julia Kristeva adopts, herself an influential French post-structuralist. She says: "A woman cannot be; it is something which does not even belong in the order of being. *It follows that a feminist practice can only be negative*, at odds with what already exists so that we may say 'that's not it' and 'that's still not it.'"[30] The problematic character of subjectivity does not mean, then, that there can be no political struggle, as one might surmise from the fact that post-structuralism deconstructs the position of the revolutionary in the same breath as it deconstructs the position of the reactionary. But the political struggle can have only a "negative function," rejecting "everything finite, definite, structured, loaded with meaning, in the existing state of society."[31]

The attraction of the post-structuralist critique of subjectivity for feminists is twofold. First, it seems to hold out the promise of an increased freedom for women, the "free play" of a plurality of differences unhampered by any predetermined gender identity as formulated by either patriarchy or cultural feminism. Second, it moves decisively beyond cultural feminism and liberal feminism in further theorizing what they leave untouched: the construction of subjectivity. We can learn a great deal here about the mechanisms of sexist oppression and the construction of specific gender categories by relating these to social discourse and by conceiving of the subject as a cultural product. Certainly, too, this analysis can help us understand right-wing women, the reproduction of ideology, and the mechanisms that block social progress. However, adopting nominalism creates significant problems for feminism. How can we seriously adopt Kristeva's plan for only negative struggle? As the Left should by now have learned, you cannot mobilize a movement that is only and always against: you must have a positive alternative, a vision of a better future that can motivate people to sacrifice their time and energy toward its realization. Moreover, a feminist adoption of nominalism will be confronted with the same problem theories of ideology have, that is, Why is a right-wing woman's consciousness constructed via social discourse but a feminist's consciousness not? Post-structuralist critiques of subjectivity pertain to the construction of all subjects or they pertain to none. And here is precisely the dilemma for feminists: How can we ground a feminist politics that deconstructs the female subject? Nominalism threatens to wipe out feminism itself.

Some feminists who wish to use post-structuralism are well aware of this danger. Biddy Martin, for example, points out that "we cannot afford to refuse to take a political stance 'which pins us to our sex' for the sake of an abstract theoretical correctness. ... There is the danger that Foucault's challenges to traditional categories, if taken to a 'logical' conclusion ... could make the question of women's oppression obsolete."[32] Based on her articulation of the problem with Foucault we are left hopeful that Martin will provide a solution that transcends nominalism. Unfortunately, in her reading of Lou Andreas-Salome, Martin Valorizes undecidability, ambiguity, and elusiveness and intimates that by maintaining the undecidability of identity the life of Andreas-Salome provides a text from which feminists can usefully learn.[33]

However, the notion that all texts are undecidable cannot be useful for feminists. In support of his contention that the meaning of texts is ultimately undecidable, Derrida offers us in *Spurs* three conflicting but equally warranted interpretations of how Nietzsche's texts construct and position the female. In one of these interpretations Derrida argues we can find purportedly feminist propositions.[34] Thus, Derrida seeks to demonstrate that even the seemingly incontrovertible interpretation of Nietzsche's works as misogynist can be challenged by an equally convincing argument that they are not. But how can this be helpful to feminists, who need to have their accusations of misogyny validated rather than rendered "undecidable"? The point is not that Derrida himself is antifeminist, nor that there is nothing at all in Derrida's work that can be useful for feminists. But the thesis of undecidability as it is applied in the case of Nietzsche sounds too much like yet another version of the antifeminist argument that our perception of sexism is based on a skewed, limited perspective and that what we take to be misogyny is in reality helpful rather than hurtful to the cause of women. The declaration of undecidability must inevitably return us to Kristeva's position, that we can give only negative answers to the question, What is a woman? If the category "woman" is fundamentally undecidable, then we can offer no positive conception of it that is immune to deconstruction, and we are left with a feminism that can be only deconstructive and, thus, nominalist once again.[35]

A nominalist position on subjectivity has the deleterious effect of de-gendering our analysis, of in effect making gender invisible once again. Foucault's ontology includes only bodies and pleasures, and he is notorious for not including gender as a category of analysis. If gender is simply a social construct, the need and even the possibility of a feminist politics becomes immediately problematic. What can we demand in the name of women if "women" do not exist and demands in their name simply reinforce the myth that they do? How can we speak out against sexism as detrimental to the interests of women if the category is a fiction? How can we demand legal abortions, adequate child care, or wages based on comparable worth without invoking a concept of "woman"?

Post-structuralism undercuts our ability to oppose the dominant trend (and, one might argue, the dominant danger) in mainstream Western intellectual thought, that is, the insistence on a universal, neutral, perspectiveless epistemology, metaphysics, and ethics. Despite rumblings from the Continent, Anglo-American thought is still wedded to the idea(l) of a universalizable, apolitical methodology and set of transhistorical basic truths unfettered by associations with particular genders, races, classes, or cultures. The rejection of subjectivity, unintentionally but nevertheless, colludes with this "generic human" thesis of classical liberal thought, that particularities of individuals are irrelevant and improper influences on knowledge. By designating individual particularities such as subjective experience as a social construct, post-structuralism's negation of the authority of the subject coincides nicely with the classical liberal's view that human particularities are irrelevant. (For the liberal, race, class, and gender are ultimately irrelevant to questions of justice and truth because "underneath we are all the same." For the post-structuralist, race, class, and gender are constructs and, therefore, incapable of decisively validating conceptions of justice and truth because underneath there lies no natural core to build on or liberate or maximize. Hence, once again, underneath we are all the same.) It is, in fact, a desire to topple this commitment to the possibility of a worldview—purported in fact as the best of all possible worldviews—grounded in a generic human, that motivates much of the cultural feminist glorification of femininity as a valid specificity legitimately grounding feminist theory.[36]

The preceding characterizations of cultural feminism and post-structuralist feminism will anger many feminists by assuming too much homogeneity and by blithely pigeonholing large and complex theories. However, I believe the tendencies I have outlined toward essentialism and toward nominalism represent the main, current responses by feminist theory to the task of reconceptualizing "woman." Both responses have significant advantages and serious shortcomings. Cultural feminism has provided a useful corrective to the "generic human" thesis of classical liberalism and has promoted community and self-affirmation, but it cannot provide a long-range future course of action for feminist theory or practice, and it is founded on a claim of essentialism that we are far from having the evidence to justify. The feminist appropriation of post-structuralism has provided suggestive insights on the construction of female and male subjectivity and has issued a crucial warning against creating a feminism that reinvokes the mechanisms of oppressive power. Nonetheless, it limits feminism to the negative tactics of reaction and deconstruction and endangers the attack against classical liberalism by discrediting the notion of an epistemologically significant, specific subjectivity. What's a feminist to do?

We cannot simply embrace the paradox. In order to avoid the serious disadvantages of cultural feminism and post-structuralism, feminism needs to transcend the dilemma by developing a third course, an alternative theory of the subject that avoids both essentialism and nominalism. This new alternative might share the post-structuralist insight that the category "woman" needs to be theorized through an exploration of the experience of subjectivity, as opposed to a description of current attributes, but it need not concede that such an exploration will necessarily result in a nominalist position on gender, or an erasure of it. Feminists need to explore the possibility of a theory of the gendered subject that does not slide into essentialism. In the following two sections I will discuss recent work that makes a contribution to the development of such a theory, or so I shall argue, and in the final section I will develop my own contribution in the form of a concept of gendered identity as positionality.

Teresa de Lauretis

Lauretis's influential book, *Alice Doesn't*, is a series of essays organized around an exploration of the problem of conceptualizing woman as subject. This problem is formulated in her work as arising out of the conflict between "woman" as a "fictional construct" and "women" as "real historical beings."[37] She says: "The relation between women as historical subjects and the notion of woman as it is produced by hegemonic discourses is neither a direct relation of identity, a one-to-one correspondence, nor a relation of simple implication. Like all other relations expressed in language, it is an arbitrary and symbolic one, that is to say, culturally set up. The manner and effects of that set-up are what the book intends to explore."[38] The strength of Lauretis's approach is that she never loses sight of the political imperative of feminist theory and, thus, never forgets that we must seek not only to describe this relation in which women's subjectivity is grounded but also to change it. And yet, given her view that we are constructed via a semiotic discourse, this political mandate becomes a crucial problem. As she puts it, "Paradoxically, the only way to position oneself outside of that discourse is to displace oneself within it—to refuse the question as formulated, or to answer deviously (though in its words), even to quote (but against the grain). The limit posed but not worked through in this book is thus the contradiction of feminist theory itself, at once excluded from discourse and imprisoned within it."[39] As with feminist theory, so, too, is the female subject "at once excluded from discourse and imprisoned within it." Constructing a theory of the subject that both concedes these truths and yet allows for the possibility of feminism is the problem Lauretis tackles throughout *Alice Doesn't*. To concede the construction of the subject via discourse entails that the feminist project cannot be simply "how to make visible the invisible" as if the essence of gender were out there waiting to be recognized by the dominant discourse. Yet Lauretis does not give up on the possibility of producing "the conditions of visibility for a different social subject."[40] In her view, a nominalist position on subjectivity can be avoided by linking subjectivity to a Peircean notion of practices and a further theorized notion of experience.[41] I shall look briefly at her discussion of this latter claim.

Lauretis's main thesis is that subjectivity, that is, what one "perceives and comprehends as subjective," is constructed through a continuous process, an ongoing constant renewal based on an interaction with the world, which she defines as experience: "And thus [subjectivity] is produced not by external ideas, values, or material causes, but by one's personal, subjective engagement in the practices, discourses, and institutions that land significance (value, meaning, and affect) to the events of the world."[42] This is the process through which one's subjectivity becomes en-gendered. But describing the subjectivity that emerges is still beset with difficulties, principally the following: "The feminist efforts have been more often than not caught in the logical trap set up by [a] paradox. Either they have assumed that 'the subject,' like 'man,' is a generic term, and as such can designate equally and at once the female and male subjects, with the result of erasing sexuality and sexual difference from subjectivity. Or else they have been obliged to resort to an oppositional notion of 'feminine' subject defined by silence, negativity, a natural sexuality, or a closeness to nature not compromised by patriarchal culture."[43] Here again is spelled out the dilemma between a post-structuralist genderless subject and a cultural feminist essentialized subject. As Lauretis points out, the latter alternative is constrained in its conceptualization of the female subject by the very act of distinguishing female from male subjectivity. This appears to produce a dilemma, for if we de-gender subjectivity, we are committed to a generic subject and thus undercut feminism, while on the other hand if we define the subject in terms of gender, articulating female subjectivity in a space clearly distinct from male subjectivity, then we become caught up in an oppositional dichotomy controlled by a misogynist discourse. A gender-bound subjectivity seems to force us to revert "women to the body and to sexuality as an immediacy of the biological, as nature."[44] For all her insistence on a subjectivity constructed through practices, Lauretis is clear that *that* conception of subjectivity is not what she wishes to propose. A subjectivity that is fundamentally shaped by gender appears to lead irrevocably to essentialism, the posing of a male/female opposition as universal and ahistorical. A subjectivity that is not fundamentally shaped by gender appears to lead to the conception of a generic human subject, as if we could peel away our "cultural" layers and get to the real root of human nature, which turns out to be genderless. Are these really our only choices?

In *Alice Doesn't* Lauretis develops the beginnings of a new conception of subjectivity. She argues that subjectivity is neither (over)determined by biology nor by "free, rational, intentionality" but, rather, by experience, which she defines (via Lacan, Eco, and Peirce) as "a complex of habits resulting from the semiotic interaction of 'outer world' and 'inner world,' the continuous engagement of a self or subject in social reality."[45] Given this definition, the question obviously becomes, Can we ascertain a "female experience"? This is the question Lauretis prompts us to consider, more specifically, to analyze "that complex of habits, dispositions, associations and perceptions, which en-genders one as female."[46] Lauretis ends her book with an insightful observation that can serve as a critical starting point:

This is where the specificity of a feminist theory may be sought: not in femininity as a privileged nearness to nature, the body, or the unconscious, an essence which inheres in women but to which males too now lay a claim; not in female tradition simply understood as private, marginal, and yet intact, outside of history but fully there to be discovered or recovered; not, finally, in the chinks and cracks of masculinity, the fissures of male identity or the repressed of phallic discourse; *but rather in that political, theoretical, self-analyzing practice* by which the relations of the subject in social reality can be rearticulated from the historical experience of women. Much, very much, is still to be done.[47]

Thus Lauretis asserts that the way out of the totalizing imprint of history and discourse is through our "political, theoretical self-analyzing practice." This should not be taken to imply that only intellectual articles in academic journals represent a free space or ground for maneuver but, rather, that all women can (and do) think about, criticize, and later discourse and, thus, that subjectivity can be reconstructed through the process of reflective practice. The key component of Lauretis's formulation is the dynamic she poses at the heart of subjectivity: a fluid interaction in constant motion and open to alteration by self-analyzing practice.

Recently, Lauretis has taken off from this point and developed further her conception of subjectivity. In the introductory essay for her latest book, *Feminist Studies/ Critical Studies,* Lauretis claims that an individual's identity is constituted with a historical process of consciousness, a process in which one's history "is interpreted or reconstructed by each of us within the horizon of meanings and knowledges available in the culture at given historical moments, a horizon that also includes modes of political commitment and struggle. ... Consciousness, therefore, is never fixed, never attained once and for all, because discursive boundaries change with historical conditions."[48] Here Lauretis guides our way out of the dilemma she articulated for us in *Alice Doesn't.* The agency of the subject is made possible through this process of political interpretation. And what emerges is multiple and shifting, neither "prefigured ... in an unchangeable symbolic order" nor merely "fragmented, or intermittent."[49] Lauretis formulates a subjectivity that gives agency to the individual while at the same time placing her within "particular discursive configurations" and, moreover, conceives of the process of consciousness as a strategy. Subjectivity may thus become imbued with race, class, and gender without being subjected to an overdetermination that erases agency.

Denise Riley

Denise Riley's *War in the Nursery: Theories of the Child and Mother* is an attempt to conceptualize women in a way that avoids what she calls the biologism/culturalist dilemma: that women must be either biologically determined or entirely cultural constructs. Both of these approaches to explaining sexual difference have been theoretically and empirically deficient, Riley claims. Biological deterministic accounts fail to problematize the concepts they use, for example, "biology," "nature," and "sex" and attempt to reduce "everything to the workings of a changeless biology."[50] On the other hand, the "usual corrective to biologism"[51]—the feminist-invoked cultural construction thesis—"ignores the fact that there really is biology, which must be conceived more clearly" and moreover "only substitutes an unbounded sphere of social determination for that of biological determination."[52]

In her attempt to avoid the inadequacies of these approaches, Riley states: "The tactical problem is in naming and specifying sexual difference where it has been ignored or misread; but without doing so in a way which guarantees it an eternal life of its own, a lonely trajectory across infinity which spreads out over the whole of being and the whole of society—as if the chance of one's gendered conception mercilessly guaranteed every subsequent facet of one's existence at all moments."[53] Here I take Riley's project to be an attempt to conceptualize the subjectivity of woman as a gendered subject, without essentializing gender such that it takes on "an eternal life of its own"; to avoid both the denial of sexual difference (nominalism) and an essentializing of sexual difference.

Despite this fundamental project, Riley's analysis in this book is mainly centered on the perceivable relations between social policies, popularized psychologies, the state, and individual practices, and she does not often ascend to the theoretical problem of conceptions of woman. What she does do is proceed with her historical and sociological analysis *without ever losing sight of the need to problematize her key concepts,* for example, woman and mother. In this she provides an example, the importance of which cannot be overestimated. Moreover, Riley discusses in her last chapter a useful approach to the political tension that can develop between the necessity of problematizing concepts on the one hand and justifying political action on the other.

In analyzing the pros and cons of various social policies, Riley tries to take a feminist point of view. Yet any such discussion must necessarily presuppose, even if it is not openly acknowledged, that needs are identifiable and can therefore be used as a yardstick in evaluating social policies. The reality is, however, that needs are terribly difficult to identify, since most if not all theories of need rely on some naturalist conception of the human agent, an agent who either can consciously identify and state all of her or his needs or whose "real" needs can be ascertained by some external process of analysis. Either method produces problems: it seems unrealistic to say that only if the agent can identify and articulate specific needs do the needs exist, and yet there are obvious dangers to relying on "experts" or others to identify the needs of an individual. Further, it is problematic to conceptualize the human agent as having needs in the same way that a table has properties, since the human agent is an entity in flux in a way that the table is not and is subject to forces of social construction that affect her subjectivity and thus her needs. Utilitarian theorists, especially desire and welfare utilitarian theorists, are particularly vulnerable to this problem, since the standard of moral evaluation they advocate using is precisely needs (or desires, which are equally problematic).[54] Feminist evaluations of social policy that use a concept of "women's needs" must run into the same difficulty. Riley's approach to this predicament is as follows: "I've said that people's needs obviously can't be revealed by a simple process of historical unveiling, while elsewhere I've talked about the 'real needs' of mothers myself. I take it that it's necessary both to stress the non-self-evident nature of need and the intricacies of its determinants, and also to act politically as if needs could be met, or at least met half-way."[55] Thus Riley asserts the possibility and even the necessity of combining decisively formulated political demands with an acknowledgment of their essentialist danger. How can this be done without weakening our political struggle?

On the one hand, as Riley argues, the logic of concrete demands does not entail a commitment to essentialism. She says: "Even though it is true that arguing for adequate childcare as one obvious way of meeting the needs of mothers does suppose an orthodox division of labor, in which responsibility for children is the province of women and not of men, nevertheless this division is what, by and large, actually obtains. Recognition of that in no way commits you to supposing that the care of children is fixed eternally as female."[56] We need not invoke a rhetoric of idealized motherhood to demand that women here and now need child care. On the other hand, the entire corpus of Riley's work on social policies is dedicated to demonstrating the dangers that such demands can entail. She explains these as follows: "Because the task of illuminating 'the needs of mothers' starts out with gender at its most decisive and inescapable point—the biological capacity to bear children—there's the danger that it may fall back into a conservative restating and confirming of social-sexual difference as timeless too. This would entail making the needs of mothers into fixed properties of 'motherhood' as a social function: I believe this is what happened in postwar Britain."[57] Thus, invoking the demands of women with children also invokes the companion belief in our cultural conception of essentialized motherhood.

As a way of avoiding this particular pitfall, Riley recommends against deploying any version of "motherhood" *as such*. I take it that what Riley means here is that we can talk about the needs of women with children and of course refer to these women as mothers but that we should eschew all reference to the idealized institution of motherhood as women's privileged vocation or the embodiment of an authentic or natural female practice.

The light that Riley sheds on our problem of woman's subjectivity is three-fold. First, and most obviously, she articulates the problem clearly and deals with it head on. Second, she shows us a way of approaching child-care demands without essentializing femininity, that is, by keeping it clear that these demands represent only current and not universal or eternal needs of women and by avoiding invocations of motherhood altogether. Third, she demands that our problematizing of concepts like "women's needs" coexist alongside a political program of demands in the name of women, without either countermanding the other. This is not to embrace the paradox but, rather, to call for a new understanding of subjectivity that can bring into harmony both our theoretical and our political agendas.

Denise Riley presents a useful approach to the political dimension of the problem of conceptualizing woman by discussing ways to avoid essentialist political demands. She reminds us that we should not avoid political action because our theory has uncovered chinks in the formulation of our key concepts.

A Concept of Positionality

Let me state initially that my approach to the problem of subjectivity is to treat it as a metaphysical problem rather than an empirical one. For readers coming from a poststructuralist tradition this statement will require immediate clarification. Continental philosophers from Nietzsche to Derrida have rejected the discipline of metaphysics in toto because they say it assumes a naive ontological connection between knowledge and a reality conceived as a thing-in-itself, totally independent of human practices and methodology. Echoing the logical positivists here, these philosophers have claimed that metaphysics is nothing but an exercise in mystification, presuming to make knowledge claims about such things as souls and "necessary" truths that we have no way of justifying. Perhaps the bottom line criticism has been that metaphysics defines truth in such a way that it is impossible to attain, and then claims to have attained it. I agree that we should reject the metaphysics of transcendent things-in-themselves and the presumption to make claims about the noumena, but this involves a rejection of a specific ontology of truth and particular tradition in the history of metaphysics and not a rejection of metaphysics itself. If metaphysics is conceived not as any particular ontological commitment but as the attempt to reason through ontological issues that cannot be decided empirically, then metaphysics continues today in Derrida's analysis of language, Foucault's conception of power, and all of the post-structuralist critiques of humanist theories of the subject. Thus, on this view, the assertion that someone is "doing metaphysics" does not serve as a pejorative. There are questions of importance to human beings that science alone cannot answer (including what science is and how it functions), and yet these are questions that we can usefully address by combining scientific data with other logical, political, moral, pragmatic, and coherence considerations. The distinction between what is normative and what is descriptive breaks down here. Metaphysical problems are problems that concern factual claims about the world (rather than simply expressive, moral, or aesthetic assertions, e.g.) but are problems that cannot be determined through empirical means alone.[58]

In my view the problem of the subject and, within this, the problem of conceptualizing "woman," is such a metaphysical problem. Thus, I disagree with both phenomenologists and psychoanalysts who assert that the nature of subjectivity can be discovered via a certain methodology and conceptual apparatus, either the epoch or the theory of the unconscious.[59] Neurophysiological reductionists likewise claim to be able to produce empirical explanations of subjectivity, but they will by and large admit that their physicalist explanations can tell us little about the experiential reality of subjectivity.[60] Moreover, I would assert that physicalist explanations can tell us little about how the concept of subjectivity should be construed, since this concept necessarily entails considerations not only of the empirical data but also of the political and ethical implications as well. Like the determination of when "human" life begins—whether at conception, full brain development, or birth—we cannot through science alone settle the issue since it turns on how we (to some extent) choose to define concepts like "human" and "woman." We cannot discover the "true meaning" of these concepts but must decide how to define them using all the empirical data, ethical arguments, political implications, and coherence constraints at hand.

Psychoanalysis should be mentioned separately here since it was Freud's initial problematizing of the subject from which developed post-structuralist rejection of the subject. It is the psychoanalytic conception of the unconscious that "undermines the subject from any position of certainty" and in fact claims to reveal that the subject is a fiction.[61] Feminists then use psychoanalysis to problematize the gendered subject to reveal "the fictional nature of the sexual category to which every human subject is none the less assigned."[62] Yet while a theorizing of the unconscious is used as a primary means of theorizing the subject, certainly psychoanalysis alone cannot provide all of the answers we need for a theory of the gendered subject.[63]

As I have already stated, it seems important to use Teresa de Lauretis's conception of experience as a way to begin to describe the features of human subjectivity. Lauretis starts with no given biological or psychological features and thus avoids assuming an essential characterization of subjectivity, but she also avoids the idealism that can follow from a rejection of materialist analyses by basing her conception on real practices and events. The importance of this focus on practices is, in part, Lauretis's shift away from the belief in the totalization of language or textuality to which most antiessentialist analyses become wedded. Lauretis wants to argue that language is not the sole source and locus of meaning, that habits and practices are crucial in the construction of meaning, and that through self-analyzing practices we can rearticulate female subjectivity. Gender is not a point to start from in the sense of being a given thing but is, instead, a posit or construct, formalizable in a nonarbitrary way through a matrix of habits, practices, and discourses. Further, it is an interpretation of our history within a particular discursive constellation, a history in which we are both subjects of and subjected to social construction.

The advantage of such an analysis is its ability to articulate a concept of gendered subjectivity without pinning it down one way or another for all time. Given this and given the danger that essentialist conceptions of the subject pose specifically for women, it seems both possible and desirable to construe a gendered subjectivity in relation to concrete habits, practices, and discourses while at the same time recognizing the fluidity of these.

As both Lacan and Riley remind us, we must continually emphasize within any account of subjectivity the historical dimension.[64] This will waylay the tendency to produce general, universal, or essential accounts by making all our conclusions contingent and revisable. Thus, through a conception of human subjectivity as an emergent property of a historicized experience, we can say "feminine subjectivity is construed here and now in such and such a way" without this ever entailing a universalizable maxim about the "feminine."

It seems to me equally important to add to this approach an "identity politics," a concept that developed from the Combahee River Collective's "A Black Feminist Statement."[65] The idea here is that one's identity is taken (and defined) as a political point of departure, as a motivation for action, and as a delineation of one's politics. Lauretis and the authors of *Yours in Struggle* are clear about the problematic nature of one's identity, one's subject-ness, and yet argue that the concept of identity politics is useful because identity is a posit that is politically paramount. Their suggestion is to recognize one's identity as always a construction yet also a necessary point of departure.

I think this point can be readily intuited by people of mixed races and cultures who have had to choose in some sense their identity.[66] For example, assimilated Jews who have chosen to become Jewish-identified as a political tactic against anti-Semitism are practicing identity politics. It may seem that members of more easily identifiable oppressed groups do not have this luxury, but I think that just as Jewish people can choose to assert their Jewishness, so black men, women of all races, and other members of more immediately recognizable oppressed groups can practice identity politics by choosing their identity as a member of one or more groups as their political point of departure. This, in fact, is what is happening when women who are not feminists downplay their identity as women and who, on becoming feminists, then begin making an issue of their femaleness. It is the claiming of their identity as women as a political point of departure that makes it possible to see, for instance, gender-biased language that in the absence of that departure point women often do not even notice.

It is true that antifeminist women can and often do identify themselves strongly as women and with women as a group, but this is usually explained by them within the context of an essentialist theory of femininity. Claiming that one's politics are grounded in one's essential identity avoids problematizing both identity and the connection between identity and politics and thus avoids the agency involved in underdetermined actions. The difference between feminists and antifeminists strikes me as precisely this: the affirmation or denial of our right and our ability to construct, and take responsibility for, our gendered identity, our politics, and our choices.[67]

Identity politics provides a decisive rejoinder to the generic human thesis and the mainstream methodology of Western political theory. According to the latter, the approach to political theory must be through a "veil of ignorance" where the theorist's personal interests and needs are hypothetically set aside. The goal is a theory of universal scope to which all ideally rational, disinterested agents would acquiesce if given sufficient information. Stripped of their particularities, these rational agents are considered to be potentially equally persuadable. Identity politics provides a materialist response to this and, in so doing, sides with Marxist class analysis. The best political theory will not be one ascertained through a veil of ignorance, a veil that is impossible to construct. Rather, political theory must base itself on the initial premise that all persons, including the theorist, have a fleshy, material identity that will influence and pass judgment on all political claims. Indeed, the best political theory for the theorist herself will be one that acknowledges this fact. As I see it, the concept of identity politics does not presuppose a prepackaged set of objective needs or political implications but problematizes the connection of identity and politics and introduces identity as a factor in any political analysis.

If we combine the concept of identity politics with a conception of the subject as positionality, we can conceive of the subject as nonessentialized and emergent from a historical experience and yet retain our political ability to take gender as an important point of departure. Thus we can say at one and the same time that gender is not natural, biological, universal, ahistorical, or essential and yet still claim that gender is relevant because we are taking gender as a position from which to act politically. What does position mean here?

When the concept "woman" is defined not by a particular set of attributes but by a particular position, the internal characteristics of the person thus identified are not denoted so much as the external context within which that person is situated. The external situation determines the person's relative position, just as the position of a pawn on a chessboard is considered safe or dangerous, powerful or weak, according to its relation to the other chess pieces. The essentialist definition of woman makes her identity independent of her external situation: since her nurturing and peaceful traits are innate they are ontologically autonomous of her position with respect to others or to the external historical and social conditions generally. The positional definition, on the other hand, makes her identity relative to a constantly shifting context, to a situation that includes a network of elements involving others, the objective economic conditions, cultural and political institutions and ideologies, and so on. If it is possible to identify women by their position within this network of relations, then it becomes possible to ground a feminist argument for women, not on a claim that their innate capacities are being stunted, but that their position within the network lacks power and mobility and requires radical change. The position of women is relative and not innate, and yet neither is it "undecidable." Through social critique and analysis we can identify women via their position relative to an existing cultural and social network.

It may sound all too familiar to say that the oppression of women involves their relative position within a society; but my claim goes further than this. I assert that the very subjectivity (or subjective experience of being a woman) and the very identity of women is constituted by women's position. However, this view should not imply that the concept of "woman" is determined solely by external elements and that the woman herself is merely a passive recipient of an identity created by these forces. Rather, she herself is part of the historicized, fluid movement, and she therefore actively contributes to the context within which her position can be delineated. I would include Lauretis's point here, that the identity of a woman is the product of her own interpretation and reconstruction of her history, as mediated through the cultural discursive context to which she has access.[68] Therefore, the concept of positionality includes two points: first, as already stated, that the concept of woman is a relational term identifiable only within a (constantly moving) context; but, second, that the position that women find themselves in can be actively utilized (rather than transcended) as a location for the construction of meaning, a place from where meaning is constructed, rather than simply the place where a meaning can be *discovered* (the meaning of femaleness). The concept of woman as positionality shows how women use their positional perspective as a place from which values are interpreted and constructed rather than as a locus of an already determined set of values. When women become feminists the crucial thing that has occurred is not that they have learned any new facts about the world but that they come to view those facts from a different position, from their own position as subjects. When colonial subjects begin to be critical of the formerly imitative attitude they had toward the colonists, what is happening is that they begin to identify with the colonized rather than the colonizers.[69] This difference in positional perspective does not necessitate a change in what are taken to be facts, although new facts may come into view from the new position, but it does necessitate a political change in perspective since the point of departure, the point from which all things are measured, has changed.

In this analysis, then, the concept of positionality allows for a determinate though fluid identity of woman that does not fall into essentialism: woman is a position from which a feminist politics can emerge rather than a set of attributes that are "objectively identifiable." Seen in this way, being a "woman" is to take up a position within a moving historical context and to be able to choose what we make of this position and how we alter this context. From the perspective of that fairly determinate though fluid and mutable position, women can themselves articulate a set of interests and ground a feminist politics.

The concept and the position of women is not ultimately undecidable or arbitrary. It is simply not possible to interpret our society in such a way that women have more power or equal power relative to men. The conception of woman that I have outlined limits the contructions of woman we can offer by defining subjectivity as positionality within a context. It thus avoids nominalism but also provides us with the means to argue against views like "oppression is all in your head" or the view that antifeminist women are not oppressed.

At the same time, by highlighting historical movement and the subject's ability to alter her context, the concept of positionality avoids essentialism. It even avoids tying ourselves to a structure of gendered politics conceived as historically infinite, though it allows for the assertion of gender politics on the basis of positionality at any time. Can we conceive of a future in which oppositional gender categories are not fundamental to one's self-concept? Even if we cannot, our theory of subjectivity should not preclude, and moreover prevent, that eventual possibility. Our concept of woman as a category, then, needs to remain open to future radical alteration, else we will preempt the possible forms eventual stages of the feminist transformation can take.

Obviously, there are many theoretical questions on positionality that this discussion leaves open. However, I would like to emphasize that the problem of woman as subject is a real one for feminism and not just on the plane of high theory. The demands of millions of women for child care, reproductive control, and safety from sexual assault can reinvoke the cultural assumption that these are exclusively feminine issues and can reinforce the right-wing's reification of gender differences unless and until we can formulate a political program that can articulate these demands in a way that challenges rather than utilizes sexist discourse.

Recently, I heard an attack on the phrase "woman of color" by a woman, dark-skinned herself, who was arguing that the use of this phrase simply reinforces the significance of that which should have no significance—skin color. To a large extent I agreed with this woman's argument: we must develop the means to address the wrongs done to us without reinvoking the basis of those wrongs. Likewise, women who have been eternally construed must seek a means of articulating a feminism that does not continue construing us in any set way. At the same time, I believe we must avoid buying into the neuter, universal "generic human" thesis that covers the West's racism and androcentrism with a blindfold. We cannot resolve this predicament by ignoring one half of it or by attempting to embrace it. The solution lies, rather, in formulating a new theory within the process of reinterpreting our position, and reconstructing our political identity, as women and feminists in relation to the world and to one another.

Notes

In writing this essay I have benefited immeasurably as a participant of the 1984–85 Pembroke Center Seminar on the Cultural Construction of Gender at Brown University. I would also like to thank Lynne Joyrich, Richard Schmitt, Denise Riley, Sandra Bartky, Naomi Scheman, and four anonymous reviewers for their helpful comments on an earlier draft of this paper.

1. It may seem that we can solve this dilemma easily enough by simply defining woman as those with female anatomies, but the question remains, What is the significance, if any, of those anatomies? What is the connection between female anatomy and the concept of woman? It should be remembered that the dominant discourse does not include in the category woman everyone with a female anatomy: it is often said that aggressive, self-serving, or powerful women are not "true" or "real" women. Moreover, the problem cannot be avoided by simply rejecting the concept of "woman" while retaining the category of "women." If there are women, then there must exist a basis for the category and a criterion for inclusion within it. This criterion need not posit a universal, homogeneous essence, but there must be a criterion nonetheless.

2. For Schopenhauer's, Kant's, and nearly every other major Western philosopher's conception of woman, and for an insight into just how contradictory and incoherent these are, see Linda Bell's excellent anthology, *Visions of Women* (Clifton, N.J.: Humana Press, 1983).

3. For an interesting discussion of whether feminists should even seek such transcendence, see Genevieve Lloyd, *The Man of Reason* (Minneapolis: University of Minnesota Press, 1984), 86–102.

4. Feminist works I would include in this group but which I won't be able to discuss in this essay are Elizabeth L. Berg, "The Third Woman," *Diacritics* 12 (1982): 11–20; and Lynne Joyrich, "Theory and Practice: The Project of Feminist Criticism," unpublished manuscript (Brown University, 1984). Luce Irigaray's work may come to mind for some readers as another proponent of a third way, but for me Irigaray's emphasis on female anatomy makes her work border too closely on essentialism.

5. Although Rich has recently departed from this position and in fact begun to move in the direction of the concept of woman I will defend in this essay (Adrienne Rich, "Notes toward a Politics of Location," in her *Blood, Bread, and Poetry* [New York: Norton, 1986]).

6. Mary Daly, *Gyn/Ecology* (Boston: Beacon, 1978), 355.

7. Ibid., 60.

8. Ibid., 59.

9. Ibid., 365 (my emphasis).

10. Adrienne Rich, *On Lies, Secrets, and Silence* (New York, 1979), 18.

11. Adrienne Rich, *Of Woman Born* (New York: Bantam, 1977), 21.

12. Ibid., 290.

13. Ibid., 21.

14. Ibid., 292. Three pages earlier Rich castigates the view that we need only release on the world women's ability to nurture in order to solve the world's problems, which may seem incongruous given the above passage. The two positions are consistent however: Rich is trying to correct the patriarchal conception of women as essentially nurturers with a view of women that is more complex and multifaceted. Thus, her essentialist conception of women is more comprehensive and complicated than the patriarchal one.

15. See Alice Echols, "The New Feminism of Yin and Yang," in *Powers of Desire: The Politics of Sexuality,* ed. Ann Snitow, Christine Stansell, and Sharon Thompson (New York: Monthly Review Press, 1983), 430–59, and "The Taming of the Id: Feminist Sexual Politics, 1968–83," in *Pleasure and Danger: Exploring Female Sexuality,* ed. Carole S. Vance (Boston: Routledge & Kegan Paul, 1984), 50–72. Hester Eisenstein paints a similar picture of cultural feminism in her *Contemporary Feminist Thought* (Boston: G. K. Hall, 1983), esp. xvii–xix and 105–45. Josephine Donovan has traced the more recent cultural feminism analyzed by Echols and Eisenstein to the earlier matriarchal vision of feminists like Charlotte Perkins Gilman (Josephine Donovan, *Feminist Theory: The Intellectual Traditions of American Feminism* [New York: Ungar, 1985], esp. chap. 2).

16. Echols, "The New Feminism of Yin and Yang," 441.

17. Ibid., 440.

18. Cherríe Moraga, "From a Long Line of Vendidas: Chicanas and Feminism," in *Feminist Studies/Critical Studies,* ed. Teresa de Lauretis (Bloomington: Indiana University Press, 1986), 180.

19. See also Moraga, "From a Long Line of Vendidas," 187, and Cherríe Moraga, "La Guera," in *This Bridge Called My Back: Writings by Radical Women of Color,* ed. Cherríe Moraga and Gloria Anzaldúa (New York: Kitchen Table, 1983), 32–33; Barbara Smith, "Introduction," in *Home Girls: A Black Feminist Anthology,* ed. Barbara Smith (New York: Kitchen Table, 1983), xix–lvi; "The Combahee River Collective Statement," in Smith, ed., 272–82; Audre Lorde, "Age, Race, Class, and Sex: Women Redefining Difference," in her *Sister Outsider* (Trumansburg, N.Y.: Crossing, 1984), 114–23; and bell hooks, *Feminist Theory: From Margin to Center* (Boston: South End, 1984). All of these works resist the universalizing tendency of cultural feminism and highlight the differences between women, and between men, in a way that undercuts arguments for the existence of an overarching gendered essence.

20. There is a wealth of literature on this, but two good places to begin are Anne Fausto-Sterling, *Myths of Gender: Biological Theories about Women and Men* (New York: Basic, 1986); and Sherrie Ortner and Harriet Whitehead, eds., *Sexual Meanings: The Cultural Construction of Gender and Sexuality* (New York: Cambridge University Press, 1981).

21. Echols, "The New Feminism of Yin and Yang," 440.

22. Hester Eisenstein's treatment of cultural feminism, though critical, is certainly more two-sided than Echols's. While Echols apparently sees only the reactionary results of cultural feminism, Eisenstein sees in it a therapeutic self-affirmation necessary to offset the impact of a misogynist culture (see Eisenstein [n. 15 above]).

23. Michel Foucault, "Why Study Power: The Question of the Subject," in *Beyond Structuralism and Hermeneutics: Michel Foucault,* ed. Hubert L. Dreyfus and Paul Rabinow, 2d ed. (Chicago: University of Chicago Press, 1983), 212.

24. This term is principally associated with Derrida for whom it refers specifically to the process of unraveling metaphors in order to reveal their underlying logic, which usually consists of a simple binary opposition such as between man/woman, subject/object, culture/na-

ture, etc. Derrida has demonstrated that within such oppositions one side is always superior to the other side, such that there is never any pure difference without domination. The term "deconstruction" has also come to mean more generally any exposure of a concept as ideological or culturally constructed rather than natural or a simple reflection of reality (see Derrida, *Of Grammatology,* trans. G. Spivak [Baltimore: Johns Hopkins University Press, 1976]; also helpful is Jonathan Culler's *On Deconstruction* [Ithaca, N.Y.: Cornell University Press, 1982]).

25. Michel Foucault, "Nietzsche, Genealogy, History," in *The Foucault Reader,* ed. Paul Rabinow (New York: Pantheon, 1984), 83.

26. This hope is evident in Michel Foucault's *The Order of Things: An Archaeology of the Human Sciences* (New York: Random House, 1973).

27. Jacques Derrida, *Spurs,* trans. Barbara Harlow (Chicago: University of Chicago Press, 1978), 49.

28. Ibid., 51.

29. Biddy Martin, "Feminism, Criticism, and Foucault," *New German Critique* 27 (1982): 11.

30. Julia Kristeva, "Woman Can Never Be Defined," in *New French Feminisms,* ed. Elaine Marks and Isabelle de Courtivron (New York: Schocken, 1981), 137 (my italics).

31. Julia Kristeva, "Oscillation between Power and Denial," in Marks and Courtivron, eds., 166.

32. Martin, 16–17.

33. Ibid., esp. 21, 24, and 29.

34. See Derrida, *Spurs,* esp. 57 and 97.

35. Martin's most recent work departs from this in a positive direction. In an essay coauthored with Chandra Talpade Mohanty, Martin points out "the political limitations of an insistence on 'indeterminacy' which implicitly, when not explicitly, denies the critic's own situatedness in the social, and in effect refuses to acknowledge the critic's own institutional home." Martin and Mohanty seek to develop a more positive, though still problematized, conception of the subject as having a "multiple and shifting" perspective. In this, their work becomes a significant contribution toward the development of an alternative conception of subjectivity, a conception not unlike the one that I will discuss in the rest of this essay ("Feminist Politics: What's Home Got to Do with It?" in Lauretis, ed. [n. 18 above], 191–212, esp. 194).

36. A wonderful exchange on this between persuasive and articulate representatives of both sides was printed in *Diacritics* (Peggy Kamuf, "Replacing Feminist Criticism," *Diacritics* 12 [1982]: 42–47; and Nancy Miller, "The Text's Heroine: A Feminist Critic and Her Fictions," *Diacritics* 12 [1982]: 48–53).

37. Teresa de Lauretis, *Alice Doesn't* (Bloomington: Indiana University Press, 1984), 5.

38. Ibid., 5–6.

39. Ibid., 7.

40. Ibid., 8–9.

41. Ibid., 11.

42. Ibid., 159.

43. Ibid., 161.

44. Ibid.

45. Ibid., 182. The principal texts Lauretis relies on in her exposition of Lacan, Eco, and Peirce are Jacques Lacan, *Ecrits* (Paris: Seuil, 1966); Umberto Eco, *A Theory of Semiotics* (Bloomington: Indiana University Press, 1976), and *The Role of the Reader: Explorations in the Semiotic of Texts* (Bloomington: Indiana University Press, 1979); and Charles Sanders Peirce, *Collected Papers,* vols. 1–8 (Cambridge, Mass.: Harvard University Press, 1931–58).

46. Lauretis, *Alice Doesn't* (n. 37 above), 182.

47. Ibid., 186 (my italics).

48. Lauretis, ed. (n. 18 above), 8.

49. Ibid., 9.

50. Denise Riley, *War in the Nursery: Theories of the Child and Mother* (London: Virago, 1983), 2.

51. Ibid., 6.

52. Ibid., 2, 3.

53. Ibid., 4.

54. For a lucid discussion of just how difficult this problem is for utilitarians, see Jon Elster, "Sour Grapes—Utilitarianism and the Genesis of Wants," in *Utilitarianism and Beyond*, ed. Amartya Sen and Bernard Williams (Cambridge: Cambridge University Press, 1982), 219–38.

55. Riley, 193–94.

56. Ibid., 194.

57. Ibid., 194–95.

58. In this conception of the proper dimension of and approach to metaphysics (as a conceptual enterprise to be decided partially by pragmatic methods), I am following the tradition of the later Rudolf Carnap and Ludwig Wittgenstein, among others (Rudolf Carnap, "Empiricism, Semantics, and Ontology," and "On the Character of Philosophical Problems," both in *The Linguistic Turn*, ed. R. Rorty [Chicago: University of Chicago Press, 1967]; and Ludwig Wittgenstein, *Philosophical Investigations*, trans. G. E. M. Anscombe [New York: Macmillan, 1958]).

59. I am thinking particularly of Husserl and Freud here. The reason for my disagreement is that both approaches are in reality more metaphysical than their proponents would admit and, further, that I have only limited sympathy for the metaphysical claims they make. I realize that to explain this fully would require a long argument, which I cannot give in this essay.

60. See, e.g., Donald Davidson, "Psychology as Philosophy," in his *Essays on Actions and Interpretations* (Oxford: Clarendon Press, 1980), 230.

61. Jacqueline Rose, "Introduction II," in *Feminine Sexuality: Jacques Lacan and the Ecole Freudienne*, ed. Juliet Mitchell and Jacqueline Rose (New York: Norton, 1982), 29, 30.

62. Ibid., 29.

63. Psychoanalysis must take credit for making subjectivity a problematic issue, and yet I think a view that gives psychoanalysis hegemony in this area is misguided, if only because psychoanalysis is still extremely hypothetical. Let a hundred flowers bloom.

64. See Juliet Mitchell, "Introduction I," in Mitchell and Rose, eds., 4–5.

65. This was suggested to me by Teresa de Lauretis in an informal talk she gave at the Pembroke Center, 1984–85. A useful discussion and application of this concept can be found in Elly Bulkin, Minnie Bruce Pratt, and Barbara Smith, *Yours in Struggle: Three Feminist Perspectives on Anti-Semitism and Racism* (Brooklyn, N.Y.: Long Haul Press, 1984), 98–99. Martin and Mohanty's paper (n. 35 above) offers a fruitful reading of the essay in *Yours in Struggle* by Minnie Bruce Pratt entitled "Identity: Skin Blood Heart" and brings into full relief the way in which she uses identity politics. See also "The Combahee River Collective" (n. 19 above).

66. This point has been the subject of long, personal reflection for me, as I myself am half Latina and half white. I have been motivated to consider it also since the situation is even more complicated for my children, who are half mine and half a Jewish father's.

67. I certainly do not believe that most women have the freedom to choose their situations in life, but I do believe that of the multiple ways we are held in check, internalized oppressive mechanisms play a significant role, and we can achieve control over these. On this point I must say I have learned from and admired the work of Mary Daly, particularly *Gyn/Ecology* (n. 6 above), which reveals and describes these internal mechanisms and challenges us to repudiate them.

68. See Teresa de Lauretis, "Feminist Studies/Critical Studies: Issues, Terms, Contexts," in Lauretis, ed. (n. 18 above), 8–9.

69. This point is brought out by Homi Bhabha in his "Of Mimicry and Man: The Ambivalence of Colonial Discourse," *October* 28 (1984): 125–33; and by Abdur Rahman in his *Intellectual Colonisation* (New Delhi: Vikas, 1983).

Sorcerer Love: A Reading of Plato's Symposium, *Diotima's Speech*

Luce Irigaray
Translated by Eleanor H. Kuykendall

In the *Symposium,* the dialogue on love, when Socrates finishes speaking, he gives the floor to a woman: Diotima. She does not participate in these exchanges or in this meal among men. She is not there. She herself does not speak. Socrates reports or recounts her views. He borrows her wisdom and power, declares her his initiator, his pedagogue, on matters of love, but she is not invited to teach or to eat. Unless she did not want to accept an invitation? But Socrates says nothing about that. And Diotima is not the only example of a woman whose wisdom, above all in love, is reported in her absence by a man.

Diotima's teaching will be very dialectical—but different from what we usually call dialectical. Unlike Hegel's, her dialectic does not work by opposition to transform the first term into the second, in order to arrive at a synthesis of the two. At the very outset, she establishes the *intermediary* and she never abandons it as a mere way or means. Her method is not, then, a propaedeutic of the *destruction* or *destructuration* of two terms in order to establish a synthesis which is neither one nor the other. She presents, uncovers, unveils the existence of a third that is already there and that permits progression: from poverty to wealth, from ignorance to wisdom, from mortality to immortality. For her, this progression always leads to a greater perfection of and in love.

But, contrary to the usual dialectical methods, love ought not to be abandoned for the sake of becoming wise or learned. It is love that leads to knowledge—both practical and metaphysical. It is love that is both the guide and the way, above all a mediator.

Love is designated as a theme, but love is also perpetually enacted, dramatized, in the exposition of the theme.

So Diotima immediately rebuts the claims that love is a great God and that it is the love of beautiful things. At the risk of offending the Gods, Diotima also asserts that love is neither beautiful nor good. This leads her interlocutor to suppose immediately that love is ugly and bad, incapable as he is of grasping the existence or instance of what is held *between,* what permits the passage between ignorance and knowledge.

If we did not, at each moment, have something to learn in the encounter with reality, between reality and already established knowledge, we would not perfect ourselves in wisdom. And not to become wiser means to become more ignorant.

Therefore, between knowledge and reality, there is an intermediary which permits the meeting and transmutation or transvaluation between the two. The dialectic of Diotima is in *four terms*, at least: the here, the two poles of the meeting, the beyond, but a beyond which never abolishes the here. And so on, indefinitely. The mediator is never abolished in an infallible knowledge. Everything is always in movement, in becoming. And the mediator of everything is, among other things, or exemplarily, love. Never completed, always evolving.

And, in response to the protestation of Socrates that love is a great God, that *everyone says so or things so*, she *laughs*. Her retort is not at all angry, balancing between contradictories; it is laughter from elsewhere. Laughing, then, she asks Socrates who this *everyone* is. Just as she ceaselessly undoes the assurance or the *closure* of opposing terms, so she rejects every ensemble of unities reduced to a similitude in order to constitute a whole:

> "You mean, by all who do not know?" said she, "or by all who know as well?" "Absolutely all." At that she laughed. (202)[1]

> ("Ce tout le monde dont tu parles, sont-ce, dit-elle, ceux qui savent ou ceux qui ne savent pas?—Tous en général, ma foi!" Elle se mit à rire.)

The tension between opposites thus abated, she shows, demonstrates, that "everyone" does not exist, nor does the position of love as *eternally* a great God. Does she teach nothing that is already defined? A method of becoming wise, learned, more perfect in love and in art [*l'art*]. She ceaselessly questions Socrates on his positions but without, like a master, positing already constituted truths. Instead, she teaches the renunciation of already established truths. And each time that Socrates thinks that he can take something as certain, she undoes his certainty. All entities, substantives, adverbs, sentences are patiently, and joyously, called into question.

For love, the demonstration is not so difficult to establish. For, if love possessed all that he desired, he would desire no more.[2] He must lack, therefore, in order to desire still. But, if love had nothing at all to do with beautiful and good things, he could not desire them either. Thus, he is an *intermediary* in a very specific sense. Does he therefore lose his status as a God? Not necessarily. He is neither mortal nor immortal: he is between the one and the other. Which qualifies him as demonic. Love is a *demon*—his function is to transmit to the gods what comes from men and to men what comes from the gods. Like everything else that is demonic, love is complementary to gods and to men in such a way as to join everything with itself. There must be a being of middling nature in order for men and gods to enter into relations, into conversation, while awake or asleep. Which makes love a kind of divination, priestly knowledge of things connected with sacrifice, initiation, incantation, prediction in general and magic.

The demons who serve as mediators between men and gods are numerous and very diverse. Love is one of them. And Love's parentage is very particular: child of *Plenty* (himself son of *Invention*) and of *Poverty*, conceived the day the birth of Aphrodite was celebrated. Thus love is always poor and

... rough, unkempt, unshod, and homeless, ever couching on the ground uncovered, sleeping beneath the open sky by doors and in the streets, because he has the nature of his mother. ... But again, in keeping with his father, he has designs upon the beautiful and good, for he is bold, headlong, and intense, a mighty hunter, always weaving some device or other, eager in invention and resourceful, searching after wisdom all through life, terrible as a magician, sorcerer, and sophist. Further, in his nature he is not immortal, nor yet mortal. No, on a given day, now he flourishes and lives, when things go well with him, and again he dies, but through the nature of his sire revives again. Yet his gain for ever slips away from him, so that Eros never is without resources, nor is ever rich.

As for ignorance and knowledge, here again he is midway between them. The case stands thus. No god seeks after wisdom, or wishes to grow wise (for he already is so), no more than anybody else seeks after wisdom if he has it. Nor, again, do ignorant folk seek after wisdom or long to grow wise; for here is just the trouble about ignorance, that what is neither beautiful and good, nor yet intelligent, to itself seems good enough. Accordingly, the man who does not think himself in need has no desire for what he does not think himself in need of.

[Socrates.] The seekers after knowledge, Diotima! If they are not the wise, nor yet the ignorant (said I), who are they, then?

[Diotima.] The point (said she) is obvious even to a child, that they are persons intermediate between these two, and that Eros is among them; for wisdom falls within the class of the most beautiful, while Eros is an eros for the beautiful. And hence it follows necessarily that Eros is a seeker after wisdom [a philosopher], and being a philosopher, is midway between wise and ignorant. (203–204)

(rude et malpropre; un va-nu-pieds qui n'a point de domicile, dormant à la belle étoile sur le pas des portes ou dans la rue selon la nature de sa mére. Mais, en revanche, guettant, sans cesse, embusqué les choses belles et bonnes, chasseur habile et ourdissant continûment quelque ruse, curieux de pensée et riche d'expédient, passant toute sa vie à philosopher, habile comme sorcier, comme inventeur de philtres magiques, comme sophiste, selon la nature de son père. De plus, sa nature n'est ni d'un mortel ni d'un immortel, mais, le même jour, tantôt, quand ses expédients ont réussi, il est en fleur, il a de la vie; tantôt au contraire il est mourant; puis, derechef, il revient à la vie grace au naturel de son pere, tandis que, d'autre part, coule de ses mains le fruit de ses expédients! Ainsi, ni jamais Amour n'est indigent, ni jamais il est riche! Entre savoir et ignorance, maintenant, Amour est intermédiare. Voici ce qui en est. Parmi les Dieux, il n'y en a aucun qui ait envie de devenir sage, car il l'est; ne s'emploie pas non plus à philosopher quiconque d'autre est sage. Mais pas davantage les ignorants ne s'emploient, de leur côté, à philosopher, et ils n'ont pas envie de devenir sages; car, ce qu'il y a precisement de fâcheux dans l'ignorance, c'est que quelqu'un, qui n'est pas un homme accompli et qui n'est pas non plus intelligent, se figure l'être dans la mesure voulue; c'est que celui qui ne croit pas être depourvu n'a point envie de ce dont il ne croit pas avoir besoin d'etre pourvu.—Quels sont donc alors, Diotime, m'écriai-je, ceux qui s'emploient à philosopher si ce ne sont ni les sages ni les ignorants?—La chose est claire, ditelle, et même déjà pour un enfant! Ce sont ceux qui sont intermediares entre ces deux extrêmes, et au nombre desquels doit aussi se trouver Amour. La sagesse, en effet, est évidemment parmi les plus belles choses, et c'est au beau qu'Amour rapporte son amour; d'où il suit que, forcément, Amour est philosophe, et, étant philosophe, qu'il est intermédiare entre le savant et l'ignorant.)

Eros is therefore *intermediary* between couples of opposites: poverty-plenty, ignorance-wisdom, ugliness-beauty, dirtiness-cleanliness, death-life, etc. And that would be inscribed in love's nature as a result of his genealogy and date of conception. And love is a philosopher, love is philosophy. Philosophy is not formal knowledge, fixed, abstracted from all feeling. It is the search for love, love of beauty, love of wisdom, which is one of the most beautiful things. Like love, the philosopher would be someone poor, dirty, a bit of a bum, always an outsider, sleeping under the stars but very curious, adept in ruses and devices of all kinds, reflecting ceaselessly, a sorcerer, a sophist, sometimes flourishing, sometimes expiring. Nothing like the representation of the philosopher we generally give: learned, correctly dressed, with good manners, understanding everything, pedantically instructing us in a corpus of already codified doctrine. The philosopher is nothing like that. He is barefoot, going out under the stars in search of an encounter with reality, seeking the embrace, the acquaintance [connaissance] (co-birthing) [(co-naissance)] of whatever gentleness of soul, beauty, wisdom might be found there. This incessant quest he inherits from his mother. He is a philosopher through his mother, an adept in invention through his father. But his passion for love, for beauty, for wisdom, comes to him from his mother, and from the date when he was conceived. Desired and wanted, besides, by his mother.

How is it that love and the philosopher are generally represented otherwise? Because they are imagined as *beloved* and not as *lovers.* As beloved Love, both like and unlike the philosopher, is imagined to be of unparalled beauty, delicate, perfect, happy. Yet the lover has an entirely different nature. He goes toward what is kind, beautiful, perfect, etc. He does not possess these. He is poor, unhappy, always in search of ... But what does he seek or love? That beautiful things become his—this is Socrates' answer. But what will happen to him if these things become his? To this question of Diotima's, Socrates has no answer. Switching "good" for "beautiful," she asks her question again. "That the good may be his," ("Qu'elles devienne siennes") Socrates repeats.

> "And what happens to the man when the good things become his?" "On this," said [Socrates], "I am more than ready with an answer: that he will be happy." (204–205)

> ("Et qu'en sera-t-il pour celui a qui il arrivera que les choses bonnes soient devenues siennes?" "Voilà, dit Socrate, à quoi je serai plus à mon aise pour répondre! Il sera heureux")

And happiness seems to put an ultimate end to this dialogical repetition between Diotima and Socrates.

*   *   *

Socrates asks: what should we call what pertains to lovers? "By what manner of pursuit and in what activity does the eagerness and straining for the object get the name of Eros? And what may this action really be?" ("Quel est le genre d'existence, le mode d'activité pour lesquels à leur zèle, à leur effort soutenu conviendrait le nom d'amour, dis-moi? En quoi peu bien consister cet acte?") And Diotima replies: "This action is engendering in beauty, with relation both to body and to soul." (205, 206) ("C'est un enfantement dans la beauté et selon le corps et selon l'âme.") But Socrates understands nothing of another, equally clear, revelation ... He understands nothing about fecundity in relation both to body and to soul:

> The union of a man and woman is, in fact, a generation; this is a thing divine; in a living creature that is mortal, it is an element of immortality, this fecundity and generation. (206)

(L'union de l'homme et de la femme est en effet un engantement et c'est une affaire divine, c'est, dans le vivant mortel, la présence de ce qui est immortel: la fécondité et la procréation.)

This statement of Diotima's never seems to have been understood. Besides, she herself will go on to emphasize the procreative aspect of love. But first she stresses the character of *divine generation in every union between man and woman,* the presence of the immortal in the living mortal. All love would be creation, potentially divine, a path between the condition of the mortal and that of the immortal. Love is fecund before all procreation. And it has a *mediumlike, demonic* fecundity. Assuring everyone, male and female, the immortal becoming of the living. But there cannot be procreation of a divine nature in what is not in harmony. And harmony with the divine is not possible for the ugly, but only for the beautiful. Thus, according to Diotima, love between man and woman is beautiful, harmonious, divine. It must be in order for procreation to take place. It is not procreation that is beautiful and that constitutes the aim of love. The aim of love is to realize the immortality in the mortality between lovers. And the expansion which produces the child follows the joy at the approach of a beautiful object. But an ugly object leads to a turning back, the shriveling up of fecundity, the painfully borne weight of the desire to procreate. Procreation and generation in beauty—these are the aim of love, because it is thus that the eternity and imperishability of a mortal being manifest themselves.

Fecundity of love between lovers, regeneration of one by the other, passage to immortality in one another, through one another—these seem to become the condition, not the cause, of procreation. Certainly, Diotima tells Socrates that the creation of beauty, of a work of art [*l'oeuvre*] (solitary creation this time?) is insufficient, that it is necessary to give birth together to a child, that this wisdom is inscribed in the animal world itself. She continues to laugh at the way he goes looking for his truths beyond the most obvious everyday reality, which he does not see or even perceive. She mocks the way his dialectical or dialogical method forgets the most elementary truths. The way his discourse on love neglects to look at, to inform itself about, the amorous state and to inquire about its cause.

Diotima speaks of *cause* in a surprising way. We could note that her method does not enter into a chain of causalities, a chain that skips over or often forgets the intermediary as generative milieu. Usually, causality is not part of her reasoning. She borrows it from the animal world and evokes it, or invokes it, with respect to procreation. Instead of allowing the child to germinate or develop in the milieu of love and fecundity between man and woman, she seeks a cause of love in the animal world: procreation.

Diotima's method miscarries here. From here on, she leads love into a schism between mortal and immortal. Love loses its demonic character. Is this the founding act of the meta-physical? There will be lovers in body and lovers in soul. But the perpetual passage from mortal to immortal that lovers confer on one another is put aside. Love loses its divinity, its mediumlike, alchemical qualities between couples of opposites. The intermediary becomes the child, and no longer love. Occupying the place of love, the child can no longer be a lover. It is put in the place of the incessant movement of love. Beloved, no doubt; but how be beloved without being a lover? And is not love trapped *in the beloved,* contrary to what Diotima wanted in the first place? A beloved who is an end is substituted for love between men and women. A beloved who is a *will*, even a *duty*, and a *means* of attaining immortality. Lovers can neither attain nor advance that between themselves. That is the weakness of love, for the child as well. If the couple of lovers cannot care for the place of love like a third term between them, then they will not remain lovers and they cannot give birth to lovers. Something gets solidified in space-time with the loss of a vital intermediary milieu and of an accessible, loving, transcendental. A sort of teleological triangle replaces a perpetual movement, a perpetual transvaluation, a permanent becoming. Love was the vehicle of this. But, if procreation becomes its goal, it risks losing its internal motivation, its fecundity "in itself", its slow and constant regeneration.

This error in method, in the originality of Diotima's method, is corrected shortly afterward only to be confirmed later on. Surely, once again, *she is not there. Socrates reports her views.* Perhaps he distorts them unwittingly and unknowingly.

The following paragraph takes up what was just asserted. It explains how it is that there is permanent renewal in us. How there is, in us, a ceaseless loss of the old, of the already dead, both in our most physical part—hair, bones, blood, our whole body—and in our most spiritual part: our character, our opinions, our desires, joys and pains, our fears. None of these elements is ever identical to what they were; some come into existence while others perish. The same is true for knowledges, which are acquired and forgotten—thus constantly renewed:

> ". ... This is the fashion in which everything mortal is preserved, not in being always perfectly identical, as in divinity, but in that the disappearing and decaying object leaves behind it another new one such as it was. By this arrangement, Socrates," said she, "the mortal partakes of immortality, both in body and all else; the immortal does so in another way. So do not marvel if everything by nature prizes its own offspring; it is for the sake of immortality that every being has this urgency and love." ... (208)

> ([C'est] de cette façon qu'est sauvegardé ce qui est mortel, non point comme ce qui est divin par l'identité absolue d'une existence eternelle, mais par le fait que ce qui s'en va, mine par son ancienneté, laisse après lui autre chose, du nouveau qui est pareil à ce qu'il était. C'est par ce moyen, dit-elle, qui ce qui est mortel participe à l'immortalité, dans son corps et en tout le reste ... Donc, ne t'émerveille pas que, ce qui est une repousse de lui-même, chaque être ait pour lui tant de sollicitude naturelle, car c'est en vue de l'immortalité que font cortège à chacun d'eux ce zèle et cet amour!)

Here, Diotima returns to her type of argumentation, including her mocking of those who suspend the present in order to search "for an eternity of time an immortal glory" ("pour l'eternité du temps une gloire immortelle"). She speaks—in a style that is loosely *woven* but never definitively *knotted*—of becoming in time, of permanent generation and regeneration here and now in each (wo)man [chacun(e)] of what is more corporeally and spiritually real. Without saying that one is the fruit of the other. But that, at each moment, we are a "regrowth" of ourselves, in perpetual increase. No more quest for immortality through the child. But in us, ceaselessly. Diotima has returned to a path which admits love as it was defined before she evoked procreation: an intermediate terrain, a mediator, a space-time of permanent *passage* between mortal and immortal.

Next, returning to an example of the quest for immortality through fame, she re-situates (the) object (of) love outside of the subject: reknown, immortal glory, etc. No more perpetual becoming-immortal in us, but rather a race toward some thing that would confer immortality. Like and unlike procreation of a child, the stake of love is placed outside the self. In the beloved and not in the lover? The lovers cited—Alcestis, Admetus, Achilles, Codros—would not have been cited unless we always remembered them. It was with the goal of eternal reknown that they loved unto death. Immortality is the object of their love. Not love itself.

> Well then (said she), when men's fecundity is of the body, they turn rather to the women, and the fashion of their love is this: through begetting children to provide themselves with immortality, renown and happiness, as they imagine—
> Securing them for all time to come.
> But when fecundity is of the soul—for indeed there are (said she) those persons who are fecund in their souls, even more than in their bodies, fecund in what is the function of the soul to conceive and also to bring forth—what is this proper offspring? It is wisdom, along with every other spiritual value. ... (208–209)

> (Cela étant, dit-elle, ceux qui sont féconds selon le corps se tournent plutôt vers les femmes, et leur façon d'etre amoureux c'est, en engendrant des enfants, de se procurer à eux-mêmes, pensent-ils, pour toute la suite du temps, le bonheur d'avoir un nom dont le souvenir ne périsse pas. Quant à ceux qui sont féconds selon l'âme, car en fait il en existe, dit-elle, dont la fécondité réside dans l'âme, à un plus haut degré encore que dans le corps, pour tout ce qui appartient à une âme d'être féconde et qu'il lui appartient d'enfanter. Or, qu'est-ce cela qui lui appartient? C'est la pensée, et c'est toute autre excellence)

What seemed to me most original in Diotima's method has disappeared once again. That irreducible intermediary milieu of love is cancelled between "subject" (an inadequate word in Plato) and "beloved reality." Amorous becoming no longer constitutes a becoming of the lover himself, of love in the (male or female) lover, between the lovers [un devenir de l'amant lui-même, de l'amour en l'amante(e), entre amants].[3] Instead it is now a teleological quest for what is deemed the highest reality and often situated in a transcendence inaccessible to our condition as mortals. Immortality is put off until death and is not counted as one of our constant tasks as mortals, as a transmutation that is endlessly incumbent on us here and now, as a possibility inscribed in a body capable of divine becoming. Beauty of body and beauty of soul become hierarchized, and the love of women becomes the lot of those who, incapable of being creators in soul, are fecund in body and seek the immortality of their name perpetuated by their offspring.

> ... By far the greatest and most beautiful form of wisdom (said she) is that which has to do with regulating states and households, and has the name, no doubt, of "temperance" and "justice." (209)

> (... de beaucoup la plus considérable et la plus belle manifestation de la pensée etant celle qui concerne l'ordonnance des Etats comme de tout éstablissement, et dont le nom, on le sait, est tempérance aussi bien que justice.)

Amorous becomings, divine, immortal, are no longer left to their intermediary current. They are qualified, hierarchized. And, in the extreme case, love dies. In the universe of determinations, there will be contests, competitions, amorous duties—the beloved or love being the prize. The lovers disappear. Our subsequent tradition has even taught us the interdiction or the futility of being lovers outside of procreation.

Yet Diotima had begun by asserting that the most divine act is "the union of man and woman, a divine affair." What she asserted then accorded with what she said about the function of love as an intermediary remaining intermediary, a demon. It seems that in the course of her speech she reduces a bit this demonic, mediumlike function of love; so that it is no longer really a demon, but an intention, a reduction to intention, to the teleology of human will. Already subjected to a doctrine with fixed goals and not to an immanent flourishing of the divine in the flesh. Irreducible mediator, at once physical and spiritual, between lovers; and not already codified duty, will, desire. Love invoked as a demon in a method toward the beautiful and good often disappears from the speech, reappearing only in art, "painting," in the form(s) love love inciting to eroticism and, perhaps, in the shape of angels. Is love itself split between *eros* and *agape?* Yet, in order for lovers to be able to love each other, there must be, between them, Love.

There remains what has been said about the philosopher-love. But why would not philosopher Love be a lover of the other? Only of the Other? Of an inaccessible transcendent? In any case, this would already be an ideal that suppresses love qua demonic. Love becomes political wisdom, wisdom in regulating the city, not the intermediary state that inhabits lovers and transports them from the condition of mortals to that of immortals. Love becomes a sort of *raison d'état.* Love founds a family, takes care of children, including the children which citizens are. The more its objective is distanced from an individual becoming, the more valuable it is. Its stake is lost in immortal good and beauty as collective goods. The family is preferable to the generation of lovers, between lovers. Adopted children are preferable to others. This, moreover, is how it comes to pass that *love between men is superior to love between man and woman.* Carnal procreation is suspended in favor of the engendering of beautiful and good things. Immortal things. That, surprisingly, is the view of Diotima. At least as translated through the words uttered by Socrates.

The beings most gifted in wisdom go directly to that end. Most begin with physical beauty and "... must love one single object [physical form of beauty], and thereof must engender fair discourses. ..." (210) (par n'aimer qu'un unique beau corps et par engendrer à cette occasion de beaux discours.") If the teaching is right, that must be so. But whoever becomes attached to one body must learn that beauty is in many bodies. After having pursued beauty in one perceptible form, he must learn that the same beauty resides in all bodies; he will

> ... abate his violent love of one, disdaining this and deeming it a trifle, and will become a lover of all fair objects. ... (210)
>
> ("[devenir] un amant de tous les beaux corps et détendra l'impétuosité de son amour à l'égard d'un seul individu; car, un tel amour, il en est venu à le dédaigner et à en faire peu de cas.")

From the attraction to a single beautiful body he passes, then, to many; and thence to the beauty residing in souls. Thus he learns that beauty is not found univocally in the body and that someone of an ugly bodily appearance can be beautiful and gentle of soul; that to be just is to know how to care for that person and to engender beautiful discourses for him. Love thus passes insensibly into love of works [oeuvres]. The passion for beautiful bodies is transmuted into the discovery of beauty in knowledges. That which liberates from the attachment to only one master opens onto the immense ocean of the beautiful, and leads to the birth of numerous and sublime discourses, as well as to thoughts inspired by a boundless love of wisdom. Until the resulting force and development permit the lover to envision a certain *unique* knowledge (210). This marvelous beauty is perceptible, perhaps, by whoever has followed the road just described, by whoever has passed through the different stages step by step. He will have, then, the vision of a beauty whose existence is "... eternal, not growing up or perishing, increasing or decreasing" ([dont] l'existence est éternelle, étrangère à la génération comme à la corruption, à l'accroissement comme au décroissement") and which, besides, is *absolutely* beautiful:

> not beautiful in one point and ugly in another, nor beautiful in this place and ugly in that, as if beautiful to some, to others ugly; again, this beauty will not be revealed to him in the semblance of a face, or hands, or any other element of the body, nor in any form of speech or knowledge, nor yet as if it appertained to any other being, or creature, for example, upon earth, or in the sky, or elsewhere; no, it will be seen as beauty in and for itself, consistent with itself in uniformity for ever, whereas all other beauties share it in such fashion that, while they are ever born and perish, that eternal beauty, never waxing, never waning, never is impaired. ... (210–211)

> (pas belle à ce point de vue et laide à cet autre, pas davantage à tel moment et non à tel autre, ni non plus belle en comparaison avec ceci, laide en comparaison avec cela, ni non plus belle en tel lieu, laide en tel autre, en tant que belle pour certains hommes, laide pour certains autres; pas davantage encore cette beauté ne se montrera à lui pourvue par exemple d'un visage, ni de mains, ni de quoi que ce soit d'autre qui soit une partie du corps; ni non plus sous l'aspect de quelque raisonnement ou encore quelque connaissance; pas davantage comme ayant en quelque être distinct quelque part son existence, en un vivant par exemple, qu'il soit de la terre ou du ciel, ou bien en quoi que ce soit d'autre; mais bien plutôt elle se montrera à lui en elle-même, et par elle-même, éternellement unie à elle-même dans l'unicité de la nature formelle, tandis que les autres beaux objets participent tous de la nature dont il s'agit en une telle façon que, ces autres objets venant à l'existence ou cessant d'exister, il n'en résulte dans la réalité dont il s'agit aucune augmentation, aucune diminution, ni non plus aucune sorte d'altération.)

To attain this sublime beauty, one must begin with the love of young men. Starting with their natural beauty, one must, step by step, raise oneself to supernatural beauty: from beautiful bodies one must pass to beautiful pursuits; then to beautiful sciences, and finally to that sublime science that is supernatural beauty alone, and that allows knowledge of the essence of beauty in isolation (211). This contemplation is what gives direction and taste to life." ... It will not appear to you to be according to the measure of gold and raiment, or of lovely boys and striplings ..." (211) ("Ni l'or ou la toilette, ni la beauté des jeunes garcons ou des jeunes hommes ne peuvent entrer en parallèle avec cette découverte.") And whoever has perceived "beauty divine in its own single nature" (211) ("le beau divin dans l'unicité de sa nature formelle"), what can he still look at? Having contemplated "the beautiful with that by which it can be seen" (211) (le beau au moyen de ce par quoi il est visible"), beyond all simulacra, he is united with it and is *really* virtuous; since he has perceived "authentic reality" ("réel authentique") he becomes dear to the divine and immortal.

This person would, then, have perceived what I shall call a *sensible transcendental,* the material texture of beauty. He would have "seen" the very spatiality of the visible, the real before all reality, all forms, all truth of particular sensations or of constructed idealities. Would he have contemplated the "nature" ("nature") of the divine? This is the support of the fabrication of the transcendent in its different modes, all of which, according to Diotima, are reached by the same propaedeutic: *the love of beauty.* Neither the good nor the true nor justice nor the government of the city would occur without beauty. And its strongest ally is love. Love therefore deserves to be venerated. And Diotima asks that her words be considered as a celebration and praise of Love.

In the second part of her speech, she used Love itself as a *means.* She cancelled out its intermediary function and subjected it to a *telos.* The power [puissance] of her method seems less evident to me here than at the beginning of her speech, when she made love the mediator of a becoming with no objective other than becoming. Perhaps Diotima is still saying the same thing. But her method, in the second part, risks losing its irreducible character and being replaced by a meta-physics. Unless what she proposes to contemplate, beauty itself, is understood as that which confuses the opposition between immanence and transcendence. An always already sensible horizon at the depths of which everything would appear. But it would be necessary to go back over the whole speech again to discover it in its enchantment.

Notes

Luce Irigaray, "L'amour Sorcier: Lecture de Platon, *Le Banquet,* Discours de Diotime. In: Luce Irigaray, 1984, pp. 27–39. Translation [originally] published by kind permission of Les Éditions de Minuit.

1. This and subsequent quotations from *The Symposium* are rendered in the English translation of Lane Cooper in Plato (1938) pp. 252–263. References in French, which follow in parentheses, are Irigaray's citations from the French translation of Léon Robin in Platon (1950).

2. In this and subsequent passages "Love" or "love" is rendered in English with the masculine pronoun—a translation required by French grammar. "L'Amour," capitalized, means "the God of Love"—Cupid or Eros, and is always masculine in French. "L'amour" uncapitalized, means "love" and is also standardly masculine in French. "Eros" and "Love" are interchangeable in English translations of most of Diotima's speech; a similar interchangeability exists in French. Historically, "l'amour" was feminine in French until it was made conventionally masculine to accord with Latin use. In poetry, uses of "l'amour" in the feminine persist to this day; but "l'amour" was not grammatically feminine in the passages from Plato that Irigaray was citing. Irigaray's argument in this essay can be read as an exploration of the ethical implications of these grammatical points. Cf. Grévisse (1964): 190–192. [Translator's note]

3. Irigaray is here exploiting the very characteristics of French grammar which exemplify her argument. "L'amant" must be masculine when any of the lovers is male; but it is also possible to specify that the lover is female, as in the title of her *Amante Marine ([Female] Lover from the Seas),* 1980. [Translator's note]

References

Grévisse, Maurice. 1964. *Le bon usage.* Gambloux: Éditions J. Duculot, S.A., 8th edition.
Irigaray, Luce. 1980. *Amante Marine.* Paris: Les Éditions de Minuit.
———. 1984. *Éthique de la différence sexuelle.* Paris: Les Éditions de Minuit.
Plato. 1938. Phaedrus, Ion, Gorgias, and Symposium, with passages from the Republic and Laws. Trans. Lane Cooper. New York: Oxford University Press.
Platon. 1950. Oeuvres Completes. Trans. Léon Robin. Paris: Gallimard (Bibliothèque de la Pléiade 58), I.

Reading the Slender Body

Susan Bordo

In the late-Victorian era, arguably for the first time in the West, those who could afford to eat well began systematically to deny themselves food in pursuit of an aesthetic ideal.[1] Certainly, other cultures had "dieted." Aristocratic Greek culture made a science of the regulation of food intake, in the service of the attainment of self-mastery and moderation.[2] Fasting, aimed at spiritual purification and domination of the flesh, was an important part of the repertoire of Christian practice in the Middle Ages.[3] These forms of "diet" can clearly be viewed as instruments for the development of a "self"—whether an "inner" self, for the Christians, or a public self, for the Greeks—constructed as an arena in which the deepest possibilities for human excellence might be realized. Rituals of fasting and asceticism were therefore reserved for the select few, aristocratic or priestly in caste, deemed capable of achieving such excellence of spirit. In the late nineteenth century, by contrast, the practices of body management begin to be middle-class preoccupations, and concern with diet becomes attached to the pursuit of an idealized physical weight or shape; it becomes a project in service of "body" rather than "soul." Fat, not appetite or desire, is the declared enemy, and people begin to measure their dietary achievements by the numbers on the scale rather than the level of their mastery of impulse and excess. The bourgeois "tyranny of slenderness" (as Kim Chernin has called it[4]) had begun its ascendancy (particularly over women), and with it the development of numerous technologies—diet, exercise, and, later on, chemicals and surgery—aimed at a purely physical transformation.

Today, we have become acutely aware of the massive and multifaceted nature of such technologies and the industries built around them. To the degree that a popular critical consciousness exists, however, it has been focused largely (and not surprisingly) on what has been viewed as pathological or extreme—on the unfortunate minority who become "obsessed," or go "too far." Television talk shows feature tales of disasters caused by stomach stapling, gastric bubbles, gastrointestinal bypass operations, liquid diets, compulsive exercising. Magazines warn of the dangers of fat-reduction surgery and liposuction. Books and articles about bulimia and anorexia nervosa proliferate. The portrayal of eating disorders by the popular media is often lurid and sensational; audiences gasp at pictures of skeletal bodies or at item-by-item descriptions of the volumes of food eaten during an average binge. Such presentations encourage a "side show" experience of the relationship between the ("normal")

audience and those on view ("the freaks"). To the degree that the audience may nonetheless recognize themselves in the behavior or reported experiences of those on stage, they confront themselves as "pathological" or outside the norm.

Of course, many of these behaviors *are* outside the norm, if only because of the financial resources they require. But preoccupation with fat, diet, and slenderness are not.[5] Indeed, such preoccupation may function as one of the most powerful "normalizing" strategies of our century, ensuring the production of self-monitoring and self-disciplining "docile bodies," sensitive to any departure from social norms, and habituated to self-improvement and transformation in the service of those norms.[6] Seen in this light, the focus on "pathology," disorder, accident, unexpected disaster, and bizarre behavior obscures the normalizing function of the technologies of diet and body management. For women, who are subject to such controls more profoundly and, historically, more ubiquitously than men, the focus on "pathology" (unless embedded in a political analysis) diverts recognition from a central means of the reproduction of gender.

This paper is part of a larger analysis of the contemporary preoccupation with slenderness as it functions within a modern, "normalizing" machinery of power in general, and, in particular, as it functions to reproduce gender-relations. For the purposes of this larger analysis, I make use of Foucault's distinction between two arenas of the social construction of the modern body—the "intelligible body" and the "useful body": (1) the representational, and (2) the practical, direct locus of social control, through which culture is converted into automatic, habitual bodily activity. The "intelligible body" includes scientific, philosophic, and aesthetic representations of the body, norms of beauty, models of health, and so forth. These representations, however, may also be seen as legislating a set of *practical* rules and regulations (some explicit, some implicit), through which the living body is "trained, shaped, obeys, and responds …;" becomes, in short, a socially adapted and "useful body."[7] So, for example, the seventeenth-century philosophic conception of body-as-machine arguably both mirrored and provided a metaphysical and technical model for an increasingly automated productive machinery of labor.

Understanding the "political anatomy" (as Foucault would call it) of the slender body requires the interrogation of both "useful" and "intelligible" arenas—interrogation of the practices or "disciplines" of diet and exercise which structure the organization of time, space, and the experience of embodiment for subjects; and, in our image-bedazzled culture, interrogation of the popular representations through which meaning is crystallized, symbolized, metaphorically encoded, and transmitted. My overall argument emphasizes the primacy of practice for evaluating the role of bodies in the nexus of power relations. In this light, we should certainly be "politically" disturbed by recent statistics on the number of young girls (80% of the nine-year-olds surveyed in one study[8]) who are making dedicated dieting the organizing principle of their days. This particular paper, however, will approach the normalizing role of diet and exercise via an examination of the representational body—the cultural imagery of ideal slenderness—which now reigns, increasingly across racial and ethnic boundaries, as the dominant body-standard of our culture.[9] More specifically, I wish to pursue here Mary Douglas's insight that images of the "microcosm"—the physical body—may symbolically reproduce central vulnerabilities and anxieties of the macrocosm—thef "social body."[10] I will explore this insight by "reading" (as the text or surface on which culture is symbolically "written") some dominant meanings that are connected, in our time, to the pursuit of slenderness.[11]

Decoding cultural images is a complex business—particularly when one considers the wide variety of ethnic, racial, and class differences that intersect with, resist, and give distinctive meaning to dominant, normalizing imagery. Even on the level of homogenizing imagery (my focus in this paper), contemporary slenderness admits of many variants and has multiple and often mutually "deconstructing" meanings. To give just one example, an examination of the photographs and copy of current fashion advertisements suggests that today's boyish body ideals, as in the 1920s, symbolize a new freedom, a casting off of the encumbrance of domestic, reproductive femininity. But when the same slender body is depicted in poses that set it off against the resurgent muscularity and bulk of the current male body-ideal, other meanings

emerge. In these gender/oppositional poses, the degree to which slenderness carries connotations of fragility, defenselessness, and lack of power over against a decisive male occupation of social space is dramatically represented.

Since it is impossible for any cultural analyst to do a full reading of the text of slenderness in the space of a single article, I will instead attempt to construct an argument about some elements of the cultural context that has conditioned the flourishing of eating disorders—anorexia, bulimia, and obesity—in our time. The first step in that argument is a decoding of the contemporary slenderness ideal so as to reveal the psychic anxieties and moral valuations contained within it—valuations concerning the correct and incorrect management of impulse and desire. In the process, I will be describing a key contrast between two different symbolic functions of body shape and size: (1) the designation of social position, e.g., marking class status or gender role; and (2) the outer indication of the state of the "soul." Next, aided by the significant work of Robert Crawford, I will turn to the "macro-body" of consumer culture, in order to demonstrate how the "correct" management of desire in that culture, requiring as it does a contradictory "double-bind" construction of personality, inevitably produces an unstable bulimic personality-type as its norm, along with the contrasting extremes of obesity and self-starvation.[12] These symbolize, I will argue, the contradictions of the "social body"—contradictions that make self-management a continual and virtually impossible task in our culture. Finally, I will introduce gender into this symbolic framework, showing how additional resonances (concerning the cultural management of female desire, on the one hand, and female flight from a purely reproductive destiny on the other) have overdetermined slenderness as the current ideal for women.

Slenderness and Contemporary Anxiety

In a recent edition of the magazine show *20/20*, several ten-year-old boys were shown some photos of fashion models. The models were pencil thin. Yet the pose was such that a small bulge of hip was forced, through the action of the body, into protuberance—as is natural, unavoidable on any but the most skeletal or the most tautly developed bodies. We bend over, we sit down, and the flesh coalesces in spots. These young boys, pointing to the hips, disgustedly pronounced the models to be "fat." Watching the show, I was appalled at the boys' reaction. Yet I couldn't deny that I had also been surprised at my own current perceptions while re-viewing female bodies in movies from the 1970s; what once appeared slender and fit now seemed loose and flabby. *Weight* was not the key element in these changed perceptions—my standards had not come to favor *thinner* bodies—but rather, I had come to expect a tighter, smoother, more "contained" body profile.

The self-criticisms of the anorectic, too, are usually focused on particular soft, protuberant areas of the body (most often the stomach) rather than on the body as a whole. Karen, in *Dying to Be Thin,* tries to dispel what she sees as the myth that the anorectic, even when emaciated, "misperceives" her body as fat:

> I hope I'm expressing myself properly here, because this is important. You have to understand. I don't see my whole body as fat. When I look in the mirror, I don't really see a fat person there. I see certain things about me that are really thin. Like my arms and legs. But I can tell the minute I eat certain things that my stomach blows up like a pig's. I know it gets distended. And it's disgusting. That's what I keep to myself—hug to myself.[13]

Or Barbara:

> Sometimes my body looks so bloated, I don't want to get dressed. I like the way it looks for exactly two days each month: usually, the eighth and ninth days after my period. Every other day, my breasts, my stomach—they're just awful lumps, bumps, bulges. My body can turn on me at any moment; it is an out-of-control mass of flesh.[14]

Much has been made of such descriptions, from both psychoanalytic and feminist perspectives. But for now, I wish to pursue these images of unwanted bulges and erupting stomachs in another direction than that of gender symbolism. I want to consider them as a metaphor for anxiety about internal processes out of control— uncontained desire, unrestrained hunger, uncontrolled impulse. Images of bodily eruption frequently function symbolically in this way in contemporary horror movies—as in recent werewolf films (*The Howling, An American Werewolf in London,*) and in David Cronenberg's remake of *The Fly*. The original *Fly* imagined a mechanical joining of fly parts and person parts, a variation on the standard "half-man, half-beast" image. In Cronenberg's *Fly*, as in the werewolf genre, a new, alien, libidinous, and uncontrollable self literally bursts through the seams of the victims' old flesh. (A related, frequently copied image occurs in *Alien*, where a parasite erupts from the chest of the human host.) While it is possible to view these new images as technically inspired by special effects possibilities, I suggest that deeper psycho-cultural anxieties are being given form.

Every year, I present my metaphysics class with Delmore Schwartz's classic "The Heavy Bear" as an example of a dualist imagination of self, in which the body is constructed as an alien, unconscious, appetitive force, thwarting and befouling the projects of the soul. Beginning with an epigraph from Alfred North Whitehead, "The withness of the body," Schwartz' poem makes "the heavy bear who goes with [him]" into "A caricature, a swollen shadow,/A stupid clown of the spirit's motive." Last year, for the first time, quite a few students interpreted the poem as describing the predicament of an obese man. This may indicate the increasing literalism of my students. But it also is suggested of the degree to which the specter of "fat" dominates their imaginations, and codes their generation's anxieties about the body's potential for excess and chaos. In advertisements, the construction of the body as an alien attacker, threatening to erupt in an unsightly display of bulging flesh, is a ubiquitous cultural image. Until the last decade, excess weight was the target of most ads for diet products; today, one is much more likely to find the enemy constructed as bulge, fat, or "flab." "Now" (a typical ad runs), "get rid of those embarrassing bumps, bulges, large stomach, flabby breasts and buttocks. Feel younger, and help prevent cellulite build-up. ... Have a nice shape with no tummy." To achieve such results (often envisioned as the absolute eradication of body: e.g., "no tummy") a violent assault on the enemy is usually required; bulges must be "attacked" and "destroyed," fat "burned," and stomachs (or, more disgustedly, "guts") must be "busted" and "eliminated." The increasing popularity of liposuction, a far from totally safe technique developed specifically to suck out the unwanted bulges of people of normal weight (it is not recommended for the obese), suggests how far our disgust with bodily bulges has gone. The ideal here is of a body that is absolutely tight, contained, "bolted down," firm (in other words, body that is protected against eruption from within, whose internal processes are under control). Areas that are soft, loose, or "wiggly" are unacceptable, even on extremely thin bodies. Cellulite management, like liposuction, has nothing to do with weight loss, and everything to do with the quest for firm bodily margins.

This perspective helps illuminate an important continuity of meaning between compulsive dieting and bodybuilding in our culture, and reveals why it has been so easy for contemporary images of female attractiveness to oscillate back and forth between a spare "minimalist" look and a solid, muscular, athletic look. The coexistence of these seemingly disparate images does not indicate that a postmodern universe of empty, endlessly differentiating images now reigns. Rather, the two ideals, though superficially very different, are united in battle against a common platoon of enemies: the soft, the loose; unsolid, excess flesh. It is perfectly permissible in our culture (even for women) to have substantial weight and bulk—so long as it is tightly managed. On the other hand, to be slim is simply not enough—so long as the flesh jiggles. Here, we arrive at one source of insight into why it is that the image of ideal slenderness has grown thinner and thinner over the last decade, and why women

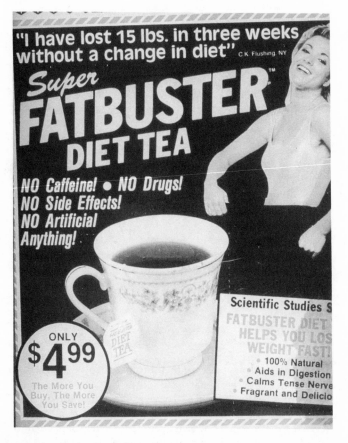

"I have lost 15 lbs. in three weeks without a change in diet" C.K. Flushing, NY

Super **FATBUSTER** DIET TEA

NO Caffeine! ● NO Drugs!
NO Side Effects!
NO Artificial
Anything!

ONLY
$**4**⁹⁹

The More You
Buy, The More
You Save!

Scientific Studies S
FATBUSTER DIET
HELPS YOU LOS
WEIGHT FAST!
● 100% Natural
● Aids in Digestion
● Calms Tense Nerve
● Fragrant and Delicio

with extremely slender bodies often still see themselves as "fat." Unless one goes the route of muscle building, it is virtually impossible to achieve a flab-less, excess-less body unless one trims very near to the bone.

Slenderness and the State of the Soul

The "moral" (and, as we shall see, economic) coding of the fat/slender body in terms of its capacities for self-containment and the control of impulse and desire represents the culmination of a developing historical change in the social symbolism of body weight and size. Until the late nineteenth century, the central discriminations marked were those of class, race, and gender; the body indicated one's social identity and "place." So, for example, the bulging stomachs of successful mid-nineteenth-century businessmen and politicians were a symbol of bourgeois success, an outward manifestation of their accumulated wealth.[15] By contrast, the gracefully slender body announced aristocratic status; disdainful of the bourgeois need to display wealth and power ostentatiously, it commanded social space invisibly rather than aggressively, seemingly above the commerce in appetite or the need to eat. Subsequently, this ideal began to be appropriated by the status-seeking middle class, as

slender wives became the showpieces of their husbands' success;[16] I will return to the gender symbolism of slenderness later.

Corpulence went out of middle-class vogue at the end of the century (even William Howard Taft, who had weighed over three hundred pounds while in office, went on a reducing diet); social power had come to be less dependent on the sheer accumulation of material wealth and more connected to the ability to control and manage the labor and resources of others. At the same time, excess body weight came to be seen as reflecting moral or personal inadequacy, or lack of will.[17] These associations are only possible in a culture of "overabundance" (that is, in a society in which those who control the production of "culture" have more than enough to eat). The moral requirement to diet depends upon the material preconditions that make the *choice* to "diet" an option and the possibility of personal "excess" a reality. Although slenderness has hitherto retained some of its traditional class-associations ("a woman can never to too rich or too thin"), the importance of this equation has eroded considerably over the last decade. Increasingly, the size and shape of the body has come to operate as a marker of personal, internal order (or disorder)—as a symbol for the state of the soul.

Consider one particularly clear example, that of changes in the meaning of the muscled body. Muscularity has had a variety of cultural meanings (until recently largely reserved for male bodies) which have prevented the well-developed body from playing too great a role in middle-class conceptions of attractiveness. Of course, muscles have symbolized masculine power. But at the same time, they have been associated with manual labor and chain gangs (and thus with lower-class and

even criminal status), and suffused with racial meaning (via numerous film representations of sweating, glistening bodies belonging to black slaves and prizefighters).
Given the racial and class biases of our culture, they were associated with the body as
material, unconscious, or animalistic. Today, however, the well-muscled body has
become a cultural icon; "working out" is a glamorized and sexualized yuppie activity. No longer signifying lower-class status (except when developed to extremes, at
which point the old association of muscles with brute, unconscious materiality surfaces once more), the firm, developed body has become a symbol of correct *attitude;*
it means that one "cares" about oneself and how one appears to others, suggesting
willpower, energy, control over infantile impulse, the ability to "make something" of
oneself. "You exercise, you diet," says Heather Locklear, promoting Bally Matrix Fitness Centre on television, "and you can do anything you want." Muscles express sexuality, but controlled, managed sexuality that is not about to erupt in unwanted and
embarrassing display.[18]

To the degree that the question of class still operates in all this, it relates to the category of social mobility (or lack of it) rather than class *location.* So, for example,
when associations of fat and lower-class status exist, they are usually mediated by
qualities of attitude or "soul"—fat being perceived as indicative of laziness, lack of
discipline, unwillingness to conform, and absence of all those "managerial" abilities
that, according to the dominant ideology, confer upward mobility. Correspondingly,
in popular teen movies such as *Flashdance* and *Vision Quest,* the ability of the (working-class) heroine and hero to pare, prune, tighten, and master the body operates as
a clear symbol of successful upward aspiration, of the penetrability of class boundaries to those who have "the right stuff." These movies (as one title explicitly suggests) are contemporary "quest myths"; like their prototype, *Rocky,* they follow the
struggle of an individual to attain a personal grail, against all odds, and through numerous trials. But unlike the film quests of a previous era (which sent Mr. Smith to
Washington and Mr. Deeds to town to battle the respective social evils of corrupt
government and big business), *Flashdance* and *Vision Quest* render the hero's and
heroine's commitment, will, and spiritual integrity through the metaphors of weight
loss, exercise, and tolerance of and ability to conquer physical pain and exhaustion.
(In *Vision Quest,* for example, the audience is encouraged to admire the young wres-
tler's perseverance when he ignores the fainting spells and nosebleeds caused by his
rigorous training and dieting.)

Not surprisingly, young people with eating disorders often thematize their own
experience in similar terms, as in the following excerpt from an interview with a
young woman runner:

> Well, I had the willpower. I could train for competition, and I could turn down food any
> time. I remember feeling that I was on a constant high. And the pain? Sure, there was
> pain. It was incredible. Between the hunger and the muscle pain from the constant
> workouts? I can't tell you how much I hurt.
>
> You may think I was crazy to put myself through constant, intense pain. But you have
> to remember. I was fighting a battle. And when you get hurt in a battle, you're proud of
> it. Sure, you may scream inside, but if you're brave and really good, then you take it qui-
> etly, because you know it's the price you pay for winning. And I needed to win. I really
> felt that if I didn't win, I would die ... all these enemy troops were coming at me, and I

had to outsmart them. If I could discipline myself enough—if I could keep myself lean and strong—then I could win. The pain was just a natural thing I had to deal with.[19]

As in *Vision Quest,* the external context is training for an athletic event. But here, too, that goal becomes subordinated to an internal one. The real battle, ultimately, is with the self. At this point, the limitations of the brief history that I presented in the opening paragraph of this paper are revealed. In that paragraph, the contemporary preoccupation with diet is contrasted to historical projects of body management suffused with moral meaning. In this section, however, I have suggested that examination of even the most "shallow" representations (teen movies) discloses a moral ideology—one, in fact, seemingly close to the aristocratic Greek ideal described by Foucault in *The Use of Pleasure.* The central element of that ideal, as Foucault describes it, is "an agonistic relation with the self"—aimed, not at the extirpation of desire and hunger in the interest of "purity" (as in the Christian strain of dualism), but at a "virile" mastery of desire through constant "spiritual combat."[20]

For the Greeks, however, the "virile" mastery of desire operated within a culture that valorized moderation. The culture of contemporary body-management, struggling to manage desire within a system that is dedicated to the proliferation of desirable commodities, is very different. In cultural fantasies such as *Vision Quest* and *Flashdance,* self-mastery is presented as an attainable and stable state; but, as I will argue in the next section of this paper, the reality of the contemporary agonism of the self is another matter entirely.

Slenderness and the Social Body

Mary Douglas, looking on the body as a system of "natural symbols" that reproduce social categories and concerns, has argued that anxiety about the maintenance of rigid bodily boundaries (manifested, for example, in rituals and prohibitions concerning excreta, saliva, and the strict delineation of "inside" and "outside") is most evident and intense in societies whose external boundaries are under attack.[21] Let me hypothesize, similarly, that preoccupation with the "internal" management of the body (i.e., management of its desires) is produced by instabilities in the "macro-regulation" of desire within the system of the social body.

In advanced consumer capitalism, as Robert Crawford has elegantly argued, an unstable, agonistic construction of personality is produced by the contradictory structure of economic life.[22] On the one hand, as "producer-selves," we must be capable of sublimating, delaying, repressing desires for immediate gratification; we must cultivate the work ethic. On the other hand, as "consumer-selves" we serve the system through a boundless capacity to capitulate to desire and indulge in impulse; we must become creatures who hunger for constant and immediate satisfaction. The regulation of desire thus becomes an ongoing problem, as we find ourselves continually besieged by temptation, while socially condemned for overindulgence. (It goes without saying that those who cannot afford to indulge, teased and frustrated by the culture, face different problems.)

Food and diet are central arenas for the expression of these contradictions. On television and in popular magazines with a flip of the page or barely a pause between commercials, images of luscious foods and the rhetoric of craving and desire are replaced by advertisements for grapefruit diets, low-calorie recipes, and exercise equipment. Even more disquieting than these manifest oppositions, however, are the constant attempts by advertisers to mystify them, suggesting that the contradiction doesn't really exist—that one *can* "have it all." Diets and exercise programs accordingly present themselves via the imagery of instant gratification ("From Fat to Fabulous in 21 Days," "Size 22 to Size 10 in No Time Flat," "Six Minutes to an Olympic-Class Stomach") and effortlessness ("3,000 Sit-Ups Without Moving an Inch ... Ten Miles of Jogging Lying Flat on Your Back," "85 pounds Without Dieting," and even, shamelessly, "Exercise Without Exercise"). In reality, however, the opposition is not so easily reconciled. Rather, it presents a classic "double-bind," in which the self is torn in two mutually incompatible directions. The contradiction is not an abstract one but stems from the specific historical construction of a "consuming passion" from which all inclinations toward balance, moderation, rationality, and foresight have been excluded.

Conditioned to lose control at the very sight of desirable products, we can only master our desires through rigid defenses against them. The slender body codes the tantalizing ideal of a well-managed self in which all is "in order" despite the contradictions of consumer culture. Thus, whether or not the struggle is played out in terms of food and diet, many of us may find our lives vacillating between a daytime rigidly ruled by the "performance principle" while our nights and weekends capitulate to unconscious "letting go" (food, shopping, liquor, television, and other addictive drugs). In this way, the central contradiction of the system inscribes itself on our bodies, and bulimia emerges as a characteristic modern personality construction, precisely and explicitly expressing the extreme development of the hunger for unrestrained consumption (exhibited in the bulimic's uncontrollable food-binges) existing in unstable tension alongside the requirement that we sober up, "clean up our act," get back in firm control on Monday morning (the necessity for purge—exhibited in the bulimic's vomiting, compulsive exercising, and laxative purges).

The same structural contradiction is also inscribed in what has been termed (incorrectly) the "paradox" that we have an "epidemic" of anorexia nervosa in this country "despite the fact that we have an overweight majority."[23] Far from paradoxical, the coexistence of anorexia and obesity reveals the instability of the contemporary personality construction, the difficulty of finding homeostasis between the "producer" and "consumer" aspects of the self. While bulimia embodies the unstable "double-bind" of consumer capitalism, anorexia and obesity embody an attempted "resolution" of that double-bind. Anorexia could therefore be seen as an extreme development of the capacity for self-denial and repression of desire (the work ethic in absolute "control"); obesity similarly points to an extreme capacity to capitulate to desire (consumerism in control). Both are rooted in the same consumer-culture construction of desire as overwhelming and overtaking the self. Given that construction, total submission or rigid defense become the only possible postures.[24]

Neither anorexia nor obesity is accepted by the culture as an appropriate response. The absolute conquest of hunger and desire (even in symbolic form) could never be tolerated by a consumer system—even if the Christian dualism of our culture also predisposes us to be dazzled by the anorectic's ability seemingly to transcend the flesh.[25] Anorectics are proud of this ability; but, as the disorder progresses, they usually feel the need to hide their skeletal bodies from those around them. If cultural attitudes toward the anorectic are ambivalent, however, reactions to the obese are not. As Marcia Millman documents in *Such a Pretty Face*, the obese elicit blinding rage and disgust in our culture, and are often viewed in terms that suggest an infant suck-

ing hungrily, unconsciously at its mother's breasts—greedy, self-absorbed, lazy, without self-control or willpower.[26] People avoid sitting near the obese; comics feel no need to restrain their cruelty; socially, they are unacceptable at public functions (one man wrote to "Dear Abby," saying that he was planning to replace his brother and sister-in-law as honor attendants at his wedding, because "they are both quite overweight"). Significantly, the part of the obese anatomy most often targeted for vicious attack, and most despised by the obese themselves, is the stomach—symbol of consumption (in the case of the obese, unrestrained consumption taking over the organism; one of Marcia Millman's interviewees recalls how the husband of a friend called hers "an awful, cancerous-looking growth").[27]

Slenderness, Self-Management and Normalization

Self-management in consumer culture, I have been arguing, becomes more elusive as it becomes more pressing. The attainment of an acceptable body is extremely difficult for those who do not come by it "naturally" (whether aided by genetics, metabolism, or high activity-level) and as the ideal becomes firmer and tauter it begins to exclude most people. Constant watchfulness over appetite and strenuous work on the body itself are required to conform to this ideal, while the most popular means of "correction"—dieting—often ensures its own failure, as the experience of deprivation leads to compensatory binging, with its attendant feelings of defeat, worthlessness, and loss of hope. Between the media images of self-containment and self-mastery and the reality of constant, everyday stress and anxiety about one's appearance lies the chasm which produces bodies habituated to self-monitoring and self-normalization.

Ultimately, the body (besides being evaluated for its success or failure at getting itself in order) is seen as demonstrating correct or incorrect attitudes toward the demands of normalization themselves. The obese and anorectic are therefore disturbing partly because they embody resistance to cultural norms. Bulimics, by contrast, typically strive for the conventionally attractive body shape dictated by their more "normative" pattern of managing desire. In the case of the obese, in particular, what is perceived as their defiant rebellion against normalization appears to be a source of the hostility they inspire. The anorectic at least pays homage to dominant cultural values, outdoing them in their own terms:

> I wanted people to look at me and see something special. I wanted to look in the face of a stranger and see admiration, so that I would know that I accomplished something that was just about impossible for most people, especially in our society. … From what I've seen, more people fail at losing weight than at any other single goal. I found out how to do what everyone else couldn't: I could lose as much or as little weight as I wanted. And that meant I was better than everyone else.[28]

The anorectic thus strives to stand above the crowd by excelling at its own rules; in so doing, however, she exposes the hidden penalties. But the obese—partiularly those who claim to be happy although overweight—are perceived as not playing by the rules at all. While the rest of us struggle to be acceptable and "normal," they must not be allowed to get away with it; they must be put in their place, humiliated, and defeated.

A number of recent talk shows make this abundantly clear. On one, much of the audience reaction was given over to disbelief, and the attempt to prove to one obese woman that she was *not* happy: "I can't believe you don't want to be slim and beautiful, I just can't believe it," "I heard you talk a lot about how you feel good about yourself and you like yourself, but I really think you're kidding yourself," "It's hard for me to believe that Mary Jane is really happy … you don't fit into chairs, it's hard to get through the doorway. My God, on the subway, forget it." When Mary Jane persisted in her assertion that she was happy, she was warned, in a viciously self-righteous tone, that it wouldn't last: "Mary Jane, to be the way you are today, you had better start going on a diet soon, because if you don't you're going to get bigger and bigger and bigger. It's true."[29] On another show, in an effort to subdue an increasingly hostile and offensive audience, one of the doctor-guests kept trying to reassure them the "fat and happy" target of their attacks did not *really* mean that she didn't *want* to lose weight; rather, she was simply tired of trying and failing. This is the construction that allows people to give their sympathy to the obese, assuming as it does the obese person's acknowledgement that to be "normal" is the most desired goal, elusive only because of personal inadequacy. Those who are willing to present themselves as pitiable, in pain, and conscious of their own unattractiveness—often demonstrated, on these shows, by self-admissions about intimate physical difficulties, orgies of self-hate or descriptions of gross consumption of food, win the sympathy and concern of the audience.

Slenderness and Gender

It has been amply documented that women in our culture are more tyrannized by the contemporary slenderness ideal than men, as they typically have been by beauty ideals in general. It is far more important to men than to women that their partners be slim.[30] Women are much more prone than men to perceive themselves as "too fat."[31] And, as is by now well known, girls and women are more likely to engage in crash dieting, laxative abuse, and compulsive exercising, and are far more vulnerable to eating disorders than males.[32] But eating disorders are not only "about" slenderness, any more than (as I have been arguing) *slenderness* is only—or even chiefly—about slenderness. My aim in this section, therefore, is not to "explain" facts about which so much has now been written from historical, psychological, and sociological points of view. Rather, I want to remain with the image of the slender body, confronting it now both as a gendered body (the slender body as female body—the usual form in which the image is displayed) and as a body whose gender meaning is never neutral. This "layer" of gender-coded signification, suffusing other meanings, overdetermines slenderness as a contemporary ideal of specifically *female* attractiveness.

The exploration of contemporary slenderness as a metaphor for the correct management of desire becomes more adequate when we confront the fact that hunger has always been a potent cultural metaphor for female sexuality, power, and desire—from the blood-craving Kali, who in one representation is shown devouring her own entrails, to the language of insatiability and voraciousness that marks the fifteenth-century discourse on witches, to the "Man-Eater" of contemporary rock lyrics: "Oh, oh, here she comes, watch out boys, she'll chew you up." This is a message, too, as I have argued elsewhere, that eating-disordered women have often internalized when they experience their battle with hunger in the gendered terms of a struggle between male and female sides of the self (the former described as "spiritual" and disciplined, the latter as appetitive and dangerous). In the anorectic's lexicon, and throughout dominant Western religious and philosophical traditions, the "virile" capacity for self-management is decisively coded as male. By contrast, all those "bodily" spontaneities—hunger, sexuality, the emotions—seen as needful of containment and control have been culturally constructed and coded as female.[33]

The management of female desire becomes a particular problem in phallocentric cultures. Women's desires are "other," mysterious, threatening to erupt and challenge the patriarchal order. Some writers have argued that female hunger (as a code for female desire) is especially problematized during periods of disruption and change in established gender-relations and in the position of women. In such periods (of

which our own is arguably one), nightmare images of what Bram Djikstra has called "the consuming woman" theme proliferate in art and literature (images representing female desire unleashed), while dominant constructions of the female body become more sylphlike—unlike the body of a fully developed woman, more like that of an adolescent or boy (images that might be called female desire unborn). Djikstra argues such a case concerning the late nineteenth century, pointing to the devouring sphinxes and bloodsucking vampires of *fin-de-siècle* art, and the accompanying vogue for elongated, "sublimely emaciated" female bodies.[34] A commentator at the time vividly describes the emergence of a new body-style, not very unlike our own:

> Women can change the cut of their clothes at will, but how can they change the cut of their anatomies? And yet, they have done just this thing. Their shoulders have become narrow and slightly sloping, their throats more slender, their hips smaller and their arms and legs elongated to an extent that suggests that bed, upon which the robber, Procrustes, used to stretch his victims …[35]

The fact that our own era has witnessed a comparable shift (from the hourglass figure of the fifties to the lanky, "androgynous," increasingly elongated slender look that has developed over the past decade) cries out for interpretation. This shift, however, needs to be interpreted not only from the standpoint of male anxiety over women's desires (Djikstra's analysis, while crucial, is only half the story), but also from the standpoint of the women who embrace the "new look." For them, it may have a very different meaning; it may symbolize, not so much the containment of female desire, as its liberation from a domestic, reproductive destiny. The fact that the slender female body can carry both these (seemingly contradictory) meanings is one reason, I would suggest, for its compelling attraction in periods of gender-change.[36]

To elaborate this argument in more detail: earlier, I presented some quotations from interviews with eating-disordered women in which they describe their revulsion to breasts, stomachs, and all other bodily bulges. At that point, I subjected these quotations to a "gender-neutral" reading. While not rescinding that interpretation, I want to overlay it now with another reading, which I have developed at greater length elsewhere.[37] The characteristic anorexic revulsion toward hips, stomach, and breasts (often accompanied by a disgust at menstruation, and relief at amenorrhoea) might be viewed as expressing rebellion against maternal, domestic femininity—a femininity that represents both the suffocating control the anorectic experiences her own mother as having had over her, *and* the mother's actual lack of position and authority outside the domestic arena. Here we encounter another reason for anxiety over soft, protuberant body-parts. They evoke helpless infancy and symbolize maternal femininity as it has been constructed over the last hundred years in the West. That femininity, as Dorothy Dinnerstein has argued, is perceived as both frighteningly powerful and, as the child comes increasingly to recognize the hierarchical nature of the sexual division-of-labor, as utterly powerless.[38]

The most literal symbolic form of maternal femininity is represented by the nineteenth-century "hourglass" figure, emphasizing breasts and hips—the markers of reproductive femaleness—against a wasp waist.[39] At the same time, the sharp contrast between the female and male form, made possible by the use of corsets, bustles, and so forth, reproduced on the body the dualistic division of social and economic life into clearly defined "male" and "female" spheres. It is not until the post-World War II period, with its relocation of women from factory to home and its coercive bourgeois dualism of the happy-homemaker-mother and the responsible, "provider" father, that such clear bodily demarcation of "male" and "female" spheres surfaces again. The era of the cinch belt, the pushup bra, and Marilyn Monroe could be viewed, for the body, as an era of "resurgent Victorianism."[40] It was also the last coercively normalizing body-ideal to reign before the beginnings of the ascendancy of boyish slenderness, in the mid-1960s.

From this perspective, one might speculate that the boys who reacted with disgust or anxiety to fleshy female parts were reacting to evocations of maternal power, newly threatening in an age when women can bring their desires out of the confinements of the home and into the public, traditionally male arena.[41] The buxom Sophia Loren was a sex goddess in an era when women were trained to channel their energy and desire into home, husband, and family. Today, it is required of that energy, loose in the public world, to be stripped of its psychic resonances with maternal power, and normalized according to the professional "male" standards of the public arena. From the standpoint of male anxiety, the lean body of the professional businesswoman today may symbolize such a neutralization. With her body and her dress, she declares symbolic allegiance to the professional, white, male world, along

with her lack of intention to subvert that arena with alternative "female values." At the same time, insofar as she is clearly "dressing up," *playing* "male" (almost always with a "softening" fashion touch to establish traditional feminine decorativeness), she represents no serious competition (symbolically, that is) to the "real men" of the workplace.

The cultural association of slenderness with reduced power and contracted social space is strikingly revealed, as I mentioned earlier, in fashion poses that juxtapose the slender female body against the currently quite solid and powerful male body ideal. But for many women, this "androgynous" ideal, far from symbolizing reduced power, may symbolize freedom (as it did in the 1890s and 1920s) from a reproductive destiny and a construction of femininity seen as constraining and suffocating. Correspondingly, taking on the accoutrements of the white, male world may be experienced as empowerment by women themselves, and as their chance to embody qualities—detachment, self-containment, self-mastery, control—that are highly valued in our culture.[42] The slender body, as I have argued earlier, symbolizes such qualities. "It was about power," says Kim Morgan, speaking of her obsession with slenderness, "that was the big thing ... something I could throw in people's faces, and they would look at me and I'd only weigh this much, but I was strong and in control, and hey *you're* sloppy. ..."[43] The taking on of "male" power-as-self-mastery is another locus where shedding pounds and developing muscles, for all their surface dissimilarities, intersect. Appropriately, the new "Joy of Cooking" takes place in the gym, in one advertisement that shamelessly exploits the associations of female bodybuilding and liberation from a traditional, domestic destiny.

In the intersection of these gender-issues and more general cultural dilemmas concerning the management of desire, we see how the tightly managed body—whether demonstrated through sleek, minimalist lines or firmly developed mus-cles—has been overdetermined as a contemporary ideal of specifically female attrac-tiveness. The axis of consumption/production is gender-overlaid, as I have argued, by the hierarchical dualism which constructs a dangerous, appetitive, bodily "female principle" in opposition to a masterful "male" will. We would thus expect that when the regulation of desire becomes especially problematic (as it is in advanced con-sumer cultures), women and their bodies will pay the greatest symbolic and material toll. When such a situation is compounded by anxiety about *women's* desires in periods when traditional forms of gender-organization are being challenged, this toll is multiplied. It would be wrong to suppose, however, that it is exacted through the simple *repression* of female hunger. Rather, here as elsewhere, power works also "from below," as women associate slenderness and self-management via the experience of newfound freedom (from a domestic destiny) and empowerment in the public arena. In this connection, we might note the difference between contemporary ideals of slenderness, coded in terms of self-mastery and expressed through traditionally "male" body symbolism, and mid-Victorian ideals of female slenderness, which symbolically emphasized reproductive femininity corseted under tight "external" constraints. But whether externally bound or internally managed, no body can escape either the imprint of culture or its gendered meanings.

Notes

1. See Keith Walden, "The Road to Fat City: An Interpretation of the Development of Weight Consciousness in Western Society," *Historical Reflections* 12:3 (1985):331–373.

2. See Michel Foucault, *The Use of Pleasure* (New York: Random House, 1986).

3. See Rudolph Bell, *Holy Anorexia* (Chicago: University of Chicago Press, 1985); and Carolyn Bynum, *Holy Feast and Holy Fast: The Religious Significance of Food to Medieval Women* (Berkeley: University of California Press, 1987), 31–48.

4. See Kim Chernin, *the Obsession: Reflections of the Tyranny of Slenderness* (New York: Harper and Row, 1981).

5. See Thomas Cash, Barbara Winstead, and Louis Janda, "The Great American Shape-up," *Psychology Today*, April 1986; "Dieting: The Losing Game" *Time*, 20 January 1986, among numerous other general reports. Concerning women's preoccupation in particular, see n. 41 below.

6. For Foucault on "docile bodies," see *Discipline and Punish* (New York: Vintage, 1979), 135–69. For an application of Foucault's ideas to the practices of diet and fitness, see Walden, "The Road to Fat City." For a Foucauldian analysis of the practices of femininity, see Sandra Bartky, "Foucault, Femininity, and the Modernization of Patriarchal Power," in *Feminism and Foucault*, ed. Irene Diamond and Lee Quinby (Boston: Northeastern University Press, 1988), 61–86.

7. Foucault (1979), 136.

8. "Fat or Not, 4th Grade Girls Diet Lest They Be Teased or Unloved," *Wall Street Journal*, 11 February 1986 (based on a University of California study). A still more recent study conducted at the University of Ottawa concluded that by age 7, a majority of young girls are anxious about their weight, and convinced they are much fatter than they are. ("Girls, at 7, Think Thin, Study Finds," *New York Times*, February 11, 1988).

9. On the "spreading" nature of eating disorders, see Paul Garfinkel and David Garner, *Anorexia Nervosa: A Multidimensional Perspective* (New York: Bruner Mazel, 1982), 102–03; and George Hsu, "Are Eating Disorders Becoming More Common in Blacks?" *The International Journal of Eating Disorders* 6:1 (January 1987):113–24. Despite these trends, resistance to the slenderness ideal persists, and should not be overlooked as a source of insight into different cultural models of beauty and the conditions that promote them.

10. See Mary Douglas, *Natural Symbols* (New York: Pantheon, 1982); and *Purity and Danger* (London: Routledge and Kegan Paul, 1966).

11. This approach presupposes, of course, that popular cultural images *have* meaning, and are not merely arbitrary formations spawned by the whimsy of "fashion," the vicissitudes of Madison Avenue, or the "logic" of postindustrial capitalism, within which (as it has been argued, by Frederick and others) a product or image's attraction derives solely from pure differentiation, from its cultural positioning, its suggestion of the novel or new. Within such a "postmodern" logic, Gail Faurschou argues, "Fashion has become the commodity 'par excellence.' It is fed by all of capitalism's incessant, frantic, reproductive passion and power. Fashion

is the logic of planned obsolescence—not just the necessity for market survival, but the cycle of desire itself, the endless process through which the body is decoded and recoded, in order to define and inhabit the newest territorialized spaces of capital's expansion;" "Fashion and the Cultural Logic of Postmodernity," *Canadian Journal of Political and Social Theory* 11:1–2 (1987):72. While I don't disagree with Faurschou's general characterization of "fashion" here, the heralding of an absolute historical break, after which images have become completely empty of history, substance, and symbolic determination, seems *itself* an embodiment, rather than a de-mystifier, of the compulsively innovative logic of postmodernity. More important to the argument of this piece, a "postmodern logic" cannot explain the magnetic cultural hold of the slenderness ideal, long after any novel juxtaposition with more fleshy forms from the 1950s has worn off. Many times, in fact, the principle of the "new" has made tentative, but ultimately nominal, gestures toward the end of the reign of thinness, announcing a "softer," "curvier" look, and so forth. How many women have picked up magazines whose covers declared such a turn, only to find that the images within remain essentially continuous with prevailing norms? Large breasts may be making a comeback, but they are attached to extremely thin, often athletic bodies. Here, I would suggest, there are constraints on the pure logic of postmodernity— constraints that this paper tries to explore.

12. See Robert Crawford, "A Cultural Account of 'Health'—Self-Control, Release, and the Social Body," *Issues in the Political Economy of Health Care,* ed. John McKinlay (New York: Methuen, 1985), 60–103. I want to stress that my own analysis is not intended to "explain" eating disorders, which, as I have argued elsewhere, are a complex, multidetermined formation requiring analysis and interpretation on many levels.

13. Ira Sacker and Marc Zimmer, *Dying To Be Thin* (New York: Warner, 1987), 57.

14. Dalma Heyn, "Body Vision?" *Mademoiselle,* April 1987, 213.

15. See Lois Banner, *American Beauty* (Chicago: University of Chicago Press, 1983), 232.

16. Ibid., 53–55.

17. See Walden, *Historical Reflections* 12:3, 334–35, 353.

18. I thank Mario Moussa for this point, and for the Heather Locklear quotation.

19. Ira Sacker and Marc Zimmer, 149–50.

20. Foucault (1986), 64–70.

21. See Mary Douglas, *Purity and Danger,* 114–28.

22. See Robert Crawford, "A Cultural Account of 'Health.'"

23. John Farquhar, Stanford University Medical Center, quoted in "Dieting: The Losing Game," *Time,* 20 February 1986, 57.

24. I discuss the construction of hunger in eating disorders more fully in "Anorexia Nervosa: Psychopathology at the Crystallization of Culture," *The Philosophical Forum* 17:2 (Winter 1985), 33–103.

25. While there has been controversy over the appropriateness of describing medieval saints as "anorexic" (see, for example, Bell, *Holy Anorexia,* and Bynum, *Holy Feast and Holy Fast* for different views on the subject), no one, as far as I am aware, has noticed that a stronger case can be made for focusing on the "spiritual" aspects of the ascetism of modern-day anorectics. As I suggest in "Anorexia Nervosa: Psychopathology as the Crystallization of Culture," it is striking how often the imagery of anorectics includes Christian/ascetic themes, with a dualistic construction of mind/matter and spirit/appetite coded in terms of purity/contamination, and the ultimate goal of cleansing the soul of desire/hunger. Thus, certain foods are seen by the anorectic as tainted, contaminating, and dangerous, while the practice of self-denial and, at times, self-mortification, is seen as purifying. "Fasting," says Clement of Alexandria (d.ca. 215), "empties the soul of matter and makes it, with the body, clear and light for the reception of divine truth" (Bynum, p. 36). A similar war against matter, and the association of the dematerialized (i.e., thin) body with enhanced and purified vision, provides common images in the self-descriptions of anorectics, where comparisons with medieval ascetism are explicitly offered. Compare, for example, the words of "a certain Daniel" from the medieval *Sayings of the Fathers:* "As the body waxes fat, the soul grows thin; and as the body grows thin, the soul by

so much waxes fat" (Bynum, p. 216) with those of a contemporary anorectic: "My soul seemed to grow as my body waned. I felt like one of those early Christian saints who starved themselves in the desert sun" (Bordo, "Anorexia Nervosa," p. 88).

26. See Marcia Millman, *Such a Pretty Face: Being Fat in America* (New York: Norton, 1980), esp. 65–79.

27. Ibid., 77.

28. Ira Sacker and Marc Zimmer, 32.

29. These quotations are taken from transcripts of the Phil Donahue show, provided by Multimedia Entertainment, Cincinnati, Ohio.

30. The discrepancy emerges very early, according to recent studies. "We don't expect boys to be that handsome," says a nine-year-old girl in the California study cited above. "But boys expect girls to be perfect and beautiful. And skinny." Her male classmate agrees: "Fat girls aren't like regular girls," he says. Many of my female students have described in their journals the pressure their boyfriends place on them to stay or get slim. They have plenty of social support for such demands. Sylvester Stallone told Cornelia Guest that he liked his woman "anorexic"; she immediately lost 24 pounds (*Time*, 18 April, 1988, 89). But few men want their women to go that far; Actress Valerie Bertinelli reports (*Syracuse Post*) how her husband, Eddie Van Halen, "helps keep her in shape": "When I get too heavy, he says, 'Honey, lose weight.' Then when I get too thin, he says, "I don't like making love with you, you've got to gain some weight."

31. The most famous of such studies, by now replicated many times, appeared in *Glamour*, February 1984; a poll of 33,000 women revealed that 75 percent considered themselves "too fat," while only 25 percent of them were above Metropolitan Life Insurance standards, and 30 percent were *below*. ("Feeling Fat in a Thin Society," p. 86). See also Kevin Thompson, "Larger than Life," *Psychology Today*, April 1986; Dalma Heyn, "Why We're Never Satisfied With Our Bodies," *McCalls*, May 1982; Daniel Goleman, "Dislike of Own Body Found Common Among Women," *New York Times*, 19 March, 1985.

32. 90 percent of all sufferers from eating disorders are female, a fact that has been explored from many clinical, historical, psychological, and cultural angles. Some of the most profound insights—insights that have become incorporated, often without adequate acknowledgement, into more recent clinical and scholarly literature—have come from Kim Chernin, *The Obsession, the Hungry Self* (New York: Harper and Row, 1981) and Susie Ohrbach, *Hunger Strike: The Anorectic's Struggle as a Metaphor for Our Age* (New York: Norton, 1986).

33. See Bordo, "Anorexia Nervosa." On female hunger as a metaphor for female sexuality in Victorian literature, see Helena Michie, *The Flesh Made Word* (New York: Oxford, 1987). On cultural associations of male/mind and female/matter, see, for instance, Dorothy Dinnerstein, *The Mermaid and the Minotaur* (New York: Harper and Row, 1977), Genevieve Lloyd, *The Man of Reason* (Minneapolis: University of Minnesota Press, 1984), and Luce Irigaray, *Speculum of the Other Woman* (Ithaca: Cornell University Press, 1985).

34. Bram Djikstra, *Idols of Perversity* (New York: Oxford University Press, 1986), 29.

35. "Mutable Beauty," *Saturday Night*, 1 February, 1902, 9.

36. Mary Jacobus and Sally Shuttleworth, pointing to the sometimes boyish figure of the "new woman" of late-Victorian literature, have suggested to me the appropriateness of this interpretation for the late-Victorian era; I have, however, chosen to argue the point only with respect to the current context.

37. Bordo, "Anorexia Nervosa."

38. See Chernin, for an exploration of thee connection between early infant experience and attitudes toward the fleshy, female body. For the impact on clinical literature of the feminist/ cultural argument about anorexia, see Susan Wooley, "Intensive Treatment of Bulimia and Body-Image Disturbance," in *Handbook of Eating Disorders*, ed. Kelly D. Brownell and John P. Foreyt (New York: Basic Books, 1986), 476–502.

39. Historian LeeAnn Whites has pointed out to me how perverse this body-symbolism seems when we remember what a pregnant and nursing body is actually like. The hourglass

figure is really more correctly a symbolic "advertisement" to men of the woman's reproductive, domestic *sphere* than a representation of her reproductive *body*.

40. See Banner, 283–85.

41. It is no accident, I believe, that Dolly Parton, now down to 100 pounds and truly looking as though she might snap in two in a strong wind, opened her new show with a statement of its implicitly antifeminist premise: "I'll bust my butt to please you!" (Surely she already has?) Her television presence is now recessive, beseeching, desiring only to serve; clearly, her packagers are exploiting the cultural resonances of her diminished physicality. Parton, of course, is no androgynous body-type. Rather, like *Wheel of Fortune's* Vanna White (who also lost a great deal of weight at one point in her career, and is obsessive about staying thin) she has tremendous appeal to those longing for a more "traditional" femininity in an era when women's public presence and power have greatly increased. Parton and White's large breasts evoke a nurturing, maternal sexuality. But after weight-reduction regimens set to anorexic standards, those breasts now adorn bodies that are vulnerably, breakably thin, with fragile, spindly arms and legs like those of young colts. Parton and White suggest the pleasures of nurturant female sexuality without an encounter with its powers and dangers.

42. See my essay, "The Body and the Reproduction of Femininity: A Feminist Appropriation of Foucault" in *Gender/Body/Knowledge: Feminist Reconstructions of Being and Knowing,* ed. Susan Bordo and Alison Jaggar (New Jersey: Rutgers University Press, 1989), for elaboration of these points.

43. "The Waist Land: Eating Disorders in America," 1985, Gannett Corporation, *MTI* Teleprograms. The analysis presented here becomes more complicated with bulimia, in which the hungering "female" self refuses to be annihilated, and feminine ideals are typically not rejected but embraced. See also Bordo, "How Television Teaches Women to Hate Their Hungers," *Mirror Images* (Newsletter of Anorexia/Bulimia Support, Syracuse, N.Y.), 4:1 (1986): 8–9.

Suggested Further Readings

Alcoff, Linda. "Cultural Feminism Versus Post-Structuralism and the Identity Crisis in Feminist Theory." *Signs: Journal of Women in Culture and Society* 13, no. 3 (1988):405–436.

Allen, Jeffner, and Iris Marion Young, eds. *The Thinking Muse: Feminism and Modern French Philosophy.* Bloomington: Indiana University Press, 1989.

Bordo, Susan. "Reading the Slender Body." In *Body/Politics: Women and the Discourses of Science,* ed. Mary Jacobus, Evelyn Fox Keller, and Sally Shuttleworth, pp. 83–112. New York: Routledge, 1990.

Butler, Judith. "The Body Politics of Julia Kristeva." *Hypatia* 3, no. 3 (Winter 1989):104–118.

Cixous, Helene. "Sorties." In *New French Feminisms,* ed. Elaine Marks and Isabelle de Courtivron, pp. 90–98. New York: Schocken Books, 1971.

De Lauretis, Teresa, ed. *Feminist Studies, Critical Studies.* Bloomington: Indiana University Press, 1986.

Duchan, Claire. *Feminism in France: From May '68 to Mitterrand.* London: Routledge and Kegan Paul, 1986.

Flax, Jane. *Thinking Fragments: Psychoanalysis. Feminism, and Postmodernism in the Contemporary West.* Berkeley: University of California Press, 1989.

Fraser, Nancy. *Unruly Practices: Power, Discourse, and Gender in Contemporary Social Theory,* pp. 69–92. Minneapolis: University of Minnesota Press, 1989.

Fraser, Nancy, and Linda Nicholson. "Social Criticism Without Philosophy: An Encounter Between Feminism and Postmodernism." In *Feminism/Postmodernism,* ed. Linda J. Nicholson, pp. 19–38. New York: Routledge, 1990.

Gallop, Jane. "The Ladies' Man." *Diacritics* 5, no. 4 (Winter 1976):28–34.

Irigaray, Luce. "When Our Lips Speak Together." *Signs: Journal of Women in Culture and Society* 6, no. 1, (1980):4–28.

_____. "And the One Doesn't Stir Without the Other." *Signs: Journal of Women in Culture and Society* 7, no. 1 (1981):60–67.

Kristeva, Julia. "Women's Time." *Signs: Journal of Women in Culture and Society* 7, no. 1 (1981):13–35.

Marks, Elaine. "Review Essay: Women and Literature in France." *Signs: Journal of Women in Culture and Society* 3, no. 4 (1978):832–842.

Marks, Elaine, and Isabelle de Courtivron. *New French Feminisms: An Anthology.* Amherst: University of Massachusetts Press, 1980.

Moi, Toril, ed. *French Feminist Thought: A Reader.* New York: Blackwell, 1987.

Sawicki, Jana. "Feminism and the Power of Foucauldian Discourse." In *After Foucault: Humanistic Knowledges, Postmodern Challenges,* ed. Jonathan Arac. New Brunswick, N.J.: Rutgers University Press, 1988.

_____. "Foucalt and Feminism: Toward a Politics of Difference." In *Feminist Interpretations and Political Theory,* ed. Mary Lyndon Shanley and Carole Pateman, pp. 217–231. University Park: Pennsylvania State University Press, 1991.

Weedon, Chris. *Feminist Practice and Poststructuralist Theory.* Oxford: Basil Blackwell, 1987.

PERSPECTIVES ON THE
INTERSECTIONS OF RACE,
CLASS, AND GENDER

Liberal, Marxist, radical, psychoanalytic, socialist, anarcha, ecological, phenomeno-logical, and postmodern feminist perspectives offer us different theoretical lenses through which we can view the complexity of women's condition. As illuminating as these lenses are, however, they are not illuminating enough. To a greater or lesser de-gree, each of them fails to see how race, ethnicity, class, religion, sexual identity, phys-ical and psychological status, and age affect any and all gender-based analyses. In-deed, it has become painfully clear that the "feminist perspectives" professors and students tend to teach and learn reflect the interests of the white, extremely well-edu-cated, and otherwise privileged Anglo-American or European women who have con-ceived them.

To be sure, a variety of feminist thinkers have tried to use more categories than gen-der in their analyses of woman's oppression and liberation. Marxist feminists have at-tended to uses of class, and radical feminists have fought the institution(s) of hetero-sexuality. Socialist feminists have struggled to say something that describes both "Woman" in general and women in the particularities, whereas postmodern feminists have sought to describe the difference(s) that women reflect. But all of these feminist thinkers, as well as those who have previously neglected matters of race and class, are eager to broaden and deepen their theories—to provide analyses that make sense to a wide variety of women ad not simply to women like themselves.

In the spirit of friendship, María Lugones honestly communicates to Elizabeth Spelman in their collaborative contribution to this volume, "Have We Got a Theory for You," what disappoints her about traditional feminist thought: It tends to treat her as the other—the Hispanic anomaly that must be fit into an Anglo framework. Lugones and Spelman challenge feminist theorists to do what has never been done before—to conceive a theory that celebrates women's different ways of thinking, doing, and being without separating women from each other on account of these differences. They also challenge feminist theorists not to write about "Woman" in general, for no such abstraction exists. Finally, they challenge feminist theorists to ferret out the racism, classism, ethnocentrism, imperialism, and heterosexism in feminist writings—"isms" that prevent women from being friends.

Lugones is particularly helpful when she describes two different ways for one woman to account for another's experience. She claims that "it is one thing for both me and you to observe you and come up with our different accounts of what you are doing (insider/outsider); it is quite another for me to observe myself and others much like me culturally and in other ways and to develop an account of myself and then use that account to give an account of you." Whereas the former strategy affords possibilities for dialogue about diverging interpretations, the latter strategy represents the imposition of one woman's experience upon another's. Anglo women, for example, have for too long simply assumed that their way of understanding women's oppression is the best way to understand not only their own oppression but also that of Hispanic women.

Lugones and Spelman call upon feminists to redo all of feminist theory. They realize the enormity of this task and wonder whether each group of women should do it *separately* or if all women should do it *jointly.* If women decide to theorize together, however, it will be hard for Anglo women to give up their privileged position. They will be able to succeed in what represents truly collaborative work only if they are properly motivated. They must not, says Lugones, be motivated either by "self-interest" (learning about the other in order to manipulate or dominate the other) or by "duty" (learning about the other because that is the proper thing for politically correct feminists to do). Rather, they must be motivated by the desire for friendship (learning about the other because the other is delightful).

Whereas Lugones and Spelman focus on the limits of feminist theory in general, Elizabeth Abel focuses on the limits of psychoanalytic feminism in particular in her essay, "Race, Class, and Psychoanalysis? Opening Questions." Even though psychoanalytic feminists have avoided most of the Freudian fathers' sins, a certain essentialism haunts their writing. Whether they follow Lacan or the exponents of object-relations theory, most psychoanalytic feminists choose to elevate a particular kind of family—heterosexual, upper-middle-class, Anglo-American, or European—into some sort of Universal Family. In so doing, says Abel, they fail to address gender relations in particular families, very few of which resemble the paradigm of the "Universal Family."

Convinced that masculine and feminine identity and behavior are substantially shaped by one's race and class, Abel shows how Hortense J. Spellers and Carolyn Kay Steedman use the categories of race and class, respectively, to politicize psychoanalytic thought. For example, she underscores Spellers's observation that whereas reproduction is "maternity" for the wife of a slave owner, it is "breeding" for the female slave. The daughter of a female slave will grow up with very different ideas about pregnancy and childbirth than will the daughter of the woman who, through her husband, owns as slaves both daughter and mother. For the slave woman, reproduction is not "female-rite/might"; it is simply the process by which the master's stock is increased. Similarly, Abel affirms Steedman's observation that a working-class daughter who witnesses her father being verbally abused by his boss will identify with her father's oppression as much as with her mother's. Even if he possesses a penis, a man is no more "masculine" than a woman is unless he is among society's commanders and controllers. The phallus, not the penis, is the source of power.

Like Abel, Patricia Hill Collins is convinced that any thorough analysis of gender must be attentive to issues of class and race. Collins contrasts "Eurocentric masculinist" epistemology with "Afrocentric feminist" epistemology in her article, "The Social Construction of Black Feminist Thought." Eurocentric masculinist epistemology (1) creates a gap between the researcher and the "object" of his or her study; (2) claims that knowledge is derived from thought, not feeling; (3) separates ethics from science; and (4) relies on an adversarial style of argument. In contrast, an Afrocentric feminist epistemology (1) refuses to distance the "subject" from the "object"; (2) insists that the emotions, no less than reason, are constitutive of knowledge; (3) claims that what is "true" cannot be separated from what is "good"; and (4) favors dialogue as the preferred path to whatever is available in the way of truth.

Although Collins's Afrocentric feminist thought bears many resemblances to Anglo-American and European feminist thought, it is not identical to these later ways of articulating women's worldview(s). There is a great need for women of color and working-class women as well as white and middle-class women to speak their own minds and express their own feelings. Feminist theory is at its best when it reflects the lived experience of particular women; when it bridges the gap between mind and body, reason and emotion, thinking and feelings; and when women, motivated by friendship, humbly identify what separates them, even as they discover what draws them together.

To be sure, there is much work to be done before feminist thought becomes multicultural, let alone global, in perspective. As it stands, many white women and women advantaged for reasons other than their race are still at the level of simply striving to add the platforms of women of color and women disadvantaged for reasons other than their race—as if the interests of the latter women were merely an interesting addendum, appendix, or footnote to the interests of the former women. The present body of feminist thought must expose itself to the healing touch of fingers whose pressures it has resisted until recently. Specifically, women who have been advantaged on account of their race or class must agree to abandon their privileged position and to move to the margins, so that those women who have been disadvantaged on account of their race or class have more space to grow. Only then will women really have the opportunity to create a cluster of intersecting perspectives on feminist thought that work together precisely because no one of them seeks to name itself as "the rule" against which all others must be measured.

Have We Got a Theory for You! Feminist Theory, Cultural Imperialism and the Demand for "The Woman's Voice"

María C. Lugones and Elizabeth V. Spelman

Prologue

(In an Hispana Voice)

A veces quisiera mezclar en una voz el sonido canyenge, tristón y urbano del porteñismo que llevo adentro con la cadencia apacible, serrana y llena de corage de la hispana nuevo mejicana. Contrastar y unir

> el piolín y la cuerda
> el traé y el pepéname
> el camión y la troca
> la lluvia y el llanto

Pero este querer se me va cuando veo que he confundido la solidaridad con la falta de diferenciea. La solidaridad requiere el reconocer, compreder, respetar y amar lo que nos lleva a llorar en distintas cadencias. El imperialismo cultural desea lo contrario, por eso necesitamos muchas voces. Porque una sola voz nos mata a las dos.

No quiero hablar por ti sino contigo. Pero si no aprendo tus modos y tu los mios la conversación es sólo aparente. Y la apariencia se levanta como una barrera sín sentido entre las dos. Sin sentido y sin sentimiento. Por eso no me debes dejar que te dicte tu ser y no me dictes el mio. Porque entonces ya no dialogamos. El diálogo entre nosotras requiere dos voces y no una.

Tal vez un día jugaremos juntas y nos hablaremos no en una lengua universal sino que vos me hablarás mi voz y yo la tuya.

Preface

This paper is the result of our dialogue, of our thinking together about differences among women and how these differences are silenced. (Think, for example, of all the silences there are connected with the fact that this paper is in English—for that is a borrowed tongue for one of us.) In the process of our talking and writing together, we saw that the differences between us did not permit our speaking in one voice. For example, when we agreed we expressed the thought differently; there were some

494

things that both of us thought were true but could not express as true of each of us; sometimes we could not say 'we'; and sometimes one of us could not express the thought in the first person singular, and to express it in the third person would be to present an outsider's and not an insider's perspective. Thus the use of two voices is central both to the process of constructing this paper and to the substance of it. We are both the authors of this paper and not just sections of it but we write together without presupposing unity of expression or of experience. So when we speak in unison it means just that—there are two voices and not just one.

I. Introduction

(In the Voice of a White/Anglo Woman Who Has Been
Teaching and Writing About Feminist Theory)

Feminism is, among other things, a response to the fact that women either have been left out of, or included in demeaning and disfiguring ways in what has been an almost exclusively male account of the world. And so while part of what feminists want and demand for women is the right to move and to act in accordance with our own wills and not against them, another part is the desire and insistence that we give our *own* accounts of these movements and actions. For it matters to us what is said about us, who says it, and to whom it is said: having the opportunity to talk bout one's life, to give an account of it, to interpret it, is integral to leading that life rather than being led through it; hence our distrust of the male monopoly over accounts of women's lives. To put the same point slightly differently, part of human life, human living, is talking about it, and we can be sure that being silenced in one's own account of one's life is a kind of amputation that signals oppression. Another reason for not divorcing life from the telling of it or talking about it is that as humans our experiences are deeply influenced by what is said about them, by ourselves or powerful (as opposed to significant) others. Indeed, the phenomenon of internalized oppression is only possible because this is so: one experiences her life in terms of the impoverished and degrading concepts others have found it convenient to use to describe her. We can't separate lives from the accounts given of them; the articulation of our experience is part of our experience.

Sometimes feminists have made even stronger claims about the importance of speaking about our own lives and the destructiveness of others presuming to speak about us or for us. First of all, the claim has been made that on the whole men's accounts of women's lives have been at best false, a function of ignorance; and at worst malicious lies, a function of a knowledgeable desire to exploit and oppress. Since it matters to us that falsehood and lies not be told about us, we demand, of those who have been responsible for those falsehoods and lies, or those who continue to transmit them, not just that we speak but that they learn to be able to hear us. It has also been claimed that talking about one's life, telling one's story, in the company of those doing the same (as in consciousness-raising sessions), is constitutive of feminist method.[1]

And so the demand that the woman's voice be heard and attended to has been made for a variety of reasons: not just so as to greatly increase the chances that true accounts of women's lives will be given, but also because the articulation of experience (in myriad ways) is among the hallmarks of a self-determining individual or community. There are not just epistemological, but moral and political reasons for demanding that the woman's voice be heard, after centuries of androcentric din.

But what more exactly is the feminist demand that the woman's voice be heard? There are several crucial notes to make about it. First of all, the demand grows out of a complaint, and in order to understand the scope and focus of the demand we have to look at the scope and focus of the complaint. The complaint does not specify *which* women have been silenced, and in one way this is appropriate to the conditions it is a complaint about: virtually no women have had a voice, whatever their race, class, ethnicity, religion, sexual alliance, whatever place and period in history they lived. And if it is as women that women have been silenced, then of course the demand must be that women as women have a voice. But in another way the complaint is very misleading, insofar as it suggests that it is women as women who have been silenced, and that whether a woman is rich or poor, Black, brown or white, etc. is irrelevant to what it means for her to be a woman. For the demand thus simply made ignores at least two related points: (1) it is only possible for a woman who does not feel highly vulnerable with respect to other parts of her identity, e.g. race, class, ethnicity, religion, sexual alliance, etc., to conceive of her voice simply or essentially as a 'woman's voice'; (2) just because not all women are equally vulnerable with respect to race, class, etc., some women's voices are more likely to be heard than others by those who have heretofore been giving—or silencing—the accounts of women's lives. For all these reasons, the women's voices most likely to come forth and the women's voices most likely to be heard are, in the US anyway, those of white, middle-class, heterosexual Christian (or anyway not self-identified non-Christian) women. Indeed, many Hispanas, Black women, Jewish women—to name a few groups—have felt it an invitation to silence rather than speech to be requested—if they are requested at all—to speak about being 'women' (with the plain wrapper—as if there were one) in distinction from speaking about being Hispana, Black, Jewish, working-class, etc., women.

The demand that the 'woman's voice' be heard, and the search for the 'woman's voice' as central to feminist methodology, reflects nascent feminist theory. It reflects nascent empirical theory insofar as it presupposes that the silencing of women is systematic, shows up in regular, patterned ways, and that there are discoverable causes of this widespread observable phenomenon; the demand reflects nascent political theory insofar as it presupposes that the silencing of women reveals a systematic pattern of power and authority; and it reflects nascent moral theory insofar as it presupposes that the silencing is unjust and that there are particular ways of remedying this injustice. Indeed, whatever else we know feminism to include—e.g. concrete direct political action—theorizing is integral to it: theories about the nature of oppression, the causes of it, the relation of the oppression of women to other forms of oppression. And certainly the concept of the woman's voice is itself a theoretical concept, in the sense that it presupposes a theory according to which our identities as human beings are actually compound identities, a kind of fusion or confusion of our otherwise separate identities as women or men, as Black or brown or white, etc. That is no less a theoretical stance than Plato's division of the person into soul and body or Aristotle's parcelling of the soul into various functions.

The demand that the 'woman's voice' be heard also invites some further directions in the exploration of women's lives and discourages or excludes others. For reasons mentioned above, systematic, sustained reflection on being a woman—the kind of contemplation that 'doing theory' requires—is most likely to be done by women who vis-à-vis other women enjoy a certain amount of political, social and economic privilege because of their skin color, class membership, ethnic identity. There is a relationship between the content of our contemplation and the fact that we have the time to engage in it at some length—otherwise we shall have to say that it is a mere accident of history that white middle-class women in the United States have in the main developed 'feminist theory' (as opposed to 'Black feminist theory', 'Chicana feminist theory', etc.) and that so much of the theory has failed to be relevant to the lives of women who are not white or middle class. Feminist theory—of all kinds—is to be based on, or anyway touch base with, the variety of real life stories women provide about themselves. But in fact, because, among other things, of the structural political and social and economic inequalities among women, the tail has been wagging the dog: feminist theory has not for the most part arisen out of a medley of women's voices; instead, the theory has arisen out of the voices, the experiences, of a fairly small handful of women, and if other women's voices do not sing in harmony with the theory, they aren't counted as women's voices—rather, they are the voices of the woman as Hispana, Black, Jew, etc. There is another sense in which the tail is wagging the dog, too; it is presumed to be the case that those who do the theory know more about those who are theorized than vice versa: hence it ought to be the case that if it is white/Anglo women who write for and about all other women, then white/Anglo women must know more about all other women than other women know about them. But in fact just in order to survive, brown and Black women have to know a lot more about white/Anglo women—not through the sustained contemplation theory requires, but through the sharp observation stark exigency demands.

(In an Hispana Voice)

I think it necessary to explain why in so many cases when women of color appear in front of white/Anglo women to talk about feminism and women of color, we mainly raise a complaint: the complaint of exclusion, of silencing, of being included in a universe we have not chosen. We usually raise the complaint with a certain amount of disguised or undisguised anger. I can only attempt to explain this phenomenon from a Hispanic viewpoint and a fairly narrow one at that: the viewpoint of an Argentinian woman who has lived in the US for 16 years, who has attempted to come to terms with the devaluation of things Hispanic and Hispanic people in 'America' and who is most familiar with Hispano life in the Southwest of the US. I am quite unfamiliar with daily Hispano life in the urban centers, though not with some of the themes and some of the salient experiences of urban Hispano life.

When I say 'we',[2] I am referring to Hispanas. I am accustomed to use the 'we' in this way. I am also pained by the tenuousness of this 'we' given that I am not a native of the US. Through the years I have come to be recognized and I have come to recognize myself more and more firmly as part of this 'we'. I also have a profound yearning for this firmness since I am a displaced person and I am conscious of not being of and I am unwilling to make myself of—even if this were possible—the white/Anglo community.

When I say 'you' I mean not the non-Hispanic but the white/Anglo women that I address. 'We' and 'you' do not capture my relation to other non-white women. The complexity of that relation is not addressed here, but it is vivid to me as I write down my thoughts on the subject at hand.

I see two related reasons for our complaint—full discourse with white/Anglo women. Both of these reasons plague our world, they contaminate it through and through. I takes some hardening of oneself, some self-acceptance of our own anger to face them, for to face them is to decide that maybe we can change our situation in self-constructive ways and we know fully well that the possibilities are minimal. We know that we cannot rest from facing these reasons, that the tenderness towards others in us undermines our possibilities, that we have to fight our own niceness because it clouds our minds and hearts. Yet we know that a thoroughgoing hardening would dehumanize us. So, we have to walk through our days in a peculiarly fragile psychic state, one that we have to struggle to maintain, one that we do not often succeed in maintaining.

We and you do not talk the same language. When we talk to you we use your language: the language of your experience and of your theories. We try to use it to communicate our world of experience. But since your language and your theories are inadequate in expressing our experiences, we only succeed in communicating our experience of exclusion. We cannot talk to you in our language because you do not understand it. So the brute facts that we understand your language and that the place where most theorizing about women is taking place is your place, both combine to require that we either use your language and distort our experience not just in the speaking about it, but in the living of it, or that we remain silent. Complaining about exclusion is a way of remaining silent.

You are ill at ease in our world. You are ill at ease in our world in a very different way than we are ill at ease in yours. You are not of our world and again, you are not of our world in a very different way than we are not of yours. In the intimacy of a personal relationship we appear to you many times to be wholly there, to have broken through or to have dissipated the barriers that separate us because you are Anglo and we are raza. When we let go of the psychic state that I referred to above in the direction of sympathy, we appear to ourselves equally whole in your presence but our intimacy is thoroughly incomplete. When we are in your world many times you remake us in your own image, although sometimes you clearly and explicitly acknowledge that we are not wholly there in our being with you. When we are in your world we ourselves feel the discomfort of having our own being Hispanas disfigured or not understood. And yet, we have had to be in your world and learn its ways. We have to participate in it, make a living in it, live in it, be mistreated in it, be ignored in it, and rarely, be appreciated in it. In learning to do these things or in learning to suffer them or in learning to enjoy what is to be enjoyed or in learning to understand your conception of us, we have had to learn your culture and thus your language and self-conceptions. But there is nothing that necessitates that you understand our world: understand, that is, not as an observer understands things, but as a participant, as someone who has a stake in them understands them. So your being ill at ease in our world lacks the features of our being ill at ease in yours precisely because you can leave and you can always tell yourselves that you will be soon out of there and because the wholeness of your selves is never touched by us, we have no tendency to remake you in our image.

But you theorize about women and we are women, so you understand yourselves to be theorizing about us and we understand you to be theorizing about us. Yet none of the feminist theories developed so far seem to me to help Hispanas in the articulation of our experience. We have a sense that in using them we are distorting our experiences. Most Hispanas cannot even understand the language used in these theories—and only in some cases the reason is that the Hispana cannot understand English. We do not recognize ourselves in these theories. They create in us a schizophrenic split between our concern for ourselves as women and ourselves as Hispanas, one that we do not feel otherwise. Thus they seem to us to force us to assimilate to some version of Anglo culture, however revised that version may be. They seem to ask that we leave our communities or that we become alienated so completely in them that we feel hollow. When we see that you feel alienated in your own communities, this confuses us because we think that maybe every feminist has to suffer this alienation. But we see that recognition of your alienation leads many of you to be empowered into the remaking of your culture, while we are paralyzed into a state of displacement with no place to go.

So I think that we need to think carefully about the relation between the articulation of our own experience, the interpretation of our own experience, and theory making by us and other non-Hispanic women about themselves and other 'women'.

The only motive that makes sense to me for your joining us in this investigation is the motive of friendship, out of friendship. A non-imperialist feminism requires that you make a real space for our articulating, interpreting, theorizing and reflecting about the connections among them—a real space must be a non-coerced space— and/or that you follow us into our world out of friendship. I see the 'out of friendship' as the only sensical motivation for this following because the task at hand for you is one of extraordinary difficulty. It requires that you be willing to devote a great part of your life to it and that you be willing to suffer alienation and self-disruption. Self-interest has been proposed as a possible motive for entering this task. But self-interest does not seem to me to be a realistic motive, since whatever the benefits you may accrue from such a journey, they cannot be concrete enough for you at this time and they may not be worth your while. I do not think that you have any obligation to understand us. You do have an obligation to abandon your imperialism, your universal claims, your reduction of us to your selves simply because they seriously harm us.

I think that the fact that we are so ill at ease with your theorizing in the ways indicated above does indicate that there is something wrong with these theories. But what is it that is wrong? Is it simply that the theories are flawed if meant to be universal but accurate so long as they are confined to your particular group(s)? Is it that the theories are not really flawed but need to be translated? Can they be translated? Is it something about the process of theorizing that is flawed? How do the two reasons for our complaint—full discourse affect the validity of your theories? Where do *we* begin? To what extent are our experience and its articulation affected by our being a colonized people, and thus by your culture, theories and conceptions? Should we theorize in community and thus as part of community life and outside the academy and other intellectual circles? What is the point of making theory? Is theory making a good thing for us to do at this time? When are we making theory and when are we just articulating and/or interpreting our experiences?

II. Some Questionable Assumptions
About Feminist Theorizing

(Unproblematically in María's & Vicky's Voice)

Feminist theories aren't just about what happens to the female population in any given society or across all societies; they are about the meaning of those experiences in the lives of women. They are bout beings who give their own accounts of what is happening to them or of what they are doing, who have culturally constructed ways of reflecting on their lives. But how can the theorizer get at the meaning of those experiences? What should the relation be between a woman's own account of her experiences and the theorizer's account of it?

Let us describe two different ways of arriving at an account of another woman's experience. It is one thing for both me and you to observe you and come up with our different accounts of what you are doing; it is quite another for me to observe myself and others much like me culturally and in other ways and to develop an account of myself and then use that account to give an account of you. In the first case you are the 'insider' and I am the 'outsider'. When the outsider makes clear that she is an outsider and that this is an outsider's account of your behavior, there is a touch of honesty about what she is doing. Most of the time the 'interpretation by an outsider' is left understood and most of the time the distance of outsidedness is understood to mark objectivity in the interpretation. But why is the outsider as an outsider interpreting your behavior? Is she doing it so that you can understand how she sees you? Is she doing it so that other outsiders will understand how you *are?* Is she doing it so that *you* will understand how you are? It would seem that if the outsider wants you to understand how she sees you and you have given your account of how you see yourself to her, there is a possibility of genuine dialogue between the two. It also seems that the lack of reciprocity could bar genuine dialogue. For why should you engage in such a one-sided dialogue? As soon as we ask this question, a host of other conditions for the possibility of a genuine dialogue between us arise: conditions having to do with your position relative to me in the various social, political and economic structures in which we might come across each other or in which you may run face to face with my account of you and my use of your account of yourself. Is this kind of dialogue necessary for me to get at the meaning of your experiences? That is, is this kind of dialogue necessary for feminist theorizing that is not seriously flawed?

Obviously the most dangerous of the understanding of what I—an outsider—am doing in giving an account of your experience is the one that describes what I'm doing as giving an account of who and how you are whether it be given to you or to other outsiders. Why should you or anyone else believe me; that is why should you or anyone else believe that you are as I say you are? Could I be right? What conditions would have to obtain for my being right? That many women are put in the position of not knowing whether or not to believe outsiders' accounts of their experiences is clear. The pressures to believe these accounts are enormous even when the woman in question does not see herself in the account. She is thus led to doubt her own judgment and to doubt all interpretation of her experience. This leads her to experience her life differently. Since the consequences of outsiders' accounts can be so significant, it is crucial that we reflect on whether or not this type of account can ever be right and if so, under what conditions.

The last point leads us to the second way of arriving at an account of another woman's experience, viz. the case in which I observe myself and others like me culturally and in other ways and use that account to give an account of you. In doing this, I remake you in my own image. Feminist theorizing approaches this remaking insofar as it depends on the concept of women as women. For it has not arrived at this concept as a consequence of dialogue with many women who are culturally different, or by any other kind of investigation of cultural differences which may include different conceptions of what it is to be a woman; it has simply presupposed this concept.

Our suggestion in this paper, and at this time it is no more than a suggestion, is that only when genuine and reciprocal dialogue takes place between 'outsiders' and 'insiders' can we trust the outsider's account. At first sight it may appear that the insider/outsider distinction disappears in the dialogue, but it is important to notice that all that happens is that we are now both outsider and insider with respect to each other. The dialogue puts us both in position to give a better account of each other's and our own experience. Here we should again note that white/Anglo women are much less prepared for this dialogue with women of color than women of color are for dialogue with them in that women of color have had to learn white/Anglo ways, self-conceptions, and conceptions of them.

But both the possibility and the desirability of this dialogue are very much in question. We need to think about the possible motivations for engaging in this dialogue, whether doing theory jointly would be a good thing, in what ways and for whom, and whether doing theory is in itself a good thing at this time for women of color or white/Anglo women. In motivating the last question let us remember the hierarchical distinctions between theorizers and those theorized about and between theorizers and doers. These distinctions are endorsed by the same views and institutions which endorse and support hierarchical distinctions between men/women, master race/inferior race, intellectuals/manual workers. Of what use is the activity of theorizing to those of us who are women of color engaged day in and day out in the task of empowering women and men of color face to face with them? Should we be articulating and interpreting their experience for them with the aid of theories? Whose theories?

III. Ways of Talking or Being Talked About That Are Helpful, Illuminating, Empowering, Respectful

(Unproblematically in María's & Vicky's Voice)

Feminists have been quite diligent about pointing out the ways in which empirical, philosophical and moral theories have been androcentric. They have thought it crucial to ask, with respect to such theories: who makes them? for whom do they make them? about what or whom are the theories? why? how are theories tested? what are the criteria for such tests and where did the criteria come from? Without posing such questions and trying to answer them, we'd never have been able to begin to mount evidence for our claims that particular theories are androcentric, sexist, biased, paternalistic, etc. Certain philosophers have become fond of—indeed, have made their careers on—pointing out that characterizing a statement as true or false is only one of many ways possible of characterizing it; it might also be, oh, rude, funny, disarming, etc.; it may be intended to soothe or to hurt; or it may have the effect, intended or not, of soothing or hurting. Similarly, theories appear to be the kinds of things that are true or false; but they also are the kinds of things that can be, e.g. useless, arrogant, disrespectful, ignorant, ethnocentric, imperialistic. The immediate point is that feminist theory is no less immune to such characterizations than, say, Plato's political theory, or Freud's theory of female psychosexual development. Of course this is not to say that if feminist theory manages to be respectful or helpful it will follow that it must be true. But if, say, an empirical theory is purported to be about 'women' and in fact is only about certain women, it is certainly false, probably ethnocentric, and of dubious usefulness except to those whose position in the world it strengthens (and theories, as we know, don't have to be true in order to be used to strengthen people's positions in the world).

Many reasons can be and have been given for the production of accounts of people's lives that plainly have nothing to do with illuminating those lives for the benefit of those living them. It is likely that both the method of investigation and the content of many accounts would be different if illuminating the lives of the people the accounts are about were the aim of the studies. Though we cannot say ahead of time how feminist theory-making would be different if all (or many more) of those people it is meant to be about were more intimately part of the theory-making process, we do suggest some specific ways being talked about can be helpful:

(1) The theory or account can be helpful if it enables one to see how parts of one's life fit together, for example, to see connection among parts of one's life one hasn't seen before. No account can do this if it doesn't get the parts right to begin with, and this cannot happen if the concepts used to describe a life are utterly foreign.

(2) A useful theory will help one locate oneself concretely in the world, rather than add to the mystification of the world and one's location in it. New concepts may be of significance here, but they will not be useful if there is no way they can be translated into already existing concepts. Suppose a theory locates you in the home, because you are a woman, but you know full well that is not where you spend most of your time? Or suppose you can't locate yourself easily in any particular class as defined by some version of marxist theory?

(3) A theory or account not only ought to accurately locate one in the world but also enable one to think about the extent to which one is responsible or not for being in that location. Otherwise, for those whose location is as oppressed peoples, it usually occurs that the oppressed have no way to see themselves as in any way self-determining, as having any sense of being worthwhile or having grounds for pride, and paradoxically at the same time feeling at fault for the position they are in. A useful theory will help people sort out just what is and is not due to themselves and their own activities as opposed to those who have power over them.

It may seem odd to make these criteria of a useful theory, if the usefulness is not to be at odds with the issue of the truth of the theory: for the focus on feeling worthwhile or having pride seems to rule out the possibility that the truth might just be that such-and-such a group of people has been under the control of others for centuries and that the only explanation of that is that they are worthless and weak people, and will never be able to change that. Feminist theorizing seems implicitly if not explicitly committed to the moral view that women *are* worthwhile beings, and the metaphysical theory that we are beings capable of bringing about a change in our situations. Does this mean feminist theory is 'biased'? Not any more than any other theory, e.g. psychoanalytic theory. What is odd here is not the feminist presupposition that women are worthwhile but rather that feminist theory (and other theory) often has the effect of empowering one group and demoralizing another.

Aspects of feminist theory are as unabashedly value-laden as other political and moral theories. It is not just an examination of women's positions, for it includes, indeed begins with, moral and political judgements about the injustice (or, where relevant, justice) of them. This means that there are implicit or explicit judgements also about what kind of changes constitute a better or worse situation for women.

(4) In this connection a theory that is useful will provide criteria for change and make suggestions for modes of resistance that don't merely reflect the situation and values of the theorizer. A theory that is respectful of those about whom it is a theory will not assume that changes that are perceived as making life better for some women are changes that will make, and will be perceived as making, life better for other women. This is NOT to say that if some women do not find a situation oppressive, other women ought never to suggest to the contrary that there might be very good reasons to think that the situation nevertheless *is* oppressive. But it is to say that, e.g. the prescription that life for women will be better when we're in the workforce rather than at home, when we are completely free of religious beliefs with patriarchal origins, when we live in complete separation from men, etc., are seen as slaps in the face to women whose life would be better if they could spend more time at home, whose identity is inseparable from their religious beliefs and cultural practices (which is not to say those beliefs and practices are to remain completely uncriticized and unchanged), who have ties to men—whether erotic or not—such that to have them severed in the name of some vision of what is 'better' is, at that time and for those women, absurd. Our visions of what is better are always informed by our perception of what is bad about our present situation. Surely we've learned enough from the history of clumsy missionaries, and the white suffragists of the 19th century (who couldn't imagine why Black women 'couldn't see' how crucial getting the vote for 'women' was) to know that we can clobber people to destruction with our visions, our versions, of what is better. BUT: this does not mean women are not to offer supportive and tentative criticism of one another. But there is a very important difference between (a) developing ideas together, in a 'pre-theoretical' stage, engaged as equals in joint enquiry, and (b) one group developing, on the basis of their own experience, a set of criteria for good change for women—and then reluctantly making revisions in the criteria at the insistence of women to whom such criteria seem ethnocentric and arrogant. The deck is stacked when one group takes it upon itself to develop the theory and then have others criticize it. Categories are quick to congeal, and the experiences of women whose lives do not fit the categories will appear as anomalous when in fact the theory should have grown out of them as much as others from the beginning. This, of course, is why any organization or conference having to do with 'women'—with no qualification—that seriously does not want to be 'solipsistic' will from the beginning be multi-cultural or state the appropriate qualifications. How we think and what we think about does depend in large part on who is there—not to mention who is expected or encouraged to speak. (Recall the boys in the *Symposium* sending the flute girls out.) Conversations and criticism take place in particular circumstances. Turf matters. So does the fact of who if anyone already has set up the terms of the conversations.

(5) Theory cannot be useful to anyone interested in resistance and change unless there is reason to believe that knowing what a theory means and believing it to be true have some connection to resistance and change. As we make theory and offer it up to others, what do we assume is the connection between theory and consciousness? Do we expect others to read theory, understand it, believe it, and have their consciousnesses and lives thereby transformed? If we really want theory to make a difference to people's lives, how ought we to present it? Do we think people come to

consciousness by reading? only by reading? Speaking to people through theory (orally or in writing) is a *very* specific context-dependent activity. That is, theory-makers and their methods and concepts constitute a community of people and of shared meanings. Their language can be just as opaque and foreign to those not in the community as a foreign tongue or dialect.[3] Why do we engage in *this* activity and what effect do we think it ought to have? As Helen Longino has asked: 'Is "doing theory" just a bonding ritual for academic or educationally privileged feminists/women?' Again, whom does our theory-making serve?

IV. Some Suggestions About How to Do Theory That Is Not Imperialistic, Ethnocentric, Disrespectful

(Problematically in the Voice of a Woman of Color)

What are the things we need to know about others, and about ourselves, in order to speak intelligently, intelligibly, sensitively, and helpfully about their lives? We can show respect, or lack of it, in writing theoretically about others no less than in talking directly with them. This is not to say that here we have a well-worked out concept of respect, but only to suggest that together all of us consider what it would mean to theorize in a respectful way.

When we speak, write, and publish our theories, to whom do we think we are accountable? Are the concerns we have in being accountable to 'the profession' at odds with the concerns we have in being accountable to those about whom we theorize? Do commitments to 'the profession', method, getting something published, getting tenure, lead us to talk and act in ways at odds with what we ourselves (let alone others) would regard as ordinary, decent behavior? To what extent do we presuppose that really understanding another person or culture requires our behaving in ways that are disrespectful, even violent? That is, to what extent do we presuppose that getting and/or publishing the requisite information requires or may require disregarding the wishes of others, lying to them, wresting information from them against their wills? Why and how do we think theorizing about others provides *understanding* of them? Is there any sense in which theorizing about others is a short-cut to understanding them?

Finally, if we think doing theory is an important activity, and we think that some conditions lead to better theorizing than others, what are we going to do about creating those conditions? If we think it not just desirable but necessary for women of different racial and ethnic identities to create feminist theory jointly, how shall that be arranged for? It may be the case that at this particular point we ought not even try to do that—that feminist theory by and for Hispanas needs to be done separately from feminist theory by and for Black women, white women, etc. But it must be recognized that white/Anglo women have more power and privilege than Hispanas, Black women, etc., and at the very least they can use such advantage to provide space and time for other women to speak (with the above caveats about implicit restrictions on what counts as 'the woman's voice'). And once again it is important to remember that the power of white/Anglo women vis-à-vis Hispanas and Black women is in inverse proportion to their working knowledge of each other.

This asymmetry is a crucial fact about the background of possible relationships between white women and women of color, whether as political coworkers, professional colleagues, or friends.

If white/Anglo women and women of color are to do theory jointly, in helpful, respectful, illuminating and empowering ways, the task ahead of white/Anglo women because of this asymmetry, is a very hard task. The task is a very complex one. In part, to make an analogy, the task can be compared to learning a text without the aid of teachers. We all know the lack of contact felt when we want to discuss a particular issue that requires knowledge of a text with someone who does not know the text at all. Or the discomfort and impatience that arise in us when we are discussing an issue that presupposes a text and someone walks into the conversation who does not know the text. That person is either left out or will impose herself on us and either try to engage in the discussion or try to change the subject. Women of color are put in these situations by white/Anglo women and men constantly. Now imagine yourself simply left out but wanting to do theory with us. The first thing to recognize and accept is that you disturb our own dialogues by putting yourself in the left-out position and not leaving us in some meaningful sense to ourselves.

You must also recognize and accept that <u>you must learn the text</u>. But the text is an extraordinarily complex one: viz. our many different cultures. You are asking us to make ourselves more vulnerable to you than we already are before we have any reason to trust that you will not take advantage of this vulnerability. <u>So you need to learn to become unintrusive, unimportant, patient to the point of tears, while at the same time open to learning any possible lessons</u>. You will also have to come to terms with the sense of alienation, of not belonging, of having your world thoroughly disrupted, having it criticized and scrutinized from the point of view of those who have been harmed by it, having important concepts central to it dismissed, being viewed with mistrust, being seen as of no consequence except as an object of mistrust.

Why would any white/Anglo woman engage in this task? Out of self-interest? What in engaging in this task would be, not just in her interest, but perceived as such by her before the task is completed or well underway? Why should we want you to come into our world out of self-interest? Two points need to be made here. The task as described could be entered into with the intention of finding out as much as possible about us so as to better dominate us. The person engaged in this task would act as a spy. The motivation is not unfamiliar to us. We have heard it said that now that Third World countries are more powerful as a bloc, westerners need to learn more about them, that it is in their self-interest to do so. Obviously there is no reason why people of color should welcome white/Anglo women into their world for the carrying out of this intention. It is also obvious that white/Anglo feminists should not engage in this task under this description since the task under this description would not lead to joint theorizing of the desired sort: respectful, illuminating, helpful and empowering. It would be helpful and empowering only in a one-sided way.

Self-interest is also mentioned as a possible motive in another way. White/Anglo women sometimes say that the task of understanding women of color would entail self-growth or self-expansion. If the task is conceived as described here, then one should doubt that growth or expansion will be the result. The severe self-disruption that the task entails should place a doubt in anyone who takes the task seriously about her possibilities of coming out of the task whole, with a self that is not as fragile as the selves of those who have been the victims of racism. But also, why should women of color embrace white/Anglo women's self-betterment without reciprocity? At this time women of color cannot afford this generous affirmation of white/Anglo women.

Another possible motive for engaging in this task is the motive of duty, 'out of obligation', because white/Anglos have done people of color wrong. Here again two considerations: coming into Hispano, Black, Native American worlds out of obligation puts white/Anglos in a orally self-righteous position that is inappropriate. You are active, we are passive. We become the vehicles of your own redemption. Secondly, we couldn't want you to come into our worlds 'out of obligation'. That is like wanting someone to make love to you out of obligation. So, whether or not you have an obligation to do this (and we would deny that you do), or whether this task could even be done out of obligation, this is an inappropriate motive.

Out of obligation you should stay out of our way, respect us and our distance, and forego the use of whatever power you have over us—for example, the power to use your language in our meetings, the power to overwhelm us with your education, the power to intrude in our communities in order to research us and to record the supposed dying of our cultures, the power to ingrain in us a sense that we are members of dying cultures and are doomed to assimilate, the power to keep us in a defensive posture with respect to our own cultures.

So the motive of friendship remains as both the only appropriate and understandable motive for white/Anglo feminists engaging in the task as described above. If you enter the task out of friendship with us, then you will be moved to attain the appropriate reciprocity of care for your and our wellbeing as whole beings, you will have a stake in us and in our world, you will be moved to satisfy the need for reciprocity of understanding that will enable you to follow us in our experiences as we are able to follow you in yours.

We are not suggesting that if the learning of the text is to be done out of friendship, you must enter into a friendship with a whole community and for the purpose of making theory. In order to understand what it is that we are suggesting, it is important to remember that during the description of her experience of exclusion, the Hispana voice said that Hispanas experience the intimacy of friendship with white/Anglo women friends as thoroughly incomplete. It is not until this fact is acknowledged by our white/Anglo women friends and felt as a profound lack in our experience of each other that white/Anglo women can begin to see us. Seeing us in our communities will make clear and concrete to you how incomplete we really are in our relationships with you. It is this beginning that forms the proper background for the yearning to understand the text of our cultures that can lead to joint theory-making.

Thus, the suggestion made here is that if white/Anglo women are to understand our voices, they must understand our communities and us in them. Again, this is not to suggest that you set out to make friends with our communities, though you may become friends with some of the members, nor is it to suggest that you should try to befriend us for the purpose of making theory with us. The latter would be a perversion of friendship. Rather, from within friendship you may be moved by friendship to undergo the very difficult task of understanding the text of our cultures by understanding our lives in our communities. This learning calls for circumspection, for questioning of yourselves and your roles in your own culture. It necessitates a striving to understand while in the comfortable position of not having an official calling card (as 'scientific' observers of our communities have); it demands recognition that you do not have the authority of knowledge; it requires coming to the task without ready-made theories to frame our lives. This learning is then extremely hard because it requires openness (including openness to severe criticism of the white/Anglo world), sensitivity, concentration, self-questioning, circumspection. It should be clear that it does not consist in a passive immersion in our cultures, but in a striving to understand what it is that our voices are saying. Only then can we engage in a mutual dialogue that does not reduce each one of us to instances of the abstraction called 'woman'.

Notes

1. For a recent example, see MacKinnon (1982).

2. I must note that when I think this 'we', I think it in Spanish—and in Spanish this 'we' is gendered, 'nosotras'. I also use 'nosotros' lovingly and with ease and in it I include all members of 'La raza cosmica' (Spanish-speaking people of the Americas, le gente de colores: people of many colors). In the US, I use 'we' contextually with varying degrees of discomfort: 'we' in the house, 'we' in the department, 'we' in the classroom, 'we' in the meeting. The discomfort springs from the sense of community in the 'we' and the varying degrees of lack of community in the context in which the 'we' is used.

3. See Bernstein (1972). Bernstein would probably, and we think wrongly, insist that theoretical terms and statements have meanings *not* 'tied to a local relationship and to a local social structure', unlike the vocabulary of, e.g. working-class children.

References

Bernstein, Basil. 1972. Social class, language and socialization. In Giglioli, Pier Paolo, ed., *Language and Social Context*, pp. 157–178. Penguin, Harmondsworth, Middlesex.

MacKinnon, Catharine. 1982. Feminism, marxism, method and the State: an agenda for theory. *Signs* 7 (3): 515–544.

Race, Class, and Psychoanalysis?
Opening Questions

Elizabeth Abel

Although psychoanalytic theory has done a great deal to improve our understanding of sexual difference, it has done little or nothing to change the concrete social conditions of sex-relations and of gender-stratification. The latter is precisely the target of feminist practice.

Rosi Braidotti, "The Politics of Ontological Difference"

It would seem fairly obvious by now that feminism's struggle to infuse into psychoanalytical theory the breath of an efficacious politics has not been a major success. Feminist approaches in recent years to Lacanian psychoanalysis, for example ... have been thwarted by the obstinacy of psychoanalytic universalist theories of subjective construction.

Paul Smith, "Julia Kristeva Et Al.; or, Take Three or More"[1]

Repudiating psychoanalysis has become a familiar gesture of contemporary feminist discourse—and with some good reasons.[2] Seduced by psychoanalytic accounts of subjectivity, much feminist theory of the 1970s has come to seem, from the vantage point of the late 1980s, to have lost its material groundings and with them the possibility of interpreting (and thereby promoting) social change. The traditional indifference of psychoanalysis to racial, class, and cultural differences, and the tendency of psychoanalysis to insulate subjectivity from social practices and discourses all run contrary to a feminism increasingly attuned to the power of social exigencies and differences in the constitution of subjectivity. It is clear that a psychoanalysis useful for contemporary feminism needs some infusion of the social—whether the "social" is construed as the technologies that regulate desire or (in this essay's terms) as the roles of race and class in a diversified construction of subjectivity.[3] It is less clear whether the resistance of psychoanalysis to the social is adventitious or intrinsic. If we agree (as I do) with Paul Smith that psychoanalysis has no innate political desire, we nevertheless can ask how labile psychoanalysis is, how far its boundaries can expand to incorporate issues of social difference into a discourse useful, if not for changing the social order, at least for theorizing this order's intervention in the production of diversely gendered subjects.

Psychoanalysis, of course, is not a monolithic discourse and has no uniform relation to the social domain. Freud's resistance to a culturally inflected psychoanalysis
is overt and infamous.[4] The recent revisions of Freud that have been more influential
for feminism, however, have opened possibilities for new negotiations between the
psychoanalytic and the social domains. Introducing the category of the social into
Lacanian discourse requires a deliberate intervention, since this discourse collapses
the social into a symbolic register that is always everywhere the same. While de-
essentializing gender by relocating it in a cultural arena that is severed from biology,
orthodox Lacanaians essentialize a dehistoricized paternal law, derived from the
symbolic Father, "the dead father of the law who ... is there however weak or absent
his real representative may be."[5] According to Jacqueline Rose, "the force of psychoanalysis is ... precisely that it gives an account of patriarchal culture as a trans-historical and cross-cultural force. It therefore conforms to a feminist demand for a theory which can explain women's subordination across specific cultures and different
historical moments."[6] By insisting that the Father's law is necessary and tantamount
to culture, however, the official Lacanian account prohibits alternative conceptualizations of culture and renders variations within patriarchal social forms (and thus
in the degree and kind of women's subordination) either inconsequential or invisible. Yet the very erasures accomplished by this discourse have pointed its most revisionist practitioners toward a reading of the ways that gender is diversely (de)con-
structed by the gaps between the social and symbolic domains.[7]

A less deliberate intervention is required within feminist object relations theory,
which explicitly locates the production of gendered subjectivity in historically specific and socially variable caretaking arrangements. To foreground these diverse social arrangements would entail not a revision of this theory but, rather, a fulfillment
of its claims to explain how the "inexorably social" self that is "constructed in a relational matrix" varies, along with that matrix, "by individual, culture, period, gender."[8] In principle, this matrix is not restricted to an invariant or insulated nuclear
family; instead, it functions as a permeable membrane through which a wide range
of changing social relations inform the evolution of the gendered subject. Jane Flax,
for example, insists: "The caretaker brings to the relationship ... the whole range of
social experience—work, friends, interaction with political and economic institutions, and so on. The seemingly abstract and suprapersonal relations of class, race,
and male dominance enter into the construction of 'individual' human development."[9] In practice, however, object relations discourse has confined itself to the
Western middle-class nuclear family and has bracketed all variables other than gender; while avoiding the homogeneity of the Lacanian symbolic, this discourse has
tended to homogenize gender by implying that children learn within the family a
single uniform masculinity or femininity. Elizabeth Spelman has mounted a powerful critique of this homogenizing tendency by arguing that "children learn what it
means to be men or women by learning what it is to be men or women of their race,
class, ethnicity" since "women mother in a social and political context in which they
not only are distinguished from men, but are, along with men of their same cultural
background, distinguished from men and women of other cultural backgrounds."[10]
But the inadequately textured accounts produced by object relations are not limitations intrinsic to the theory. In her response to a methodological debate on *The Reproduction of Mothering*, Nancy Chodorow invites further research into "class and
ethnic differences, differences in family and household structure, differences in sex-

ual orientation of parents, and historical and cross-cultural variations in these relationships" and claims that if she were to write a new *Reproduction of Mothering* she
would "examine the link between what seems exclusively gender related and the construction of other aspects of society, politics, and culture."[11] This is not the direction
her own work has pursued; but there is no intrinsic incompatibility between the governing principles of object relations theory and socially inflected qualifications of
that theory.[12]

Posing the question of the social enables us to redraw the map of psychoanalytic
feminism, so sharply and hierarchically split over the last decade between Lacan and
object relations. Both psychoanalytic discourses now seem guilty, either in theory or
in practice, of privileging a decontextualized gender as the constitutive factor in subjectivity; and both discourses are (diversely) subject to revision. When difference is
interpreted within a social as well as a linguistic framework, moreover, the Lacanian
critique of the unitary subject loses some of its special edge, and the heterogeneity of
the Lacanian subject seems insufficiently textured and less radically different from
the intersubjectively constituted self of object relations.[13] Most importantly, the urgency of theorizing subjectivity within a range of social contexts has made it less productive to reiterate the old oppositions within psychoanalytic feminism, or between
psychoanalysis and contemporary feminism, than to image more fluid intersections.

Toward this end, I want to ground this essay in a reading of two dense and brilliant
texts that address the intersections of gender with race or class from perspectives
both indebted to and critical of psychoanalysis. Both published in this country in
1987, Hortense J. Spillers's "Mama's Baby, Papa's Maybe: An American Grammar
Book," a psychoanalytically informed meditation on the devastations wrought by
slavery on African-American kinship and gender structures, and Carolyn Kay
Steedman's *Landscape for a Good Woman: A Story of Two Lives,* a reading of class
analysis against and with psychoanalysis, are teasingly and deliberately polyphonic
texts. Although Spillers works primarily with Lacan, and Steedman primarily with
object relations, each asserts and subverts a range of psychoanalytic and social discourses and propels them into provocative and complicated play.

II

*Is the Freudian landscape an applicable text (say nothing of appropriate) to social and his-
torical situations that do not replicate moments of its own cultural origins and involvements?*

**Hortense J. Spillers, " 'The Permanent Obliquity of an In[pha]llibly
Straight': In the Time of the Daughters and the Fathers"[14]**

"Mama's Baby, Papa's Maybe: An American Grammar Book" offers a qualified yes
to the question of the applicability of psychoanalysis to the African-American social
landscape, although, as the shift from the epigraph's spatial metaphor to the figure of
the "grammar book" suggests, Lacanian rather than Freudian discourse is at issue
here. The essay's title also offers an intertextual clue to one function of Lacanian theory in Spillers's own discourse. In "Interstices: A Small Drama of Words," an earlier
essay, Spillers introduces the folksay "Mama's baby, papa's maybe" to signal the im-

portance of the "hidden and impermissible" paternal origins of feminist analysis in the dominant culture's master discourses, whose boundaries feminism can explode while exploiting an extended heritage of discursive strategies.[15] In "Mama's Baby, Papa's Maybe: An American Grammar Book," a discourse on the "grammar" of the European-American eradication of African kinship structures serves to destabilize Anglo-American universalizations of gender difference, to ally black feminist analyses of degendering under slavery with the larger theoretical project of poststructuralism, and to recast the Lacanian symbolic in the terms of cultural domination. Overtly, a Lacanian discourse politicized through the African-American context authorizes a critique of an Anglo-American feminism identified with object relations and dismissed as "the reproduction of mothering"—as an account, that is, of female gender transmission entirely irrelevant to the brutally disrupted kinship bonds of persons in captivity. Nevertheless, as the essay's title indicates, there is a contradictory (although largely disavowed) alliance with the mother—both with the biological mother whose determinative role in the social definition of the slave child complicates Spillers's allegiance to the paternal discourse and the Name of the Father it privileges, and, consequently, with the discursive mother (an Anglo-American feminism allied with object relations) that, despite its different social context, also underscores the mother's centrality. This discursive genealogy is both irreducibly heterogeneous and necessary to Spillers's project of specifying the complex (de)constructions of gender under slavery.

Spillers invokes the Lacanian divorce between biology and culture in order to subvert the assumption she ascribes to Anglo-American feminism that shared biology entails a common gender, that all biological females participate in a single womanhood reproduced across the generations. In quite an orthodox Lacanian claim, she asserts that " 'gendering' takes place within the confines of the domestic, an essential metaphor that then spreads its tentacles for male and female subjects over a wider ground of human and social purposes. Domesticity appears to gain its power by way of a common origin of cultural fictions that are grounded in the specificity of proper names, more exactly, a patronymic."[16] Violently dislocated from their own kinship (and consequently gender) structures and situated outside the domestic realm in the New World, captive persons in Spillers's account are deprived of gender. This pulverization is also played out on the body. It is not only that gender is severed from biology but also that "biology" shifts in this account from the arena of sexual difference to the Lacanian zone of the fragmented body imperfectly effaced by our illusions of coherence.[17] During both slavery and the Middle Passage (for Spillers, at once a horrific historical reality and a metaphor of the slave's perpetually suspended social definition), violent assaults deprived the captive person's body of any integrity and, consequently, of gender. Distinguishing the socially conceptualized "body" from the undifferentiated, ungendered "flesh" subtending it, Spillers argues that the European capture of African bodies constituted "high crimes against the *flesh*. ... If we think of the 'flesh' as a primary narrative, then we mean its seared, divided, ripped-apartness, riveted to the ship's hole, fallen, or 'escaped' overboard," or with "eyes beaten out, arms, backs, skulls branded, a left jaw, a right ankle, punctured; teeth missing, as the calculated work of iron, whips, chains, knives, the canine patrol, the bullet" (67). Torture deliberately undoes, and thus exposes the factitiousness of, the integrated body.

Spillers reads the degendering of captive persons through Lacan, but she also politicizes Lacan by focusing on the sites of cultural domination at which kinship, gender, and bodies are deconstructed. Rather than detailing a universal law of culture to
which all speaking beings are "subjected," she examines relations of power among
cultures, the encounters between different symbolic orders instead of the passage
from infancy to culture. By delineating the practices of cultural domination, she renders their violence palpable: the slave's abused flesh bears "the marks of a cultural
text whose inside has been turned outside" (67). These inscriptions are in turn perpetuated across generations by the symbolic substitutions of language, as violent (in
this account) as the slaveowner's branding iron: "Sticks and bricks *might* break our
bones, but words will most certainly *kill* us" (68). It is not, as for Lacan, that "language" speaks "us" but that a dominant symbolic order marks the bodies of its cap-
tives. For the African-American female, seizing the power to name within this system is both an imperative of survival and the condition of possibility for a new social
subject undetermined by either the dichotomy phallus/castration that has vexed the
efforts of Lacan's feminist heirs to theorize the place of "the feminine" in "language"
or by the conventions of domesticity that have produced the Anglo-American "gendered female."

Spillers also politicizes Lacan by highlighting the fissures between the social and
symbolic realms within the culture of slavery, in which the Name of the Father
establishes not gender but property. Since slavery prohibits the African-American
male from participating in "the prevailing social fiction of the Father's name, the Father's law," slave children (and their heirs) in Spillers's argument have a distinctive
relation to the patriarchal symbolic register, a relation in which masculinity, constituted through a "dual fatherhood ... comprised of the African father's *banished*
name and body and the captor father's mocking presence," is inevitably divided (80).
Within this fractured configuration, moreover, the position of the enslaved mother
acquires special prominence. Probing the gaps between the social and symbolic
fields opens a space for the mother and the mode of feminism that orthodox
Lacanian rhetoric critiques.

Overtly, the enslaved mother is the locus of Spillers's sharpest distinction between
biology and gender, between ungendered black "female bodies in the raw" and the
white "gendered female" defined preeminently in terms of a revered maternity (75).
Reproduction under slavery is breeding, not maternity; denied all maternal claims to
her children, the enslaved mother simply increases her owner's stock; "'motherhood'
as female blood-rite/right" is destroyed (75). Nevertheless, Spillers accords the slave
mother a critical, albeit transient, role in the formation of her children's subjectivity.
Working from Frederick Douglass's account of the impact of his enforced early separation from his mother, which he claims eventually dissolved his sense of kinship
with his siblings. Spillers locates the experience of kinship in the presence of the
mother: "If the child's humanity is mirrored initially in the eyes of its mother, or the
maternal function, then we might be able to guess that the social subject grasps the
whole dynamic of resemblance and kinship by way of the same source" (76). Using a
language of mirroring reminiscent of D. W. Winnicott, Spillers relocates the origin of
the social subject in the maternal rather than the paternal function.[18] To underscore
the eradication of kinship under slavery, Spillers envisages a maternal function that
slavery (imperfectly) destroys.

By the end of the essay, where the subversive matricentric discourse culminates, it is clear that some maternal imprint survives the master culture's attacks. Unmediated by a father empowered by the Father's name, the enslaved child's relation to the mother gains an almost tangible proximity. Spillers carefully differentiates this relationship from the pathological structure that the Moynihan Report ascribes to the black family, since the mother's absolute disempowerment precludes any presumption of matriarchy; but at the same time that "motherhood as female blood-rite is outraged, is denied … it becomes the founding term of a human and social enactment" (80). According to the American slave code, the "condition" of the mother determines that of "'all her remotest posterity'" (79). But, Spillers asks, "What is the 'condition' of the mother? Is it the 'condition' of enslavement the writer means, or does he mean the 'mark' and the 'knowledge' of the *mother* upon the child that here translates into the culturally forbidden and impure?" (79). This culturally forbidden maternal mark is a redemptive antidote to the marks the patriarchal symbolic order inscribes on the bodies of its slaves. Spillers examines the consequences of this marking for the African-American male, who "has been touched, therefore, by the *mother, handed* by her in ways that he cannot escape, and in ways that the white American male is allowed to temporize by a fatherly reprieve. … It is the heritage of the *mother* that the African-American must regain as an aspect of his own personhood—the power of 'yes' to the 'female' within" (80).

This invocation of androgynous African-American masculinity—seemingly a regendering rather than a degendering—introduces at the end of Spillers's text an anomalously Anglo-American discourse of "personhood" and gender that raises some important unanswered questions. Does the African-American mother mark her son and her daughter identically? If the mother's mark on her son enables some access to the "'female' within," what does it enable for the daughter? Why is the daughter so conspicuously absent from this text? Shrouded in silence, she enters only as a double of the delegitimated African-American father, the mirroring pair with which the essay begins, and in apposition to the mother, as if mother and daughter were indistinguishable: "the African-American woman, the mother, the daughter" (80).[19] Allowed, like the son, no "fatherly reprieve," does the daughter merge with the mother—as she does in Chodorow's account of female identity formation in mother-centered (i.e., normative Western) families? Does the context of slavery, with its enforced alienation of the father, undo the fluidity of mother-daughter boundaries that Chodorow represents as the "reproduction of mothering," or, as Toni Morrison's *Beloved* suggests, does it exaggerate this loss of boundaries? Must the daughter be banned from Spillers's text to ward off the threat that possible gender differences between son and daughter pose to a discourse on degendering?

Addressing these questions directly might have complicated in productive ways Spillers's already dazzlingly complex analysis. Perhaps the contradictions involved in representing both an undoing and a redoing of gender in a language informed by the Lacanian critique of the subject and by the Anglo-American valorization of the female—a language (dis)loyal to both the identity-subverting Name of the Father and to the boundary-transgressing body of the mother—should be asserted and analyzed more fully as the necessary heteroglossia of a discourse bridging race, gender, psychoanalysis, and history.

III

Class and gender, and their articulations, are the bits and pieces from which psychological selfhood is made.

Carolyn Kay Steedman, *Landscape for a Good Woman*[20]

More self-consciously polyphonic, *Landscape for a Good Woman: A Story of Two Lives* takes a different contradiction for its subject. Written from the perspective of the daughter, this extraordinary hybrid text splices a double biography (the narrator's and her working-class mother's) with a feminist psychoanalytic critique of cultural criticism and a class critique of feminist psychoanalysis. The text gains its power from dizzying reversals that undo its own neatly mapped social and discursive landscape, bifurcated by a gate dividing an affluent terrain of "bourgeois household[s] where doors shut along the corridor"—the landscape that generates, and thus is rendered normative by, our dominant narratives of childhood subjectivity (psychoanalysis and fairy tales, affiliated forms in Steedman's account)—from the working-class terrain of the narrator's own childhood, the council houses of South London's long streets, "the world outside the gate" that has been represented only in the discourses of class (77). Despite the construction of these clear oppositions, the boundaries of class and discourse frequently dissolve. There is no stable narrative perspective: the adult narrator's ambiguously classed voice both merges with and ironically echoes the working-class child's, which itself frequently mimics her mother's. No individual discourse can adequately represent the complexity of feeling and class positioning. Overtly repudiated for its class specificity, psychoanalysis re-enters through a carefully crafted subtext of fairy tales that disclose the unruly features of the narrator's subjectivity, and through the narrative structure of the text, which, like a case history (Steedman's own analogy for it), "presents the ebb and flow of memory, the structure of dreams, the stories that people tell to explain themselves to others" (21). More provocative than the text's articulated claims are its unstated but clearly signaled contradictions and self-critiques, which open a different narrative scene.

Direct feminist psychoanalytic challenges to class analysis are the least successful aspect of this text. Steedman's most emphatic project is to grant her mother the subjectivity denied by the conventions of a (masculine) cultural criticism that construct the working-class mother as "'Mum, the formidable and eternal Mum, virago, domestic law giver, comforter and martyr'" (92).[21] Stereotyped and misdescribed (Steedman insists on her mother's nondomestic roles as worker and economic provider), the figure of "our mam" epitomizes the absence of individuality in (even sympathetic) representations of the working class. "When the sons of the working class, who have made their earlier escape from this landscape of psychological simplicity, put so much effort into accepting and celebrating it ... then something important, and odd, and possibly promising of startling revelation, is actually going on. This refusal of a complicated psychology to those living in conditions of material distress is a central theme of this book" (12). Writing as a daughter of the working class, Steedman strives to articulate and to validate her mother's desires, to fill in the psychological content absent from the accounts of such cultural critics as Jeremy

Seabrook and Richard Hoggart, to revise a canonical class perspective through the lenses of gender and psychoanalysis. But her portrait has its own monolithic features. By insisting on the overriding centrality and legitimacy of her mother's craving for "the things of the earth," on her unresigned response to material deprivation, Steedman circumscribes the subjectivity whose complexity she asserts but does not demonstrate. The metonymic series that characterizes her mother's desire tends to unfold within a single register. "From a Lancashire mill town and a working-class twenties childhood she came away wanting: fine clothes, glamour, money; to be what she wasn't" (6).[22] Sexuality, love, loneliness, and loss barely inflect this story of thwarted desire and legitimate envy. Psychological complexity reduces in this context to a more nuanced narrative of class consciousness.

Privileging the politics of envy constricts the psychoanalytic complication of working-class maternal subjectivity; class, however, powerfully and variously revises psychoanalysis, most succinctly in two "primal" scenes that crystallize the narrator's childhood relation to her parents. In both these scenes, as in Freud's primal scene, the narrator is an observer rather than a participant: watching from the sidelines is *the* working-class child's position in this text. What she sees, in contrast to the scenario witnessed by the Freudian child, however, is a class rather than a sexual encounter, for her developmental task entails negotiating subjectivity between class as well as gender positions. The first (chronologically) of these scenes revises Lacan's revision of Freud in a way that suggests a daughterly counterpart to Spillers's analysis of African-American fathers and sons. The narrator's father takes his three-year-old daughter for a walk in the bluebell wood. After gathering the flowers, they are suddenly accosted by an angry forest-keeper who reprimands the father for picking the flowers and, snatching them from his hands, scatters them on the ground, "their white roots glimmering, unprotected" (50). Recalling "the roots and their whiteness, and the way in which they had been pulled away, to wither exposed on the bank," the narrator remembers her father as "the loser, feminized, undone" by "the very solid and powerful" forest-keeper (50–51).

Recasting oedipal conflict in terms of class, the scene dramatizes the narrator's perception of her father's "castration" and her consequent disbelief in the equation of power with masculinity: "the iron of patriarchy didn't enter into my soul" (19). Like Spillers, and *contra* Lacan, Steedman argues that the disenfranchised father's difference from the Name of the Father critically shapes his child's gender and sexuality. (And like Spillers, Steedman depicts a situation of illegitimacy, in which the father can't legally transmit his family name.) If the African-American son, in Spillers's account, has access, through the gap between the African-American father and the Name of the (symbolic) Father, to an intimacy with the "'female' within," the working-class daughter, in Steedman's account, undergoes a different form of gender blurring by identifying with, rather than desiring, a socially castrated father. The narrator is called by one of her father's names for her, Kay, which Steedman signs here (and in no other text) as her middle name. As a young girl, she identifies with her father's body rather than her mother's: "A little girl's body, its neat containment, seems much more like that of a man that it does of a woman. ... His body was in some way mine" (94). Without power as a gender differential, without the phallus giving meaning to the penis, genital differences lose their significance. Defined through neither opposition nor attraction to masculinity, the narrator's working-class femininity positions her outside the dominant psychoanalytic narratives, and their affiliated fairy tales, of heterosexuality. "In the fairy-stories the daughters love their fathers because they are mighty princes, great rulers, and because such power seduces. The modern psychoanalytic myths posit the same plot, old tales are made manifest: secret longings, doors closing along the corridors of the bourgeois household. But daddy, you never knew me like this ... the iron didn't enter into the soul" (61). In her own household the mother, not the father, is the potent presence behind closed doors; marginalized both outside the family and (partially as a consequence) within, the father is an object of the daughter's pity rather than desire.[23]

Through the other primal scene, given far more weight than the one with the father and preceding it in the narrative (although, chronologically, it occurs a few months later), the narrator's relation to her mother calls into question the construction of femininity within different psychoanalytic discourses. As in the scene in the bluebell wood, the child is a spectator rather than a participant; once again, she observes a class encounter between two same-sex adults, here, her mother (who has just given birth to the narrator's sister) and a health visitor who censors the mother's provision of physical—and, by implication, psychological—nurture: " 'This house isn't fit for a baby' " (2).[24] In both scenes, a disciplinary figure bearing class authority intervenes in the narrator's relation to a parent and introduces a difference within gender. Watching from the curtainless window as the health visitor recedes, the child makes a silent pact of class solidarity with her mother, articulated by the adult narrator's vow: "I will do everything and anything until the end of my days to stop anyone ever talking to me like that woman talked to my mother. ... I read a [middle-class] woman's book, meet such a woman at a party (a woman now, like me) and think quite deliberately as we talk: we are divided. ... I know this and you don't" (2). The interaction simultaneously revises and conflates oedipal and preoedipal scenarios, for it is the middle-class woman (rather than the father) who both interrupts and consolidates the mother-daughter bond. The daughter's identification with her mother is not produced in a dyadic sphere created by the mother's mirroring gaze but through a common position at the window and a shared perception of a third term. Identification with the mother is disidentification with the health visitor; it is triadic rather than dyadic and triangulated by class instead of patriarchy.

To defend her mother from the middle-class critique personified by the health visitor, the narrator must avoid participating in psychoanalytic discourses that might signal her complicity with this critique. As a child, she approvingly echoes her mother's class-appropriate definition of good mothering—"we'd never gone hungry; she went out to work for us; we had warm beds to lie in at night"—and insists on the sufficiency of a purely material mothering (1). As an adult, she both reiterates this definition, with some ironic distance, and displaces it with Winnicott's notion of good enough mothering (in her one eager unequivocal appropriation of psychoanalysis) to argue that her own childhood desire to have children demonstrates, as Winnicott suggests, her mother's adequacy; but her case is unconvincing, and perhaps intentionally so, since her childhood desire for two children, one resembling herself and the other her mother, just as plausibly attests to a longing to repair insufficient mothering by remothering both her mother and herself. What the class configuration consistently inhibits is the direct articulation of anger and the endorsement of psychoanalytic accounts of childhood ambivalence that might seem, through their contaminating association with the health visitor's judgment, to blame the (maternal) victim. The middle-class intervention thus shapes the mother-daughter bond both by disallowing ambivalence and by seemingly resolving it through providing an alternative focus for the daughter's anger, deflecting it away from the mother. This female triangle enables a version of the splitting that Melanie Klein attributes to the infant, who divides the inevitably frustrating mother into a "good" breast and "bad" breast: the "bad" breast, by drawing anger to itself, preserves the idealization of the mother.[25] But rather than overtly asserting her ambivalence (which she occasionally enacts indirectly through sudden unexplained outbursts of tears), Steedman's narrator represents ambivalence as the psychic property of the working-class mother who loves her children but simultaneously resents the hardships they impose. Steedman renders maternal ambivalence as a temporal structure produced by economic exigencies (although the imagery seems, as I shall argue later, to return ambivalence to the child): "What came free could be given freely, like her milk: loving a baby costs very little. But feeding us during our later childhood was a tense struggle between giving and denial. We never went hungry, we were well nourished, but fed in the cheapest possible way. I knew this, I think, when I conjured her under the kitchen table, the thin wounds across her breasts pouring forth blood, not milk" (93). In contrast to her apostrophe to her father, the narrator never blames or even retrospectively addresses her mother. The only overt sign of trouble is a brief unexplained allusion to a nine-year period when the adult narrator refused to see her mother.

Declining to theorize the daughter's ambivalence both invokes and revokes the discourse of Klein; insisting on the mother's ambivalence differentiates Steedman's account from that of Klein's most influential feminist descendant, Nancy Chodorow, whom Steedman faults for the middle-class assumption that mothers identify and merge with daughters, who themselves become mothers in order to reproduce the original merger with their own mothers. There is a primary identification with the mother in this text—"she, myself, walks my dreams"—but no normative reproduction of mothering, most obviously because the narrator deliberately does not become a mother (61). (Her sister, however, does become a mother, in an untold story that haunts the fringes of this text.) More importantly, this daughter internalizes from her mother not relationality and fluid ego boundaries but stoicism in the face of inequality. What she learns from her mother's response to the health visitor—"she [the mother] had cried. ... And then she stopped crying, my mother, got by, the phrase that picks up after all difficulty"—she learns again through the story of her great-grandmother, sent from home at age eleven to work as a maid in a distant town: "She cried, because tears are cheap; and then she stopped, and got by, because no one gives you anything in this world" (1–2, 31). The femininity (re)produced through this working-class female genealogy has more to do with self-sufficiency than with relationality. Replacing the tears that figure fluid boundaries is a maternal voice commanding self-restraint; under her mother's tutelage, the narrator learns to dry her "sentimental" tears over nineteenth-century accounts of child labor, as well as any tears she might shed for herself. The withholding, not the offer, of empathic merger here structures female subjectivity. In her description of her final visit to her mother, two weeks before her mother's death, the narrator represents this withholding as an inevitable function of a class position that makes its members feel endangered and illegitimate, threatened by emotions that are perilous for victims and denied the self-esteem that enables mirroring: "I was really a ghost who came to call. That feeling, the sense of being absent in my mother's presence, was nothing to do with illness, was what it had always been like. We were truly illegitimate, outside any law of recognition: the mirror broken, a lump of ice for a heart" (142).

Steedman's metaphors, however, signal a different discourse, with a less forgiving account of broken mirroring. The disavowed story of daughterly ambivalence returns through the middle-class discourse of fairy tales, ingeniously manipulated to encode a subversive psychoanalytic subtext to the daughter's faithful narrative of class. Never represented as coherent narratives, but nonetheless evoked through recurrent allusions, two interwoven fairy tales, "The Snow Queen" and "The Little Mermaid," create a violent imaginary of class, mirrors, ice, tears, milk, and blood. By depicting scenarios in which the mother, absent from the family, assumes a terrifying mythic guise (as the Snow Queen and the sea witch), these tales call into question the narrator's legitimatization of working-class mothering.

"The Snow Queen" offers the least threatening and most explicit counternarrative, in which the narrator openly identifies with the (male) protagonist who shares her name, Kay. In the opening section of the fairy tale, the devil makes a distorting mirror that transforms beauty into ugliness; it falls and breaks into hundreds of millions of billions of pieces which pierce people's eyes, distorting their vision, and penetrate their hearts, turning them to ice. During a snowstorm, Kay (who lives with his grandmother) is visited by the Snow Queen, whose power he has defied by boasting he would melt her on the stove. "She was delicately lovely, but all ice, glittering, dazzling ice ... her eyes shone like two bright stars, but there was no rest or peace in them."[26] After this visit, two splinters from the devil's mirror suddenly enter Kay's eyes and heart; his vision transformed and his heart frozen, he becomes the Snow Queen's icy subject. Only the empathic tears of his devoted playmate, Gerda, who travels to the Snow Queen's arctic palace in search of him, melt Kay's frozen heart, and his tears of gratitude wash the splinters from his eye. Steedman's recurrent allusions to this story—"the mirror breaks ... and a lump of ice is lodged in the heart" (97)—indict the mother she overtly justifies. The stoical voice, from this perspective, is a frozen voice; the repudiation of tears, a form of death rather than of strength. The fairy tale intimates the unstated cost of "getting by" without emphathic mothering. What the broken mirror (re)produces is a frozen heart.

Through its story of chosen mutilation, "The Little Mermaid" introduces a more violent psychoanalytic discourse, which replaces the Winnicottian language of mirroring with a Kleinian language of passion and blood.[27] Although the story itself focuses on the heterosexual romance between the mermaid and the prince, Steedman's choice of images highlights the relationship of the mermaid and the sea witch, whom the mermaid begs to transform her fishtail into legs in order to win the prince's love. The witch warns her: "It hurts; it is as if a sharp sword were running through you. ... Every step you take will be as if you were treading upon sharp knives, so sharp as to draw blood" (132). As payment for this service, to be rendered through a potion made with her own blood, the witch demands the mermaid's beautiful voice: "She [the witch] punctured her breast and let the black blood drop into the caldron ... thereupon she cuts off the tongue of the little mermaid, who was dumb now and could neither sing nor speak" (133–34). Although these sacrifices prove futile in the fairy tale, they constitute the central symbolic episode of Steedman's text, which circulates the images of knives and sacrifice without specifying who is cutting whom. Whereas the mermaid elects her sacrifice to gain the love of the prince, the violent sacrificial relationships in Steedman's text bind mothers and daughters, not women and men: "Somehow the iron of patriarchy didn't enter into my soul. ... in the dreams it is a woman who holds the knife, and only a woman can kill" (19). (Steedman's final description of her dying mother as looking "like a witch" [140]—thin, dark, gaunt—secures the connection to the fairy tale.) During her first reading of the two fairy tales, at age seven, the narrator imagines her parents naked under the kitchen table, holding sharp-edged knives with which they "cut each other, making thin surface wounds like lines drawn with a sharp red pencil, from which the blood poured. ... Downstairs I thought, the thin blood falls in sheets from my mother's breasts; she was the most cut, but I knew it was she who did the cutting. I couldn't always see the knife in my father's hand" (54). By the time she is twelve, her father has dropped out of the picture and sexual warfare has become self-dramatized maternal self-mutilation, as the narrator reimagines "the knife in my mother's hand, and the thin red lines of blood drawn across her breasts: displaying to my imagination the mutilation involved in keeping and feeding us" (82). Lacing milk with blood, the imagery reveals at once the narrator's guilty conviction that she has, however in advertently, bloodied her mother's breasts, and her anger at her mother's self-display. Through the parallel scene from "The Little Mermaid," it is clear that the sacrifice is mutual: the witch mother mutilates herself to enable the mermaid/daughter's upward mobility (to the land/to the middle class), and in exchange the daughter relinquishes her voice, parroting instead her mother's working-class discourse on good mothering. Instead of being mirrored by her mother, the daughter faithfully echoes her voice.

Through the fairy-tale subtext, then, Steedman launches a subversive psychoanalytic critique of her own class-based critique of psychoanalysis. Both discourses are necessary to represent the subjectivity produced by a position straddling the class divide, for the narrator (in contrast to the mother with whom she so strongly identifies) is not confined to the working-class world of her childhood: she gains continued access, through education, to the middle-class culture she began at age seven to consume through fairy tales. Steedman doesn't speculate whether a contemporary child rooted entirely in the working class feels anger at her mother; instead, she demonstrates the prohibitions on that child's recognition of her anger and subtly devises strategies for representing her own complex position on the boundary.

She figures this position most deftly through the contrast between two narratives: the story of the little watercress girl recounted by Henry Mayhew in *London Labour and the London Poor* and the story of "Dora" recounted by Freud, the story "we" know intimately because it is "*the* story ... of the bourgeois household and the romances of the family and the fairy-tales that lie behind its closed doors" (137–39). These narratives mark the range of her contradictory identifications: between working-class femininity (defined by labor) and middle-class femininity (defined by sexuality), between harmonious and disharmonious mother-daughter relationships, between history and psychoanalysis, and between coherent and hysterical (contradictory, disrupted) narrative modes. Steedman valorizes the story of the little watercress girl for resisting our dominant cultural narratives and insists that she finds a mirror image in this "good and helpful child, who eased her mother's life" (141); but her own troubled story far more closely resembles Dora's inconclusive tale. (The narrator's childhood failure to come home from rehearsing a school play in time to buy the watercress her mother wants for tea underlines her distance from the dutiful watercress girl.) For all its incoherence, Dora's narrative is legible to the narrator, while the watercress girl's remains opaque. Insisting that lives "outside the gate" be allowed to preserve their inscrutability, Steedman refuses to recuperate the watercress girl's story to familiar (psychoanalytic) narratives. But her own heterogeneous narrative, as full as Dora's of gaps, contradictions, repetitions, and revisions that interrupt and interlard the exposition, unfolds within a psychoanalytic register that seemingly operates for the person on the boundary as well as the one inside the gate.

IV

However unfeasible and inefficient it may sound, I see no way to avoid insisting that there has to be a simultaneous other focus: not merely who am I? but who is the other woman? How am I naming her? How does she name me?

Gayatri Chakravorty Spivak, "French Feminism in an International Frame"[28]

Steedman's focus on the boundary affiliates her with a current trend in readings of class and psychoanalysis. The boundary is the critical position in these readings, for it both destabilizes and extends the psychoanalytic enclosure, as Jane Gallop and Mary Poovey suggest in their investigations of the threshold figure of the governess, who exists at once outside and inside the middle-class family.[29] As a duplicate mother who is "castrated" by passing through the circuit of money, the governess disrupts the imaginary wholeness of the middle-class family and of psychoanalytic theory. Yet psychoanalysis is well suited to describe this disruption, which Gallop represents as an intervention of the symbolic in the imaginary. Poovey depicts psychoanalysis as the most appropriate discourse for articulating the splits, identifications, and displacements that characterize both the person on the boundary and the current historical situation of feminist criticism itself, positioned "between the powerful guardians of culture, among whom we do and do not belong, and a vast, heterogeneous majority who feel excluded from what we say, and between an outdated ideology of individualism and an ideology of decentered subjects whose hour is not yet here."[30]

Poovey's account of feminism's double loyalties returns us to Spillers's representation of feminism's discursive genealogy. Like Steedman, Gallop, and Poovey, moreover, Spillers locates psychoanalysis (as well as feminism) at the boundaries, rather than exclusively on either side. When she explicitly invokes psychoanalysis (as opposed to the analogies she implies between the effects of the Lacanian symbolic and of cultural domination), it is in relation to negotiations across racial and gender boundaries. Spillers examines a specific discursive moment in the representation of slavery, Harriet Jacobs's *Incidents in the Life of a Slave Girl*. Written by an escaped female slave and dictated to a woman abolitionist, Jacobs's text succinctly embodies these negotiations through the representation of a triangulated scene between Linda Brent, the autobiographical protagonist, and Mr. and Mrs. Flint, the white couple that owns her. By acting out her husband's desire for the captive woman, Mrs. Flint dissolves the boundaries of gender on both sides of the racial divide, "degendering" both herself and Linda Brent by subjecting Brent to female as well as male sexual desire (and thereby contrasting her to the "gendered female," who is defined by a relation of vulnerability solely to the male). There is an identification, however, not only between the Anglo-American woman and man but also between the Anglo-American and African-American woman and man but also between the Anglo-American and African-American women, "twin actants on a common psychic landscape" created by the sovereignty of the Anglo-American male: "Neither could claim her body and its various productions—for quite different reasons, albeit—as her own ... we cannot unravel one female's narrative from the other's, cannot decipher one without tripping over the other" (77). These multiple interwoven identifications make this scene resemble "casebook narratives from psychoanalysis" (76). It is less the experience of captive persons themselves than the "'threads cable-strong' of an incestuous interracial genealogy [that] uncover slavery in the United States as one of the richest displays of the psychoanalytic dimensions of culture before the science of European psychoanalysis takes hold" (77).

Spillers and Steedman share (along with Gallop and Poovey) a preference for delineating situations and figures at the boundary and a reticence about representing the subjectivity of persons entirely dominated by oppression. Steedman explores her own liminal position and refuses to interpret the watercress girl's story; Spillers details the positioning, but not the subjectivity, of persons in captivity and suggests that the twentieth-century "black woman," rather than the captive person, constitutes the "profoundest revelation" of the "split subject that psychoanalytic theory posits" (65). Their caution raises a critical question about the limits of psychoanalysis. How do we know when social and cultural boundaries should be crossed, when "naming" the "other woman," as Spivak and others have exhorted us to do, simply appropriates "her" to "us"?[31] Rather than groping after some definitive answer, I want to end by gesturing toward a countertext that crosses, instead of lingering at, a boundary, a text that has been a kind of subtext to my own. *Beloved* deliberately represents captive persons as subjects rather than as objects of oppression, and does so primarily in a discourse on the hunger, passion, and violence generated in the "too thick" mother-daughter bond produced by the conditions of slavery.[32] This extraordinary project has its attendant risks, of course, discernible perhaps in the novel's enormous popularity with women readers across racial lines. But the text circumvents any easy delimitation of the boundaries of psychoanalysis.

It is too early for feminism to foreclose on psychoanalysis. Vast cultural terrains unfold beyond the boundaries of this essay, and beyond those of psychoanalysis as well, undoubtedly. But rather than fixing those boundaries, my goal has been to forestall the sense that we know exactly where they lie and what they necessarily exclude. Psychoanalysis has been resistant to the social, but it need not always, uniformly, be. It is better for feminism to challenge that resistance than to renounce psychoanalysis entirely or succumb to its seductions.

Notes

1. Rosi Braidotti, "The Politics of Ontological Difference," in *Between Feminism and Psychoanalysis*, ed. Teresa Brennan (London: Routledge, 1989), pp. 97–98. Paul Smith, "Julia Kristeva Et Al.; or, Take Three or More," in *Feminism and Psychoanalysis*, ed. Richard Feldstein and Judith Roof (Ithaca: Cornell University Press, 1989), pp. 84–85.

I am grateful to Marianne Hirsch and Evelyn Fox Keller for their boundless patience and support during the composition of this essay. I am also grateful for Mary M. Childers's helpful criticism, which I have been able only in part to incorporate into this version of the essay.

2. There are diverse reasons for the pervasive current disrepute of psychoanalysis, ranging from the politics of academic discourse, in which the hegemony of psychoanalysis within "theory" has been displaced by more historical and socially nuanced discourses, to the politics of public discourse on the family, in which psychoanalysis has been tainted by its alleged complicity in the cover-up of child abuse. The exemplary case of the latter charge is Jeffrey Moussaieff Masson, *The Assault on Truth: Freud's Suppression of the Seduction Theory* (New York: Farrar, Straus, and Giroux, 1984). See also Judith Lewis Herman, with Lisa Hirschman, *Father-Daughter Incest* (Cambridge, Mass.: Harvard University Press, 1981) and Louise DeSalvo, *Virginia Woolf: The Impact of Childhood Sexual Abuse on Her Life and Work* (Boston: Beacon Press, 1989). These diverse discursive arenas share a perception of the social irresponsibility of psychoanalysis. For a response to this charge, see Jacqueline Rose, "Where Does the Misery Come From? Psychoanalysis, Feminism, and the Event," in *Feminism and Psychoanalysis*, pp. 25–39. For a similar attempt to rescue psychoanalysis for feminism, see Rachel Bowlby on the gendered implications of "repudiation," in "Still Crazy After All These Years," in *Between Feminism and Psychoanalysis*, pp. 40–60.

3. For an integration of psychoanalysis and the social realm under the aegis of Foucault, see Julian Henriques, Wendy Hollway, Cathy Urwin, Couze Venn, Valerie Walkerdine, *Changing the Subject: Psychology, Social Regulation and Subjectivity* (London and New York: Methuen, 1984).

4. *Totem and Taboo* is devoted to demonstrating that all culture originates in patricide, which is universally preserved in the psyche as the oedipus complex. In "Mother-Right and the Sexual Ignorance of Savages" Freud's British representative Ernest Jones defends the universality of the oedipus complex against the cultural relativism of Bronislaw Malinowski by arguing that only "primordial Oedipus tendencies" could generate the denial of paternity enabling the matrilinear Melanesian societies Malinowski studied. See Sigmund Freud, *Totem and Taboo* [1913–14], *The Standard Edition of the Complete Psychological Works of Sigmund Freud*, trans. and ed. James Strachey (London: Hogarth Press, 1953–66), vol. 13; Ernest Jones, "Mother-Right and the Sexual Ignorance of Savages" [1924], in *Essays in Applied Psycho-Analysis*, 2 vols. (London: Hogarth Press and the Institute of Psycho-Analysis, 1951), 2:170; and Bronislaw Malinowski, *Sex and Repression in Savage Society* (1927; Chicago: University of Chicago Press, 1985).

5. Juliet Mitchell, *Psychoanalysis and Feminism: Freud, Reich, Laing, and Women* (New York: Random House, 1974), p. 395.

6. Jacqueline Rose, *Sexuality in the Field of Vision* (London: Verso, 1986), p. 90. Here, and in her essay "Where Does the Misery Come From?" (see n. 2 above), Rose mounts the most eloquent defenses of the utility of Lacanian psychoanalysis for feminism.

7. This revision has emerged only from theorists with primary commitments to questions of race and class. In the Lacanian anthology *Between Feminism and Psychoanalysis*, for example, the editor, Teresa Brennan, comments in her Introduction that "real changes in either parenting patterns or the social position of women and men must have consequences for the symbolic" (p. 3), but neither the Introduction nor the rest of the anthology examines these changes or their consequences. Despite Brennan's claim that the anthology unsettles the "relation of psychical structures to the political realities of women's social conditions" (p. 12), all of the essays (except for Rosi Braidotti's overt critique of psychoanalysis) either define the "social," the "political," and the "historical" within the terms of psychoanalysis (so that the "social" is coterminous with the death drive, for example) or circumscribe them radically (the only social context analyzed, for example, is the academy). The anthology bears witness to Paul Smith's charge that psychoanalysis cannot generate political desire and has tended to deplete that of feminism—unless, I would argue, feminism demands that psychoanalysis address specific social configurations.

8. Nancy J. Chodorow, *Feminism and Psychoanalytic Theory* (Cambridge: Polity Press, 1989), pp. 157, 159. Object relations theory has consistently emphasized the social context of development, in opposition to the intrapsychic terrain of drive theory; some slippage between the "social" as the narrowly interpersonal and as a more inclusive historical field has bolstered the discourse's political claims. For a recent critique, from an entirely different perspective, of the place of the social in object relations, see Daniel N. Stern, *The Interpersonal World of the Infant: A View From Psychoanalysis and Developmental Psychology* (New York: Basic Books, 1985).

9. Jane Flax, *Thinking Fragments: Psychoanalysis, Feminism, and Postmodernism in the Contemporary West* (Berkeley and Los Angeles: University of California Press, 1989), p. 122. This position is also presented in various ways throughout Nancy Chodorow's *Feminism and Psychoanalytic Theory*.

10. Elizabeth V. Spelman, *Inessential Woman: Problems of Exclusion in Feminist Thought* (Boston: Beacon Press, 1988), pp. 95, 157. For a recent critique of Chodorow's "cultural essentialism" from a Lacanian perspective that faults the assumptions that gender is constant within the subject and that psychological differences between the sexes are universal, see Toril Moi, "Patriarchal Thought and the Drive for Knowledge," in *Between Feminism and Psychoanalysis*, pp. 189–205. For a related critique of Chodorow from a Foucauldian perspective, see Cathy Urwin's contribution to *Changing the Subject*, which insists on the ways that the mother's response to her child, and hence the child's perception and internalization of the mother's gender, is always mediated by the mother's own "positioning within particular discourses which enter into the constitution of her role" (p. 320).

11. Chodorow, "On *The Reproduction of Mothering*: A Methodological Debate," *Signs* 6, no. 3 (Spring 1981): 514. At the end of her early essay "Family Structure and Feminine Personality" (in *Woman, Culture, and Society*, ed. Michelle Zimbalist Rosaldo and Louise Lamphere [Stanford: Stanford University Press, 1974]), Chodorow launches this cross-cultural work by drawing from ethnographies of Java and East London to contrast the pathological dimension of the mother-daughter bond in Western middle-class families with the higher self-esteem transmitted from mother to daughter in cultures in which mothers have authority and important connections with other women both outside and within the home. The complaint that Chodorow privileges (rather than simply represents) Western middle-class femininity seems to me based on a misperception.

12. Hence the recurrent claim that object relations theory is intrinsically inapplicable to diverse social configurations seems misguided to me. Recent explorations of multiple mothering in extended African-American families, for example, seem perfectly congruent with Chodorow's emphasis on the psychological consequences of female caretakers. See, for example, Patricia Hill Collins, "The Meaning of Motherhood in Black Culture and Black Mother/ Daughter Relationships," in *Sage: A Scholarly Journal on Black Women* 4, no. 2 (Fall 1987): 3–10.

13. On the insufficiency of the Lacanian subject for a feminist politics, see Teresa de Lauretis, "Feminist Studies/Critical Studies: Issues, Terms, and Contexts," in *Feminist Studies/Critical Studies*, ed. Teresa de Lauretis (Bloomington: Indiana University Press, 1986), pp. 1–19. In her Introduction to *Between Feminism and Psychoanalysis*, Teresa Brennan eloquently argues for undoing the hierarchized polarization of object relations and Lacan. For a reading of object relations theory as incorporating, rather than opposing, some basic principles of deconstruction, see Leslie Wahl Rabine, "A Feminist Politics of Non-Identity," *Feminist Studies* 14, no. 1 (Spring 1988): 11–31. For a partially comparable project, in another arena, of undoing the opposition between Anglo-American and French feminisms, see Betsy Draine, "Refusing the Wisdom of Solomon: Some Recent Feminist Literary Theory," *Signs* 15, no. 1 (Autumn 1989): 144–70. Reworking the opposition sometimes generates reversals. In *Thinking Fragments*, Jane Flax argues surprisingly that "Object relations theory is more compatible with postmodernism that Freudian or Lacanian analysis because it does not require a fixed or essentialist view of 'human nature'. ... As social relations and family structures change, so would human nature" (p. 110). This assertion is based on privileging history as the *only* form of dif-

ference and on overlooking the radically disruptive, de-essentializing function of the unconscious in Lacan; it is important to remember that the intersubjectively constituted and historically variable self of object relations remains more integrated than the split subject of Lacan.
Nevertheless, Flax's assertion usefully calls into question the oversimplified opposition between the allegedly unitary self of object relations and the heterogeneous Lacanian subject.

14. Hortense J. Spillers, "'The Permanent Obliquity of an In[pha]llibly Straight': In the
Time of the Daughters and the Fathers," in *Daughters and Fathers*, ed. Lynda E. Boose and
Betty S. Flowers (Baltimore: Johns Hopkins University Press, 1989), p. 158.

15. Hortense J. Spillers, "Interstices: A Small Drama of Words," in *Pleasure and Danger*, ed.
Carol Vance (Boston: Routledge and Kegan Paul, 1984), p. 88.

16. Hortense J. Spillers, "Mama's Baby, Papa's Maybe: An American Grammar Book," *diacritics* 17, no. 2 (Summer 1987): 72; subsequent citations of this work will be placed in parentheses in the text. For a non-Lacanian account of the ways that slavery undoes the meaning of
domesticity, see Hortense J. Spillers, "Changing the Letter: The Yokes, the Jokes of Discourse,
or, Mrs. Stowe, Mr. Reed," in *Slavery and the Literary Imagination*, ed. Deborah E. McDowell
and Arnold Rampersad (Baltimore: Johns Hopkins University Press, 1989), pp. 25–61.

17. See Jacques Lacan, "The Mirror Stage as Formative of the Function of the I," *Ecrits: A
Selection*, trans. Alan Sheridan (New York: W. W. Norton, 1977), pp. 1–7.

18. See D. W. Winnicott, "Mirror-role of Mother and Family in Child Development," *Playing and Reality* (Harmondsworth, Middlesex: Penguin Books, 1971). I cite Winnicott rather
than Lacan (whose essay on the mirror stage influenced Winnicott) because Spillers's emphasis on the child's humanity and the social implications of the mother's responsive gaze are
much closer to the discourse of object relations than to Lacan's insistence on the alienating
structure of the ego produced by the mirror stage. For Lacan, the social subject is produced by
the symbolic.

19. In "'The Permanent Obliquity of an In[pha]llibly Straight': In the Time of the Daughters and the Fathers," Spillers offers a detailed analysis of the African-American father-daughter relationship, which has captured her attention more fully than the mother-daughter relationship.

20. Carolyn Kay Steedman, *Landscape for a Good Woman: A Story of Two Lives* (London: Virago, 1986; New Brunswick: Rutgers University Press, 1987), p. 7; subsequent citations of this
work will be to the American edition and will be placed in parentheses in the text. I am grateful to Tricia Moran for calling this text to my attention.

21. From Jeremy Seabrook, *What Went Wrong?* (London: Victor Gollancz, 1978), cited by
Steedman.

22. Or note another characteristic example: "Born into 'the old working class,' she wanted: a
New Look skirt, a timbered country cottage, to marry a prince" (p. 9). Rather than introducing a new direction, the last term in these series encompasses the others.

23. As Julie Abraham points out in her review of *Landscape for a Good Woman* in the *Wom-
en's Review of Books* 5, no. 9 (June 1988), Steedman is reticent about her own sexuality. Her
story, however, puts her at a distance form the dominant narratives of heterosexuality. Although as a daughter she desires to be marked by the father, or by the law he (inadequately)
represents, she expresses no desire for the person that he is.

24. Steedman represents the boundaries of the working-class home as more permeable than
the locked doors of the middle-class houses behind the gate. Curtainless windows and un-
locked doors characterize the narrator's family home, whose domestic boundaries are also
subverted by the frequent presence of boarders. That the marginalized father, who sleeps in
the attic, is sometimes mistaken for another border underlines the blurring of the inside-out-
side dichotomy. On the psychoanalytic fiction of the insular middle-class family, see Jane Gallop, *The Daughter's Seduction: Feminism and Psychoanalysis* (Ithaca: Cornell University Press,
1982), p. 144.

25. See Melanie Klein, *"Love, Guilt, and Reparation" and Other Works, 1921–45* (New York: Dell, 1975). Conspicuously absent (repressed?) from Steedman's text, Klein is mentioned only in relation to the pathologization of envy, never in relation to the mother-daughter bond.

26. Dulac's *"The Snow Queen" and Other Stories from Hans Andersen* (Garden City: Doubleday, 1976), p. 16; subsequent citations of "The Snow Queen" will be placed in parentheses in the text. Citations of "The Little Mermaid" will also be to this edition and will be placed in parentheses in the text.

27. On the evolution of object relations from the Kleinian emphasis on hunger and aggression to Winnicott's more benign accounts of mother-infant mirroring, see Jay R. Greenberg and Stephen A. Mitchell, *Object Relations in Psychoanalytic Theory* (Cambridge, Mass.: Harvard University Press, 1983); Judith M. Hughes, *Reshaping the Psychoanalytic Domain: The Work of Melanie Klein, W. R. D. Fairbairn, and D. W. Winnicott* (Berkeley and Los Angeles: University of California Press, 1989); and D. W. Winnicott, "A Personal View of the Kleinian Contribution," in *The Maturational Processes and the Facilitating Environment* (London: Hogarth Press, 1965), pp. 171–78.

28. Gayatri Chakravorty Spivak, "French Feminism in an International Frame," *Yale French Studies* 62 (1981): 179.

29. Jane Gallop, *The Daughter's Seduction: Feminism and Psychoanalysis* (Ithaca: Cornell University Press, 1982), pp. 141–48; Mary Poovey, "The Anathematized Race: The Governance and *Jane Eyre*," in *Feminism and Psychoanalysis*, pp. 230–54.

30. Poovey, "The Anathematized Race," p. 254.

31. Spivak's line has been cited in numerous places. See especially Jane Gallop, "The Monster in the Mirror: The Feminist Critic's Psychoanalysis," in *Feminism and Psychoanalysis*, pp. 13–24; Jane Gallop, "Annie Leclerc Writing a Letter, with Vermeer," in *The Poetics of Gender*, ed. Nancy K. Miller (New York: Columbia University Press, 1986), pp. 137–56; and Helena Michie's extremely interesting comparison and critique of these two essays in "Not One of the Family: The Repression of the Other Woman in Feminist Theory," in *Discontented Discourses: Feminism/Textual Intervention/Psychoanalysis*, ed. Marleen S. Barr and Richard Feldstein (Urbana: University of Illinois Press, 1989), pp. 15–28.

32. Toni Morrison, *Beloved* (New York: Knopf, 1987), p. 164. "Too thick" is the charge made by Paul D and does not, of course, represent Morrison's perspective. The whole question of *Beloved* and psychoanalysis is, obviously, the subject of another essay.

The Social Construction
of Black Feminist Thought

Patricia Hill Collins

Sojourner Truth, Anna Julia Cooper, Ida Wells Barnett, and Fannie Lou Hamer are but a few names from a growing list of distinguished African-American women activists. Although their sustained resistance to Black women's victimization within interlocking systems of race, gender, and class oppression is well known, these women did not act alone.[1] Their actions were nurtured by the support of countless, ordinary African-American women who, through strategies of everyday resistance, created a powerful foundation for this more visible Black feminist activist tradition.[2] Such support has been essential to the shape and goals of Black feminist thought.

The long-term and widely shared resistance among African-American women can only have been sustained by an enduring and shared standpoint among Black women about the meaning of oppression and the actions that Black women can and should take to resist it. Efforts to identify the central concepts of this Black women's standpoint figure prominently in the works of contemporary Black feminist intellectuals.[3] Moreover, political and epistemological issues influence the social construction of Black feminist thought. Like other subordinate groups, African-American women not only have developed distinctive interpretations of Black women's oppression but have done so by using alternative ways of producing and validating knowledge itself.

A Black Women's Standpoint

The Foundation of Black Feminist Thought

Black women's everyday acts of resistance challenge two prevailing approaches to studying the consciousness of oppressed groups.[4] One approach claims that subordinate groups identify with the powerful and have no valid independent interpretation of their own oppression.[5] The second approach assumes that the oppressed are less human than their rulers and, therefore, are less capable of articulating their own standpoint.[6] Both approaches see any independent consciousness expressed by an oppressed group as being not of the group's own making and/or inferior to the per-spective of the dominant group.[7] More important, both interpretations suggest that oppressed groups lack the motivation for political activism because of their flawed consciousness of their own subordination.

Yet African-American women have been neither passive victims of nor willing ac-complices to their own domination. As a result, emerging work in Black women's studies contends that Black women have a self-defined standpoint on their own op-pression.[8] Two interlocking components characterize this standpoint. First, Black women's political and economic status provides them with a distinctive set of experi-ences that offers a different view of material reality than that available to other groups. The unpaid and paid work that Black women perform, the types of commu-nities in which they live, and the kinds of relationships they have with others suggest that African-American women, as a group, experience a different world than those who are not Black and female.[9] Second, these experiences stimulate a distinctive Black feminist consciousness concerning that material reality.[10] In brief, a subordi-nate group not only experiences a different reality than a group that rules, but a sub-ordinate group may interpret that reality differently than a dominant group.

Many ordinary African-American women have grasped this connection between what one does and how one thinks. Hannah Nelson, an elderly Black domestic worker, discusses how work shapes the standpoints of African-American and white women: "Since I have to work, I don't really have to worry about most of the things that most of the white women I have worked for are worrying about. And if these women did their own work, they would think just like I do—about this, anyway."[11] Ruth Shays, a Black inner city resident, points out how variations in men's and wom-en's experiences lead to differences in perspective: "The mind of the man and the mind of the woman is the same. But this business of living makes women use their minds in ways that men don't even have to think about."[12] Finally, elderly domestic worker Rosa Wakefield assesses how the standpoints of the powerful and those who serve them diverge: "If you eats these dinners and don't cook 'em, if you wears these clothes and don't buy or iron them, then you might start thinking that the good fairy or some spirit did all that. ... Blackfolks don't have no time to be thinking like that. ... But when you don't have anything else to do, you can think like that. It's bad for your mind, though."[13]

While African-American women may occupy material positions that stimulate a unique standpoint, expressing an independent Black feminist consciousness is prob-lematic precisely because more powerful groups have a vested interest in suppressing such thought. As Hannah Nelson notes, "I have grown to womanhood in a world where the saner you are, the madder you are made to appear."[14] Nelson realizes that those who control the schools, the media, and other cultural institutions are gener-ally skilled in establishing their view of reality as superior to alternative interpreta-tions. While an oppressed group's experiences may put them in a position to see things differently, their lack of control over the apparatuses of society that sustain ideological hegemony makes the articulation of their self-defined standpoint diffi-cult. Groups unequal in power are correspondingly unequal in their access to the re-sources necessary to implement their perspectives outside their particular group.

One key reason that standpoints of oppressed groups are discredited and sup-pressed by the more powerful is that self-defined standpoints can stimulate oppressed groups to resist their domination. For instance, Annie Adams, a southern Black woman, describes how she became involved in civil rights activities.

> When I first went into the mill we had segregated water fountains. … Same thing about the toilets. I had to clean the toilets for the inspection room and then, when I got ready to go to the bathroom, I had to go all the way to the bottom of the stairs to the cellar. So I asked my boss man, "What's the difference? If I can go in there and clean them toilets, why can't I use them?" Finally, I started to use that toilet. I decided I wasn't going to walk a mile to go to the bathroom.[15]

In this case, Adams found the standpoint of the "boss man" inadequate, developed one of her own, and acted upon it. In doing so, her actions exemplify the connections between experiencing oppression, developing a self-defined standpoint on that experience, and resistance.

The Significance of Black Feminist Thought

The existence of a distinctive Black women's standpoint does not mean that it has been adequately articulated in Black feminist thought. Peter Berger and Thomas Luckmann provide a useful approach to clarifying the relationship between a Black women's standpoint and Black feminist thought with the contention that knowledge exists on two levels.[16] The first level includes the everyday, taken-for-granted knowledge shared by members of a given group, such as the ideas expressed by Ruth Shays and Annie Adams. Black feminist thought, by extension, represents a second level of knowledge, the more specialized knowledge furnished by experts who are part of a group and who express the group's standpoint. The two levels of knowledge are interdependent; while Black feminist thought articulates the taken-for-granted knowledge of African-American women, it also encourages all Black women to create new self-definitions that validate a Black women's standpoint.

Black feminist thought's potential significance goes far beyond demonstrating that Black women can produce independent, specialized knowledge. Such thought can encourage collective identity by offering Black women a different view of themselves and their world than that offered by the established social order. This different view encourages African-American women to value their own subjective knowledge base.[17] By taking elements and themes of Black women's culture and traditions and infusing them with new meaning, Black feminist thought rearticulates a consciousness that already exists.[18] More important, this rearticulated consciousness gives African-American women another tool of resistance to all forms of their subordination.[19]

Black feminist thought, then, specializes in formulating and rearticulating the distinctive, self-defined standpoint of African-American women. One approach to learning more about a Black women's standpoint is to consult standard scholarly sources for the ideas of specialists on Black women's experiences.[20] But investigating a Black women's standpoint and Black feminist thought requires more ingenuity than that required in examining the standpoints and thought of white males. Rearticulating the standpoint of African-American women through Black feminist thought is much more difficult since one cannot use the same techniques to study the knowledge of the dominated as one uses to study the knowledge of the powerful. This is precisely because subordinate groups have long had to use alternative ways to create an independent consciousness and to rearticulate it through specialists validated by the oppressed themselves.

The Eurocentric Masculinist
Knowledge-Validation Process[21]

All social thought, including white masculinist and Black feminist, reflects the interests and standpoint of its creators. As Karl Mannheim notes, "If one were to trace in detail … the origin and … diffusion of a certain thought-model, one would discover the … affinity it has to the social position of given groups and their manner of interpreting the world."[22] Scholars, publishers, and other experts represent specific interests and credentialing processes, and their knowledge claims must satisfy the epistemological and political criteria of the contexts in which they reside.[23]

Two political criteria influence the knowledge-validation process. First, knowledge claims must be evaluated by a community of experts whose members represent the standpoints of the groups from which they originate. Second, each community of experts must maintain its credibility as defined by the larger group in which it is situated and from which it draws its basic, taken-for-granted knowledge.

When white males control the knowledge-validation process, both political criteria can work to suppress Black feminist thought. Since the general culture shaping the taken-for-granted knowledge of the community of experts is one permeated by widespread notions of Black and female inferiority,[24] new knowledge claims that seem to violate these fundamental assumptions are likely to be viewed as anomalies.[25] Moreover, specialized thought challenging notions of Black and female inferiority is unlikely to be generated from within a white-male-controlled academic community because both the kinds of questions that could be asked and the explanations that would be found satisfying would necessarily reflect a basic lack of familiarity with Black women's reality.[26]

The experiences of African-American women scholars illustrate how individuals who wish to rearticulate a Black Women's standpoint through Black feminist thought can be suppressed by a white-male-controlled knowledge-validation process. Exclusion from basic literacy, quality educational experiences, and faculty and administrative positions has limited Black women's access to influential academic positions.[27] Thus, while Black women can produce knowledge claims that contest those advanced by the white male community, this community does not grant that Black women scholars have competing knowledge claims based in another knowledge-validation process. As a consequence, any credentials controlled by white male academicians can be denied to Black women producing Black feminist thought on the grounds that it is not credible research.

Those Black women with academic credentials who seek to exert the authority that their status grants them to propose new knowledge claims about African-American women face pressures to use their authority to help legitimate a system that devalues and excludes the majority of Black women.[28] One way of excluding the majority of Black women from the knowledge-validation process is to permit a few Black women to acquire positions of authority in institutions that legitimate knowledge and to encourage them to work within the taken-for-granted assumptions of Black female inferiority shared by the scholarly community and the culture at large. Those Black women who accept these assumptions are likely to be rewarded by their institutions, often at significant personal cost. Those challenging the assumptions run the risk of being ostracized.

African-American women academicians who persist in trying to rearticulate a Black women's standpoint also face potential rejection of their knowledge claims on epistemological grounds. Just as the material realities of the powerful and the dominated produce separate standpoints, each group may also have distinctive epistemologies or theories of knowledge. It is my contention that Black female scholars may know that something is true but be unwilling or unable to legitimate their claims using Eurocentric masculinist criteria for consistency with substantiated knowledge and Eurocentric masculinist criteria for methodological adequacy.

For any particular interpretive context, new knowledge claims must be consistent with an existing body of knowledge that the group controlling the interpretive context accepts as true. The methods used to validate knowledge claims must also be acceptable to the group controlling the knowledge-validation process.

The criteria for the methodological adequacy of positivism illustrate the epistemological standards that Black women scholars would have to satisfy in legitimating alternative knowledge claims.[29] Positivist approaches aim to create scientific descriptions of reality by producing objective generalizations. Since researchers have widely differing values, experiences, and emotions, genuine science is thought to be unattainable unless all human characteristics except rationality are eliminated from the research process. By following strict methodological rules, scientists aim to distance themselves from the values, vested interests, and emotions generated by their class, race, sex, or unique situation and in so doing become detached observers and manipulators of nature.[30]

Several requirements typify positivist methodological approaches. First, research methods generally require a distancing of the researcher from her/his "object" of study by defining the researcher as a "subject" with full human subjectivity and objectifying the "object" of study.[31] A second requirement is the absence of emotions from the research process.[32] Third, ethics and values are deemed inappropriate in the research process, either as the reason for scientific inquiry or as part of the research process itself.[33] Finally, adversarial debates, whether written or oral, become the preferred method of ascertaining truth—the arguments that can withstand the greatest assault and survive intact become the strongest truths.[34]

Such criteria ask African-American women to objectify themselves, devalue their emotional life, displace their motivations for furthering knowledge about Black women, and confront, in an adversarial relationship, those who have more social, economic, and professional power than they. It seems unlikely, therefore, that Black women would use a positivist epistemological stance in rearticulating a Black women's standpoint. Black women are more likely to choose an alternative epistemology for assessing knowledge claims, one using standards that are consistent with Black women's criteria for substantiated knowledge and with Black women's criteria for methodological adequacy. If such an epistemology exists, what are its contours? Moreover, what is its role in the production of Black feminist thought?

The Contours of an Afrocentric Feminist Epistemology

Africanist analyses of the Black experience generally agree on the fundamental elements of an Afrocentric standpoint. In spite of varying histories, Black societies reflect elements of a core African value system that existed prior to and independently of racial oppression.[35] Moreover, as a result of colonialism, imperialism, slavery, apartheid, and other systems of racial domination, Blacks share a common experience of oppression. These similarities in material conditions have fostered shared Afrocentric values that permeate the family structure, religious institutions, culture, and community life of Blacks in varying parts of Africa, the Caribbean, South America, and North America.[36] This Afrocentric consciousness permeates the shared history of people of African descent through the framework of a distinctive Afrocentric epistemology.[37]

Feminist scholars advance a similar argument. They assert that women share a history of patriarchal oppression through the political economy of the material conditions of sexuality and reproduction.[38] These shared material conditions are thought to transcend divisions among women created by race, social class, religion, sexual orientation, and ethnicity and to form the basis of a women's standpoint with its corresponding feminist consciousness and epistemology.[39]

Since Black women have access to both the Afrocentric and the feminist standpoints, an alternative epistemology used to rearticulate a Black women's standpoint reflects elements of both traditions.[40] The search for the distinguishing features of an alternative epistemology used by African-American women reveals that values and ideas that Africanist scholars identify as being characteristically "Black" often bear remarkable resemblance to similar ideas claimed by feminist scholars as being characteristically "female."[41] This similarity suggests that the material conditions of oppression can vary dramatically and yet generate some uniformity in the epistemologies of subordinate groups. Thus, the significance of an Afrocentric feminist epistemology may lie in its enrichment of our understanding of how subordinate groups create knowledge that enables them to resist oppression.

The parallels between the two conceptual schemes raise a question: Is the worldview of women of African descent more intensely infused with the overlapping feminine/Afrocentric standpoints than is the case for either African-American men or white women?[42] While an Afrocentric feminist epistemology reflects elements of epistemologies used by Blacks as a group and women as a group, it also paradoxically demonstrates features that may be unique to Black women. On certain dimensions, Black women may more closely resemble Black men, on others, white women, and on still others, Black women may stand apart from both groups. Black feminist sociologist Deborah K. King describes this phenomenon as a "both/or" orientation, the act of being simultaneously a member of a group and yet standing apart from it. She suggests that multiple realities among Black women yield a "multiple consciousness in Black women's politics" and that this state of belonging yet not belonging forms an integral part of Black women's oppositional consciousness.[43] Bonnie Thornton Dill's analysis of how Black women live with contradictions, a situation she labels the "dialectics of Black womanhood," parallels King's assertions that this "both/or" orientation is central to an Afrocentric feminist consciousness.[44] Rather than emphasizing how a Black women's standpoint and its accompanying epistemology are different than those in Afrocentric and feminist analyses, I use Black women's experiences as a point of contact between the two.

Viewing an Afrocentric feminist epistemology in this way challenges analyses claiming that Black women have a more accurate view of oppression than do other groups. Such approaches suggest that oppression can be quantified and compared and that adding layers of oppression produces a potentially clearer standpoint. While it is tempting to claim that Black women are more oppressed than everyone else and therefore have the best standpoint from which to understand the mechanisms, processes, and effects of oppression, this simply may not be the case.[45]

African-American women do not uniformly share an Afrocentric feminist epistemology since social class introduces variations among Black women in seeing, valuing, and using Afrocentric feminist perspectives. While a Black women's standpoint and its accompanying epistemology stem from Black women's consciousness of race and gender oppression, they are not simply the result of combining Afrocentric and female values—standpoints are rooted in real material conditions structured by social class.[46]

Concrete Experience as a Criterion of Meaning

Carolyn Chase, a thirty-one-year-old inner city Black woman, notes, "My aunt used to say, 'A heap see, but a few know.'"[47] This saying depicts two types of knowing, knowledge and wisdom, and taps the first dimension of an Afrocentric feminist epistemology. Living life as Black women requires wisdom since knowledge about the dynamics of race, gender, and class subordination has been essential to Black women's survival. African-American women give such wisdom high credence in assessing knowledge.

Allusions to these two types of knowing pervade the words of a range of African-American women. In explaining the tenacity of racism, Zilpha Elaw, a preacher of the mid-1800s, noted: "The pride of a white skin is a bauble of great value with many in some parts of the United States, who readily sacrifice their intelligence to their prejudices, and possess more knowledge than wisdom."[48] In describing differences separating African-American and white women, Nancy White invokes a similar rule: "When you come right down to it, white women just *think* they are free. Black women *know* they ain't free."[49] Geneva Smitherman, a college professor specializing in African-American linguistics, suggests that "from a black perspective, written documents are limited in what they can teach about life and survival in the world. Blacks are quick to ridicule 'educated fools,' … they have 'book learning' but no 'mother wit,' knowledge, but not wisdom."[50] Mabel Lincoln eloquently summarizes the distinction between knowledge and wisdom: "To black people like me, a fool is funny—you know, people who love to break bad, people you can't tell anything to, folks that would take a shotgun to a roach."[51]

Black women need wisdom to know how to deal with the "educated fools" who would "take a shotgun to a roach." As members of a subordinate group, Black women cannot afford to be fools of any type, for their devalued status denies them the protections that white skin, maleness, and wealth confer. This distinction between knowledge and wisdom, and the use of experience as the cutting edge dividing them, has been key to Black women's survival. In the context of race, gender, and class oppression, the distinction is essential since knowledge without wisdom is adequate for the powerful, but wisdom is essential to the survival of the subordinate.

For ordinary African-American women, those individuals who have lived through the experiences about which they claim to be experts are more believable and credible than those who have merely read or thought about such experiences. Thus, concrete experience as a criterion for credibility frequently is invoked by Black women when making knowledge claims. For instance, Hannah Nelson describes the importance that personal experience has for her: "Our speech is most directly personal, and every black person assumes that every other black person has a right to a personal opinion. In speaking of grave matters, your personal experience is considered very good evidence. With us, distant statistics are certainly not as important as the actual experience of a sober person."[52] Similarly, Ruth Shays uses her concrete experiences to challenge the idea that formal education is the only route to knowledge: "I am the kind of person who doesn't have a lot of education, but both my mother and my father had good common sense. Now, I think that's all you need. I might not know how to use thirty-four words where three would do, but that does not mean that I don't know what I'm talking about ... I know what I'm talking about because I'm talking about myself. I'm talking about what I have lived."[53] Implicit in Shays's self-assessment is a critique of the type of knowledge that obscures the truth, the "thirty-four words" that cover up a truth that can be expressed in three.

Even after substantial mastery of white masculinist epistemologies, many Black women scholars invoke their own concrete experiences and those of other Black women in selecting topics for investigation and methodologies used. For example, Elsa Barkley Brown subtitles her essay on Black women's history, "how my mother taught me to be an historian in spite of my academic training."[54] Similarly, Joyce Ladner maintains that growing up as a Black woman in the South gave her special insights in conducting her study of Black adolescent women.[55]

Henry Mitchell and Nicholas Lewter claim that experience as a criterion of meaning with practical images as its symbolic vehicles is a fundamental epistemological tenet in African-American thought-systems.[56] Stories, narratives, and Bible principles are selected for their applicability to the lived experiences of African-Americans and become symbolic representations of a whole wealth of experience. For example, Bible tales are told for their value to common life, so their interpretation involves no need for scientific historical verification. The narrative method requires that the story be "told, not torn apart in analysis, and trusted as core belief, not admired as science."[57] Any biblical story contains more than characters and a plot—it presents key ethical issues salient in African-American life.

June Jordan's essay about her mother's suicide exemplifies the multiple levels of meaning that can occur when concrete experiences are used as a criterion of meaning. Jordan describes her mother, a woman who literally died trying to stand up, and the effect that her mother's death had on her own work:

> I think all of this is really about women and work. Certainly this is all about me as a woman and my life work. I mean I am not sure my mother's suicide was something extraordinary. Perhaps most women must deal with a similar inheritance, the legacy of a woman whose death you cannot possibly pinpoint because she died so many, many times and because, even before she became your mother, the life of that woman was taken. ... I came too late to help my mother to her feet. By way of everlasting thanks to all of the women who have helped me to stay alive I am working never to be late again.[58]

While Jordan has knowledge about the concrete act of her mother's death, she also strives for wisdom concerning the meaning of that death.

Some feminist scholars offer a similar claim that women, as a group, are more likely than men to use concrete knowledge in assessing knowledge claims. For example, a substantial number of the 135 women in a study of women's cognitive development were "connected knowers" and were drawn to the sort of knowledge that emerges from first-hand observation. Such women felt that since knowledge comes from experience, the best way of understanding another person's ideas was to try to share the experiences that led the person to form those ideas. At the heart of the procedures used by connected knowers is the capacity for empathy.[59]

In valuing the concrete, African-American women may be invoking not only an Afrocentric tradition, but a women's tradition as well. Some feminist theorists suggest that women are socialized in complex relational nexuses where contextual rules take priority over abstract principles in governing behavior. This socialization process is thought to stimulate characteristic ways of knowing.[60] For example, Canadian sociologist Dorothy Smith maintains that two modes of knowing exist, one located in the body and the space it occupies and the other passing beyond it. She asserts that women, through their child-rearing and nurturing activities, mediate these two modes and use the concrete experiences of their daily lives to assess more abstract knowledge claims.[61]

Amanda King, a young Black mother, describes how she used the concrete to assess the abstract and points out how difficult mediating these two modes of knowing can be:

> The leaders of the ROC [a labor union] lost their jobs too, but it just seemed like they were used to losing their jobs. ... This was like a lifelong thing for them, to get out there and protest. They were like, what do you call them—intellectuals. ... You got the ones that go to the university that are supposed to make all the speeches, they're the ones that are supposed to lead, you know, put this little revolution together, and then you got the little ones ... that go to the factory everyday, they be the ones that have to fight. I had a child and I thought I don't have the time to be running around with these people. ... I mean I understand some of that stuff they were talking about, like the bourgeoisie, the rich and the poor and all that, but I had surviving on my mind for me and my kid.[62]

For King, abstract ideals of class solidarity were mediated by the concrete experience of motherhood and the connectedness it involved.

In traditional African-American communities, Black women find considerable institutional support for valuing concrete experience. Black extended families and Black churches are two key institutions where Black women experts with concrete knowledge of what it takes to be self-defined Black women share their knowledge with their younger, less experienced sisters. This relationship of sisterhood among Black women can be seen as a model for a whole series of relationships that African-American women have with each other, whether it is networks among women in extended families, among women in the Black church, or among women in the African-American community at large.[63]

Since the Black church and the Black family are both woman-centered and Afrocentric institutions, African-American women traditionally have found considerable institutional support for this dimension of an Afrocentric feminist epistemology in ways that are unique to them. While white women may value the concrete, it is questionable whether white families, particularly middle-class nuclear ones, and white community institutions provide comparable types of support. Similarly, while Black men are supported by Afrocentric institutions, they cannot participate in Black women's sisterhood. In terms of Black women's relationships with one another then, African-American women may indeed find it easier than others to recognize connectedness as a primary way of knowing, simply because they are encouraged to do so by Black women's tradition of sisterhood.

The Use of Dialogue in Assessing Knowledge Claims

For Black women, new knowledge claims are rarely worked out in isolation from other individuals and are usually developed through dialogues with other members of a community. A primary epistemological assumption underlying the use of dialogue in assessing knowledge claims is that connectedness rather than separation is an essential component of the knowledge-validation process.[64]

The use of dialogue has deep roots in an African-based oral tradition and in African-American culture.[65] Ruth Shays describes the importance of dialogue in the knowledge-validation process of enslaved African-Americans: "They would find a lie if it took them a year ... the foreparents found the truth because they listened and they made people tell their part many times. Most often you can hear a lie. ... Those old people was everywhere and knew the truth of many disputes. They believed that a liar should suffer the pain of his lies, and they had all kinds of ways of bringing liars to judgement."[66]

The widespread use of the call and response discourse mode among African-Americans exemplifies the importance placed on dialogue. Composed of spontaneous verbal and nonverbal interaction between speaker and listener in which all of the speaker's statements or "calls" are punctuated by expressions or "responses" from the listener, this Black discourse mode pervades African-American culture. The fundamental requirement of this interactive network is active participation of all individuals.[67] For ideas to the tested and validated, everyone in the group must participate. To refuse to join in, especially if one really disagrees with what has been said is seen as "cheating."[68]

June Jordan's analysis of Black English points to the significance of this dimension of an alternative epistemology.

Our language is a system constructed by people constantly needing to insist that we exist. ... Our language devolves from a culture that abhors all abstraction, or anything tending to obscure or delete the fact of the human being who is here and now/the truth of the person who is speaking or listening. Consequently, *there is no passive voice construction possible in Black English.* For example, you cannot say, "Black English is being eliminated." You must say, instead, "White people eliminating Black English." The assumption of the presence of life governs all of Black English ... every sentence assumes the living and active participation of at least two human beings, the speaker and the listener.[69]

Many Black women intellectuals invoke the relationships and connectedness provided by use of dialogue. When asked why she chose the themes she did, novelist Gayle Jones replied: "I was ... interested ... in oral traditions of storytelling—Afro-American and others, in which there is always the consciousness and importance of the hearer."[70] In describing the difference in the way male and female writers select significant events and relationships, Jones points out that "with many women writers, relationships within family, community, between men and women, and among women—from slave narratives by black women writers on—are treated as complex and significant relationships, whereas with many men the significant relationships are those that involve confrontations—relationships outside the family and community."[71] Alice Walker's reaction to Zora Neale Hurston's book, *Mules and Men,* is another example of the use of dialogue in assessing knowledge claims. In *Mules and Men,* Hurston chose not to become a detached observer of the stories and folktales she collected but instead, through extensive dialogues with the people in the com-

munities she studied, placed herself at the center of her analysis. Using a similar process, Walker tests the truth of Hurston's knowledge claims: "When I read *Mules and
Men* I was delighted. Here was this perfect book! The 'perfection' of which I immediately tested on my relatives, who are such typical Black Americans they are useful for
every sort of political, cultural, or economic survey. Very regular people from the
South, rapidly forgetting their Southern cultural inheritance in the suburbs and
ghettos of Boston and New York, they sat around reading the book themselves, listening to me read the book, listening to each other read the book, and a kind of paradise was regained."[72]

Their centrality in Black churches and Black extended families provides Black
women with a high degree of support from Black institutions for invoking dialogue
as a dimension of an Afrocentric feminist epistemology. However, when African-
American women use dialogues in assessing knowledge claims, they might be invoking a particularly female way of knowing as well. Feminist scholars contend that
males and females are socialized within their families to seek different types of autonomy, the former based on separation, the latter seeking connectedness, and that
this variation in types of autonomy parallels the characteristic differences between
male and female ways of knowing.[73] For instance, in contrast to the visual metaphors
(such as equating knowledge with illumination, knowing with seeing, and truth with
light) that scientists and philosophers typically use, women tend to ground their
epistemological premises in metaphors suggesting speaking and listening.[74]

While there are significant differences between the roles Black women play in their
families and those played by middle-class white women, Black women clearly are affected by general cultural norms prescribing certain familial roles for women. Thus,
in terms of the role of dialogue in an Afrocentric feminist epistemology, Black
women may again experience a convergence of the values of the African-American
community and woman-centered values.

The Ethic of Caring

"Ole white preachers used to talk wid dey tongues widdout sayin' nothin', but Jesus
told us slaves to talk wid our hearts."[75] These words of an ex-slave suggest that ideas
cannot be divorced from the individuals who create and share them. This theme of
"talking with the heart" taps another dimension of an alternative epistemology used
by African-American women, the ethic of caring. Just as the ex-slave used the wisdom in his heart to reject the ideas of the preachers who talked "wid dey tongues
widdout sayin' nothin'," the ethic of caring suggests that personal expressiveness,
emotions, and empathy are central to the knowledge-validation process.

One of the three interrelated components making up the ethic of caring is the emphasis placed on individual uniqueness. Rooted in a tradition of African humanism,
each individual is thought to be a unique expression of a common spirit, power, or
energy expressed by all life.[76] This belief in individual uniqueness is illustrated by the
value placed on personal expressiveness in African-American communities.[77]
Johnetta Ray, an inner city resident, describes this Afrocentric emphasis on individual uniqueness: "No matter how hard we try, I don't think black people will ever develop much of a herd instinct. We are profound individualists with a passion for self-
expression."[78]

A second component of the ethic of caring concerns the appropriateness of emotions in dialogues. Emotion indicates that a speaker believes in the validity of an ar-

gument.[79] Consider Ntozake Shange's description of one of the goals of her work: "Our [Western] society allows people to be absolutely neurotic and totally out of touch with their feelings and everyone else's feelings, and yet be very respectable. This, to me, is a travesty. ... I'm trying to change the idea of seeing emotions and intellect as distinct faculties."[80] Shange's words echo those of the ex-slave. Both see the denigration of emotion as problematic, and both suggest that expressiveness should be reclaimed and valued.

A third component of the ethic of caring involves developing the capacity for empathy. Harriet Jones, a sixteen-year-old Black woman, explains why she chose to open up to her interviewer: "Some things in my life are so hard for me to bear, and it makes me feel better to know that you feel sorry about those things and would change them if you could."[81]

These three components of the ethic of caring—the value placed on individual expressiveness, the appropriateness of emotions, and the capacity for empathy—pervade African-American culture. One of the best examples of the interactive nature of the importance of dialogue and the ethic of caring in assessing knowledge claims occurs in the use of the call and response discourse mode in traditional Black church services. In such services, both the minister and the congregation routinely use voice rhythm and vocal inflection to convey meaning. The sound of what is being said is just as important as the words themselves in what is, in a sense, a dialogue between reason and emotions. As a result, it is nearly impossible to filter out the strictly linguistic-cognitive abstract meaning from the sociocultural psycho-emotive meaning.[82] While the ideas presented by a speaker must have validity, that is, agree with the general body of knowledge shared by the Black congregation, the group also appraises the way knowledge claims are presented.

There is growing evidence that the ethic of caring may be part of women's experience as well. Certain dimensions of women's ways of knowing bear striking resemblance to Afrocentric expressions of the ethic of caring. Belenky, Clinchy, Goldberger, and Tarule point out that two contrasting epistemological orientations characterize knowing—one, an epistemology of separation based on impersonal procedures for establishing truth, and the other, an epistemology of connection in which truth emerges through care. While these ways of knowing are not gender specific, disproportionate numbers of women rely on connected knowing.[83]

The parallels between Afrocentric expressions of the ethic of caring and those advanced by feminist scholars are noteworthy. The emphasis placed on expressiveness and emotion in African-American communities bears marked resemblance to feminist perspectives on the importance of personality in connected knowing. Separate knowers try to subtract the personality of an individual from his or her ideas because they see personality as biasing those ideas. In contrast, connected knowers see personality as adding to an individual's ideas, and they feel that the personality of each group member enriches a group's understanding.[84] Similarly, the significance of individual uniqueness, personal expressiveness, and empathy in African-American communities resembles the importance that some feminist analyses place on women's "inner voice."[85]

The convergence of Afrocentric and feminist values in the ethic-of-care dimension of an alternative epistemology seems particularly acute. While white women may have access to a women's tradition valuing emotion and expressiveness, few white social institutions except the family validate this way of knowing. In contrast,

Black women have long had the support of the Black church, an institution with deep roots in the African past and a philosophy that accepts and encourages expressiveness and an ethic of caring. While Black men share in this Afrocentric tradition, they must resolve the contradictions that distinguish abstract, unemotional Western masculinity from an Afrocentric ethic of caring. The differences among race/gender groups thus hinge on differences in their access to institutional supports valuing one type of knowing over another. Although Black women may be denigrated within white-male-controlled academic institutions, other institutions, such as Black families and churches, which encourage the expression of Black female power, seem to do so by way of their support for an Afrocentric feminist epistemology.

The Ethic of Personal Accountability

An ethic of personal accountability is the final dimension of an alternative epistemology. Not only must individuals develop their knowledge claims through dialogue and present those knowledge claims in a style proving their concern for their ideas, people are expected to be accountable for their knowledge claims. Zilpha Elaw's description of slavery reflects this notion that every idea has an owner and that the owner's identity matters: "Oh, the abominations of slavery! ... every case of slavery, however lenient its inflictions and mitigated its atrocities, indicates an oppressor, the oppressed, and oppression."[86] For Elaw, abstract definitions of slavery mesh with the concrete identities of its perpetrators and its victims. Blacks "consider it essential for individuals to have personal positions on issues and assume full responsibility for arguing their validity."[87]

Assessments of an individual's knowledge claims simultaneously evaluate an individual's character, values, and ethics. African-Americans reject Eurocentric masculinist beliefs that probing into an individual's personal viewpoint is outside the boundaries of discussion. Rather, all views expressed and actions taken are thought to derive from a central set of core beliefs that cannot be other than personal.[88] From this perspective, knowledge claims made by individuals respected for their moral and ethical values will carry more weight than those offered by less respected figures.[89]

An example drawn from an undergraduate course composed entirely of Black women, which I taught, might help clarify the uniqueness of this portion of the knowledge-validation process. During one class discussion, I assigned the students the task of critiquing an analysis of Black feminism advanced by a prominent Black male scholar. Instead of dissecting the rationality of the author's thesis, my students demanded facts about the author's personal biography. They were especially interested in concrete details of his life such as his relationships with Black women, his marital status, and his social class background. By requesting data on dimensions of his personal life routinely excluded in positivist approaches to knowledge validation, they were invoking concrete experience as a criterion of meaning. They used this information to assess whether he really cared about his topic and invoked this ethic of caring in advancing their knowledge claims about his work. Furthermore, they refused to evaluate the rationality of his written ideas without some indication of his personal credibility as an ethical human being. The entire exchange could only have occurred as a dialogue among members of a class that had established a solid enough community to invoke an alternative epistemology in assessing knowledge claims.[90]

The ethic of personal accountability is clearly an Afrocentric value, but is it feminist as well? While limited by its attention to middle-class, white women, Carol

Gilligan's work suggests that there is a female model for moral development where women are more inclined to link morality to responsibility, relationships, and the ability to maintain social ties.[91] If this is the case, then African-American women again experience a convergence of values from Afrocentric and female institutions.

The use of an Afrocentric feminist epistemology in traditional Black church services illustrates the interactive nature of all four dimensions and also serve as a metaphor for the distinguishing features of an Afrocentric feminist way of knowing. The services represent more than dialogues between the rationality used in examining biblical texts/stories and the emotion inherent in the use of reason for this purpose. The rationale for such dialogues addresses the task of examining concrete experiences for the presence of an ethic of caring. Neither emotion nor ethics is subordinated to reason. Instead, emotion, ethics, and reason are used as interconnected, essential components in assessing knowledge claims. In an Afrocentric feminist epistemology, values lie at the heart of the knowledge-validation process such that inquiry always has an ethical aim.

Epistemology and Black Feminist Thought

Living life as an African-American woman is a necessary prerequisite for producing Black feminist thought because within Black women's communities thought is validated and produced with reference to a particular set of historical, material, and epistemological conditions.[92] African-American women who adhere to the idea that claims about Black women must be substantiated by Black women's sense of their own experiences and who anchor their knowledge claims in an Afrocentric feminist epistemology have produced a rich tradition of Black feminist thought.

Traditionally, such women were blues singers, poets, autobiographers, storytellers, and orators validated by the larger community of Black women as experts on a Black women's standpoint. Only a few unusual African-American feminist scholars have been able to defy Eurocentric masculinist epistemologies and explicitly embrace an Afrocentric feminist epistemology. Consider Alice Walker's description of Zora Neale Hurston: "In my mind, Zora Neale Hurston, Billie Holiday, and Bessie Smith form a sort of unholy trinity. Zora *belongs* in the tradition of Black women singers, rather than among 'the literati.' ... Like Billie and Bessie she followed her own road, believed in her own gods, pursued her own dreams, and refused to separate herself from 'common' people."[93]

Zora Neale Hurston is an exception for, prior to 1950, few Black women earned advanced degrees, and most of those who did complied with Eurocentric masculinist epistemologies. While these women worked on behalf of Black women, they did so within the confines of pervasive race and gender oppression. Black women scholars were in a position to see the exclusion of Black women from scholarly discourse, and the thematic content of their work often reflected their interest in examining a Black women's standpoint. However, their tenuous status in academic institutions led them to adhere to Eurocentric masculinist epistemologies so that their work would be accepted as scholarly. As a result, while they produced Black feminist thought, those Black women most likely to gain academic credentials were often least likely to produce Black feminist thought that used an Afrocentric feminist epistemology.

As more Black women earn advanced degrees, the range of Black feminist scholarship is expanding. Increasing numbers of African-American women scholars are

explicitly choosing to ground their work in Black women's experiences, and, by doing so, many implicitly adhere to an Afrocentric feminist epistemology. Rather than
being restrained by their "both/and" status of marginality, these women make creative use of their outsider-within status and produce innovative Black feminist
thought. The difficulties these women face lie less in demonstrating the technical
components of white male epistemologies than in resisting the hegemonic nature of
these patterns of thought in order to see, value, and use existing alternative
Afrocentric feminist ways of knowing.

In establishing the legitimacy of their knowledge claims, Black women scholars
who want to develop Black feminist thought may encounter the often conflicting
standards of three key groups. First, Black feminist thought must be validated by ordinary African-American women who grow to womanhood "in a world where the
saner you are, the madder you are made to appear."[94] To be credible in the eyes of
this group, scholars must be personal advocates for their material, be accountable for
the consequences of their work, have lived or experienced their material in some
fashion, and be willing to engage in dialogues about their findings with ordinary, everyday people. Second, if it is to establish its legitimacy, Black feminist thought also
must be accepted by the community of Black women scholars. These scholars place
varying amounts of importance on rearticulating a Black women's standpoint using
an Afrocentric feminist epistemology. Third, Black feminist thought within academia must be prepared to confront Eurocentric masculinist political and epistemological requirements.

The dilemma facing Black women scholars engaged in creating Black feminist
thought is that a knowledge claim that meets the criteria of adequacy for one group
and thus is judged to be an acceptable knowledge claim may not be translatable into
the terms of a different group. Using the example of Black English, June Jordan illustrates the difficulty of moving among epistemologies: "You cannot 'translate' instances of Standard English preoccupied with abstraction or with nothing/nobody
evidently alive into Black English. That would warp the language into uses antithetical to the guiding perspective of its community of users. Rather you must first
change those standard English sentences, themselves, into ideas consistent with the
person-centered assumptions of Black English."[95] While both worldviews share a
common vocabulary, the ideas themselves defy direct translation.

Once Black feminist scholars face the notion that, on certain dimensions of a
Black women's standpoint, it may be fruitless to try to translate ideas from an
Afrocentric feminist epistemology into a Eurocentric masculinist epistemology, then
the choices become clearer. Rather than trying to uncover universal knowledge
claims that can withstand the translation from one epistemology to another, time
might be better spent rearticulating a Black women's standpoint in order to give African-American women the tools to resist their own subordination. The goal here is
not one of integrating Black female "folk culture" into the substantiated body of academic knowledge, for that substantiated knowledge is, in many ways, antithetical to
the best interests of Black women. Rather, the process is one of rearticulating a preexisting Black women's standpoint and recentering the language of existing academic discourse to accommodate these knowledge claims. For those Black women
scholars engaged in this rearticulation process, the social construction of Black feminist thought requires the skill and sophistication to decide which knowledge claims
can be validated using the epistemological assumptions of one but not both frame-

works, which claims can be generated in one framework and only partially accommodated by the other, and which claims can be made in both frameworks without violating the basic political and epistemological assumptions of either.

Black feminist scholars offering knowledge claims that cannot be accommodated by both frameworks face the choice between accepting the taken-for-granted assumptions that permeate white-male-controlled academic institutions or leaving academia. Those Black women who choose to remain in academia must accept the possibility that their knowledge claims will be limited to those claims about Black women that are consistent with a white male worldview. And yet those African-American women who leave academia may find their work is inaccessible to scholarly communities.

Black feminist scholars offering knowledge claims that can be partially accommodated by both epistemologies can create a body of thought that stands outside of either. Rather than trying to synthesize competing worldviews that, at this point in time, may defy reconciliation, their task is to point out common themes and concerns. By making creative use of their status as mediators, their thought becomes an entity unto itself that is rooted in two distinct political and epistemological contexts.[96]

Those Black feminists who develop knowledge claims that both epistemologies can accommodate may have found a route to the elusive goal of generating so-called objective generalizations that can stand as universal truths. Those ideas that are validated as true by African-American women, African-American men, white men, white women, and other groups with distinctive standpoints, with each group using the epistemological approaches growing from its unique standpoint, thus become the most objective truths.[97]

Alternative knowledge claims, in and of themselves, are rarely threatening to conventional knowledge. Such claims are routinely ignored, discredited, or simply absorbed and marginalized in existing paradigms. Much more threatening is the challenge that alternative epistemologies offer to the basic process used by the powerful to legitimate their knowledge claims. If the epistemology used to validate knowledge comes into question, then all prior knowledge claims validated under the dominant model become suspect. An alternative epistemology challenges all certified knowledge and opens up the question of whether what has been taken to be true can stand the test of alternative ways of validating truth. The existence of an independent Black women's standpoint using an Afrocentric feminist epistemology calls into question the content of what currently passes as truth and simultaneously challenges the process of arriving at that truth.

Notes

Special thanks go out to the following people for reading various drafts of this manuscript: Evelyn Nakano Glenn, Lynn Weber Cannon, and participants in the 1986 Research Institute, Center for Research on Women, Memphis State University; Elsa Barkley Brown, Deborah K. King, Elizabeth V. Spelman, and Angelene Jamison-Hall; and four anonymous reviewers at *Signs*.

1. For analyses of how interlocking systems of oppression affect Black women, see Frances Beale, "Double Jeopardy: To Be Black and Female," in *The Black Woman*, ed. Toni Cade (New York: Signet, 1970); Angela Y. Davis, *Women, Race and Class* (New York: Random House, 1981);

Bonnie Thornton Dill, "Race, Class, and Gender: Prospects for an All-Inclusive Sisterhood," *Feminist Studies* 9, no. 1 (1983): 131–50; bell hooks, *Ain't I a Woman? Black Women and Feminism* (Boston: South End Press, 1981); Diane Lewis, "A Response to Inequality: Black Women, Racism, and Sexism," *Signs: Journal of Women in Culture and Society* 3, no. 2 (Winter 1977): 339–61; Pauli Murray, "The Liberation of Black Women," in *Voices of the New Feminism,* ed. Mary Lou Thompson (Boston: Beacon, 1970), 87–102; and the introduction in Filomina Chioma Steady, *The Black Woman Cross-Culturally* (Cambridge, Mass.: Schenkman, 1981), 7–41.

2. See the introduction in Steady for an overview of Black women's strengths. This strength-resiliency perspective has greatly influenced empirical work on African-American women. See, e.g., Joyce Ladner's study of low-income Black adolescent girls, *Tomorrow's Tomorrow* (New York: Doubleday, 1971); and Lena Wright Myers's work on Black women's self-concept, *Black Women: Do They Cope Better?* (Englewood Cliffs, N.J.: Prentice-Hall, 1980). For discussions of Black women's resistance, see Elizabeth Fox-Genovese, "Strategies and Forms of Resistance: Focus on Slave Women in the United States," in *In Resistance: Studies in African, Caribbean and Afro-American History,* ed. Gary Y. Okihiro (Amherst, Mass.: University of Massachusetts Press, 1986), 143–65; and Rosalyn Terborg-Penn, "Black Women in Resistance: A Cross-Cultural Perspective," in Okihiro, ed., 188–209. For a comprehensive discussion of everyday resistance, see James C. Scott, *Weapons of the Weak: Everyday Forms of Peasant Resistance* (New Haven, Conn.: Yale University Press, 1985).

3. See Patricia Hill Collins's analysis of the substantive content of Black feminist thought in "Learning from the Outsider Within: The Sociological Significance of Black Feminist Thought," *Social Problems* 33, no. 6 (1986): 14–32.

4. Scott describes consciousness as the meaning that people give to their acts through the symbols, norms, and ideological forms they create.

5. This thesis is found in scholarship of varying theoretical perspectives. For example, Marxist analyses of working-class consciousness claim that "false consciousness" makes the working class unable to penetrate the hegemony of ruling-class ideologies. See Scott's critique of this literature.

6. For example, in Western societies, African-Americans have been judged as being less capable of intellectual excellence, more suited to manual labor, and therefore as less human than whites. Similarly, white women have been assigned roles as emotional, irrational creatures ruled by passions and biological urges. They too have been stigmatized as being less than fully human, as being objects. For a discussion of the importance that objectification and dehumanization play in maintaining systems of domination, see Arthur Brittan and Mary Maynard, *Sexism, Racism and Oppression* (New York: Basil Blackwell, 1984).

7. The tendency for Western scholarship to assess Black culture as pathological and deviant illustrates this process. See Rhett S. Jones, "Proving Blacks Inferior: The Sociology of Knowledge," in *The Death of White Sociology,* ed. Joyce Ladner (New York: Vintage, 1973), 114–35.

8. The presence of an independent standpoint does not mean that it is uniformly shared by all Black women or even that Black women fully recognize its contours. By using the concept of standpoint, I do not mean to minimize the rich diversity existing among African American women. I use the phrase "Black women's standpoint" to emphasize the plurality of experiences within the overarching term "standpoint." For discussions of the concept of standpoint, see Nancy M. Hartsock, "The Feminist Standpoint: Developing the Ground for a Specifically Feminist Historical Materialism," in *Discovering Reality,* ed. Sandra Harding and Merrill Hintikka (Boston: D. Reidel, 1983), 283–310, and *Money, Sex, and Power* (Boston: Northeastern University Press, 1983); and Alison M. Jaggar, *Feminist Politics and Human Nature* (Totowa, N.J.: Rowman & Allanheld, 1983), 377–89. My use of the standpoint epistemologies as an organizing concept in this essay does not mean that the concept is problem-free. For a helpful critique of standpoint epistemologies, see Sandra Harding, *The Science Question in Feminism* (Ithaca, N.Y.: Cornell University Press 1986).

9. One contribution of contemporary Black women's studies in its documentation of how race, class, and gender have structured these differences. For representative works surveying African-American women's experiences, see Paula Giddings, *When and Where I Enter: The Impact of Black Women on Race and Sex in America* (New York: William Morrow, 1984); and Jacqueline Jones, *Labor of Love, Labor of Sorrow: Black Women, Work, and the Family from Slavery to the Present* (New York: Basic, 1985).

10. For example, Judith Rollins, *Between Women: Domestics and Their Employers* (Philadelphia: Temple University Press, 1985); and Bonnie Thornton Dill, "'The Means to Put My Children Through': Child-Rearing Goals and Strategies among Black Female Domestic Servants," in *The Black Woman*, ed. LaFrances Rodgers-Rose (Beverly Hills, Calif.: Sage Publications, 1980), 107–23, report that Black domestic workers do not see themselves as being the devalued workers that their employers perceive and construct their own interpretations of the meaning of their work. For additional discussions of how Black women's consciousness is shaped by the material conditions they encounter, see Ladner (n. 2 above); Myers (n. 2 above); and Cheryl Townsend Gilkes, "'Together and in Harness': Women's Traditions in the Sanctified Church," *Signs* 10, no. 4 (Summer 1985): 678–99. See also Marcia Westkott's discussion of consciousness as a sphere of freedom for women in "Feminist Criticism of the Social Sciences," *Harvard Educational Review* 49, no. 4 (1979): 422–30.

11. John Langston Gwaltney, *Drylongso: A Self-Portrait of Black America* (New York: Vintage, 1980), 4.

12. Ibid., 33.

13. Ibid., 88.

14. Ibid., 7.

15. Victoria Byerly, *Hard Times Cotton Mill Girls: Personal Histories of Womanhood and Poverty in the South* (New York: ILR Press, 1986), 134.

16. See Peter L. Berger and Thomas Luckmann, *The Social Construction of Reality* (New York: Doubleday, 1966), for a discussion of everyday thought and the role of experts in articulating specialized thought.

17. See Michael Omi and Howard Winant, *Racial Formation in the United States* (New York: Routledge & Kegan Paul, 1986), esp. 93.

18. In discussing standpoint epistemologies, Hartsock, in *Money, Sex, and Power*, notes that a standpoint is "achieved rather than obvious, a mediated rather than immediate understanding" (132).

19. See Scott (n. 2 above); and Hartsock, *Money, Sex, and Power* (n. 8 above).

20. Some readers may question how one determines whether the ideas of any given African-American woman are "feminist" and "Afrocentric." I offer the following working definitions. I agree with the general definition of feminist consciousness provided by Black feminist sociologist Deborah K. King: "Any purposes, goals, and activities which seek to enhance the potential of women, to ensure their liberty, afford them equal opportunity, and to permit and encourage their self-determination represent a feminist consciousness, even if they occur within a racial community" (in "Race, Class and Gender Salience in Black Women's Womanist Consciousness" [Dartmouth College, Department of Sociology, Hanover, N.H., 1987, typescript], 22). To be Black or Afrocentric, such thought must not only reflect a similar concern for the self-determination of African-American people, but must in some way draw upon key elements of an Afrocentric tradition as well.

21. The Eurocentric masculinist process is defined here as the institutions, paradigms, and any elements of the knowledge-validation procedure controlled by white males and whose purpose is to represent a white male standpoint. While this process represents the interests of powerful white males, various dimensions of the process are not necessarily managed by white males themselves.

22. Karl Mannheim, *Ideology and Utopia: An Introduction to the Sociology of Knowledge* (New York: Harcourt, Brace, 1936, 1954), 276.

544 *Patricia Hill Collins*

23. The knowledge-validation model used in this essay is taken from Michael Mulkay, *Science and the Sociology of Knowledge* (Boston: Allen & Unwin, 1979). For a general discussion of the structure of knowledge, see Thomas Kuhn, *The Structure of Scientific Revolutions* (Chicago: University of Chicago Press, 1962).

24. For analyses of the content and functions of images of Black female inferiority, see Mae King, "The Politics of Sexual Stereotypes," *Black Scholar* 4, nos. 6–7 (1973): 12–23; Cheryl Townsend Gilkes, "From Slavery to Social Welfare: Racism and the Control of Black Women," in *Class, Race, and Sex: The Dynamics of Control,* ed. Amy Smerdlow and Helen Lessinger (Boston: G. K. Hall, 1981), 288–300; and Elizabeth Higginbotham, "Two Representative Issues in Contemporary Sociological Work on Black Women," in *But Some of Us Are Brave,* ed. Gloria T. Hull, Patricia Bell Scott, and Barbara Smith (Old Westbury, N.Y.: Feminist Press, 1982).

25. Kuhn.

26. Evelyn Fox Keller, *Reflections on Gender and Science* (New Haven, Conn.: Yale University Press, 1985), 167.

27. Maxine Baca Zinn, Lynn Weber Cannon, Elizabeth Higginbotham, and Bonnie Thornton Dill, "The Cost of Exclusionary Practices in Women's Studies," *Signs* 11, no. 2 (Winter 1986): 290–303.

28. Berger and Luckmann (n. 16 above) note that if an outsider group, in this case African-American women, recognizes that the insider group, namely, white men, requires special privileges from the larger society, a special problem arises of keeping the outsiders out and at the same time having them acknowledge the legitimacy of this procedure. Accepting a few "safe" outsiders is one way of addressing this legitimation problem. Collins's discussion (n. 3 above) of Black women as "outsiders within" addresses this issue. Other relevant works include Franz Fanon's analysis of the role of the national middle class in maintaining colonial systems, *The Wretched of the Earth* (New York: Grove, 1963); and William Tabb's discussion of the use of "bright natives" in controlling African-American communities, *The Political Economy of the Black Ghetto* (New York: Norton, 1970).

29. While I have been describing Eurocentric masculinist approaches as a single process, there are many schools of thought or paradigms subsumed under this one process. Positivism represents one such paradigm. See Harding (n. 8 above) for an overview and critique of this literature. The following discussion depends heavily on Jaggar (n. 8 above), 355–58.

30. Jaggar, 356.

31. See Keller, especially her analysis of static autonomy and its relation to objectivity (67–126).

32. Ironically, researchers must "objectify" themselves to achieve this lack of bias. See Arlie Russell Hochschild, "The Sociology of Feeling and Emotion: Selected Possibilities," in *Another Voice: Feminist Perspectives on Social Life and Social Science,* ed. Marcia Millman and Rosabeth Kanter (Garden City, N.Y.: Anchor, 1975), 280–307. Also, see Jaggar.

33. See Norma Haan, Robert Bellah, Paul Rabinow, and William Sullivan, eds., *Social Science as Moral Inquiry* (New York: Columbia University Press, 1983), esp. Michelle Z. Rosaldo's "Moral/Analytic Dilemmas Posed by the Intersection of Feminism and Social Science," 76–96; and Robert Bellah's "The Ethical Aims of Social Inquiry," 360–81.

34. Janice Moulton, "A Paradigm of Philosophy: The Adversary Method," in Harding and Hintikka, eds. (n. 8 above), 149–64.

35. For detailed discussions of the Afrocentric worldview, see John S. Mbiti, *African Religions and Philosophy* (London: Heinemann, 1969); Dominique Zahan, *The Religion, Spirituality, and Thought of Traditional Africa* (Chicago: University of Chicago Press, 1979); and Mechal Sobel, *Trabelin' On: The Slave Journey to an Afro-Baptist Faith* (Westport, Conn.: Greenwood Press, 1979), 1–76.

36. For representative works applying these concepts to African-American culture, see Niara Sudarkasa, "Interpreting the African Heritage in Afro-American Family Organization," in *Black Families,* ed. Harriette Pipes McAdoo (Beverly Hills, Calif.: Sage, 1981); Henry H. Mitchell and Nicholas Cooper Lewter, *Soul Theology: The Heart of American Black Culture* (San Fran-

cisco: Harper & Row, 1986); Robert Farris Thompson, *Flash of the Spirit: African and Afro-American Art and Philosophy* (New York: Vintage, 1983); and Ortiz M. Walton, "Comparative Analysis of the African and the Western Aesthetics," in *The Black Aesthetic,* ed. Addison Gayle (Garden City, N.Y.: Doubleday, 1971), 154–64.

37. One of the best discussions of an Afrocentric epistemology is offered by James E. Turner, "Foreword: Africana Studies and Epistemology; a Discourse in the Sociology of Knowledge," in *The Next Decade: Theoretical and Research Issues in Africana Studies,* ed. James E. Turner (Ithaca, N.Y.: Cornell University Africana Studies and Research Center, 1984), v–xxv. See also Vernon Dixon, "World Views and Research Methodology," summarized in Harding (n. 8 above), 170.

38. See Hester Eisenstein, *Contemporary Feminist Thought* (Boston: G. K. Hall, 1983). Nancy Hartsock's *Money, Sex, and Power* (n. 8 above), 145–209, offers a particularly insightful analysis of women's oppression.

39. For discussions of feminist consciousness, see Dorothy Smith, "A Sociology for Women," in *The Prism of Sex: Essays in the Sociology of Knowledge,* ed. Julia A. Sherman and Evelyn T. Beck (Madison: University of Wisconsin Press, 1979); and Michelle Z. Rosaldo, "Women, Culture, and Society: A Theoretical Overview," in *Woman, Culture, and Society,* ed. Michelle Z. Rosaldo and Louise Lamphere (Stanford, Calif.: Stanford University Press, 1974), 17–42. Feminist epistemologies are surveyed by Jaggar (n. 8 above).

40. One significant difference between Afrocentric and feminist standpoints is that much of what is termed women's culture is, unlike African-American culture, created in the context of and produced by oppression. Those who argue for a women's culture are electing to value, rather than denigrate, those traits associated with females in white patriarchal societies. While this choice is important, it is not the same as identifying an independent, historic culture associated with a society. I am indebted to Deborah K. King for this point.

41. Critiques of the Eurocentric masculinist knowledge-validation process by both Africanist and feminist scholars illustrate this point. What one group labels "white" and "Eurocentric," the other describes as "male-dominated" and "masculinist." Although he does not emphasize its patriarchal and racist features, Morris Berman's *The Reenchantment of the World* (New York: Bantam, 1981) provides a historical discussion of Western thought. Afrocentric analyses of this same process can be found in Molefi Kete Asante, "International/Intercultural Relations," in *Contemporary Black Thought,* ed. Molefi Kete Asante and Abdulai S. Vandi (Beverly Hills, Calif.: Sage, 1980), 43–58; and Dona Richards, "European Mythology: The Ideology of 'Progress,'" in Asante and Vandi, eds., 59–79. For feminist analyses, see Hartsock, *Money, Sex, and Power.* Harding also discusses this similarity (see chap. 7, "Other 'Others' and Fractured Identities: Issues for Epistemologists," 163–96).

42. Harding, 166.

43. D. King (n. 20 above).

44. Bonnie Thornton Dill, "The Dialectics of Black Womanhood," *Signs* 4, no. 3 (Spring 1979): 543–55.

45. One implication of standpoint approaches is that the more subordinate the group, the purer the vision of the oppressed group. This is an outcome of the origins of standpoint approaches in Marxist social theory, itself a dualistic analysis of social structure. Because such approaches rely on quantifying and ranking human oppressions—familiar tenets of positivist approaches—they are rejected by Blacks and feminists alike. See Harding (n. 8 above) for a discussion of this point. See also Elizabeth V. Spelman's discussion of the fallacy of additive oppression in "Theories of Race and Gender: The Erasure of Black Women," *Quest* 5, no. 4 (1982): 36–62.

46. Class differences among Black women may be marked. For example, see Paula Giddings's analysis (n. 9 above) of the role of social class in shaping Black women's political activism; or Elizabeth Higginbotham's study of the effects of social class in Black women's college attendance in "Race and Class Barriers to Black Women's College Attendance," *Journal of Ethnic Studies* 13, no. 1 (1985): 89–107. Those African-American women who have experienced the

greatest degree of convergence of race, class and gender oppression may be in a better position to recognize and use an alternative epistemology.

47. Gwaltney (n. 11 above), 83.

48. William L. Andrews, *Sisters of the Spirit: Three Black Women's Autobiographies of the Nineteenth Century* (Bloomington: Indiana University Press, 1986), 85.

49. Gwaltney, 147.

50. Geneva Smitherman, *Talkin and Testifyin: The Language of Black America* (Detroit: Wayne State University Press, 1986), 76.

51. Gwaltney, 68.

52. Ibid., 7.

53. Ibid., 27, 33.

54. Elsa Barkley Brown, "Hearing Our Mothers' Lives" (paper presented at the Fifteenth Anniversary Faculty Lecture Series, African-American and African Studies, Emory University, Atlanta, 1986).

55. Ladner (n. 2 above).

56. Mitchell and Lewter (n. 36 above). The use of the narrative approach in African-American theology exemplifies an inductive system of logic alternately called "folk wisdom" or a survival-based, need-oriented method of assessing knowledge claims.

57. Ibid., 8.

58. June Jordan, *On Call: Political Essays* (Boston: South End Press, 1985), 26.

59. Mary Belenky, Blythe Clinchy, Nancy Goldberger, and Jill Tarule, *Women's Ways of Knowing* (New York: Basic, 1986), 113.

60. Hartsock, *Money, Sex and Power* (n. 8 above), 237; and Nancy Chodorow, *The Reproduction of Mothering* (Berkeley and Los Angeles: University of California Press, 1978).

61. Dorothy Smith, *The Everyday World as Problematic* (Boston: Northeastern University Press, 1987).

62. Byerly (n. 15 above), 198.

63. For Black women's centrality in the family, see Steady (n. 1 above); Ladner (n. 2 above); Brown (n. 54 above); and McAdoo, ed. (n. 36 above). See Gilkes, "'Together and in Harness'" (n. 10 above), for Black women in the church; and chap. 4 of Deborah Gray White, *Ar'n't I a Woman? Female Slaves in the Plantation South* (New York: Norton, 1985). See also Gloria Joseph, "Black Mothers and Daughters: Their Roles and Functions in American Society," in *Common Differences: Conflicts in Black and White Feminist Perspectives,* ed. Gloria Joseph and Jill Lewis (Garden City, N.Y.: Anchor, 1981), 75–126. Even though Black women play essential roles in Black families and Black churches, these institutions are not free from sexism.

64. As Belenky et al. note, "Unlike the eye, the ear requires closeness between subject and object. Unlike seeing, speaking and listening suggest dialogue and interaction" (18).

65. Thomas Kochman, *Black and White: Styles in Conflict* (Chicago: University of Chicago Press, 1981); and Smitherman (n. 50 above).

66. Gwaltney (n. 11 above), 32.

67. Smitherman, 108.

68. Kochman, 28.

69. Jordan (n. 58 above), 129.

70. Claudia Tate, *Black Women Writers at Work* (New York: Continuum, 1983), 91.

71. Ibid., 92.

72. Alice Walker, *In Search of Our Mothers' Gardens* (New York: Harcourt Brace Jovanovich, 1974), 84.

73. Keller (n. 26 above); Chodorow (n. 60 above).

74. Belenky et al. (n. 59 above), 16.

75. Thomas Webber, *Deep Like the Rivers* (New York: Norton, 1978), 127.

76. In her discussion of the West African Sacred Cosmos, Mechal Sobel (n. 35 above) notes that Nyam, a root word in many West African languages, connotes an enduring spirit, power,

or energy possessed by all life. In spite of the pervasiveness of this key concept in African humanism, its definition remains elusive. She points out, "Every individual analyzing the various Sacred Cosmos of West Africa has recognized the reality of this force, but no one has yet adequately translated this concept into Western terms" (13).

77. For discussions of personal expressiveness in African-American culture, see Smitherman (n. 50 above); Kochman (n. 65 above), esp. chap. 9; and Mitchell and Lewter (n. 36 above).

78. Gwaltney (n. 11 above), 228.

79. For feminist analyses of the subordination of emotion in Western culture, see Hochschild (n. 32 above); and Chodorow.

80. Tate (n. 70 above), 156.

81. Gwaltney, 11.

82. Smitherman, 135 and 137.

83. Belenky et al. (n. 59 above), 100–130.

84. Ibid., 119.

85. See ibid., 52–75, for a discussion of inner voice and its role in women's cognitive styles. Regarding empathy, Belenky et al. note: "Connected knowers begin with an interest in the facts of other people's lives, but they gradually shift the focus to other people's ways of thinking. ... It is the form rather than the content of knowing that is central. ... Connected learners learn through empathy" (115).

86. Andrews (n. 48 above), 98.

87. Kochman (n. 65 above), 20 and 25.

88. Ibid., 23.

89. The sizable proportion of ministers among Black political leaders illustrates the importance of ethics in African-American communities.

90. Belenky et al. discuss a similar situation. They note, "People could critique each other's work in this class and accept each other's criticisms because members of the group shared a similar experience. ... Authority in connected knowing rests not on power or status or certification but on commonality of experience" (118).

91. Carol Gilligan, *In a Different Voice* (Cambridge, Mass.: Harvard University Press, 1982). Carol Stack critiques Gilligan's model by arguing that African-Americans invoke a similar model of moral development to that used by women (see "The culture of Gender: Women and Men of Color," *Signs* 11, no. 2 [Winter 1986]: 321–24). Another difficulty with Gilligan's work concerns the homogeneity of the subjects whom she studied.

92. Black men, white women, and members of other race, class, and gender groups should be encouraged to interpret, teach, and critique the Black feminist thought produced by African-American women.

93. Walker (n. 72 above), 91.

94. Gwaltney (n. 11 above), 7.

95. Jordan (n. 58 above), 130.

96. Collins (n. 3 above).

97. This point addresses the question of relativity in the sociology of knowledge and offers a way of regulating competing knowledge claims.

Suggested Further Readings

Ammott, Teresa L., and Julie A. Matthaei. *Race, Gender, and Work: A Multicultural Economic History of Women in the United States.* Boston: South End Press, 1991.

Davis, Angela Y. *Women, Race and Class.* New York: Random House, 1981.

hooks, bell. *Ain't I a Woman: Black Women and Feminism.* Boston: South End Press, 1981.

_____. *Feminist Theory: From Margin to Center.* Boston: South End Press, 1984.

_____. *Yearning: Race, Gender, and Cultural Politics.* Boston: South End Press, 1990.

Hull, Gloria T., Patricia Dell Scott, and Barbara Smith, eds. *But Some of Us Are Brave.* Old Westbury, N.Y.: Feminist Press 1982.

Joseph, Gloria, and Jill Lewis. *Common Differences: Conflicts in Black and White Feminist Perspectives.* New York: Anchor, 1981.

Lorde, Audre. *Zami: A New Spelling of My Name.* Watertown, Mass.: Persephone Press, 1982.

_____. *Sister Outsider.* Trumansburg, N.Y.: Crossing Press, 1984.

Moraga, Cherríe, and Gloria Anzaldúa, eds. *This Bridge Called My Back: Writings of Radical Women of Color.* Watertown, Mass.: Persephone Press, 1981.

Omolade, Barbara. "Black Women and Feminism." In *The Future of Difference,* ed. Hester Eisenstein and Alice Jardine, pp. 247–257. Boston: G. K. Hall, 1980.

Rich, Adrienne. "Disloyal to Civilization: Feminism, Racism, and Gynephobia." *Chrysalis: A Magazine for Women's Culture* 7 (1978) 9–27.

Smith, Barbara. "Notes for Yet Another Paper on Black Feminism, or Will the Real Enemy Please Stand Up?" *Conditions: Five—The Black Women's Issue* 2, no. 2 (Autumn 1979): 123–127.

Spelman, Elizabeth. "Theories of Race and Gender: The Erasure of Black Women." *Quest* 5, no. 4 (1980): 36–62.

About the Book and Editors

The past twenty years have seen an explosion of work by feminist philosophers and several surveys of this work have documented the richness of the many different ways of doing feminist philosophy. But this major new anthology is the first broad and inclusive selection of the most important work in this field.

There are many unanswered questions about the future of feminist philosophy. Which of the many varieties of feminist philosophy will last, and which will fade away? What kinds of accommodations will be possible with mainstream non-feminist philosophy? Which will separate themselves and flourish on their own? To what extent will feminists change the topics philosophers address? To what extent will they change the very way in which philosophy is done?

However these questions are answered, it is clear that feminist philosophy is having and will continue to have a major impact on the discipline of philosophy. This volume is the first to allow the scholar, the student, and other interested readers to sample this diverse literature and to ponder these questions for themselves.

Organized around nine traditional "types" of feminist philosophy, *Feminism and Philosophy* is an imaginatively edited volume that will stimulate readers to explore many new pathways of understanding. It marks a defining moment in feminist philosophy, and it will be an essential text for philosophers and for feminist theorists in many other fields.

Nancy Tuana is professor of philosophy at the University of Oregon. She is the author of *Woman and the History of Philosophy* and *The Less Noble Sex: Scientific, Religious, and Philosophical Conceptions of Woman's Nature* and editor of *Feminism and Science* and *Feminist Interpretations of Plato*. **Rosemarie Tong** is Thatcher Professor of the Medical Humanities at Davidson College. She is author of *Feminine and Feminist Ethics; Women, Sex, and the Law;* and *Feminist Thought.* Her current interest is feminist medical ethics.